ITALY

From Revolution to Republic

1700 to the Present

Fourth Edition

Spencer M. Di Scala

Westview
PRESS

A Member of the Perseus Books Group

Text design by Trish Wilkinson
Set in 10-point Minion by the Perseus Books Group

Library of Congress Cataloging-in-Publication Data

Di Scala, Spencer.
    Italy : from revolution to republic, 1700 to the present / Spencer M. Di Scala.
— 4th ed.
        p.   cm.
    Includes bibliographical references and index.
    ISBN 978-0-8133-4413-3 (pbk. : alk. paper)
    1. Italy—History—18th century. 2. Italy—History—19th century.
3. Italy—History—20th century. 4. Italy—History—21st century. I. Title.
DG545.D5 2009
945—dc22   2008046711

10   9   8   7   6   5   4   3   2   1

Contents

List of Maps

Preface and Acknowledgments

ALTHOUGH ITALY HAS A DISTINGUISHED PAST, THE COUNTRY'S MODERN history generates controversy. The ideas that the general public has about Italians are frequently contradictory and based on insufficient knowledge and on stereotypes. Fascism, communism, terrorism, and crime—these images vie with those of a fashionable, sophisticated, and fun-loving people. Academic interpretations of modern Italy frequently reflect, imperfectly, the Italian political milieu. Thus, the Risorgimento, once interpreted as a heroic struggle to liberate the peninsula, came under criticism because it allegedly failed to involve the masses. The Christian Democrats (DC), praised by the U.S. government for keeping Italy out of the Soviet bloc, were condemned by professors for excluding the "different" Italian Communists from power.

This book has its own point of view, but it provides readers with different interpretations of Italian history even where they might disagree with mine. To provide the flavor of historical controversies, I have brought diverse viewpoints into the text and the bibliographical essay; put events into historical context; compared them, where warranted, with similar developments in other countries; and informed readers of the views of protagonists of the time. For example, within the context of the times, the masses did have a significant role in Italian unification and, under Socialist guidance, in late nineteenth- and early twentieth-century Italian society and politics. I have also supplied whatever detail is necessary to achieve clarity and understanding, for example, in my account of Italian participation in the world wars, where I saw historical misconceptions.

I have structured the book to include periods that are usually not considered at length in a single volume. The book begins in the eighteenth century, after an introduction covering the end of the Renaissance, because that is where the modern age began for Italy, not with unification in 1861; I have also devoted much attention to periods other than the Risorgimento and fascism, which are sometimes covered in other works almost to the exclusion of other, fundamental, eras. One of the lessons of history, I think, is continuity despite apparent breaks. I have stressed links through culture, society, and economics. Sometimes periods that broke politically with previous times demonstrate continuity in other ways—for example, economically. This is the case with the Fascist period, whose continuity with the republic, on levels other than the political, is sometimes striking. In the early 1990s, Italy underwent major changes in its political system owing to a major corruption scandal and the end of international communism, but here again, continuity stands out. Even after 1992, when the corruption scandal swept away the old parties and most observers were expecting a radical break with the past, the continuity over the following years in certain areas was uncanny. By 2008, the country remained in flux because of an unsettled political picture, increasing immigration, globalization, a stagnating population, a declining economy, and international terrorism—areas to which this edition pays particular attention—but Italians struggled to maintain their traditions.

∽o∾

I owe debts to many people from whose help I benefited. Steve Catalano, my former editor at Westview Press, encouraged me to do this fourth edition, while Brooke Kush worked hard to see it through; I profited much by their suggestions. Roy Domenico offered important ideas for improvement that I was glad to accept. I owe much to the librarians at the University of Massachusetts Boston, who kept me constantly updated on the new technology that has revolutionized research. As always, I owe the greatest debt to my wife, Laura, and as was the case with the previous editions, I dedicate this book, with love, to my daughter Ashley.

Spencer M. Di Scala
Boston, Massachusetts
May 2008

The Setting

A CURSORY GLANCE AT A MAP OF ITALY REVEALS IMPORTANT GEOGRAPHICAL features that have profoundly influenced the boot-shaped peninsula's history. The most striking aspect is the mountainous and hilly terrain. To the north, the Alps—cited by the poet Dante as being the natural border of Italy—crown the peninsula and form Italy's boundaries with France, Switzerland, Austria, and Slovenia. Pockmarked by more than a thousand glaciers and with peaks of over 13,000 feet, the Alps give a picture of rugged beauty. The most famous peaks include Monte Bianco (15,771 feet), Monte Rosa (15,203 feet), and the Matterhorn (14,692 feet). The Alps affect the country's climate by blocking the northern and western winds and have been an important factor in the area's military history by making control of the few passes essential. In modern times, the starkly beautiful terrain has given rise to the important skiing and tourist industries. Besides the Alps, a long mountain range runs down the entire length of the peninsula. With their highest peak at 9,560 feet, the Apennines are lower than the Alps but are 745 miles long and extend practically to the sea. A recent geological formation, the Italian Peninsula is subject to earthquakes and volcanic activity. The country includes Europe's three active volcanoes (Vesuvius, Etna, and Stromboli), and various forms of volcanic action are visible in areas such as the Campi Flegrei and Pozzuoli, outside Naples, and on islands such as Ischia in the Bay of Naples. Depending on location, these volcanic phenomena produce thermal springs—a source of revenue because of their supposed therapeutic effects—gas emissions, and unpleasantly abrupt alterations in ground levels.

Mountains and hilly areas represent 77 percent of the peninsula's territory; plains make up 23 percent. Arable land is strictly limited and has contributed to a high population density in the cities and towns and to vast emigration. The peninsula once included an abundance of unhealthful marshlands, especially in the Veneto, Tuscany, and Lazio. Drained relatively recently, they were hotbeds of malaria and other diseases and hampered the peninsula's economic development.

Fertile plains are practically restricted to the Po River Valley in the North and to small areas around such southern cities as Naples and Catania. The climate, which is cool and wet in the North and hot and dry in the South, also favors the Po Valley, which grows large quantities of rice, wheat, maize, and sugar beets. The fertile but tiny southern plains produce tomatoes and citrus fruits, both of which are important export crops.

Different climates and terrain help explain diverse dietary habits, products, and economic developments. The North historically produced more meat and dairy products. Northerners thus cooked with butter. Rice, introduced about five hundred years ago and favored by the wet conditions, became a staple instead of the pasta characteristic of the South. Soil and weather conditions in the Center and the South favor olive trees, and thus olive oil is featured in these regional cuisines and has become one of Italy's principal agricultural exports. Along with the production of olive oil, Italy's climate and soil favor wine-producing grapes, which grow well over the entire peninsula. Wine goes well with both pasta and rice—which is "born in water and dies in wine." Italy is the world's largest wine exporter, a status that has frequently created trade tension with France and Spain. As befits a country with wide climatic diversity, Italian wines range greatly. In the northern area of Piedmont, robust wines such as Barolo, Barbera, and Gattinara match the best French red wines in quality and are suitable for aging. The South produces wine of lower quality but of high alcoholic content; these wines, because they can be cut in various ways to create a less-expensive beverage, historically have found a foreign and domestic market among the lower classes. Good local wines, best consumed on the spot, contribute to a thriving industry.

Climatic and geographical characteristics have also produced differences, however, that are more crucial to modern economies. Italy is very poor in natural resources, having no substantial deposits of the coal, iron ore, or petroleum necessary for industrial economies. Given this situation, the North has had important advantages over the South. It is closer to northern Europe, and its plains facilitated the building of roads and easier communications with the rest of Europe; because of the mountainous southern terrain, for example, a highway linking the entire South with northern Italy and Europe was not completed until the 1960s. The North has numerous rivers and large lakes that can be utilized for hydroelectric power—and industry—but southern rivers run dry during the summer and are ill suited for making electricity. Although these advantages favored the development of an industrial base in the North in the late nineteenth century, the lack of an important energy source and poor communications help account for the South's failure to industrialize and to modernize its economy.

Besides economic disequilibrium, the difficult terrain facilitated the peninsula's division into many independent political units and hampered political, social, and linguistic unification. In ancient times, Roman military force unified the peninsula. This unity survived the fall of the empire in the West (A.D. 476), but ended with the Lombard invasions of the sixth century. With the revival of trade in Europe, which began during the tenth century, Italians took advantage of their strategic location in the central Mediterranean Sea and their proximity to the Middle East to dominate European trade with the more advanced Arab world. The four maritime republics (Venice, Genoa, Pisa, and Amalfi) restored the Mediterranean to Western control and made it safe once again for European traders. Thanks to their strategic location and trading skills, Venetian and Genoese merchants gained vast economic concessions among the Arabs and traveled as far as China. Merchant-dominated Italian cities such as Florence, Venice, and Milan boomed, reaching unheard-of populations of 80,000 to 100,000. The cities achieved economic hegemony in Europe—especially in banking—overthrew medieval religious domination, and acquired secular political aspects that resembled modern times. The cities produced goods such as woolen cloth and arms and also tamed the land: around Milan, the largest irrigation project since the fall of the Roman Empire was undertaken around 1100 and was worked on by Leonardo da Vinci in the fifteenth century. According to British historian Stuart Woolf, "By the twelfth and thirteenth centuries, the cities of northern and central Italy, as much of the countryside, had already acquired that characteristic physiognomy of towers and civic buildings, of markets and economic bustle, which amazed all foreign visitors and distinguished Italy from the rest of Europe." Italy had become "the land of the hundred cities" and embarked upon that remarkable cultural domination of Europe that culminated in the Renaissance.

Within this context, Italian political units assumed different forms. In areas such as Lombardy, large cities expanded to take over the myriad smaller cities and towns and became organized as regional states. Cities such as Rome and Naples dominated several regions, whereas others shared political control of a single region (Parma and Modena). Tucked in the peninsula's northwestern corner (Piedmont), the Savoy dynasty busily gathered feudal possessions that it eventually organized as a highly centralized state in the seventeenth century.

By 1494, when the foreign invasions that spelled the end of Italian independence began, the peninsula, shaped by geography and history, had crystallized into several different states that lasted until unification occurred between 1861 and 1870.

Introduction:
From "School of Europe"
to Conquered Land

During the eighteenth century, Europe's most famous philosophe, Voltaire, summed up Renaissance Italy: "The Italians had everything, except music, which was still in its infancy, and experimental philosophy, which was unknown everywhere until Galileo finally introduced it into the world." Yet in the eyes of many observers, within a hundred years of Emperor Charles V's sack of Rome in 1527, Italy appeared to be a "land of the dead." Is this view of post-Renaissance Italy accurate, and if so, how do historians explain this rapid decline?

THE INVASIONS

During the Middle Ages, Italy was divided into many independent political entities that eventually coalesced into five major states—Naples, Florence, Rome, Venice, and Milan—and several minor ones. Although the Swiss historian of the Renaissance, Jacob Burckhardt, argued that these states were the first in Europe with modern attributes, none of them developed enough strength to conquer and unify the entire peninsula.

Peculiar to Italy and marking its entire history was the Papal State, which the popes considered essential to ensure their independence from secular rulers anxious to dominate the Church. For centuries popes battled the German-based Holy Roman Empire, which claimed Italy and the authority to intervene in Church affairs.

The fight between papacy and empire enabled the Italian states to remain independent. Over the centuries, the empire steadily declined, but during the "Babylonian Captivity" and the "Great Schism" between 1308 and 1417, when the French nominated the popes and competing pontiffs claimed the allegiance of the faithful, the papacy's power decreased as well. The threat of political domination of Italy by either the Holy Roman Empire or the pope receded.

By 1454, the Italian states had consciously established a balance of power. This equilibrium meant that none of the major states could dominate the entire peninsula because the others would ally against it. In effect, the territorial division of Italy had been officially recognized, guaranteed a multistate system on the peninsula, and made Italian unification impossible.

This development contrasted with events in France, Spain, and England that resulted in strong national monarchies. In 1494, the Milanese ruler Ludovico il Moro, his power threatened by other Italian monarchs, invited French King Charles VIII into Italy to aid him. This move introduced a strong contender for European preponderance into the Italian equation. When France's rival, Spain, also entered Italy, the peninsula became a major battleground between the two great powers.

Although Ludovico's policy proved ill fated, great-power intervention was probably just a matter of time. Italy had been a battleground since ancient days, and only the decline of the two great medieval powers—the Church and the Holy Roman Empire—had produced political independence. During the Renaissance "the Italians had everything"—rich cities and cultural, financial, and commercial superiority—but, separately, none of the small states could compete militarily with their newly united neighbors. Too weak to prevail militarily over either France or Spain, and too divided to act in concert and heed Machiavelli's "exhortation to take Italy and free her from the hands of the barbarians," the Italian states combined now with one, now with the other great power, in a vain attempt to salvage their independence through the application of balance-of-power principles. The savage fighting brought destruction, economic decline, and misery to the entire peninsula. The Spanish won the contest, and in 1559 the Treaty of Cateau-Cambrésis consigned Italy to Spain.

ITALY DURING THE SPANISH DOMINATION

Two major interpretive trends dominate historical views of post-Renaissance Italy. Not surprisingly, observers during the nineteenth-century Italian national revival viewed the period as a break with the preceding one and blamed Italy's "decadence" on war, foreign domination, and religious reaction. Subsequently adopted and honed by Marxist historians, this explanation became the standard interpretation. Proponents agree that, resting upon direct control of Milan and Naples, Spanish domination until 1713 favored important economic and social developments that, though less rapid, produced more serious alterations than did the political changes.

Most important, in the late sixteenth and seventeenth centuries, the tendency of merchants to make large investments in land increased drastically. The prosperity of medieval and Renaissance Italy had been based on commerce, which military operations rendered very risky. Though less spectacular, the profits from land were safer. In Milan, Florence, Venice, and other once-flourishing commercial centers, the urban upper classes gradually became transformed into a landed aristocracy that adopted the Spanish nobility's attitude of viewing commerce as an undignified activity. Furthermore, always needing money, the Spanish authorities sold fiefs, noble titles, and the right to perform public services, such as collecting taxes and dispensing justice, to families once devoted to trade. According to these historians, this policy "refeudalized" Italy.

This process helps explain the near absence of an enterprising Italian bourgeoisie interested in change, as developed in France. It also encouraged the overcrowding of cities because peasants moved into urban areas to take advantage of the aristocratic wealth concentrated there by engaging in such activities as begging. This movement resulted in extremely poor living conditions and an imbalance between city and countryside. The cities consumed the food produced on the land without providing anything in return, such as capital.

International trends intensified the decline. Increased trade with the Americas and new routes around Africa shifted trade away from Italian cities such as Venice and toward French, Spanish, and English Atlantic ports. Furthermore, since Spain was constantly involved in wars against the "infidel" Turks, Italian insertion into the Spanish orbit increased Italy's exposure to naval attacks and piracy; shipborne commerce was devastated and coastal areas depopulated, while increased taxation to pay for the fighting further impoverished the Italian Peninsula. Operas such as Antonio Vivaldi's *La Fida Ninfa* (first produced in January 1732) illustrate a lingering concern with the effects of piracy. Finally, Spain's military championship of the Counter-Reformation, combined with the papacy's struggle to reestablish Catholic supremacy in Europe, accelerated Italy's decline by stifling the country's cultural life.

REFORMATION AND COUNTER-REFORMATION

The attempt of Martin Luther and other European reformers to purify the Catholic Church found many sympathizers among Italian theologians and intellectuals.

Italian historian Delio Cantimori described the rich and suggestive ideas of these thinkers, which were so widespread that the future Pope Paul IV complained: "At that time it seemed that one could not be considered a proper noble or courtier if one did not have some heretical or erroneous opinions."

Given the papacy's influence, the power of Spain, the weakness of the bourgeoisie, and the economically depressed peasantry, these Reformation ideas could not be transformed into a mass movement. Initially concentrating on the necessity to end corruption as a way to combat heresy, the Church rapidly turned to repression and doctrinal conservatism.

"If our own father had been a heretic," stated Pope Paul IV, "we would personally have carried the wood needed to burn him at the stake." In line with his strong beliefs, Paul IV increased the Inquisition's powers, purged the Church hierarchy, imprisoned anyone vaguely suspected of harboring heretical ideas, and encouraged completion of the Index of Forbidden Books. Book shipments into Italy were scrutinized for offensive material, and book burnings became regular events. In 1573, the Inquisition summoned painter Paolo Veronese, criticized him for including "buffoons, drunken Germans, dwarfs, and other such absurdities" in a painting of the Last Supper, and ordered him to correct the picture at his own expense. In 1600, philosopher Giordano Bruno was burned at the stake for his ideas. In 1616, Galileo submitted to the Inquisition's order to stop teaching that the earth orbits the sun. Religious confraternities were important in politics and in maintaining social order, while papal politics became increasingly complex.

As a result of these persecutions, many intellectuals fled Italy, a diaspora that greatly impoverished the country and enriched the rest of Europe. At first this emigration affected religious reformers such as Bernardino Ochino, precursor of unitarianism, and Fausto and Lelio Sozzini, who greatly influenced the Reformation in eastern Europe. In the seventeenth century, this "brain drain" became a flood that included artists, musicians, diplomats, statesmen, and specialized artisans.

During the same period, at the behest of King and Holy Roman Emperor Charles V of Spain, the Church convened the Council of Trent (1545–1563). This council reaffirmed all the Church's doctrines, conforming with the ideas of Charles's son Philip II and making him the Church's champion.

At the same time, the Church distorted Italian cultural life. Through its propaganda activities, domination of education, and political influence, the Church identified the glories of Italy with those of Catholicism and attributed to the Italians the historical function of safeguarding Catholic tradition and the Church's "liberty." This identification of Italian greatness with the Church inspired a "Guelph" spirit in Italian culture that remained influential into the nineteenth century, when an Italian confederation with the pope as its head became one option for a united Italy. (During the Middle Ages, the Guelphs supported the papacy against the empire, hence the term's identification with the Church.)

THE DEBATE

This synopsis may be considered the standard view of post-Renaissance Italy, but it has been increasingly challenged by historians. According to these revisionists, careful research reveals "refeudalization" as a myth. Furthermore, they believe, Charles V established a new order in alliance with the Italian states, not against them. Instead of misery, this Spanish "consolidation" supposedly produced a measure of peace and a new economic, commercial, industrial, and agricultural prosperity.

Furthermore, instead of viewing the Counter-Reformation as a Spanish-inspired suffocation of Renaissance humanism, these observers praise it as a religious revival with deep Italian roots. Rather than interpreting the Counter-Reformation as a subversion of Italian culture by the Church, revisionists emphasize a new and more modern definition of the nation during this period and point to an emerging nationalism. Just as they see no break in the economic sector, the revisionists discern not decadence but continuity in the secular culture of the high Renaissance. Indeed, their analysis of the age's artistic, literary, and scientific creativity is the keystone of their argument. In recent years, a rich historical literature has emphasized society and culture in the different states. Indeed, consideration of the development of the individual states is a crucial aspect of understanding future Italian events if history is not to be distorted.

Both the standard and revisionist views have merit. It would seem an error to define as decadent the mannerist style of art and the Baroque Age that, between 1550 and 1750, produced Claudio Monteverdi, who brought opera from its primitive to its developed form, world-class artists such as the painters Annibale Carracci and Caravaggio, the poet Torquato Tasso, the sculptor Gian Lorenzo Bernini, and the religious thinker Paolo Sarpi. On the other hand, the revisionists do not deny that a relative decline in all fields occurred, but they tend to push it back, blame it on war and disease, and explain it in European rather than in Italian terms. And yet, the destruction, the suppression of ideas, the intellectual exodus, the subordination of Italian to Spanish interests under Philip II, and the repression of Paolo Sarpi's advanced ideas on the relationship between church and state all occurred. Whether these events can best be explained by direct Spanish and papal intervention or by indirect pressure or trends that had Italian origins, as the revisionists believe, seems a less important issue.

Although the essence of the post-Renaissance era will continue to be debated, several facts seem clear. Although continuity should be emphasized over a break, and gradualism over a drastic shift, the Italian decline of the late sixteenth and seventeenth centuries seems both real and serious in all sectors. Italy not only lost its position as prime innovator and leader of the Western world but also regressed economically and politically. The peninsula remained, however, intimately linked to western Europe, played a key role in the cultural developments of the eighteenth century, and was profoundly influenced by European events.

PART ONE

Enlightenment and French Revolutionary Italy

CHAPTER ONE

The Italian
Enlightenment

THE EIGHTEENTH-CENTURY EUROPEAN ENLIGHTENMENT USED IDEAS AS "intellectual weapons" to alter the existing religious, political, and social situation. The intellectuals of this age, the philosophes (*illuministi* in Italian), aimed to transform their traditional, rigid, and inequitable society into a world that enjoyed greater justice. They utilized "reason," critical judgment that corroded the "myths" underpinning the existing political and social structure. By employing reason, they could analyze society, learn the principles governing behavior, and achieve a more perfect and rational world by applying these principles through education and influence upon powerful "Enlightened monarchs."

In short, the philosophes applied physicist Isaac Newton's scientific methodology to the study of society, reversing the prevailing attitude of reverence for the past and aiming for perfection in the future rather than lamenting the loss of the past's golden age. Newton had influence also in Italy. Using the rules of evidence, they questioned everything, destroyed the historical basis of the old regime, and set the stage for the "Age of the Democratic Revolution" in Europe and America.

In practice, the philosophes advocated eliminating the Church's political power, judging government by a utilitarian yardstick, rationalizing the economy by eliminating feudal vestiges and by establishing an equitable tax system, opening careers to talent instead of birth, drafting constitutions to limit the power of governments, securing civil rights, and reforming the justice system.

RECIPROCAL INFLUENCES

France's position as the center of the Enlightenment sometimes causes observers to overlook the crucial contributions of Italian, German, English, Russian, and other thinkers, and Marxist analyses of the movement as the expression of a rising bourgeoisie have downplayed the Enlightenment's revolutionary character outside France. In Italy during the 1920s and 1930s, the Fascists encouraged interpretation of the Italian Enlightenment as a purely native movement foreshadowing the Risorgimento—the movement for Italian unification. After World War II, Italian historian Franco Venturi refuted this nationalistic view by demonstrating the Italian Enlightenment's richness and its integration within the "Atlantic" movement. Newtonian ideas, for example, influenced the Italian Enlightenment, and the Italian intellectual diaspora had effects on northern European culture.

Although intellectual developments in France stimulated discussion in Italy, Italians also influenced European Enlightenment thinkers. The works of Alberto Radicati di Passerano, an exile from the intolerant Kingdom of Sardinia (Piedmont), dealt with several issues dear to Enlightenment intellectuals. After a bold analysis of religious leaders, for example, he wryly concluded that "it would be better . . . to be an atheist than to worship a Being chargeable with such enormous crimes and iniquities." Like French philosophe Denis Diderot, Passerano chipped away at the concept that governments enforce ethical behavior established by God, a prime source of their authority, and argued that ethical concepts originate in social habit and custom.

If Passerano's ideas dealt with the more subtle aspects of the "myths" holding existing society together, writer Girolamo Tartarotti undermined grosser ones. In the 1740s, he struck a blow against prejudice and superstition by demolishing the belief in witches; such beliefs, he argued, contradicted morality and the scientific precepts of the new age. His work stimulated a vast debate over magic and touched off a general attack in France, Austria, and Germany on the supposed existence of witches, vampires, and ghosts.

The work of a Milanese thinker, Pietro Verri, is another example of this reciprocal influence. His *Meditations on Political Economy* (1771) caused a commotion in Europe by criticizing the Physiocrats, influential economists who advocated taxes on all land as the only source of new wealth. Verri argued that Physiocratic ideas would keep out foreign produce, working against the beneficial free trade that the Physiocrats intended their program to produce. Translated into French, German, and Russian, Verri's book stirred discussion among the most famous philosophes and provided Europe with a taste of the fundamental issues being engaged by Italian intellectuals.

But it was another Milanese thinker who had the most international influence. Cesare Beccaria's *Of Crimes and Punishments* (1764) was translated into many languages (the French edition bore a famous commentary by Voltaire). In examining justice during his time, Beccaria made compelling arguments for speedy trials, for informing the accused of their crimes, for limiting the power of judges, for proportioning the punishment to the crime, for equalizing punishments for the same crime, and for treating offenders equally regardless of social class; he denounced torture and the death penalty. Beccaria placed jurisprudence on a modern footing in Europe and America.

THE LONG PEACE

Besides these intellectual aspects, political currents also intertwined in eighteenth-century Italy. Historians seem to agree that the 1730s mark the depth of the Italian post-Renaissance crisis and that the decade witnessed a slow revival of the political, economic, and intellectual fortunes of the country.

They divide the century into two periods. From 1700 to 1748, the precipitous decline of Spain and the desire to pluck Spanish spoils in Italy provoked major conflicts. During the War of Spanish Succession (1700–1713), the French attempted to take over the entire Spanish Empire, including Italy, while Austria hoped to substitute its hegemony for Spain's on the peninsula. In the end, Austrian domination replaced Spanish, a development that made the Italian diplomatic situation more fluid.

The Austrians controlled only Lombardy (Milan) directly, even though they had indirect power in Tuscany (Florence). Spain retained influence in Naples, Sicily, and Parma through Bourbon rulers, but these states regained their independence. To obtain a consensus in their newly acquired possessions, the rulers adopted important reforms based on the prevailing Enlightenment culture. These attempts had the powerful support of Italian intellectuals, many of whom played an active role in the government and thus gained valuable governmental experience. A good example of Hapsburg activities in this sense can be seen in Trieste, where the Austrians established a free port and granted tolerance to the Jews.

With the decline of Spain and the emergence of a new European balance, the Italian diplomatic equation underwent major changes. The major beneficiary was Piedmont. Tucked in the northwest corner of Italy, and pursuing the expansionist aims of its ruling Savoy dynasty, this state ably exploited the differences between France and Austria, new rivals for supremacy in Italy. Because of England's emergence as a Mediterranean power and its policy of preserving Piedmontese independence to counterbalance France and Austria, and because of its value to France and Austria as a buffer state, Piedmont gained diplomatic maneuverability. Smaller Italian states acquired some diplomatic maneuverability as well. By exploiting its privileged position, Piedmont acquired the large island of Sardinia, increased its mainland possessions, and won recognition as a kingdom. Thus, the eighteenth century witnessed the growth in prestige and size of the state that, a century and a half later, would accomplish Italian unification.

MAP 1.1   Eighteenth-Century Italy

European developments produced a long peace in Italy. Following the War of Austrian Succession (1740–1748), the rivals for control of Italy—France and Austria—became allies. Consequently, European conflicts did not involve the peninsula until 1792, when revolutionary France and conservative Austria battled anew. For fifty years, the Italian states could concentrate on internal affairs. Different conditions in various sections guaranteed mixed results, but the reform attempts were always interesting in their own right and helped determine the future course of the various Italian regions.

THE NORTH

Enlightened reforms and their effects on social and economic development placed Lombardy, despite its subjection to Austria, in the forefront of the Italian states.

The Austrian Hapsburg queen, Maria Theresa (1740–1780), initiated a reform policy on practical grounds, not on Enlightenment principles. Emerging from a war designed to dismember her disparate empire, Maria Theresa understood that only by streamlining the financial and administrative structure of her dominions could she increase production and the population's capacity to pay more taxes. In practice, this policy meant a campaign against the remnants of Lombard feudalism, which hampered production—a goal that secured the cooperation of the Lombard *philosophes*.

The most crucial reform proved to be the vast land survey initiated by Maria Theresa's father and completed by the empress in 1759. This survey allowed the state to impose a fairer tax on land belonging to all classes, including the nobility. Besides addressing the equity issue, the survey ensured fiscal stability by imposing definitive taxes, thus stimulating agricultural production. A typical but rarely implemented Enlightenment demand, this reform pleased Pietro Verri and the Lombard *illuministi*, ensuring their collaboration in the reforms that followed.

During the seventeenth century, the Spanish had sold to landlords the right to collect certain taxes and tolls. Between 1760 and 1786, the Austrians returned direct control of these taxes and tolls to the state. As a result, the economic position of nobles suffered. Since the reform presented the nobility with the choice of either a reduction in income or a return to business activity, part of the Lombard aristocracy engaged in improving its lands for profit. In short, this reform dealt a death blow to the residues of Lombard feudalism and created the basis for its legal abolition in 1797, results that went beyond the government's intentions. Furthermore, redemption of indirect taxes and tolls permitted Lombardy in 1776 to declare freedom of internal trade in grains and, ten years later, to permit their free export. Lombardy thus carried out a series of important reforms that had long been advocated by European philosophes but that countries such as France had been unable to achieve.

In other areas of reform, such as administration, the Church, and education, the Austrians achieved mixed success, but on balance, the reform policy yielded permanent results. In the fertile Lombard lowlands, the great noble estates began breaking up, the land going to persons—noble and not—who founded vibrant agricultural firms. Intent on increasing production and profits, the agricultural bourgeoisie introduced new production methods and products such as cheese. This activity reversed the previous parasitic role of the city and created an equilibrium between city and country, as may be seen in the cultivation of the silkworm in the country while the towns invested capital and produced finished silk products. The population spurt in the smaller Lombard cities signaled a new dynamism unknown in Lombard society since the Renaissance.

The emerging middle class favored by Austrian policy created a climate for greater participation in politics to further its economic interests, although this was expressed only with the arrival of the French in 1796. At this critical point, however, the Austrians reversed their policy of cooperation with the Italians. The circumstances of Maria Theresa's accession to the throne had forced her to collaborate with her subjects, but her son pursued a policy of centralization throughout his empire. After his mother's death in 1780, Joseph II strengthened his control over Lombard officials; by 1790, collaboration with intellectuals and the middle class had ended. Historian Alexander Grab emphasizes the limits of Austrian reform policy and believes that "Joseph II lacked a commitment to a deep economic reform program"; according to Grab, for further significant economic change to occur, "other political upheavals and a stronger bourgeoisie were necessary." Thus the Austrian fracture with the Lombard illuministi and the middle class transformed collaboration into permanent conflict and ensured a receptive audience for French revolutionary ideas.

No reform activity of the kind noted in Lombardy marked adjoining Piedmont. This state lacked the stimulus of a new ruling house eager to establish itself and did not follow a reform policy. Indeed, the Savoy dynasty judged reform dangerous to its control and persecuted Enlightenment culture. The travails of an important Piedmontese writer, Vittorio Alfieri, symbolize the poor relationship of this state with its intellectuals.

Other differences from the Italian pattern also show up. Piedmontese origins lay not in a large commercial city that had swallowed surrounding territory but in a collection of medieval fiefs over which the Savoy house had succeeded in imposing a centralized command after 1559. The government accomplished this aim by taming the unruly aristocracy and by converting it into a "service nobility" of the Prussian type that was closely bound to the monarchy. Loss of its fiscal privileges did not transform the Piedmontese nobility into a business class, as had partially occurred in Lombardy, but into a military, bureaucratic, and diplomatic caste; it thus retained its social status and its landed character.

This development did not improve Piedmontese agriculture, which remained backward. Industrial activity did not develop because the government failed to encourage commerce through the eradication of feudal conditions and because Piedmont lacked large cities. While Piedmontese rulers made weak attempts to improve the economy, they rejected the Enlightenment reforms that would have encouraged industry and commerce.

Piedmont achieved military and diplomatic successes in the eighteenth century, but it would not emerge as a serious candidate to lead the movement for Italian unification in the next century until it had moderated the less progressive aspects of its society, economy, and politics.

The fate of Venice and Genoa, once important mercantile republics, may be considered together. Venice emerged exhausted from the numerous attempts to destroy it during the late Renaissance and from a century-long conflict with the Turks. The discovery of America had pushed Venice into a long economic decline; by the eighteenth century, the republic had dwindled to diplomatic insignificance, even though its governmental structure remained an object of study and admiration for the philosophes.

The Venetian nobility abandoned commerce for landed activity and concentrated wealth into a few hands while retaining the severe restrictions for entry into the ruling class that had existed in its glory days. These factors prevented the emergence of a commercial middle class and provided little incentive for the aristocracy to engage in commerce once more. Enlightenment ideas did penetrate and some industry did develop, but not to a significant degree.

Similar to Venice in its restrictive governmental structure, Genoa also presents interesting dissimilarities. Given Genoa's small size and poor hinterland, the nobles continued to lend money to the great powers, but this money-lending never developed into modern investment activity, nor did it stimulate industrial growth. Only in the ports of Leghorn and Genoa did mercantile activity expand; this commercial development gave rise to a vocal bourgeois class that was impatient with noble privileges and that later supported Italian unification.

THE CENTER

The government of the Grand Duchy of Tuscany, the area surrounding Florence, conducted the most serious experiment in Enlightenment reform. When Francis of Lorraine, husband of Maria Theresa, became the grand duke in 1737, he brought Tuscany under indirect Austrian control and initiated the reform process that their son, Peter Leopold (1765–1790), greatly accelerated.

Peter Leopold inherited an agricultural region that primarily produced grain, wine, olive oil, and fruit. The bourgeoisie was weak, and the land belonged mostly to the nobility, the ruling family, the Church, or to special orders of knights founded to fight the Turks. The peasants worked the land as sharecroppers to produce for themselves and the landowners, not for a market. The absence of a market, combined with the large tracts of unhealthy marshland, created a depressed peasant class perpetually indebted to the landlords and subject to frequent famines.

As in Lombardy, the new Austrian dynasty collaborated with the illuministi to bring about a series of reforms. Expanding on a 1767 provision, Peter Leopold allowed unlimited exportation and importation of agricultural products in 1775. Eight years later, he eliminated internal tariffs and tolls, fulfilling in Tuscany the philosophes' dream of free commerce. In addition, between 1747 and 1789, freedom to buy and sell land arrived through strict limits on mortmain (perpetual ownership of land by the Church and other institutions forbidden to sell it). Between 1770 and 1781, the government, in the hope of eliminating serious obstacles to production, abolished the obsolete privileged corporations that had once dominated the Florentine economy.

During the same period, Peter Leopold limited the power of the central administration by giving greater autonomy to local government and adopted fiscal reforms. He replaced the many confusing taxes with one land tax, which was to be paid by all landholders, and reduced the sharecroppers' burden by limiting the percentage of this tax that could be passed on to them. In addition, tax privileges enjoyed by ecclesiastical orders and privileged corporations ceased.

However, a land survey that would have ensured the effectiveness of the reforms could not be completed, and the government's attempt to create a small landholding class failed. The grand duke broke up vast governmental holdings into small plots and arranged for their sale to peasants under easy terms. Unfortunately, these buyers proved too poor to meet the conditions of sale and consequently sold the land either to rich city dwellers or to noble landholders. In a related area, the government achieved only mixed success in reclaiming marshland, including the Maremma, an area so unhealthy, a popular song proclaimed, that birds lost their tails if they flew over it.

The government partially succeeded in limiting the Church's influence by curbing mortmain, abolishing fiscal privileges, ending the Inquisition, and suppressing the Jesuits. But when Peter Leopold tried to introduce Jansenism—policies to "purify" the Church favored by the philosophes—he failed. When he attempted to reform religious orders by abolishing perpetual vows, simplifying religious ceremonies, cutting the number of feast days, reducing the pope's authority, and forbidding the veneration of relics, he encountered hierarchical and popular resistance; riots broke out, and the grand duke backed off.

Despite its intensity and the collaboration of the illuministi, Peter Leopold's reform effort had slight effect; his failure illustrated the difficulty of producing real change against a recalcitrant social structure. In Tuscany, as in the other Italian states, the government reached the point when it had to decide whether to force greater reform at the risk of revolution or give up the effort.

The chief stimulus for reform was removed when Peter Leopold succeeded his brother Joseph as the Austrian emperor in 1790. The French Revolution had already begun, and Peter's successors abandoned reform. This increased conservatism of the Tuscan rulers made Tuscan intellectuals more receptive to revolutionary ideas. Like Lombardy, Tuscany confronted a crisis situation at the end of the eighteenth century.

The Papal State faced greater problems than Tuscany and lacked its reform fervor. The pope's temporal domain, sliced in two by the Apennine Mountains, consisted of several disparate regions. Large noble and ecclesiastical landholdings and stagnant marshlands characterized the most backward areas to the south, such as Lazio, where the sharecroppers lived a particularly depressed life, even if they resisted the power of the local magnates. In these regions, there was little commerce in the cities, which served mainly as administrative centers. Rome was important not as an economic center but as the capital of Christendom and as a center of the arts; indeed, its ability to siphon gold from the Catholic world dampened its rulers' will to undertake reforms. Northern regions, such as the Romagna, enjoyed a more resilient economy because of better communications with the North; silk and hemp stimulated industrial production, the University of Bologna maintained intellectual contact with Europe, and fairs and ports spurred trade. Even there, however, depressed agricultural conditions forced sharecroppers into the cities to beg, and a stunted, economically weak bourgeoisie remained subservient to the aristocracy.

Consisting of a mix of ancient feudal families, "nephews" descended from past popes and cardinals, and dignitaries of the papal court, the ruling class ran the papal government and the Church for its own benefit. Strengthened by the imposition of a fairly centralized papal authority in the sixteenth century, this group resisted Enlightenment culture so successfully that the reform initiated with severe criticism of papal policy from abroad. Slowly the papal government introduced some measures such as the abolition of taxes and tolls in 1793, but these were too late and too inadequate to avert the crisis of the state in the late eighteenth century.

The little Duchies of Parma and Modena round out this survey of the Center. Both areas were centers of Enlightenment reform and culture, Modena being particularly noted for the activities of Ludovico Antonio Muratori, the historian of Italian cultural unity.

THE SOUTH

In the South, the Kingdoms of Naples and Sicily were home to Enlightenment writers who were of high quality but were defeated in the long run by a feudalistic social structure and the unwillingness of the rulers to adopt the drastic reform measures necessary to redress the poor economic and social conditions. Although these two kingdoms had the same ruler, they were administratively distinct and will be discussed separately.

Surveying his new possessions from his capital in Naples, the king, Charles of Bourbon (1734–1759), would have observed the most disparate kingdom on the peninsula. It consisted of six regions, each of which lacked a commercial and industrial base, possessed few roads, and organized agricultural production only for local markets. With a population of almost 410,000, the city of Naples, the largest city in Italy and one of the biggest in Europe, dominated the entire state. Naples, however, owed its size to its position as the seat of government, its appeal as a residential center for a nobility that refused to manage its lands, and its attraction for enormous numbers of peasants abandoning the land to find work as servants or to beg. Very little commerce or industry existed in the city, which lived off the countryside and best illustrated the economic disequilibrium that afflicted the kingdom.

In addition, Charles's Spanish forebears had bequeathed him a mixed heredity where the nobility was concerned. They had drastically reduced the nobility's governmental role at the center, but in the countryside the nobles had increased their power, retaining crucial functions such as tax collection and the dispensing of justice. In addition, out of two thousand towns, Charles had jurisdiction over fewer than fifty.

Rural economic and social conditions varied, but they were among the worst in Italy. Except in areas suitable for growing fruits, vegetables, grapes, and olives, extensive agriculture characterized by the primitive production of cereals alternated with long periods of leaving the land fallow. Tenant farmers worked large baronial holdings under miserable living conditions, with many forced to become day laborers or to leave the land.

Important trends, which might have signaled possible changes, did not alter this dismal picture. Europe throughout the eighteenth century witnessed enormous inflation. The Neapolitan barons, living in Naples and straining to keep up with the social requirements of a brilliant court, incurred large debts; to increase their income, they raised the peasants' fees and dues and, when that did not raise enough money, either sold off parcels of their land or "rented" them to overseers. This new group—small property holders, merchants, moneylenders, administrative employees—opposed the feudal interests of the nobility and created a new tension in the countryside. But because the new class failed to develop new products and methods of production, the struggle neither created an agrarian bourgeoisie nor substantially weakened the nobility.

This disappointing result occurred despite the collaboration of notable illuministi with Charles's chief minister, Bernardo Tanucci, and his successors. Enlightenment intellectuals such as Antonio Genovesi and Gaetano Filangieri sought to eliminate the worst aspects of feudalism, but Neapolitan monarchs reacted weakly to the resistance of the privileged classes, and Tanucci did not agree with the more extreme measures the philosophes suggested. In 1741, for example, Charles ordered a land survey, but poor implementation of reform policies ensured that the barons did not pay their fair share of taxes; the poor would continue carrying the major burden of taxation, which was exacerbated by an expensive military policy. The kingdom remained economically backward; it exported unfinished products such as raw silk, olive oil, and grain and imported finished products while running a very high deficit.

The Neapolitan Enlightenment probably succeeded best in its Church policy. With a disproportionately large number of priests, vast landholdings, important fiscal and legal privileges, and the government's inability to block the flow of vast sums to the pope, the Church presented a more serious problem in Naples than it did in other Italian states.

Energetic action to restrict Church influence began early. In 1741, a new concordat (an agreement regulating relations between Church and State) limited the Church's fiscal privileges and the authority of Church courts. Soon thereafter the Inquisition was abolished, and Tanucci suppressed many monasteries, abolished mortmain for new acquisitions, expelled the Jesuits, confiscated their property, and abolished ecclesiastical tithes (taxes). The Church's power was still significant at the end of the century, but it had greatly diminished.

Ferdinand IV succeeded Charles but left policy to his Austrian wife, Queen Maria Carolina, and to her English adviser, John Acton. Reform policies continued until 1792, when, fearful that Enlightenment ideas would produce a revolution as they had in France, the two reversed course.

Despite the high intellectual quality of the Neapolitan Enlightenment and its strong international ties, it produced fewer results than the Enlightenment movement in either Lombardy or Tuscany. Illuminista collaboration ended in Naples, as it had in the other Italian states, on a note of failure and resentment that would plunge the kingdom into a greater crisis.

In the other Bourbon-controlled kingdom, Sicily, the social situation resembled that of Naples, but because low consumption allowed high grain exportation, the nobility retained a stronger economic position than its Neapolitan counterpart. Moreover, the Sicilian nobles had won important political privileges from the previous Spanish rulers. A small bourgeois class existed in some cities, but its lack of capital condemned it to perpetual weakness and dependence on English capital, for example, for the development of the wine industry in Marsala. Finally, an active baron-dominated Parliament rounded out the noble advantage.

Although Neapolitan administrators cooperated with the barons until 1781, this changed with the arrival of Domenico Caracciolo, an energetic philosophe who

MARIA CAROLINA
Queen of Intrigue

⟡⟡⟡

Born on August 13, 1752, in Vienna, Maria Carolina married Ferdinand IV of Naples in 1768. She did not love Ferdinand and felt frustrated at being excluded from the kingdom's ruling Council of State because she had given birth to three daughters but not to a son. She took a string of lovers and, in 1775, bore a male heir and joined the ruling Council. She dominated the government and became "in reality, the King of Naples."

Maria Carolina strengthened Austria's influence to Spain's detriment. She fired the capable Bernardo Tanucci and brought in new ministers, many of whom were her lovers. A folk song about her includes the line: "You're a whore and everyone knows it." Nevertheless, during this period Maria Carolina's brothers, Joseph in Austria and Peter Leopold in Tuscany, attempted to bring about reforms favored by the French Enlightenment. The queen demonstrated herself sympathetic to a similar policy; Enlightenment intellectuals favoring reform regarded her positively, and a period of reform began in Naples.

However, the French Revolution in 1789 scared Maria Carolina into ending reform measures. After the beheading of her sister, Marie Antoinette, on October 16, 1793, she lived in terror. Along with her English minister and lover, Lord Acton, she hunted down anyone she suspected of favoring the hated French,

imprisoning or executing them. Because the English fleet protected the kingdom, she became close to the English ambassador's wife, Emma Hamilton, Admiral Horatio Nelson's lover. In 1798, her army defeated by the French-dominated Roman Republic, she, the king, and the court fled to Sicily under the British fleet's protection.

In 1799, Cardinal Fabrizio Ruffo overthrew the Neapolitan Republic that had replaced the kingdom. He made an agreement that spared the lives of the revolutionaries if they would surrender. Maria Carolina, however, would have none of it. She prepared a list of persons she wanted dead and gave it to Emma Hamilton. Hamilton passed it on to Admiral Nelson; he pressured Ruffo to go back on his word to the revolutionaries. In an incident that shocked all Europe, the restored regime executed everyone on Maria Carolina's list.

In 1806, Napoleon conquered the Kingdom of Naples. Maria Carolina fled to Sicily once again. The queen wanted to try a comeback one more time, but her husband concentrated on his mistress rather than politics. On February 2, 1814, with Napoleon about to fall, Maria Carolina went to Vienna to ask the allies to return her throne. On September 7, the answer came: no—they feared a repeat of 1799. Maria Carolina, her heart (it is said) unable to take the shock, died the same day.

had lived in Paris. His ambitious program would have weakened Sicilian feudalism by limiting the barons' power to confiscate goods and dispense justice, eliminating their political and financial control of the towns, establishing a mechanism to redeem feudal rights, and attacking the barons' financial privileges.

The barons fought back by portraying the Neapolitans as new conquerors attempting to abolish the ancient rights of the Sicilian "nation." Following a pattern all too typical of the eighteenth century, the barons won the support of the very people who would have benefited from the projected reforms. In addition, by gradually transforming their fiefs into free land, members of the nobility converted themselves into large landowners while preserving their economic and social privileges.

DAILY LIFE

As might be expected, living conditions at this time varied greatly depending on social class and region. In the towns, luxurious Renaissance villas, monuments, theaters, fountains, and monumental stairs built for gala occasions (for example, the Spanish Steps in Rome) contrasted with very poor housing. And despite a demographic recovery that allowed Rome to reach 163,000 and Florence 72,000, low population density characterized urban centers. In smaller towns, convicts used cart-drawn water barrels to clean the streets, which were unpaved and unnamed and on which stood unnumbered houses. Mild weather encouraged people to live outdoors: they sold wares and cooked food on the street, washed clothes in the fountains, and relieved themselves in the courtyards. Because of the heat, people rose early and ceased all activity at noon; everyone slept during the afternoon and resumed their tasks only after the sun had gone down. They had dinner very late and retired even later.

Tradespeople and shops concentrated in specific areas, which eventually took the names of their trades. Wooden signs bearing a symbol of the trade identified the shops. For example, a brass plate identified a Roman barber, and since men with high-pitched voices took the place of women in musical performances, he proudly advertised: "Here we castrate the singers in the Papal chapels."

Travelers remarked upon how well tended the land in the countryside seemed, despite the extreme poverty of the peasants. German poet Goethe wrote: "It would seem impossible to see better-kept fields." In the North, fertile lands, irrigation networks, and landowner interest eased the sharecroppers' lot, but in the South an adverse climate, absentee landlords, isolation, and the lack of public works crushed the sharecroppers. Peasants lived in huts with only a hole in the roof to let out the smoke. In Sicily, most men possessed only a short, brown, sleeveless waistcoat, with a heavy brown or black wool cloak for the winter; women wore dresses of black linen or serge, a handkerchief on their heads, and, on Sundays, a white mantle if they owned one.

As might be expected, peasants and the poor in general did not receive an education because the Italian states did not establish a public school system. Occasionally a priest who noticed a boy of uncommon intelligence might teach him or arrange for his education in a seminary (not necessarily to become part of the clergy), but the lack of an educational system accounts for the very high illiteracy rate that later afflicted modern Italy. In the middle of the nineteenth century, illiteracy in the South was at 80 percent, but a hundred years earlier it was probably higher and more diffused.

Southern peasants frequently rebelled against their situation. A popular song dating from the fourteenth century demanded: "You promised me six 'handkerchiefs' [pieces of land], and I'm here to claim them . . . for that which you carry on your back [own] is not yours." In the seventeenth century, serious revolts shook the region, but the lack of a strong middle class hampered the evolution of these revolts into revolution. Until the famine of 1763–1764, agricultural conditions probably remained static or even improved. That development, however, worsened the conditions of the sharecroppers and tenants. Lacking reserves, technical skill, and the ability to resist a nobility that imposed harsher conditions of land tenure, and forced to borrow money that they could never repay, many of these peasants became day laborers or found other means of subsistence. These developments help explain the great increase in begging that observers report in the eighteenth century.

In the cities, the government's control of food prices and tendency to restrain the worst abuses of the nobility mitigated the poverty there. Begging was rife, but the poor had a better hope of receiving charity and of finding employment in the guilds or as servants in the many palaces owned by the aristocracy or the Church hierarchy.

Not all nobles fared better than the common folk. Foreign tourists reported that poor aristocrats resided in large palaces that they could not afford to heat, but luckily, the wealthy nobles were usually generous to foreigners. This was a boon to travelers like Goethe, who was warned to avoid the "Golden Lion" in Catania: "It is worse than if you had fallen into the clutches of the Cyclops, the Sirens, and the Scyllas all at the same time."

Governments subjected wealthy nobles to dress codes appropriate to their station in life. In Venice, nobles had to wear a toga based upon the dress of the ancient Roman Senate. When capes became fashionable in the seventeenth century, a law punished noblemen caught wearing them in public with five years' imprisonment and a heavy fine. Noblewomen who wore colors other than black suffered a similar fate, since only prostitutes wore bright colors and rouge. These attempts at control failed, especially during the eighteenth century, when magazines introduced French and English fashions.

Noblemen hired tutors, usually clergy, to educate their sons, but these were mostly useless. Serious sons of the nobility and the middle class went to Jesuit academies, which were fairly widespread throughout the peninsula. The Jesuits imparted strict discipline and religious instruction to their charges, in addition to a solid grounding in Latin and the classics. After the suppression of the Jesuit order in 1773, the Jansenist-influenced Congregation of Pious Schools became more important. These fathers introduced subjects more appropriate to the eighteenth-century interest in economic and agricultural affairs. Italian was also a more important part of the curriculum, and many later supporters of Italian independence came out of these schools.

As might be expected, the increasing importance given to education did not extend to women. Daughters of well-off families generally went off to convents to await marriage, and they were educated primarily in the acquisition of social and domestic skills. Sometimes they learned some reading and writing, but generally parents, who believed it dangerous for women to know how to read because they might be misled by bad books, felt that learning the rosary was far more appropriate. Despite these limitations on their education, there are interesting reports of highly cultivated women in eighteenth-century Italy, and in the major Italian cities, salons run by women—usually noble—were, as in France, major centers of culture.

In eighteenth-century Europe, women were excluded from the recently founded scientific academies—following a long-established practice in the universities. "In Italy, however, a few women succeeded in carving out a niche for themselves. They were excluded neither from the universities and the scientific academies nor from the knowledge expounded by those universities." In fact, Laura Bassi Verati was granted a lectureship at the University of Bologna (in the Papal State) on October 29, 1732, and eventually received one of the highest salaries at the institution—1,200 lire a year.

As a rule, however, women led restricted lives. They did not go out, except to church, and chaperones always accompanied them. Their parents chose their husbands without taking their wishes into consideration, even though the bridegroom was sometimes expected to make some ritual show of love. In Venice, women could dissolve marriages for such reasons as "barbarous treatment by the husband," but during the divorce proceedings they had to retreat to a convent. Venice prohibited public affection between husbands and wives, a ban that contributed to the evolution of the *cicisbeo*, a noble "servant." Frequently encountered in Carlo Goldoni's plays and a staple of upper-class Venetian marriage contracts, the cicisbeo accompanied the noblewoman everywhere, was present during her most intimate functions, but was never her lover. As a Venetian satirist described it, his duty was "to stay constantly by the side of the wife of a third party and by express contract and obligation to be bored by her for days at a time."

Religious attitudes differed greatly from those in modern times. During church services, people chatted, walked around, gathered in crowds, and conducted their business. Religious festivals also provided entertainment. People appeared genuinely attached to their religion—many attended mass daily, recited the rosary nightly, and observed Lent—but they saw no reason to alter their behavior. Brothels burned candles to the Virgin Mary and charged an extra fee to have masses said on special occasions. People gave in to their passions, went to confession, and began all over again.

This pattern shocked no one. Goethe observed a rich nobleman famous for his expensive vices begging for money to ransom slaves captured by the Barbary pirates. When the poet remarked upon the contradiction, he received the following response: "But we are all like that! We gladly pay for our own follies ourselves, but others are expected to provide the money for our virtues." When it came time to reap the rewards of a virtuous life, the funerals of the rich were lavish, and the deceased were remembered with the grandiose monuments that decorate Italian churches. In Sicily, the corpse was frequently dressed in the deceased's finest garments and brought seated into the decorated church as musicians played their instruments. In the states most affected by the Enlightenment, however, a reaction against these customs set in; states such as Lombardy and Tuscany regulated funerals even to the point of restricting the number of candles families could display (depending on their social status) and forbidding the use of coffins except for high clergy and nuns.

CULTURE AND CRISIS

Whereas contradiction characterized private life, the interaction of philosophy and politics and the manifest failure of reform marked the public life of eighteenth-century Italy. Enlightenment philosophy, however, precluded a return to old methods, spurring the illuministi instead to examine the causes of their failure and to take new action.

European and Italian philosophes had counted upon rulers imbued with their ideas—"Enlightened monarchs"—to reform their countries and in the process justified their leaders on the basis of utilitarianism. The philosophes eventually realized that the monarchs ruled for their own benefit. At this point, they replaced "Enlightened monarchy" as a basis for rule with Jean-Jacques Rousseau's "general will," a difficult political concept that easily translated into "majority rule." In France, a country with an economically powerful and politically sophisticated bourgeoisie, this transition helped produce the Revolution. In Italy, the bourgeoisie's strength varied, but nowhere attained that of its French counterpart. Thus the collapse of Enlightenment reform due to the withdrawal of government support could not immediately lead to revolution, but it did produce a crisis that made Italian intellectuals receptive to radical social, economic, and political solutions, including the idea of national cohesion.

In Naples, Tanucci rejected the ideas of Antonio Genovesi, a professor of political economy, to free the grain trade and to eliminate government interference in the economy as a means of modernizing the state, alleviating rural poverty, and preventing such terrible catastrophes as the famine of 1763–1764. Famine also hit Tuscany in the 1760s, but by the 1790s the reform movement had petered out or failed. Italy approached the end of the eighteenth century in a severe economic and moral crisis characterized by widespread discontent.

If indeed "a substantial part of the Italian Enlightenment debate can properly be read as testimony to the scale of pauperism," it is comprehensible that with the failure of reform, revolutionary ideas current in the rest of Europe should become attractive to Italian intellectuals. In the 1770s and 1780s, for example, the appeal of Freemasonry to growing numbers of Italian intellectuals signaled their withdrawal from conventional politics. In the South especially, faith in radical, egalitarian, and communistic methods of solving Italy's problems increased. Influential Neapolitan philosophe Gaetano Filangieri might remain basically optimistic, but he forcefully identified Europe's paramount problem as the minority's monopoly on wealth; "the remedy to be aimed at," he asserted, was to make certain that "everything be in the hands of the many."

The search for new solutions produced faith not only in egalitarianism and republicanism of the American type but also in a revival of national feeling, the idea that the lot of Italians would improve if the peninsula were united and if the people could work together. But what made the Italians one people? Discussion centered on several elements that emphasized pride and national character. In their quest to understand the relationship between language and nationality, intellectuals debated the ideas of Neapolitan philosopher Giambattista Vico, a philosophical giant of the age. Vico's student, Genovesi, challenged his colleagues by lecturing at the University of Naples in Italian. Genovesi's reasoning was double-edged: as long as Latin, incomprehensible to most Italians, dominated education, there could be no mass education and no national solidarity, and no nation could develop an independent culture so long as its most important works were written in a foreign language. Accordingly, Genovesi and other scholars wrote in Italian and convincingly argued for the scholarly stature of Italian.

During the same period, "history also became a source of national pride," and Italians turned their emphasis from European to Italian history. Ancient Rome, whose language had dominated the cultural life of the peninsula but now hindered the view of Italians as one people, was deemphasized. In Modena, Ludovico Antonio Muratori investigated the Middle Ages as the source of modern Italy. He published majestic, accurate collections of medieval documents designed to demonstrate the continuity of Italian history through the ages. One historian believes that, because of this kind of activity, "a national feeling resulting from a recognition of a common cultural heritage, common historical traditions, common economic interests, and common language" made progress during the eighteenth century.

This view does not contradict the cosmopolitan essence of the Italian Enlightenment, but it suggests the multiple antecedents of the Risorgimento. Between 1700 and 1789, European influences found quick acceptance in Italy, despite the resistance of an older culture, and transformed the static situation of the previous century into a dynamic one. Historian Giorgio Candeloro believed that the political, social, economic, and cultural conditions that emerged during the period combined with the impetus of the French Revolution to create a necessary "preface" to the Risorgimento.

In short, the Italian and European cultural strains, and their complex interaction with Atlantic society and politics, must be understood to analyze the Italian Enlightenment on its own merits and to appreciate its implications.

CHAPTER TWO

Italy and the French Revolution

THE FRENCH REVOLUTION'S IMPACT ON ITALY HAS AROUSED FIERCE debate. Did the Risorgimento originate during the Enlightenment, the dawn of national awareness, or was it another nineteenth-century spin-off of the French Revolution? Historians have not reached a consensus on this question, but many believe that the social and political changes induced by the Revolution, and therefore its influence on the Risorgimento, would have been impossible without the Enlightenment.

GREETING REVOLUTION

The last chapter described how Enlightenment measures stimulated only the limited development of a modern bourgeoisie. The growth of groups profiting from inflationistic economic trends and antifeudalistic governmental action through the acquisition of land, the management of noble holdings, or rents—a "primitive" capitalism—increased tensions with the ruling classes and contributed to the impoverishment of many peasants. In addition, because of the Europe-wide price rise, real wages dropped and poverty increased dramatically. This social crisis coincided with the cultural and political crisis, the growth of radical ideas, and the new emphasis on cultural and linguistic unity.

Thus, the Italian situation had become critical by 1789, when the French Revolution exploded. Between then and 1795, the Revolution found popular support and a warm welcome from disillusioned Italian intellectuals. Disorders erupted in several states, as in Naples, where demonstrators wished "to do as the French are doing," or Piedmont, where crowds shouted, "Long live France!" The intellectuals had already gone beyond cultural considerations by advocating Italian political revival. Piedmontese playwright Vittorio Alfieri, who dedicated one of his works to "the American liberator," George Washington, symbolized this feeling.

Intellectuals published draft constitutions, favored French ideals, and transformed Masonic lodges into Jacobin organizations. The turmoil caused by the Revolution favored the intellectuals' activities by exacerbating the economic crisis: prices rose, trade difficulties increased, and the fiscal burden worsened as arms spending increased. Furthermore, the governments responded to French developments by truncating reform policies, allying with the Church, and repressing the opposition. Intellectuals and governments set upon a collision course, but Italians imbued with French revolutionary principles could make slight headway without outside help.

STATECRAFT IN A REVOLUTIONARY ERA

The wars of the French Revolution that began in 1792 ended the long peace between France and Austria, which once more fought for supremacy in Italy. One important difference, however, marked this struggle. Frightened by revolution, Italian monarchs did not negotiate for advantages but allied with Austria. Despite French attempts to secure Piedmontese support, this state quickly joined Austria in fighting France. In short, contrary to its policy in the seventeenth century, Piedmont threw away its strategic advantage and allowed itself to be exploited diplomatically by Austria. Naples and Tuscany preferred to remain neutral, but the British coerced them into war. French policy appeared torn between traditional diplomatic initiatives and revolutionary aims. While French agents attempted to convert Italian dissatisfaction into revolution, their government acted to exploit revolutionary fervor for expansionist ends.

The primary reason for this development was the course of the French Revolution itself. The Revolution's "moderate" phase ended in late 1792, and a radical period followed. The Jacobins seized control and held power until July–August 1794. When the French overhauled their form of government in 1795, they set up the Directory, a government that consisted of five directors chosen by two councils. These changes had important effects on Italy. The Directory pursued conservative domestic policies and exploited French revolutionary ideals to extend French influence abroad. This course created the premise for a fight with the Italians because they remained committed to Jacobinism after its defeat in France and resented French expansionism. In addition, France and the conservative European powers continued fighting during the years the Directory remained in power. These conflicts had important effects on Italy because the French first became dominant on the peninsula, then met defeat, and then returned for several years until their definitive downfall. A host of shifting territorial arrangements in Italy during the French revolutionary and Napoleonic periods reflected these events.

After war broke out in 1792, the French quickly occupied Savoy and Nice, but then the French army bogged down. In March 1796, however, Napoleon Bonaparte, who was from the formerly Genoese island of Corsica, became the French commander on the Italian front. On April 12, he unloosed a campaign that broke through enemy lines, defeated the Piedmontese, and chased the Austrians out of Italy. He came within seventy-five miles of Vienna before the Treaty of Campoformio was signed in 1797. With the Austrian defeat, Napoleon controlled the entire peninsula.

ITALIAN JACOBINISM

The French conquerors made a host of complex, constantly shifting territorial alterations in Italy. They established several republics governed by a directory (as was the case in France between 1795 and 1799) that included areas that were previously part of different states. This change provided many Italians with the important experience of living, working, and governing together.

In the North, Napoleon established the short-lived Cispadane Republic (consisting of the papal legations of Bologna and Ferrara and the Duchy of Modena) and the Transpadane Republic (which included the Duchies of Milan and Mantua), later merged into the Cisalpine Republic. By October 1797, the Cisalpine Republic was enlarged and included 3.5 million inhabitants who had formerly been the subjects of several states. The French reorganized Genoa into the Ligurian Republic and, in February 1798, incorporated the pope's domains into the Roman Republic. This last development provoked a Neapolitan attack, with Austrian and British support, resulting in a Bourbon defeat, the royal family's escape to Sicily, and the establishment of a Neapolitan Republic in January 1799.

Unlike France, the peninsula was pervaded by Jacobin influence during this period. Indeed, informed scholars from Giorgio Vaccarini to Stuart Woolf agree that the staunchly republican Italian Jacobins, or "patriots," posed the question of Italian revival in political and social terms, calling for unity, independence, and a republic. Giorgio Candeloro argued that a pan-Italian "Jacobin-patriotic" movement formed between 1789 and 1795 posed the Italian problem in political terms; he sees this development as the beginning of the Risorgimento.

The story of the French revolutionary impact in Italy, therefore, could not be linear because the French discouraged an Italian revolution for domestic and diplomatic reasons. Although heavily influenced by France, the republics of this era were characterized by significant intellectual independence, a degree of political autonomy, and a complex relationship with the French.

Even before the French conquest, for example, Piedmontese Jacobins conspired with Filippo Buonarroti. Buonarroti, a law graduate of the University of Pisa, a former official of the French Jacobin government, and a participant in Gracchus Babeuf's communistic "conspiracy of the equals" in 1796, would become the major European conspiratorial figure in the early nineteenth century. Buonarroti and his Italian friends planned a Piedmontese uprising that would gain popular support by attacking feudalism and instituting a republic as the first step in the liberation of Italy.

This plan failed because of the conspirators' arrests in Paris and Napoleon's rapid advance. The conspiracy had negative repercussions on France's Italian policy because it branded Italians as radical followers of Babeuf. Ironically, French officials concluded that they should not "republicanize" Italy because the Italian youth, "excited and carried away by ideas borrowed from our revolution, . . . want to stir things up, without knowing how, without calculating their resources, without any clear and balanced ideas about what sort of thing they want to set up." In the debate about Italy's future, in which the Jacobins demanded an independent and unified Italian republic, the Directory favored conservative currents and viewed the peninsula as an area to be exploited economically to pay for France's wars; indeed, after the initial pro-French euphoria, this attitude caused many Italians to turn against the French and support the counterrevolutionary movements of 1799.

Napoleon's political ambition also proved critical. His military successes gave him a great deal of independence from Paris, and he used it to gain support. This meant allowing the Italians some freedom to debate the crucial issues but not allowing these ideas to be translated into action. At the same time, Napoleon controlled the conquered areas, intervened in the republics' domestic affairs, and drew their boundaries to ensure continued Italian military dependence on France. Napoleon's decision to award the Venetian Republic to Austria despite the protests of Italian patriots was the most clamorous example of this policy.

Within the context of French revolutionary Italy, therefore, Italian Jacobin ideas had little chance of being realized; nevertheless, they had an important effect on the future. Although they differed on the process, composition, and political form a united Italy would assume, the Jacobins never wavered in their total commitment to a unified, independent Italian republic. They also believed that French revolutionary ideals would free Italy and regenerate Italian society, but they identified these ideals in the most radical phase of the French Revolution, which had ended in France. Italian Jacobins had absolute faith in education as a means of eliminating Church influence and inspiring egalitarian democracy, and they viewed the creation of a small, independent, peasant property-holding class as essential to the future of their country. But how were they to create such a class, and how could they eliminate poverty? Here debate raged, as it had in France. Jacobin Melchiorre Gioia advocated cutting up Church estates for distribution to the poor; others wanted the equal distribution of land, an imposition of a maximum income, or the abolition of property. All supported state intervention on behalf of the poor through public assistance.

Within this context, Italian Jacobins stirringly debated the meaning of "democracy," a term that frequently appeared in the titles of their newspapers. For them, democracy and republicanism were inseparable. More interesting, they agreed with moderate political philosopher Charles Louis Montesquieu and favored representative government over the precepts of Rousseau, the thinker who most influenced French Jacobins. Though Jacobinism has come to be identified with totalitarianism, some observers find the origins of the "making of Italian democracy" in this "Jacobin triennium."

But Italian Jacobinism ran into difficulty as early as 1797. Jacobins advocating the liberation and regeneration of Italy and humanity called for French evacuation of their country so that a revolution could proceed in a unified republic without foreign interference. Napoleon responded by repressing patriotic exponents and organizations. By 1798, leading Jacobins had flocked out of Lombardy, the radical center, admitting defeat by moving on to Rome and Naples.

The Early Republics

Practical developments in the various republics set up by the French reflected the badly divided Italian situation. The French government and, eventually, Napoleon lumped together as enemies the "reactionaries" who favored the old order and the "anarchistic" Jacobins arguing for radical change and Italian unity. Furthermore, the confusing rival claims of Italian cities and regions tried their patience, as did Italian attempts at independent policies designed to further patriotic aims. By now, the French were primarily interested in exacting payments from the Italians to help finance their wars, coercing the republics to raise their own armies for French ends, and taxing to pay for French forces stationed on Italian soil.

The French imposed moderate governments that would follow these policies. When the Cispadane Republic in the North proved unruly, Napoleon abolished it, reordered its territory, and established the Cisalpine Republic. The constitutions of this and the other republics reflected the French governmental setup: an executive consisting of five directors and a legislature composed of two houses elected by a restricted suffrage. Rigid administrative centralization was also imported from revolutionary France, and Napoleon personally named the highest officials. But he still faced fierce opposition from democrats influenced by French Jacobin ideals who demanded social justice measures such as price controls and progressive taxation.

In Milan, the heart of the Cisalpine Republic, the financial crisis caused by French exactions and Napoleon's hostility defeated advanced democratic demands, but a series of reforms paralleling those of the early French Revolution—the abolition of feudalism, tithes, and primogeniture; the confiscation of Church lands; the institution of civil matrimony; and the declaration of equality of men and women—were undertaken. As had happened in France, these measures generally favored the middle class and the peasants.

The more moderate southern Jacobins obtained fewer results. In Rome the Jacobins could operate primarily through their political clubs and newspapers, and in Naples the French quickly eliminated the more democratic leaders. Indeed, in Naples the failure to implement significant reforms beyond the abolition of primogeniture was disastrous for the Parthenopean Republic.

COUNTERREVOLUTION

Because France's overly powerful position disrupted the balance of power, the European war resumed in 1799. The allies of the "Second Coalition" aimed to reduce French dominance in Italy. At the same time, French exactions, the plundering of wealth and artworks, the identification of Italian Jacobins as pro-French traitors, and revolutionary anticlericalism inflamed the common people. In addition, the reception accorded to French reforms was not uniform; in many circles they provoked cultural conflict, resentment, and resistance. These elements produced an explosion, at the same time popular and reactionary, against the French invaders and their Italian supporters.

This development had its most important manifestation in Naples. Proclaimed on January 22, 1799, the Parthenopean Republic moved rapidly to give Naples an administration of the French type, but it acted on a law that abolished feudalism only on April 25, when the peasants had already risen against it. This procrastination proved to be the republic's undoing.

In January, Cardinal Fabrizio Ruffo had already organized the Armata cristiana e reale, also called the Army of the Holy Faith (Sanfedista), to retake Naples. He landed in Calabria, and by playing upon the peasants' blind faith, loyalty to the king, and hatred of taxes, he provoked a mass uprising against the republic. The peasants' extraordinary marching song proclaimed themes that motivated them:

> *To the sound of the beating drum*
> *Long live the little people;*
> *To the sound of tambourines*

the poor have risen.
To the sound of bells
long live the populace;
To the sound of violins
death to the Jacobins.
As for French revolutionary principles:
The French arrived
they taxed us;
Liberté . . . egalité
you rob me
I rob thee!

In April 1799, Austrian victories in Lombardy placed French forces in jeopardy, and they withdrew from Naples, leaving the Neapolitan Jacobins to fend for themselves. Ruffo marched north and took the capital after a heroic resistance. "Defenceless men, women, and children were butchered in hundreds by the laz- zaroni [lower classes]," wrote historian R. M. Johnston. After resisting valiantly, the patriots signed a capitulation that guaranteed their lives. In July, however, King Ferdinand IV, pushed by Admiral Horatio Nelson of England and Queen Maria Carolina, unilaterally declared the agreement null and void. In a move condemned in all Europe, the restored government slaughtered the flower of the Neapolitan intelligentsia with a ruthlessness remembered to the present day.

The Neapolitan counterrevolution, the most famous incident of its kind, raises interesting questions and had important implications. The most important question is, why did the revolutionary government fail to achieve popular sup- port? The answer seemingly lies in the failure to abolish the vestiges of feudalism quickly and the underestimation of the depth of popular feeling, but the skill with which Ruffo played upon peasant religious devotion and hatred of foreign- ers and high taxes was also important. According to the classic account of the counterrevolution by Vincenzo Cuoco, the intellectuals themselves concluded that the people were misled and that there existed "two peoples, divided by two different climates and two centuries of history." Also, "nowhere else has a mon- arch ever sentenced to prison, death, and exile prelates, gentlemen, generals, admirals, writers, scientists, poets, philosophers, jurists, and nobles—the intellec- tual and spiritual flower of the country." Revenge and a desire to decapitate future revolutions explain Ferdinand's action, but Nelson aimed to destroy French in- fluence and guarantee future British dominance over Naples and its strategic ports—in addition to impressing his mistress.

Finally, what were the implications of the institution of a republic in Naples and of its dramatic fall? During the Parthenopean Republic's brief life, culture flourished. In the *Monitore napoletano,* the major vehicle of intellectual discussion, Jacobins such as Eleonora De Fonseca Pimentel, one of the reaction's most illustrious victims, analyzed Neapolitan conditions and debated crucial reforms. The republicans also considered the fate of all Italy. In June 1799, in coordination with Italians from different parts of the peninsula, an appeal for the proclamation of a "single, indivisible, and independent Italian Republic" came to an unfriendly French Directory. Later declarations blamed its failure to endorse this goal as a reason for France's defeat in Italy.

Philosopher and historian Benedetto Croce stressed the importance of failed experiments with the nobility consecrated by tragic defeats as a prime motivating force in history. He argued that the massacre of the Neapolitan patriots had enduringly positive consequences for the peninsula. In the South, it "created a revolutionary tradition and education by example," and it forced the Neapolitan monarchy to rely upon the plebeian element, "transforming the Enlightened monarchy of Charles of Bourbon into the paupers' monarchy" that ended in 1860. It taught modern Italian liberals not to rely on the word of foreign governments. And, most important, it "planted the first seeds of Italian unity" by making Italians understand the need for a revolutionary movement based on the cooperation of the most "cultured" classes from all parts of Italy.

French-dominated northern Italy fell under a combined Austro-Russian assault in 1799, and elements similar to the Neapolitan counterrevolution could be discerned elsewhere, especially in Tuscany and Lombardy. Although some reforms of the early French Revolution were adopted, the Directory's Italian policy had failed. The French government's rapaciousness had alienated the people, and French hostility to the idea of Italian unification had diminished loyalty to France.

NAPOLEON IN ITALY

The Directory's domestic policies and its foreign failures produced the coup d'état of 18 Brumaire (November 9, 1799), which brought Napoleon Bonaparte to power in France. His Italian origins and his professed special interest in Italy hinted at support for its future unification. The French ruler had no intention of favoring independence, but his rhetoric reinforced the nationalist ideals of the French Revolution. In addition, by consolidating Italy into a few states, he brought together the former inhabitants of different political constituencies and provided them with the opportunity to work together. Along with French reforms, this development created a more efficient political class, one that was unattached to the old regimes and would play an important role in the early

PORTRAITS

ELEONORA DE FONSECA PIMENTEL
Poet and Martyr

—❧❧—

Born in Rome on January 13, 1852, of noble Portuguese parents, Eleonora De Fonseca Pimentel moved with her family to Naples at age ten. She received an excellent education, studying Latin and Greek, and corresponded with the most important French and Italian writers of the age.

In 1778, Pimentel married a Neapolitan army officer in what turned out to be a very unhappy union. In 1779, she lost a son aged only eight months. Shortly afterwards, she lost an unborn baby because of a severe beating at the hands of her husband. She managed to separate from him in 1786.

In 1792, she came under the influence of French revolutionary ideas advocating liberty and progress for the lower classes. On October 5, 1798, the police arrested her, but she was liberated following the flight of the king and his court to Sicily in 1798.

In January 1799, Neapolitan Jacobins formed a republic; they did so to the verses of a poem Pimentel had composed in prison, "L'inno alla libertà" (The Hymn to Liberty). Pimentel was the most visible leader of the Neapolitan Republic during its brief existence, founding, editing, and writing for the *Monitore napoletano*, the most important, influential, and historically significant newspaper in Italy.

During the counterrevolution led by Cardinal Fabrizio Ruffo, Pimentel was among the rebels who agreed to surrender in return for their freedom and whom Ruffo betrayed. The government sentenced her to die by hanging and rejected her appeal to be beheaded instead of hanged because she did not belong to the Neapolitan nobility. They also turned down her request to have her skirts tied together so they would not open when her body hung in the air. She faced death with dignity, asking for a coffee before she went to her execution, which took place on August 20, 1799, and saying in Latin: "Perhaps, one day, it will be useful to remember all of this."

For a whole day, the authorities left her body hanging in Piazza Mercato while the crowd intoned, "Lady Eleonora . . . now dances in the Market," and thanked the "Holy Pope" for helping them defeat the Jacobins. Eleonora De Fonseca Pimentel's body was buried in a nearby church that was later torn down. Her remains were moved but, despite the best efforts of historians, have never been found.

Risorgimento. The increased economic opportunities created by wider markets and the experience of fighting in the same army under the same flag explains how the idea of Italian unity made a qualitative leap forward during the Napoleonic period. In fact, creation of an Italian army, even if primarily used as an instrument of French expansionism, favored Italian nationalism by being directed against the Austrians.

Prudent historians, however, will consider the negative aspects as well. Despite the existence of native states that struggled to formulate independent policies, the peninsula remained a conquered land that had a subordinate place in Napoleon's schemes of empire. The need to subsidize French military costs and the "Continental System," which favored French industry, limited economic opportunities. And though armies may convey a feeling of national glory, the draft, the expenses, the casualties, and the recognition that Italian soldiers were fighting for foreign aims caused resentment.

After taking power, Napoleon addressed foreign affairs. He defeated Austria in the Battle of Marengo in northern Italy on June 14, 1800; further victories produced the Treaty of Lunéville with Austria (February 9, 1801), which recognized French dominance on the peninsula. Thereafter, until his fall, Napoleon retained control of Italy, except for the islands of Sicily and Sardinia, where the exiled kings of Naples and Piedmont remained under British protection.

Napoleon's territorial reorganization of the peninsula occurred in two phases, from 1800 to 1802 and from 1805 to 1809. Practical considerations concerning the empire as a whole, not continuity in Napoleon's thought or action toward Italians, dictated the changes. At first, Napoleon reestablished the old republics, then reorganized them into the Italian Republic and named himself president. As usual, the French-dominated states reflected French governmental organization and became kingdoms after Napoleon declared himself emperor in 1804. Increasing tension marked Napoleon's relationship with the pope. In 1803, Napoleon and the pope signed a concordat that regulated relations between France and the Church, but Napoleon quickly moved to take control of Church affairs. In 1804, Napoleon invited the pope to crown him emperor, but then crowned himself. In Italy, relations were strained by an intense cultural struggle between Pius VII and the emperor, leading to a famous quarrel between the two and to the pope's arrest. By 1809, Napoleonic Italy had taken its final form, with the Kingdom of Italy in the North, the Kingdom of Naples in the South, and large areas (including Piedmont and the city of Rome) ruled directly as parts of imperial France.

THE ITALIAN REPUBLIC AND THE KINGDOM OF ITALY

Following an abortive attempt at reviving the Cisalpine Republic, Napoleon created the Italian Republic in the North (1802). Once again, the republic's constitution paralleled the French Constitution imposed by Napoleon and reserved all power to him. Napoleon made himself president of the new republic, but chose as his vice president Francesco Melzi d'Eril, a prominent Milanese patrician of

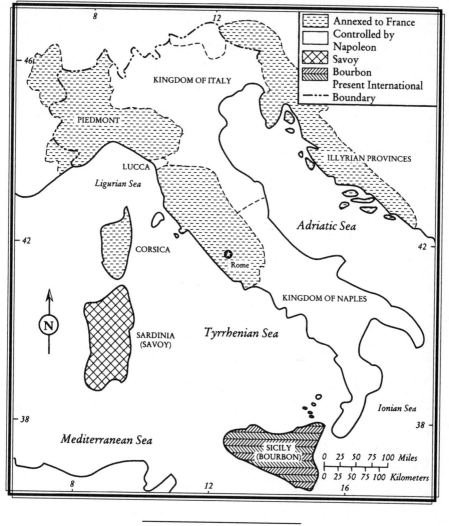

MAP 2.1   NAPOLEONIC ITALY, 1812

moderate liberal views who was deeply hostile to Jacobinism and strongly supported property rights and Italian independence. Napoleon delegated a fair amount of autonomy to Melzi, but disputes still occurred because of the vice president's support of Italian independence.

Melzi imposed French-inspired governmental institutions and laws and relied on the wealthy landowning class to make them function. Representative bodies modeled on Napoleonic France were instituted at the center, and a French-style administrative structure was established at the local level. Melzi considered an efficient state structure essential for eventual independence, but he did not favor the radicals and found it difficult to secure active involvement by the wealthy classes even though his economic policies favored them. He had some success in creating a political personnel, a new tax system, and an effective police force, but his suspicion of critics limited his effectiveness and facilitated Napoleon's intervention. Thus, although the Italians worked on comprehensive legislation, delays caused the French to impose their own law codes; this legislation, among the most advanced in Europe, created a definitive break with the old regime, but certain aspects, such as reintroduction of the death penalty, caused resentment.

Church policy also provoked disputes. Napoleon's imposition, in 1803, of the concordat that France had signed with the pope two years before violated Melzi's Enlightenment conception of church-state relations. The concordat gave the pope and cardinals more authority over the Church and increased prestige in the state. An irritated Melzi issued a decree restating the validity of earlier laws that, in the Jansenist tradition, had curbed the Church's power. In this manner, he attenuated the concordat's effect until Napoleon quarreled with the pope and set off another power struggle with the Church.

Melzi also had a different conception of the role that an Italian army would play. He and other Italians considered an independent army indispensable to the development of Italian national consciousness and independence—exactly what Napoleon feared. The French ruler favored a military force, but only as an instrument of imperial policy. Despite many difficulties—not the least of which was the lack of homogeneity and desertions—Melzi introduced a military conscription system, and a republican army took shape and became a focus of patriotic fervor.

Within its circumscribed sphere, Melzi's diplomacy challenged Napoleon. Perhaps as a step toward eventual unification, Melzi hoped to expand the republic's frontiers, especially in Venetia, and undertook talks to achieve that end. Napoleon disapproved of this activity and stopped it. In fact, Napoleon limited Melzi's options when he refused the Italian Republic permission to exchange diplomatic representatives with other states and obliged it to go through French diplomats; in addition, French involvement of the republic in wars without consultation further revealed the republic's dependent status.

In 1804, Napoleon proclaimed himself emperor. Even more than before, he enforced uniformity upon his client states, removing their leaders if they resisted his orders. He transformed the Italian Republic into the Kingdom of Italy and named as viceroy his stepson, Eugène Beauharnais, who was much more subservient than the independent Melzi. French institutions and policies were introduced with greater determination than previously, but Napoleon's subordination of the kingdom's interests to his own and the increasing pace of his wars created enormous cracks in the structure.

The landowners had profited from Melzi's policies, which had brought stability, allowed them to buy public lands cheaply, and liberated them from the incubus of Jacobinism. Furthermore, the price rise of agricultural goods had more than compensated them for tax increases and the loss of feudal privileges. The commercial and industrial bourgeoisie had benefited from the establishment of a large state free of customs barriers, the unification of weights and measures, the existence of a single currency, the expenditures of the Italian and French armies, and the building of new roads. The textile and silk industries boomed, and Italian products found markets in England, France, Germany, Austria, and Switzerland.

Napoleon's desire to subordinate the Kingdom of Italy economically to France and his attempt to ruin the British economy through the prohibition of trade with his enemy (the Continental System) eventually suffocated these promising economic developments. French economic policies favored the French landowners and bourgeoisie by blocking the exportation of Italian products to France, favoring the importation of French products, and disrupting old patterns of trade by annexing parts of Italy to France. The Continental System exacerbated the effects of this discrimination by closing Italy to trade with Britain and by subjecting it to a British blockade. As in other parts of the empire, the Continental System provoked economic disaster and turned property owners and merchants against Napoleon.

In addition to economic factors, French military policy also provoked opposition. The positive effects of an Italian army have already been noted, but the constant use of that force in all parts of Europe for the benefit of the French Empire and the great number of casualties made conscripts—most of whom were peasants—less eager to serve. In the later years of the kingdom, the increase in draft-dodging and desertions provided greater impetus to the banditry that afflicted the state.

Adding to this phenomenon was the unhappiness of the lower classes, whose lives had not substantially improved during the Napoleonic domination. Indeed, the conservative policies, both of the Italian Republic and of the Kingdom of Italy, that had strengthened the landowners had done little for the poor. Although there was a widespread revolt in 1809, the lower classes seem to have been characterized by an increasingly "passive awaiting of events which sooner or later would have decided the fortunes of Europe and of Italy."

This attitude had its counterpart even in the middle class and among noble moderates who had benefited by government jobs. Napoleon's desire to surround himself with technicians who would execute orders without elaborating independent programs prevented the formation of a reform party such as had existed in the eighteenth century, despite the existence of a large state that might have been the nucleus of a united Italy. As time went on, French policies deprived proponents of independence of all hope. Despite Napoleon's attempt to fire their enthusiasm through official organizations, they dropped out of politics.

These elements made the Napoleonic Kingdom of Italy a structure with little content, destined to disappear with its creator.

THE KINGDOM OF NAPLES

In southern Italy, the Bourbon monarchy restored by the *lazzaroni* in 1799 punished the nobility because some of its elements had supported the Parthenopean Republic but failed to deliver promised fiscal reforms or to break up feudal property. The monarchy's ambiguous foreign policy, which alienated the large powers, mirrored its failure to garner mass support. The precarious situation of Naples allowed Napoleon to declare Ferdinand IV deposed, and a French army occupied the capital in February 1806. The king and his court fled once again to Sicily, from where Ferdinand encouraged a repeat of the 1799 uprising. This effort presented a serious problem to the French because the attempt became embroiled with brigandage. Strong government forces put down the revolt, but brigandage remained an endemic problem.

Napoleon's brother Joseph became the first French king of Naples until he left to be king of Spain in May 1808. A French cavalry general and Napoleon's brother-in-law, Joachim Murat, replaced Joseph in July of the same year.

As had happened in northern Italy, both men introduced reforms of the French type. Indeed, these measures, many of which had been discussed during the Enlightenment but had not been adopted, affected southern Italy more than the Napoleonic regimes influenced the North. Because of the South's less advanced starting point, however, these reforms could not bring the region's social structure to the North's level in the years of French rule from 1806 to 1814. Indeed, although the Napoleonic reformers—French and Neapolitan—struggled to improve economic and social conditions, they opposed radical action to modernize southern society.

As usual, the new rulers applied Napoleonic legislation to Naples. They instituted law codes and rationalized and simplified the fiscal system, which gained a modern footing. They abolished feudalism, and many Church lands were confiscated and sold to the benefit of the bourgeoisie and other wealthy landowners. Although these developments improved the lot of the provincial bourgeoisie, they did not result in the modernization of southern agriculture. The southern peasant remained poor, and land hunger continued to be the region's major problem.

Despite these issues, the Napoleonic regimes in Naples seem to have aroused a greater energetic response than their northern counterparts. To consolidate themselves, the rulers sought compromises with leading Neapolitan exponents by bringing them into their governments in important positions. Under Napoleon's brother Joseph, the French element predominated and the king closely followed Napoleon's policies. Murat, however, gave predominance to the Neapolitans, achieved semi-autonomy from Napoleon, and worked toward independence. He balanced the budget, helped industry, spurred education, and, most important, developed a well-trained army out of which issued many future patriots. He also established communication with patriots hoping to unify Italy.

As a result, unlike in northern Italy, government functionaries formed in Napoleonic Naples did not "drop out" of politics. On the contrary, they became ever more active and even entered the numerous secret societies formed during the period in the hope of gaining a greater participation in government. Murat opposed the creation of an effective parliament, but his desire for greater Neapolitan autonomy and, later, his support of Italy's independence proved an important meeting ground. For all its weaknesses, during this period the Kingdom of Naples kept alive the hope for Italian unity and independence.

CHAPTER THREE

The First War
for Italian Unity

B y the time Napoleon invaded Russia in 1812, he faced passive or outright opposition throughout his empire. A guerrilla war raged in Spain, while in Italy widespread dislike of the Napoleonic order affected all regions and classes. The Continental System suffocated the middle class, which had initially been stimulated by Napoleon's economic and legislative reforms. Napoleon's desire to create loyal, apolitical functionaries and his aversion to persons with potential political programs alienated the rich bourgeoisie and nobility, the bedrock of his social stability policies; his fight with the Church culminated in the pope's arrest and alienated the clergy. The peasantry, damaged by a pro-landowner and high tax policy, was now further exasperated by conscription and the heavy casualties of the Napoleonic Wars.

Nevertheless, French reforms and Italian reaction to them helped significantly in extending the principles of unity and independence for the peninsula. Italy remained rural, the peasants uneducated, and most Italians lacked a national consciousness, but if the desire for unity had previously taken root among radicals and influential intellectuals, it now spread to at least part of the middle class and would soon take on a life of its own. By creating new states, no matter how dependent, the French raised Italian national consciousness. Although it would not be true to say that the desire for unification was widespread among Italians, by 1812 they understood that a larger trading area brought economic benefits and that France exploited a conquered Italy for its own purposes. For intellectuals at least, it would not be a large jump from there to a demand for unification.

The Growth of the Secret Societies

Since the Napoleonic police prevented open opposition, Italians formed secret societies. Originating in eighteenth-century Freemasonry, these societies had diverse political orientations, organizations, and rituals, but they became conspiratorial after 1794. This development first occurred in France among groups eager to restore either Jacobinism or the monarchy. In Italy, reactionary societies also existed, but the nationalistic-patriotic societies had particular importance because many active fighters for Italian unification would emerge from them. Especially active in the South during the Napoleonic period, they were the first widespread, influential groups advocating independence and a constitution.

Members of the Society of the Rays, dissolved in 1802, initiated these clandestine liberal groups in which, despite usually vague programs, republican, Buonarrotian, and French revolutionary ideas predominated. The largest such society was the Carboneria, or society of the charcoal burners (*carbonari*), most active in the South because of the prodigious activity of a French official who served both Joseph Bonaparte and Murat. Indeed, Murat and his government had contacts with the Carboneria during its early years; a break occurred only in 1813 to 1815, when—influenced by British agents who were whipping up feeling against the French—the carbonari demanded a liberal constitution that Murat refused to grant.

THE FAILURE OF THE "PURE ITALIANS"

By December 1812, the consequences of Napoleon's Russian defeat had become clear. Of the Kingdom of Italy's 27,000-man army, for example, only 1,000 survived. This disaster increased underlying anti-Napoleon feeling and contributed to a growing sentiment for independence. But many negative factors conspired against the realization of this hope.

In 1812, the British had forced the Bourbons to issue a constitution in Sicily, a move that bolstered the false claim that the reactionaries favored a constitution and independence. Furthermore, though the secret societies desired a constitution, they lacked a well-defined program and a coordinated organization. They operated in an atmosphere of war weariness and mistrust that, given their clandestine nature, they could not hope to overcome. Under these circumstances, the patriots first faced a problem that would recur throughout the Risorgimento: how to utilize a constituted state—and its bureaucracy, army, and diplomacy—for their goal of uniting Italy.

In the North, the patriotic movement was especially fragmented. The "pure Italians," led by Count Federico Confalonieri, had a particularly unrealistic program. With Napoleon tottering, they hoped to eliminate French influence, gain British support to prevent an Austrian restoration, and obtain the Kingdom of Italy's independence by accepting any king agreeable to the allies. When Napoleon abdicated, Eugène Beauharnais's supporters convoked the Senate, hoping to peti-

PORTRAITS

EUGÈNE DE BEAUHARNAIS
Step-relative

⋙∼⋘

Eugène de Beauharnais always hovered around monarchs, but never quite entered the club himself. Eugène was born in Paris on September 3, 1781, the son of a general and Josephine Tascher de la Pagerie. His father had served in the American Revolutionary War but was executed on June 23, 1794, by the French revolutionary government for failing to achieve his objectives. In March 1796, his widow married an as-yet-unknown Napoleon Bonaparte, arousing the resentment of Eugène and his sister Hortense (who later married Napoleon's brother Louis). Napoleon, however, treated him kindly, and Eugène helped him and his mother reconcile during difficult periods. Eugène helped Napoleon come to power in 1799.

In 1804, Napoleon formally declared France an empire, took the title King of Italy, and named Eugène his viceroy. In 1806, Napoleon formally adopted him. Although Eugène had no rights of succession in France, Napoleon slated him to become king if the emperor should die without a second son (the first would have inherited the French throne). Napoleon also gave him a generous annual stipend of 200,000 francs. In 1806, Eugène married the king of Bavaria's daughter, Princess Augusta Amelia.

Eugène ruled the Kingdom of Italy well and faithfully for his stepfather. He fought with Napoleon and steadily collected titles and estates.

With the defeat of Napoleon's regime in 1814, Eugène lost his Italian possessions, but the allies treated him well. They continued to address him as viceroy and made provisions for him outside France. He kept his Italian, German, and French estates and on November 14, 1817, received the titles of Duke of Leuchtenberg and Prince of Eichstatt. Eugène watched several of his descendants become sovereigns. His nephew, the son of his sister Hortense and Napoleon's brother Louis, ruled France as president from 1848 until 1852, and then as Emperor Napoleon III until 1870. Eugène's son Auguste married the queen of Portugal, two daughters married kings, and another son narrowly missed becoming king of Belgium in 1831.

Eugène himself, once so important for Italy, disappeared from the peninsula's history. He lived comfortably at his father-in-law's Bavarian court and died in Munich on February 21, 1824.

tion the allies to recognize him as sovereign of an independent kingdom, but the senators refused. Despite this setback, Eugène prepared to declare himself king, but provoked a mass revolt led by Confalonieri and his friends. Austria used this pretext to intervene. As the Austrians moved into Lombardy, a depressed Eugène handed the area over to them.

Since British officials had favored Lombard independence, Confalonieri appealed to Lord Castlereagh, in charge of foreign affairs, to support an independent and constitutional North Italian regime. Tied to an Austrian alliance, Castlereagh refused. His statement that the Lombards had nothing to fear from a "paternal Austrian government" provoked a defiant statement from Confalonieri announcing that Italians would never accept Austrian domination. On June 12, 1814, Austria officially annexed Lombardy, signaling the swift failure of the "pure Italians."

MURAT AND THE WAR FOR UNITY

Like Prince Eugène, Joachim Murat fought in Russia at Napoleon's side, but unlike Eugène, Murat criticized Napoleon and, despite some hesitation about turning against the emperor, was determined to save his Neapolitan throne. At the end of his ill-fated Russian expedition in December 1812, Napoleon left Murat in charge of his defeated army and went to raise a new force in France; anxious to take charge of his own kingdom during a delicate diplomatic moment, however, Murat suddenly relinquished this command to Eugène and returned to Naples.

Murat had been distancing himself from Napoleon for some time. Influenced by his Neapolitan councilors, King Joachim had resisted carrying out the emperor's orders when they adversely affected the Neapolitan people. Furthermore, Pietro Colletta, a contemporary observer, testified that these advisers had previously convinced Murat that he should adopt a policy favoring Italian independence and perhaps unity. Seeking to remain in Italy as an independent sovereign after Napoleon's defeat, Murat initiated negotiations with the Austrians and the British.

As talks dragged on, a faltering Napoleon remained powerful enough to pressure Murat to aid Eugène in northern Italy. In August 1813, Murat did so, but without his army and leaving his wife Caroline (Napoleon's sister) to continue negotiations with the allies. Following Napoleon's defeat at the Battle of Leipzig in November 1813, Murat returned to Naples; in December and January, he occupied Tuscany and large parts of the Papal State. Irritated by Murat's diplomatic and military actions but preoccupied by Napoleon's continued resistance, the allies finally reached agreement with Murat. Austria recognized him as King of Naples and promised territorial gains at the pope's expense; in turn, Murat renounced his claim to Sicily and promised to join the war against Napoleon by attacking Eugène. The British also concluded an armistice with the Neapolitan king.

Murat declared war on Eugène, but remained psychologically incapable of engaging his former friends on the battlefield; since he was not a major factor in the final defeat of the Napoleonic regime in Italy, he had little say in the peninsula's disposition. While he procrastinated, the Austrians and British defeated Eugène and brought the old Italian rulers back in their train. To avoid alienating the allies, Murat returned to the pope the occupied areas of the Papal State and, at this crucial point, found himself facing a serious revolt in his own realm.

Murat's foreign policy may be criticized as ambiguous or praised as realistic, but historians agree that he made a fundamental error in domestic policy: his apparent refusal to compromise on the demand by the carbonari for a constitution. Clearly, such a move would have caused problems with the Austrians, but Murat incorrectly calculated his action's potential within Italy. Indeed, despite his contacts with the Carboneria, he not only proved incapable of gaining its support but also alienated the burgeoning movement based upon the secret societies, leaving the field free to British and Bourbon agents who emphasized a constitution and freedom from the French. The result was widespread revolt, which Murat ruthlessly suppressed. Continuous revolts by the carbonari in October 1813, in March and April 1814, and in March 1815 enveloped several southern regions and gravely weakened Murat's negotiating and military positions vis-à-vis the British and Austrians. Murat promised a constitution too late; timely promulgation of an instrument the Neapolitans already possessed in draft form would have advanced the Italian cause immeasurably.

With the opening of the Congress of Vienna, at which the great powers discussed the shape of post-Napoleonic Europe, Murat's position deteriorated. The British distrusted him, and the Russians and the restored French Bourbons pressed to restore the Neapolitan Bourbons. The Austrians had recognized Murat, but only for strategic reasons that were no longer operative after Napoleon's defeat. In fact, the Austrian foreign minister and architect of Restoration Europe, Clemens von Metternich, also favored the return of the more pliable Ferdinand IV, but Metternich, because he sponsored the sanctity of contracts as the basis of a new European order, would not take unprovoked action against Murat. Murat, however, provided Metternich with the pretext for intervention after March 1815.

During that month, Napoleon escaped from exile in Elba and made a bid—the Hundred Days from March 20 to June 29, 1815—to become sovereign of France once more. Murat believed that Napoleon's return would tie down the great powers in northern Europe for a long time and that he could gain territorial concessions in return for Neapolitan neutrality. In fact, Murat communicated with Napoleon's followers before the emperor escaped, but his calculations turned out to be wrong on both counts.

Murat declared war on the Austrians and moved into the Papal State. In Rimini, he issued a famous proclamation promising a constitution and exhorting the Italians to join him in a war for independence and unity. This appeal failed because of war weariness, a lack of coordination with the patriotic movement, and Murat's poor track record on the constitutional question. A series of military defeats quickly followed. On May 12, 1815, too late, Murat finally issued a constitution. Less than a week later, he left for exile in Corsica. Metternich then restored the Bourbons.

In October 1815, Joachim Murat landed once more on Neapolitan soil, seeking to reconquer his "beautiful Kingdom." He was immediately captured and shot, but as a soldier, he asked permission to command the firing squad and died a hero's death: "Courage, good soldiers, shoot!" Fearing a popular reaction, the Neapolitan authorities suppressed news of the execution.

In the church where Murat was buried, townspeople heard the sounds of chains, observed the building suddenly illuminate itself, and heard King Joachim try to leave his tomb. Fear filled the village until a holy woman told the people that an angel had informed her that Saint George, whose church Murat had rebuilt, knew that the king would soon die and had called him to martyrdom to save his soul. "Knowing that they had been the instrument of salvation, the people calmed themselves."

Murat and the "Italian Question"

The historiographic debate regarding Murat's role in Italian history has followed the course of his ghost—at first it was agitated, and then it disappeared. This first war for Italian unity, however premature, deserves special mention as the first concrete step in a long process.

An attempt to secure as much independence as possible from Napoleon and a policy directed at bolstering the pride of his Italian subjects marked Murat's reign in Naples. These factors explain why Murat's actions went beyond the usual French administrative reforms of the period. King Joachim not only attempted to construct a modern state and to stimulate agriculture and industry but also zealously brought about important educational measures ranging from the elementary to the university level. He hoped to revive the kingdom's cultural pride by encouraging artistic endeavors, archaeological research, the study of ancient languages, and the rebuilding and beautification of cities. These measures demonstrated a genuine desire to restore the kingdom's ancient glory, a change that could subsequently serve as a springboard for political revival. In fact, the British reported that his actions made him very popular in all Italy.

Indeed, as a result of his policies, word spread in Murat's own domains and in Italy that he wished to unify Italy. By 1812, he had begun preparations for a war to be fought "under the French flag, but, who knows, perhaps under the Neapolitan flag." This attitude alienated the allies and Napoleon. Historian Angela Valente argued that the British were ready to leave him undisturbed in Naples had he not insisted on uniting Italy. She also discovered letters to Napoleon, written in 1813, in which Murat suggests that the emperor could save himself by heading a popular movement for Italian independence and unity: "It is the road to salvation and will ensure enduring glory to the great Napoleon." Murat's belief that the Italians would rise en masse should Napoleon proclaim a war for Italian unification peppers Neapolitan documents of the period and appears to be the origin of Murat's own war for Italian unity.

Why did Murat's appeal fail to raise the Italians? Among the reasons already mentioned, historians emphasize the early failure to promulgate a constitution. Valente suggested that Murat was much more concerned with this issue than previously believed. She discovered a draft of a Neapolitan constitution that Murat ordered drawn up in May 1814, along with evidence of the king's continuing interest in this subject. She wrote that only Murat's fear of a violent Austrian reaction at a time of delicate political negotiation prevented him from issuing the document and thus winning the support of the southern patriotic movement.

Would this support have made a difference? Historians think not. They emphasize the rural nature of Italian society at this time and the vague and sometimes contrasting hopes of the patriotic movement at this early stage. Crystallized in the secret societies, the patriots' desire for independence had become identified with their anti-French feelings, despite Murat. Their Jacobin origins were muted by conservative elements, and the mixture emerged as a vague constitutional feeling. Ironically, this state of affairs allowed the allies to exploit the patriotic movement for the purpose of restoring the old regimes and keeping Italy divided.

In 1815, the international and the Italian situations did not appear mature for Italian independence and unity, but the first war for both had been fought. This was a particularly important event in Italian history. Despite the very real divisions among Italians of different regions, dating from the fall of Rome in 1870 to the present, Neapolitan policy favoring unity and the kingdom's willingness to engage in a war on behalf of the peninsula's independence, especially at this early date, was remarkable. That this policy was initiated by a Frenchman and would have greatly strengthened his personal power is less remarkable, even though it helps explain the historiographical silence on the issue. After all, Italian unification would finally be accomplished by a dynasty of French origins more honed in the subtle ways of power than the dashing and impetuous French revolutionary cavalry general.

PART TWO

Restoration Italy

CHAPTER FOUR

A
"Geographical Expression"

HISTORY PROVIDES FEW EXAMPLES OF THE SINGLE-MINDED DETERMINATION
with which the victorious allies of the anti-French coalition applied their
policy after Napoleon's defeat. Metternich and other statesmen tried to restore
the political order as it had existed before the French Revolution insofar as it was
possible, but in the long run conservatives could not suppress the national and
constitutional aspirations unleashed in Europe by the French. In their attempts
to contain the effects of the economic, social, and legislative changes of the revolutionary era, the restored rulers met with little success. However, Austria proved
remarkably successful in keeping control of the areas in which it had established
its political domination—in Italy until 1860 and in Germany until 1866.

In Italy and the rest of Europe during the Restoration, the tension between an
evolving society and a repressive political order drove events. With the industrial
revolution's progress and the spread of liberalism, how quickly a particular society changed and to what extent governments endeavored to block the political
ramifications of that evolution became crucial variables determining the history
of different areas.

GENERAL PRINCIPLES

Even before the Final Act of the Congress of Vienna (June 9, 1815), Austria, England, Russia, and Prussia had established a twenty-year alliance against possible
renewed French aggression in the postrevolutionary era in the Treaty of Chau-
mont (March 9, 1814). The powers supplemented this pact with the Holy Alliance
(September 1815). Originally based on the vague mysticism of Russian Czar
Alexander I, this agreement became a prime instrument of antirevolutionary intervention under Metternich's influence. With Castlereagh's cooperation, the
great powers instituted the Concert of Europe, which called a series of congresses

47

in the 1820s and sanctioned the powers' intervention against revolts shaking the smaller states. This mechanism allowed the Austrians to crush Italian patriotic revolutions and to continue dominating Italy. The Restoration's antirevolutionary and balance-of-power policies found their major challenge on the Italian Peninsula. The conflict caused numerous revolutions throughout the nineteenth century and, in the unification process of 1859 to 1861, the European balance's first substantial modification after the Congress of Vienna.

As in the rest of Europe, the social, political, and administrative situation generated turmoil in the restored Italian states. Despite loyalty problems, the restored rulers retained the essence of French revolutionary reforms as well as the natives who had made up the Napoleonic bureaucracy because they could not dispense with the efficiency of either. But to ensure their power, the restored absolutistic regimes handed over control of the army and the administration to their noble allies. An alliance with the large landowners and the Church further bolstered the nobility's strong position. Although noble domination conflicted with the economic and political growth of the industrial and commercial bourgeoisie, immediately after the Napoleonic Wars overproduction and a price collapse temporarily weakened the bourgeoisie and favored the reactionary elements in European society. The years after 1818, however, saw an extraordinary acceleration in economic growth, which was stimulated by railway building; this economic development set the stage for a renewed political challenge to the reactionary ruling groups by a bourgeoisie harboring liberal and national aspirations.

Austrian Domination and Its Limits

Balance-of-power politics signified strengthening the victorious allies and the small countries ringing France. In Italy, this meant handing over Genoa to Piedmont, and Venice to Austria. These changes violated "legitimacy," one of the Congress of Vienna's vaunted watchwords, since both republics had a centuries-long history. The Congress's other precept, "compensation," strengthened Austria's control of the peninsula.

Venice went to Austria because the empire had given up the Austrian Netherlands, a strategic liability, to the Kingdom of Holland. The Venetian hinterland, now geographically linked to Austria, made the empire more powerful. In addition, the monarchs of three small Italian states were tied to the Austrian dynasty, and the papacy viewed Austria as its prime protector. The King of Naples had been restored by Austrian intervention against Murat, and a friendship treaty mandating an Austrian commander for the Neapolitan army and prohibiting a constitution bound the monarch to Austria. Finally, control of strategic cities in

Lombardy-Venetia, known as the "quadrilateral," completed the Austrian military domination of Italy.

Although Austria had practical control over Italian affairs, two elements limited its domination. With the restoration of a European balance after Napoleon's defeat, Piedmont regained not only its independence but also the great-power guarantee of its territorial integrity that it had enjoyed in the eighteenth century—whereby neither France nor Austria could reduce it to subservience. In the early nineteenth century, the Savoy dynasty followed a conservative, pro-Austrian policy, but its Italian aspirations remained active, and internal changes would later catapult Piedmont to the forefront of the unification movement.

In addition, the patriots could focus on one country as the enemy of Italian independence and unity. While the debate over the future shape of an Italian state waxed furious and lacerated the national movement, the patriots united to fight against the Austrian Empire.

Restoration Italy: Shape and Substance

With the exception of the disappearance of Venice and Genoa, the map of Restoration Italy superficially appeared similar to that of the eighteenth century. In the South, Austria had initially recognized Murat as the Neapolitan king and the Bourbons had to await Murat's defeat to be restored. The Papal State resumed its previous shape thanks to the diplomacy of Cardinal Ercole Consalvi.

In the North, the breakup of the Napoleonic Kingdom of Italy caused major disruptions. Its territory went to four states, and both political and economic frontiers were reestablished. Whereas during the Napoleonic period it had been possible to exchange goods freely, customs barriers now reappeared, a development that dealt a bitter blow to commerce. For a time, these restored barriers even hampered internal trade between Lombardy and Venetia, both Austrian possessions, and between the various regions of the Piedmontese state.

Despite economic handicaps, the Lombard economy boomed thanks to the continued development of new products and the engagement of the aristocracy in business enterprises. Lombardy also profited from the long peace after 1815, but the Austrians allowed the Lombards no autonomy and absorbed two-thirds of their economic surplus to offset the Austrian Empire's chronic deficits. This situation helps explain the intense hatred that the Lombards had for their rulers and the disorders that periodically shook the area.

In Piedmont, the government's cultural and political repression was one reason the Kingdom of Sardinia shared only minimally in the economic boom occurring to its east. While in the rest of Italy Enlightenment measures influenced by French revolutionary principles replaced Napoleonic legislation, the Savoys restored preexisting measures uncontaminated by modern ideas. They allowed the Jesuits to return (the order had been dissolved in the eighteenth century), and they discriminated against religious minorities. King Victor Emanuel I refused to wear clothes styled after the beginning of the French Revolution. Piedmontese Joseph De Maistre became the theoretician of the European reaction, and patriotic intellectuals such as Silvio Pellico were forced into exile. One result of the Piedmontese repression, however, was the growth of secret societies opposing the government.

The Papal State witnessed a struggle between moderates and reactionaries but eventually reverted to its old ways. Pius VII's government included a real statesman willing to judge French revolutionary legislation on its merits: Cardinal Consalvi. He refused to restore the personal privileges of the barons and, for the most part, recognized the sale of Church lands that had occurred during the French occupation, even though former owners were often partially indemnified for their losses. In considering papal-Austrian relations during this period, Alan Reinerman has made an interesting argument for Consalvi's cooperation with Metternich against the reactionary party, the Zelanti; in effect, Consalvi's moderate policy coincided with Metternich's views because Metternich was convinced that obscurantist policies would produce a "church-state conflict that was sure to weaken the conservative front and open the way for liberal gains." In the long run, however, neither collaboration with the Austrian leader nor European recognition of his statesmanlike qualities saved Consalvi after Pius VII's death. In 1823, Pope Leo XII was elected with Zelante backing against Metternich's opposition, and Consalvi's reforms were undone. Reinerman has described some of the measures that followed as "not merely reactionary but truly medieval."

In contrast to Piedmont and the Papal State, the Tuscan Restoration took the form of Ferdinand III's moderate conservatism: laws and the rule of men influenced by the Tuscan Enlightenment. Napoleonic legislation was repealed, but advanced Tuscan laws replaced it. On the whole, tolerance marked the Restoration in Florence, and only Vienna's intervention blocked the grand duke from issuing a constitution.

Surprisingly, Naples also returned to its Enlightenment tradition instead of practicing repression. No massacre of the 1799 type occurred, nor was it even contemplated, and Prince Canosa, the police minister, lost his position through resentment against his persecution of carbonari, Muratists, and Freemasons. The king's principal adviser, finance minister Luigi de' Medici, encouraged cooperation between Bourbon loyalists and Muratists. A concordat with the Church was not as harsh as early negotiations had indicated it would be. French legislation and reforms remained practically intact, and feudalism was not reestablished.

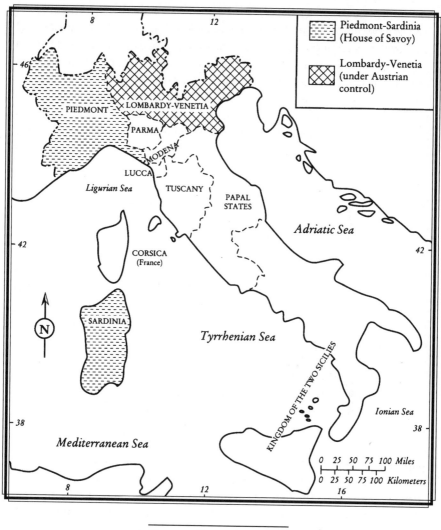

MAP 4.1   RESTORATION ITALY

Indeed, with the administrative absorption of Sicily by Naples, creating the Kingdom of the Two Sicilies (Ferdinand IV now became Ferdinand I), the Bourbon government extended French reforms to the island.

Combined European and Italian elements thus characterized the Restoration. Depending on the area, renewed territorial division, intensified Austrian domination, and the return of embittered or resigned dynasties created either an oppressive or a languid atmosphere. The nobility, reinforced by large landowners and the new rich of the Napoleonic era, kept the struggling commercial and industrial bourgeoisie in a subordinate position, while the Church increased its economic power and its influence over education and culture. But though Italy lagged behind France and Belgium, the development of productive forces in agriculture, industry, and commerce—aided by the survival of French Revolution–inspired reforms and institutions—could not be halted. This economic activity would make a powerful contribution to the alteration of the Restoration's political and social structure.

Restoration Culture

A constant struggle of intellectual tendencies—none of which achieved dominance—cultural resistance, and the slow but steady breakdown of old currents of thought marked the culture of the Italian Restoration.

As in the rest of Europe, romanticism emerged in Italy during this period. The most important review advocating romantic ideas was the Milanese *Il Conciliatore*, and Ugo Foscolo, a poet best known for his masterpieces *Dei Sepolcri* and *Le ultime lettere di Jacopo Ortis*, made artistic activity an important component of national identity. In Florence, the *Antologia*, edited by Gian Pietro Vieusseux, was more oriented toward the social sciences and accepted contributions from all schools, although romanticism eventually set the tone for the magazine. Politically, the moderate liberals who ran the review hoped to link up with reform elements in the Tuscan government and to do battle with the official culture of Restoration Italy. For this reason, the emphasis on historical studies never produced a reactionary or conservative outlook in the country's romantic movement, as it did in France and Germany. Indeed, attracted by French historian Victor Cousin's concept of conciliating order and liberty, and emphasizing gradual but progressive reform against Jacobin radicalism, Italian thinkers stressed a moderate monarchical liberalism that would become the Risorgimento's winning card.

The most important thinker of this moderate liberal current, Gian Domenico Romagnosi, evolved a program for a national monarchy in which the royal prerogative would be counterbalanced by the nation. Cesare Balbo, a young man destined for an important role in the Risorgimento, also implied that constitutional liberty derived from the restoration of ancient liberties and institutions, not from the votes of constituent assemblies. Important currents of political thought that had long-term effects appeared during the Italian Restoration, as they did during the Restoration monarchy in France.

A similar development occurred in the religious thought of the Restoration. Catholicism's hostility to the legacies of the Enlightenment and the French Revolution contributed to the repressive atmosphere, but some religious thinkers dreamed of reconciling liberty and authority. The most authoritative figure here was Antonio Rosmini, a priest who struggled with the "Christian" concern of protecting the human person against the "despotism" of modern society, which he considered more efficient than that of the old regime. Primarily concerned with social equilibrium and social justice, Rosmini would produce a draft for a papal constitution in 1848. In short, the Restoration was the seedbed of liberal Catholicism, a movement that made a major contribution to the Risorgimento, and historian Giorgio Spini has stressed the influence of Italian Protestants, whose concept of life as a duty and history as a mission spurred Italians to view national problems in "religious" terms.

A straight line connects liberal Catholicism with the most successful writer of the period, Alessandro Manzoni, a consummate practitioner of the historical novel so popular during this period. Beginning as an anticlerical, and not officially a romantic, Manzoni was attracted to Catholicism as a moral imperative.

Manzoni's masterpiece, *The Betrothed*, tells the tale of Renzo and Lucia, lovers caught up in the political and social vicissitudes of Spanish-dominated seventeenth-century Milan. Here "we have a fusion of themes—the political or patriotic conscience mingles with the Catholic conscience." Contemporaries easily associated the Spaniards with the repressive Austrians, but the novel explores two other levels important for Italian history. Manzoni recounts the history of an age through the eyes of the victims of grand politics and explains what individuals armed with little but faith in God must do to survive. The novel has been seen as the history of the Italian people: oppressed but able to retain their dignity and vitality.

The other reason for the novel's importance is Manzoni's conscious and successful development of an Italian language that could serve as "a means of communication for all sorts of concepts for all the Italians." Historian Giuliano Procacci emphasized that when writers of the period wished to paint a true picture of popular characters, they had to use their local dialects, but Manzoni created a vibrant Italian language that could be understood by all—not just intellectuals—without being dialectical or provincial. And according to literary critic Christopher Cairns, Manzoni consolidated "linguistic theories about the Italian language in art, the modern analogue, in this sense, of the *Divine Comedy*." Manzoni's work, which was begun in eighteenth-century Naples (and was discussed in Chapter 1), capped the process of trying to elevate the Italian language to a scholarly level. Besides its historical significance, *The Betrothed* survives as a literary masterpiece that has become an integral part of every cultured Italian's heritage.

PORTRAITS

GIACOMO LEOPARDI
Escape

Giacomo Leopardi, Italy's world-class romantic poet, led a life from which he constantly tried to escape, but he could take flight only in poetry.

Born in Recanati, a backwater town in the Marche (Papal States), on June 29, 1798, Leopardi was unlucky from the beginning because of his parents and his ill health. His mother's frugality reached legendary proportions, and his father tried to spend the family fortune; luckily, his prize possession benefited his son: a vast library consisting of 20,000 books. Otherwise, his father was a reactionary who loathed liberals and tried to force his son to become a priest.

Instead of playing as a child, Giacomo Leopardi buried himself in books. By age fifteen, he had learned Greek, Latin, Hebrew, and several modern languages. He studied philosophy, history, and the natural sciences; translated classical texts; wrote on astronomy; and wrote a poem in ancient Greek. He wrote several tragedies and works that exhibited his strong liberal politics. He began his *Zibaldone*, a sort of diary of his thoughts on literature and philosophy that eventually numbered 4,500 pages. At age eighteen, Leopardi turned to writing the poetry that would make him famous. Throughout his life, he sought to escape from his family and Recanati. His family would not let him go out on his own until age twenty, and

he tried and failed to run away. He finally left his hometown thanks to his poetry.

During his brief, unhappy life, he fell in love continuously, but the affairs were poetic, not physical. Because he was unattractive and in poor health, women never returned his love. Leopardi had very poor eyesight, suffered from scoliosis, was misshapen, had asthma, and lived in constant pain. He sardonically described himself as a "walking tomb." In 1818, he published *All'Italia* and *Sopra il monumento di Dante*, which established his literary reputation and his patriotic credentials, but it is the passion of his love poems that makes him a universally recognized romantic poet of the first order, in a class with Byron, Keats, and Shelley.

Leopardi's growing fame, literary production, and collaboration with important publishers allowed him to leave Recanati in 1825. He traveled to Milan, Florence, Bologna, and Pisa, falling in love and writing. In 1833, Leopardi settled in Naples with a friend and became infatuated with a married woman. The police confiscated some of his poetry, but he continued to write as his health deteriorated. A fatal attack of asthma killed him on June 14, 1837. Originally buried in the Church of San Vitale in Naples, Giacomo Leopardi was moved in 1839 to a tomb called that of the Roman poet Virgil in the Margellina section of Naples.

A world-class poet also worked in Restoration Italy: Giacomo Leopardi, the hunchback son of a virulent reactionary, fit the European mold of a melancholy and suicidal romantic. It is hardly surprising that Leopardi, who lived under terrible personal circumstances, differed from many other romantics in considering nature a hostile force that had to be dominated by humanity. Leopardi recalled Italy's past glory, lamented the country's fate, and denounced the Austrians and the French. His overtly patriotic poems are not his best work, but these themes are reflected in all his poetry; they "provide a consummation, in a sense, of the ideas of that generation of writers which launched the Italians on the idealist path toward the *Risorgimento*."

Other Italian novelists, poets, and playwrights of the period could not match the towering literary stature of either Manzoni or Leopardi, but they infused with national feeling the models they adopted from the Italian Renaissance, German romanticism, and English literature. Influencing the content of these writings were the memoirs of Italians who had fought with Napoleon. Unwilling to rest on their laurels, these memorialists emphasized the distinction and honor with which Italians had fought in the most arduous Napoleonic campaigns; they aimed to redress Italy's modest military tradition in recent times and suggested that Italians could redeem themselves on the battlefield. Throughout the Restoration and the Risorgimento, this military theme dominated a steady stream of literary works dealing with the foreign invasions to which the peninsula had been subjected over the centuries. The most famous included Giovanni Battista Niccolini's *Giovanni da Procida* (1817) and *Arnaldo da Brescia* (1837); Tommaso Grossi's *I Lombardi alla prima crociata* (1826), transformed into a popular and patriotic opera by Giuseppe Verdi in 1843; Massimo d'Azeglio's *Ettore Fieramosca* (1833) and *Niccolò de' Lapi* (1841); Giovanni Berchet's *Fantasie* (1829); and Domenico Guerrazzi's *L'assedio di Firenze* (1836).

Besides literature, opera became a patriotic weapon that had to be disguised to elude the period's heavy censorship. Gioacchino Rossini's *William Tell* (1829), a story of heroic resistance against oppression, clearly alluded to the Italian political situation. A haunting aria in Vincenzo Bellini's *I Puritani* (1835) describes the hardship of the exile, a common figure who emerged from the many Italian revolutions of the age; in this opera, a stirring duet concludes: "It is beautiful to confront death while shouting: Liberty!" The musical heir of these composers, Verdi, included choruses in his operas during the Risorgimento—such as "Va, pensiero" in *Nabucco*—that were easily susceptible to patriotic interpretation. The letters of his name separated by periods (*Long Live* V.E.R.D.I.) stood in Italian for "Victor Emanuel King of Italy."

Although the Restoration was not a particularly brilliant period for the plastic arts, it did produce a world-class sculptor in Antonio Canova. His most significant work related to a patriotic theme, *Tomb to Vittorio Alfieri* (1810), and dates from shortly before Napoleon's fall. It shows a crowned "Italia" that some consider the first iconographical treatment of "Italy," pointedly made during the French occupation. Writer and Risorgimento hero Massimo d'Azeglio, in addition to the work previously mentioned, painted romantic landscapes, some of which have been interpreted as antiforeign.

And so Art became enlisted in the struggle for independence.

CHAPTER FIVE

Failed Revolutions:
The 1820s and 1830s

A LTHOUGH GOVERNMENTS IN SOME ITALIAN STATES PURSUED MODERATE
policies after 1815, all ignored vital changes in the political mentality and the
social and economic conditions that had occurred during the French revolutionary and Napoleonic periods. Continued fear of losing their power made the
rulers partners of a reactionary Austria. The revolutionary principles that dominated nineteenth-century Europe continued in the form of nationalism and liberalism. Both concepts posed a mortal threat for the Austrian Empire because
nationalism implied independence for all nationalities and liberalism advocated
constitutional limitations on the sovereign's power.

Italy represented a major threat to Austria because the desire for independence
and unity that the French Revolution had stimulated among "Jacobin-Patriotic" intellectuals from different parts of the Italian Peninsula had spread beyond radical
circles. Italian liberals and radicals of the 1820s and 1830s set off a series of revolutions and looked to France for help. The disorders failed, but they produced some
important lessons. First, the ideological underpinning of unity had to become less
vague, and it had to give a picture of the future Italy to create favorable Italian and
European pressure essential to Italian liberty. The debate on this issue produced
three major "models," which are discussed in the next chapter. Second, the failures of
the 1820s and 1830s—along with the events of 1848–1849—demonstrated to Italian
patriots that the European revolutionary movement would not or could not come to
their aid. Half a century of disappointment would drive most Italian revolutionaries
to unify their country by seizing the realistic options that opened to them in the
1850s. The revolutions of the 1820s and 1830s were important stages in this evolution.

THE NEAPOLITAN REVOLUTION

In 1820, a military revolution against King Ferdinand VII of Spain proclaimed the
Spanish Constitution of 1812, which became a model for Italian liberals of this

period. This constitution presented an overwhelming problem for the rulers of the period, however, even if they had been inclined to accept constitutions: it greatly weakened the monarch's power. Thus, even when a ruler declared his acceptance under revolutionary pressure, it was understood that he could never sanction a document that turned him into a virtual figurehead. Ferdinand VII was typical in biding his time until French troops could rescue him in 1823.

The Spanish Revolution had profound effects in Italy, especially in the Kingdom of the Two Sicilies. In July 1820, Luigi Minichini, a carbonaro priest, touched off a revolution based on the Spanish model. At first the revolution secured the support of Guglielmo Pepe, a general in the Neapolitan army who had previously served Murat. Bourbon efforts to stop the revolt failed because the carbonari had infected the army. Furthermore, the king had retained many officials who had held office under Murat because the kingdom needed their experience. Called "Muratists" because they favored a policy of moderate reform such as had been pursued by King Joachim, they were no carbonari. But Muratist leaders ultimately proved unreliable because they disliked the government's subservience to Austria, its hostility to constitutions, and its reduction of the public works budget.

Unlike the Muratists, the carbonari were confused and divided, but they strongly exhibited Jacobin tendencies. Many members of the secret society yearned for a constitution, and the most progressive leaders strongly favored independence and unity for all Italy. Moreover, there were regular contacts between the Neapolitan carbonari and members of the same and other sects in the Papal State and northern Italy, and their vague constitutional stirrings had solidified into a specific demand for the Spanish Constitution of 1812. Beyond this desire, it would be an error to attribute much social, political, or organizational cohesion to the Carboneria, but its spectacular growth after the withdrawal of Austrian troops in 1817 and the constant, if ineffectual, planning for insurrectional activity demonstrated dissatisfaction with the restored regime. In the South, carbonari lodges have been seen as the successors of eighteenth-century Freemasonry, previously discussed; like Freemasonry, the Carboneria society was strong primarily in the provinces and attracted small businessmen, small property owners, minor officials, and members of the local militias. Estimates of membership in the lodges have varied from 300,000 to 1 million. Although these estimates are certainly exaggerated (after all, the nature of secret societies is to be secretive), they do indicate that the carbonari achieved a significant measure of popular support.

Muratist complicity made the Carboneria formidable beyond its inherent strength because the involvement of the Muratists gave an impression of coherence and consistency that the society lacked. But the strongly democratic carbonari tendencies made the Muratists uncomfortable, and they also disapproved of the Spanish Constitution as too radical. Consequently, they kept tabs on the carbonari, refused to join the society, and hoped to exploit the carbonari for their own purposes.

This scheme failed because the carbonari seized the initiative and forced the more prestigious Muratist leaders to follow. The rebels marched on the capital, and on July 13, 1820, Neapolitan King Ferdinand I swore allegiance to the Spanish Constitution with the same enthusiasm as his Spanish namesake. When a Muratist-dominated government took power amid popular rejoicing, the Neapolitan Revolution seemed to have succeeded and to have achieved genuine popularity.

The speed of the changes pointed to widespread support for a constitutional regime, but within nine months the revolution had been ignominiously defeated. Victory revealed the intrinsic weaknesses of the constitution, the carbonari, and the Muratists. The carbonari followed up their initial success with democratic measures, including tax reductions and partial decentralization, but Muratists used their influence in the bureaucracy and the army to oppose rapid change. In the newly elected Parliament, democratic carbonari-backed deputies maintained an uneasy equilibrium with the Muratist-landowner majority by resorting to popular pressure.

These divisions and the opposition of the great powers sealed the revolution's fate. Because constitutions weakened the royal power holding together the Austrian Empire, Metternich opposed them—and he particularly objected to Neapolitan developments for the example they would set in North Italy. A secret treaty with the Bourbons gave Austria the right to intervene if Naples granted a constitution, but the 1820 events had caught the Austrian statesman by surprise and he was short of troops on the peninsula. Moreover, he faced competition from France and Russia, both interested in reducing Austrian dominance in Italy. However, Metternich had an advantage: his rivals adamantly opposed the Spanish Constitution as well.

In attempting to take advantage of the diplomatic situation and forestall Austrian intervention, Muratist leaders assured the great powers that they had no intention of "exporting" the revolution. Understanding the danger posed to the revolution by the Spanish Constitution, the Muratists also tried to modify that document, but the carbonari would not allow the sacred instrument to be touched. The inability to alter the Spanish Constitution ensured Ferdinand's continued hostility, despite his public acceptance of the revolution, and enhanced Metternich's capacity to exploit the issue. Furthermore, as proof that they did not wish to spread disorder abroad, the Muratists refused to transform the revolution into a campaign for national unity. This decision proved a major blunder: Metternich intended to crush the revolution once he had cleared away the diplomatic obstacles. Given the circumstances, the revolutionaries had few chances of succeeding, but linking the Neapolitan Revolution to national unity might have mobilized the peninsula into action at a time when Austria was momentarily weak. This course might have furthered the cause of unity and, even if it had failed, would have strengthened the southern image in the future unified Italy. Patriots in Piedmont and Lombardy were sympathetic to unification and stood ready to act. The course of the Neapolitan Revolution demonstrated that without the guiding principle of national unity, Italian revolutions of this period could only be dead ends.

Sicilian events bolster this conclusion. Unhappiness with the loss of autonomy (1816), economic crisis, reforms, hatred of Neapolitans, and the demand for the Sicilian Constitution of 1812—as opposed to the Spanish Constitution—stimulated a revolt against the Neapolitan Revolution, fierce fighting among different Sicilian factions, and Neapolitan military intervention. Conversely, the conviction of many Sicilians that only by becoming part of a wider *Italian* movement could Sicily attain autonomy from the Neapolitans represented a step forward for the patriots.

Sicilian developments supplied Metternich with a strong argument for intervention. After smoothing out the diplomatic kinks (Congress of Troppau, October 1820, and Congress of Laibach, January 1821), and once King Ferdinand managed to leave Naples, Metternich moved his troops into the kingdom and easily suffocated the revolution in March 1821.

THE PIEDMONTESE REVOLT

In northern Italy, Neapolitan events encouraged a conspiracy in late 1820 that had strong national overtones. Rumors of an imminent invasion of Naples encouraged a concerted plan for an uprising against Austrian domination of the peninsula in the Kingdom of Sardinia and Austrian-controlled Lombardy-Venetia. Despite the different problems of North and South and the divisions among the revolutionaries, the events of 1820–1821 illustrate the strict interdependence of Italy's most diverse regions and the capacity of Italians to initiate their own revolutionary activity.

The Restoration's harshness in the North stimulated opposition among the middle classes and the aristocracy, and the carbonari remained active in the region. In Piedmont, Victor Emanuel I recognized the failure of his reactionary policy and briefly flirted with reform before ending the attempt out of fear of the Neapolitan and Spanish revolutions. When widespread dissatisfaction spread among liberal aristocrats—including the influential Massimo d'Azeglio and Cesare Balbo—many converted to an alliance with middle-class carbonari who advocated adopting the Spanish Constitution. As in Naples, this demand and the inability of liberal aristocrats to moderate the stance of their radical allies would prove fatal.

In Piedmont, the conspirators hoped to enlist the House of Savoy in their activities by appealing to its dynastic ambitions. As the Austrian army prepared to move against Naples from Lombardy-Venetia, conspirators hoped to coordinate simultaneous revolts in Piedmont and Lombardy-Venetia, declare a constitution, drive Austria out of Italy, and establish a strong northern Italian kingdom under the Savoy monarchy. The aggrandizement of Piedmont, they reckoned, would ensure Victor Emanuel's collaboration and induce him to swallow a constitution. As insurance, the conspirators also negotiated with Charles Albert, heir to the throne after Victor Emanuel's reactionary brother Charles Felix.

This plan found ardent supporters in Lombardy-Venetia who chafed under Austrian repression and who believed they needed a regular army such as the Piedmontese could provide to drive out their oppressors. Emperor Francis ruled his Italian kingdom with an iron fist: German reigned as the official language; Austrians and Slavs ran the civil service and officered Italian military units, raised by conscription; severe restrictions discriminated against Italian products if they competed with Austrian goods, and other regulations practically prohibited Italians from traveling; modern history was a forbidden subject at the university; only the official newspaper could appear as a daily; censors examined cultural reviews before they were printed or brought into the country; and the government banned many authors.

These conditions bred conspiracies among the aristocracy, the middle class, professionals, and businessmen. The Austrians responded with legislation that forbade secret societies, instituted the death penalty for taking part in revolutions, and mandated hard labor for life for failing to prevent revolution or for neglecting to denounce persons engaging in revolutionary activities. These measures permitted the police to arrest persons suspected to be members of secret societies and to extort information. By 1820, just as Piedmontese and Lombard liberals planned their revolt, mass arrests and trials had become the norm, making it difficult for conspiracies to succeed. In October, the Austrian police arrested two important leaders, Count Federico Confalonieri and Silvio Pellico. The two men had founded *Il Conciliatore*, a literary review that mixed romanticism with patriotic ideals in a necessarily subtle manner; this approach, however, did not prevent their becoming police targets. Such methods wiped out the Lombard part of the conspiracy, but not the greater opposition. Sentenced to fifteen years of hard labor, Pellico published *My Prisons* in 1832, a classic account of his incarceration at the Spielberg prison; Confalonieri had his death sentence commuted to life at hard labor. Pellico's book and Confalonieri's dramatic story as told by his wife inspired the Risorgimento generation to struggle against Austrian domination.

Despite the arrest of their Lombard coconspirators, the Piedmontese rebels pushed ahead with their plans. On March 9–10, 1821, Alessandria, the kingdom's chief fortress and a city known for its democratic tendencies, rebelled; the rebels proclaimed the Spanish Constitution and support for Italian unity and independence. At this point, Victor Emanuel caused the conspirators' plan to go awry when he suddenly abdicated. Charles Albert became regent because the new king, Charles Felix, was out of the country. As already mentioned, the conspirators had been in contact with Charles Albert and claimed they had his support (whether this was true has been debated ever since), but the regent subsequently proved to be an unreliable ally. As rebellion spread throughout the kingdom, Charles Albert succumbed to pressure and officially proclaimed the Spanish Constitution, but his tortuous reasoning and halting justification revealed his fear of Charles Felix—who turned against him anyway—and his willingness to submit to the new king's orders. When Charles Felix ordered Charles Albert to retire to a loyal fortress, he meekly complied instead of leading the revolution as the rebels had hoped. Charles Felix promptly requested the Austrians to intervene, and they crushed the Piedmontese revolt in April 1821.

Historians rightly emphasize the contradictions that doomed the Piedmontese Revolution. However, the episode marked the entrance into the fray of a moderate party that wished to achieve Italian unity and independence in conjunction with the Savoy dynasty. Although radical democrats dominated the unification movement for the next twenty years, the failed revolutions of 1820–1821 converted many moderate liberals to the cause. The native rulers had proved powerless before an overwhelming desire for change, but Austria had demonstrated its hostility toward constitutions and its ability to maintain domination by military means. Italian moderates who wished to apply the principles of French and British liberalism to Italy now recognized the need for independence from Austria as a prerequisite for Italian constitutional development. This realization proved decisive in the long struggle for unification.

CONTINUOUS REVOLUTION

Events following the agitation of 1820–1821 confirmed the existence of two "parties" favoring Italian unification—democratic-republican and moderate-liberal-monarchical. The Austrian crackdown and the intense Italian reaction of the 1820s and 1830s produced not only radical-democratic but also moderate exiles such as Santorre di Santarosa, who was implicated in the Piedmontese events. Influenced by French liberals such as Victor Cousin, the moderates preferred a constitution similar to the French Charter of 1814 rather than the Spanish Constitution of 1812,

PORTRAITS

SILVIO PELLICO
Gentle Revolutionary

❧❧

Silvio Pellico, a gentle, highly religious person, did more to damage Austria's cause in Italy than any battle. He did it by means of a slim book in which he described his suffering and his faith.

Pellico, the son of a government employee, was born in Saluzzo, a city about twenty miles from the Piedmontese capital of Turin, on June 24, 1788. A precocious child, he composed a play at age ten and performed it with his friends in his home. His family moved to Milan, where Silvio received a position teaching in a school for the orphaned children of soldiers. He entered into contact with the most famous Italian and European romantic writers of the period. In 1815, he wrote a successful play, *Francesca da Rimini*, which is his second most important work.

In Italy, the Restoration was an era of political and literary ferment in which Italians contested Austrian domination of their country, and Pellico did not escape his times. He took a job in the home of Count Luigi Porro Lambertenghi tutoring his children. Porro, a leading opponent of the Austrians, was among the founders of *Il Conciliatore*. Pellico threw himself into the editing of this review and attracted the suspicion of the police. He also became involved with the carbonari, members of a secret society that plotted against the Austrians. In 1820, the police arrested Pellico. On February 24, 1822, the Austrians sentenced him to death, but commuted his sentence. Pellico was transferred from a Venetian prison to serve fifteen years of hard labor at the harshest Hapsburg jail, the Spielberg in Moravia.

Pellico served his time with resignation; he was bolstered by his strong Catholic faith and aided by a priest who ministered to his spiritual needs. In 1830, with seven years left on his sentence, the Austrians released him.

In 1832, there appeared *Le Mie Prigioni* (My Prisons), a description of Pellico's life in the various jails he had passed through. He wrote about his experiences in a simple, clear manner and without displaying venom toward his jailers. Pellico described his daily life in a matter-of-fact, even gentle, way; in one episode, he described how he had trained a spider to eat out of his hand. Rather than display bitterness, this brief book exhibits the feelings of a pious Catholic who accepts his fate as the will of God. His extraordinary memoir revealed Pellico as one of the finest Italian writers of the period. More important from the standpoint of Italian history, it laid bare the tyranny of the Austrian regime for all to see and greatly contributed to turning Italian and international opinion against that regime.

Probably because he had been broken by his prison experiences, Pellico did not participate in politics after the publication of his book. He lived quietly, working as a librarian for a noble family in Turin. Silvio Pellico died in Turin on January 31, 1854, after a long illness. His last words were reputed to have been: "To Paradise, to Paradise, I am leaving! I have been very fortunate to die after I have expiated my sins on this earth."

especially after the Spanish Revolution's defeat in 1823. The decade of the 1820s, which witnessed a diaspora of Italian intellectuals throughout Europe, created a new "liberal" political emigration paralleling the radical-republican-democratic one that had existed since French revolutionary days. These moderates interacted with Europeans of a like persuasion and, through their contacts and writings, made the Italian cause "respectable" and gained support for it.

Furthermore, Italian exiles of different political colors won sympathy for their own cause by fighting and dying for liberty in countries such as Spain and Greece. The recognition of Greek independence in 1830, which was particularly popular in Europe, suggested that Austria could be isolated diplomatically and its policies defeated by international pressure—a lesson skillfully exploited by Italian patriots.

Besides the exiles' contacts with foreigners, in the 1820s and 1830s the exiles and conspirators within Italy also increased their communication enormously. For example, the old revolutionary Filippo Buonarroti was still alive and appeared to the police to be pulling the strings of numerous European radical conspiracies. In 1828, Buonarroti published his recollections of Babeuf's failed communist conspiracy of 1796, which was the model for the secret society's modern form. But despite his European prominence and his historical importance in introducing "the ideology of state communism and dictatorship" into European socialism, Buonarroti's influence in Italy was probably limited to the Apofasimeni (desperate ones). The significance of this group is primarily associated with Carlo Bianco di Saint Jorioz, its organizer, and his influence on Giuseppe Mazzini, one of the nineteenth century's most prominent revolutionaries.

In 1830, another wave of revolutions surged over Europe: the French overthrew the Bourbons and replaced them with the more liberal Louis Philippe, and the Belgians successfully declared their independence from Holland. For a brief time, it seemed to European democrats that France might resume its role as revolutionary guide. Spurred by the possibility of French aid, the "July Revolution" encouraged Italian patriots to act.

Geographically limited to the Duchies of Modena and Parma and the Papal State, the 1831 Italian revolutions are important because they stated the desire of all patriotic factions for unity and independence more explicitly than had the previous revolutions. The late 1820s had seen confused plots involving liberals and princes, such as Francis IV of Modena and Napoleon's descendants, who, some patriots believed, could be hitched to the patriotic cause. By 1830, however, the Modenese liberal Ciro Menotti had organized revolutionary committees in several cities with the purpose of achieving "the independence, the unity, and the liberty of all Italy" through a "representative monarchy" and a king chosen by a national assembly. To strengthen his hand, Menotti made contact with Italian exiles in Paris, but, dominated by Buonarroti, these exiles demanded "the Italian Republic, one and indivisible, from the Alps to the Sea."

When revolutions erupted in central Italy in February 1831, the tricolor of Italian unity (green, white, and red) appeared everywhere, and many papal and ducal troops deserted to the patriotic cause. The idea of unity, at least, seemed to have been consolidated, but not the form that an eventual Italian state would assume. In Paris, the exiles once again called for a republic and warned Italians against the wiles of kings who would try to divide the people by offering them constitutions. But the monarchical "party" lacked a candidate to be king of a united country.

The revolutions of 1831 failed, as had those of 1820–1821. Rome itself did not revolt, and the revolutionaries hesitated to attack that city for fear of precipitating Austrian action—a vain hope. France had been hinting that it would not help the revolutionaries, and when Louis Philippe's government explicitly declared that French blood would be spent only for France, the myth of the revolutionary fatherland willing to do battle for Italian independence collapsed. In the meantime, Metternich's successful diplomatic maneuvering allowed Austrian military intervention to crush yet another Italian revolution. More would follow.

PART THREE

The Risorgimento

CHAPTER SIX

Three Models
for Unification

FROM THE 1830S UNTIL UNIFICATION, ITALIAN INTELLECTUALS ARDENTLY discussed not whether the peninsula would be unified but how unification might take place and what its future would be. In interweaving these questions, they produced responses that further stimulated the desire for independence and unity.

THE ENDURING MYTH

By the early 1830s, progress toward unification had reached a peak, but then stagnated. The idea of unity had achieved widespread acceptance among Italian opinion makers, but the means of achieving this goal remained elusive. The Carboneria and other secret societies had demonstrated their capacity to overthrow existing governments, but not to challenge Austrian hegemony; their opposition to current conditions appealed to large numbers of people, but their lack of a rigorous ideology failed to galvanize them and their elaborate rituals masked ineffectiveness.

The man who would reinvigorate the struggle for Italian liberty, Giuseppe Mazzini, became a carbonaro in 1827, the same year he earned a law degree. A sickly child who later became the epitome of the romantic revolutionary, and given to playing the guitar and smoking cigars, Mazzini had aimed at a career in medicine, like his father, but gave up that hope after feeling faint while observing an operation. Supported by a devoted mother, and having basked early in the revolutionary recollections of his father, he seemed destined to become a revolutionary. The elder Mazzini pushed his son to choose literature as a vocation but encountered the stubborn resistance of his wife. Giuseppe's mother regarded her son as a messiah, fueling the mythical quality that came to surround him. She recounted that at age eleven, her son ran up to a beggar, threw his arms around him, and asked her to give the man something. The beggar exclaimed, prophetically, "Love him dearly, signora. He is one who will love the people." All this happened in front of a church, as befitted the man whose slogan would become "God and the People."

Another story of mythical proportions is commonly invoked to explain Mazzini's entrance into the struggle for Italian liberty. On a Sunday in April 1821, defeated revolutionaries, planning to sail for Spain to continue the struggle for liberty, crowded around a dock in Genoa. They asked for money from Maria Mazzini and her teenage son—an incident that remained etched in the boy's memory forever. Giuseppe Mazzini—dressed in black, in mourning for his country, driven into exile, condemned to death, a man who continually conspired for Italy's freedom, who struck fear in the hearts of the continent's police, and who inspired the most heroic events of 1848 and of Risorgimento hero Giuseppe Garibaldi—could not avoid having his life take on the mythical attributes that underpin great movements.

As a carbonaro, Mazzini encountered only disappointment, outdated rituals, ridiculous missions, and intractable old leaders. The secret society's failure during the disorders of 1830 was the last straw for him. A senior member of the society betrayed him, and the police arrested Mazzini in November. In jail, he encountered once again the emphasis on ritual rather than action when a fellow prisoner tapped him rhythmically on the head, conferring a higher Masonic dignity upon him instead of providing contacts to aid in resisting their captors. Finally convinced of the old society's irrelevance, Mazzini abandoned it and established a new organization as the instrument of Italian unification, Giovine Italia (Young Italy).

At a time when the national movement's failures caused many patriots to doubt the possibility of unifying the peninsula, Mazzini proclaimed that Italy had to be free and independent, with Rome as its capital.

THE THEORY

Influenced by the revolutionary atmosphere of the 1830s, Mazzini insisted on greater autonomy and dignity for the Italian movement by carving a niche for it in the European revolutionary-philosophical context.

The idea of progress animated Mazzini's philosophical system, as it had enlivened that of the eighteenth-century philosophes, but unlike them, Mazzini tied progress as a historical law to God's will and nationality. In a kind of "left" romanticism, Mazzini argued that individuals and nations had a special "mission" within God's universal plan for humanity's improvement. Each nationality, therefore, had to have control of its own affairs in order to fulfill God's will. There could be no doubt about the existence of an Italian nation, which twice before had led the world, even though it now found itself prostrate because of foreign domination and the weakness of its citizens. Acquiring knowledge of their mission and devoting all their energies to it became a moral imperative, a faith, a duty, for Italians as for other peoples.

Although faith in God's idea of progress stalled during the Restoration under reactionary hammer blows and the exhaustion of the French revolutionary generation, Mazzini argued that the romantic era had rebelled against authority and he preached moral renewal. Even if that movement had itself become lost in the meanderings of medieval mysticism, its appeal to youth had produced a ferment that could not be blocked. The nineteenth century, with youth as its watchword, would overwhelm conservatives who erroneously concluded that Louis Philippe's triumph in France had ended social revolution. Far from killing "the great social revolution," the French Revolution of 1830, Mazzini believed, had merely announced it.

It was the duty of the young to overthrow systematic repression in Europe, which blocked the moral education of the people and the progress willed by God. In describing the atrocious conditions that prevailed not only in Italy but in most of Europe—censorship, the threat of capital punishment for reading proscribed books and foreign newspapers, the closing of universities—Mazzini asked, "Who will give progress to this people?" His answer: "Insurrection is the only course . . . possible; a general, determined rising of the multitude: the holy war of the oppressed." The slogan: "God and the People."

Unlike other forms of nationalism, Mazzini's religious-romantic-nationalism placed all nationalities on an equal footing because God had anointed each with a special mission. His nationalism was devoid of the intolerance toward other nationalities that marred, for example, German nationalism and the ideas of some Italian moderates. Considering the ill repute into which nationalism later fell, it would be unjust not to recall the progressivism of Mazzini's brand, which defended the dignity of all nationalities and their obligation to eliminate the shackles binding them and others. Mazzini insisted that the "European revolution today will be made in the name of national independence." These national revolutions would produce a new map of Europe, which Mazzini sketched, coinciding with the existing geographical distribution of thirteen or fourteen identifiable national groups; the details he wisely left to "the future and the people's vote." Once terminated, the European struggle for freedom would create equal political entities that would be based on popular sovereignty and prepared to fulfill their special missions within God's plan for humanity's progress. Empires such as the Austrian, the Russian, and the Turkish, powered by the tyrannical and selfish domination of diverse nationalities destined to develop in different directions, would disappear.

Italy's mission was intimately bound up with the country's history and its struggle for liberty. It had to lead the way to the new order because its fight for national unity was the quest for the unity of humanity. In seeking this unity, the Italian nation had to overcome two powerful obstacles—Austria and the papacy. In destroying the first, Italy would advance the cause of oppressed nationalities, encourage the formation of independent states, create the premise of a future European federation, and promote God's cause. Italians could free themselves only by freeing others.

If Austria's collapse would bring liberty, obliterating the papacy would create a new unity. In the past, the Eternal City had united humankind twice, under the Caesars (Action) and under the popes (Spirit); the "Third Rome," that of the people, the successor of both, would "unite, in a faith that will make Thought and Action one, Europe, America and every part of the terrestrial globe." Thus Mazzini's religious fervor should not be confused with organized religion; in his view, neither popes nor priests interpret God's law, but the people do—and their religion is progressive nationalism.

Historian Gaetano Salvemini wrote that, despite the weaknesses that may be discerned in the Italian patriot's philosophy, by fusing medieval utopian ideas, Rousseau's *Social Contract*, and the doctrines of nineteenth-century French thinker Saint-Simon, Mazzini emphasized "many democratic ideas that belong to our own time." But Mazzini's modernity emerges more fully when we pose the question of how he would unite Italy. Neither a military strategist nor a tactician, Mazzini did not create the method by which he advocated the physical destruction of Austrian power, but he made an extraordinary selection from among the available methods and enriched it with his own ideology.

Mazzini's philosophy, in fact, found its military complement in the ideas of Carlo Bianco di Saint Jorioz. Bianco had been part of the Piedmontese agitation of 1821, after which he participated in the Spanish Revolution. After a period of imprisonment there, he traveled to other parts of Europe and settled in Paris. In 1830, he published *Della guerra nazionale d'insurrezione per bande applicata all'Italia* (The National Insurrectionary War by Means of Guerrilla Bands, Applied to Italy). This work, the first theoretical treatise on guerrilla warfare, drew from the lessons of the Spanish uprising against Napoleon and of the Greek war for independence. According to Bianco, a popular uprising using the methods of guerrilla warfare was the only way to free Italy. Despite Bianco's closeness to Buonarroti at this time, Mazzini, with whom Bianco later collaborated, made Bianco's military concepts an integral part of his own system and publicized them. It can be argued that Bianco's ideas animated the military aspects of the 1848 revolutions and the 1860 expedition of "The Thousand," which culminated in unification.

The program of Mazzini's Young Italy (1831), after emphasizing national insurrection and intimately tying it to the education of the people, made the following extremely significant methodological statement: "Insurrection—by means of guerrilla bands—is the true method of warfare for all nations desirous of emancipating themselves from a foreign yoke. This method of warfare supplies the want—inevitable at the commencement of the insurrection—of a regular army; it calls the greatest number of elements into the field, and yet may be sustained by the smallest number. It forms the military education of the people, and consecrates every foot of the native soil by the memory of some warlike deed."

It seems ironic that English-language writers neglect this full-blown antecedent of what have become known as "wars of national liberation," which have been successful in China, Cuba, and Vietnam. Italian historians, although aware of this aspect of Mazzini's thought, generally fail to emphasize it. The inner contradictions of a desperate populace rising up against foreign occupiers, yet failing to turn against native grandees, as Marxists did, perhaps helps to explain this attitude. But Mazzini's overwhelming desire to liberate Italy and prevent the national struggle from degenerating into a divisive social conflict prompted him to stress the military aspects of liberation and even to adopt practical measures against its transformation into a class war.

To this fundamental reason must be added Mazzini's differences with Buonarroti, the period's chief champion of social revolution. For Buonarroti, the French Jacobin experience of the 1790s demonstrated how revolutions generate class warfare, and the French Revolution of 1830 confirmed it; the poor therefore had to organize themselves militarily to prepare for the coming social war. The leadership of revolutions consequently devolved to an elite, a concept that introduced a dictatorial principle into class action. This idea also worked for Buonarroti on the international level, France being the general and less-advanced countries such as Italy the soldiers. Though Mazzini recognized that an insurrection had to be prepared in secret by a few leaders, to avoid dictatorship and terror he emphasized the people's role. Do not, he wrote, "condemn the yearning masses to inertia; do not delude yourselves into thinking that you operate for them; do not entrust to only one class the great work of national regeneration." Even more important in the Italian context, Mazzini acknowledged that there could be revolutionary collaboration between France and Italy, but insisted that the Italians had to take the lead in the struggle to free themselves; this was at the core of the nation's larger mission. This last point applied more to the Italian situation than did Buonarroti's, energized the peninsula's patriotic movement, and eclipsed Buonarroti's influence. In fact, Mazzini's thesis originated the slogan of the 1848 revolutions: *L'Italia fará da sé* (Italy will do it by itself).

Mazzini's challenge to Buonarroti has made it seem to some modern commentators, especially of the left, that the Italian thinker neglected the social question.

Indeed, for the reasons already discussed, Mazzini did not address the issue as directly as Buonarroti did. Mazzini emphasized national revolutions—essentially political movements that would avoid class warfare but create the conditions for social change and the material progress of the masses. These developments could occur exclusively in a republic. Only republican institutions, he believed, could enact the social legislation that would embody the law of God and humanity that people be "free, equal, and brothers," because they guaranteed free expression of the "general will." Monarchies "necessarily" injected privilege and an intermediate element, aristocracy, into the national equation, thus undermining equality and liberty. Mazzini considered monarchies obsolete.

If Italy should not be unified as a kingdom, neither should it be a federation, which would weaken the nation, make it a prey to its neighbors, and "strike at the root of the great mission Italy is destined to accomplish towards humanity." Mazzini emphasized that unity signified neither administrative centralization nor the destruction of local autonomy, but that "political organization" should be "one and central."

Like his demand that Italians take the lead in their own liberation, Mazzini's dogmatic insistence that without unity there could be no nationality brought about a qualitative change in the Italian national movement. Unlike other patriots, who believed that unification was preferable to a divided peninsula, Mazzini advocated unity as an indivisible entity because he believed it to be the only solution to the Italian problem. According to Mazzini, the entire history of the peninsula tended toward unity. Although, on analysis, his evidence for this concept can be disputed, it is true that developments since the eighteenth century had been working against the peninsula's division into separate states and that progressive forces advocating change worked for national unity. Mazzini lent fire to this tendency by injecting it with the passion born of religious, philosophical, historical, and national conviction and, consequently, the inevitability of success.

In this manner, Mazzini evolved his powerful model of the new Italy: a democratic, socially compassionate, indivisible republic based on popular sovereignty and distinguished by a duty to lead other nations in achieving the liberty that would permit them to fulfill their God-given missions. This model caught the imagination of the patriotic movement and of future generations.

PRACTICE

After Mazzini's arrest in November 1830, Piedmontese authorities gave him the choice of living either in exile or in a small town. Mazzini left his country for Marseilles. There he founded Young Italy, a practical expression of his revolutionary ideas.

Young Italy surpassed the Carboneria thanks not only to its goals, which were outlined earlier, but also to its modern organization. At the top, the Central Group, consisting of Mazzini and his closest associates, named three-person provincial groups for every Italian province. These groups appointed organizers who recruited two categories of members, the Federals and the Federal-Propagators, in each of the province's cities. The Federal-Propagators, chosen from persons who possessed "heart [courage] and mind," had the task of initiating the Federals, selected from persons who had the "heart" but not the "mind" to choose appropriate people. Each member had to take a nom de guerre with which to be recognized within the Young Italy society and swear an oath reaffirming the organization's ideology. Except for secret signals permitting members to recognize each other, this oath was Young Italy's only ritual. At first, membership was restricted to persons under forty, but Mazzini later modified this condition by allowing admission to persons who "had sucked the aspirations of the century"—that is, he made youth dependent upon spirit. Mazzini hoped in this manner to distinguish his organization from the Carboneria, which was paralyzed by a timid membership and complex, meaningless rituals.

Immediate, resolute action also distinguished Young Italy from the Carboneria. To prepare the field for revolution, Mazzini signed an agreement (September 1832) with Buonarroti. But the old conspirator had reorganized his Italian societies with the aim of gaining control of Mazzini's movement, and the rivalry between the two leaders marred Young Italy's revolutionary debut. In addition, their conflicting ideas on social revolution and Buonarroti's conviction that an Italian revolution should not be attempted unless France took the lead produced a complete break between Mazzini and Buonarroti in 1834.

Between 1830 and 1832, Mazzini's organization quickly found adherents in several Italian regions, especially Liguria (Genoa), Piedmont, Lombardy, Venetia, and, to a lesser extent, Tuscany, the Kingdom of the Two Sicilies, and the Papal State. Mazzini chose Piedmont for his first revolutionary action. The insurrection there was to be based on the army and coordinated with an uprising in Genoa and revolutionary incursions from Switzerland and France. These ambitious plans went awry almost immediately. The Piedmontese government discovered the conspiracy in the army almost by accident in April 1833 and resorted to torture and execution to maintain control. Despite this serious setback, Mazzini doggedly pushed ahead, but prompt military action thwarted the Genoa uprising; in Switzerland, the general entrusted by Mazzini to lead the revolutionary invasion gambled away the money raised to arm one thousand volunteers. Other patriots gathered, but the Swiss authorities disarmed them. A revolutionary column invading from France was defeated by the Piedmontese *carabinieri*.

The fizzle of Mazzini's first revolutionary challenge created a crisis for his organization, a death sentence in absentia, and flight to England, but not failure. An

English historian put it best: "The immediate result of Mazzini's teaching was to fan to a blaze the embers of Italian nationality." Patriots later important in the national movement had responded to his call to action. These included Giuseppe Garibaldi, who made his revolutionary debut in the projected Genoese uprising, and Vincenzo Gioberti, the priest who was sent into exile for his Mazzinian sympathies and who would later make the Risorgimento respectable. For this reason, even though Mazzini's "titanic" model for a future Italy could not be adopted, "nonetheless he made Italy."

THE ITALIAN PRIMACY

Mazzini argued that Italy should be united to fulfill a God-given mission. But both the mission and its methods were radical. Furthermore, Mazzini's intimately religious temperament detested the traditional religious forms that dominated the peninsula. These views made Mazzini the mortal enemy of Italian moderates who believed in unification for economic and other reasons but abhorred Mazzini's revolutionary ideology. In short, "the great mass of educated Italians, who had too much common sense or too little courage for Mazzini's gospel, were looking for a milder creed which would reconcile patriotism and prudence."

From the beginning, this "moderate" party split into two factions. One predominantly Catholic faction was centered in Lombardy, thanks to the cultural influence of Manzoni and Rosmini, but a Turinese priest emerged as its most powerful spokesman.

Vincenzo Gioberti's youthful flirtation with Mazzini's ideas ended with the taming of the Mazzinian mission for Italy. Italians indeed had a special "mission" Gioberti argued in his extremely influential *On the Civil and Moral Primacy of the Italians* (the *Primato*, 1843)—the spiritual leadership of the Catholic world. Gioberti tied Italy's greatness to the Church—a familiar tenet—but brilliantly linked the Church to unification, thus removing the radical edge that Mazzini and Buonarroti had given Italy's "mission" while retaining the crucial concept that Italy necessarily had to be the "redeeming" nation. Before Gioberti, the demand for unification had been the province of revolutionaries; by single-handedly inventing "neo-Guelphism," Gioberti gave the independence movement respectable ideological credentials. Gioberti achieved this by tying the papacy's regeneration to Italy's resurrection. He attributed the papacy's decline to the split between religion and civil society caused by the French Revolution; the resurgence of Italy and the papacy together would heal this division by reconciling the Church with liberty and progress. As Mazzini had done, Gioberti provided the Risorgimento with a universal aspect, but one that deemphasized revolution and caught the imagina-

PORTRAITS

VINCENZO GIOBERTI
New-Style Guelph

~∞~

The priest who seemed to revive the Catholic Church's political fortunes in the midnineteenth century was born on April 5, 1801. Vincenzo Gioberti's parents came from a modest background and died while he was still young. Gioberti studied theology at the University of Turin and earned a doctorate there on January 9, 1823. Ordained a priest two years later, he became a court chaplain and a professor in the theological college.

Despite his links with the establishment, moderate liberal political ideas attracted Gioberti, and he seems to have joined several secret societies. He had republican sympathies and wrote for Giuseppe Mazzini's newspaper *Giovane Italia*, but he never joined the Genoese revolutionary's organization because he considered it too violent. In May 1833, he came under suspicion as a subversive and was arrested. The authorities forced him into exile. He went first to Paris and then to Brussels, where he lived from 1834 to 1845. The published philosophical collection of his works totals thirty-five volumes.

Gioberti remains most famous for his 1843 *Del primato civile e morale degli italiani*—dedicated to Silvio Pellico—in which he proposed that Italy unite as a federation of states under the presidency of the pope, an idea known as "neo-

Guelphism." Gioberti achieved instant fame with this book, especially because it coincided with the election and reforms of Pius IX, but in April 1848 came Pius's allocution in which he rejected any role for the papacy in Italian unification.

By 1848, however, many other changes had also taken place. The Piedmontese government, once hostile to Gioberti, had granted a constitution, and Gioberti emerged as very influential. He returned in triumph to Turin in April 1848, successfully ran for Parliament, and became prime minister on December 16. Gioberti resigned as prime minister on February 20, 1849, and retired to private life in Paris.

Gioberti became less moderate as he got older. Already in the mid-1840s he had bitterly attacked the Jesuits, who opposed his neo-Guelphism, in several tracts. In 1851, he published another influential work, *Del rinnovamento civile d'Italia* (On the Civil Renewal of Italy). This book marked the definitive death of his brainchild, neo-Guelphism, at his own hands. In the book, Gioberti advocated liberalism and the unification of Italy under the leadership of the king of Piedmont-Sardinia.

Vincenzo Gioberti died in Paris soon after publication of this work, on November 26, 1852.

tion of moderate liberals by mandating cooperation between the Church and the national movement. He thus provided a vehicle of political expression for well-off groups such as wealthy landowners, progressive nobles, and liberal clergy who were eager to revive the peninsula's fortunes but unwilling to throw over their religion, social status, and traditional values. Gioberti's lasting importance lies in his mobilization of these influential groups for unification, not in his model for an independent Italy.

Gioberti reconciled Italy's political independence with its spiritual mission by envisioning a loose confederation of existing states under the pope's presidency. His unification model consisted of an economic union with consultative institutions open to moderate reform. Thus Gioberti hoped not only to eliminate the serious divisions among Italians concerning Italy's future makeup but also to win the support of Italian rulers for unity. However, this proposed neo-Guelph confederation stood out for its impracticality. The current pope, Gregory XVI, inspired confidence in no one; indeed, Gioberti himself acknowledged that only a new pope could carry out his program. It is a tribute to the stunning boldness of Gioberti's project that his ideas influenced the election of a pope who seemed capable of realizing his plan. Although the unexpected election of a "liberal" pope briefly breathed life into Gioberti's vision, it would quickly become exposed for the impossible dream it was, and even Gioberti would abandon the conceptual model of a unified Italy as expressed in the *Primato*.

But liberals had been fired by Gioberti's vision of moderate leadership for the national movement. Instead of the pope, they focused on the Piedmontese monarch as the only ruler with the energy and perhaps the will to free Italy while preserving traditional values.

"Hamlet," or the Quandary of Moderates

In his bid to win the support of the princes for his unification model, Gioberti appealed to King Charles Albert of Piedmont-Sardinia to help free the Italians. Although welcoming Gioberti's role in gaining respectability for the independence movement, Piedmontese moderates had no faith in the papacy's ability to reform itself or to lead the independence movement. The strength of the Piedmontese moderate movement resided in its connection with the government. Many liberals were statesmen and bureaucrats proud of their traditions. They resented Austrian domination of the peninsula and papal interference in their government and agreed that unity could greatly enhance Piedmont's power. They did not favor unification on Mazzinian terms but instead called on Turin to fight for a federated Italy, complete with a customs union.

As with the previous two models, influential literary works stimulated the idea of unification under Savoy leadership. Terenzio Mamiani's *Nostro parere intorno alle cose italiane* (Our Opinion on Italian Things, 1841) argued that Italians could unify themselves by fighting for their freedom under an Italian monarch. Given the disparity of forces in the field, the struggle would have to await a moment of

Austrian weakness. In the meantime, Italians had to prepare themselves by initiating the patriotic education of the masses, winning over the wealthy and the clergy to the movement, and implementing a program of educational, religious, and social reforms. Mamiani advocated agreement between liberals and Catholics but disagreed with Gioberti's emphasis on a paramount position for the Church.

Whereas Mamiani's tract illustrates the moderates' prevailing skepticism of Gioberti's concrete solution to the Italian problem, Cesare Balbo's *Le speranze d'Italia* (The Hopes of Italy, 1844) had an important influence on the liberal milieu. As with Mamiani, Balbo's dialogue with Gioberti confirms moderate disagreement with the ideas of the Turinese priest. A Catholic who was sympathetic to Gioberti's views, Balbo pronounced them impossible to apply practically. Balbo gave four possible unification scenarios, each dependent on the elimination of an Austrian role in Italian affairs: concerted action by Italian monarchs; a popular insurrection; foreign intervention; and the satisfaction of Austrian appetites outside of Italy. For Balbo, the first three were impossible or dangerous. He therefore held out the hope that with the decline of the Turkish Empire the Western powers would hand over Ottoman territory to Austria to bolster it against Russia, which they all feared, and as an inducement to the Austrians to withdraw from Italy. Capping this diplomatic deal, Piedmont would absorb Lombardy and Venetia to form a strong northern Italian kingdom and create an Italian confederation free from Austrian domination.

Although Balbo's solution to the Italian problem may appear unrealistic today, it had an important impact when he proposed the idea because it expressed the feelings of the Piedmontese ruling circles with whom he had close connections. The Savoys had long wanted to absorb Lombardy and Venetia, a goal Piedmontese diplomats never abandoned. Furthermore, Piedmontese moderate liberals and conservatives both favored Austrian expansion at Turkish expense, a plan that had French encouragement. This solution would not only resolve the Italian problem and expand Piedmontese power but also reinforce Catholic Austria against eastern Orthodox Russia. Unlike Mazzini, neither Balbo nor the Piedmontese government sympathized with the national aspirations of eastern Europeans under Austrian domination. For Balbo and the Piedmontese rulers, who with Gioberti identified civilization with the advance of Catholicism, the plan approached perfection.

Thus, although it might have seemed puerile to hope that Austria could be made to give up Italian territory, Balbo viewed the decline of the Ottoman Empire as important in connecting two significant problems threatening the peace of Europe. Although his plan did not work out, Balbo emphasized the importance of Piedmontese and European diplomacy in attaining a solution to the peninsula's problems and linked Piedmontese expansionism and Italian independence in a nonrevolutionary manner.

But the major obstacle to Piedmontese guidance of the national movement was none other than King Charles Albert himself, the person to whom Balbo's entire book was a veiled appeal. The indecisiveness Charles Albert showed in the 1821 conspiracy would characterize the monarch throughout his life. His uncle, the conservative Charles Felix, never forgave Charles Albert's role in that revolution and favored denying him the throne, until persuaded otherwise by Metternich. This uncertainty made the Piedmontese court a center of intrigue and left its mark on the heir to the throne after he became king.

Because of his past, Charles Albert ascended the throne to serious doubts at home and abroad as to his future performance. Mazzini greeted him with a strange appeal to support the national cause, which he followed up in 1833 with an attempted revolution. Reactionary policies characterized the new reign's first years. Charles Albert supported the attempts of French conservative monarchists to overthrow King Louis Philippe and signed a military convention with Austria. He discouraged moderates looking to him for leadership of the national movement, and the violence with which he repressed the revolutionaries of 1833 ranks as one of the Risorgimento's worst chapters. The psychologically unstable, physically delicate ruler led a strange life, adopting peculiar diets, falling prey to quacks, and fueling intense political and religious intrigue. He is supposed to have remarked that he stood "between the dagger of the Carbonari and the poisoned chocolate of the Jesuits."

Despite the inauspicious start to his reign, Charles Albert resisted becoming the tool of reactionaries. A strong factor that helps explain this resistance was his family background and youthful experience: his father fought with Napoleon, and his mother entertained French troops while he was being educated in Geneva on a stipend from Napoleon. Reinforcing these factors, probably his strong Piedmontese patriotism and his stubborn commitment to good government accounts for his resistance to the reactionaries. He strengthened his kingdom through a series of administrative and legislative reforms that partially satisfied the bourgeois demand to modernize the economy while retaining the Crown's prerogatives. Some of his economic reforms and a desire to reduce Piedmontese dependence on Austria brought the two countries to the brink of war. He unleashed an attack on Church power, considered a prime reason for Piedmontese backwardness. He gradually weeded out conservative ministers from his government, replacing them with moderate liberals, and suggested that he might grant a constitution. He encouraged nationalists by stating that he would strike a blow for Italy when the opportunity came and by remarking: "If Piedmont lost Austria she would gain Italy, and then Italy would be able to act for herself."

Despite these developments, Charles Albert never overcame the fundamental ambivalence of his character. As his "liberalism" increased his standing among his subjects, he seemed fearful of his growing popularity. When war with Austria seemed imminent, he hastily retreated and sought arbitration. He accompanied his actions against the Church with a promise to the Jesuits that they would be safe. In sum, it remained unclear whether Charles Albert would respond to the appeal of moderate liberals to become the champion of Italian independence. To patriots, he was truly "the Hamlet of Italy."

Even with this uncertainty, an important change occurred in the Italy of the 1830s and 1840s: Italian moderate opinion now favored independence. This stance signaled a crucial break—one that enormously advanced the cause of independence—in the conservative-reactionary front that had allowed Austria and its Italian allies to reassert their dominance in 1815, 1821, and 1831. In this sense, a "cultural revolution" had indeed occurred.

This development was represented not only by writers such as those examined in this chapter but also by a wider cultural phenomenon. Between 1839 and 1847, scientists and technicians from all parts of the peninsula met together in congresses. These meetings advanced the cause of unity by discussing common Italian problems, by contributing to the elaboration of a moderate national program, and by helping build the country's future ruling class. The popularity of scientific meetings and associations was so strong that even Metternich had to permit them, and Charles Albert sympathized with the movement.

By the 1840s, the dominant political culture in Italy demanded independence. Except for Mazzini's, the other models called for a confederation, but Mazzini's radical democratic ideas alarmed the moderates, who rejected the weak pope as the leader of the national movement and instead turned to Piedmont. Charles Albert vacillated but gave timid promises to help.

The people, the pope, and Piedmont represented the three best hopes for independence and unification. In retrospect, it seems clear which one had the best chance for success, but historical events usually unfold in unexpected ways.

CHAPTER SEVEN

The Revolutions of 1848: The Great Shakeout

PRISCILLA ROBERTSON, AUTHOR OF A CLASSIC WORK ON THE 1848 revolutions in Europe, wrote this about the Italians: "In habit and attitude . . . they were the most democratic people in Europe, except possibly for the Swiss." Behavior in two areas bolsters Robertson's arguments: the relationship among the classes and the position of women.

With regard to the first, Robertson notes the courtesy and respect with which the aristocracy treated the lower classes, contrasting this behavior with that in other parts of Europe. Robertson wrote that ownership of property by the common people and the great economic strides that had been made in the North accounted for this relationship. The remarkable influence of women in Italian life accounted for this "easy friendliness and self-respect" of the workers. Robertson emphasizes the political commitment and the prominence of women in Italian society, which exceeded that of women in France, Germany, and England.

Among the major European revolutionaries, Mazzini alone denounced limits on women's equality with men in the revolutionary movement. Women not only participated in the Risorgimento but were its "fiercer patriots." Among them were Giuditta Bellerio Sidoli, Mazzini's lover and "intellectual passion," and Anita Garibaldi, who fought alongside her husband and died in the field. The fictional heroine in Camillo Boito's *Senso*—made into a film by Luchino Visconti—was caught up in the passions of sex, and the Risorgimento exacted a terrible price for her betrayal by an Austrian soldier. The *London Times* correspondent observed that "it was hard for Englishmen to allow for the freedom of manners which Italian women enjoyed, coupled with perfect respectability."

These aspects of Italian society illustrate the democratic climate of the 1848 revolutions that attempted to put Mazzini's preaching into action.

PORTRAITS

GIUDITTA BELLERIO SIDOLI
Patriot

Giuditta Bellerio, daughter of a magistrate of the Napoleonic Kingdom of Italy and born in Milan in 1804, may serve as a model of the kind of suffering endured by the women who participated in the struggle to liberate Italy. At age sixteen, she married Giovanni Sidoli, a patriot and a member of the Carboneria. Besides love, wife and husband shared a strong desire to liberate Italy. After the revolutionary wave of 1820–1821, Giovanni Sidoli fled to Switzerland, where, following the birth of a daughter, his wife joined him. In 1828, in Swiss exile, Giovanni Sidoli died from a lung ailment.

Despite her husband's death, Giuditta Bellerio Sidoli continued her subversive activities against the Austrians and the native Italian rulers. In the late 1820s, tensions in Italy increased; in 1830–1831, a wave of revolutions struck central Italy. One of the epicenters of the disorders was the Duchy of Modena, where Giuditta Sidoli joined Ciro Menotti as an important revolutionary protagonist; wearing the Italian tricolor, she led demonstrations in the main square. When the Austrians defeated the revolution, Sidoli fled, once again, for Swiss exile.

In 1832, Giuditta Sidoli settled in the French city of Marseilles; there, her apartment served as a meeting place for Italian exiles dreaming of Italian liberation after having been banished from their homes and chased by the police of Europe. Among the exiles congregating there was "Pippo"—Giuseppe Mazzini. The two became lovers and, together, founded a new society: Young Italy, of which Sidoli handled the finances. In 1833, Mazzini fled from the French police to Geneva, and Sidoli followed in his wake, nursing him during a period of declining health. Sidoli, however, soon became overwhelmed by a desire to return to Italy to see her children again.

In 1833, she left for Italy under an assumed name, hoping that the police would allow her to enter the country. However, they either blocked her from entering, expelled her, or threw her into prison. She led this life from 1833 to 1852, when she settled in Turin. In the Piedmontese capital, intellectuals and nobility frequented her salon where, despite her age, they found her fascinating and beautiful. Mazzini had once told her: "Smile at me always! It is the only smile that comes to me from life." Their love affair, however, had long ended by the time she went to Turin, and they saw each other only occasionally.

On March 28, 1871, aged sixty-seven, Giuditta Sidoli died of pneumonia. She refused the last rites because, she said, she did not believe in the God of the Catholic Church—only in the God of exiles and the downtrodden.

Economics

Besides the development of a cultural and ideological milieu favoring unification, the peninsula's participation in Europe's rapid economic and commercial growth after 1820, discussed in chapter 4, reinforced the demand for national independence. But economic development proceeded unevenly and at a slower pace than in other parts of Europe. The patriots attributed the lag to the political order and the territorial divisions that Austria had imposed on the peninsula.

Lombardy led in economic growth. Building on eighteenth-century reforms, production had become capitalist, and the aristocracy engaged in business to a greater extent than in other parts of the peninsula. Prosperity varied according to the region's zones, but the value of silk exports, for example, more than quadrupled between 1814 and 1841. The cotton, metallurgical, and mechanical industries all got their starts during this period, and the expansion of banking testifies to the growth of capital accumulation.

Even though Lombard economic progress outstripped the rest of Italy, it trailed more advanced parts of Europe. Lombard capitalism was still primarily based on landownership, and growing Asian competition and the vagaries of foreign demand increasingly threatened the chief export and source of wealth: silk. Of all the peninsula's regions, Lombardy came closest to developing, but had not yet achieved, a modern economy based on production as a response to increasing internal demand. Lombardy's status as an Austrian colony blocked this qualitative leap, for although Lombards benefited from some positive aspects of Austrian rule, such as good roads, decent administration, and a measure of local autonomy, they suffered serious economic and tariff discrimination, which favored Austrian-owned enterprises and hampered Italian-owned businesses. Furthermore, the peninsula's division into small states protected by tariff barriers deprived fledgling Lombard industries of natural markets and stunted their future development. Finally, Lombards watched helplessly as the Austrians drew one-third of their empire's revenue from Lombardy (which accounted for only one-sixth of the population) and unofficially shut them out of the best government jobs.

These factors explain why widespread anti-Austrian feeling agitated the richest part of Italy. Patriots attributed Lombardy's economic growth primarily to Italian enterprise against overwhelming odds and emphasized the severely negative aspects of Austrian rule. Moreover, they believed that future industrial development in Lombardy depended on the region's economic integration with the rest of Italy and free trade for the entire peninsula. But as long as foreign rule continued, Austrian protectionist concerns took precedence over Italian economic development. Indeed, the more Lombard economic activity accelerated, the greater the dispute with Austria became. Economic growth in Lombardy before 1848, therefore, stimulated revolutionary feelings and decisively contributed to the struggle for Italian independence.

Piedmont enjoyed the next-fastest-growing economy in Italy. This was an important change from past years and greatly enhanced the Risorgimento's cause. Economic progress in Piedmont stemmed from administrative and legislative reforms, the encouragement of free trade, and other economic reforms advocated by patriots and European economists. Charles Albert reversed his predecessor's protectionist policies by eliminating export duties on raw silk, lowering the tariff on grain and other products, and signing twenty-six commercial treaties with foreign states. These measures, put into effect between 1840 and 1847, favored the growth of modern credit institutions, spurred greater economic activity among the bourgeoisie, intensified the rate at which capitalist firms transformed economic relationships on the land, and encouraged the progress of new industries. Economic development also stimulated research, the exchange of information, congresses of scientists, and the creation of groups such as the Agricultural Association in 1842. Most active in these developments were moderate liberals such as Count Camillo Benso di Cavour, future leader of the national movement.

As with his politics, innumerable contradictions accompanied Charles Albert's economic policies. The king hoped to stimulate the economy without relinquishing his absolutistic power, a goal that made it more difficult to eradicate old methods and ideas. With all their limits, however, the Piedmontese reforms of this period prepared the ground for the economic policy of Cavour during the next decade and contributed greatly to the momentum favoring unification.

Economic growth failed to reconcile patriots to Italy's dependent political status, however, and stagnation in the South confirmed their desire for unity and independence. Rome was a prime example of this feeling. Between 1823 and 1846, Popes Leo XII and Gregory XVI blocked the minimum reforms that the changes in nineteenth-century Italian, European, and even Roman society required. Metternich and the European powers, anxious to strengthen the papacy, pressured the government for reforms to no avail. The extremist Zelanti continued to determine policy, propped up by the Austrians and irregular paramilitary terrorist formations that "came to bear an increasing resemblance to the *squadristi* of Fascist Italy, performing the same function of intimidating political opponents by arbitrary extralegal violence, and causing at times similar concern to their supposed masters."

Italians and Europeans attributed the worst poverty, economic degradation, and financial stagnation in Italy to the nature of papal government, which was controlled by a narrow political class of prelates who perceived reform as a dire threat to their power. Despite Gioberti's theories, the Papal State appeared as an anachronism whose survival depended on continual Austrian military intervention against frequent attempts to overthrow an oppressive government. In a perverse way, the extent of governmental mismanagement and the revolutionary agitation that the government's reactionary policies provoked significantly influenced the Risorgimento; mismanagement transformed the problem of the Papal State into a common Italian matter and focused European attention on Italy's plight.

Farther south, in the Kingdom of the Two Sicilies, Enlightenment and Napoleonic reforms had failed to transform a landed and money-lending bourgeoisie into a modern productive class engaged in business and industry. King Ferdinand II pursued protectionist and reform policies aimed at mollifying the bourgeoisie, not at stimulating economic changes that might threaten his absolutistic rule. For the patriots, the problem was that the southern bourgeoisie's landed character paralyzed the liberal national movement. Southern patriots sought to change the government, but the bourgeoisie relied on it for economic favors and for protection from the brigandage exacerbated by widespread poverty. Although a strong desire for unification characterized southern intellectuals, the kingdom's social and political structure limited their options to insurrection. A moderate movement might have hoped to collaborate with the king, but no such movement developed as it had in the North. Thus the Bourbon dynasty coupled with a backward economy precluded the South from assuming leadership in the Risorgimento and cost the region dearly after unification.

RUMBLINGS

As in the rest of Europe, numerous rumblings preceded the "year of revolutions" on the peninsula. In Italy, unlike in other areas, the overwhelming demand for national independence, not economic factors, drove events. Moreover, the disorders in different parts of the country did not remain isolated but influenced each other. Eventually the events of 1848–1849 spurred the intervention of Italians from the entire peninsula and of all political persuasions.

After the initial defeat of his insurrectionary activities, Mazzini withdrew in 1834 to London, where he suffered a period of doubt. When he reemerged, his faith was unscathed and his ideology unchanged. Painfully rebuilding his conspiratorial organization, Mazzini amplified the social dimension of his activities by devoting more attention to the workers, but his radicalism still made him anathema to many progressives who otherwise might have supported him.

At the same time, exiles influenced by Mazzini but not controlled by him linked up with local opponents of the pope and the Bourbons and initiated several important but ill-fated insurrections. Forced to emigrate after the numerous Italian revolutions, these exiles had become freedom fighters for liberal causes in Europe and America and hoped to exploit their military experience in the struggle to free their homeland. They focused on the Papal State and the Kingdom of the Two Sicilies because these states had been shaken since 1834 by endemic rebellions. Harsh measures and frequent executions failed to quell the ongoing disturbances. Hoping to organize resistance, exiles from Spain and Malta converged on the Romagna and the Bourbon domains in 1843. Mazzini had advised against the action because he judged its preparation insufficient; the capture and execution of the conspirators proved him correct. The brutality of the repression that followed the disorders in the Papal State inspired the Bandiera brothers, sons of an admiral and sailors in the Austrian navy, to start a revolution in the South. Betrayed by spies, they refused an Austrian offer of clemency and "invaded" the Kingdom of the Two Sicilies with only nineteen men. They were captured by Bourbon troops and executed.

The revolutionary attempts of this period demonstrated a misunderstanding of Mazzini's tactics; he advocated insurrection to stimulate guerrilla warfare but did not believe that isolated patriot bands could incite insurrection. Nevertheless, the desperate activism of Italian patriots characterized the Italian situation in the years leading up to 1848, and the patriots' sacrifice won Italian and foreign sympathy for the national cause.

In 1845–1846, the rebellions in the South also increased moderate influence on the governments that were not directly affected by the uprisings but were fearful that the agitation would spread to their states. The continual failure of revolutionary agitation in the Papal State caused liberals to investigate whether a more peaceful means of change existed. Massimo D'Azeglio, an intimate friend of Cesare Balbo's who had impeccable social connections, was dispatched to the Romagna to determine whether he could advance the moderate liberal cause there. D'Azeglio's mission was a discreet success despite widespread skepticism about Charles Albert. Soon after D'Azeglio's departure, however, a new revolt erupted. The participants made several mild requests, which were refused. This emphasized the unreasonableness of a papal government that forced its subjects to take up arms to achieve minimal change.

Upon his return to Turin, D'Azeglio reported the details of his visit to Charles Albert. The monarch's astounding response: "Tell them to be quiet and not move, since, for now, nothing can be done; but also let them be certain that, when the occasion presents itself, *my life, the lives of my children, my arms, my treasure, my army, everything will be spent for the Italian cause.*" Given Charles Albert's past history, even D'Azeglio sounded a cautionary note, but this time the king would make good on his promise.

D'Azeglio kept the momentum going. Encouraged by the king, he published his ideas on the Italian situation as it related to the Papal State. The resulting *Degli ultimi casi di Romagna* (On the Last Incidents of the Romagna, 1846) was one of the Risorgimento's most influential works. D'Azeglio explained his reasoning in his memoirs: "Revolution, no. We already have had enough. War, no, because we have neither the means nor the strength. . . . Therefore, put the question in a camp where every individual always has some force, . . . the camp of opinion and publicity."

D'Azeglio attacked the papal government. He stated that it had lost all popular support, that it remained in power thanks only to the Austrians, and that it had to reform or perish. He paid homage to the patriots who had sacrificed their lives in the many uprisings, but argued that the revolutionaries had no right to speak on behalf of the people. He urged them to renounce conspiracies and violence and to fight for independence by developing a vast public opinion movement at home and abroad—a "conspiracy in the sunlight"—supplemented by military discipline to be employed when the opportunity presented itself. In short, no more secret conspiracies but, instead, a vast "open conspiracy."

D'Azeglio's lively, influential, and widely read pamphlet completed the liberal moderate program, even though, characteristically, Charles Albert refused the author permission to publish it in Turin. The appeal to public opinion invested the moderates with a "democratic" aura with which to combat radical influence, and the Piedmontese would soon supply the Risorgimento with an efficient army and a well-organized diplomatic corps. Moreover, D'Azeglio's work had the enthusiastic endorsement of the other moderate leaders. Even Mazzini commented: "The great national idea is expressed with decision, without reticence, and with admirable courage." And Mazzini had the most to lose.

THE SURPRISE POPE

Although these considerations would become clear over the next few years, in 1846 different models for unification competed, and, amazingly, the least likely suddenly became the most probable.

On June 1, 1846, the "retrograde, stubborn, lazy, reactionary to the highest degree" Pope Gregory XVI died. Ironically, the ideas expressed in Gioberti's *Primato* and by the liberal moderates had penetrated the highest ranks of the clergy. Furthermore, popular pressure in the form of petitions and the crisis of the Papal State itself convinced several cardinals that Gregory's policies had to end. These men engineered the election of the cardinal from Imola as a compromise at a conclave that had originally pitted a highly favored conservative against an opponent considered overly liberal.

The new fifty-four-year-old pope, Pius IX, or Pio Nono (Giovanni Maria Mastai-Ferretti), came from the Romagna and favored change. He was reasonable rather than liberal, counted among his friends those of a moderate political persuasion, and had read Gioberti, Balbo, and D'Azeglio. It is not surprising, therefore, that moderate and neo-Guelph ideas influenced him. His election stunned Metternich and the Austrians.

In his first official act, Pius IX appointed a commission to study an amnesty for political prisoners, demanded by popular opinion. Although conservative prelates served on this commission, it included the novel presence of influential liberals, and on July 16 it granted the amnesty. Variously judged as generous and limited, the amnesty was important because of the context in which it was issued: the most reactionary state in Europe seemed to have made a complete turnaround.

The resulting explosion of popular joy and Gioberti's famous prophecy created the myth of Pio Nono. The people of the Eternal City saluted him with a torchlight parade, continuously begged for his blessing, and detached his horses from his carriage so they could pull it themselves. Similar tumultuous scenes repeated themselves in other cities, in churches, and in theaters, and Bologna's central piazza echoed with the strains of a hymn Rossini had composed and directed in the pope's honor. The peninsula witnessed an extraordinary chorus of enthusiasm for the pope and Italy. Where Mazzini had failed to raise the people, Pio Nono had succeeded; what the moderates had judged as extremely difficult, and perhaps dangerous, Pius IX had done effortlessly. An observer has noted that these events of 1846 "initiated the national revolution of 1848."

But a fundamental reality remained: Pius IX was not a liberal, and although historians have argued that he sympathized with Italian independence and unity, he was unwilling to lead the movement. In addition, he was indecisive: he supported reforms, but not to the extent demanded by the patriots who gained control of the Roman crowd and nudged it from neo-Guelphism to radical democracy. In his biography of the pope, historian Frank Coppa quotes Pius as saying, "We will cede as long as our conscience permits us, but arriving at the limit which we have already pre-established, we will not, with the help of God, go beyond it by one step, even if they tore [*sic*] us to pieces."

Gradually, the joyful exhibitions turned into demonstrations for measures about which Pius IX was lukewarm or that he did not wish to address. Pressed by the people throughout 1847, and either "inebriated by the applause" or lacking the strength to oppose it, Pius only emboldened the crowd as he yielded to its pretensions. When he found the conviction to stop the process, the neo-Guelph bubble burst.

THE PEOPLE'S REVOLUTION

The strong involvement of the masses in the Risorgimento characterized not only Rome but other parts of Italy during this period. In the repressed South, where no Pio Nono appeared to save the day, patriots and exiles planned coordinated uprisings in Naples, Palermo, and other areas, in addition to Tuscany and the Papal State.

In this conspiratorial context, and against the dramatic Roman backdrop, the revolution of 1848 exploded in Palermo on January 8. Despite their appearance of being isolated and yearning for independence from Naples, Sicilian patriots had solid contacts with the national movement. Simultaneously, a revolt began on the Continent; the Neapolitan king granted some concessions and fired his hated police chief, actions that heartened rather than satisfied the rebels. Popular demonstrations for a constitution ensued. Ferdinand II angled for Austrian intervention and, when he failed to receive it, published on January 29 a constitution based on the French Constitution of 1830. Even though this act inspired some southern moderates to hope for an alliance with Ferdinand II to free Italy, fear and a desire to split Neapolitans and Sicilians (who supported a different constitution) motivated the king.

Ferdinand's action brought pressure on other Italian rulers to follow suit. When news of the Neapolitan Constitution reached Piedmont, massive demonstrations occurred in the kingdom's two chief cities, Turin and Genoa. These events finally forced Charles Albert to choose; he had been following a policy of encouraging the liberals on the independence issue while granting administrative reforms but retaining political power in his own hands. The demand for a constitution meant that he could no longer pursue that policy; indeed, the king opposed a constitution because it weakened his position and because he had promised his predecessor that he would never grant one. Conservatives encouraged him to hold fast, but his advisers argued that it would be wise to grant a constitution speedily rather than be forced to do so under the popular pressure that would inevitably build up. A moderate commentator exposed the contradictions of those opposing a constitution: "Those of you who do not wish to diminish the King's authority by allowing the Nation's participation through political representation, those of you who oppose written guarantees or sanctions against the abuse of power, those of you who say that public opinion is a sufficient check, have you thought about which guarantee you count on? That of revolution, neither more nor less." Under the force of these arguments, Charles Albert's resistance waned; finally, he received a dispensation from the oath he made to Charles Felix that he would not agree to a constitution. On February 8, the government published the *Statuto*, also based on the French Constitution of 1830; this instrument, discussed in chapter 8, became the constitution of united Italy.

The people greeted the Statuto's promulgation with great enthusiasm. Widespread demonstrations of support quickly turned anti-Austrian and anti-Jesuit. The new constitutional order mandated the replacement of the current government with one more acceptable to the liberals, and in March a cabinet headed by Balbo took office.

Demonstrations had caused the government to plan reforms in Tuscany as well. News from Naples and Turin, however, forced the grand duke to go beyond reforms and to publish a constitution on February 17.

These events brought about repercussions in Rome. As previously mentioned, patriots there had been pushing Pius to speed the pace of reform and to increase support for the national movement. The papal government initiated talks with Charles Albert about creating a customs union but refused Piedmont's offer of an alliance directed against Austria. The renewed agitation in Italy found Roman patriots and demonstrators increasingly disenchanted with the slow pace of reform and Pius IX becoming more upset with his subjects' demands, but once again the two misunderstood each other. On February 10, Pius issued a statement attributing past reforms to his own benevolence, not to the rights of the people. He called for calm, invited the Romans to desist from making requests not conforming to his duties (a constitution?), and sought to defuse a demand for military reorganization directed against the Austrians by denying there was danger of war. Pius nullified his stern message, however, by ending with an eloquent call upon God to bless *Italy*. The pope intended to end the continuous demonstrations demanding support for the national movement, but given the Italian context and the gathering revolutionary storm that would soon break out over Europe, everyone interpreted the pope's message as conferring his benediction on the patriotic movement. That evening, enthusiastic demonstrators cheered the pope, who, once more, tried unsuccessfully to clarify his position. He wound up the evening by blessing all Italy once again.

The concession of constitutions in Naples, Turin, and Florence, a mounting petition drive in the Papal State, and increasing European disorder convinced members of the papal government that it had become necessary to grant a constitution, despite Pio Nono's initial opposition. At the same time, a debate occurred on which qualities would best combine democratic principles with the Papal State's religious nature, but the pope ignored this discussion. On March 14, Pius published a constitution establishing two legislative houses but giving the pope and the College of Cardinals supreme power over legislation. The constitution also banned the secular legislature from passing laws in matters of mixed secular-ecclesiastical concern—extremely difficult to define—and conferred political rights only on practicing Catholics. Under the circumstances, these weaknesses went unnoticed, and popular ecstasy greeted the constitution's promulgation and raised Pius's popularity to new heights.

By the time Pius issued his constitution, revolution had radically altered the European landscape. In late February, King Louis Philippe had been overthrown and the Second Republic established in France. In mid-March, the revolution spread to Vienna, an event that proved crucial for Italy and other Austrian-dominated areas.

The events of early 1848 resulted in constitutions for all the major Italian states except Lombardy-Venetia. Convinced that concessions to constitutionalism or nationalism would end in the breakup of their polyglot empire, the Austrians harshly repressed the slightest sign of national feeling in their Italian possessions. They arrested well-known leaders in Lombardy and Venetia, but the struggle's novel aspect was that it spread into the popular consciousness, at least in urban areas. Austrian officials and their subjects engaged in an imaginative "cold war" calculated to inflict maximum irritation on each other. The most famous of these events was the antismoking campaign. In an effort to deprive the government of revenues from its tobacco monopoly, the Milanese gave up smoking and pressured anyone not participating in the boycott to follow their example. Austrian authorities distributed free cigars to their soldiers, who sauntered down the streets blowing smoke in the faces of citizens; when fights ensued, Austrian troops killed and maimed unarmed civilians.

With the outbreak of the Viennese revolution and Metternich's ignominious flight from his capital, the Italian possessions exploded. The Austrians had poured reinforcements into Italy, but they were unprepared for the fierce street fighting that broke out in Milan on March 18—the "Five Days." This uprising seems to have begun spontaneously but was rapidly transformed into a guerrilla war directed by a War Council. This council had as its guiding light Carlo Cattaneo, a federalist republican who had believed in gradual progress toward independence but who concluded that the national feeling demonstrated by the uprising made his ideas obsolete. On March 22, when the Austrian commander, Joseph Radetzky, was forced to pull his army out of Milan, Mazzini's theory that civilians could defeat professional armies was realized. Encouraged by similar developments throughout Austria's Italian dominions—especially the expulsion of the Austrians from Venice—and the news that volunteers from Naples, the Papal State, and Tuscany were rushing to aid the Lombards, Cattaneo and the War Council proposed raising a democratic volunteer army to drive the Austrians out of the peninsula as a prerequisite to a definitive political solution. Unfortunately, the conversion of Cattaneo, the "reluctant revolutionary," to something uncomfortably resembling Mazzini's "people's war" raised an alarming specter and compromised the national independence movement.

THE DIVIDED WAR FOR LIBERATION

Although their desire to liberate themselves from Austrian domination and their support for a "free Italy" unified the rebels, politics divided them. Differences existed among republicans, including Cattaneo and Mazzini; the latter was more radical but willing to subordinate everything to achieve unity. Bad blood, however, split Lombard republicans from aristocrats who favored Charles Albert and advocated the fusion of Lombardy with Piedmont. Led by Count Gabrio Casati, the aristocratic party feared not only the Austrians but also the radical-democratic implications of a popular war. Lombard moderates formed a provisional government and appealed to Charles Albert to intervene. The Piedmontese king consented but arrived after the Milanese had driven out the Austrians.

This tardiness made the republicans even more suspicious of Charles Albert. The king's indecisiveness has already been noted, but Cattaneo had a simpler explanation for his motives. He believed that Charles Albert had intervened for dynastic reasons, "to save the most retrograde part of Italy" and to transform the conflict from a "people's war" into a "safe" conventional one. The Piedmontese army, therefore, had come to replace the Austrians, not to save the Lombards.

In sum, with the Austrian army still intact, the Italians began squabbling about issues such as fusing Lombardy-Venetia with Piedmont and about where the capital would be located. Cattaneo conducted a campaign to block fusion by calling for the election of assemblies to decide that and other questions. He condemned as treason Mazzini's attempt to reach a compromise with the king and later denied any validity to a May referendum overwhelmingly favoring fusion, which clearly indicated popular support for the Piedmontese solution. Cattaneo's memoirs graphically illustrate republican suspicion of Charles Albert's motives, and the fulminations found there symbolize the republican-monarchist split in the national movement. This republican hatred of the "royal war" culminated in the fragmentation of Mazzini-oriented groups, the revival of local rivalries, and the proclamation of small independent republics. The Piedmontese, in turn, resorted to self-destructive stratagems to block these tendencies. For example, because Venice had proclaimed itself a republic under the leadership of Daniele Manin, the Piedmontese refused to move against Austrian reinforcements in an attempt to frighten Venetia into declaring union with Piedmont.

Because these divisions sabotaged the "war for national liberation" before Austrian influence on the peninsula could be eliminated, the conflict was transformed into a conventional one between armies. This change and the recovery by the conservatives in Vienna shifted the military advantage to the Austrian commander Radetzky, who retreated into impregnable fortresses and regrouped.

Other aspects of the Italian situation also favored Austria. Spurred by popular enthusiasm, Rome, Florence, and Naples had sent troops to aid the national cause. As hegemony of the national movement passed to Piedmont, however, the frightened rulers of these states withdrew their forces. In Rome, Pius finally found the courage to oppose the reform movement, and the Kingdom of the Two Sicilies fell prey to disorders and secession. Suspicious of possible French aid, the Piedmontese, having refused an Austrian offer to content themselves with Lombardy, faced the Austrian army alone. Furthermore, Charles Albert continued his contradictory policies by allowing conservatives suspicious of the national movement space to maneuver. After several small victories, the Piedmontese lost the Battle of Custoza in July. A slow retreat and the loss of Milan followed on August 6, 1848, and an armistice was signed three days later.

Anger and accusations of betrayal directed at Charles Albert followed the loss of Lombardy. In Turin, a Gioberti government took command, but was soon replaced with a more democratic cabinet. Eager to vindicate himself as soon as possible, Charles Albert wished to resume the war, and the government agreed. Because of his previous defeats, the king relinquished command of his dispirited and politically divided army to Polish General Wojciech Chrzanowski. On March 23, 1849, the Piedmontese once again met defeat at the Battle of Novara. Failing to find the death he sought on the battlefield, Charles Albert abdicated in favor of his son, who took the name of Victor Emanuel II, and left for Portugal. "There are moments which redeem an entire life," said a contemporary observer; Charles Albert finally found redemption at Novara.

THE ROMAN REVOLUTION

Even as the national revolution began unraveling, dramatic events occurred in Rome. Pius was shocked by the commander of his troops, who told his soldiers that they were waging a new crusade. Reports of a possible schism with Catholics in Austria and southern Germany also alarmed the pope. As a result, on April 29, 1848, Pius issued the famous allocution making his position clear. He declared that, as leader of all the Catholics, he would not wage war on the Catholic Austrians.

Pius had finally distinguished between his sympathies as an Italian and his duty as pope, but the reaction was immediate, sharp, and unanimous. "He has betrayed us," tearfully declared Angelo Brunetti, known as Ciceruacchio, chief tribune of the people. Instability followed the allocution, and Pius's appointment of moderate Pellegrino Rossi to head a government failed to stem it. Rossi's energetic reform policies and resistance to demands that he support the national cause alienated conservatives and democrats alike. On November 15, a fanatic stabbed him to death. Demonstrations ensued, and the crowd imposed a cabinet committed to Italian independence. On November 24, Pio Nono fled to Gaeta, in the Kingdom of the Two Sicilies.

The Catholic powers vowed to save the pope. Naples and Spain, even republican France, offered Pius military assistance while the Romans exulted to Verdi's patriotic *La Battaglia di Legnano*, deposed the pope, and declared a republic. Verdi's opera tells how the Italian city-states routed German Emperor Frederick

Barbarossa in 1176; with the defeat of the national movement in the North, the Eternal City became the center of the Risorgimento. Freedom fighters poured into Rome, including Giuseppe Garibaldi, who had spent years fighting in South America.

The Roman Republic put itself into the hands of Giuseppe Mazzini, who revealed himself an excellent organizer capable of winning the people's support. Despite difficult conditions, hardly any disorders marred the republic's existence. The Romans discussed and adopted the most democratic constitution of the period and carried out a series of significant social reforms. The republic abolished the Inquisition, special courts, clerical control of schools and universities, and censorship. On February 21, 1849, the republican Assembly mandated the takeover of Church property by the state and passed measures to ensure that the land would actually reach the peasants. The republic also introduced the concept of a paid clergy.

These measures encountered criticism, but they dramatically illustrate the competence and courage of Rome's democratic administration. Mazzini's party showed great promise in resolving the Papal State's ancient ills and, given more time, might have transformed its economy in a manner that the popes had perennially demonstrated themselves incapable of doing.

THE PEOPLE DEFEATED

But time had run out for the national movement's democratic wing. By 1849, reactionaries had regained control in Austria and Germany. Italian liberals had negotiated for French help, but republican France was too radical for the Piedmontese and too conservative for the democrats. In May and June 1848, French radicals who might have supported Italian liberty suffered defeat. The election of Napoleon I's nephew, Louis Napoleon, as president of the Second Republic encouraged some Italian democrats, but he was primarily interested in strengthening his own position. In Tuscany, where the people had expelled Leopold II, the Austrians intervened ferociously. The restored grand duke reinstituted absolutistic rule and, on May 6, 1852, revoked the constitution he had granted in 1848. In the Kingdom of the Two Sicilies, Ferdinand II suspended the Neapolitan Parliament forever on March 13, 1849. The king then proceeded to reconquer Sicily, which had previously declared its independence. By the end of May, all resistance to the Bourbons had ceased.

These events and the Austrian siege of Venice left the Roman Republic as the only beacon of hope for Italians. Garibaldi organized Rome's defense in the expectation of an Austrian attack. Naples and Spain sent troops to restore the pope, but they proved too weak to accomplish the mission. Indeed, Garibaldi planned to invade Neapolitan territory to revive the Neapolitan Revolution. Hoping to avoid exacerbating the diplomatic situation, Mazzini successfully opposed the move. He believed that rivalry with the Austrians and republican sympathies might encourage the French to aid the Romans. Instead, the French president hoped to strengthen himself internally by exploiting the Italian situation. Louis Napoleon gambled on garnering domestic Catholic as well as liberal support by restoring the pope but pressuring him to retain the constitution he had previously granted. A heroic defense defeated Louis Napoleon's army at first, but its commander violated an armistice and sneaked in reinforcements. Thus the French destroyed the Roman Republic and restored Pio Nono.

The patriots scattered from Rome and the other defeated revolutionary states. Garibaldi escaped from the French in a desperate attempt to reach Venice, but many of his men were captured and executed, and his wife died in his arms. On August 26, following a tenacious defense that won the respect of its Austrian besiegers, Venice finally capitulated. The people's revolution had been crushed.

With the exception of France, all the rulers who were overthrown in the gigantic European revolutionary movement of 1848 were restored. This fact has led observers to ask whether or not the revolutions of 1848 constituted a "turning point."

In Italy, they had a clarifying effect by eliminating two models for unification from contention. Neo-Guelphism turned out to be an illusion. The 1848 events demonstrated that no matter how sympathetic individual popes might be to Italian national issues, they would subordinate their feelings to their role as international leaders of the Catholic world and would call in foreign powers to intervene on their behalf. Moreover, the papacy reverted to its ancient role as a major obstacle to the peninsula's unity because the restored Pius IX no longer toyed with liberal ideas.

Mazzini's model also emerged fatally wounded from the events of 1848. Although Mazzini did not plan the uprisings, his ideas inspired and marked them. He had theorized the revolution of the people as the answer to military occupation. From a military viewpoint, 1848 proved him correct, but "there was an immense gap between the people as dreamed of by Mazzini and as awakened by revolution." The victorious people failed to carry out his ideal of a free, united, and indivisible Italy, reviving instead class and local divisions. Furthermore, whereas Mazzini had demonstrated prudence and a keen awareness of the Italian and European diplomatic context, republican leaders such as Cattaneo had demonstrated an inflexibility and suspiciousness that alienated the national movement's moderate wing. In addition, the developments of 1848–1849 revealed the limitations of Mazzini's methods. They might succeed in overthrowing princes but could not defeat the great powers. Indeed, 1848 proved that Italy could not "do it by itself"; the national movement needed Europe's help against Austria, and only an established power had a chance of securing that aid. Mazzini, the sworn enemy of the European establishment, could never institute a dialogue with the powers. Although Mazzinian ideals continued to fascinate part of the national movement and exercised a pull far into the future, support for Mazzini greatly diminished over the next few years. Even his sympathizers became convinced that Mazzini lacked the practical qualities necessary to free the peninsula from foreign domination.

The destruction of neo-Guelphism and the decline of Mazzinianism left the moderate model for independence under Piedmontese leadership as the most plausible solution to the Italian problem. Charles Albert's abdication removed a major obstacle to Piedmont's leadership, and the Statuto, the only surviving Italian constitution, quickened the kingdom's evolution into a liberal state. Absolutism had returned to Rome, Naples, and Tuscany, eliminating them as centers of the Risorgimento; those governments could no longer pretend to enjoy real popular support, buttressed as they were by Austrian or French armies. With the Austrians exacting as well a terrible price from the inhabitants of Lombardy-Venetia—where they also unsuccessfully attempted to stimulate a class war—Piedmont attracted the sympathies of Italians comparing their situation to that of the only independent state on the peninsula.

The revolutions of 1848 had brought independence within sight, despite local differences and political divisions. In 1849, this dream had suffered defeat but remained alive. Indeed, the revolutions had simplified the terms of the Italian problem and had set into motion a process that culminated in unity and independence.

CHAPTER EIGHT

Cavour and the Piedmontese Solution

I N 1848, THE ITALIANS HAD LED EUROPE IN REVOLUTION, AND IN 1849 THEIR heroic resistance against overwhelming French and Austrian force won the admiration of Europeans. In the 1850s, amid all the gloom, unification was forcefully posed as a European problem and Piedmont had been converted to the cause of independence.

THE "SECOND RESTORATION"

The restored regimes clamped down hard on their populations. In Lombardy-Venetia, military authorities under Radetzky ruled until 1857 and imposed a harsh repression: persons discovered with arms in their possession faced summary execution, and suspected patriots were beaten. On August 12, 1849, the Austrians gave an amnesty for all but the most compromised patriots, but the police retained wide powers to crush suspected opposition. No dialogue between the imperial government and its Lombard and Venetian subjects existed, and physical force alone kept the Austrians in power.

The Lombard economy stagnated. Diseases debilitating the silk and wine-making industries caused great hardship, but Austrian administration was primarily responsible for the downturn because it increased taxes to make the Italians pay for the 1848 revolutions and for an increased share of the empire's enormous deficit. The Austrians failed to encourage railway building, the engine of economic development, and subordinated Lombardy's economic well-being to their strategic goals. In the decade following 1848, Lombards looked wistfully at the economic growth of Piedmont and concluded that independence was the necessary prerequisite for progress.

Conditions in Rome and Naples also deteriorated. With the support of Europe's Catholics, Pius IX revoked the 1848 constitution, vigorously opposed liberalism and democracy, and broke with the national movement. Reaction gripped the state, corruption reigned in the economic sphere, and reform ended. In the religious area, the Curia attacked liberal Catholicism and rejected reform. The Jesuits spearheaded the antiliberal campaign through their new review *La Civiltà Cattolica*. Discontent among all classes grew, and conspiracy flourished, but French troops in Rome and Austrian soldiers holding down the outlying areas made a fresh revolution unlikely. After the brief parenthesis of Pio Nono's "liberal" biennium, the Papal State had reverted to its old self.

The same happened in the Kingdom of the Two Sicilies, where the reaction matched that of 1799 in ferocity, if not in bloodshed. The kingdom languished economically because the king would not consider reforms, which he thought might stimulate another revolution. Worsening economic conditions fueled numerous antigovernment conspiracies.

Though on a superficial level the "second restoration" resembled the one following 1815, European and Italian conditions were different. On the diplomatic side, the unity that had characterized the Vienna settlement cracked. The 1848 revolutions had encouraged a Prussian move to become preeminent in Germany, and Russia hoped that its suppression of the Hungarian Revolution on behalf of Austria and Austria's embroilment in Germany would result in a free hand in Turkey. The revival of Bonapartism in France, where Louis Napoleon seized dictatorial power in 1851, compounded these changes. In 1854, the Crimean War broke out because France and England struggled to contain an expanding Russia. These changes altered the European equilibrium and furthered the Italian cause.

As usual, economics contributed to the changing European diplomatic picture. Italy's economy stagnated, but in the rest of western Europe the period up to 1873 witnessed a general price rise, rapid economic development, increased pressure for free trade, and the shift of political power from the aristocracy to the bourgeoisie. England favored a peaceful continent that would favor trade. Economic interests contributed to diplomatic resolutions of issues such as the "Italian problem," which had generated so much disorder. The decline of revolutionary influence and the growing attraction of a moderate solution to the Risorgimento favored this scenario.

MAZZINI AND HIS ENEMIES

Despite his defeat in 1849, Giuseppe Mazzini remained optimistic about the ultimate success of revolution. He established the Central Committee for European Democracy in England and the National Association in Italy to further his cause, but in fact he was fast losing support among both radicals and moderates.

Radicals such as Giuseppe Ferrari, an associate of Cattaneo's during the 1848 Milan revolution, influenced by the new socialist ideas circulating among European intellectuals, proclaimed that liberty and independence were "only lies where the rich crush the poor"—a position with which Mazzini could never agree. Socialist thinker Carlo Pisacane attributed the failure of the 1848 revolutions to class warfare and to Mazzini's emphasis on unity rather than on liberty. The ideas of this young Neapolitan, tragically killed in 1857 during the struggle for independence, provide crucial testimony to the rising importance of social issues in the Risorgimento. The heated discussions among Italian radicals ended the possibility of unified action by radical patriots.

After 1849, the moderates as well were distancing themselves from Mazzini. His revolutionary ideology fostered conspiracies all over Italy, but they culminated in failed revolutions, such as the one in Milan in February 1853, which revealed serious splits between the Milanese bourgeoisie and popular classes. This defeat polarized the national movement and increased criticism of Mazzini from friends who were losing faith in him. They proposed the union of all patriotic forces, which would require postponing until after unity a decision on whether Italy should be a republic or a monarchy. In effect, this meant collaboration with Piedmont. The intransigent Mazzini responded by forming the Action Party, a fighting group committed to immediate combat, unity, and a republic. The hemorrhaging in Mazzini's camp had already begun when Piedmontese developments accelerated it.

Cavour and the Transformation of Piedmont

In 1849, the liberal transformation of Piedmont appeared most unlikely. Thrust on the throne by the abdication of Charles Albert, Victor Emanuel II had not been groomed to succeed his father, perhaps because of persistent rumors about his paternity and because his mother and his wife were Hapsburgs. Notwithstanding his nickname, "the Gentleman King," his long-running affair with an earthy drum major's daughter, popularly known as "la bella Rosina," scandalized his subjects, and his manners shocked Queen Victoria.

According to legend, Victor Emanuel earned his appellative by refusing to revoke the Statuto despite pressure by Radetzky to do so, but English historian Denis Mack Smith casts doubt on this story. He believes that the new monarch promised to revoke the constitution, asking for and receiving a pledge of Austrian support. The urgency of peace at any price after the disastrous Battle of Novara and Victor Emanuel's success in securing a good deal from Radetzky, however, fuel suspicion that the young king shrewdly manipulated the Austrians. Facing military collapse, a revolution in Genoa, and the insistence by Piedmontese democrats that the war be continued, the new monarch could hardly withdraw the Statuto.

The evolution of the conservative Statuto in a liberal direction marked the decade from 1849 to 1859. The Statuto reserved to the king absolute power to name and dismiss his ministers. It bolstered the Crown's position by failing to establish the office of prime minister, by creating a Chamber of Deputies elected by restricted suffrage and lacking the power to confirm or dismiss governments, and by instituting a Senate appointed by the king that could veto legislation passed by the Chamber. Yet unlike the French Constitution of 1830, on which it was patterned, the new constitutional order permitted liberal political expression and the emergence of liberal statesmen.

The elections of July 15, 1849, produced a majority to the left of the king and of his government headed by Massimo D'Azeglio. As a result, the Chamber of Deputies quarreled with the government over ratifying the peace treaty with Austria. The king dissolved the Chamber in late November and issued a critical statement asking for support. In this famous "Moncalieri Proclamation," authored by D'Azeglio, Victor Emanuel complained about the Chamber's "hostile" acts toward him. He stated that if the voters failed to elect a favorable majority, they, and not he, would be responsible for any future disorders and other consequences.

Although this proclamation established a precedent encouraging future intervention in elections, it produced positive results. Elections held on December 9 gave the government a two-thirds majority, but a high percentage of voter participation was the key reason for this outcome. The Moncalieri Proclamation revitalized Parliament by encouraging the middle classes to become involved in politics and ending conservative suggestions to demote the Chamber to a consultative assembly. The electoral debate also reenergized the patriotic movement, and the constitution proved crucial in attracting patriotic supporters from all over Italy.

The constitutional system propelled onto the political scene a remarkable individual who would set the future course of Piedmontese liberalism and Italian independence: Camillo Benso, Count of Cavour. Cavour was born on August 10, 1810, the second son of Marquis Michele Benso, the police chief of Turin from 1835 to 1847, and Adele de Sellon, a Protestant from Geneva who later converted to Catholicism. His father's flexibility as a conservative who adapted well to more liberal times seems to have influenced the young Cavour's intense intellectual life. Cavour also interacted with Swiss and French intellectuals related to his mother. Cavour was attracted to moderate liberalism as a young man.

Cavour pursued a military career but found the army ill suited to his character. After being punished for defending the July Revolution in France, Cavour resigned his commission in November 1831. He traveled widely in Britain, France, and Switzerland, familiarizing himself with the western European political tradition and economic system and applying his knowledge to Piedmontese commerce and agriculture. He participated in various business enterprises, including banking, railway construction, stock market investments, candle manufacturing, and commerce in wheat and rice—in addition to gambling. His most spectacular endeavor took place at his estate in Leri, where he established a showplace of modern agricultural and business methods. In 1842, he helped found the influential Agrarian Association; by 1848, he had achieved fame as a businessman with a reputation as a serious student of Piedmontese economic affairs. He decided to enter politics, in which he had always been interested.

Cavour was a supreme pragmatist who believed in a middle road. He supported gradual change and favored cooperation among the bourgeoisie, the progressive nobility, and a monarchy sensitive to the nation's wishes. He rejected radical democracy, socialism, and communism and dismissed the romantic nationalism propagated by Mazzini and Gioberti; for him, the Risorgimento was simply a movement to raise Italy to the level of the most advanced European countries.

Thus Cavour aimed to modernize Piedmont's economic system, address pressing social issues, and make the kingdom into a major player in the European diplomatic constellation. Cavour forcefully brought the Italian problem to the attention of the powers in ways they could comprehend. He brought to the moderate model for independence a necessary element that it had always lacked: a brilliant statesman operating within a viable constitutional system. Cavour's qualities appeared just as Gioberti's neo-Guelphism and Mazzini's radical democracy were faltering and proved irresistible to the national movement.

Because his middle stance alienated both the right and the left of the Piedmontese political spectrum, Cavour faced a difficult struggle, but he was a major influence in the operation of the constitutional system. When he entered politics, some Piedmontese conservatives, along with leftists and moderates, believed that the Church's excessive power should be curbed, and clashes between the reactionary Catholic hierarchy and the government made resolution of this question urgent. In late 1849, Cavour supported Count Giuseppe Siccardi's nomination as minister of justice and ecclesiastical affairs. In February 1850, Siccardi presented bills reducing the Church's influence. These laws liberalized Piedmont's ecclesiastical legislation by eliminating antiquated Church privileges and, by splitting conservatives and moderates, made an anti-Statuto alliance impossible. More important, Cavour distinguished himself in the debate by boldly pressing the government for further reforms. His action constructed the foundation for an agreement between the moderates and the left in the Chamber of Deputies.

Between October 1850 and 1852, Cavour served in two cabinet posts and guided Piedmont's economic and financial affairs. A convinced free-trader, he negotiated commercial treaties with Britain, France, Belgium, Austria, and other countries. Passed against conservative opposition, these agreements eliminated protectionism, increased trade, helped modernize the economy, and placed Piedmontese economic policy on a par with other European countries. Cavour encouraged an ambitious program of railway building, key to the country's further modernization and to increasing business activity. His attempted banking reform was rejected, but he succeeded in reorganizing the state's financial administration. Cavour sought to bring Piedmont's growing budget deficit under control by increasing taxes on business and in other areas, but his opposition to progressive income taxes, heavy borrowing for railway building, and the cost of rearmament made him less successful in keeping the deficit low.

In carrying out his economic program, Cavour ran into opposition from conservatives in the Chamber, and most of his measures passed because of support from moderate leftists led by Urbano Rattazzi. This de facto cooperation provided the basis for a future political alliance. The head of the government, D'Azeglio, had allowed Cavour relative freedom but opposed the state's further liberalization, a development that Cavour considered essential. This stalemate suggested a new majority composed of Cavour's moderate right and Rattazzi's moderate left, a change spurred as well by foreign developments. On December 1–2, 1851, President Louis Napoleon Bonaparte assumed dictatorial power in France, causing Austria to seek a rapprochement with it. An Austro-French agreement would have squeezed Piedmont between two reactionary powers and favored Piedmontese conservatives opposing the progressive evolution of the state. This scenario seemed to be playing out when French and Austrian pressure forced the government to present a bill imposing press restrictions. As a cabinet member, Cavour could not openly oppose the bill, but he differentiated his position from the government's and made a pact with Rattazzi in which the two statesmen promised to support the constitution, independence, and further liberalization.

This *connubio*, or "marriage," favored the liberal development of Piedmont by creating a new majority powerful enough to block conservative backsliding and to support progressive legislation. By allying with a party intimately identified with the Risorgimento and the 1848 revolutions, Cavour announced Piedmont's paramount role in the independence struggle. The connubio incarnated a new alliance between the bourgeoisie, which favored independence, and sympathetic segments of the nobility that undermined conservative and extreme Left influence and became a pole of attraction for patriots.

The delicate political operation furthered both the Risorgimento and the liberal transformation of a state that had been among the peninsula's most reactionary. As with all great political compromises, this one had costs. In the maneuvering that produced a Cavour cabinet in November 1852, for example, the Piedmontese statesman agreed not to use all the power at his disposal to pass a bill instituting civil marriage because Victor Emanuel opposed it. The measure met defeat in the Senate by one vote and had to wait until 1865 to be enacted. These concessions to Piedmont's political and social realities were so small in comparison to Cavour's achievement in rooting constitutionalism in Piedmont that English historian Denis Mack Smith's criticism of Cavour's alleged "transformism" and of his high-handedness misses the mark. (A term usually applied to post-unification politics, and discussed in Chapter 10, "transformism" indicates the abandonment of one's principles for political gain.)

Indeed, Piedmont's liberal political, economic, and Church policies during Cavour's stewardship propelled the northern state into becoming the national movement's undisputed leader. Cavour made agricultural loans easier to obtain, modernized the credit industry, ended residual feudal dues, and reformed the law on joint-stock companies; all these changes greatly aided business. With regard to the Church, Cavour launched the attractive slogan: "A free Church in a free state." In 1855, a law dissolved all religious corporations not devoted to teaching, preaching, or caring for the sick, raised the stipends of the lower clergy, and provided pensions for disabled clergy through a tax on benefices. Victor Emanuel opposed this legislation and intervened against Cavour in concert with the Church and Pius IX, but Cavour outfoxed them both and ensured continued liberal leadership of the country.

In the ten years after the 1849 defeat of the national movement, Cavour's policies put Piedmont at the head of Italy in economic development and political progressivism. Free trade spurred agricultural development and the silk industry and put textile and cast-iron manufacturing on a modern footing; banking reforms created the basis for a future centralized banking system. The major stimulus for nineteenth-century economic activity, railway building, showed a tremendous jump. In 1848, Piedmont had 8 kilometers of railway, compared to 357 in the other Italian states. By 1859, Piedmont counted 850 kilometers in operation and an additional 250 under construction, including work on the major Frejus tunnel through the Alps, compared with a total of 986 for the rest of the peninsula. The railways were built either by the state or with state subsidies.

The prodigious economic activity brought with it an improvement in the conditions of life for the bourgeoisie, and the right of association, recognized by the Statuto, allowed the growing number of workers to organize. Since this economic and political development occurred during a decade of stagnation for the rest of Italy, Piedmont became an example to emulate and a magnet for other Italians because it demonstrated the economic benefits of independence and unity.

A "STERNER PLAN"

Cavour's successes contrasted with continued failures in the Mazzinian camp that left independence under Piedmont's guide as the only practical option for patriots. As many as 50,000 exiles from the Risorgimento's disruptions made their homes in Piedmont. One of them, Marquis Giorgio Pallavicino-Trivulzio, a democrat from Lombardy and survivor of Austrian prisons, proved particularly important as the moving force in the transmigration of republicans to the monarchical camp. Pallavicino insisted that patriots should downplay their republicanism because Italian independence was the most important issue, and only monarchist Piedmont offered any real hope of freeing Italy. He convinced many exiles from the 1848 revolutions to drop Mazzini and come over to Piedmont. Paris exile Daniele Manin, hero of the Venetian Republic and well connected within the European liberal milieu, was Pallavicino's most influential convert. In 1855, Manin stated that the republicans stood ready to sacrifice their demand for a republic if the House of Savoy led the fight for Italian independence.

Piedmontese foreign policy began favoring independence at a time when European diplomats seemed ready to support an enlarged Piedmont, but only as a way of blocking unification. Despite his own sympathy for unification, Cavour the realist believed that it could not be achieved. He supposedly told Giuseppe La Farina, an influential leader of the democrats-turned-monarchists: "If the Italians demonstrate themselves mature for unity, I hope that the opportunity will not be long in coming; but I warn you that of all my political friends, none believe in the possibility and that its approach would compromise me and the cause we believe in."

Mazzini sought compromise with Pallavicino, but his followers continued their conspiratorial activities. Between 1853 and 1857, several Mazzini-inspired revolts occurred—including Pisacane's famous landing in southern Italy—but all failed. The resulting discredit of his tactics brought about a deep crisis in Mazzini's Action Party and the founding of the rival National Society in August 1857. This organization represented the definitive defection of democrats once influenced by Mazzini to Cavour. The Society's manifesto, approved by Cavour, subordinated all questions to Italian independence and unification. The Society stated that it supported the Savoy dynasty and the Piedmontese government as long as they supported Italian freedom and unity. Besides this moral support, the Society delivered over to Cavour a network of former Mazzinians that covered all Italy. The National Society proved invaluable in the creation of public opinion favorable to unity, in the calling of volunteers, and in the referenda and other actions that produced a united Italy in 1861. Historian Raymond Grew remarked: "Its [the National Society's] formation was the most dramatic sign that republicans were turning to Cavour, that nationalists would accept unification under Piedmontese monarchy, that the era of Mazzini was really over."

DIPLOMATIC INITIATIVES

The Italian situation cleared up just as crucial diplomatic alterations occurred in Europe. The conjunction of the two provided Cavour with the opportunity to demonstrate himself a master statesman capable of exploiting the European diplomatic system on behalf of his aims on the peninsula—despite the enormous disproportion in power between Piedmont and the large states.

The European situation was fluid. The continued decline of Turkey and the weakness demonstrated by Austria during the 1848 revolutions emboldened Russia. Czar Nicholas I believed that gratitude for his intervention against the Hungarian Revolution and the time required to recover from the 1848 revolutions would induce Austria to give him a free hand in Turkey, and that the French regime's weakness caused by recent domestic changes would prevent Napoleon III from interfering with his Turkish ambitions. But Nicholas miscalculated. Rapid economic development reinvigorated France; the British feared that Russian successes in Turkey would lead to Russian hegemony in Europe; and Austria's gratitude did not diminish its opposition to Russian gains in Turkey or its fear that cooperation with Russia would induce France and Britain to encourage a Piedmontese move against Austria's Italian possessions. When Nicholas moved against Turkey, the British and French declared war (March 27, 1854) to contain Russian expansionism.

The French and British needed allies and hoped for Austrian assistance to wage a war that stretched their lines of communication to the limit. Knowing that if they were engaged in a conflict in the East the Italians would revolt, the Austrians requested a French guarantee for their Italian possessions. The French seemed willing, but Austria chose instead to create a "neutral" bloc with Prussia and the German states. Austria then exploited this bloc to gain Turkish territory. In the meantime, French and British forces became bogged down. Given their desperate situation, the allies still attempted to draw in Austria and agreed to support the Italian status quo while the war continued in the East.

Piedmont and the Italian cause thus risked being crushed in the high-stakes great-power maneuvers. As the eastern crisis simmered, Piedmontese liberals, including Cavour, interpreted it as an ideological struggle between liberalism and conservatism that would result in a reordering of Europe on national lines. A broad consensus favoring Piedmontese participation on the side of Britain and France against reactionary Russia and Austria existed in Piedmont, but the British and French preferred an Austrian alliance that would prove dangerous to the Italian cause. As the hope for Austrian intervention faded, the allies approached Piedmont to join in the conflict; Cavour was displeased with British and French recalcitrance to accept Piedmontese conditions, while the king favored intervention at any cost. This set up a dangerous situation as Victor Emanuel prepared to dismiss Cavour and replace him with a conservative minister. Getting wind of the plan and convinced that nothing further could be done to alter the diplomatic realities, Cavour cleverly got himself named foreign minister and brought Piedmont into the conflict.

Cavour managed this complicated situation so well that the historical literature frequently portrays him as having planned Piedmont's intervention in the Crimean War. He took advantage of the conflict, domestically, by preventing a conservative involution of Piedmontese politics, maintaining a liberal constitutional system, and strengthening his links with the national movement. Externally, even though the allies preferred Austrian intervention, Cavour successfully used Piedmont's status as a belligerent to increase its prestige. After the conflict, Cavour cleverly exploited his position to gain greater influence beyond that of the leader of a second-rate power. He could never have "planned" all these developments. Historian A. William Salomone wrote: "Perennially on the job, restlessly ready to begin again after every bad turn, he was keen-eyed enough to learn the secret of extracting the potential of success from almost every failure." Cavour's brilliance, like Otto von Bismarck's, the artificer of German unity, lay in his ability to adapt to adverse conditions and to make rapid decisions, even though he had a less powerful state to work with. Unlike Bismarck, however, he used these qualities to preserve liberalism, not destroy it, and to integrate the dynasty into the Italian national fabric, not dominate it.

Although Piedmont's participation in the peace conference after the Crimean War was initially uncertain, Cavour succeeded in participating in the Congress of Paris as an equal, but he found the great powers unwilling to act against Austria on Italy's behalf. Cavour put forward several schemes to strengthen Piedmont's territorial and dynastic position, all of which went nowhere. On April 8, however, over Austria's objection, the participants discussed the Italian problem and criticized Austria. Both contemporaries and historians judged this debate very important, but Cavour came away dissatisfied. During Cavour's trip to Paris, Napoleon III asked him to draft a memorandum on the Italian situation. The direct contact established with the emperor and the Austro-Russian split were the chief results of the Congress of Paris and the Crimean War. At home, Parliament enthusiastically approved Cavour's diplomatic activity, enhancing his political position. Cavour announced that Piedmont's liberal system had put the state on a collision course with Austria.

On January 14, 1858, an event occurred that focused European attention on the Italian problem: Felice Orsini attempted to assassinate Napoleon. Orsini's desperate act aroused sympathy for the Italian cause, including, strangely enough, that of Napoleon. Napoleon allowed Orsini to turn the trial into a showpiece for the Italian cause, asking in return that Orsini publish a letter renouncing assassination and appealing for Napoleon's aid. The Orsini affair reinforced Napoleon's fear that the Italian situation encouraged revolutionary activities that threatened his throne. Apparently the attempt on his life encouraged him to unite with Piedmont as a means of defusing the revolutionary movement in Italy.

Cavour's contacts with Napoleonic circles culminated in a meeting between Napoleon and Cavour at Plombières, which Cavour detailed for Victor Emanuel in a memorandum on July 24, 1858. At this meeting, Napoleon declared himself ready to help Piedmont expel Austria from Italy. A condition of such action was that Austria declare war and that the struggle not become a "revolutionary" conflict. The two men settled on the acceptance by Victor Emanuel of an appeal by the people of Massa-Carrara, which would provoke a crisis with Piedmont, Piedmontese military preparations, and an Austrian ultimatum.

The two men then discussed the peninsula's postwar appearance. Piedmont would take Lombardy-Venetia and part of the Papal State to form a strong northern Italian kingdom; the pope would retain Rome and its surrounding territory; Tuscany and the remaining papal territory would be united into the Kingdom of Central Italy; the Kingdom of the Two Sicilies would remain intact to appease Russia (it had supported Russia during the Crimean War), although Napoleon ventilated the idea of placing Joachim Murat's son on the throne if the Neapolitans should revolt. Finally, to compensate the pope, he would be made head of an Italian confederation. France would be compensated with the Piedmontese regions of Savoy and perhaps Nice. To complete the new French order on the peninsula, Napoleon requested the hand of Victor Emanuel's daughter, Clotilde, for his cousin Jerome, nicknamed Plon-Plon. Reflecting the concerns of the age, the major part of the memorandum concerned Cavour's attempt to convince the king to accept the marriage of his religious fifteen-year-old daughter to the thirty-six-year-old playboy.

The Plombières agreement illustrates the complicated nature of Italian, French, and European diplomacy of the period. The agreement would not plan a united Italy, which would have damaged French interests; as it was, it conflicted with the policies of professional French diplomats, causing Napoleon to conduct the talks on a personal level, in secret, and against the wishes of his pro-Austrian foreign minister, Count Alexandre Walewski.

What did Napoleon hope to achieve? First, there were personal factors. As a young man, Napoleon had participated in the central Italian revolutions of 1831,

PORTRAITS

FELICE ORSINI
Criminal Conspirator or Freedom Fighter?

∽∘∾

In all battles for liberation, there are people who will argue that violence is necessary for the cause. Their activities usually throw doubt on their choice of tactics, even if they successfully contribute to the attainment of lofty goals. This was true of Felice Orsini.

Orsini, born at Medola, Forlì (near Imola), in the Papal States on December 10, 1819, came from a family that had served the Napoleonic regime and had ties with the Carboneria. Raised by his uncle, Orsini first got into serious trouble at age seventeen, when he killed his uncle's cook. An investigation showed that the murder resulted from a dispute over a woman. Women found Orsini fascinating, and they helped him throughout his life. After the murder, for example, two women hid him from the police until his uncle could intervene. His uncle, a great friend of Cardinal Mastai-Ferretti, the future Pius IX, got him into a seminary, but he was expelled because of his romantic involvement with two women. Later, he was implicated with his father in trying to overthrow the Papal State; he was arrested and given a life sentence in 1844, but was soon released by Pius IX.

During the 1848 uprisings, Orsini fought against the Austrians and the pope. In 1854, Mazzini dispatched him on a secret mission to Hungary. Caught by the Austrians, he spent two years in a prison at Mantua. Again, his way with women helped him escape. Orsini's breakout and subsequent adventures were so dramatic that an English publisher paid him to tell his story.

In Turin after his escapade, Orsini became convinced that French Emperor Napoleon III had blocked Italian unity and led the European reaction. Orsini and some friends went to Paris and, on January 14, 1858, threw three bombs at the emperor and his wife while they were on their way to the theater. The conspirators missed their targets, but the bombs killed 8 and wounded 156 in the crowd. Captured and sentenced to death, Orsini was given permission by Napoleon to publish a letter addressed to him. Orsini wrote: "Your Majesty, do not reject the supreme request of a patriot on his way to the gallows: Free my Fatherland and the benedictions of 25 million citizens will follow you everywhere and always."

On March 13, 1858, Felice Orsini calmly went to his death amid the tears of the women in the crowd and crying, "Long live Italy! Long live France!"

The press presented Orsini as a hero, and his letter moved the emperor. Cavour reemphasized that neither Napoleon nor Europe would ever find peace until the Italian powder keg was defused. Napoleon asked Cavour to meet with him secretly so they could plot to expel the Austrians from Italy and liberate the country. Felice Orsini had paid for his actions with his life, but his sacrifice contributed to Italy's liberation.

and his elder brother had died during one of them, so he had a personal interest in Italy. The emperor also viewed himself as carrying on the imperial tradition of his uncle, Napoleon I, who had been active in Italy. The desire to end revolutionary turmoil on the peninsula was a major factor. Most importantly, however, Napoleon aimed at making French influence predominant in Italy, the glory of which would strengthen his throne—thus the need to expel Austria and create a northern Italian kingdom tied to a France that would dominate the peninsula. The connection with progressive-oriented French rule instead of reactionary Austria would stabilize the Italian states and make them less susceptible to revolution.

Cavour recognized the benefits that would accrue to Napoleon, but exhorted Victor Emanuel to endorse the Plombières agreement. If the plan worked, Cavour wrote: "Your Majesty, sovereign in law over the richest and most powerful part of Italy, would be sovereign in fact over the whole peninsula." But Cavour's reasoning went beyond the dynastic argument he had to employ for the king's benefit. Even though the agreement did not envision a unified Italy, Austria's expulsion would rearrange the age-old order on the peninsula and make a native state supreme. Given the level of anti-Austrian feeling in Italy, it also seemed unlikely to Cavour that the war would not stimulate revolutions—and his links with the National Society and moderates all over Italy ensured Cavour's ability to deal favorably with the eventuality without letting the revolutions get out of hand. In addition, the French initiative presented the only opportunity to alter the Italian situation. Cavour calculated that French control would be temporary because the suspicious great powers feared an attempt to rebuild Napoleon I's empire and would curb French domination of the peninsula. The final element in Piedmont's favor was its vigorous liberal political system, which powerfully attracted the peninsula's bourgeoisie in a manner Napoleon's absolutism, despite its progressive elements, could not do.

This key point allowed Cavour to adjust his policies and maintain support for them during the unpredictable, unforeseen, and complex developments of 1859 and 1860 that created a united Italy. In sum, Napoleon unwittingly constructed a favorable context for unification, but this achievement required Cavour's "métier of the real politico, of the genuine statesman, of a maker of states."

THE 1859 WAR AND ITS AFTERMATH

The war issuing from the Plombières meeting was fought against a confused and changing backdrop; the conflict's favorable outcome for the Italians illustrates Cavour's diplomatic skills and the maturity that the national movement had achieved.

After Plombières, the anxious Austrian ambassador to Paris asked: "What sort of deal have these two conspirators made?" In a meeting with the diplomatic corps on New Year's Day 1859, Napoleon startled the Austrian ambassador by telling him that he regretted that relations between their two countries "are not as good as I would have hoped." On January 10, Victor Emanuel made the famous "cry of anguish" discourse to Parliament stating that he could not remain insensitive to the pain of his fellow Italians. This speech, coordinated with Napoleon, set the stage for the conflict, aroused great enthusiasm on the peninsula, and stimulated the movement of volunteers from all over the peninsula to aid Piedmont in the coming war for independence.

On January 26, France and Piedmont signed an "offensive-defensive" alliance. Piedmont was obliged to pay the costs of the operation and cede Savoy and Nice, but at least the treaty nailed down the size of the French military contribution. In February, the Piedmontese Parliament authorized the government to contract a loan to pay for the conflict, while in France a pamphlet directly inspired by Napoleon gave his solution for the "Italian problem." But though the plan for war seemed on track, Napoleon made the first of his several clamorous reversals.

Except for Napoleon, the French establishment opposed the Piedmontese alliance. Bankers making loans to Austria and the Italian states feared for their present and future investments. Catholics fretted about the possible loss of papal territory. Diplomats considered it folly to weaken Austria because it would signify the rise of Prussia and possible German unification under that state. In addition, the conflict threatened a wider war in which memories of Napoleon Bonaparte would trigger a great-power alliance against France.

These fears proved unfounded. Both Russian and British public opinion sympathized with the Italian national movement, and the issues were not strong enough for either country to intervene. Britain, however, attempted to mediate the dispute, and Napoleon got cold feet. As Piedmont went on a war footing, British mediation produced an agreement for a congress, which Austria would not attend unless Piedmont disarmed. Despite Cavour's vehement protest, France and Britain successfully pressured Piedmont to do so.

This development spelled disaster for Cavour. The proximity of a war for independence had inflamed Italy, and the sudden collapse of nationalistic expectations would certainly have been directed against Cavour. Informed of Napoleon's decision at 1:30 AM, Cavour jumped up on his bed and exclaimed: "There is nothing left for me to do but to get a pistol and blow my head off!" The Austrians, however, refused to discuss the Italian situation as equals with Piedmont at a congress. Misinterpreting the Italian problems as a Piedmontese plot, fearing to appear weak and jeopardize their position in Germany, alarmed at the economic consequences of remaining on a war footing during protracted negotiations, and convinced they could knock out Piedmont before the French army arrived, the Austrians on April 21 delivered Piedmont an ultimatum demanding immediate disarmament. Cavour refused the ultimatum, and the war began. "It was one of those jackpots you win only once in a century," commented Massimo D'Azeglio.

Besides French assistance, the crucial factor in this "Second War for Independence," when compared to the conflict of 1848–1849, was the unity of the Italians. In Piedmont, patriotic feelings and dynastic loyalty replaced political division. Unlike 1848, the republicans played a minor role. Mazzini put demands for a republic on the back burner and accepted the war against Austria under Piedmont's guidance on the grounds that Austria was the enemy of all Italian development. Volunteers joined the military effort, and Garibaldi was given a command of his own. The National Society acted as an auxiliary organization for Cavour and intensified its actions throughout Italy, ensuring that the political divisions of 1848 did not reappear.

The military effort during this conflict was not particularly notable, except that the railway was used for the first time in great strategic maneuvers. The opposing armies fought two significant battles, Magenta and Solferino, both Franco-Piedmontese victories. Then, all of a sudden, Napoleon reversed himself. Without informing Cavour, on July 11 Napoleon met with the Austrian emperor at Villafranca and ended the war. The agreement provided that Lombardy would be ceded to France, which would hand it over to Piedmont. Venice would remain under Austrian suzerainty and would join a confederation to be established under the pope's presidency. The rest of Italy would return to the situation that had existed before the war.

A complex interplay of international relations and Italian developments explain Villafranca. Prussia had mobilized, and France could not ignore this potential threat, even though the Prussians aimed at weakening Austria in Germany. From the military viewpoint, the war was far from over despite the French victories. But the main reasons for Napoleon's actions are to be found in Italian developments. His hope of containing revolutions proved illusory. Insurrections occurred in Tuscany, Parma, Modena, and the eastern part of the Papal State. With the divisions of 1848 gone, these areas requested annexation to Piedmont, which Cavour initially deferred because of French disapproval. Napoleon saw the Italian situation as out of control and believed that, if the war continued, he could not prevent the annexation of central Italy to Piedmont. Instead of French hegemony over the peninsula, he faced the prospect of a strengthened state on his border and so called the war off.

Cavour resigned in protest at this new manifestation of Napoleonic "treachery," but instead of reestablishing the old order, Villafranca proved the last, failed attempt of the powers to arrange the peninsula according to their plans and without the consent of its inhabitants. Villafranca could be enforced only through the use of arms. For reasons of prestige, France could neither use force nor allow Austria to do so. Napoleon made this clear from the beginning to the Austrians and Italians alike. Also crucial in this equation, Britain and Russia judged Austria's position in Italy as lost and favored an Italy independent of foreign influences.

Given the lack of a military option, central Italian leaders such as Bettino Ricasoli in Tuscany acted with considerable political skill in a confusing and complex environment. In close cooperation with the National Society, the patriots skillfully demonstrated the support that unity had among the people. The affected areas elected assemblies that voted overwhelmingly for annexation to Piedmont in August and September 1859. In December, Napoleon, convinced of the impossibility of enforcing Villafranca, aimed at cession of Nice and Savoy in return for his agreement to the annexation of central Italy. In January, Cavour returned to power in Piedmont and conducted the negotiations.

After agreement had been reached, the question was put to the people, and in March 1860 the former states of central Italy chose annexation by large majorities. Plebiscites were also held in Nice and Savoy, which voted for annexation to France. Questions have been raised about the fairness of the central Italian plebiscites, but by the standards of the day those gauges of popular opinion seemed convincing.

On March 25, 1860, elections for the Chamber of Deputies took place in the old Piedmontese domains and in the new territories. They produced an overwhelming victory for Cavour. In a stunning turnaround, the war of 1859 had produced an enlarged liberal northern Italian kingdom, but the surprises had by no means ended.

GARIBALDI AND THE THOUSAND

Cavour demonstrated consummate diplomatic skill in managing the events of 1859 and 1860, but they had achieved a larger northern Italian kingdom, not unification. It was the romantic spirits within the national movement who pressed forward in this quest.

With the absorption of northern Italy by Piedmont, attention focused on the South. Mazzini launched the idea of regaining the initiative for the republicans through action in the South. Francesco Crispi, a follower of Mazzini, traveled to Sicily in July and August 1859 to contact antigovernment conspirators there and to organize a revolution. When the revolt failed, Crispi turned to Giuseppe Garibaldi, the premier guerrilla fighter, and asked him to lead a Sicilian revolution. Garibaldi answered that he would do so only if the aim of the revolt was

Italian unity under Victor Emanuel. Garibaldi's attitude reflected that of Sicilian patriots. This position was widespread even among the democrats, and Mazzini himself had acknowledged the impossibility of attaining a republic.

In early April 1860, a revolution erupted in Palermo, and outside of that city it assumed the aspect of a guerrilla war. It did not go well, however, and Crispi urged Garibaldi to intervene. Garibaldi vacillated, but on May 11, 1860, he set sail with 1,000 volunteers amid myriad difficulties, having been forced to leave with outmoded weapons and without ammunition (which he picked up later). Cavour feared diplomatic repercussions if Piedmont aided the expedition, and a serious disagreement with Victor Emanuel II ensued.

Landing on the island at Marsala, Garibaldi found Sicily defended by a force of 25,000 that was well disciplined and well armed, but that was also engaged in fighting the revolution. Garibaldi's tactical and strategic brilliance, the military experience of his volunteers, the support of anti-Bourbon rebels, and the inefficiency of the Bourbon military command explain his victories. The crucial battle occurred at Calatafimi, where a fierce *garibaldino* bayonet attack offset enemy superiority in arms. Soon thereafter, a brilliant feint sent some of the best Bourbon troops on a wild goose chase while Garibaldi moved into Palermo on May 27. The city promptly rose, and Garibaldi held on to the capital despite a fierce artillery bombardment. The city was abandoned by the Neapolitans, and Garibaldi proceeded to reduce the rest of the island.

Cavour reacted cautiously. Not daring to oppose the wave of favorable popular opinion the expedition had generated, he allowed the various committees collecting funds to resupply the general. Modern rifles, volunteers, and medical supplies were sent to Sicily on ships that the American consul-general in Genoa had reflagged as American. This operation saved Cavour from diplomatic embarrassment, but the harsh European reaction Cavour expected because of Garibaldi's adventure never materialized. The powers had become used to the idea of Italian unity, and European public opinion was very favorable. Nonetheless, serious political, social, and diplomatic problems brewed.

Faced with his dynasty's destruction, Neapolitan King Francis II promised a constitution and installed a new cabinet. These measures fell flat, and an insurrection began in Naples. Francis's timid and ineffectual action had reinforced the "annexationist" party among moderates on the continent, and social issues ensured its dominance. In Sicily, the alliance between Garibaldi and the insurrectionary bands was breaking down as the common objective of expelling the Bourbons came within reach. The peasants saw an opportunity to achieve their ancient goal of land redistribution, but the nobles and bourgeois had jumped on Garibaldi's bandwagon because, with the crumbling of the old order, they wished to stop social change: "If we want things to stay as they are, things will have to change," says a character in the novel *The Leopard*. "D'you understand?" In Sicily, garibaldini leaders participated in the crackdown, while on the continent, where peasants had similar demands, liberals concluded that a quick unitary solution under Piedmont offered the best hope for stable and efficient government.

Cavour found it difficult to react because the Neapolitans considered Garibaldi a hero and were anxiously awaiting him. Cavour pushed for a quick annexation of Sicily, but Garibaldi hoped to exploit the island as a base for operations on the continent. Once again, Cavour feared the diplomatic consequences of this operation. The French especially opposed Garibaldi's threat to eliminate the Kingdom of the Two Sicilies and sought British cooperation in blocking an attempt by Garibaldi to cross the Strait of Messina. British refusal removed that obstacle, but the duel between Cavour and Garibaldi continued on other fronts.

Cavour understood that Garibaldi's spectacular success had suddenly and dramatically shifted the initiative to the Action Party. Seizure of continental Neapolitan territory would greatly enhance Garibaldi's prestige and transform Victor Emanuel into the popular general's appendage. In addition, Garibaldi was determined to attack Rome after he had taken Naples, and Mazzini also encouraged him to move against Venice, still under Austrian control. These actions would risk bringing in the French and the Austrians against the national movement and destroy what the Risorgimento had accomplished. In mid-August, the redshirts crossed onto the Continent and fought their way up the Italian boot. Cavour had thought of several schemes to neutralize Garibaldi's appeal and finally decided to advance through papal territory to the northern border of the Kingdom of Naples while promising Napoleon that Rome would remain inviolable.

This move would result in annexation of papal Umbria and the Marche, contributing to the restoration of Piedmontese prestige and moderate control of the national movement. Furthermore, the Piedmontese army would be in a position to intervene in the South, if necessary, preventing Garibaldi from moving on Rome. Cavour's plan to checkmate the democrats depended on Napoleon's consent, which would ensure French neutrality and block Austrian intervention to save the pope. Napoleon understood that Cavour's action would probably produce a unified Italy, but if Garibaldi attacked Rome, the French monarch would have to choose between losing face by abandoning the Eternal City or fighting alongside a French Catholic who commanded the papal volunteers but who was an opponent of Napoleon. If a unified Italy was in the cards, the emperor preferred that it be controlled by moderates over whom he had some influence. When Cavour's envoys explained the plan to him, therefore, he answered: "Do it, but do it quickly."

In September 1860, Cavour stimulated revolts that served as the royal Piedmontese army's pretext for crossing the papal frontier. On September 18, the

Piedmontese defeated the papal army at Castelfidardo, accomplishing Cavour's goals. Cavour announced that Piedmont supported a unitary solution to the Italian question, thereby stealing the democrats' thunder. Garibaldi was furious about not being able to proceed on to Rome, but he was considerably weakened militarily by the Battle of the Volturno in October, when he barely contained a large Bourbon army, and by a serious pro-Bourbon insurgence behind his lines. When Victor Emanuel crossed into the Kingdom of Naples, Garibaldi greeted him at Teano as "King of Italy." Speculation that Garibaldi wavered as to whether to hand over the South seems to be contradicted by a conversation with Mazzini in late September indicating that Garibaldi had decided not to make problems on this score and to put off an eventual expedition to Rome or Venice. Garibaldi's sole request of the king was to ask him to fire Cavour, but the Gentleman King refused. Garibaldi was furious with Cavour because of the Roman question and because Cavour had ceded Garibaldi's birthplace, Nice, to France, but the general could do nothing because Cavour had Parliament's confidence.

The major remaining question was whether the South would be "annexed" to Piedmont, as central Italy had been, or whether a constituent assembly would be convoked and present conditions for union. Since Garibaldi had retained legal and military control of the area, the second option seemed a possibility. Mazzini urged Garibaldi to insist upon an elected assembly that would draw up a "national pact" and shake moderate control of the national movement. Cavour, however, outmaneuvered the democrats on this question because such a course might have jeopardized the most important goal of the democrats themselves—unity. Moreover, Cavour skillfully exploited the desire of the southern bourgeoisie to bring a rapid end to the unsettled situation through annexation. He presented a bill in the Piedmontese Parliament "accepting" annexation and pledging to work for unity with Rome and Venice. Meanwhile, the moderates maneuvered to hold plebiscites in Sicily and on the Neapolitan mainland. On October 21, Naples and Sicily voted overwhelmingly for union. Marche and Umbria followed suit on November 4.

After the final destruction of Bourbon forces, the flight of Francis II, and the ironing out of minor diplomatic problems, Parliament officially proclaimed the Kingdom of Italy on March 17, 1861.

THE DEBATE

Even though Venice and Rome did not become part of the new kingdom until 1866 and 1870, Italian unification had been achieved. The culmination of a long and complex process, and of high drama involving the participation of colorful individuals, the Risorgimento could not fail to become a favored subject of historians. As might have been expected, the first reflections glorified the party that had been successful in uniting the peninsula. Although the "losers"—Mazzini and the Action Party—condemned the manner in which unification had occurred, early historiography exalted Cavour, Victor Emanuel, and other important players on the moderate side. Historians concentrated on the "heroic" developments of 1859 and 1860 that had produced a unified state and not on the Risorgimento's roots or its slow development. Cavour's glorification transformed him from a statesman who could profit brilliantly from his errors into the perfect manipulator of European diplomacy who unified Italy according to a plan. Instead of being seen as persons with opposing ideologies, the heroes of the Risorgimento became collaborators: Mazzini "the pen," Cavour "the mind," and Garibaldi "the sword" of unification.

Like all important historical events, the Risorgimento was exploited by different political groups. Since Italy did not become a dominant power, influential Italian intellectuals became highly critical of the way Italy had been unified. Over the next fifty years, this attitude produced numerous and vicious denunciations of the parliamentary system and the policies of the new state. In the 1920s, the Fascists exploited this corrosive criticism in their successful drive for power, denying the liberal nature of Cavour's work, the real accomplishments of the state produced by the Risorgimento, and even claiming some Risorgimento patriots as precursors of fascism.

At that point, philosopher and historian Benedetto Croce rose to the Risorgimento's defense. Croce emphasized the progress made by the Kingdom of Italy after unification and argued that Italian unification was "the masterpiece" of European liberalism. In arguing against the Fascist interpretation of Italian history, Croce certainly gave an overly optimistic view, but opponents of fascism understood the historical context of his interpretation, and, in general, Croce's version prevailed.

After World War II, however, Marxist historians criticized Croce. The Marxist "school" condemned the Risorgimento for uniting Italy with little popular participation. The impetus for this development was the publication of Antonio Gramsci's prison notebooks. Gramsci, a founder of the Italian Communist Party, argued that to combat the moderates, the Action Party had to create an alternative economic and social program of the radical Jacobin type that would have appealed to the rural masses making up 80 percent of the peninsula's population. But, he wrote, the democrats retained a partially agrarian character that limited their freedom of action with regard to the landholding classes. In other words, the Actionists no less than the moderates feared a degeneration of the Risorgimento into "communism." Since Austria occupied Italy, it was easy enough for the democrats to emphasize the national struggle and neglect the social character of the revolution to create unity. Gramsci believed that, despite the difficulties, an alliance with the peasants was possible and that the Risorgimento was "a failed revolution."

This view seems motivated by the desire of leftist Italian intellectuals to shake free from Croce's enormous cultural influence, by the persistence of the "southern problem," and by an effort to discredit the existing political system. The "failed revolution" concept not only seems unhistorical but also appears illogical, even from a Marxist viewpoint. If the revolutionary aspects of the Risorgimento were so easily put aside, existing conditions did not favor victorious peasant agitation of a modern kind. Consequently, only dictatorial methods could have ensured a radical "Jacobin" solution; leaving aside the central issue of the long-term consequences of such methods, those favoring this kind of force at the time lacked the means to carry out "revolutionary" policies. Furthermore, activists must and do choose priorities when making political decisions, and the first priority in the 1800s could only have been to expel the Austrians, even at the cost of social reform. The Communists made a similar choice during World War II when they put aside social revolution to join with a reactionary Italian government to drive out the Nazis. Applying the failed revolution principle to other events would reduce history to an absurd series of missed opportunities. As for the southern problem, which indeed persisted, it seems unclear that a constituent assembly would have resolved the question, although it might have jeopardized unification. The major criticism here is that the Piedmontese extended their laws and administrative system to the South. Aside from the plausible argument that the newly united country had to take that course to prevent Italy from falling apart after unification, the differences between the Piedmontese and the Neapolitan administration do not appear as great as commonly supposed, since both originated in the centralizing tendencies of revolutionary France.

Gramsci's emphasis on an agricultural revolution as a means of generating capital accumulation for industrialization, and the resulting criticism of the Risorgimento because this revolution did not occur, derives from the Marxist interpretation of the French Revolution. Liberal historian Rosario Romeo contested this model. In analyzing Italy's economic and political history, Romeo insisted on emphasizing the constraints faced by Italian statesmen during and after the Risorgimento. Employing statistics as a means of proving his point, Romeo argued that the 1860s and 1870s saw significant increases in capital and that the capital thus accumulated went first into building basic services such as a railway network. Capital investment in industry followed and stimulated economic growth after this essential process. Romeo does not deny that these economic developments occurred at first through a political compromise between the bourgeoisie and the semifeudal landowners at the expense of rural areas and the

South, but he believes that these conditions were temporary and characterized industrialization everywhere. Although some of Romeo's statistics have been called into question, his thesis stands as an attractive alternative to Gramsci's.

It seems legitimate for historians to analyze errors, as does Marxist Giorgio Candeloro in pointing to the Risorgimento's failure to enlarge the electoral system or to elaborate a new administrative system suited to the integration of different parts of the peninsula; they can plumb with Raymond Grew the roots of how and why the persons who made the Risorgimento "narrowed" its political focus by reducing popular participation; and they can sympathize with the defeated personages. But historians "cannot reduce the Italian national revolution merely into a function of the unrealized potentialities of the Risorgimento."

In tracing the origins of problems, historians must also take care not to burden one age with the mistakes of future eras. It is more reasonable to emphasize the successes of a movement, in addition to its failures, not in absolute terms but in relation to similar movements during the same period. For example, in comparing Italian and German unification, it is clear that no figure comparable to Mazzini gained such prominence in Germany, and no one wielded influence the way he did, either at the time or in the future. In like manner, even though Cavour can be criticized for his constitutional shortcomings, Piedmont's past as Italy's most reactionary state and the distance it covered toward liberalism during his tenure must also be emphasized. Furthermore, Italian unity resulted from the interplay of actions taken by Piedmontese liberals and the democratic movement based on a revolutionary ideology, even though they conflicted; whereas a conservative dedicated to raw power and unwilling to make concessions to more liberal forces guided the Prussian military and diplomatic activities that unified Germany on the basis of Prussian and dynastic supremacy and an exasperated nationalism. In Prussia, as in Piedmont, a moderate liberal movement was under way before Bismarck came to power, but he definitively defeated it, while Cavour stimulated liberalism in his country.

These different aspects of Italian and German unification would determine the different roads taken by the united countries, despite superficial similarities. From a social viewpoint, in Italy the gulf between aristocracy and bourgeoisie had been considerably narrowed. Although the nobility maintained a powerful position in the army and the diplomatic corps of united Italy, it also engaged fully in commercial and banking activities, and the bourgeoisie, even though linked to the land, engaged in commerce and the professions. In Germany, the nobility remained a closed and compact class of landholders that preserved some feudal privileges and retained political control of Prussia and the unified state; the German bourgeoisie, although economically better off than its Italian counterpart because of greater resources and the faster formation of a national market, had less influence in the political arena. United Germany was more politically backward than united Italy, despite the problems of the Italian constitution, which will be elaborated upon in the next chapter. Although they resembled each other in the late eighteenth century, Piedmont emerged from the unity movement radically different from Prussia because of the cultural and political revolution brought about by the Risorgimento. Risorgimento statesmen achieved ministerial responsibility for united Italy, even if imperfect, but Bismarck eliminated that possibility for united Germany, severing it from Western constitutional development. In a few years after unification, Piedmont became integrated into Italy, whereas Prussia dominated Germany up to 1918 at least. Northern domination of southern Italy can be partially explained by objective economic reasons; politically, however, cabinets had to be geographically balanced, and by 1887 the country had a southern prime minister.

Finally, even in defeat the democratic ideals of Mazzini and the example of Garibaldi continued to ferment in Italy and to maintain a European and worldwide influence down to present times. In this sense, these activists no longer appear as the "losers" of the Risorgimento.

PART FOUR

The "Age of Prose"

CHAPTER NINE

Cavour's Heirs: The "Right" Reigns

O N JUNE 6, 1861, CAMILLO CAVOUR DIED AT AGE FIFTY. UPON HEARING OF his death, Napoleon said: "The driver has fallen from the box; now we must see if the horses will bolt or go back to the stable."

This statement expressed Europe's doubts that Italy would hold together. The "driver" had died at a crucial time. The peninsula had been united after centuries of political division, which had produced different customs, traditions, and dialects. Venice and Rome remained out of the kingdom, and making them part of Italy presented numerous diplomatic difficulties. Melding the disparate parts of the peninsula and building a single state out of long-divided areas would prove formidable. Risorgimento wars and the takeover of the debts of the old states created enormous financial problems for the new state. Besides these issues, the question of whether the more socially backward parts of the peninsula could successfully make the transition to liberal institutions remained a question mark. Given these challenges, the new state's inability to become a great power hardly comes as a surprise.

COMPLETING UNIFICATION

When Cavour died of "fever," the Kingdom of Italy had been declared, but unification remained incomplete. Cavour's heirs—the "Right"—had to integrate the peninsula into one state, and that was a qualitatively different and less heroic job than the exhilarating struggle for independence. As Victor Emanuel II remarked, the age of poetry had given way to an age of prose.

European politics had determined the manner in which Italy had been unified and strongly influenced its future political development. The annexations excluded a federal structure, while the threat of political disputes leading to foreign intervention and collapse made calling a constituent assembly dangerous. The different parts of the peninsula had been attached to preexisting states that had their own dynasties, constitutions, and administrative structures. It is hardly surprising that Cavour and his successors—anxious to forestall complications that could undo the unification so painfully achieved—extended Piedmont's political system, its economic policies, and its administration to the rest of Italy. By amalgamating political and economic liberalism with a rigid administrative structure, Cavour and the Right created a strong state that survived the shocks of postunification but that did not solve the southern or social questions.

With a social structure similar to that of Piedmont, the North adapted fairly well to the new legislation, but the South did not. Moderate leaders had assumed that the passage of power from the Bourbons and Garibaldi into their hands would resolve the South's problems, but the real issue was the disparity in the economic and social development between the two regions. For example, unlike Piedmont, Bourbon tariff policy had been protectionist. After unification, the new rulers extended free trade policies to the South without regard to southern conditions or to the economic emergency that existed in the area. These policies exacerbated the South's crisis and contributed to the brigandage there, which was part protest and part pro-Bourbon revolt. Adding to the insensitivity of the northerners, the new state dissolved Garibaldi's volunteer army under unfavorable conditions; this move created resentment and deprived the government of a valuable and committed military force that could have been employed against the "brigands." After unification, Italy committed 100,000 troops to fight a stubborn guerrilla-type war against southern brigands and to put down a revolution in Sicily.

In addition to confronting the southern problem, the Right had pledged to incorporate Venice and Rome into Italy. Of the two, Venice seemed the greater problem because of Austria's military strength. Before his death, Cavour concentrated on making Rome the new state's capital. The rationale for the Papal State's existence had always been to protect the pope's independence. With only a rump area still belonging to the pontiff, however, Cavour believed this argument no longer held. He hoped to convince the pope to give up Rome in return for a guarantee by Italy that he would retain freedom of action. Both Pius IX and his minister, Cardinal Giacomo Antonelli, refused.

The opportunity to take Venice came in 1866 as the struggle between Austria and Prussia for control of Germany came to a head. Italy and Prussia signed an alliance providing for an Italian attack on Austria's Italian possessions if war broke out between the two Germanic powers. The problems of the Italian military in amalgamating previously separate forces, the failure of central command, and the "sectional conflict, personal animosities and partisan conflict" resulted in two Italian defeats: on land at Custoza and on the sea at Lissa. Prussia, however, defeated Austria in the conflict, known as the Seven Weeks' War, and Italy received Venice as a result.

PORTRAITS

CARDINAL GIACOMO ANTONELLI
Layman Loyalist

〜◦〜

In his opposition to Italian unification and later the Italian state, Pius IX could call on an authoritative helper who allowed the Church to make the best of a bad situation and to survive the political upheavals of the mid and late nineteenth century. Giacomo Antonelli, the last lay cardinal, turned down the opportunity to become a priest, but he served the Church with greater effectiveness than most of its religious retinue.

Giacomo Antonelli's father, Domenico, made his fortune through construction contracts for the Papal State. A strict disciplinarian, Domenico decided that the third of his eight children, Giacomo, born on April 2, 1806, should enter the priesthood. Giacomo received his degrees in canon and civil law from the University of Rome and served Pope Gregory XVI and later Pius IX in a number of important capacities. However, he chose not to become a priest.

During the upheavals of 1848 and 1849, Antonelli found himself in a delicate position. He had an important part in issuing the 1848 constitution, given by Pius on March 10, and then headed the constitutional government. Antonelli advocated close cooperation with the other Italian states and an end to Austrian intervention in the peninsula's affairs. Radicals called upon him to participate in the fight against the Austrians, but Pius did not wish to do so. The compromise solution—to send a papal army north, but only for defensive purposes—satisfied no one. When, on April 29, 1848, Pius declared that he would not support the war against Austria, Antonelli resigned.

From then on, things in Rome got worse, and Antonelli advised Pius to flee to Gaeta. When the radicals set up a republic, Antonelli responded by calling for the intervention of the Catholic powers. When the French restored Pius in April 1850, Antonelli followed his orders in resisting their pressure for constitutional reforms. Furthermore, he implemented the pope's conservative policies for the next twenty-six years, running both the papal government and its diplomacy.

When Pius refused to leave Rome after the capital fell to the Italians on September 20, 1870, and declared himself a "prisoner in the Vatican," the decisions were widely attributed to Antonelli's influence. Most important, through his negotiating and economic abilities, Antonelli put the now-reduced papacy on a sound financial basis. This achievement allowed the pope to refuse the Law of Papal Guarantees, Italy's offer to settle the "Roman Question."

During his lifetime and after, Cardinal Antonelli was bitterly denounced as the architect of the conservative policies followed by Pius and as the stimulus for the *Syllabus of Errors* and the doctrine of papal infallibility. Recent research has tended to moderate this view, suggesting that the policies were Pius's and that Antonelli implemented them. Above all, Antonelli was a loyalist.

Cardinal Giacomo Antonelli remained a "prisoner in the Vatican" with Pius and died there on November 6, 1876.

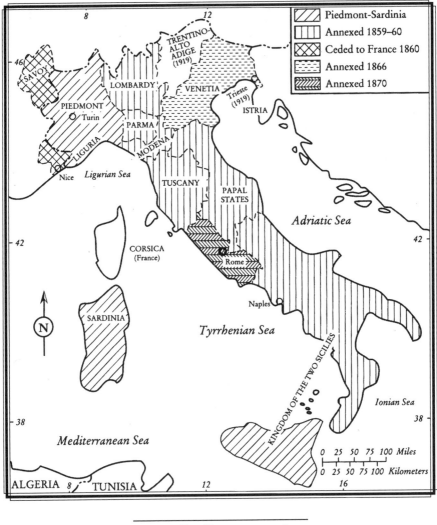

MAP 9.1 THE UNIFICATION OF ITALY

Rome proved the harder nut to crack. Despite bad blood between Napoleon and the pope, French honor and the presence of French troops, originally sent in 1849, forced France to protect the Holy City. Complicating the diplomatic situation, Garibaldi's pledge to take Rome, if honored, would have provoked military intervention not only by France but by the Catholic powers and volunteers. The

Right negotiated a French evacuation, which it could only achieve by guaranteeing Rome's borders while contemporaneously coveting the city for Italy's capital; it feared both the diplomatic consequences of an attack by Garibaldi and a popular backlash if forced to intervene against the hero. In 1864, an agreement secured the withdrawal of French troops and removal of the capital from Turin to Florence as a pledge of good faith. During this period, Garibaldi attempted to take Rome twice; the second time French troops returned, and a French minister declared that Italy would "never" get Rome. With the outbreak of the 1870 Franco-Prussian War, however, the French withdrew their garrison and the Italians took Rome, which became the capital.

FINANCES

The new kingdom was burdened with a heavy debt that caused an enormous deficit, for the 1861–1865 period, of 47 percent over receipts. Expenditures in connection with Piedmont's modernization after 1848 and loans contracted in 1859–1860 by the provisional regimes that later became part of the kingdom accounted for two-thirds of the new state's debt. Swelling this Risorgimento "bill" were the country's military and other spending after unification. Between 1861 and 1865, the public debt doubled.

The governments of the Right hoped to remedy this situation in several ways. First they resorted to selling public buildings and land on a vast scale. This property flooded the market; the result: low prices created a windfall for the rich, who could afford to buy. In 1867, the lands of monastic orders were confiscated and sold, with the same results. The government also sold state railways, but private companies could not make a profit, and the state had to buy them back. In addition, direct and indirect taxes alike were increased. Before 1865, direct taxation, paid by the rich, increased by 54 percent, and transfer taxes increased 40 percent. In comparison, taxes on consumption increased only 11 percent, while revenues from state monopolies grew by 25 percent. Up to 1865, then, the burden of paying for the deficit increased more for the wealthy than the poor.

Thanks to a continuing inability to stem the deficit and an economic crisis in 1866, however, the burden shifted. The Right hoped to eliminate the deficit through stringent spending controls and by the orthodox economic methods advocated by finance minister Quintino Sella. In 1869, the Right increased several taxes and, most important, instituted the hated *macinato* (grist mill) tax. This measure hit the poor hardest because it taxed the grinding of grains, especially wheat, essential for making the bread and other food products that represented a large percentage of the lower class's budget. In comparing tax revenues in 1865 and in 1871, it has been calculated that while direct and transfer taxes increased 63 and 50 percent, respectively, taxes on consumption, paid primarily by the lower classes, increased 107 percent. The grist mill tax provoked agitation throughout the country, especially in the North, but it proved essential in solving the financial crisis. On the other hand, not only was the tax unfair, but it put Italy on the road to becoming the highest-taxed country in Europe, and it greatly increased social tensions.

Besides increasing taxes, the Right resorted to an important financial measure to improve Italy's economic position: the inconvertibility of bank notes. At this time, European currencies could be exchanged for gold on demand, but in 1866 the Italians eliminated this practice for the lira. This *corso forzoso* proved remarkably successful; because of the difficulty of securing gold to pay for imports, the country was forced to reduce imports dramatically, while exports increased. Besides this salutary effect, the policy put the lira on a sound footing and got Italians used to paper money. These results could be seen after 1881, when convertibility was reintroduced and there was little demand for gold and no appreciable inflation.

From the fiscal viewpoint, the Right's policies proved so successful that their political opponents—supposedly more sensitive to lower-class concerns—perpetuated those measures even though they placed the major economic burden on the poor.

THE CHURCH

In addition to the grave financial problems it faced, the Right confronted the Church's hostility. The Church greeted unification with anger because the new state had absorbed most of the papal possessions. Pius excommunicated the Piedmontese leaders responsible for annexing papal territory and punished the priest who, despite this expulsion, had given Cavour the last rites.

After the Kingdom of Italy's birth, the pope concentrated on saving Rome. He walked a tightrope between the Italian state and Garibaldi, both hoping through either diplomacy or force to secure Rome for Italy, and while Napoleon III pledged to protect the Holy City for political reasons, he was uncomfortable with the commitment. As the pope's political power waned, he reinforced himself in the spiritual realm. In 1864, the withdrawal of the French contingent provided the occasion for publication of the *Syllabus of Errors*, a controversial condemnation of modern civilization, and when the Italians took Rome in 1870, a Church council declared the pope infallible when officially defining Church doctrine (*ex cathedra*). These measures indicated the pope's desire to do battle with secular states and strengthened his influence among the Italian clergy.

The Church's hostility to the new state had major effects in two distinct but ultimately linked areas. In domestic affairs, the Church announced the *Non expe-*

dit in February 1868. This decree ordered Italian Catholics not to participate in Italian political life and to boycott national elections. This meant that there would be no organized national Catholic Party in Italy, although, in effect, Catholics did engage in politics through the Opera dei Congressi, political committees tightly controlled by priests. On the one hand, the official Church boycott exacerbated an important weakness of the new kingdom by reducing the already low level of political participation on the national level, caused, above all, by the high illiteracy rate. (There were some property qualifications, but it was the literacy requirement that excluded most men from attaining the right to vote; as in most countries, women could not vote.) On the other hand, the boycott muffled the effects of Church hostility in Parliament at a particularly delicate time in the nation's life.

With the fall of Rome on September 20, 1870, the Italian clergy intensified its attacks on the government from its pulpits and the Pope plotted to get Rome back. The government retaliated by prohibiting Church services when they became openly political manifestations. In addition, the government ordered inspections at seminaries to ensure that the education taking place there conformed with the "fundamental necessities" of culture, and a law was passed allowing for the conscription of priests. The same period witnessed Bismarck's anti-Catholic *Kulturkampf* (struggle for civilization) in Germany, compared to which the Right's campaign was a policy of pinpricks. In fact, Italian leftists admired Bismarck's anti-Church policy and objected to the mildness of the Italian measures.

Diplomatic considerations, however, obliged the Right to pursue a cautious policy toward the Church. The Vatican pressed European Catholic powers to intervene against Italy and restore the Papal State, but Napoleon's overthrow in 1870 as a result of the Franco-Prussian War created problems for Italy. During its early days, the Third French Republic, which replaced the Second Empire, was very conservative and subject to clerical influence. This development caused bad blood between France and Italy—exacerbated by what the French perceived as "ungratefulness" in Italy's failure to intervene on France's side in the recent war and by resentment against the Italians for having taken Rome when the French withdrew their troops to fight the Germans. Public opinion whipped up by French bishops brought the two countries close to an open break.

The Italian government sought to mollify France and the other European powers. Rejecting concessions that might have given Rome an international character because of possible diplomatic complications and papal intransigence, Prime Minister Giovanni Lanza's cabinet presented the "Law of Papal Guarantees" to Parliament on January 23, 1871. This bill proposed resolving the Church problem through the separation of church and state and a guarantee of liberty and independence for the pope and the Church. Consequently, the state gave up various rights it had vis-à-vis the Church, made the pope a practical sovereign in

Italy, instituted punishment for assassination attempts and insults against his person, arranged for the diplomatic immunity necessary to fulfill his mission, allowed full freedom to use papal buildings and Roman churches, and appropriated a yearly budget equal to what the pope had received as income from the former Papal State. The law provoked protests among Italian anticlericals because, they argued, it gave the pope a special position within the Italian constitutional order that no other individual or religious institution enjoyed. This opposition, however, did not prevent successive governments of the Right and the Left from enforcing the law, finally passed on May 13, 1871.

Although the pope rejected this settlement because it was an internal Italian law that Italy could unilaterally revoke at any moment, the legislation achieved its purposes. Despite the pope's continued opposition and the clergy's propaganda, it defused European diplomatic hostility as it became clear that Pius had real freedom, even though he proclaimed himself a "prisoner" in the 11,000-room Vatican. A representative of a government friendly to the pope summarized the diplomatic situation when he said: "This old man, who every week flings insults in your face . . . does you far more good in Europe's eyes than all the honesty and moderation which you have demonstrated in your policies toward the Papacy! Those speeches prove that the Pope remains the freest and most independent man on earth." The Right had shrewdly made the papacy seem unreasonable in European eyes, thus reducing tensions on this issue.

In the domestic arena, the Law of Papal Guarantees did not separate church and state, but it regulated church-state relations in Italy for fifty years according to the best political compromise that could be achieved at the time. Pius IX's successors kept the dispute alive, but the Vatican tacitly accepted the law and claimed most of the rights that the state granted it under the legislation. The Left, which denounced and denigrated the law, made no move to repeal the measure after it came to power and, on the contrary, vigorously enforced it. By enabling the new state successfully to get past a delicate issue threatening its fragile existence so soon after unification, the Law of Papal Guarantees represents a monument to the wisdom of the Right.

Fall of the Right

During its tenure in power, the Right was dogged by the serious political opposition of the Left. The Left was composed of former Mazzinians who had abandoned the Genoese republican and gone over to the Piedmontese camp in the 1850s to make unification possible. The old Risorgimento question of whether Italy should be united as a monarchy or a republic constituted the original distinction between these two political groupings and persisted in the newly formed kingdom. In 1865, a new break occurred between Mazzini and some of his most important followers: Francesco Crispi, Benedetto Cairoli, and Agostino Bertani. In a famous letter to Mazzini, Crispi wrote that the Italian Constitution could be reformed and that he preferred to enact Mazzini's principles into law rather than use the insurrectionary method that, Crispi believed, divided leftists. In his words: "The monarchy unites us, but the republic would divide us." Thus, Crispi and his friends dropped the fight for a republic, but not for an extension of liberty and social legislation by legal means. This was the basis on which the Left fought the Right in Parliament.

Before 1870, the major issue dividing Left and Right was Rome. Influenced by its anticlerical and revolutionary origins, the Left criticized the Right's "timid" Roman policy. The Left advocated storming the Holy City, making an idealistic appeal to the people, and gloriously avenging French suppression of the Roman Republic in 1849, whereas the Right counted on diplomatic maneuvering. When Lanza took Rome as the result of the French withdrawal, the Left attacked him for entering the city in a supposedly embarrassed, unheroic, and almost apologetic manner. Subsequently, the Left blasted the Right on the Law of Papal Guarantees, arguing that the measure violated freedom of conscience and set up Catholicism as a "state religion." The Left rejected the Right's diplomatic objective on the ground that the pope would never accept the loss of his temporal power.

The two groups also fought bitterly over other issues, especially tax policy and the detested macinato. The Left denounced the measure and promised to repeal it immediately once it came to power. The Right also neglected Italy's pressing social problems, the Left insisted, and failed to widen the country's electoral base. At the same time, a debate erupted on the government's free trade policies, which had gravely damaged the South. Indeed, in the South the Left gathered strength because of increasing resentment against the Right's "Piedmontization" of the area, poor treatment of Garibaldi's volunteers after unification, the free trade regime that crippled the region, and frequent use of the police to quell social agitation. These policies increased opposition to the new state to such an extent that socialistic ideologies flourished, and in 1874 anarchists led by Russian revolutionary Mikhail Bakunin tried to overthrow the government.

Ironically, despite these disputes and its bitter denunciation of the Right, the Left had little substantially different to offer. In fact, the two groups resembled each other: their members came from the same social class, and they were well-off, educated, eloquent patriots who had participated in the Risorgimento and who had overthrown old states, princes, and laws, including the pope's temporal power. Neither group was reactionary—a losing policy identified with the Austrians and the old states. In addition, the Right included important proponents of progressive policies identified with the Left—widening of the suffrage, extension of civil liberties, and government intervention on the side of the poor—and opponents to those ideas existed within the Left. Furthermore, when the Left came to power, it either delayed changing or did not touch legislation passed by the Right and thus set the basis for a historic compromise.

The Left's constant hammering and the South's decisive support produced a major change in the 1874 elections. The Right won 275 seats, preserving a slight majority, but the parliamentary "arithmetic" opened the possibility of negotiations that would produce an eventual majority for the Left. Neither Right nor Left was a "party" in the modern sense; both were divided into many groups that, centered on prominent individuals, could suddenly shift their political allegiance. On March 18, 1876, a cabinet of the Right headed by Marco Minghetti lost a vote on the macinato question when a group of Tuscan deputies who disagreed with his railway policy deserted him. A government of the Left replaced Minghetti, and in November new elections were held. The new interior minister, Giovanni Nicotera, brought the government's power to bear in favor of the Left. As a result, the Right won only about 20 percent of the seats in the Chamber. It never rose again.

Despite the criticisms that could be leveled against the Right and the polemics of which it was made the object during its rule, the Right had significant accomplishments to its credit. It completed unification and ended the pope's temporal power, even if not in the "heroic" manner envisioned by the Left and by historians. At the same time, the Right set the tone for church-state relations for half a century through the Law of Papal Guarantees. It also steered a successful course in foreign policy on the papal issue, shattering the pope's hopes to restore his temporal power. Finally, the Right did achieve a balanced budget under difficult economic conditions. When the Left came to power, its actions demonstrated that it appreciated the value of those achievements, even if its words never did.

CHAPTER TEN

Two
"Parliamentary Dictators"

BETWEEN 1876 AND 1896, LEFTIST LEADERS AGOSTINO DEPRETIS AND Francesco Crispi dominated Italian politics. Both had been Risorgimento heroes and followers of Garibaldi, but the similarity ends there. Depretis, calm, prudent, and calculating, frequently shared power with the well-meaning but politically inept Benedetto Cairoli. The fiery, temperamental, and controversial Crispi governed from 1887 to 1896. His own worst enemy, Crispi stormed back from a period of political "exile," caused by his allegedly bigamous marital status, to implement domestic and foreign policies that still stir debate and impede a serene discussion of this period.

DEPRETIS AND HIS POLICIES

Although the term "revolution" with which contemporaries greeted the Left's coming to power in 1876 is overblown, the event should not be undervalued. Recalling the Left's origins in Mazzini's republicanism and the revolutionary antecedents of its leaders, contemporaries debated whether the king would turn the government over to his former enemies. That he did so is a positive comment on the monarch's flexibility, the parliamentary state's solidity, and the Left's capacity to evolve politically.

As the end of the Right's term approached, a debate arose within the Left. Deploring the continued stagnation of the South's economy, Giovanni Nicotera proposed breaking off from the Left and allying with groups from the Right sympathetic to southern aspirations. Depretis responded by presenting a comprehensive program in a speech at Stradella on October 10, 1875 (reiterated the next year). He hoped to meet Nicotera's objection by promising, when the Left came to power, free, compulsory, and secular elementary education, expanded suffrage, and the expenditure of public funds to address the problems of the country's areas that had suffered most under the "misgovernment" of the old states or that were unable to improve economic conditions by themselves. By making these proposals, Depretis sought to demonstrate that the Left had a wider social base than the Right.

When the Left achieved power, however, it discovered that its program could not be carried out as originally drafted. As previously stated, leftist leaders had denounced the Law of Papal Guarantees and demanded its immediate repeal. Faced with diplomatic realities, however, the Left now rigorously enforced it. Depretis stated that although he would give no further concessions to the Church, neither would he withdraw past concessions. Furthermore, anticlerical legislation proposed by the Left did not depart from the guidelines set down by the Right. Even when the Left passed a law providing for free and compulsory school attendance in 1877, it made provisions for religious instruction if parents requested it.

Nor could the Left radically depart from the financial policies of the Right. Out of power, the Left had promised an immediate repeal of the hated macinato tax, but it found that financial considerations prohibited quick action. Leftist cabinets did eliminate the macinato, but only gradually by 1884. More important, although the Left reduced some other taxes as well, it made no major alterations in the tax system. In addition, the Left did not keep its promise to spur economic development in the South by spending significantly more public funds there, although it did promote an important inquiry into the problems of the South by Stefano Jacini and Sidney Sonnino. From then on, Italian officials understood the importance of the southern problem and realized that rebuilding the South's economy would take decades.

Continuing the work of the Right, the Left vigorously promoted the building of railways, which were essential for the country's economic development, and their purchase by the state. But unlike members of the Right, Depretis championed giving concessions to private businessmen to run them.

The Left acted as well in two other important areas: civil liberties and suffrage extension. Giuseppe Zanardelli, a minister in several governments of this period, forcefully argued in favor of the right of assembly and association. He opposed preventive action by the government, defended the right of people to be free from arrest until they actually violated a law, and courageously argued his case against critics who accused him of being soft on law and order. In 1878, an assassination attempt against the king and other disturbances forced the Cairoli cabinet, of which Zanardelli was a part, to resign, but he successfully drafted a progressive penal code that went into effect in 1890.

In the related area of suffrage extension, which Depretis had promised in his Stradella program, several governmental crises, financial problems, and a fear of opposition by the Right postponed action. In 1881, however, Zanardelli introduced a bill giving the right to vote to literate males over twenty-one who paid at least nineteen lire a year in taxes. The number of persons eligible to vote under the new law rose from 600,000 to 2 million (from 2.18 percent of the population to 6.97 percent). The reform increased the influence of the urban lower-middle classes, many of whom knew how to read and write, and encouraged the formation of new working-class parties. The change acknowledged the growing importance of the urban industrial, intellectual, and commercial classes of the North as opposed to the landowning classes. The legislation went as far as it was possible to go without extending the suffrage to illiterates and to women.

Depretis and the Left expected a hard fight from the Right on all these issues, but with the exception of civil liberties, the struggle did not materialize. It has already been mentioned that members of the rival groups had similar social origins; the large majority in favor of the suffrage law revealed that two distinct parties advocating radically different programs no longer existed. Groups nominally belonging to the Right frequently discovered themselves voting for leftist government proposals when members of the Left voted against them.

In 1882 Depretis took official notice of this development. He announced that the Right had evolved to the point that it had become indistinguishable from the Left. Since the Right had become "transformed," its leaders would be welcomed in his cabinets. Objecting that it had been the Left that had been transformed, the Rightists accepted Depretis's offer. From then on, when leaders of the "Left" or "Right" formed cabinets, they included representatives of the "opposition" faction. In fact, the Chamber of Deputies now consisted of a large liberal party, underpinned by the middle bourgeoisie, whose factions collaborated but kept the titles "Right" and "Left." Only the Extreme Left (Estrema Sinistra) and, later, the Socialists separated themselves from this party by an ill-defined and flexible line. This grouping of minority political organizations became the only pole of opposition in Parliament. The term "transformism," however, acquired a connotation of betrayal of principle and corruption that it retains.

On the whole, Depretis's tenure had positive effects on the country. He was known for being a parliamentary "dictator," and Felice Cavallotti, colorful leader of the Extreme Left, accused him of being corrupt, suppressing liberty, colluding with industrialists, and making secret deals with the Church, but though Depretis had mastered the art of maneuvering deputies and taking full advantage of any means to achieve his goals, he was no dictator. Giuseppe Marcora, a radical deputy, saw him as "individually honest, a liberal, and an enemy of all excesses"; Marcora concluded that Depretis was "much better than his reputation." Indeed, Depretis's pragmatism and calming effect on the Chamber of Deputies helped win backing for his reform program. Depretis also piloted the new country through the traumatic time of Victor Emanuel II's death in 1878 and, unlike his successor, avoided major foreign adventures. This prudence made Depretis unacceptable to intellectuals who asserted Italy's greatness, and his transformism made him unpopular with the people.

PORTRAITS

AGOSTINO DEPRETIS
"Transformist"

❧∞❧

In Italian history, the term "transformism" has a negative connotation, signifying selling out one's principles for political gain. The policy's founder was supposed to be Agostino Depretis, several times prime minister of Italy. However, is the common meaning of the term correct, and did the person with whom it is most closely associated deserve his reputation?

Agostino Depretis was born at Mezzana Corti (now Bressana Bottarona), near Pavia, on January 31, 1813, and died at Stradella on July 29, 1887. He studied the law and, in his youth, participated in the Risorgimento as a follower of Mazzini. He entered the Piedmontese Parliament in 1848 as a Democrat, winning a string of sixteen elections to both the Piedmontese and the Italian Chamber of Deputies that succeeded it.

Depretis had a successful political career. Elected vice president of the Chamber of Deputies five times between 1849 and 1866, he served as minister of public works, minister of the navy, and finance minister. He made a name for himself on the Left as a practical politician, and when its leader, Urbano Rattazzi, died in 1873, Depretis succeeded him. In 1876, he headed the new Leftist cabinet. He held new elections in November of the same year and won an overwhelming victory.

In reality, the 1876 elections resulted in a hodgepodge of fragmented parliamentary factions and convinced Depretis that he needed to move slowly on the reforms he had promised. He required the support of groups of his rivals of the Right to pass them. In fact, not all those groups opposed his ideas; some had expressed similar notions and stood ready to cooperate with him.

Depretis remained in power for the next eleven years with only brief breaks. He pushed through several important reforms the country needed, but found it necessary to compromise. In doing so, he encountered the ire of members of his own party who believed that he was not doing enough and who objected to collaborating with elements of the Right, no matter how liberal. Although conceding his personal honesty, his critics accused him of avoiding problems and denounced him because, they charged, his transformism corrupted Italian politics. "Transformism" thus became a dirty word in Italian politics.

In reality, both Right and Left had compromised, which was the essence of democratic politics: Depretis had sought support for his progressive platform, and elements on the Right had provided it. The lack of party discipline in the Chamber of Deputies—during Depretis's time and in the future—made alternation between two approximately equal parties representing different principles difficult. This difficulty has remained a hallmark of Italian politics, and so has "transformism."

CRISPI'S DOMESTIC LEGISLATION

Among Depretis's possible successors, Francesco Crispi distinguished himself. A prominent Risorgimento fighter, radical, and friend of Garibaldi's, Crispi scaled the heights of political power in the new state as minister of the interior, but his personal life caused scandal. In 1878, he married in a civil ceremony Lina Barbagallo, the woman he loved dearly and with whom he had been living, and the mother of his children. Unfortunately, Crispi, always drawn to beautiful women, had in 1854 married a woman who followed him into exile during his Risorgimento days. Agostino Depretis was a witness to the marriage and had purchased the wedding ring for the bride. Crispi declared that the earlier ceremony was invalid because it had been conducted by a Jesuit without proper authorization, that he had entered the union out of a sense of duty, and that the subsequent strange behavior of his first wife had ended the union, but a virulent press campaign made him a political pariah.

Despite this incident, Crispi made a slow comeback. He emerged as leader of the "Pentarchy," a group of deputies demanding that Depretis pursue a more energetic African policy. In January 1887, a column of 500 Italian soldiers was destroyed at Dogali, an incident that gave credence to Crispi's criticism. In July 1887, an already ill Depretis brought Crispi into his cabinet as minister of the interior, thus designating him as his successor. Upon Depretis's death, King Humbert I asked Crispi to form a government.

Mixed emotions greeted the controversial Crispi's rise to power. The Vatican feared him as a staunch anticlerical, and his uncompromising antagonism toward the Right alarmed the leaders of that group. Tired of Depretis's prudence and welcoming Crispi's passion and boldness, however, many leftists hailed his accession. In fact, although Crispi took serious action against neither the Church nor the Right, his government listened to the country's progressive lobby. And although he took a hard turn to the right during his later years as prime minister, a series of progressive measures that had a lasting influence mark his early tenure.

Most important, his government overcame the previously mentioned opposition to Zanardelli's penal code that the statesman from Iseo, now Crispi's justice minister, implemented in 1890. The code abolished the death penalty; partially addressed the changing economic and social structure of the country and the political demands of the lower classes by reducing punishment for crimes against property; and tacitly admitted the legality of strikes by not declaring them illegal. This last provision, however, did not prevent governments from intervening in favor of employers. On the issue of preventive detention that had caused so much debate in 1878, the new code compromised. Police regulations spelling out the Zanardelli code maintained restrictive measures requiring groups to notify the police twenty-four hours before meetings and allowed law enforcement officials to dissolve associations. In addition, *domicilio coatto* (internal exile), by which the police could forcibly send "dangerous" persons to remote areas of the country without a trial, remained in the code; police officials favored this weapon against the growing anarchist and socialist movements, discussed in chapter 11. Reflecting the tensions between church and state during the period, the penal code also established sanctions against priests who attacked the state and its institutions and who violated its laws.

Despite obvious compromises, the Zanardelli penal code and the regulations governing police behavior significantly liberalized Italian law and lasted until the Fascists replaced them with more restrictive laws in 1926 and 1930.

Besides the penal area, other legislation during the Crispi period attempted to address lower-class interests and to modernize the country. His treasury minister, Giovanni Giolitti, believed that in modern democracies economic issues are paramount and must be resolved in favor of the people, whose participation is the hallmark of such regimes. As a result, in 1889 Giolitti piloted a law through the Chamber of Deputies that modified the procedures for the awarding of public works contracts, thus allowing cash-strapped workers' cooperatives to compete more evenly with well-heeled private companies. In 1888, another measure extended local autonomy. It enlarged the right to vote in local elections and permitted the city councils of provincial capitals and of towns over 10,000 to elect their mayors. (By 1896, all towns could elect their mayors.) A special commission, presided over by an appointed officer of the central government, the prefect, limited actual control, but the legislation dramatically expanded participation in local government. Crispi also established a system of appeals against administrative incompetence and abuses, on the national and local levels, which became the basis of continued Italian practice in this area. Attempts to adopt this system since the 1870s had failed before Crispi succeeded in 1889 and 1890. In a series of laws passed in 1887 and 1888, Crispi further strengthened the prime minister's office and its control over the bureaucracy. The government received wider powers to replace and retire prefects and to institute or abolish ministries. A law also abolished the office of secretary general, an administrative position in each ministry that had become highly politicized, and replaced it with that of undersecretary, a member of the government who acted as a vice minister.

Finally, two laws rounded out this prodigious legislative activity: a public health law and one reorganizing charitable institutions. Adopted in 1888, the first law set the basis for future Italian legislation in the field, and the second reorganized and modernized charitable institutions, simplifying their complex structure and secularizing many of them. Crispi's legislative activity in the domestic sphere thus left a permanent mark on the country. His foreign policy and its internal implications, however, have remained controversial.

Foreign Policy

Even during the Right's tenure before 1876, relations between Italy and France had soured. The Franco-Prussian War had caused the overthrow of Napoleon III's empire and its replacement by the Third Republic. Dominated by conservatives during its initial phase, the new regime believed Italy had not demonstrated gratitude for French help in the unification struggle and resented the Italian takeover of Rome after the withdrawal of French troops. This resentment and a rapprochement with the Church made France fertile ground for the pope's maneuvers against Italy over the issue of his lost territory. As a result, the Right began casting around for allies and turned to the strongest European power, Germany.

The Left's rise did not alter this major shift, despite the closer cultural links of leftist statesmen with France and the victory of parliamentarianism there in 1877. Until 1881, however, a distaste for Bismarck's Austrian allies and the priority the German statesman gave to that tie hindered an Italo-German pact. That year, colonial competition caused Franco-Italian relations to worsen dramatically. Given the proximity of Tunisia to Sicily, many Italians had emigrated there, and the Italian government had pursued a policy of economic penetration as a prelude to bringing the North African territory under its control. This policy brought Italy into conflict with the French, who wished to attach the area to their Algerian protectorate next door. When the Italians lost the struggle for Tunisia, they attributed the loss to their lack of powerful allies and determined to seek a German alliance. Bismarck made it clear that the road to Berlin ran through Vienna, so the Italians swallowed their pride and made up with Austria-Hungary (as the empire became known after 1867). Although relations between the two Risorgimento enemies remained poor beneath the surface and became progressively more poisoned, in 1882 Italy joined Austria-Hungary and Germany in the Triple Alliance.

Crispi's accession in 1887 exacerbated relations with the French. Although Italian democrats in his party admired France, Crispi loathed it. Moreover, Crispi had excellent relations with Bismarck, France's archenemy, and the press hailed the Italian leader as Bismarck's close adviser. The French suspected an Italo-German plot to attack them. As tensions between Italy and France escalated, each followed a policy of pinpricks. Taking seriously information fed to him by a secret informer, Crispi set off a war scare by telling the British that the French were about to attack Italy and prompting the dispatch of British warships to Genoa. This situation caused a rapid increase in military expenses and the budget deficit. Although a shooting war never came off, a ten-year "tariff war" caused by the protectionist policies of France and Italy erupted in 1888. Both countries increased duties and imposed quotas on each other's goods, but the Italians were no match for the economically more powerful French.

Crispi's anti-French policies left no permanent mark on relations between the two nations, but his foreign adventurism and diplomatic miscalculations brought further misery to the country. Despite his friendship with Bismarck, Crispi misunderstood the fundamental function of the Triple Alliance as a conservative instrument designed to preserve the European status quo, and he attempted to use the pact to win a colonial empire. This policy necessitated downplaying Italian interests in Europe, especially in the Balkans and in the Irredenta, the Italian-speaking territories that remained part of Austria. Consequently, Crispi pursued a friendly policy toward Austria that raised the ire of newly allied France and Russia and alienated domestic opinion. Because of his mistaken interpretation of the Triple Alliance, the expected payoff—German and Austrian support for Italian colonial ventures—never came. In 1890, the French strengthened their protectorate over Tunisia; Crispi protested—but he failed to secure substantial German-Austrian support against the move. When Crispi sought diplomatic aid for his expansion plans in East Africa (Ethiopia) by getting the Germans to pressure the French and British, he received this rebuke: "The Triple Alliance is a conservative pact, not a profit-making company." After Bismarck left the scene in 1890, the European diplomatic situation shifted in favor of France, which, in addition to concluding a Russian alliance, moved closer to England. This emerging "camp" would not miss the opportunity to strike at the Triple Alliance through Italy.

Despite the lack of diplomatic support and the economic problems of his country, Crispi doggedly pushed ahead with his plans to take Ethiopia. Between February 1891 and November 1893, the Crispi government was replaced by cabinets headed by Antonio Di Rudinì and Giovanni Giolitti. Both men were cool to Crispi's African venture and wished to patch up relations with France, but their brief tenure did not permit any real changes in foreign policy. Furthermore, domestic problems, including banking scandals and a revolt in Sicily, increased the temptation, upon Crispi's return to office (the reasons for Giolitti's fall and Crispi's return are discussed later), to undertake a foreign adventure to distract the nation from these problems.

In East Africa, Crispi had already laid the groundwork for expansion of the existing Italian colonies and the conquest of Ethiopia. In typical European fashion, the Italians hoped to take advantage of complex internal disputes and on May 2, 1889, signed the Treaty of Uccialli with Menelik, a local contestant for power. The Italians believed that they had secured a protectorate over the area, but they had succeeded only in uniting the local forces against them. Hostilities broke out over the differing interpretations of the Uccialli treaty. In 1895, the Italian commander Oreste Baratieri requested reinforcements, but Crispi refused because of opposition from the northern bourgeoisie, ironically allied with antiwar radicals and

Socialists. Although the European bourgeoisie generally favored colonialism, in Italy the industrial revolution had just begun in the North, necessitating a period of peace and stability, and the industrialists opposed "squandering" resources in Africa. As a result, their representatives in the government, particularly treasury minister Sidney Sonnino, refused to sanction further aid for the military effort in Africa. Crispi's support came not from the dynamic groups building a new industrial base in the North but from the southern bourgeoisie tied to the central administration and eager for new opportunities in the colonies.

In addition, Crispi interfered in the military operations. Contradictory orders from Rome reached Africa, and the soldiers, many of whom had political aspirations, argued among themselves. On March 1, 1896, separated Italian columns confronted a vastly superior native force and met defeat at the Battle of Adowa. About 4,000 Italians and 2,600 native troops died, along with 9,000 Ethiopians. The resulting demonstrations and political backlash ended Crispi's long tenure in office.

Military factors alone do not explain the defeat. Crispi's plan to exploit the Triple Alliance as a cover for African expansion produced a misguided policy of Austrian appeasement that damaged Italian interests in the Balkans and irritated the Russians—who joined the French in supplying the Ethiopians and encouraging native resistance to the Italians. In addition to the diplomatic failure, Crispi misjudged the power of new domestic forces within Italy, which, ironically, gained impetus from economic measures passed by his administration; he also underestimated the capability of these groups to ally against his policies, despite their differences. In Milan, the center of modern economic activity, industrialists and persecuted Socialists joined forces against him. Emerging from a social and economic crisis, the nation was in no mood to engage in colonial adventures. It understood that the government followed a colonial policy to gain prestige and to imitate the big powers and that no economic gains or attractive areas of settlement were to be won.

The military events, however, created a desire for revenge that burned more brightly the farther Adowa receded and would come to full fruition under the Fascist regime of Benito Mussolini. Indeed, Nationalists would later praise Crispi, and in an unfortunate development, Fascists claimed him as a forerunner. Both Crispi and Mussolini attempted to impart dynamism to Italian foreign policy, but in the end, with their inability to adapt Italian foreign policy to the country's level of domestic economic and social development and their erroneous interpretation of the European diplomatic situation, they had only their mistakes in common.

CHAPTER ELEVEN

Social and Economic Dilemmas

I N JUDGING ITALIAN SOCIAL AND ECONOMIC POLICIES AFTER UNIFICATION, historians frequently fail to emphasize the difficulties of creating a unified state. The patriots had been too preoccupied in forging unity to devote much attention to the economic and social issues that would confront them afterward. Furthermore, the Italian peninsula presented unique problems. It was probably more disparate than any other European country. The old states had a long, ingrained history and entrenched separate administrations, economic policies, systems of law, mentalities, and dialects. Although standard Italian had been the first language to establish itself after the Middle Ages and intellectuals knew it, ordinary people spoke dialects that were frequently unintelligible to inhabitants of different regions.

After unification, Piedmont resolved these problems in perhaps the only viable manner, given international conditions: by extending its administrative, economic, and legal structures to the rest of the peninsula. This policy caused long-term resentment and revolts, but crucial short-term questions had to be solved immediately. Consider the basic issue of budgeting, which affected all areas of social and economic life: "No one knew, for example, how much tax evasion there was; only an oracle could have forecast what military expenditures would be to cope with brigandage or keep an army at fighting trim for fear of international complications; and even a supernatural power would have been hard pressed to know how much the founding fathers would pay out for public works, especially railroads."

During the first forty years after unification, a complex economic web threatened the new state. Italian statesmen understood the need for a modern infrastructure to create a national market and to link the country to Europe, and they substantially completed that task by 1880. This accomplishment brought notable trade increases, but did not resolve the major economic imbalances of the peninsula that had existed for centuries. The weakest parts of the country dragged down the economy, which brought about dire social and political repercussions. As in other nations, pressure groups and compromises affected government policies, both positively and negatively.

NORTH AND SOUTH: THE GREAT DIVIDE

Although lack of raw materials, especially the coal and iron crucial to the "first" industrial revolution, was the most critical factor inhibiting industrialization and hampering the nation's ability to attract the capital necessary for faster economic growth, it was not the only element in the complex economic story of post-unification Italy.

Another inhibiting factor was the population problem. Italy's population had steadily increased since the eighteenth century, and in 1881 it reached almost 28.5 million. A drastic change in demographics did not occur during the first twenty years after unification, which was characterized by the high birth and death rates typical of pre-industrial societies. After 1880, improvements in public health measures and better food and living conditions pushed average annual population increases over 10 percent, owing to a decrease in the death rate and an increased birthrate. But then emigration exploded, especially after 1895, the "take-off" period for the Italian economy (see Table 11.1).* From 1900 to 1914, emigration averaged almost 616,000 per year—bringing the annual population increase on the peninsula down to 0.7 percent during the nation's industrial takeoff and becoming an essential ingredient in its social and economic equilibrium. By 1901, the population stood at 32 million, considerably less than it would have been without emigration.

Generally, with industrialization the birthrate decreases as living conditions improve and emigration declines, but in Italy neither occurred. The lopsided nature of the country's industrialization, which took place only in the Northwest, explains this difference. Accompanying this factor, emigration changed character: before the 1870s, it had been seasonal, directed toward Europe, and involved the entire country; afterward, it became southern and permanent, focused on the Americas. In short, the country experienced not only incomplete industrial and economic development but also a seriously unbalanced one that accentuated the differences between North and South. The dualistic nature of Italian society and its economy can be explained by the complex interaction of history, the international agricultural crisis of 1880 to 1895, and government policies.

---

*As will be noticed throughout this work, different sources provide slightly different statistics.

Table 11.1

Italian Emigration: Annual Average Before World War I

1861–1870	121,040*
1871–1880	35,764**
1881–1890	187,920*
1901–1913	601,500***

* No figures available for return immigration.
** Figure is net of return immigration.
***No figures available for return immigration from European and Mediterranean countries.

Exacerbating the problem, extreme regional differences marked Italian agriculture. Lombardy continued building on the Enlightenment reforms of the eighteenth century, which had encouraged transformation of its agriculture into a capitalistic system. Piedmont benefited from economic reforms in the nineteenth century, which contributed to its leading role in the Risorgimento. To the south, around Bologna, the Emilean marshes were being drained and the capitalistic transformation of the land had begun, poising the region for a rapid economic development.

In other Italian regions, such hopeful conditions did not prevail. In the North, Venetian agriculture remained backward, with sharecroppers and tenant farmers primarily producing raw silk for exportation and maize. Poor living conditions and widespread pellagra, a disease caused by niacin deficiency, spurred emigration. In the central regions of Tuscany, Umbria, Marches, and Lazio, the nobility and city bourgeoisie retained their power by maintaining sharecropping. Nonetheless, the peasants of these regions fared better than Venetians and southerners by applying improved methods to the production of wine, olives, and fruit, for which there was an increased demand in Italy and abroad. The profits went primarily to the landlords, and the areas lagged behind Lombardy and Piedmont, but the products at least allowed peasants to enjoy a healthier diet than the people of Venetia and the South.

The South suffered the worst social and economic conditions. The reforms of the eighteenth century had either failed or produced half-capitalistic enterprises based on exploitation of the peasants. Conditions varied according to the geographical features of the regions. Living and working were harshest in the mountains, calculated at 40 percent of the old Kingdom of the Two Sicilies. Economic changes had cut the profitability of sheep herding, a major activity. In the 1870s, the population began growing, increasing pressure on the already poor soil and water; coinciding with this development, emigration to America began. In proportion to their population, the mountainous regions of the South (Calabria, Basilicata, Molise, and the Abruzzi) lost the greatest number of people to emigration.

The flatter areas devoted primarily to extensive cultivation of cereals and shepherding (about 30 percent) suffered severe droughts and lacked irrigation. Primitive cultivation methods prevailed on large latifundia and small plots. These *latifondi* consisted of large holdings accumulated by landlords over the years from the former possessions of feudal lords, from the Church during the Napoleonic and post-unitary period, and from usurped domain lands that had once belonged to the state. On the continent, the latifundia generally belonged to the bourgeoisie, and in Sicily to the nobles. The owners usually did not live on the land but rented it to people who had it worked by day laborers and salaried peasants. The extremely low salaries produced low yields per acre but high profits for latifundia owners and renters, thus discouraging investment and technological innovations on the land. Misery and lack of investment produced a harvest of social agitation and peasant demands for a share in the former state lands that the owners had usurped. This unrest contributed to the brigandage following unification, but after its defeat the peasant had no escape except emigration. Fearing a decline in the labor supply, large landowners first enlisted government aid to slow emigration, to no avail, then realized its importance as a "safety valve" and encouraged it.

In Sicily, poor social and economic conditions strengthened the Mafia. In the eighteenth and nineteenth centuries, nobles stimulated a misplaced patriotism to sabotage Enlightenment reforms and the Bourbon administration and employed criminal elements to maintain their power. This alliance survived unification, and the new state found it easier to accept than to destroy the local power structure. After unification, the Mafia flourished. In the words of Denis Mack Smith, "It was used by landowners who needed strong-arm men to collect rents and intimidate labour; and by the *gabellotti* [people who profited from renting land from the owners and having it worked by others] who, as well as coercing their workers, had to intimidate the owners in order to rent the *latifondi* on easy terms." In addition, liberal democratic institutions, combined with a voting base narrowed by illiteracy and poverty, increased the difficulties of combating the existing system. With a restricted electorate of only about 1 percent, landowners and their peers manipulated elections through Mafia influence. The police could not intervene unilaterally, as it had during Bourbon rule, so the liberal system "offered a better field for bribery and intimidation than autocratic government had ever done." In 1861, for example, a new law gave considerable influence to village notables, constraining Italian prefects to work with local "Grand Electors" with Mafia connections to help the government win elections. If the prefect failed to deliver electoral victories, the government would transfer him, and if he tried to keep the elections honest, local bosses with Mafia connections would use their influence to remove him; if both failed, the Mafia would resort to assassination. The new state's weakness strengthened the Mafia in Sicily and enhanced the political influence of other southern Italian criminal "organizations" such as the Camorra and the 'Ndrangheta.

Despite the prevalence of the latifundia, numerous landowning peasants persisted in the South. They possessed several small parcels of land, distant from each other and usually insufficient to support a family. They made long treks daily to work their own land and, at least part of the year, the land of others. Unlike northern peasants, they did not live on the land but in large towns from which they would set out each day.

Well-watered parts of the region alleviated this dismal picture of southern agriculture to a limited extent. More fortunate areas produced specialized products for export to foreign countries and to northern and central Italy. These sections, estimated at about 25 percent of the South, included parts of Campania, Sicily, and Puglia. Their products included wine, olives, and citrus fruits. The most notable early development occurred around the cities of Bari and Lecce, the first to be connected by rail to the rest of Italy and Europe. The Bari-Lecce area profited from the free trade system imposed by Piedmont after unification that devastated most of the South's agriculture by exporting wine to France. In 1880, phylloxera had hit French vines, but the disease spared this region for about the next twenty years. Even these more fortunate areas, however, suffered from the vagaries of politics and economics. With the outbreak of the tariff war in 1888, the French retaliated against Italian agricultural products, and wine exports did not reach the level of the 1880s even after the "war" ended.

Although total Italian agricultural production increased between 1866 and 1875 because of better communications with the rest of Europe, this increase did not alter the fundamentally backward nature of the country's agriculture. Investors preferred to put their money into bonds the government issued to service the huge debt, rather than invest in technical innovations on the land. Southern landowners accumulated more property by buying expropriated Church and domain property, rather than introduce technical innovations, because existing social conditions allowed them to make substantial profits using outmoded methods of cultivation. The state's fiscal policies exacerbated matters by weighing heaviest on the poorest areas.

In his 1881 investigation of agricultural conditions, Stefano Jacini drew a gloomy conclusion when he cited the low production of land, the antiquated methods, the heavy taxation policies, and the misery of the peasants: "Agricultural

Italy presents itself to us as a chronic and cancerous patient." Jacini suggested government intervention and reducing the fiscal burden to help agriculture, but international developments and domestic problems would make this solution impossible.

AGRICULTURAL CRISIS AND EMIGRATION: THE SOUTHERN PROBLEM

The international agrarian crisis that hit Italy between 1881 and 1894 had its roots in long-term technological trends. By the 1870s, completion of the American railway network and improvements in steamship transportation allowed American grain and other cereals grown inexpensively on its vast plains to reach Europe and to be sold there for less than the Europeans could produce it. European prices of wheat, corn, and other agricultural products plummeted, threatened farmers with ruin, and presented European governments with a dilemma. If they did nothing, the cheaper prices would favor urban consumers. That policy had two disadvantages: it provoked intense opposition among politically powerful large landowners who could threaten the government's viability and left countries vulnerable to starvation if war broke out. But raising the tariff would alienate industrialists who would have to pay their workers more to cover increased food prices. As a result of these considerations, European countries erected protective barriers to protect farmers and industry alike and intensified their colonial expansion to find markets. The crisis had different but crucial results in all countries, including Italy.

The Italian crisis first appeared in a drastic price decline for grains and corn, accompanied by a jump in grain imports and price stabilization at a lower level during the 1876 to 1880 period. The imports declined with passage of a new tariff in 1887. After 1900, imports increased again, this time owing to the rising food needs of the population and Italy's inability to meet them. In addition to grain prices, the price of other Italian agricultural goods—including wine, olive oil, and raw silk—dropped as well.

A debate ensued on how to protect the country. The Risorgimento generation favored free trade, but the calls for trade protection in order to meet the crisis intensified. The inquiry into agricultural conditions undertaken by Jacini (1877–1884) called for direct government intervention and tax cuts to improve technology and favor more private investment on the land. Following a debate on these issues, a quick switch to protectionism seemed unlikely. In 1887, however, the situation changed. In that year the Italians suffered a colonial defeat at Dogali, a defeat that forced Prime Minister Depretis to modify his government by taking in Crispi, the major proponent of colonialism. Depretis had to request more funds for an army better equipped to pursue a vigorous colonial policy, to be financed by increasing the tariff (definitively passed on June 21, 1887). As a result, the government could not afford to cut taxes and increase services for agriculture. The desire of the Italians to play a great-power role in international affairs, combined with the poverty of their country, meant that Italy devoted a greater percentage of its income to military expenditures than did more advanced countries, and these expenditures siphoned scarce resources away from the domestic sector.

Furthermore, the tariff had important social and economic implications. It ensured that emigration would continue by permitting the latifundia to survive the onslaught of cheap American grain. The emigration "safety valve" contributed to the rescue of large landowners by lessening the social tensions that might otherwise have exploded into revolt. In 1888, a law supported by the Meridionalisti (advocates for the South) allowed free emigration. The southern bourgeoisie profited by acting as recruiting agents for the steamship lines that transported emigrants to the United States under appalling conditions.

Some emigrants returned with their American savings to buy land, joining their land-hungry compatriots to continue the struggle against the landlords, but the fight had been lost. The agrarian crisis and government policies ensured the survival of the inefficient latifundia, low production, and social inequities and blocked new types of land tenure, greater production, and better wages—which would have reduced emigration and created greater wealth for the entire country. Instead, poor agricultural conditions in the South helped limit the country's industrial growth to the Northwest and greatly intensified the severe economic imbalance between North and South.

INDUSTRIAL DEVELOPMENT AND PROTECTIONISM

Economic historians agree that important gains in agricultural production per unit precede or accompany rapid industrial expansion and continued growth. Increased agricultural productivity allows a country to export more products and thus earn more foreign exchange that can be invested; raises per capita income so that investment capital becomes more available; and expands the domestic market for industrial products as machinery becomes crucial to further increase productivity.

The backwardness of southern agriculture ensured that productivity increases in the agrarian sector would not occur. During the 1870s, the cost of establishing the new state, the expense of building an infrastructure, the low savings rates, the price declines of industrial products, and the technical changes in heavy industry that gave the edge to older, more experienced, and better-capitalized foreign firms help explain the failure of Italian industry to develop more rapidly. But why did the country lag so far behind the rest of Europe from 1880 to 1896, after the government had built an infrastructure and emigration had reduced population pressure, and despite the existence of important nuclei of engineers, technicians, and skilled laborers? Here, agricultural backwardness appears to have been a main culprit in restricting the domestic market so that it could not support a sustained takeoff in the areas crucial to the industrial revolution—iron and textiles. Confirming this explanation are the following events: the industrial takeoff in the North after 1896 coincided with a great increase in agricultural productivity in Lombardy, Piedmont, and Emilia, but the South did not experience this development and failed to follow suit in the industrial sector.

In 1880, industry represented a small part of the total economy. Agriculture dominated, followed by the service sector (such as commerce and finance), which had increased after unification and tied the peninsula more closely to the rest of Europe. Because of the favorable treatment accorded to it in the tariff of 1878, cotton manufacturing developed rapidly but, thanks to the head start of the older industrialized countries, could not play the role of leader. Also accorded favorable treatment in 1878, wool had a notable, if slower, development. The silk industry remained important but was handicapped by plant illnesses, Asian competition, and concentration on the production of semifinished items for export. Because the government and foreign capitalists placed orders for cheaper iron products and locomotives abroad, railway and ship building did not stimulate these industries.

The lack of a policy to industrialize the country reflects an important debate. It took time for statesmen of the period to understand that Italy had to industrialize rapidly if it was not to regress. Although most agreed that action favorable to some industries had to be taken, they believed in a balanced development of the country, with agriculture leading the way and industry playing a supporting role. After this idea was abandoned, a new debate began. The proponents of a modern iron and steel industry demanded a general protective tariff for iron products. Their antagonists, however, argued that the costs of implanting the iron sector would be prohibitive; they believed in the free importation of iron products to provide cheap material to the mechanical industry, where, they argued, Italy could compete with foreign countries. They also called for a protective tariff on machine products and government orders to stimulate the industry.

The 1887 tariff gave the victory to the partisans of a strong iron and steel industry. The machine industry received some added protection, but not enough, according to economic historian Alexander Gerschenkron, who argued persuasively that the mechanical sector could have competed with its rivals had it received greater support. As it had done in Germany ten years earlier, the tariff signaled the alliance of industrialists and large landowners to secure protection for their products. In another parallel with Germany, the government stimulated the metal and mechanical sectors by placing orders for a big navy. Under the leadership of navy minister Benedetto Brin (1884–1891), the leading proponent of large warships, Parliament appropriated huge sums and advanced the money to large firms created to exploit the new opportunities. The government also boosted spending for railways, and this time was partially successful in its attempt to ensure that domestic industry filled the new orders. These operations encouraged financial firms to reorient their investments from government paper to the industrial sector. But the banking system was poorly organized and regulated, and in 1893–1894 it collapsed amid charges of widespread corruption. Its subsequent reorganization on modern lines, however, and the creation of something like a central bank set the stage for further industrial development.

Thus the state emerged as a major player in the country's industrialization, but it paid a high price. Industry became inordinately dependent on government contracts, and though it profited, it also suffered because of the vagaries of state orders and indirect subsidies. Taxpayers and consumers footed the bill for expensive Italian products, and all Italians paid more for foodstuffs. The government policies that produced the rapid, though lopsided, industrialization of 1896 to 1914 also increased the already high political and social tensions that marked the century's end. Protectionism played an important role in the industrialization of most countries, but it cost the Italians more.

EDUCATION

Linking social and economic problems with political tensions and intensifying the North-South imbalance were schooling and education. Modern industrial democracies depend heavily on literacy, and here Italian educational policies turned in a mixed performance.

The illiteracy rate declined after unification, but slowly. In 1871, the illiteracy rate for the entire population was 72.9 percent. In 1881, the percentage had declined to 67.3. Illiteracy was higher in the South than in the North, but the statistics reveal a more significant discrepancy: a tendency for illiteracy to drop faster in the cities. The 1901 census showed that illiteracy fell over a nineteen-year period by 27.6 percent in urban areas but only by 20 percent in the countryside. The rural nature of the South and the greater illiteracy there caused its high rate to persist longer. For example, those areas that had the lowest illiteracy in 1861 (Lombardy and Piedmont) dropped below 50 percent in ten years and below 25 percent by 1901; the South, including the islands and part of the Center, still had an illiteracy rate of more than 50 percent in 1901.

The most important factor in bringing down illiteracy is elementary education, and the old governments had done little to encourage public education. A law named after Count Gabrio Casati and passed in Piedmont in 1859 intended to encourage education was extended to all Italy after unification. The law struck at clerical influence and reorganized education on the European model; that is, it was concerned primarily with the education of elites in the secondary schools. It paid only rudimentary attention to elementary education, obliging the towns to provide free education for two years (four years for towns that had populations of more than 4,000 or that had a secondary school), and it provided minimum wages for teachers. The law obliged fathers to send their children "of both sexes" to school under punishment of law. Besides the insufficient time provided to teach literacy to children who knew only the local dialect, many towns (prevalently in the South) could not afford to meet their obligations to finance the schools, and the law provided no sanctions for fathers who did not send their children to school. In addition, because of the need to work the land to help their families, many children could not afford to go to school.

The Left recognized the inadequate nature of the law, and a debate ensued after 1870 in which the Left pushed for free, compulsory education similar to that of other European nations. In 1877, Parliament passed the Coppino law providing for three years of compulsory education for children of both sexes from ages six to nine and sanctions for parents who did not comply. Because the new law made insufficient provision for financing the schools, many children received only two years' schooling. Over the years, governments of the Left greatly increased appropriations for education in many areas, including school construction and teachers' salaries. Nonetheless, the quality of elementary education and attendance remained low, and the formulas for distributing the funds helped the richer North and worked against the South.

The country fared better in the quality of public secondary and higher education. The number of students increased substantially but remained well below the proportions of other European countries. Public education overshadowed private and was highly centralized and geared to producing professionals. In the secondary schools, the state paid the most attention to educating the elite through a rigorous classical education. Technical education remained inferior, to the point that future Prime Minister Luigi Luzzatti overhauled it in 1869. This reform, untouched until 1923, improved matters but did not eliminate the subordination of the technical schools, which remained a weak link in Italy's industrialization effort.

THE CATHOLIC SOCIAL MOVEMENT

Education had been an old battleground between the Church and the secular power in Europe. In Italy, the Church had retained control of education in the old states with the major exception of Piedmont. The Casati law had anticlerical aspects but did not eliminate religious teaching by priests in the public schools. When the debate over compulsory education began after 1870, intransigent Catholics opposed it because their schools could not compete with free public education and because, they argued, public schools taught liberal values. After unification, when the Coppino law established obligatory schooling but did not abolish religious instruction, major polemics arose between Catholics and proponents of lay education as some local jurisdictions retained religious instruction and others abolished it. The fight fueled the introduction of "positivist" philosophies and empirical programs into Italian schools as a means of combating Catholic "spiritualism."

The battle over education illustrated the anticlerical aftermath of the Risorgimento: the Church's unwillingness to accept unification, its order requiring Catholics to abstain from national politics, and the pope's appeal for the intervention of foreign powers. The state struck back in 1866 and 1867 by extending to all Italy the earlier Piedmontese legislation expropriating Church property not used for religious purposes, by instituting a special tax on most of the rest, and by punishing Church interference in political activities. Economics more than religious persecution spurred the government to confiscate Church property, and the authorities handed out mild punishments when they acted against the Church. Furthermore, affiliation with the Catholic Church shut no one out of a career in state service.

These factors favored reconciliation between church and state. Despite the political intransigence of Church authorities, a healing process between state and church began as many Catholics accepted the reality of unification and tried to reconcile their faith and patriotism. With the death of Pius IX in 1878 and the election of Leo XIII, an attempt at cooperation with the national government replaced hostility. Although a policy of cooperation was adopted most clearly in Germany and France, Italy moved in the same direction even though the particular problems caused by the country's being the site of the papacy's center caused the policy to be implemented unofficially and with caution.

Forbidden from overt participation in national politics, the Catholic movement dedicated itself to social concerns. The Church's centuries-long tradition encouraged this development, as did the rising threat from a new atheistic and radical force: socialism. Moreover, the Catholic movement's strength created the premise of an alliance with the liberals, who also feared socialism. The new century would witness a muting of the old disputes with the state and a partnership between Catholics and liberals based on antisocialism.

The North, where Socialist organizations proliferated, remained the Catholic focus. Respect for property, the denial that an inherent struggle existed between owners and employees, a lack of aggressiveness, an emphasis on Christian cooperation instead of struggle based on economic interests, and a failure to challenge the existing system marked the Catholic social movement. Although they were extremely active in charitable activities and championed the dignity of labor and its right to decent wages, the Catholics hesitated to organize unions and favor strikes, activities that would have alienated their rich noble and bourgeois supporters. Catholics romanticized the past, emphasizing cooperation and corporate medieval institutions; they debated the feasibility of mixed unions consisting of employees and employers. They devoted their considerable energies to creating a vast network of economic and social organizations to help peasants and workers: mutual aid societies, cooperatives, and rural savings banks (culminating in the Bank of Rome, the Vatican's financial arm). Coordinating these economic activities and local political initiatives was the Opera dei Congressi, a lay organization, controlled by the Church, whose efficiency no political party could match. The Opera ensured that its religious view permeated Catholic social activity and that no radical ideas would germinate from it.

In 1891, Leo XIII's encyclical *Rerum Novarum* gave theoretical unity to these social activities. It modernized the Church's mission by declaring that labor was not just another commodity whose value depended on supply and demand, opposing the exploitation of workers, emphasizing justice in economic relationships, and arguing for protection of child and female labor. The encyclical also reaffirmed the Church's traditional role as defender of the poor, stated its preference for a corporate organization of society, argued against the extension of the state's powers over society, and condemned liberalism and socialism.

Rerum Novarum established the foundation for Italian Christian democracy. A professor at the University of Pisa, Giuseppe Toniolo, theoretician of Church primacy in social and economic activity, organized a congress of Catholic intellectuals in October 1892 and founded a review devoted to the social sciences. Committed to providing a "scientific" basis to Catholic activities, as Marx and Engels had done for the Socialists, Toniolo advocated social legislation and measures favoring workers and the poor, but on a foundation of class cooperation, not class struggle.

Don Romolo Murri, the priest who was the real founder of Italian Christian democracy, hoped to defeat socialism by linking the already strong Catholic social activism to politics. In 1898, Murri founded *Cultura Sociale*, a title that recalled the Socialist *Critica Sociale*. Murri believed the Catholics would be the real winners in the struggle between the Socialists and the state because the Catholic social movement could mobilize much larger masses than their rivals. Toniolo and Murri both believed that true democracy translated into a great victory for Christian democracy, but whereas Toniolo understood that the Church would not condone a political campaign designed to destroy the liberal state and believed it would collapse of its own weight, Murri had absorbed Socialist rhetoric about the destruction of liberal institutions. Murri condemned the liberal state as an expression of the evil bourgeoisie and therefore as antithetical to Catholic principles. As he wrote to Filippo Meda, a Catholic leader willing to enter into a dialogue with the state, he believed in "the necessity of a reorganization [of society] from below, inspired by the Church, and therefore in opposition to the mission of the modern state."

Murri did not push revolution as a means of destroying the state, but he did advocate Catholic political intransigence beyond that authorized by the Vatican to destroy the state in the name of Christ. Thus, ironically, Christian Democrats (DC) rejected the state and favored a harder opposition than the more vocal clerical intransigents, who, though they opposed Italian governments because of anticlerical legislation, favored an eventual accommodation. Indeed, peace discussions between church and state began and were advanced by that noted anticlerical, Francesco Crispi.

When the talks fell apart, the government misidentified the clericals as the state's most tenacious opponents. During the 1898 riots, the government arrested clerical intransigent leaders such as Don Davide Albertario along with Socialists and anarchists. Shocked at being lumped with the leftist opponents of the state, the Church slowly changed its policy to one of cooperation with the government against their common Socialist enemies. The Catholic social movement went along, but Christian Democratic opposition to real reconciliation represented a major weakness for the liberal state.

ANARCHISTS AND SOCIALISTS: THE "SOCIAL QUESTION"

Italy's economic dislocations during the late nineteenth century prompted opposition by those most affected. This movement condemned bourgeois power and the organization of society that exploited the working class. Radicals preached the destruction of bourgeois-controlled governments and the passage of power to workers.

The working-class movement was divided into two broad currents: anarchism and socialism. Anarchists advocated immediate social revolution without giving much thought to analyzing the conditions that would favor it or what the new society might look like. Mikhail Bakunin, a Russian anarchist, disseminated Socialist ideas in Italy on behalf of the London-based International Workingmen's Association in the 1860s. He destroyed the influence of Mazzinianism among Italian workers and gained the allegiance of many Italian intellectuals against Marx during the 1860s and 1870s. Persons of high quality who joined the movement included Carlo Cafiero, whose wealth financed the anarchist movement; Errico

Malatesta, its longtime leader; lawyer Francesco Saverio Merlino, later a Marxist revisionist; Andrea Costa, who would create a forerunner of the Italian Socialist Party; and Russian revolutionary Anna Kuliscioff, Costa's lover, a future founder of the Socialist Party, and the "Signora" of Italian socialism.

Bakunin advocated the immediate overthrow of the state by violence. In 1874 and 1877, anarchist bands attempted to spark a nationwide revolution, but the police had little trouble suppressing their activities because of the lack of popular support. After 1877, prominent leaders deserted the anarchist movement when it became clear that its methods had failed. In 1878, Anna Kuliscioff pointed out that miserable social conditions are the prerequisites for revolts, but that revolutions must issue from the people and cannot be made without them. In August 1879, a famous letter from Andrea Costa pronounced anarchism a failure because it had neglected the economic conditions and needs of the people, "and when we raised the flag of revolt, the people did not understand us and we were left alone."

Costa advised his comrades to enter Parliament, and in 1883 he became the first Socialist to serve there. But he remained an anarchist at heart, advocating the destruction of existing political institutions by infiltrating and undermining them rather than transforming them into tools that the proletariat could use. He proposed the union of all Socialist factions in Italy and the broadening of the movement's base by establishing a political party. In 1881, he founded the Partito Socialista Rivoluzionario di Romagna, intended to be the nucleus of a nationwide political organization, but the party failed to achieve this aim.

In 1882, workers in Milan founded the Partito Operaio Italiano (Italian Workers' Party, POI), the Italian Socialist Party's direct forerunner. This organization hoped to take advantage of the recently widened suffrage and signaled the shift in working-class influence from the artisan Romagna to what would become the Italian industrial heartland. Although Socialist intellectuals around the Milanese newspaper *La Plebe* had a hand in founding the organization, the party distrusted "bourgeois" Socialists and restricted membership exclusively to workers, a policy that proved disastrous. In 1886, the government dissolved the party after seizing upon a dispute with the popular leader of the Radical Democrats, Felice Cavallotti, who feared POI competition. Although *operaista* leaders reorganized, their organization never recovered. It had reached a membership of 40,000.

The task of creating a Socialist party now fell to Filippo Turati and Anna Kuliscioff. A former Radical Democrat and poet who had been part of an important artistic movement in Milan, Turati had converted to Marxism. Turati and Kuliscioff had fallen in love in Naples after her affair with Costa cooled down; returning to Milan, they lived together until her death in 1925. Together, they founded the Milanese Socialist League, a "cell" that enunciated the principles that would inspire the future Italian Socialist Party, and, in 1891, *Critica Sociale*, the review that spread Marxist ideology in Italy.

PORTRAITS

ANDREA COSTA
Precursor

༄༅࿐

A ndrea Costa could serve as the model for the idealist youth of late nineteenth-century Italy who were attracted to radical ideologies. Born in Imola on November 30, 1851, he studied at the University of Bologna with the Nobel Prize–winning poet Giosuè Carducci, but was attracted to anarchism. Anarchists advocated assassination and revolution as their primary weapons. The anarchists tried to spark two revolutions in Italy, but they failed miserably. Costa founded several anarchist newspapers in his home region of the Romagna and participated in revolutionary activities. Arrested in 1874, Costa was released from prison in 1876 and left for Paris.

In Paris, Costa met Anna Kuliscioff, a Russian revolutionary anarchist who had fled to France. After the two became lovers, they had a daughter, whom they named Andreina after him. In the meantime, the French police arrested Kuliscioff. She was expelled from France and went to Italy, where she became disillusioned with violence. She argued that the classic anarchist method of sparking revolution to change society would always be a failure because it did nothing to gain the support of the people. The year was 1879, and in August, Costa, influenced by Kuliscioff, wrote a letter to his friends from his prison cell that has remained famous in Italian radical annals.

In the letter, Costa renounced violence, as Kuliscioff had done. He advised his friends to run for office and enter Parliament. From that platform, Costa wrote, they could infiltrate, undermine, and destroy existing political institutions. Released from prison, he returned to the Romagna and in 1881 founded the Revolutionary Socialist Party of the Romagna. In 1882, he became the first Socialist elected to the Chamber of Deputies. Despite his willingness to change, however, Costa never fit the mold of a typical social democrat and remained a revered figure and a romantic revolutionary with little influence.

By 1885, his love affair with Anna Kuliscioff had long since cooled down, and she had become the companion of Filippo Turati, Italy's most notable Socialist politician. They lived in Milan and raised Andreina together. Andreina—the daughter of two atheistic anarchists, raised by her rebellious mother and an unwavering Socialist—married a conservative Catholic industrialist from Milan, much to her mother's chagrin. Her son, Andrea's grandchild, became a monk. Andrea Costa died in Imola on January 19, 1910. Rumors circulated that he converted on his deathbed, but this seems an unlikely scenario.

Turati and Kuliscioff believed in a nonviolent, gradual road to socialism in which socialist ideas would penetrate all the institutions of the old society. Violence was irrelevant and illusionary because the proletariat itself had absorbed bourgeois principles and because it had been held in subjection and ignorance for so long. If the workers were so "backward," as many Socialist leaders claimed, how could the working class lead the way to the higher organization of society represented by socialism? From the beginning, Turati denounced the "dictatorship of the proletariat," which he claimed introduced an oligarchic principle into socialism that he predicted would produce a dictatorship of intellectuals against the proletariat. Only by promoting a spiritual growth through educating the workers and enacting social legislation to mitigate the terrible conditions under which they labored could that fate be avoided. Social and economic reforms could be achieved in Parliament; this goal required the establishment of a Socialist party to coordinate political action, not only to pass social legislation but also to defeat reactionary governments hostile to the proletariat's progress and to help extend the democracy necessary for socialism. Self-redemption and autonomous political action would teach workers their own best interests and how to organize to achieve them. The "revolution," therefore, would be the culmination of a great evolutionary movement.

These ideas initially won out, but the left wing, or the "revolutionaries," opposed them in the Italian as in the other European Socialist parties. The revolutionaries argued that there were no distinctions among bourgeois groups and viewed governments and parliaments as merely "ruling committees" of the bourgeoisie. For that reason, revolutionaries advocated the violent overthrow of the existing government because they believed that social legislation bettering working conditions would only reconcile workers and capitalists.

But the social and economic crises of the late nineteenth century masked these divisions. By the early 1890s, anarchist influence had declined, and the Socialists had clarified their social, economic, and political goals. Despite opposition by Marxist philosopher Antonio Labriola, who argued that Italy had not developed to the point where a viable Socialist party was possible, Turati and Kuliscioff succeeded in founding one in October 1892. At a congress of working-class organizations held in Genoa, they achieved enough support from workers to defeat both the old POI leaders and the anarchists. The victory over the POI meant that Socialist intellectuals participated fully in the new party (although the worker-intellectual feud continued), and the anarchists were expelled from the movement. Over the next three years, the party perfected its organization—making it the first centralized, disciplined, modern Italian political party on the model of the German Socialist Party (SPD)—and adopted the name Partito Socialista Italiano (PSI).

The PSI bore Turati's stamp—a social and economic commitment to "the immediate improvement of working-class conditions (hours, salaries, factory rules, etc.)" and "a wider struggle having as its goal the conquest of the organs of public power (state, commune, public administrations, etc.)" to transform them from oppressive institutions "into instruments of economic and political expropriation of the dominating class." But divisions over political alliances remained, even if, as a compromise, the party did not immediately allow understandings with bourgeois parties. For Turati, alliances could not be admitted for the moment for practical purposes; for the revolutionaries, the reasons were ideological.

The Italian political situation seemed favorable for Socialist affirmation in 1892. A cabinet headed by Giolitti and friendlier to the workers than Crispi's took office in May. Giolitti's attitude allowed the PSI to expand its membership and support but got the government into trouble with the Right and Crispi, who was especially alarmed at Socialist growth in Sicily. In 1893, several incidents combined to topple Giolitti: the bank scandals and resulting corruption charges against the prime minister; disturbances after the murder of several Italian workers in France; and finally, a revolt in Sicily headed by the *fasci siciliani*, peasant leagues considered to be under Socialist influence. Giolitti resigned and Crispi returned. He proclaimed martial law and established military tribunals on the island. Repression spread to the entire country as agitation increased and Crispi received full powers. In June 1894, he secured passage of "exceptional" laws that allowed the persecution of anarchists and Socialists, and in October he dissolved the PSI.

Crispi's policies set off an important debate within the PSI: his colonialism had already alienated northern industrialists; should the Socialists modify their political intransigence and present a united antigovernment front with Crispi's bourgeois opponents? Turati and Kuliscioff had no ideological objection to alliances but had to move cautiously not to alienate their Socialist comrades. In January 1894, Kuliscioff wrote to Engels and secured his support for political alliances with the bourgeoisie. In July, Turati and Kuliscioff brought their group into the bourgeois-led anti-Crispi League for the Defense of Liberty and negotiated an alliance with non-Socialist radicals for the February 1895 local elections. This move completed the powerful alliance of Crispi opponents known as the "State of Milan," which took the lead in toppling Crispi after the Adowa defeat in 1896.

Turati's moves in Milan violated official party policy, and though the Milanese leader won modification of the strict electoral policy and an exception for Milan, he failed to secure an endorsement of political alliances in principle. He clearly believed in them, wished to make them a feature of Socialist policy, and remained ready to oppose his comrades if he believed alliances would further Socialist aims.

Government repression briefly paused after Crispi's fall but worsened in 1898 as the protective tariff, the country's poor social conditions, and international dislocations produced nationwide riots. This crisis developed into a political threat to the country's parliamentary system that lasted until 1901. Until then, the Socialists remained unified to protect the basic liberties necessary for the party and the labor movement to survive. But when that threat receded, the division between Socialists who wished to improve the lot of peasants and workers through existing institutions and those who wanted an immediate overthrow of the state exploded with full force. As with the Catholics, the left wing threatened the existence of the liberal state, but unlike the Catholics, no Vatican kept a lid on the Socialist dispute.

CHAPTER TWELVE

The Rise of Socialism and the Giolittian Era

DEPRESSED PRICES AND POOR ECONOMIC CONDITIONS PLAGUED EUROPE from the early 1870s to the 1890s, but higher prices and prosperity marked the years between 1896 and 1914, despite a sharp 1907–1908 recession. Protectionism increased prices for agricultural goods, industrialists worked together to raise prices for their products, and gold discoveries in South Africa and the Klondike expanded the money supply. The demand for industrial products increased because of the arms race, the growth of the middle class, the opening of colonial markets, higher wages, and governmental stimulation of the economy through increased spending. Most important, technological advances in electricity, chemicals, and the internal combustion engine created new industrial sectors and touched off the "second" industrial revolution.

These changes allowed Italy to become the first Mediterranean country to move into the advanced industrial arena, despite regional imbalances. Economic changes drastically affected the country's political and social life. Requiring more freedom and less political tension, the growing and increasingly powerful northern bourgeoisie displayed less tolerance for Crispi and leaders who failed to recognize the paramount importance of their goals, who favored foreign adventures, and whose recalcitrance stimulated social unrest that interfered with the country's economic development. During the early years of the twentieth century, industrialists reached necessary but limited understandings with their opponents. The Socialists also were committed to liquidating the repressive mentality of late nineteenth-century government leaders, a tendency demonstrated by the Milanese alliance between radicals and business leaders against Crispi. Between 1901 and World War I, the converging interests of bourgeoisie and proletariat outweighed ideology and had positive if limited effects. However, in both camps the groups criticizing this practical "politics of things" gained strength, and as war exploded in 1911 with Turkey and in 1914 in Europe, the compromise responsible for Italy's political, social, and economic advances ruptured.

From End-of-Century Crisis
to "Liberal Springtide"

Antonio Di Rudinì succeeded Crispi. A Sicilian leader of the Right, Rudinì had failed to live up to the promise he had demonstrated as a young man during the Risorgimento; he had been a boy wonder, one unkind critic commented, and then "the wonder disappeared but the boy remained."

The Milanese industrialists who had opposed Crispi supported Rudinì but felt ill at ease with his social and administrative reform projects. They favored drastic cuts in unproductive government expenses to stimulate northern industrial activity. To satisfy them, Rudinì retreated from Ethiopia following the Adowa defeat, but the funds saved by this withdrawal satisfied no one. The war minister's plan to reduce the army's size while increasing its efficiency ran into King Humbert I's staunch opposition, and fearing that his government would fall, Rudinì sabotaged it. The prime minister hoped to increase his support in the country by favoring agrarian interests, strengthening the executive power against Parliament, and meeting some of the workers' demands through social legislation. This "conservative decentralization" program included granting towns under 10,000 the right to elect their own mayors, permitting local referenda on tax matters, and creating a system of voluntary accident insurance.

Elements of this program resembled Bismarck's attempt to undercut the German Socialists by meeting some working-class demands, and it did appeal to moderates on the left. However, the program alienated the Extreme Right, which advocated strong measures to meet the threat from the Extreme Left. In 1897, Sidney Sonnino published a famous article arguing that over the past fifty years the Statuto had evolved in a democratic direction unforeseen by its framers. Sonnino condemned the Italian parliamentary system as too liberal and argued that political practice should conform to the letter of the constitution. This reasoning would have allowed the king to name or dismiss ministers without Parliament's intervention.

Besides his troubles with the Right, Rudinì alienated the Socialists, many of whose leaders had been imprisoned by Crispi and remained in jail despite a partial amnesty. Filippo Turati denounced government repression of the Socialist press and Socialist associations as unconstitutional. The Socialists warned that government tariff policy would produce dramatic increases in the price of food, which would increase the risk of revolts. In the elections of March 1897, the Socialist parliamentary delegation increased from ten to fifteen, signaling the failure of the government anti-Socialist campaign.

In February, food riots in Sicily left ten demonstrators dead. After an eerie two-month calm, the disorders suddenly flared up and spread throughout the country, made worse by high prices, a bad harvest, and the disruption of trade caused by the Spanish-American War. The unrest culminated in Milan, where the army used artillery to fire at demonstrators. The indiscriminate shooting caused 80 civilian deaths and 500 wounded, according to official statistics, but unofficial estimates claimed 400 dead and 1,000 wounded. After the firing stopped, the arrests began. The police detained leaders who had opposed the government—Socialists, Catholics, Radicals, and Republicans. The government shut down the opposition press, somehow missing the Socialist daily, *Avanti!*, and handed out long prison sentences. Conservatives explained the Milanese disorders as a conspiracy of the most disparate enemies to destroy the state.

Rudinì's crackdown failed to save his cabinet. In Parliament, conservatives blamed Rudinì's moderate policies for encouraging the disorders. On June 18, Rudinì resigned. While opposition leaders were hauled before military courts, General Luigi Pelloux headed a new cabinet. Pelloux had liberal credentials, and a reactionary wave seemed to have been avoided when he withdrew restrictive bills proposed by his predecessor. Pelloux, however, received temporary emergency powers and then asked for permanent legislation that would have severely restricted constitutionally guaranteed freedoms of the press, association, and assembly. He came under the influence of Sonnino, who led the floor fight for the bills. This development aroused the suspicion of the moderates, but they adopted a wait-and-see attitude.

The Socialists attacked the Pelloux-Sonnino alliance because Sonnino seemed positioned to carry out his proposed constitutional revisions and end the country's democratic evolution. Convinced that socialism could not develop without democracy, the Socialists changed from opponents of a Statuto they deemed too restrictive into defenders of the constitution "repudiated by the bourgeoisie." The party had officially rejected Turati's alliance policy even though it had made an exception for Milan; now it dropped its refusal to cooperate with all "bourgeois" groups and coordinated its political efforts in the country and in Parliament with the Radicals and Republicans. This action solidified cooperation in Parliament among the Estrema Sinistra (Extreme Left).

In the Chamber of Deputies, the Estrema could count on only about 67 deputies out of 508, but that body's rules allowed a determined group to delay business indefinitely. Estrema deputies resorted to "obstruction"—long speeches, myriad amendments, numerous votes. Sonnino proposed limiting debate by changing the rules—against which the Estrema filibustered. The government's supporters then circumvented the Chamber by embodying the original bills in royal decrees issued by the king. This procedure irritated moderates who were philosophically opposed to the Estrema's methods and contributed to an understanding between them and the Estrema. By July 1899, almost half the deputies opposed Pelloux. In the country, jailed opposition leaders were elected to the Chamber and reelected when declared ineligible, and widespread agitation for an amnesty forced the government to grant several pardons. Tempers flared in Parliament and fistfights broke out on the Chamber floor.

Faced by an impossible situation, the king ended the session and attention shifted to a court case appealing the government's enforcement of the royal decrees as law. In February 1900, Italy's highest court ruled against the government, forcing it to seek approval of the decrees in Parliament. Realizing that their majority had been slowly dissolving, Pelloux and Sonnino resorted to illegal procedures to limit debate, further alienating the moderate deputies. Although they succeeded in having the rules changes formally adopted as a result of these methods, the action failed to end the Estrema's resistance, and the government's only choice was to hold new elections.

The elections of June 3 and 10, 1900, spelled disaster for Pelloux. Despite government interference in the balloting, it lost the popular vote and won only a slim and uncertain majority in the Chamber of Deputies. The Socialist delegation doubled, and the Estrema swelled to 95. Pelloux's resignation as a result of these elections effectively ended the reaction of 1898–1900.

The end-of-century crisis spurred debate among contemporaries and historians: Turati's Socialist opponent, Arturo Labriola, interpreted Pelloux as the front man in a royal plot to undermine parliamentary institutions. In 1975, Umberto Levra viewed the crisis as a successful bourgeois coup d'état against the proletariat because it resulted in the triumph of Turati's ideas within the Socialist Party. Leaving aside Levra's ideological bias, the fact remains that by cooperating with other parties of the Extreme Left, the Socialists defeated the reaction of 1898–1900; in a similar situation during 1920 to 1924, the leftist parties chose an isolationist course that contributed to the victory of fascism in Italy.

After Pelloux's resignation, the king asked the eighty-one-year-old president of the Senate, Giuseppe Saracco, to form a government. A wag commented: "When Italy most desperately feels the need for a lusty male to impregnate her, she consummates a union with an old man already betrothed to Death." On July 29, 1900, an Italian anarchist returned to Italy from Paterson, New Jersey, to assassinate King Humbert. Humbert's twenty-nine-year-old son, Victor Emanuel III, chose a conciliatory course over confrontation. The country rapidly returned to normal, but had less tolerance for government arbitrariness. Following a labor dispute in Genoa, Saracco authorized the dissolution of the local Chamber of Labor. In response, a massive general strike paralyzed Italy's largest port city, and sympathy strikes occurred in other parts of the country. In February 1901, Saracco resigned.

Victor Emanuel III lacked the physical presence of his predecessors, and his short stature made him fair game for political cartoonists throughout his reign. In his personal life, he was cold, as his son frequently complained. Unlike Victor Emanuel II and Humbert I, he eschewed relationships with women and reserved his passion for his vast coin collection. Emotionally he was insecure. He frequently seemed weak and tended to waver, to play his cards too close to the chest, and to follow the path of least resistance. These qualities brought him and his country to grief, contributing to the rise of fascism and the end of his dynasty in 1946.

Finding a replacement for Saracco presented unusual difficulties because the Chamber of Deputies gave no clear indication of a successor. To the cheers of the Left, the king appointed the liberal Zanardelli to form a government, despite indications that the Chamber preferred Sonnino. Although this solution pleased the Left, it was fraught with long-term implications. Presented with an opportunity to designate the prime minister, the Chamber meekly relied on the monarch to make the choice. The king chose Zanardelli, who would come to power with Giovanni Giolitti, because Zanardelli and Giolitti's ideas were popular in the country despite their doubtful majority in the Chamber of Deputies. The king did not approve of Giolitti, an advocate of tax reform, because fiscal reform would lead to fewer funds for the army. The king handled the dilemma shrewdly: he opted for Zanardelli and Giolitti, but made cuts in military expenses impossible by exercising his right to name the ministers for war and the navy and to influence the choice of foreign minister. At the same time, a secret agreement committed Italy to sending six army corps to Germany in case of war with France, making it impossible to reduce the army below the current twelve corps. In short, he presented Giolitti with the option of joining the government with few chances for reform or of fighting for tax reforms outside of it. Giolitti entered the cabinet believing that the need for a liberal government that would initiate a dialogue between Socialists and business outweighed fiscal reform. The Estrema had little choice but to support the Zanardelli-Giolitti cabinet out of fear that Sonnino would come to power. Significant fiscal reform never came off the back burner.

For the Socialist delegation, Giolitti's presence as interior minister guaranteed the country protection against repression and compensated for the cabinet's imperfections. In a well-publicized speech in October 1899, Giolitti had announced the bankruptcy of reaction and outlined a program that included respect for civil rights, an overhaul of the judicial and administrative systems, and fiscal reform. He criticized fixed and indirect taxes and protective tariffs and advocated proportional taxation. The fiscal parts of his program would remain largely unfulfilled, but Giolitti believed that the government could no longer be at the service of "restricted cabals." It had to cease intervening on the side of employers in labor disputes, grant labor's reasonable demands, and encourage higher wages, as befitted an advanced economy. As interior minister, he ended the government's long-standing policy of breaking strikes.

The coming of the Zanardelli-Giolitti cabinet encouraged workers to strike, especially on the land. Socialists formed agricultural leagues and unions that demanded improved wages and working conditions. On the land, the number of strikes increased from 27 involving 12,517 participants in 1900 to 629 with 222,985 participants in 1901.

Predictably a conservative counterattack began in Parliament in April 1901. Sonnino denounced the cabinet for its supposed subordination to the Socialists and called for a strong government to restore "discipline." Giolitti countered that the Chamber had to choose between liberty and repression. A dispute erupted among the Socialists about whether the deputies should vote confidence in the government; without a positive vote from the Socialist delegation, the cabinet would fall and be replaced by a Sonnino-led coalition. The Socialist Party Directorate ordered its deputies not to vote confidence in the government, but Turati persuaded the deputies to do otherwise. On June 22, 1901, the entire Estrema, led by the Socialists, voted in favor of the Zanardelli-Giolitti government, keeping it in power by a 264-to-184 margin—"the victory of liberty," *Avanti!* commented of the first Italian government to receive Socialist votes. The Socialists had saved "the Liberal Springtide."

POLITICS, ECONOMICS, AND SOCIETY IN THE GIOLITTIAN ERA

Between the turbulence of the reactionary movement that ended in 1901 and the forces set in motion by the Libyan War of 1911–1912, the Giolittian age appears as an oasis of political stabilization. Giolitti, a calm and collected Piedmontese nurtured in the bureaucracy, consistently outmaneuvered his conservative enemies and seemed prepared to open negotiations with new forces previously excluded from the political process and from a reasonable share in the nation's growing wealth. His sympathy for the political and economic platforms of these groups stopped well short of agreeing with their aims, but his willingness to support some of their demands exposed him to attacks from the right.

Giolitti drew an important lesson from the 1900 elections, which had increased the representation of the Left. In 1903, he invited Turati to join his new cabinet, but because of internal party opposition, Turati refused. For the next decade, PSI leaders argued about whether cooperating with Giolitti would end with their "absorption" into the bourgeois political system. Weakened by serious divisions, as was the case in most European countries, Italy's Socialists won concessions but failed to enter the inner circle directing the country's policies.

The Radicals and Republicans—other leftist organizations—also debated "domestication." The Radicals were divided, but some accepted cabinet posts at different times. The Republicans remained more adamant, but given the country's liberal direction, they failed to convince Italians why replacing the monarchy with a republic would make a substantial difference for the country.

In 1904, Italy's first general strike occurred, but Giolitti, correctly calculating that the movement would fall apart after a few days, did not intervene. Although his conduct provoked criticism from disgruntled conservatives demanding strong action, he shrewdly used the strike to bolster his position by calling new elections that produced a majority more favorable to him in the Chamber of Deputies.

The general strike alarmed the Catholics and helped shape a new policy. The election of politically moderate Pope Pius X in 1903, the dissolution of the Opera dei Congressi in 1904, and the influence of Lombard industrial and banking groups over Catholic economic organizations battered the Christian Democrats, who opposed any accommodation with the state. Buffeted by the rise of anticlericalism in France and alarmed by the growth of socialism in Italy, the Vatican entered the Italian political fray on the moderate side, as desired by Catholic banking and industrialist interests.

Catholics did not formally repudiate the *Non expedit* policy but participated for the first time in the 1904 national elections in an organized manner on the side of the government and in defense of the existing order. In the 1909 elections, their participation increased, and in 1913 their leader, Count Ottorino Gentiloni, concluded a "pact" by which Catholics voted for liberal candidates in return for a pledge of support for the Church's position on Catholic education, religious instruction in public schools, and divorce. When Gentiloni claimed that a majority of the Chamber had been elected under these conditions, a scandal broke out that provoked the resignation of Radical representatives from the cabinet and Giolitti's resignation.

But this situation was only the iceberg's tip. Counting on support from northern industrialists and southern landowners, as well as electoral manipulation in the South, Giolitti stayed in power between 1903 and 1913, a long stretch interrupted only by two Sonnino cabinets in 1906 and 1909, lasting three months each, and by governments headed by his stand-ins, Alessandro Fortis and Luigi Luzzatti. Under Socialist prodding, Giolitti moved toward quasi-universal manhood suffrage, which gave the vote to illiterate males at age twenty-one if they had served in the army, and at age thirty if they had not. The reform strengthened Catholics and Socialists alike. At the same time, Italy's growing industrialization stimulated interest in colonies as sources of raw materials and markets, and a nascent but vocal Nationalist Association demanded colonies as an expression of national activism and prestige. The "Gentiloni Pact" represented Giolitti's attempt to accommodate the Catholics and draw upon their support in the first elections held under male universal suffrage while placating industrialists and Nationalists by undertaking a war against Turkey to acquire Libya.

The war signaled a defeat for Giolitti's domestic policy. Left-wing Socialists unhappy with Giolitti took over the PSI and expelled Leonida Bissolati, who was friendly to the prime minister, and his supporters. The Nationalists had advocated a heroic war and viewed Giolitti's military conduct as timid. Conservatives objected to Giolitti's leftward turn in domestic affairs, while industrialists discovered that they could not gain much from Libya and were drawn to economic penetration of the Balkans. The Gentiloni Pact alienated the Extreme Left, anticlericals, and anyone who believed that the Church should not have a privileged position in modern society. As World War I drew closer, the "Giolittian system" seemed in shambles.

The political stabilization achieved by Giolitti until 1913 has been cited as the most important ingredient in the remarkable economic development that Italy achieved in the decade before World War I. The series of technical changes cited in the following discussion have as their premise the political advances made during the Giolittian era.

According to economic historian Valerio Castronovo, Italy's industrial progress during this period "would be inconceivable without . . . the maturation of new political orientations in the country. From here [one can understand] the . . . centrality of the Giolittian age also for the nation's economic evolution to the extent that there occurred the most serious post-unitary effort to widen the base of the bourgeois liberal state by reabsorbing, within the context of continuing national integration, the historic Catholic and Socialist oppositions."

This process meant the liquidation in 1901 of "strong governments." This crucial development had important results and could not have occurred without reformist Socialist support. With the defeat of reaction, more progressive business forces bent on maximizing the economic changes taking place came to the fore. More sympathetic to healing the fractures within Italian society, these forces supported government intervention to stimulate industry, spending for public works, social legislation, and reasonable labor demands. Progressive bourgeoisie and reformist Socialists alike had their focus in the North, which brought about an unofficial but real loosening of the coalition between northern industrialists and reactionary southern landowners. The lopsided industrial development previously described continued apace as reformists aided the more progressive northern bourgeoisie and neglected or misunderstood southern problems, contributing to tensions and strains within the Socialist movement. Whether, within the Italian context, the policy was the only or the best choice remains a matter of debate. Certainly, however, it contributed significantly to the country's political democratization, to its industrialization, to increased employment for workers and better salaries, to greater unionization and the freedom to negotiate contracts, to the diffusion of education, to the emancipation of day laborers from middlemen, and to universal suffrage. Furthermore, this "legalitarian" evolution of Italy's Socialists and their cooperation with a more liberal bourgeoisie until the Giolittian system fell apart coincides with a similar development in France and Germany.

It has been calculated that the percentage of net investment of Italian national income increased from 3.5 percent during 1896 to 1900, to 6.7 percent in 1901 to 1905, and to 10.2 during 1906 to 1910. According to a conservative estimate, the average increase in industrial production, which had been 1.1 percent in the 1880s, spurted to 4.3 percent. Manufacturing doubled in fifteen years, and from a Mediterranean backwater, Italy made its entrance into the western European industrial area.

Besides the political changes, other factors help explain this development. The international economic depression of the 1870s and 1880s ended and was followed by an international boom in production and trade. More important, the depression and the introduction of new products, processes, and financial organization ended the industrial domination of Britain, giving greater space to the United States and Germany and, to a lesser extent, to countries such as Italy. New industries such as the electrical, chemical, and automobile sectors boomed, while radical reorganization of the credit industry by trusts, cartels, and banks made more credit available.

In Italy, the generation of hydroelectric power increased dramatically because the country needed a source of cheap energy. In finance, the bank scandals of 1893–1894 resulted in the reorganization of the banking industry and the creation, for all intents and purposes, of a central bank; the Bank of Italy fostered discipline and an enormous growth of credit, which was essential for industrial development in old and new sectors of the economy. As previously discussed, despite its high cost for consumers and its other imperfections, the 1887 tariff spurred significant growth in the metallurgical and other industries. The mechanical, textile, automobile, and chemical industries became more important for their number of workers, capital investment, and production. Even though agriculture remained the economy's most important element and Italian industry did not reach world-class levels until World War I, the Giolittian period set the basis for that development (see Table 12.1).

Table 12.1

Average Annual Growth Rate of Gross Domestic Product for Italy, France, Germany, and the United Kingdom, 1896–1913

Italy	2.8
France	1.9
Germany	3.2
United Kingdom	1.7

A prerequisite for this remarkable economic activity was the end of the agricultural crisis in the North after 1895. During the early twentieth century, Lombard agriculture developed at a faster pace than ever before and reached advanced European levels, producing more capital for investment. Energetic state activity in the economic sphere contributed to this development. Increased taxes and spending cuts during the late nineteenth century created budget surpluses that allowed the government to stimulate the economy through spending for public works, the navy, and the merchant marine. The budget amount devoted to public works rose from 17.2 percent during 1897 to 1902 to 21 percent from 1903 to 1907, and military expenditures increased from 20.1 percent to 22.1 percent. In 1905, the government made another crucial contribution to economic development by taking over operation of the railways, improving service, and calming serious labor agitation in the vital transportation sector.

These economic advances made government and industrialists better able to meet workers' demands, brought forward primarily by reformist Socialists. Even though Italy lagged behind the advanced industrial nations, in the northwestern "industrial triangle" bounded by Milan, Turin, and Genoa working conditions improved substantially. Unions protected workers' rights, and workers' cooperatives competed for lucrative government contracts. In 1902, a law established a Labor Office and a Superior Council of Labor. Consisting of representatives of all classes, this last institution collected statistics and proposed measures to alleviate poor working-class conditions. Parliament passed legislation providing for or extending old-age sickness and accident insurance and a measure to protect women and children from industrial hazards. Other legislation protected emigrants, aided malaria- and pellagra-stricken areas of the country, promoted land reclamation, and instituted a medal honoring labor. The Chamber also responded to agitation demanding reduction of the workday and longer weekends. By 1913, most metal workers benefited from a shortened, ten-hour workday, and some worked shorter hours.

In the great northern cities and Rome, municipal administrations took over and ran essential services such as transportation and utilities. In Milan, a famous charitable institution, the Società Umanitaria, ministered to the spiritual and physical needs of the poor, and Socialists sponsored free libraries (using the Boston Public Library as a model) and free educational programs. Progressive employers interested in the welfare of their employees supported these activities, bringing them into frequent contact with the Socialists and labor leaders with whom the owners cooperated.

This activity brought the standard of living in the North close to that of industrialized Europe. In 1905, skilled workers with good earnings received 3 lire a day, and, in exceptional circumstances, 5. Women earned from 1 lira to 1.5 daily, and children less. Compared with the South, these wages were substantial. In that region the peasant received less remuneration than either a northern industrial worker or a day laborer in the Po Valley. Between 1901 and 1914, real wages for industrial workers rose 26 percent compared to a national increase of 17 percent. In short, the struggle between the classes changed in nature during the Giolittian period because, whereas at the end of the previous century the oppressed southern peasant had been the protagonist of massive popular agitation, now "social conflict and political confrontation . . . had as their epicenter the great cities and the countryside of the North, i.e., the structures of the Italian economy and capitalism which were the most advanced or, at any rate, the least fragile."

Southerners shared little of this prosperity. The government did dramatize the South's plight and invested more in the region than it received from the area in taxes, but it continued to make political deals with large landowners and their supporters to ensure the government's majority in the Chamber of Deputies and therefore had little incentive to alter existing social and political conditions. The government hoped that the expansive potential of northern capitalism could resolve the southern problem, and it did support sporadic industrial and agricultural projects in the area, but these attempts failed to alter conditions in the South. The gap between North and South increased in the early twentieth century, representing a major failure of the Giolittian era. In the South, emigration accelerated, and support grew for the conquest of African colonies where southern peasants might satisfy their land hunger under the Italian flag.

Even though the substantial and real legislative activity, accomplishments, and developments of the Giolittian age created "the first profile of an industrial society," many areas of the country did not share in the progress. Southern illiteracy remained at 60 percent, elementary education was still deficient, and public spending stayed at late nineteenth-century levels. Despite his accomplishments, Giolitti missed a solid opportunity to knit the "two Italies" together.

Dilemmas of Italian Socialism

The previous sections illustrate the crucial importance that the Italian Socialist movement attained at the beginning of the twentieth century and retained throughout the Giolittian era. The Socialist vote in favor of the Zanardelli-Giolitti cabinet in June 1901 firmly established the "liberal springtide" in the country. As if to mock the opening of a new era, however, shortly after the vote soldiers fired into a crowd of striking agricultural workers in a town near Ferrara, killing three and wounding thirty. In addition to touching off a parliamentary duel that threatened the cordial relations between Socialist deputies and the government, the incident made the reformists vulnerable to a violent onslaught by the Socialist revolutionary left wing.

PORTRAITS

FILIPPO TURATI
Cassandra

⟅∾⟆

Filippo Turati, the most important Socialist leader of the Giolittian era, labored under a curse similar to that of Cassandra, the mythological figure who could see the future but whom nobody believed.

Turati was born in Canzo, a lake town north of Milan, on November 25, 1857. He came from a comfortable family, and his mother doted on him. Turati attended the University of Bologna and participated in the *scapigliatura*, a movement of artists, writers, and bohemians centered in Milan. He wrote poetry and lived a disordered life. He wrote "The Workers' Hymn," a poem that, put to music, became the most famous protest song of the era. Turati later remarked about his lyrics that he should have been executed for the murder of the Italian language.

Turati wrote many prescient political articles and published an important sociological work tracing the roots of crime to society. He met Anna Kuliscioff in Naples in 1885, and the two became lovers and political allies for the rest of their lives. They founded the Italian Socialist Party in 1892. The government persecuted the couple and jailed both during the 1898 disorders. To stop the repression that he considered a feature of Italian society, Turati advocated voting for a liberal government, touching off divisions between his reformists and the revolutionaries, who endorsed the taking of power by violent means. Italian revolutionaries denounced reformists as traitors to the Socialist cause for a hundred years, but then finally scrambled to describe themselves as reformists.

Turati and Kuliscioff lived in an apartment in the Galleria, overlooking Milan's Duomo. With Kuliscioff presiding over her salon from her green couch, they influenced the country's most famous intellectuals. After Turati's election to Parliament, Kuliscioff sent him daily letters full of political advice; she would rush to post her letters in a mailbox carried by a tram so he could receive them in Rome the next morning.

Turati believed Italian politics to be vulnerable to reactionary lurches and strongly denounced the Socialist culture of violence. He predicted that the Socialist emphasis on violence would cause violence to be used against them. He fought Benito Mussolini's policy of violence in 1912 and argued against Italy's entrance into World War I. In 1919, he warned the Socialist Party not to follow the Bolsheviks in calling for the violent overthrow of the government, predicting that such a policy would boomerang. His prediction proved accurate.

In 1926, Turati fled Italy for Paris, where he became the most powerful symbol of antifascism among the exiles and led an important resistance organization. He warned that fascism would spread to other countries, but European leaders ignored him.

Filippo Turati died in Paris on March 29, 1932, while Adolf Hitler marched to power. On October 11, 1948, a day resplendent with sunshine, Turati's remains were transferred from Paris to Milan's Cimitero Monumentale and interred next to Kuliscioff's.

The dispute illustrates the dilemmas faced by Italian Socialist leaders. Interclass alliances had been accepted during the 1898–1900 crisis, but whereas the revolutionaries considered them exceptions to the general rule of intransigence, Kuliscioff and Turati considered alliances a permanent feature of future Socialist policy. They argued that Italy was a special case in Marxist terms. Given the country's industrial backwardness and the bourgeoisie's failure to transform the political and social structure, the Socialist Party would have to assume, temporarily, the role of the democratic left and ensure the survival of democracy, socialism's prerequisite. Furthermore, in an intuition reminiscent of Eduard Bernstein's revisionism of the same period, Turati argued that the bourgeoisie was not a monolithic entity and that Socialists could implement a policy of flexible alliances with advanced groups to win reforms for the proletariat. Turati had made this argument in Milan in 1894 and in November 1899 had identified Radical leader Ettore Sacchi and Giovanni Giolitti as national leaders with whom the Socialists could cooperate. Following the crisis of 1898–1900, the reformists accentuated their alliance policy, while leftist Socialists insisted it be dropped.

These contrasting positions found ideological expression in July 1901. Writing in *Critica Sociale*, Turati argued that the increasing industrialization of society was the basic cause of socialism, a gradual development about which parties could do very little. Socialists had to spur the transformation of "the thinking, the habits, and the capacities of the proletarian masses" by training workers for political power through the gradual conquest of government institutions; thus the defense of basic freedoms necessary for the workers' development, in concert with liberal bourgeois groups, became the Socialists' overriding concern. Political intransigence, demanded by the revolutionaries, meant rejecting reforms and weakening democracy; seizing power would not advance socialism because it would not change society.

This position proved extremely difficult to sustain. If the Socialists had continued to win significantly higher wages, improved working conditions, and political and fiscal reforms, they might have resisted the onslaught of their revolutionary comrades. By late 1902, however, the vast strike movement had spread to the public service industries, a development Giolitti could not sanction. Moreover, in response to higher wages, landowners brought in new machinery that cost the workers jobs. A rollback in salaries occurred, and many agricultural leagues collapsed. These developments favored a new Socialist faction that challenged the reformists in their Milanese stronghold. Revolutionary syndicalism advocated an ever-escalating spiral of strikes that would culminate in a general strike mystically conceived as the "Revolution." The combination of the government's rightward drift and increased opposition within the PSI forced the Socialist deputies to withdraw their support from the Zanardelli-Giolitti government in 1903. Zanardelli's death and Giolitti's invitation to Turati to join his cabinet in the same year put the Socialists in a quandary.

Turati's acceptance would have formally split the party, increasingly dominated by revolutionaries. Rebuffed by the Left, Giolitti found support to his right, and the Socialist influence over his actions petered out. As mentioned, in 1904, a general strike exploded in response to more killings by soldiers; the strike not only alienated public opinion but shattered the revolutionary syndicalist mystique. Giolitti seized the occasion to hold new elections that accelerated the entry of Catholics into national politics. The result was a significantly more conservative Chamber of Deputies. During the next several years, the reformists slowly reconquered the party, retook control of the labor movement, and, in 1906, founded the first national labor organization, the General Confederation of Labor (Confederazione Generale del Lavoro, CGL). The defeated revolutionary syndicalists abandoned the party, but the traditional left wing remained in the PSI and planned a comeback. Its leaders took advantage of the reformists' inability to win spectacular political reforms, while Giolitti switched allies and shifted across the political spectrum with great alacrity in his successful bid to stay in office. Though Socialists contributed to the passage of significant legislation, they remained seriously underrepresented because of the lack of proportional representation; this ensured that they would not achieve a structural reorganization of Italian society and fueled revolutionary criticism of reformist action.

In addition to the schism between the right and left wings, the reformists split among themselves. Historian and southern leader Gaetano Salvemini argued that political corruption and the literacy requirement guaranteed that the government would always win an overwhelming number of seats in the South. When this was combined with the support Giolitti enjoyed in the North, Socialist hopes of winning a majority in the Chamber and passing significant reforms were futile. Salvemini's solution: extending the suffrage to illiterates. Turati objected because he wished to retain the link between literacy and the vote as a means of eradicating illiteracy and because he believed that divorcing the two would benefit the Catholics. The dispute ballooned into a full-fledged war between the two reformist leaders in which Salvemini charged that a North-South split existed also in the Socialist Party. Much to Salvemini's ire, Turati argued for northern economic investments and political guidance in leading the South out of its predicament. Salvemini condemned the reformists for allegedly sacrificing the South to Giolitti because they wished to protect the northern "workers' elites" who received government contracts. In 1911, Salvemini left the party.

Besides the Salvemini-Turati split, other cracks appeared in the reformist facade. A spat with his companion Anna Kuliscioff over immediate extension of the vote to women soon blew over, but a serious debate between Turati-Kuliscioff and their close friend Leonida Bissolati had ominous consequences. Bissolati wished to import the British Labor Party model into Italy, according to which the PSI would deemphasize Marxist ideology and concentrate on the immediate problems and demands of the labor movement: higher wages and better working conditions.

The two reformist factions also disagreed over escalating military expenses. European Socialists assumed that there could be no major wars in the future because workers made up the bulk of the huge conscript armies, and workers would turn their guns on their own officers if a "bourgeois" war broke out. In 1905, Bissolati led an Italian Socialist delegation to Trieste to coordinate antiwar action with his Austrian counterparts in case of a conflict between Italy and Austria. The Italians pledged to take concrete measures to sabotage a conflict, but the Austrians refused to make any commitments. Bissolati concluded that a war was likely and worried that an Austro-German victory would destroy democracy in Europe. As a result, he quarreled with Turati and supported the government's military and diplomatic policies.

In the negotiations for his 1911 cabinet, Giolitti tried to get Socialist support by extending the vote to illiterates, nationalizing the life insurance industry, and giving Bissolati a cabinet post. Bissolati was tempted, but Turati dissuaded him from accepting the offer. Bissolati seriously compromised the reformist image by refusing to oppose a war with Turkey for the conquest of Libya that broke out in 1911. Bissolati was convinced that Italy had to be strengthened in view of a future conflict with the Austro-Germans. This position made the reformists seem to support a colonial conflict despite Turati's principled stand against it. The revolutionaries had reorganized to seize control of the party and profited from popular opposition to the war. At the party's Congress of Reggio Emilia in July 1912, the left wing won a stunning victory.

Rage against the war brought a new kind of Socialist leader to the fore—one who oversimplified issues, glorified violence, and polarized the political struggle. The Reggio Emilia congress starred Benito Mussolini, a revolutionary from the Romagna who had distinguished himself by his violent style and whose arrest because of antiwar activities brought him national prominence. At the conclusion of a fiery antiwar speech, Mussolini successfully proposed the expulsion of Bissolati and his group for their support of the war.

Traditional revolutionaries distrusted this upstart, but Mussolini's performance thrust him into the forefront of Socialist politics and propelled him toward editorship of *Avanti!*, which he achieved in December 1912.

This change occurred just as the economic system turned down. The Libyan conflict produced credit restrictions, an interruption of Middle Eastern trade, price increases, and unemployment. Worsening economic conditions and political protest provoked strikes against which the authorities responded by firing upon the demonstrators. Mussolini organized the Socialist Party and the million members in its collateral organizations and appealed directly to the Socialist masses through the newspaper rather than depending on the party apparatus that opposed him.

In January 1913, at Rocca Gorga, a conflict between the police and demonstrators left seven dead and ignited a violent campaign by Mussolini's *Avanti!* against "proletarian massacres." Using language that foreshadowed that of the terrorists of the 1970s, Mussolini labeled the killings "state assassinations" and accused the government of "massacre politics." He advocated a general strike and claimed that the proletariat had an innate right to revolt, to employ violence, and to kill anyone who murdered workers.

The reformists were unable to dislodge Mussolini, who forced them to fight on emotional issues that negated their rational approach. Neither the reformists nor Mussolini's traditional leftist opponents could take effective action against him because Mussolini's demagogic approach appealed directly to the party rank and file and the masses, both of which considered him the premier Italian revolutionary. At the Congress of Ancona in 1914, Mussolini strengthened himself at the expense of his left-wing antagonists. After that assembly, *Avanti!* wrote that Italian socialism had become "ever more class and ever less democracy," reflecting Mussolini's disdain for democracy.

In searching for deeply felt issues capable of galvanizing the masses, Mussolini emphasized antimilitarism. Military expenses had long drained the treasury while the army aroused great hostility because it was the primary internal peacekeeper. (A modern police force did not come into existence until after World War I when Il Duce created it.) In 1914, *Avanti!* initiated a vigorous campaign against the army. In Ancona, a city in the Marche, local Socialists, Republicans, and anarchists mounted a strong protest over two soldiers who had been disciplined for political reasons. The authorities responded by prohibiting public meetings. A clash between soldiers and demonstrators left three dead and five wounded. The signal for "Red Week"—June 7–14, 1914—had been given.

Mussolini's *Avanti!* headlined "Workers of Italy, Strike!" Accustomed to strikes and violence, the nation did not at first comprehend the changed situation. In some areas, the strike followed a normal course, but in the Romagna it assumed an insurrectionary character. Socialists, Republicans, and anarchists organized action committees. All over the region, strikers attacked troops, invaded gun shops, sacked churches and government offices, and burned trains in the stations. Revolutionaries on bicycles and motorcycles linked rebel strongholds. A revolutionary roadblock netted a general on inspection who was forced to surrender his sword to the revolution. Strikers occupied sensitive points with military precision, raised barricades and roadblocks, isolated cities, and sealed off the region from the rest of the country.

Giolitti had been replaced in office by Antonio Salandra, a member of the Right. Salandra denounced Red Week as a "criminal conspiracy," even though the movement clearly lacked planning and surprised the national working-class leaders. The railway workers, crucial elements in any revolutionary design, remained aloof, and CGL leaders called a halt to the strike. The army encountered little resistance when it moved into the Romagna to reestablish control. Mussolini exalted the strike's effectiveness, but soon recognized reality: he admitted that the CGL had been correct in calling off the action because the insurrection had been doomed from the beginning. Salandra stated that the disorders had lasted as long as they had because the government wished to avoid bloodshed.

In fact, the masses had surprised their own leaders, none of whom had come to terms with the concrete possibility of a revolution. No plan of action existed because the revolutionaries had not believed that the masses would revolt. When Mussolini realized that Red Week had failed, he demanded ideological changes to work out the details of future revolutionary action. Even before Red Week, Mussolini had argued that the revolution needed the support of at least part of the army to succeed, a lesson he took seriously during his Fascist period. Red Week nevertheless revealed the masses' profoundly revolutionary mentality: "Italy needs a revolution," Mussolini wrote in his review, *Utopia*, "and will have it." What kind of revolution would it be, he asked? Incredibly he answered: "It doesn't matter. Every political revolution, Karl Marx said, is also a social revolution." From then on, for Mussolini, revolution in itself became the ultimate goal; above all, revolutionaries must prepare for revolution.

Mussolini had reduced revolution to a power struggle that the masses could win if they were united, organized, armed, and ruthless. Immediately after Red Week, he planned to strengthen the unity of groups dedicated to revolutionary action, but in August 1914, World War I erupted and completely altered the situation. Republicans and revolutionary syndicalists believed that the conflict would provoke a revolution and championed Italian intervention in the war, but the Socialist masses' deeply rooted pacifism forced Mussolini to adopt a neutralist course. Challenged by his revolutionary syndicalist friends to change his position in light of events, Mussolini recognized the war's revolutionary potential and switched to interventionism as the fastest means of achieving revolution.

In an emotionally charged gathering in Milan on November 24, 1914, the PSI expelled Mussolini, but the party and its aims had become irrelevant. Red Week had rooted in Mussolini and influential Italian intellectuals the desire for action at any cost, the triumph of activism over ideology, the glorification of violence, the compulsion to greet revolution at any moment, the constant state of tension typical of revolutionary foot soldiers, the cynical use of ideology, ideological confusion, and a propensity for demagogy. The Giolittian era's beginning had signaled a new political civility, but its twilight witnessed the metamorphosis of the debates among Socialists into fratricidal warfare.

"MINISTER OF THE UNDERWORLD" OR "ITALIAN DEMOCRACY IN THE MAKING"?

Once a neglected area of study, the historical interpretation of the Giolittian period increased in importance after the Fascist dictatorship was established in Italy (1922–1926). Seeking to bolster their regime, the Fascists argued that pre-Fascist Italy, exemplified by Giolitti, had done nothing to develop the country. This charge brought a response from philosopher-historian Benedetto Croce, who, in his 1928 *History of Italy from 1871 to 1915*, argued that the nation had made great progress during the Giolittian era.

In their attacks on Giolitti, the Fascists pointed to the many criticisms made by Giolitti's opponents during his long tenure. The most famous of these came in 1910: Gaetano Salvemini's *Il ministro della mala vita* (The Minister of the Underworld). Salvemini condemned Giolitti because his "control" of southern elections ensured him a majority in the Chamber. Salvemini's pamphlet vividly described the stuffing of ballot boxes, the cooperation between police and criminals, and the terrorizing of political opponents undertaken during Giolitti's tenure. These tactics, Salvemini wrote, resulted in the South's returning 150 of Giolitti's 250 staunch parliamentary supporters. Giolitti refrained from using these methods in the North because the larger number of voters there made such techniques more difficult to apply than in the South, where the literacy requirement excluded most people from voting and where a change of a few hundred ballots could decide an election. Salvemini's remedy for the problem was to extend universal suffrage to the South. Salvemini's "Minister of the Underworld" epithet stuck. In historical memory, Giolitti's accomplishments receded and the unsavory methods described by Salvemini were remembered.

After the Fascist victory in Italy, Salvemini went into exile. He became a professor at Harvard University, where, in 1943, a young scholar, A. William Salomone, sent him a manuscript on Giolittian Italy and asked him to comment on it. Salomone subtitled the work *Italian Democracy in the Making* because, he argued, "whatever the defects and limitations of his methods, Giolitti had represented a constructive moment in the development of pre–1914 Italy toward a genuine liberalization of the Italian national structure and conscience." The book contradicted Salvemini's well-known ideas and may have been expected to elicit an unfavorable reaction from him.

Two years later, the book appeared, and in it was a surprising "Introductory Essay" written by Salvemini. In the essay, Salvemini accepted the author's conclusions. Allowing for the imperfections of the Piedmontese statesman, Salvemini admitted that his experiences in foreign countries and with the regime that followed Giolitti had caused him to reassess his previous views. In comparing Giolitti with American and British politicians, he dismissed the charge that Giolitti had been a "dictator." He wrote:

> My knowledge of the men who came after Giolitti in Italy as well as of countries in which I have lived during the last twenty years has convinced me that if Giolitti was not better, neither was he worse than many non-Italian politicians, and he was certainly less reprehensible than the Italian politicians who followed him. For while we Italian crusaders attacked him from the Left accusing him of being—and he was— a corrupter of Italian democracy in the making, others assailed him from the Right because he was even too democratic for their taste. Our criticism thus did not help to direct the evolution of Italian public life toward less imperfect forms of democracy, but rather toward the victory of those militarist, nationalist, and reactionary groups who had found even Giolitti's democracy too perfect.

Stung by later, rosier interpretations of Giolitti inspired by this apparent recantation, Salvemini altered his vision of the Piedmontese statesman to emphasize his description of him as a "corrupter" of "Italian democracy in the making." Later historians, however, have attempted a more neutral assessment by delving into the details of Giolitti's policies, by seeking a more balanced view of his long tenure, and by examining the workings of Italian society and politics of the time. To some extent, these historians have reduced the passions that the calm and collected Giolitti stirred, and the historical debate seems to have settled somewhere between the two extremes.

PART FIVE

War and Fascism

CHAPTER THIRTEEN

The Culture
of the New Italy

ITALY AFTER UNIFICATION FELT THE INFLUENCE OF EUROPE MORE STRONGLY
than before. No longer obsessed by the fight for freedom, the Italians created an
economic infrastructure intimately linking the peninsula to the rest of Europe. In
the North, this development stimulated industrialization and created social conditions closely resembling the more advanced European countries. In the cultural
arena, the free circulation of ideas allowed the country to participate vigorously in
both the constructive and destructive intellectual currents of the age. In the South,
industry developed sporadically, but southern intellectuals had an important role
in the country's culture. The intermixture of modern and ancient, a continuation
of old traditions, and the introduction of new trends characterized Italian society
and thought during the late nineteenth and early twentieth centuries.

PRIVATE LIVES

Before the 1848 revolutions, Italian family life was provincial, formal, and static.
Children addressed their parents in the polite form (*Lei*). Parents decided the
trade or profession their children would pursue, and negotiations between families determined marriage partners. Girls typically married at sixteen, and boys,
who were in danger of being drafted, at nineteen. Young middle-class couples
spent their marriage night not on a honeymoon but in the house of the bride's
family. The houses of the middle class were usually large enough for a room
with a double bed to be reserved for the bride and groom, an area that would
later serve as their children's birthplace. On the morning following the wedding
night, the relatives congregated to congratulate the newlyweds and bring gifts
such as chocolate and snuffboxes. Poorer households usually lived together in
one large room, but sometimes there was a bedroom that parents and children
shared.

Extended families generally consisted of parents, children, grandchildren, and unmarried sisters. Women usually gave birth to eight or ten children. The father ran the household as a patriarch and wielded complete authority over the family, but his wife had a great deal of unofficial influence.

Midnineteenth-century homes lacked modern comforts. The fireplace predominated in the kitchen, a beautiful room that housed numerous pots and pans, many made of gleaming copper. No running water existed, not even pumps, and water had to be drawn from wells and hauled in a pail. Some buildings had primitive bathrooms consisting of a hole that led to a cesspool, usually one toilet every three floors. Specially designed chairs supplemented the bathrooms. The furniture was varied and lasted a lifetime. Many households owned contemporary ornate furniture, but often beautiful antique Renaissance pieces were mixed in with the middle- or lower-class household's possessions. Since laundry had to be hand-washed in public fountains, household furniture included huge closets to hold the many linens and to allow women to delay washing as long as possible.

Houses were uncomfortable. Although romantic, fireplaces produced insufficient warmth. Paper lit from an oil lamp lit fires, but after 1856 matches came into use. Since they were very expensive, the father kept them under lock and key; when he was ready to use them, the children gathered round to enjoy the spectacle. To heat their hands, women used *scaldini*, commonly called "husbands"— terra cotta or copper vases containing lighted charcoal. Charcoal also filled braziers that the family placed under tables. Before retiring, family members used special kinds of braziers, nicknamed "priests," to heat cold beds.

Women worked hard. They spent long hours in the kitchen, cooking three- and four-course meals for eighteen or twenty, not counting children. They prepared sauces, bread, preserves, and the liquors. They usually made the soap. Although middle-class families hired maids to help them, all women ironed, sewed, and folded laundry. Irons had to be heated in a fire; the invention of irons in which women could insert lighted coals was a later improvement. Hoop skirts and related paraphernalia might take a full day to iron. At night, the women gathered around the light of an oil lamp until midnight to "relax"—talking, sewing, or knitting clothes for the children or for a trousseau. Women would continue this activity during pregnancy and nursing of children, who were generally breast-fed up to age one.

Women usually went out only on Sundays, when they dressed as elegantly as possible. On rare occasions, and only when accompanied, they went for a walk or shopped. Stores, which were long, narrow warehouses, had no display windows. Middle-class women still wore hoop skirts, crinoline, ribbons, lace, and hats. Because fur coats had not yet been widely imported from northern Europe, mantles served as protection against the cold. Fashion for men dictated tight suits, long tails, light-colored pants, striped vests, starched collars, big ties, and either a felt or a top hat. Beards and sideburns were de rigueur, and around 1880 waxed mustaches became popular.

Before midcentury, middle-class males seldom led a more exciting life than females. Their usually authoritarian fathers sent them away to boarding school at age seven or eight. When male offspring attended university, to avoid spoiling them fathers would give them low allowances. The father of a young male typically arranged a marriage for his son, without consultation, and kept him economically dependent as long as possible. Males engaged in little or no physical activity, except fencing, an essential skill because the typical university student fought several duels before he graduated. If he entered politics, it was a good idea to keep practicing. Dashing Radical leader Felice Cavallotti fought over ninety duels and died in an 1898 encounter; Socialist leaders Filippo Turati Claudio Treves and Benito Mussolini also faced challenges.

The wars of the Risorgimento, 1848 to 1870, brought changes in the social situation. Fired by the fight for independence, many young men and women ran off to join the struggle, frequently spending time in exile. Their participation in the cause exposed them to new countries, conditions, and attitudes. This altered mentality, combined with improving economic conditions, especially in the 1890s, spurred many couples to move out on their own and caused extended families to break up.

Salaries were still low, but so were expenses. In 1869, a typical professional such as a university professor earned 2,000 lire a year (a lira was worth about 20 cents). A four-room apartment plus kitchen cost 200 to 300 lire a year. At that salary, maids were affordable; they earned from 3 to 4 lire a month and were mostly peasant women who preferred this form of work to heavy labor in the fields. Middle-class women still bore many children, but this cheap labor supply enabled them to go out more often. Newly installed street lighting (gas illumination at midcentury, electric lighting later) made evening excursions safer, and the increased number of coffeehouses and the introduction of lower-priced theater seats made them more pleasant. In Milan, the city government subsidized its famous La Scala opera house, making performances more affordable. Couples customarily took a stroll (*passegiata*), exploiting the nightly occasion to comment on the outfits other people wore and to gawk at the rich returning from the races. Afterward, a couple could rent a chair (4 *centesimi*, or cents) and sit in the piazza, buy a sherbet (1 cent) or ice cream from the carts (2 or 4 cents), and enjoy the free band music supplied by the municipality. In Bologna, with the change from a 10-cent piece, one could buy a newspaper for 2 cents. (*Il Resto del Carlino*—"the change from the dime"—still publishes.)

Under the circumstances, the common people mingled with the day's famous personalities more often than they do today. In Rome, philosopher Antonio Labriola gave impromptu harangues on Marxist philosophy at the Café Aragno (now transformed into a more banal fast-food place). Prime Minister Giovanni Giolitti strolled to his office past the train station, escorted only by his friends, and engaged in lively conversation. In Milan, Socialist leaders planned their moves in popular restaurants and cafés, where they gathered with workers to drink wine and discuss politics. A lowly factory worker could show up at a local party meeting and argue policy with the most famous chieftain—and did. On the midnight trams, Turati and Kuliscioff rode home, hand in hand, after those meetings and rallies. A citizen wishing to ensure that a letter reached Rome the next morning would deposit it in a mailbox carried by the same tram. In the city's "parlor," the Galleria, politicians animatedly discussed pressing issues. A few steps away, under the portico at number 23, the "Signora" of Italian socialism, Anna Kuliscioff, sat on a green couch before a magnificent window overlooking the Duomo and presided over the country's most famous salon. To attend Kuliscioff's salon, Benito Mussolini, newcomer to Milan, had to walk only a short distance from his lodgings in the shadow of the Sforza Castle, but his rejection there rankled him for the rest of his life. On his visits to Naples, Gabriele D'Annunzio frequented the same *pizzerie* as the common folk. The poet appeared in the company of the most famous journalist couple of the day, Matilde Serao and Edoardo Scarfoglio, soon the object of popular curiosity owing to their clamorous breakup. Contemporaries report that D'Annunzio was always elegant, his outfit complemented by a fashionable straw hat, canary yellow gloves, a walking stick made from precious wood, and a fresh flower in his lapel. The royal family also enjoyed the city's most famous dish. In 1889, on royal stationery, Queen Margherita wrote to pizza maker Raffaele Esposito that "the three kinds of pizza which you made for His Majesty were found to be excellent." The queen herself especially appreciated the kind made with tomatoes, mozzarella, and basil; Esposito personally created it for her, and it is still called "pizza Margherita."

During the same period, the increasing ease of travel within and outside cities sweetened life. Electric trams replaced horse-drawn ones and ran to the suburbs, where one could get away for the weekend. In 1885, there were as yet no fixed stops and trams would wait patiently for passengers who hailed them from their windows. The need for independent travel stimulated the bicycle's development from a crude machine to a comfortable mode of transportation. With rubber wheels and other innovations, the bicycle evolved into the major means of private transportation before the advent of the automobile. For long-distance travel, nothing could beat the railway: it reduced fares for special occasions and offered smoking and nonsmoking compartments, compartments for women only, and good food. The construction of a railway network and the improving economy enabled the middle class, especially mothers and children, to take summer vacations. During the same period, the cult of sports invaded Italy from England. People engaged in swimming and canoeing and mountain climbing, spurred by the example of Finance Minister Quintino Sella, who was famous for his alpine skills.

New inventions had a great impact as the new century opened. In the North, newly built houses featured central heating, flush toilets, and, sometimes, elevators. A telephone network fostered efficient communication and, along with it, police wiretapping. Economical stoves using a variety of fuels, the vacuum cleaner, the icebox, and the electric iron appeared. Frozen meat arriving from Argentina and exotic fruits such as bananas, coconuts, dates, and pineapples reached the market, stimulating dietary variety. The typewriter arrived from the United States, its appearance making it easier for women to find jobs outside the home.

By the 1890s, women saw important changes in their lives. In the North, they went out alone to shop in modern stores featuring display windows and ready-to-wear merchandise. They enjoyed their own magazines. By 1900, "hundreds" had earned university degrees in the same fields as men, including medicine. Fashion reflected this newfound mobility as skirts shortened, up to the ankle, and clothes became more practical for both sexes. Many obstacles still hindered the professional lives of women, and most remained oriented to the family, but women rebelled against chaperones, objected to arranged marriages, married much later, practiced birth control, and bore fewer children.

Despite this real progress, however, women still suffered from an inferior economic, legal, and social status. They were denied the vote, despite a radical feminist movement and women's associations of various political shades. Courts annulled marriages in which the bridegroom discovered that his bride was not a virgin. Only women could be punished for adultery—a legal provision that lasted until after World War II. A woman needed her husband's permission to open a bank account or administer property. Socialists, Radicals, and some liberals (such as Zanardelli) supported divorce, but bills that would have instituted divorce were regularly defeated by politicians, who argued that divorce would destabilize society, and by the Church, acting in concert. As late as 1913, a female law professor at the University of Rome was denied admission to the bar. During the early twentieth century, women usually became either schoolteachers or telephone operators, the main choices open to them. Working conditions in the elementary and secondary schools were so bad that Gaetano Salvemini felt compelled to lead the charge in improving the schoolteachers' lot, and the telephone operators' plight was the focus of one of Matilde Serao's most famous novels.

As might be expected, changes came more slowly in the South. In 1905 in Sardinia, for example, a man and a woman staying together at a hotel—even if married—still caused scandal. In parts of the South, men had to do the shopping because people frowned on women who left the house alone. But despite uneven progress, Italian life generally improved during the early twentieth century, even for the poor. Age-old diseases such as pellagra and malaria diminished, and wealth increased. Along with the rest of Europe, Italy lived the "Belle Époque"— the Continent's last self-confident moment.

ARTS AND SCIENCES

Although modern trends in society entered Italy during this period, traditional values continued in the arts. The peninsula's different dialects had developed a robust literature, which continued to be produced, read, and performed. The most recent examples of this rich legacy were the Neapolitan plays of Edoardo De Filippo, which achieved international prominence after World War II. The same might be said of folk or regional music, a rich source of social and religious commentary.

Since Italian opera continued to dominate Europe, it is not surprising that this art form attracted the most talented musicians. Of the four great nineteenth-century composers, Vincenzo Bellini and Gaetano Donizetti died before unification. Gioacchino Rossini, best known for his brilliant and iconoclastic *Barber of Seville* and his patriotic *William Tell*, had stopped composing. Giuseppe Verdi had fully participated in the patriotic cause by his actions and his music; besides *Nabucco*, *The Battle of Legnano* told about the victory of Italian city-states over the German Holy Roman Emperor Frederick Barbarossa in 1176, and *Rigoletto* ridiculed the aristocracy to such a degree that Austrian censors intervened. After unification, Verdi wrote his three greatest works, *Aida*, *Otello*, and *Falstaff*; *Aida* was still concerned with patriotic themes, whereas the last two, based on Shakespearean plays, helped import the German "music drama" into Italy. Verdi was appointed a life senator in 1875 and died in 1901.

Verdi's refinement of the music drama illustrates the vitality of opera composition in Italy. Arrigo Boito championed this music form through his activities and through a brilliant concrete example, *Mefistofele*. Boito quarreled with Verdi over the music drama but later collaborated with him as the librettist for Verdi's last two operas. Boito also wrote the libretto for Amilcare Ponchielli's *La Gioconda*, which remains an extremely popular work thanks to such excerpts as the "Dance of the Hours," used in Walt Disney's *Fantasia*. The dire suffering of Ponchielli's heroine seemed to signal a trend in opera; it incorporated a concern with social problems, known as realism in France and *verismo* in its Italian version. Pietro Mascagni appropriated *Cavalleria Rusticana*, a work of the most famous practitioner of this art, Giovanni Verga, and turned it into an operatic masterpiece, and Ruggiero Leoncavallo produced *I Pagliacci*, another tragic story about ordinary people. The most famous opera composer after Verdi, however, was Giacomo Puccini, who, like Verdi, was also a successful businessman. Puccini continued the "realistic" trend in such works as *La Bohème* and *Madama Butterfly*, but also ranged into the historical and the fantastic with *Tosca* and *Turandot*. Presented posthumously at La Scala in 1926, this last opera illustrates Puccini's incorporation of "modern music" into his work.

Although operatic music dominated the Italian scene, the late nineteenth and early twentieth centuries produced greater interest in symphonic music. Important societies and reviews promoted this art form, and by the 1880s the major cities supported symphonic orchestras. This activity produced important conductors such as Giuseppe Martucci and Ottorino Respighi, perhaps the country's most famous symphonic composer. In addition, Ferruccio Busoni pioneered polyphonic music and has been called the first modern composer.

Literature during this period seemed especially attuned to modern concerns. In the 1870s in Milan, a movement of Bohemian writers, poets, and artists known as the *scapigliatura* favored trends important in other countries. Perhaps because of the Church's role in opposing unification, Pius IX's condemnation of modern civilization in the *Syllabus of Errors*, and the Vatican's continued opposition to the Italian state, writers were preoccupied with antireligious themes. The country's best poet, Nobel Prize winner Giosuè Carducci, scandalized Italy with his *Inno a Satana* (Hymn to Satan), an attack on the Church at a time when it opposed unification. His reputation rests on such works as *Odi Barbare* and *Rime Nuove*. After the death of this "poetic dictator," a "Triumvirate" dominated the Italian poetic world: Antonio Fogazzaro, Gabriele D'Annunzio, and Giovanni Pascoli. The poetry of the first two is still read, but their reputations rest on their novels and plays. Pascoli's best work makes the point that the poet has a special sensibility and understands life better than the philosopher or the scientist. The nation's most famous woman poet, Ada Negri, was influenced by the Socialist atmosphere of Milan and wrote poetry calling for social justice for the proletariat.

A new movement, futurism, influenced poetry, although it had a more profound effect on painting and sculpture. Determined to bring Italian culture into the industrial age, the Futurists glorified technology, hailed speed, and designed modernistic cities. They were especially taken with fast cars and composed hymns to coal and electricity. The iconoclastic movement's founding father, poet Filippo Tommaso Marinetti, was its best-known spokesman. The Futurist manifesto, published in Paris in 1909, declared that futurism was anti-everything and that its followers believed only in violence because energy and dynamism were born of struggle, a principle that led them to favor war: "We want to glorify war," their manifesto said, "sole hygiene of the world." They demanded a "cynical, astute, and aggressive" foreign policy. They called for the rejuvenation of Italy by destroying its values and traditions, its monuments, its museums, and its libraries. Their "futurist evenings," which usually degenerated into chaos and fistfights, have remained famous.

The Futurist penchant for dangerous living, modernity, and violence made them precursors of the later Fascists. Writer Piero Gobetti believed that fascism was no more than the "social continuation" of futurism. The Futurists were the precursors of the destructive artistic and intellectual forces sweeping Europe during the early twentieth century and had a major impact on Italian cultural life through their publications and the journal *Lacerba* (1913). They had influence as far away as Russia.

At the opposite pole from the Futurists were the *crepuscolari*, best represented by Guido Gozzano. This school took its name from the Italian word for "twilight" because they believed the world to be at an end. Tired and pessimistic, these poets pictured life in somber tones. Instead of fading out, however, Italian poetry renewed itself in a remarkable burst of new life. The years between 1880 and 1901 witnessed the birth of four poets whose work during and after World War I would be hailed by critics as among the best in the world: Giuseppe Ungaretti, Umberto Saba, Eugenio Montale, and Salvatore Quasimodo.

Besides poetry, the Italian novel underwent a profound period of renewal after unification. Influenced by French realism and English positivism, novelists in the 1870s and 1880s attempted to portray life as it really was; they concentrated on small areas and described the life of ordinary people in every detail.

This *Verismo*, or the social novel, counted several distinguished practitioners. These included Luigi Capuana, a Sicilian who wrote about theory and produced a splendid example in his *Marchese di Roccaverdina*. Another Sicilian, Giovanni Verga, produced this school's best novels: *I Malavoglia* and *Mastro-Don Gesualdo* are magnificent descriptions of social conditions in Sicily. The novels of the country's first important female journalist, Matilde Serao, also provide an excellent social history of the time. She applied her journalistic talents to describing the life and foibles of the people—from gambling to the plight of early telephone operators, from political corruption to the miserable life of a nun no longer sheltered by the convent. One of her most famous books, *Il ventre di Napoli*, describes life as lived by the Neapolitan poor during the cholera epidemic of 1883. According to persistent rumors, her last, anti-Fascist, novel caused Mussolini to veto her nomination for the Nobel Prize. Another woman did win the Nobel Prize. Grazia Deledda's novels are also concerned with social conditions, particularly in her native Sardinia. Similar to these women, Emilio De Marchi has remained famous for his description of Milanese life. His masterpiece, *Demetrio Pianelli*, graphically examines the exploitation of public workers.

Antonio Fogazzaro is famous for *Piccolo mondo antico*, which takes place during the Risorgimento, and *Piccolo mondo moderno*. His most controversial novel,

MATILDE SERAO
Reality

∞

Italy's first important woman journalist, Matilde Serao was born on the Greek island of Patras of a Greek mother of noble descent, Paolina Borelly, and Francesco Serao, a lawyer and Risorgimento patriot. The family returned to Italy with the fall of the Bourbon dynasty and settled in Naples. Matilde Serao worked as a telegraph operator for four years while publishing several stories during that period. Her work experience served as the basis for a novel, *Telegrafi di Stato*, one of several works describing the condition of women.

Serao went to Rome in 1882, where the quality of her early stories allowed her to enter the hectic world of late nineteenth-century Italian journalism. She contributed to the most fashionable periodicals and met another famous journalist, Edoardo Scarfoglio. High-strung and nervous, Scarfoglio did not seem a good match for the plain-looking Serao, but the two married in 1885. Serao bore four children to Scarfoglio (one stillborn) and raised another daughter of his with another woman (who dropped the daughter off and then committed suicide). She wrote prolifically and, with her husband, founded a newspaper, the *Corriere di Roma*. This venture failed economically, but in the meantime the pair had met Matteo Schilizzi, a rich banker from Leghorn who financed a new newspaper, the *Corriere di Napoli*, which made a fortune when it published a scandalous D'Annunzio novel that other publishers would not touch—*L'Innocente*. When the venture ceased, the couple left with a large amount of money. They established *Il Mattino*, still the largest paper in the South.

The relationship with Scarfoglio, always stormy, definitively broke down in 1903. Serao left him to live with a lawyer named Giuseppe Natale. She had a fifth child with Natale, but did not marry him, even following Scarfoglio's death in 1917. In 1904, she founded another newspaper in Naples, *Il Giorno*, the newspaper of the petit bourgeoisie and small businesspeople of the city, which she edited until she died at her desk of a heart attack on July 27, 1927.

In addition to her vast journalistic production, Matilde Serao wrote about forty full-length novels, many of them translated into English. Her journalism greatly influenced her fictional works. Her most successful books faithfully describe the colorful and contradictory social conditions of Naples. The most important of these works is *Il paese di cuccagna*. Another important work, *Il ventre di Napoli*, graphically describes one of the cholera epidemics that periodically hit the city. She successfully portrayed the position of women in Italian society of the period in *Telegrafi di Stato*, *Suor Giovanna della Croce*, a novel about aged nuns, and in love novels such as *Fantasia* and *Cuore Infermo*. She wrote: "From the time I began writing, I have never wanted to nor have I known how to be other than a faithful and humble chronicler of my memory."

Her honesty and fidelity to reality cost her the Nobel Prize, which Mussolini vetoed when her last novel denounced nationalism.

Il Santo, supported the religious reform movement known as modernism; later condemned by Pope Pius X, the book was placed on the Index. Gabriele D'Annunzio, poet and playwright, found fame as a writer of sensuous and decadent novels, such as *Il Piacere* and *Il trionfo della morte*. In addition to his writings, his private and political life electrified Italy and Europe.

As the nineteenth century closed, the psychological novel made its entrance, culminating in the work of Italo Svevo. *Senilità* (1898) was so far ahead of its time that critical condemnation caused the author to quit writing. Later, encouraged by James Joyce, who taught English in Trieste, Svevo produced a second masterpiece, *The Conscience of Zeno*.

Another important genre during this period was the children's novel. The most famous novels in this tradition are Carlo Collodi's *Le avventure di Pinocchio* and Edmondo De Amicis's story about schoolchildren, *Cuore*.

In drama, D'Annunzio treated the most sensational topics, but the best dramatist was Luigi Pirandello, winner of the Nobel Prize. Married to a woman who suffered from psychological disorders, his pessimistic plays investigate the question, what is reality? His most famous plays are still performed in many languages—*Six Characters in Search of an Author*, *Henry IV*, and *Right You Are, If You Think You Are*.

Literary trends also provide a clue to the philosophical concerns of the age. In the 1880s, English positivism dominated Italian philosophical circles, greatly influencing young students who later became the leaders of Italian socialism. During the 1890s, German philosophy became more important, especially Hegelianism. Naples became a leading European center of Hegelian philosophy thanks to Benedetto Croce. A leading philosopher and historian of his time, Croce's influence was felt throughout the Western world. In Italy, he dominated Italian culture to such an extent that Italian thinkers have been revolting against him ever since.

Two areas once the province of Italian artists seemed to languish during this period. Antonio Canova, the last European-class sculptor, died in 1821. The best sculptors between unification and the 1890s were the Neapolitan Vincenzo Gemito and the Milanese Medardo Rosso, the latter known particularly for his innovative impressionist style. The country did not produce first-class sculptors such as Marino Marini and Giacomo Manzù until the 1920s.

Immediately following unification, a school called the Macchiaoli (from *macchia*, "spot," a technique that employed patches of color) dominated Italian painting. Concerned with picturing the world as it really was, critics consider these painters interesting rather than important, although the best representatives, such as Giovanni Fattori, have recently enjoyed a revival, and the entire school is being reevaluated. At the same time, the "Posillipo school" flourished in Naples, and Ferrara produced a great portraitist in Giovanni Boldini, who was noted for his painting of Verdi but achieved his greatest fame in Paris.

Futurism had its greatest impact on painting between 1900 and 1914. Affected by the accelerating industrialization of society, Futurist painters focused on speed and energy and attempted to portray their concrete "decomposition" on canvas. Some of the most important Italian painters of this school produced works that had an impact on European painting. Giacomo Balla, an older painter, inspired the Futurists and showed the way. The best Futurist painters include Carlo Carrà, Gino Severini, and Umberto Boccioni, whose devotion to action got him killed in World War I. The works of this school are amply represented in the Museum of Modern Art in New York, but the most extensive collection is in Milan's Villa Palestro.

Futurists had a major impact on Italian artists before and after World War I, although it is difficult to group them into schools. Carrà, for example, later became a prime exponent of "metaphysical" painting, along with Giorgio De Chirico. The list of avant-garde painters affected in different ways by Futurist principles and techniques includes Amedeo Modigliani, Giorgio Morandi, Ottone Rosai, Filippo De Pisis, Mario Sironi, Scipione (a pseudonym for Gino Bonichi), and Massimo Campigli.

The period before World War I witnessed the beginning of a new art form influenced by scientific developments: motion pictures. Italians pioneered this art with the French and Americans. In 1896, the first documentary appeared for which admission was charged. These early films experimented with methods that went beyond still photography, which characterized early cinematic development. Italians produced different types of films, but the most popular and profitable were historical and costume dramas. In 1905, Vittorio Calcina produced *The Conquest of Rome*, which portrayed the Risorgimento's last episode. The most famous of these historical epics, however, were Mario Caserini's *The Last Days of Pompeii* (1913), Enrico Guazzoni's *Quo Vadis?* (1912), and Giovanni Pastrone's *Cabiria* (1914). Memorable for its enormous cost of 1 million lire and for D'Annunzio's collaboration, the extravaganza *Cabiria* remained unsurpassed during the silent film era for its historical accuracy and craftsmanship. To give a sense of wide space and to move from long to short shots, Pastrone invented the dolly, which became standard equipment for modern filmmaking. His lighting opened a new era, and his hand coloring of scenes gave the effect of a color motion picture. As might be expected, the Futurists also produced a manifesto on film and made movies.

Concentrated in Rome and Turin, the film industry formed a major production company in 1906 that briefly allowed Italy to dominate the world market. Film historian Pierre Lephrohon has called the years between 1909 and 1916 Italy's "golden age" of cinema. The film industry declined in the 1920s, primarily because of American competition, but would enjoy an artistic renaissance following World War II.

Besides the arts, the activity in the sciences was also notable. The peninsula had lost the preeminent position it had held during the seventeenth century as the cradle of the scientific revolution, but it maintained an important position in science. Mathematicians made significant contributions to their field, but carrying on the tradition of Galileo and Alessandro Volta, Italian physicists excelled. Volta, who died in 1823, had concentrated on the practical applications of electromagnetism—along with classical mechanics, the pillar of pre-twentieth-century physics—and invented the "voltaic pile," forerunner of the battery. Antonio Pacinotti also investigated electromagnetism and the application of electricity to motors. Besides Pacinotti's research on continuous current, Galileo Ferraris contributed to the understanding of alternating current. In a related field, Augusto Righi's work on electromagnetic waves stimulated the research of Guglielmo Marconi, who shared a Nobel Prize in 1909 for his accomplishments in the field of "wireless telegraphy." Marconi had successfully sent the world's first wireless transmission at Sasso Marconi, near Bologna. In the 1920s, Marconi experimented with short waves, successfully sending radio signals over vast distances and linking the entire world together. In the culmination of the work on electromagnetism begun by Volta, Marconi made fundamental contributions that had great practical and theoretical significance for modern applications such as radar.

Biology as well was an active field for inquiry on the peninsula. Carlo Matteucci's research on the connection between electrical and biological phenomena proved important for the later invention of such diagnostic tools as the electrocardiogram and the electroencephalogram. At the same time, biologists conducted studies that contributed to the understanding of the agents that cause deadly diseases such as pneumonia, meningitis, syphilis, malaria, and African sleeping sickness.

POLITICAL CULTURE

In addition to the arts and physical sciences, social sciences such as sociology received wide attention. This interest had its greatest impact on rightist intellectuals, who did not enjoy a wide following. Nevertheless, these intellectuals discussed ideas that had lasting political effects in Italy and Europe.

The failure of the great expectations of a "Third Rome" seems to have been at the root of this rightist political culture. Intellectuals denounced the inability of their leaders to re-create Italian greatness. The death of Victor Emanuel II and the monarchy's declining prestige under his son Humbert I quickly inspired acid criticism of Italy's "unheroic" status and touched off, in Richard Drake's felicitous phrase, "the politics of nostalgia."

PORTRAITS

GUGLIELMO MARCONI
Wireless

∽∾∾

The inventor of one of the most revolutionary technologies in human history, the wireless (the basis for the radio), Guglielmo Marconi did not have a formal education. Born in Bologna on April 25, 1874, the son of an Italian gentleman and an Irish mother, he showed little interest in schooling but had a keen talent in physics that a private teacher, Vincenzo Rosa, carefully developed. At age twenty, Marconi became intrigued by the possibility of sending signals without wires. He began a series of experiments in the attic of the family home that brought him quickly to the invention of the wireless. At first, he succeeded in sending signals over several yards; then he invented new kinds of apparatus that dramatically increased the distance over which signals could be sent. He transmitted wireless signals across the attic, the garden, and his father's estate, between cities, over the English Channel, and, finally, across the Atlantic Ocean.

On February 12, 1896, having offered his invention to the Italian postal service and been turned down, Marconi went to England, where his cousin introduced him to the chief engineer of the British post office, William Preece. Preece gave him full support, and there followed a series of spectacular public demonstrations of Marconi's invention that caught the imagination of the British public. On December 20, 1902, Marconi sent signals from Newfoundland to Cornwall, England, and, on January 18, 1903, from Cape Cod, Massachusetts. These transmissions not only electrified the scientific community, which did not believe it could be done, but also demonstrated that the signals were not affected by the curvature of the earth. In 1909, he received the Nobel Prize in physics.

Marconi, who had established his own company in 1897 and patented his invention in 1900, conducted new experiments between 1902 and 1912. He made new breakthroughs, sent signals from ships, opened up the first commercial wireless service in 1907, and extended his business all over the world. By 1914, over 1,500 ships carried wireless equipment as further research improved broadcasting capabilities, increased safety, and enhanced communications. Marconi outfitted a famous yacht, the *Elettra*, as a floating laboratory from which he conducted numerous experiments with electromagnetic waves and microwaves; in 1922, he predicted the coming of radar.

During World War I, he served in the Italian army and navy, visited the United States as a member of an Italian mission, and was sent as a plenipotentiary delegate by his country to the Paris Peace Conference. Marconi received many distinctions and honors and was named a senator by Italy in 1914. Guglielmo Marconi, father of modern communications, died in Rome on July 20, 1937.

A poet, dramatist, novelist, great lover, and European celebrity, Gabriele D'Annunzio symbolized these restless intellectuals' desire to perform great deeds. Crashing upon the literary scene at age sixteen, abandoning the Right for the Left in the Chamber during the parliamentary crisis of 1898, and proclaiming, "I go toward life!," D'Annunzio, who was a hero of the army, navy, and air force during World War I and a Fascist precursor afterward, moved in the tradition of a European school that drew strength from the mystical, irrational, and unexplainable sources of life. Consequently, in his art he attempted no elevation of human dignity or deep analysis of moral values. Only pure power and a love of action at any cost stimulated him. "D'Annunzio declaimed upon the beauty of fire and destruction, the voluptuous attractions of power and glory, he sang of the Nietzschian superman," A. William Salomone has written. A line from D'Annunzio's 1908 play *La Nave* succinctly epitomizes his philosophy: "Arm the prow and set sail toward the world!"

Socialism could only briefly attract D'Annunzio and other writers drunk with the desire for violence. They resented the patient work advocated by the party's reformist leaders, but above all they hated Giovanni Giolitti, the prosaic leader who understood that the country could not immediately be transformed by bombast and who blocked the ascent of brilliant intellectuals to the power they craved. D'Annunzio and his friends prodded the country to act heroically to take its rightful place among the great powers not only in name but in deed. In condemning the Italian government, these intellectuals denounced the parliamentary system, the source of Giolitti's power. From Sonnino's influential 1897 article "Let's Return to the Constitution" and before, there had been a long tradition of parliamentary criticism in Italy. In the late nineteenth and early twentieth centuries, sociologists Gaetano Mosca, Vilfredo Pareto, and Robert Michels (a German Socialist influenced by Italian politics who taught at Turin and later turned to the right) modernized these beliefs. No matter what the political system, they wrote, the organized minority—the political class or "elite"—always rules over the disorganized majority. Regardless of the scientific value of their studies or their own views, extreme rightists incorporated these sociologists into their ideologies first to delegitimize the parliamentary regime and then, after World War I, to justify the wielding of power by Fascists who considered their minority status a badge of pride.

Action at any cost, delegitimizing the liberal regime as a national representative, and justifying elites—these were the elements that underpinned the Italian nationalism of the early twentieth century, a movement radically different from the one that had produced unification. Influenced by these currents, Enrico Corradini, Giuseppe Prezzolini, and Giovanni Papini established the influential review *Il Regno* (1903–1905), dedicated to fighting Giolitti, democracy, socialism, liberalism, and pacifism and to reestablishing authority. They glorified war, power, and imperialism as ends in themselves.

In 1908, Prezzolini and Papini modified their ideas in a new journal, *La Voce*. Prezzolini believed that the country's moral life could be reformed by joining culture and politics. The journal aimed to purge politics of the rhetoric that Prezzolini claimed contaminated the country's political life and hoped to end what he considered Italian provincialism. The review brought together in its pages the most influential Italian and European intellectuals.

La Voce opposed the Nationalist movement in the name of a "true" nationalism, but it had little influence beyond restricted intellectual circles. In 1910, Corradini established the Nationalist Association, an organization that reasserted the themes expressed in *Il Regno*. Nationalists and Futurists linked up to emphasize the principles of power connected to the "beauty" of war. The Futurists had declared: "We exalt aggressiveness . . . and the fist." For Nationalists, war had become the chief instrument of national policy and, as it had for the Futurists, necessary for the health of nations, a kind of national Darwinism and a means of maintaining eternal youth. Furthermore, Corradini had evolved a view of Marxism that both criticized and co-opted it in a manner that produced profound effects.

Corradini believed in the class struggle, but among classes of nations, not social classes. Rich nations dominated "proletarian" ones not only in an economic but also in a cultural sense. Rich countries possessed colonies, essential for markets and raw materials. They exported capital, whereas the proletarian nations, bereft of economic resources and colonies, had to export labor to survive. This labor was exploited in third countries by exported capital. Thus, British capital making a profit for its owners in New York exploited Italian labor building the subways. A revolution was necessary and would come in the form of a revolutionary war of the proletarian nations against the capitalist ones. Italy, the proletarian nation par excellence, would lead the other proletarian countries on this modern-day crusade for justice.

To prepare for this war, Italy needed colonies and had to reach a new level of unity. Corradini and the Nationalists demanded that Giolitti seize Libya, which Nationalist propagandists pictured as a grand oasis filled with raw materials, a perfect alternative to America as a goal for emigration; they recalled Rome's heritage there and exploited the fear that other countries might soon take it over. Although they were not solely responsible for pushing Giolitti into war in 1911, their campaign created the pressure that forced the government to act. To reach internal unity, Corradini criticized Marxism as the great dividing force: it split Italian workers and employers. Socialists emphasized the commonality of interests of Italian and foreign workers against Italian and foreign employers, but Corradini argued that workers in the rich nations made only a show of opposing their capitalists. They could have stopped imperialism, but allowed it to continue because they benefited from it; French workers opposed social security for Italian emigrant workers in France, and Belgian workers attacked the Italian workers forced to toil in their country. Marxism for Corradini was a kind of capitalist plot. Italian workers needed to cooperate with their employers to prepare for the coming revolutionary war. Out of this unity would emerge fresh pride, a new culture based on ancient Rome, and a new efficiency; the trains would run on time, he said, and a new architecture based on Rome's rounded arch would flourish.

The Libyan War was too limited to qualify as the overarching conflict dreamed of by the Nationalists. When World War I erupted, they demanded Italian intervention in the conflict despite the opposition of Parliament. Nationalists viewed the struggle at once as a revolutionary war that would redeem Italian honor and get rid of Giolitti. Afterwards, their ideology dovetailed nicely with Fascist practice and style. Unlike the Nationalists, Mussolini hailed from the revolutionary left, but as discussed in chapter 12, after Red Week he too exalted violence for its own sake. By severing the revolution from its Marxist goal of redeeming the proletariat, he made his antidemocratic ideals, his taste for action, his authoritarian tendencies, and his "will to power" ends in themselves. By the time Mussolini came to power, the Nationalists had already worked these elements into an ideology that he could and did accept. In this manner, Nationalist antidemocratic ideals won out in postwar Italy.

CHAPTER FOURTEEN

World War I
and the Red Biennium

A FTER 1870, THE EUROPEAN DIPLOMATIC SCENE CHANGED DRAMATICALLY. Italian and German unification ended the balance created by the Vienna settlement of 1815 and destabilized the Continent. If united Germany threatened the supremacy of Britain and France, united Italy served as an example to the minorities in Austria fighting for new rights. For Serbia, an independent Slav state wishing to attract Slavs living under the Hapsburg monarchy and create a large country, Piedmont was the ideal model.

The Austrians had never accepted their Italian defeat and resolved never to let it happen again: if their minorities followed the Italian example, the empire would disappear.

DIPLOMACY

Bismarck, the statesman who made Germany, set the tone for European diplomacy before World War I. He aimed at preventing a conjunction of France and Russia, which could trap Germany between them if war came, through a series of alliances. However, cracks appeared in Bismarck's diplomatic edifice because of Austro-Russian competition in the Balkans and because Russia supported Serbia. With Germany closely allied to Austria, Bismarck attempted various expedients to keep Russia satisfied, but even before Emperor William II forced him to retire in 1890, the Bismarckian system had begun to unravel. The diplomatic recovery of France, the struggle in the Balkans, and the German drive for world influence marked European diplomacy during the early twentieth century.

The circumstances under which the Italians joined the Triple Alliance in 1882 have previously been discussed. The Italians conceived of the alliance as defensive and made clear from the beginning their desire to maintain good relations with Britain. The British controlled the Mediterranean, and the long Italian coastline made the peninsula vulnerable, but cultural considerations came into play as well. Relations with France improved when tensions over Tunisia ended and after Crispi's resignation in 1896. The Italians settled their problems with the French over Tunis (1896) and ended the "tariff war" with a commercial agreement (1898).

In their effort to escape the diplomatic isolation imposed by Bismarck, the French cultivated their southern neighbor through their skilled ambassador to Italy, Camille Barrère. In 1902, Italy and France agreed to remain neutral in case either was attacked by other powers, even if they should be provoked into declaring war (the Barrère-Prinetti Accord). France recognized Italy's freedom of action in Libya, and Italy did the same for France in Morocco.

This understanding may have conflicted with Italy's obligations under the Triple Alliance, just as a similar agreement between Germany and Russia (the Reinsurance Treaty, 1887–1890) may have done. In response to German concerns, Foreign Minister Giulio Prinetti offered an early renewal of the Triple Alliance; during the talks, he sought but failed to receive official guarantees on the defensive nature of the alliance, support for Italian interests in Libya and the Balkans, and commercial concessions. Luigi Albertini, who knew Prinetti, "several times asked himself whether the man would have concluded the agreement of 30 June 1902 with France, had Berlin and Vienna allowed him to boast of having his proposals, more formal than substantial as they were, accepted in the renewal of the alliance."

Important as personalities were, this diplomatic activity occurred within the context of a power realignment. Russia and France had already come to an agreement, and France and Britain had settled their colonial problems. England had emerged from its "splendid isolation," and the Triple Entente (France, Britain, and Russia) was being forged to counter the German threat. This altered power situation, in addition to cultural considerations, hostility to the Central Powers (Germany and Austria-Hungary) on the part of the Italian democratic left, and persistently poor relations with Austria, sapped Italian loyalty toward the Triplice. The Italian minority in the Irredenta, the "unredeemed lands" (Trent, the Trentino, and Trieste), remained subject to physical attack and abuse, and Franz Conrad von Hotzendorf, chief of the Austrian General Staff, missed no occasion, such as a crippling earthquake in Sicily in 1909, to advocate a preventive war on Italy.

As participants in the diplomatic initiatives of the period, the Italians followed the expansionistic policies common to European powers of this era, even if proportioned to their status as the weakest of the great powers. As in the rest of Europe, Italy's industrial development spurred this activity, especially in the Balkans, where Italy came into conflict with Austria-Hungary. In 1903, during one of the Balkan crises, Prinetti sought guarantees that Italian interests would be protected, because Article VII of the alliance, negotiated in 1887, promised Italy compensation for Austrian changes in the area. Instead of responding to the concerns of its ally, however, Austria reacted by concluding a secret agreement with the Russians directed against Italy, as the Russians revealed to the Italians in 1909.

Austrian disregard for Article VII caused continuous problems for the Triple Alliance and produced strains with Germany that strengthened Italy's good relations with France and Britain. During the Moroccan crisis of 1905–1906, for example, Germany asked for diplomatic support at an international conference but was irritated when the Italian representative, Emilio Visconti Venosta, failed to provide it because Morocco did not come within the purview of the Triple Alliance and because blundering German policy alienated the powers. Shortly afterward, a peevish Kaiser William II told the Austrians that "in case Italy should show hostility to Austria-Hungary," he would "seize with real enthusiasm" the opportunity to join in a military attack on the kingdom. Under the circumstances, the Italians were not about to go beyond their formal commitments under the alliance.

During the next year, the Italians and Austrians tried to patch up their precarious relationship, but in late 1908 the situation deteriorated. Reacting to events in Turkey that threatened their military occupation of Bosnia-Herzegovina, the Austrians formally annexed the area. This action produced a European crisis. The Italians asked for compensation under Article VII. The Austrians refused but promised concessions to the empire's Italian minority; Italy never received compensation or concessions. In 1909, an earthquake killed more than 100,000 people in Messina, Sicily. Austrian Chief-of-Staff Conrad advocated an attack on the Italians while they were absorbed in massive relief operations, causing more bad blood between the allies. In 1909, the Italians reached a secret agreement with Russia at Racconigi in which the Russians pledged support for Italian interests in the Balkans and Libya. This accord rounded out an increasingly friendly Italian relationship with the entente powers. Later in 1909, the Italians and Austrians patched up relations; Austrian refusal to compensate Italy under Article VII, however, encouraged the Italians to comply with the letter of the Triple Alliance but not its spirit.

Why did Italy not simply abandon the Triple Alliance? The primary reason seems to have been fear of a war between the two old enemies if they did not remain linked in an alliance. Even pro-German Foreign Minister Antonino di San Giuliano commented in 1914 that Italy would probably leave the alliance in a few years. Several years earlier, another foreign minister, Tommaso Tittoni, when asked by a Russian diplomat why Italy did not denounce the Triple Alliance, replied: "We shall come out someday, but it will be to go to war."

During the Libyan War, 1911–1912, Italy's allies provided no help, and Austria-Hungary created obstacles to the Italian war effort. Germany and Austria had long recognized Italy's freedom of action in Libya, but Germany was wooing Turkey and hoped that Italy would become bogged down and embroiled with France over colonial issues. The Italians occupied the Dodecanese Islands, off the Turkish coast, but opposition by the great powers to decisive military action against their homeland allowed the Turks to continue the conflict longer than otherwise would have been possible. Taking advantage of the conflict, Russian diplomats put together a coalition of small Balkan states that prepared to attack Turkey, causing the Turks to end the war.

The Balkan Wars that followed the Libyan conflict in 1912 and 1913 resulted in an aggrandizement of Serbia at Turkey's expense. In July 1913, the Austrians considered what to do if the settlement after the Second Balkan War transformed Serbia into an irresistible pole of attraction for Slavs living in the empire, as Piedmont had become a model for Italians. Austrian officials concluded that they must absolutely eliminate the threat. The Germans cooled the Austrians down momentarily, but the Austrian attitude alarmed the Italians, who believed that an Austrian attack against Serbia would set off a European conflagration. Prime Minister Giolitti warned his allies that Italy would never follow them into an offensive war against Serbia, because the Triple Alliance would not apply, and that the consequences of a wider war would fall squarely on the Austrians. Foreign Minister San Giuliano told his allies: "It would be impossible in this eventuality to want to invoke the Triple Alliance which is purely defensive in character and has been so interpreted by all the statesmen of the three allied countries ever since it has existed." The foreign minister assured his allies that Italy would loyally fulfill its duty should they be attacked, but "no Italian Government could recognize the *casus foederis* in an Austrian war of aggression on Serbia."

San Giuliano's reasoning found no interlocutor among Italy's allies, who took advantage of his clarity to cut the Italians out of the alliance's decision-making mechanism, another violation of the treaty's letter and spirit. When, at the end of the Second Balkan War in 1913, Serbia occupied Albania, giving it access to the sea and increasing its prestige enormously, the Austrians sent an ultimatum demanding Serbian evacuation of Albania. Aware of San Giuliano's position, the Austrians informed Italy only after sending the ultimatum, an action they would repeat in June 1914. Determined to crush the Serbian threat, the Austrians expected Italy to join them without having been informed or having consented to Austrian actions. In 1914, fearing that Italy would either veto action or demand compensation, Germany and Austria-Hungary kept the Italians in the dark about their moves following the assassination of Archduke Francis Ferdinand, which touched off World War I. As a result, when the war broke out, Italy stated that the terms of the Triple Alliance obligating it to join Germany and Austria-Hungary had not been fulfilled because its allies had taken the offensive. Italy declared its neutrality and, under Article VII, requested compensation for Austrian gains in the Balkans.

Given their stormy diplomatic relationship, Austro-German violation of the Triple Alliance's terms, the popular hostility to Austria, and the absurdity of rendering aid to the Central Powers—which, if successful, would only strengthen their hereditary enemy—the Italians followed the only rational course: neutrality. While the Allies sought to woo the Italians into the conflict on their side, San Giuliano opened negotiations to compensate Italy for Austrian changes in the Balkans. The empire's Italian-speaking areas became the chief focus of the talks, which the Germans encouraged the Austrians to undertake. Unfortunately, San Giuliano died in October 1914, depriving Italian diplomacy of a sophisticated practitioner. Negotiations continued under Prime Minister Antonio Salandra and Foreign Minister Sidney Sonnino according to the guidelines set down by San Giuliano. The manner in which they conducted these negotiations, however, amounted to a public relations disaster.

NEUTRALISTS AND INTERVENTIONISTS

What was the domestic context of these foreign policy developments? In 1914, Italy had overcome the worst of an economic recession that started two years earlier. Politically, however, the country was still in political turmoil because of changes brought about by the institution of universal male suffrage. The Extreme Left emerged strengthened but more split than usual. To win a majority, Giolitti had had to cooperate with the Catholics by stipulating the so-called Gentiloni Pact. When news of the "pact" emerged, Giolitti resigned, indicating he would allow the rightist liberals the opportunity to rule. On March 21, 1914, Antonio Salandra formed a new government with the support of the Giolittian majority. Undoubtedly, Giolitti planned to return at the appropriate moment, as he had in the past, but four months later World War I erupted.

The Italian people favored keeping the country out of the conflict, but well-organized political minorities and industrial groups that would profit from intervention advocated entrance into the war. How did the battle shape up?

Although the Socialists and their organizations had grown significantly in numbers, the war found the Socialist movement seriously split between the reformists and Mussolini's revolutionary wing. The Socialists greeted the declaration of neutrality with relief. However, while official party policy did not budge from "absolute neutrality," many Socialists came to believe that this position would isolate the party from the country's mainstream in the midst of great events. Moreover, after reports of German atrocities in Belgium and France, "absolute neutrality" came under attack as effectively favoring the Central Powers—a devastating charge because Italian leftists sympathized with the Triple Entente.

Moreover, influential party members had converted to interventionism. The party's inflexible neutralism isolated it from the "democratic interventionists"—Republicans, Radicals, and independent Socialists—"Wilsonian" precursors who, like most Socialists, believed that the Central Powers had to be defeated to save democracy and produce a peaceful world free of militarism and authoritarianism. One of these democratic interventionists, Gaetano Salvemini, wrote: "It is necessary that *this* war kill *all* war." By defining the war as a bourgeois conflict that did not concern them, however, the Socialists cut themselves off from a vital issue dominating Italian and world concern in 1914 and in the future.

Even antiwar leftist Socialists moved toward interventionism, and they gained momentum during the resulting debate. After some hesitation, Benito Mussolini publicly advocated a change in party policy. Mussolini agreed with revolutionary syndicalist leader Alceste De Ambris that the war would lead to revolution. Nationalists and Futurists first advocated intervention on the German side against the French, but then, realizing that this policy had little chance of succeeding, demanded war against Austria because it would make Italy supreme in the Adriatic—a line allowing them to link up with Salandra. It is impossible to overestimate the activity and influence of these groups, even though their membership was small; they included all the live intellectual forces that had produced the country's avant-garde reviews as well as its most visible artists, such as Gabriele D'Annunzio. Mussolini's switch to interventionism caused the Socialists to expel him. Under the slogan "Neither support nor sabotage," the PSI signaled that it would not support the war effort even if the country entered the conflict. Party discipline prevented many Socialists from supporting interventionism, but at the cost of leaving them open to the charge that they had betrayed their country.

The country's liberal establishment initially agreed to keep the country neutral and to avoid instability by retaining the present government. This broad liberal "party" consisted of two groups: left liberals who were Giolitti followers, and right liberals who were Sonnino-Salandra supporters. Giolitti believed that a war would be long and costly and that Italy could attain the Italian-speaking parts of Austria under Article VII of the Triple Alliance in return for its neutrality. He had the votes to become prime minister, but as a known neutralist, he felt that he would have less credibility if he threatened war in the event that Austria did not give up the territories.

By early 1915, Salandra and Sonnino had become convinced that Italy could not remain neutral and be a player in the postwar European world. Preoccupied primarily with the Adriatic and the Balkans, they reasoned that if Italy did not intervene and Austria won, it would gain supremacy in those areas. If Austria was defeated without Italian participation, an enlarged Serbia backed by a pan-Slavist Russia would dominate and perhaps even annex the Italian-speaking areas of Austria. In March 1915, with Austria refusing to give up its Italian-speaking territories, Foreign Minister Sonnino negotiated the Pact of London with the Triple Entente pledging Italian intervention within one month. Within Italy, the rightist liberal group of Salandra and Sonnino was backed by Luigi Albertini's *Corriere della Sera*, the country's most influential newspaper, and the liberal press. Behind this press were industrialists who stood to gain from war. Finally, as Giolitti's neutralist stance hardened, the liberals of the Right, along with the revolutionaries and Nationalists who had chafed under Giolitti, seized the opportunity to get rid of him by defeating his line on the war.

A strong neutralist bloc that might have blunted these forces and helped keep the country out of the war never materialized. Different sympathies toward the warring sides marked Catholics. Some favored Austria as a Catholic bulwark against the Orthodox Slavs, others supported the entente as the hope of European democracy, and some saw the conflict as God's punishment. In practice, Italian Catholics agreed with Pope Benedict XV's opposition to the conflict and favored staying out of it. Politically, however, Catholics remained subordinate to the liberals and did not take the initiative. Catholics stood ready to follow their government's decision, whatever it might be. Unlike the Socialists, when Italy intervened the Catholics supported the war effort.

Before Italy could enter the war, the Pact of London had to be ratified by Parliament. This was no easy task. Parliament had not been informed, and Giolitti commanded a majority. Including the Socialists, war opponents numbered about 400 out of 508 and could have refused to accept the agreement. However, "spontaneous" demonstrations took place against Giolitti, the Socialists, and a "decrepit" Parliament. In May 1915, handfuls of demonstrators rushed through the piazzas shouting for war and cheering the oratory of Italy's poet-warrior, D'Annunzio. The interventionist press magnified the size of the demonstrations, and the police suppressed Socialist organization of counterdemonstrations. When Giolitti learned of the pact's existence, he believed that honor committed the country to adhere to it, ratified or not, and he exited the scene. His majority then went over to Salandra.

On May 20, 1915, the Chamber convened to ratify war against Austria. Because the official reason for war was mistreatment of the Italian minority, Parliament declared war only on Austria-Hungary and not Germany. The manner in which the Chamber had been maneuvered by Salandra, Sonnino, and the king into declaring war against the sentiments of the majority of the population debilitated democracy, confirmed the disdain of Parliament's critics, and produced terrible fruits.

WORLD WAR I

The conflict with Turkey two years before had left Italy militarily unprepared. Nonetheless, the country mounted a massive war offensive against Austria in mountain terrain that made the Italian front the most difficult of the war. In addition, the lack of coordination between the supreme commander and the cabinet hampered the war effort. Intervention also came at the crucial time when the war turned in favor of the Central Powers. Italy failed to deliver Austria a swift knockout punch, and the Italians bogged down in the trenches, as had their French and British allies on the western front. In 1916, the Italians survived a concentrated offensive of crack troops designed by Conrad to drive them out of the war—the Strafexpedition. Numerous battles exacted a tremendous toll from Austrians and Italians alike, but until 1917, neither side made much headway. Nevertheless, by summer 1917, the Austro-Hungarian army appeared worn down and unable to withstand another Italian offensive, planned for the next spring. To prevent defeat, the Austrians turned to their German allies and proposed a great offensive before the winter to knock Italy out of the conflict. The Germans consented, transferring experienced troops and generals to the Italian front.

Despite evidence that reached him, Italian commander Luigi Cadorna refused to believe that a major offensive was in the works. He failed to take adequate defensive measures and kept his forces in an offensive posture. The well-thought-out Austro-German plan had surprise on its side when the battle known as Caporetto began on October 24, 1917. Rapid movement and local military superiority allowed the Austro-Germans to wipe out important units, while bad communications contributed to the false impression of a rout. Believing the war over, many soldiers threw down their weapons and streamed home. This information, combined with the well-known Socialist opposition to the war, caused Cadorna and interventionists to blame the defeat on Socialist propaganda. Even though the Socialists came out in favor of defending the country during this battle, the supposed Socialist "betrayal" of the war effort later caused many Italians to sympathize with the Fascists. Moreover, a distorted impression of the Italian war effort created by Cadorna himself led the Allies to denigrate Italy's contribution to the victory over the Central Powers. This view contributed to a peace settlement whose provisions regarding Italy were resented by the Italians, as well as to the rise of fascism.

In the domestic arena, the fight between neutralists and interventionists continued throughout the war. Italian Socialists participated prominently in the international Socialist conferences of Zimmerwald (1915) and Kienthal (1916) to bring peace. The Catholics declared that they would do their duty, but the pope's attempts to end the war caused many to question their support for the conflict. These opinions, which the fairly mild censorship allowed to circulate freely, sapped enthusiasm among large strata of the population and, consequently, the soldiers, and drew interventionist fulminations.

Economic and social developments as a result of the war also had important consequences. Aided by new production techniques, war-related heavy industry expanded tremendously, and Italy acquired the capacity to make a major contribution to the Allied war effort. Production of electric power doubled, and steel production increased 50 percent. The development of a modern engineering industry had implications for the country's industrial advance after the war, and the sector's percentage share of manufacturing rose from 21.6 to 31.8 percent. This expansion stimulated the growth of giant firms such as Ilva, Fiat, and, especially, Ansaldo. These companies tightened their relationship with big banks and created a major problem for the government because they were in a position to dominate large sectors of the economy. On the other hand, the government felt obliged to support these giant industrial complexes because they were necessary for the war effort. Since they profited from the war, the owners of these firms also presented their activities and attempts to expand into the banking sector as patriotic endeavors. Anyone who put obstacles in their path was branded as unpatriotic. Besides these problems, the distortion of the Italian economy caused major disruption after the conflict ended and war matériel was no longer needed.

These and other war-related developments provoked dissatisfaction and disorder among the population. Industrial workers toiled sixteen hours a day, but to keep production high the government favored the employers. Consequently, workers had to put up with strict discipline, compulsory arbitration, and close surveillance. Real wages of industrial workers dropped with inflation by 27 percent from 1913 to 1917, while the average profits of the industrial companies increased from 4.26 percent to 7.7 percent. Wartime inflation also cut the income of the middle class, but war profiteers flourished. Despite tax increases, the government was reluctant to crack down on them. The ostentation with which these profiteers exhibited their newfound wealth caused resentment among all sectors of the population. The worst-off sector was the peasantry. Exemptions from military service were given more freely for industrial workers than for peasants. To keep production high, women took the place of men in the fields, but real agricultural wages suffered greater decreases than industrial salaries. The obvious shift of wealth from the countryside to the city further dampened enthusiasm for the war.

These resentments, fanned by shortages, overcrowding, and the Russian Revolution of March 1917, brought disorders that began in the spring of 1917. Disturbances frequently led by women affected parts of northern Italy, but the explosion hit Turin in August. Because of the increase in their bargaining power during the war, workers in the engineering sector there had achieved unofficial recognition of elected factory committees by the state. Some of these institutions had come to be dominated by intransigent Socialists, who, spurred by events in Russia, intensified their antiwar campaign. Antiwar demonstrations erupted during a visit by a Russian delegation in August 13. On August 22, temporary bread shortages touched off protests that quickly developed into massive demonstrations against the war. The rioters attacked stores and police stations, burned churches, and threw up barricades. The army appeared the next day, bringing in tanks and machine guns. Socialist leaders called for calm and refused demands for a nationwide strike. By August 28, Turin returned to normal.

These wartime events had important effects on the government. Salandra's cabinet had fallen on June 10, 1916, because of discord with the high command over how the war was being conducted, interventionist dissatisfaction with his performance, and neutralist resentment over his outmaneuvering of Giolitti to pull Italy into the conflict. Seventy-eight-year-old Paolo Boselli replaced him. Boselli was chosen because of his supposed ability to bring concord among the country's leaders. His cabinet represented a wide coalition, including liberals of the right and left, democratic interventionists, Radicals, a Republican, a Catholic, and a Giolittian representative. The Boselli government was criticized by the interventionists for its lack of energy, its inefficiency, and its reluctance to crack down on political activity of the kind that had led to the Turin disorders. Demonstrations demanded a new and efficient war cabinet and better coordination between the home and fighting fronts. Better control of antiwar activity was instituted, but on October 25, 1917, the Boselli cabinet was brought down.

Vittorio Emanuele Orlando replaced Boselli. Orlando had been criticized by the interventionists for being too lenient toward "defeatists" as interior minister, but he defended himself by arguing that a country fighting for liberty had to be sensitive to civil rights. To Parliament's credit, Orlando was confirmed because of his pledge to combine a more efficient war effort with concern for civil rights.

With the Orlando government, Italy reorganized itself and pursued the war with greater vigor. Orlando created a war council consisting of military and naval leaders and civilian ministers. This council directed the war effort with greater efficiency, created harmony between government and high command, and established effective political supervision of the army. The high command was reconstituted to rectify the weaknesses from which it had previously suffered. Special units known as the Arditi were created to infuse a greater war spirit into the fighting forces. Recruited from young volunteers, usually middle-class and university graduates, these pampered units enjoyed special privileges and distinctive uniforms— black shirts and distinctive insignia. They received special training and were employed for the most dangerous and visible military operations. Unlike the rest of the infantry, who were primarily interested in staying alive, the Arditi loved fighting for its own sake and lived for war. After the war, these shock troops could not forget conflict and supplied the Fascists with their most warlike squads.

The Italian military effort in the war's most difficult sector eventually proved that the Caporetto defeat had military, not political, roots and that it was a tem-

MAP 14.1   ITALY AFTER WORLD WAR I

porary setback. Caporetto resembled the defeats suffered by all sides during the war. The battle's real significance is that the Austro-German objective of driving Italy out of the conflict failed, the enemy captured no major city, and the Italian army stopped it on the Piave. Under its new commander, Armando Diaz, the army reorganized and within a year unleashed a great offensive of its own that broke the Austro-Hungarian army at Vittorio Veneto. The only Allied forces to end the war on enemy soil, the Italians signed an armistice on November 3, 1918. A week later, an armistice on the western front ended all hostilities, but not the consequences of the war.

AFTERMATH: THE "RED BIENNIUM"

According to official statistics, 571,000 Italian soldiers died in combat during World War I, to which must be added 57,000 prisoners of war who died and

60,000 missing in action who never returned; the disabled totaled almost 452,000. This was a lower proportion of the population than was the case with the other major European combatants, but about the same considering that Italy entered the war ten months after it began.

The Italians believed that their effort went unappreciated and uncompensated by their allies. The conflict's enormous cost had led the government to raise expectations: it claimed Fiume, an Italian-speaking city in the Austrian Empire not included in the Pact of London. The postwar settlement gave Italy Trent, the Trentino, Trieste, and, because of strategic considerations, the Austrian-populated South Tyrol (Alto Adige) up to the Brenner Pass, but a dispute broke out regarding the Adriatic coast of what became Yugoslavia. Italians had settled the area centuries before, but because they lived in the cities, the Austrians had encouraged Slavic immigration into the hinterland. After having given in to British and French demands to modify his "Fourteen Points" in their favor, President Woodrow Wilson resisted Italian requests for Fiume and other territory that would have put Slavic minorities in Italy. In fact, there was a basic contradiction in the Italian position at the Paris Peace Conference. Foreign Minister Sonnino claimed fulfillment of the Pact of London on strategic grounds, even though it put German-speaking minorities in Italy, but Prime Minister Vittorio Emanuele Orlando claimed Fiume on the basis of self-determination. The Italians believed that Wilson was pro-Yugoslavia and biased against them. A dispute broke out on this issue, and the Italian representatives withdrew from the Paris Peace Conference.

This break heightened the resentment toward the war snaking through Italy. The country also failed to reap other rewards promised by the entente in 1915. The root of this situation was the inability of Italian diplomacy to exploit the traditional balance of power that the war had eliminated by prostrating Germany and making France supreme on the Continent. The French and the British divided the German and Turkish colonial holdings among themselves using a method that galled the Italians: League of Nations "mandates," given to advanced countries to instruct the natives in democracy. Italian statesmen scoffed at this new system as an effort to refurbish the old colonialism in response to a war whose magnitude had made it necessary to justify imperialism in idealistic terms. The lack of mandates given to Italy impugned the country's democratic credentials and denigrated its role in fighting "to make the world safe for democracy."

Domestically, the resentment transformed the postwar Paris settlement into the "mutilated victory." Powerless to alter the international situation, the forces that had supported intervention blamed the Socialists for having scuttled the country's efforts to reap the rewards of its sacrifices. Lumped in with the Socialists were the democratic interventionists, who advocated a just rather than a harsh peace as necessary to avoid a future conflict, who repudiated colonialism and nationalism, and who wished to give up claims to Adriatic areas inhabited by Slavs. Interventionists responded that the neutralists had "sabotaged" the war effort and now wished to renounce the rightful fruits of the country's sacrifices. This extremist argument produced a debate on the war similar to the "stab in the back" debate in Germany and would justify the later Fascist campaign against the Left.

The war's tremendous economic, social, and political dislocation, however, initially caused a reaction that favored former neutralist forces rather than the Right. As in other countries, the enormous expense of fighting the war fueled inflation, which reached spectacular proportions by 1919. Total note circulation, under 3.6 billion lire in 1914, hit almost 18.6 billion (values are in lire of the period). The lira collapsed, its exchange rate with the dollar dropping to 4.97 cents in 1920 from 19.30 cents in 1913. The cost of living soared from a base of 100 in 1913 to 268.1 in 1919, and the wholesale price index reached 366. Real wages plunged. The budget went wildly out of kilter. In 1919–1920, the state took in 15,207 million lire and spent 23,093 million, and the situation worsened the next year.

As in the other nations engaged in World War I, the conflict had brought a shift in Italy away from peacetime industry to a concentration on heavy industry and weapons production. At war's end, the trend abruptly ended; major industries went into crisis, and massive unemployment followed. As in the other belligerent countries, the hasty demobilization of the army worsened the unemployment problem.

These conditions created chaos in the country. On the land, man-days lost to strikes increased from 3,270 in the last year of the war to more than 3.4 million in 1919, and to 14.1 million in 1920. Promised land if they continued fighting, returning peasant soldiers invaded large estates when the government failed to fulfill its pledge. The left-liberal cabinets proposed compromises but did not halt the movement—thus alienating the landowners and making them susceptible to being attracted to the paramilitary groups that promised to defend their property.

In the cities, a similar situation existed. Membership in the Socialist labor union, the largest, exploded from 249,000 in 1918 to 1,159,000 in 1919, and to 2,320,000 in 1920. Man-days lost to strikes increased dramatically from 906,000 in 1918 to 14.2 million in 1919. The militant metalworkers won the eight-hour day in February 1919. To the consternation of industrialists, "factory councils" of workers demanded a dominant voice in management. Strikes turned into disorders and attacks on citizens and former soldiers. In major cities, workers established "Soviets" on the Russian model and sacked shops. Future Communist Party founder Antonio Gramsci compared Italy to Kerensky's Russia—the last regime before the Communist Revolution.

Influenced by the Communist Revolution, the Socialist Party seemed poised to overthrow the government. Turati argued that a revolution in Italy alone was impossible, but at its 1919 Bologna Congress the party denounced the reformists, now reduced to a small minority, repudiated its 1892 program, and adopted one advocating violence on the Soviet model. Regardless of whether or not revolutionary conditions existed in postwar Italy, the new "maximalist" majority led by Giacinto Menotti Serrati was revolutionary in rhetoric only. Maximalists denounced existing institutions but ran for Parliament and did not attempt to organize a revolution. At the same time, they frightened the middle class and drove it to seek salvation on the right.

The effect of this confused situation was tragic. In the parliamentary elections of 1919, the Socialists tripled their vote to become the largest party in the Chamber with 156 seats. The Catholics had formed their own independent Italian Popular Party (Partito Popolare Italiano, PPI), led by the left-leaning sociologist-priest Don Luigi Sturzo, and won 100 seats. These forces combined would have commanded a majority, but the Catholics would not cooperate with the PSI, and the radicalized Socialists collaborated with no one. The liberals were split, and proportional representation fractionalized the Chamber. These conditions made it extremely difficult to put together governments, which, during this period, depended on Catholic support and produced continual cabinet reshufflings. For about a year, economist and historian Francesco Saverio Nitti headed governments brought to their knees by the labor agitation and civil disorders. On June 9, 1920, Nitti definitively resigned on the issue of reducing the expensive state subsidy for bread.

To many deputies, it appeared that only the country's senior statesman, Giovanni Giolitti, could resolve the political crisis. On October 12, 1919, Giolitti had already proposed a leftist program but had modified it to gain support on the right in order to gain a stable majority and restore Parliament's ability to govern. In the economic sphere, he proposed legislation to increase taxes on the rich—including a war profits tax and the registration of stocks and bonds in owners' names so they could be taxed. He hoped to reduce government subsidies, end inflation, and balance the budget. The strenuous opposition of the bourgeoisie and the Catholic party—alienated especially by the proposal to tax stocks and bonds—combined with Socialist lack of support, caused his project to fail. Domestic and foreign problems intertwined as well to weaken Giolitti. In late June 1920, the government was forced to abandon Albania when army units, under orders to leave for that country to consolidate Italian control there, mutinied. This development increased the hostility to Giolitti on the right.

Giolitti's tenure and the "Red Years" culminated in August and September 1920 with the factory occupations. This crisis had its origins in the demand for salary increases by workers in the metallurgical industry. This sector had been hard hit by the postwar decline in demand for its products, and its spokesmen

DON LUIGI STURZO
The Catholic Party

་ལ

The assumption that Catholic political parties must necessarily be conservative is not confirmed by history. The first national Catholic party founded in Italy, ancestor of the Christian Democratic Party that dominated Italian politics for forty-five years after World War II, was founded by a progressive priest.

Born in Caltagirone (Catania), Sicily, on November 26, 1871, Luigi Sturzo came from a devout Catholic family of the rural aristocracy and entered the seminary at an early age. He hoped to become a professor of philosophy and went to Rome to complete his university education; in the Holy City, he discovered a vocation for politics. He is said to have decided to enter politics on Holy Saturday in 1895 when he went to bless some houses for Easter in the poorest sections of Rome and was struck by the poverty he saw. The Christian Social thought of another priest, Don Romolo Murri, whom Sturzo met during this period, greatly influenced him. He began writing articles in journals discussing the Church's mission to help the poor.

In 1902, Sturzo entered politics at the head of a small Catholic group in his native Caltagirone. By 1905, he had become mayor, a position he held for fifteen years. After the Vatican formally revoked its *Non expedit* policy in 1918, Sturzo founded a national Catholic party on January 18, 1919. Sturzo did not wish the party to be dependent on Vatican dic-tates, nor to have the word "Catholic" in its title, so it took the name Partito Popolare Italiano (Italian Popular Party, PPI). It advocated widespread landownership, women's suffrage, social legislation, disarmament, proportional representation, and an elected Senate.

The Vatican considered Sturzo too liberal and clashed with him over his approach to Benito Mussolini, whom Sturzo opposed and with whom the Vatican wished to reach an accommodation. After 1922, the Vatican turned against the PPI and forced Sturzo into exile. Some historians argue that the Vatican wished to protect Sturzo; others believe that it wished to protect itself. Sturzo left for London, where he was active in anti-Fascist circles. In 1940, he went to New York, where he spent World War II continuing his anti-Fascist campaign.

Sturzo returned to Italy in September 1946. In the meantime, the Christian Democratic Party, descendant of Sturzo's PPI, had been founded, with Alcide De Gasperi as its leader. Sturzo disapproved of the new Catholic organization; at age seventy-five, he had become more conservative and believed that the Christian Democrats inclined toward socialism. In 1952, President Luigi Einaudi named him a senator for life.

Don Luigi Sturzo died on August 8, 1959, and was buried in Rome. In July 1962, his body was moved to a mausoleum in his native city.

refused all raises. The adamant stance of the industrialists appears to have been politically motivated and formed part of an industrial counteroffensive begun several months before. By provoking a strike, the metal industry hoped to defeat the metalworkers' union, FIOM (Federazione Italiana Operai Metallurgici), one of the country's most aggressive, and take the steam out of the workers' movement. The owners aimed to weaken Giolitti by forcing his government to intervene if violence occurred. At the same time, they hoped to bargain with the government, exchanging some salary increases for an increase in tariff protection for their hard-hit industry. Finally, the owners hoped to obtain significant concessions from Giolitti on his fiscal policy of increased taxation for the rich.

As the workers organized a slowdown, their leaders and government officials worked to avert a strike, but the industrialists remained inflexible on wage increases. FIOM had already announced that in the event of lockouts the workers would remain in the factories. On August 30, the Alfa Romeo automobile factory in Milan staged a lockout. Since Alfa Romeo belonged to Ilva, among the most intransigent industrial groups, the industrialists probably wished to provoke government intervention on the emotional ground of property rights violations. A FIOM order to occupy 300 factories followed. The workers formed Red Guards to protect against police intervention and attempted to continue production in an orderly manner, but lack of technicians, supplies, capital, and markets made continued production unfeasible. As with the 1904 general strike, Giolitti did not use force but limited the police to patrolling outside the factories. Giolitti stated that he had warned the industrialists not to provoke the occupations, that all the country's police would have been necessary to occupy the factories before the workers did so, and that then there would have been no one to safeguard public order against the hundreds of thousands of enraged workers left outside. Giolitti also noted the union leaders' declaration that the factory occupations had economic and not political significance. Giolitti believed that once the workers realized that they could not run the factories, the affair would be settled without bloodshed, as in fact happened in September.

The factory occupations had incalculable and ironic results. Probably conditions during the Red Biennium did not amount to a revolutionary situation, but if they had, after September 1920 the danger of revolution no longer existed. The maximalist leadership of the Socialist Party had continually proclaimed its desire to organize a revolution in Italy, but its failure to take concrete action, while abandoning the struggle within the existing political system at a time when it could have pushed that system in a progressive direction, resulted in paralysis. The maximalists squandered the Socialist Party's reformist heritage, built upon patient work over two decades, and replaced it with nothing. Their rhetoric and lack of action also alienated the communistic left wing, which moved toward secession.

Their support of continuous strikes and disorder without any positive result estranged the lower-middle classes, alienated former Socialist sympathizers, depressed the workers, and provoked a strong bourgeois reaction.

Even though the factory occupations involved 600,000 workers and produced better working conditions, disillusion over the lack of political results killed worker militancy. In 1921, man-days lost because of strikes dropped by more than half in industry and by more than 90 percent on the land. The Fascist counterattack had begun by then, but this decline is only in part attributable to Fascist violence.

Furthermore, the change of mood caused by the occupations may be traced in the disappointing results for the Socialists in the local elections of November 1920 and by the definitive turn of industrialists and landowners to the paramilitary Fascist movement to protect their interests just when the danger of a Socialist-Communist revolution diminished. Socialists won a majority in 2,022 communes (out of 8,346) and in 26 provincial councils (out of 69), but lost clamorous battles in big cities such as Turin, Genoa, Rome, Florence, Naples, and Palermo to "national" and "patriotic blocs" formed by liberals, democrats, Nationalists, and Fascists. The Socialists won big against the national bloc in Bologna, which, for that reason, became the flash point for Fascist violence against the Left. In Milan, the Socialists squeaked to a narrow victory that boded ill for the future because Catholics supported the national bloc without a formal alliance. On its own, the PPI won a majority in 1,613 communes and 10 councils; varied coalitions of liberals and democrats controlled 4,665 communes and 33 provincial councils.

So the reaction began in late 1920. The maximalists had wasted a unique opportunity to steer the country in a progressive direction and had helped foster conditions that destroyed Italian democracy.

CHAPTER FIFTEEN

The Rise of Fascism

I N DESCRIBING THE EVENTS OF 1921–1922 IN ITALY, THE *DAILY MAIL'S* special correspondent and Fascist apologist Sir Percival Phillips wrote: "The Fascisti went about their grim work with a scornful calm. . . . They meted out punishment with the inexorable demeanour of an executioner."

During 1919 and 1920, the Left's influence in Italy contrasted starkly with the conservative wave in Britain and France. Alarmed by what seemed the likelihood of domination by the Left, the Italian middle classes and political Right struck back with a ferocity unknown in western Europe up to that time.

EARLY FASCISM

Who were the Fascists? Fascism had its start with leftist Socialist leader Benito Mussolini. The son of a poor schoolteacher and a Socialist blacksmith, Mussolini was born on July 29, 1883, in the village of Predappio in the Romagna region. He exhibited violent tendencies in his youth, and in an attempt to calm down her unruly son, his mother sent him to a Catholic boarding school. The harsh discipline there made things worse, and he got into trouble for fighting and stabbing a fellow student. Mussolini had declared himself a Socialist while still at school. Thanks to his Socialist contacts, he was able to find a position teaching elementary school after graduation, but could not hold on to his job because of a clamorous love affair. In 1902, he expatriated to Switzerland. He tried working at construction, but the labor was too hard. When he ran out of money, he linked up with Italian Socialists and began writing for Socialist newspapers, including the revolutionary syndicalist organ *Avanguardia Socialista*. He got into trouble with the Swiss authorities because he advocated strikes and violence. The Swiss expelled him in 1903, but the Italian police had no reason to hold him, and he slipped back into Switzerland. There he continued his political activities, fell in love, claimed to engage in intellectual pursuits, and, he said, attended the lectures of Italian sociologist Vilfredo Pareto. Mussolini was due to report for the draft in

1904, but changed the date on his passport to show that it expired in 1905. In January 1905, perhaps suffering from homesickness, Mussolini returned to Italy, taking advantage of an amnesty, and began serving his term in the army. After 1906, his army time up, he spent several years teaching, engaging in political agitation, and writing for an Italian newspaper in Trent, then part of the Austrian Empire.

By 1910, he was back in Italy organizing the local Socialists of Forlì and editing their newspaper, *Lotta di classe* (Class Struggle). He advocated violent revolution and denounced parliamentarianism, as he had in the past. He condemned war and joined his revolutionary comrades in attempting to dislodge the Socialist Party's reformist leadership. The outbreak of the Libyan War in 1911 and his arrest for antiwar activities brought him a prison term and national attention. At the Congress of Reggio Emilia in 1912, he successfully presented a motion demanding the expulsion of reformist leaders who had not denounced the conflict. Four months later, he became editor of the Socialist daily newspaper *Avanti!*

When World War I broke out, Mussolini went along with the Socialist interpretation of the conflict as a "bourgeois" war, but, influenced by his revolutionary syndicalist friends, he came to believe that it had revolutionary potential; at any rate, he argued, the Socialists were becoming isolated from the country's vital cultural currents by their intransigent position in favor of absolute neutrality. He attempted to alter Socialist Party policy from his newspaper pulpit but failed. As a result, Mussolini lost his position as editor and was expelled from the PSI for advocating Italian intervention. To implement his ideas, Mussolini accepted financial support from industrialists, who stood to make money from the war, to found a newspaper, *Il Popolo d'Italia*. His former colleagues accused him of betrayal, a charge that historians still debate. A consummate newspaperman, Mussolini kept his publication alive after the war with industrialist help.

The newspaper established Mussolini as a leading interventionist; it solidified his reputation among groups that resented Socialist Party opposition to the conflict and considered the PSI's late, lukewarm support as "defeatist." These associations shared a nationalistic, anti-Socialist, antiparliamentarian, and authoritarian outlook—and a propensity for violence. The groups included the Nationalist Association, already mentioned, and new organizations such as the "futurist fasci [bands]," the first to incorporate a military arm composed of war veterans from special combat units—the Arditi, or storm troops, devoted to violence. Under the leadership of Mussolini and poet Filippo Marinetti, these bands set a dangerous precedent by rioting to prevent Leonida Bissolati from delivering a foreign policy speech in Milan on January 11, 1919. At this time, Allied and Yugoslav opposition to Italian demands for Dalmatian territory infuriated these small violent groups. Since they had fought in the war, they believed that they had earned the right to determine Italy's future, and they denounced anyone advocating the "renunciation" of Italian claims after the country's victory in World War I.

Linked to these groups by his newfound nationalism, Mussolini, saying he was still a Socialist, attempted to found a labor party. This effort fizzled, but he insisted on creating a movement that was both "National" and "Socialist." Responding to his call in *Il Popolo d'Italia*, on March 23, 1919, about 300 journalists, war veterans, former revolutionary interventionists, and some Republicans and dissident Socialists accepted his invitation to meet in Milan's Piazza San Sepolcro. There, the "Fascists of the first hour" organized themselves in the *fasci di combattimento* (combat groups).

These *fasci* (a member of which was a *fascista*) fit the pattern of the nationalist, violent groups previously described, except that the fasci incorporated a leftist program to appeal to the masses and claimed that they were not elitist. Mussolini's rhetoric was nationalist and anti-Socialist, and his methods violent, but the Fascist program published in June 1919 demonstrated Mussolini's leftist heritage. Its demands included: universal suffrage; lowering of the voting age to eighteen; the right of women to vote and to hold office; abolition of the conservative Senate; election of a National Assembly to determine Italy's future constitutional makeup; an eight-hour workday; a minimum wage; worker participation in industrial management; lowering of the retirement age from sixty-five to fifty-five; nationalization of all arms factories; a heavy graduated income tax, "which will take the form of a true partial expropriation of wealth"; the confiscation of all property belonging to religious congregations; and the confiscation of 85 percent of war profits.

Even though it aimed at gathering votes, this platform cannot be dismissed as demagogy. Mussolini later realized that he could never come to power if he pressed these demands, and he dropped them. In 1919, this program represented his views, but even after that the "leftist" Italian Fascist strain remained prominent. Fascist hierarchs such as Italo Balbo referred to Italy as "the Great Proletariat," and at least claimed to act on behalf of the masses; others urged Mussolini to unleash the "second wave" of the "Fascist revolution" to destroy the bourgeoisie after the necessary compromises to achieve power, while others supported worker demands.

In the 1919 elections, it became clear to Mussolini that he could not compete with the Socialists on a leftist program. No Fascist won election to the Chamber of Deputies, and at the end of the year all the fasci together counted only 870 members. Mussolini had to change or become politically irrelevant.

Furthermore, Mussolini faced more prominent rivals on the right, the most important of whom was Gabriele D'Annunzio, poet and war hero. After the Allies had denied Fiume to Italy, D'Annunzio led an expedition of volunteers to take the city in September 1919. From Fiume, D'Annunzio invented much of the symbolism and spirit later used by fascism, conspired against the Italian government, and, also enjoying mass appeal, attempted to absorb the nascent Fascist movement. Mussolini

PORTRAITS

ITALO BALBO
Murdered by Mussolini?

～∞∞～

Benito Mussolini always made certain that none of his collaborators would ever be in a position to rival him. He failed with only one person. The fearless and handsome air marshal Italo Balbo died under mysterious circumstances that gave rise to persistent, yet unresolved, rumors that the Duce had him murdered.

Italo Balbo was born on June 6, 1896, in Quartesana (Ferrara) of a modest family of schoolteachers. Balbo enjoyed arguing in the cafés of Ferrara and Milan with other intellectuals, including Benito Mussolini. Balbo fought in World War I with the Alpini (elite mountain troops) and was promoted to captain because of his courage under fire. His service record gives a hint of the qualities—courage, determination, independence—that made him a hero to the Italian people and an irritant to the Duce.

In 1921, with fascism clearly on the ascendant, Balbo became political secretary of the Ferrara Fascist organization, supporting the large landowners who wished to destroy the Socialist agricultural labor unions. Balbo used his military experience to organize the squads to extend Fascist paramilitary activities to the rest of the Po Valley, to conduct dry runs for the March on Rome, and to prepare the groundwork for a Fascist militia. He also helped organize the March on Rome in October 1922.

Balbo's career flowered when Mussolini named him undersecretary and then, from 1929 to 1933, minister of aviation. He became an international celebrity on the order of Charles Lindbergh, Amelia Earhart, and other aviation pioneers by personally leading a mass flight of twenty-four seaplanes from Italy to Chicago and back again. The city of Chicago named a main thoroughfare after him. Balbo tried and failed to convince Mussolini to construct a powerful air arm. Besides the rival claims of the army, the dashing Balbo had become so popular that the Duce perceived him as a threat and "exiled" him by appointing him governor of Libya.

Arriving in Tripoli in January 1934, Balbo worked to make the colony into a viable area of Italian colonization. In the meantime, he disagreed with Mussolini's increasingly close association with Hitler. When informed of the German alliance by the foreign minister, he stormed out of the meeting, slammed the door, and exclaimed: "You will all wind up shining the shoes of the Germans!" He was the only Fascist hierarch who courageously objected to Mussolini against the German alliance and Italy's entrance into World War II, but he accepted appointment as commander of Italian forces in North Africa.

In the skies of Tobruk on June 28, 1940, Balbo's plane prepared to land after a reconnaissance flight when Italian guns brought it down. Balbo's wife and critics of the Duce rejected the official explanation of a "friendly fire" mistake; they charged that Mussolini had given the order to shoot down the plane. In 1997, the Italian press published an interview with a gunner who claimed that he had shot down Balbo's plane because he identified it as an enemy target. This assertion seemed unconvincing to those who continued to believe that Mussolini had Balbo murdered. Whatever the truth, Balbo's death eliminated a dangerous rival to the Duce.

avoided this peril until Giolitti dislodged D'Annunzio by military means in December 1920. Mussolini ably deserted D'Annunzio while maintaining his own reputation. More important, however, the incident prompted an informal accord with Mussolini, whose neutrality Giolitti considered necessary to avoid domestic repercussions of his attack on D'Annunzio. The Fascists were allowed to participate with the liberals in the national blocs for the 1920 local elections, gaining important advantages. Furthermore, the simultaneous failure of the factory occupations convinced Mussolini of the impossibility of a Socialist revolution. He aimed to absorb D'Annunzio's followers and intensified his violent attacks on the leftists in conjunction with rightist forces.

AGRARIAN FASCISM

Politicians in postwar Italy knew that the country faced a severe political, social, and economic crisis, but believed it could be overcome. In the struggle for normality, Giolitti achieved some important victories, such as defusing D'Annunzio and settling the factory occupations. But in confronting for the first time a radically militant new movement blending right and left that was bent on achieving power and headed by a brilliant, unprincipled tactician-opportunist, liberal statesmen committed the error of conducting politics as usual. In the past, Giolitti had cooperated with politically unruly forces to teach them responsibility by giving them a taste of power; he tried the same technique with Mussolini, but this aided fascism's explosive growth in 1920–1921.

The economic crisis following World War I reached an acute phase in those years, when the failed factory occupations had taken the steam out of the labor movement. Industrial giants such as Ilva and Perrone-Ansaldo and big banks either crashed or slumped dangerously. Faced by falling investments, skyrocketing business failures, and growing unemployment, Giolitti mollified the business community by delaying implementation of his fiscal policy; combined with the decline in power of the unions, the economic crisis favored rampant reaction, especially on the land.

One of the most dramatic scenes in Bernardo Bertolucci's film *1900* occurs when a Fascist passes around the hat for landowner contributions to finance violence against the peasants. Indeed, the reaction began in the Emilia (around Bologna), a rich agricultural area in which the Socialists had founded the modern peasant movement in the 1890s. In 1919–1920, the Socialist-led leagues achieved control of labor and local political institutions. Their domination allowed the leagues to set wages and impose lower prices. This policy angered the large landowners; they found willing allies among small landowners and the petite bourgeoisie, who had supported intervention and been alienated by Socialist antiwar ideology, violence, and intimidation favoring the poorest peasants.

In the fall of 1920, these nationalist, anti-Socialist, and antiworker sentiments fueled the spread of fascism on the land. The agrarian bourgeoisie financed the reaction and supported it politically. In contrast with the movement's slower urban development, the number of rural fasci mushroomed, flanked by armed "action squads" composed of Arditi, former military officers, young people, students, former legionnaire followers of D'Annunzio, and mercenaries who joined from the ranks of the unemployed and the shiftless. The squads unleashed a campaign of violence against Socialists, Communists, and anarchists, destroying property belonging to the leagues, leftist parties, and working-class institutions—Chambers of Labor, cooperatives, meeting halls, newspapers. They beat and killed Socialists and their sympathizers, and they forced opponents to drink large quantities of castor oil. (Federico Fellini's film *Amarcord* includes a scene that illustrates the debilitating physical and psychological effects of this novel tactic.) Mussolini and his men argued that their opponents had opposed entrance into the war and then stood ready to "renounce" the gains made by the soldiers' sacrifices. They developed the idea that those who had fought in World War I—a "trenchocracy"—deserved to rule the country.

With many unemployed workers returning to the countryside because of the economic crisis, and dispirited by the fate of the factory occupations, divided, lacking central direction, and not organized to respond to violence, the agrarian leagues could not hold on to their economic gains and began to succumb to the Fascist offensive. Local authorities—prefects, police, magistracy, carabinieri, and army—sympathized with the anti-Socialist forces and either turned a blind eye to the violence, supplied arms and transportation for Fascist "punitive expeditions," repressed the unsystematic efforts of the Left to react, or arrested the victims.

One incident illustrates Fascist tactics, the level of agitation, and the attitude of local authorities. To protest the escalating violence, on November 21, 1920, the Bologna Socialists called for a great demonstration on the occasion of the swearing in of the newly elected Socialist mayor and city government. The Fascists vowed to take action, and when the day came, several hundred of them opened fire when the mayor spoke; instead of stopping the Fascists, the police joined in the shooting at city hall. From inside the building, a Socialist responded by hurling hand grenades, increasing the panic. Shots struck a minority member of the city council—a nationalist and war hero. The press blamed the "Bolsheviks" for his death and for the incident. The national government dissolved the city administration, and Fascist squads attacked their opponents in the city and outside. Fascist violence spread like wildfire from Bologna to other provinces, increasing in intensity in areas with strong peasant movements, Socialist or Catholic. Fascists conducted "punitive expeditions" with ever-greater boldness, terrorizing towns, destroying property belonging to leftist organizations, invading homes to beat and kill their enemies, and implanting new fasci to keep control of the conquered areas. Hundreds of dead and wounded were left in the squads' wake.

Although these raids were primarily conducted on the local level and financed by the local bourgeoisie in cooperation with local authorities, the national government indirectly supported the Fascist hordes. Giolitti condemned the violence and told authorities to be evenhanded in dealing with it, but took little practical action against the Fascist movement. According to Arturo Labriola, a member of the governments of this period, with the Socialist Party still powerful but uncooperative in Parliament, Giolitti hoped to exploit fascism to weaken the Socialists, after which he would have presumably offered them a deal. Tragically, he misunderstood the nature of the Fascists, who, as Alexander De Grand has written, "did not gain support because they promised subversion, but because they promised revenge against the Reds and restored social discipline."

In accordance with his plan and with the argument that the country's political mood had changed since 1919, Giolitti dissolved the Chamber of Deputies in April 1921 and called new elections. In preparation for the vote, which he hoped would diminish PSI and PPI strength, he fostered the creation of national blocs consisting of liberals, democrats, and Fascists. Between March and May 1921, the fasci had grown from 317 to 1,001, and their adherents from 80,500 to 187,100. They had become a force to be reckoned with.

THE COMMUNIST SPLIT

The bourgeois counteroffensive had important effects within the Socialist movement. As violence escalated, the reformist position that the PSI had to cooperate with political forces willing to preserve Italian democracy and support a national government that promised to enforce the law against Fascist atrocities gained more support. Giolitti ultimately aimed at Socialist collaboration; given the intransigence of the majority, he expected a PSI split on the right, after which he could reach an agreement with a new reformist party. The reformists, however, aimed at maintaining the party's contractual power intact by altering the PSI's policy and bringing the entire organization into a coalition. Such a task would be difficult. Taking note of the weakened Socialist position, the maximalist majority modified its view on the imminence of revolution and recognized the necessity for unity, but still shunned collaboration with non-Socialist forces.

At the same time, the PSI's left wing (Communist) wanted the reformists expelled. In July and August 1920, the Second Congress of the Third International (also called the Communist International, or Comintern) established a centralized structure. Parties wishing to join the International had to accept the so-called

Twenty-One Conditions subjecting the national organizations to the control of an executive committee. These demands included the expulsion of "social democrats" such as Turati, a change of party name to "Communist," and a new party directorate to have a two-thirds majority of people who were Communists before formulation of the Twenty-One Conditions.

Maximalist leader Giacinto Menotti Serrati objected to the mechanical acceptance of these demands on the ground that each country had different traditions and conditions. He believed that Italy needed unity in case of revolution or to fight reaction. He also objected to the name change because it would disorient the masses, who were familiar with the PSI's glorious tradition. Serrati's objections were based on his recognition that a PSI majority adamantly opposed the expulsions and the name change.

The disillusion caused by the factory occupations and the reaction's effects convinced maximalist leaders that a split would be fatal. Between September and November 1920, a series of meetings established that Serrati's viewpoint had majority support. There were two Communist factions, one led by Antonio Gramsci, who headed Turin's Ordine Nuovo group, which was more flexible, and the other headed by Neapolitan engineer Amedeo Bordiga, who advocated a disciplined Leninist revolutionary party on the Soviet model and unconditional acceptance of the Twenty-One Conditions. In a meeting of the Communist current on November 28–29, Bordiga won out.

The setting had been prepared for a split that would exclude the Communists and leave the squabbling reformist and maximalist wings in the same organization—the worst possible solution. This occurred at the Congress of Livorno on January 15, 1921. The Communist motion mandating rigid implementation of the Twenty-One Conditions went down to defeat against a maximalist proposal allowing them to be applied with "autonomy." The Communists walked out and founded the Communist Party of Italy (PCdI, later PCI, Italian Communist Party).

Although it may be argued that the split was a long time coming, resulted in an ideologically pure organization, and created a party that had a crucial role in Italian history, the immediate effects were disastrous. The schism divided the Italian working-class movement at the reaction's height, further damaging its capacity to resist fascism. The PCI attracted fewer adherents than its founders anticipated and was less compact than appeared; forced to compete with the larger PSI for the same political space, Communists targeted Socialists, not Fascists, as the primary enemies.

Furthermore, neither the Communist nor the Socialist Party could contest the Fascist drive toward power. The schism did not clarify the ideological situation in the PSI, which meant that the reformists failed to alter intransigent party policy in favor of one supporting a government pledged to defend democracy, a fight that made for continuing paralysis and a fresh split in 1922. Nor was the new Communist Party any more effective. Under Bordiga's leadership, it remained extremist, and Gramsci's view that revolution was the only possible answer to Fascist reaction delayed an appropriate analysis of fascism and consequently "of the means to combat it efficiently."

From Giolitti's Fall to the Fascist Coup d'État

The general elections of May 1921, designed by Giolitti to bolster his cabinet, doomed it instead. Of the two parties whose representation Giolitti had hoped to reduce, the Socialists declined only slightly and the Catholics picked up eight seats. At the same time, the Communists won fifteen seats and the Fascists thirty-five. Despite their limited representation, the Fascists could count on aid from Nationalists and right-liberal groups. Giolitti had hoped the elections would provide him with a stable majority based on Center and Center-Right liberals, but his rule remained dependent on the lukewarm support of the PPI and heterogeneous factions in the Chamber. As a result of this unstable situation, he resigned on June 27, 1921.

Ivanoe Bonomi replaced him. Bonomi, a moderate Socialist expelled from the PSI in 1912 with Bissolati, had links with the Right and the non-Socialist Left thanks to his past as a democratic interventionist. He hoped to end the country's turmoil through a "Pact of Pacification" negotiated between Fascists and Socialists. Mussolini, afraid the growing reputation of fascism as a violent movement would isolate it and block its acceptance as a legitimate mass political movement, favored the pact because it demonstrated Fascist goodwill. As difficult negotiations proceeded, in July the police and population in Sarzana fired on a Fascist column bent on freeing jailed comrades. This incident showed that, sufficiently provoked, the police would attack Fascists and that workers and peasants could unite against fascism. Mussolini pressed his people to reopen talks, and the pact was signed on August 2, 1921.

The pacification pact brought to the surface divisions between Mussolini and agrarian fascism—the political and military strains. Mussolini hoped to gain political advantage by inserting fascism into parliamentary maneuvers, by distinguishing it from the extreme conservative right, and even by considering agreements with leftists and the labor movement. Reflecting their alliance with large landholders, agrarian Fascists wanted to wipe out peasant leagues and organizations, not only Socialist, Communist, and anarchist but Catholic and Republican as well.

Agrarian Fascists used violence less subtly than Mussolini and admired D'Annunzio too much, but they represented the movement's major force. As a result, a regional congress of Fascists from Emilia-Romagna rejected the pact and advocated calling a national congress. Because Fascist leaders Italo Balbo, Roberto Farinacci, and Dino Grandi were present at the gathering, Mussolini responded to the challenge by resigning as a member of the Fascist Executive Commission.

But none of the leaders wished to weaken fascism by splitting it, so the leadership buried its differences. Mussolini emphasized transforming the movement into a party, more easily subject to control, and the Fascist National Council rejected Mussolini's resignation. Meanwhile, the pact had proved inapplicable, rendering the difference of opinion over it moot. Over the next few months, Mussolini concluded that it was inopportune to continue challenging agrarian fascism, gave it free rein, and formally denounced the dead pacification pact.

In return, the third Fascist Congress (November 7–11, 1921) formally established the National Fascist Party (Partito Nazionale Fascista, PNF). This congress revealed the major changes that had occurred since fascism's birth in 1919. According to statistics unveiled at the meeting, the party consisted of 2,200 fasci composed of 320,000 members. Unlike early fascism, this membership hailed primarily from the landowning and middle classes; farmworkers in the party were probably forced to join, but the organization counted numerous tradesmen, civil servants, and professionals. Reflecting this shift in membership, the congress abandoned the 1919 platform and adopted a "new program" emphasizing laissez-faire and nationalist principles instead of the "socialistic" ones of 1919. The 1921 program demanded the end of taxes on inheritances and bondholders, the abolition of public service strikes, a large standing army, freedom for the Catholic Church to perform its spiritual duties, and, paralleling Parliament, National Technical Councils enjoying legislative powers.

While Fascist leaders demonstrated flexibility in submerging their differences, their enemies persisted in misinterpreting and undervaluing fascism. The Socialists erred in signing the pact because they misjudged the government's commitment to crack down on fascism should its leaders violate its terms. The agreement provided an excuse for the authorities to dismantle the Arditi del Popolo, a leftist military organization created to defend against the squads. The reformists, strong supporters of the pact, drew the logical consequences of its failure by seriously posing the question of Socialist collaboration in a cabinet committed to defend democracy against the Fascist onslaught, but the maximalists remained inflexible. Encouraged by the divisions among Fascists, they interpreted fascism as an extreme bourgeois reaction that would simplify the class struggle and lead to the dictatorship of the proletariat. The PSI Directorate saw collaboration with governments, not fascism, as the major threat to socialism and declared "incompatible the presence within the party of those who affirm the collaborationist principle." Serrati opposed expelling the reformists, but his refusal to consider governmental collaboration, the agreement of Socialist representatives at the Moscow Congress of the Communist International (June 22–July 12, 1921) to press for expulsion against Serrati's wishes, the consequent creation of a new "third internationalist" faction within the PSI bent on ejecting the reformists, and the maximalist victory at the Eighteenth PSI National Congress, October 10–15, 1921, all set the stage for a new split in 1922.

The Catholic PPI, another potentially powerful Fascist opponent, also made a series of errors during this crucial period. Just as the Socialists suffered from a left-right division, so did this organization. Represented by Don Luigi Sturzo, a sociologist, and Guido Miglioli, a northern peasant organizer, the Catholic left staunchly opposed fascism but found itself weakened by Pope Pius XI's support of the right wing. Despite the Left's desire for a strong statement against fascism, the PPI congress of October 20–23 avoided condemning it and delivered a weak statement on the possibility of collaborating with the Socialists in a governmental coalition. Noted for his staunch antifascism, Sturzo seemed not to comprehend how close fascism was to achieving power and had no practical plan for thwarting it. Even more serious, and for reasons still hotly debated, Sturzo opposed the return of Giolitti to power after Bonomi's fall. Since even Mussolini believed that Giolitti would have used the army to defeat a Fascist attempt at a coup d'état had he been at the government's helm in 1922, and given that the PPI was the linchpin for cabinets during this era, Sturzo's "veto" of the Piedmontese statesman was crucial to fascism's success.

Although Giolitti's past anticlericalism and his advocacy of registering securities in the names of their owners irritated Sturzo, a different conception of politics probably accounts for the PPI's opposition. Sturzo favored negotiating with the other political forces to achieve agreement on a cabinet's program and composition before its installation, whereas Giolitti insisted upon making the major decisions himself. The Catholic conception reflected the evolving mass party basis of Italian politics; although bargaining became standard procedure after World War II, in 1922 half the deputies belonged to ill-defined "parties" with vague programs and slight ideological commitment better represented by Giolitti's style. Furthermore, as events would demonstrate, the PPI lacked alternatives to a Giolitti cabinet, made impossible by its policy. Along with the other parties, the Catholics underestimated Mussolini's impending threat to democracy.

On February 2, 1922, Bonomi resigned, done in by the pacification pact's failure and his refusal to bail out the Banca Italiana di Sconto, a large bank linked to the Perrone industrial group. Although Bonomi acted to prevent major economic repercussions, and although other measures taken by his government and the previous Giolitti government eventually reversed the dismal economic situation, rightist groups that supported Perrone and had clamored for government intervention to save the bank turned against Bonomi. Democrats representing irate depositors and moderate-liberal groups pressing for Giolitti's return joined them.

A drawn-out crisis followed Bonomi's fall. Many prominent politicians failed to win support that would permit them to govern. Socialist reformist parliamentarians proposed a cabinet that would pursue an anti-Fascist policy, but they received no response from the PPI or democratic groups, only a dressing-down from their own party. The Catholics vetoed Giolitti and refused to take the helm themselves. Finally, on February 25, a temporary solution allowed a government to form under Giolitti's lieutenant, Luigi Facta, who tacitly agreed to resign when a more permanent agreement could be reached. An unsteady coalition of Catholics and liberal democratic groups supplied the majority, despite Sturzo's displeasure.

Facta's weakness encouraged a great Fascist offensive in the spring and summer of 1922, coinciding, oddly enough, with the burgeoning of the Fascist labor movement. In January 1922, previously autonomous Fascist labor organizations organized in a centralized federation linked to the PNF. A former revolutionary syndicalist and organizer of Italian workers in the United States, Edmondo Rossoni, took charge of the movement, which, for reasons that will be discussed, grew to an amazing 458,000 members by June 1922. Despite Rossoni's sincerity and skill in mobilizing workers, the labor movement contradicted fascism's real nature. In fact, Fascist labor leaders faced constant embarrassment, especially on the land where they had the most support, by the propensity of owners to violate agreements even after workers had taken cuts because of the economic situation. Fascist leaders shrewdly resolved their problem by organizing vast actions to wring concessions from an increasingly weak state. September 1921 had witnessed a "march" on Ravenna in imitation of D'Annunzio's Fiume exploit; organized as a pilot project by Italo Balbo, *Ras* (a term referring to Fascist bosses in the provinces and taken from Ethiopian chieftains) of Ferrara Province, the march proved that Fascists could solve the logistical problem of moving large masses of people. In May 1922, 60,000 peasants protected by Fascist squads occupied Ferrara and forced the government to make appropriations for public works. Later the same month, 20,000 Fascists occupied Bologna for five days in a move against a prefect who had instituted measures prohibiting the importation of workers competing with Socialist leagues; giving in to Fascist demands, the government transferred the official, Cesare Mori. By moves of this kind, Fascists cleverly protected landowner interests by focusing worker demands against an enfeebled government.

Fascist inroads on the labor movement did not depend solely on these tactics. Besides the respect that the experienced Rossoni commanded, Fascist labor leaders enunciated a series of progressive demands, including an eight-hour day, a worker share in management, and worker representation in personnel decisions. Fascist labor leaders emphasized balancing the interests of workers and the nation; this concept appealed to peasants who rejected the Marxist emphasis on the class struggle and who favored practical means to increase production, opposed public service strikes, and trusted in the capitalists to lead the way out of the economic crisis. Fascist labor organizations took the name "corporations" from D'Annunzio, which conveyed the idea of solidarity. Reflecting fascism's split personality, in September 1922, Mussolini's newspaper stated that it could do without the proletariat's support, but the idea of a partnership to rescue the country appealed to many workers.

Facta's failure to act against Fascist violence, and the de facto complicity of local officials, encouraged local Fascist leaders to escalate the violence. Punitive raids struck many cities, but culminated on July 13. Squads led by Roberto Farinacci occupied the Cremona city hall, terrorized their opponents, and destroyed the homes of prominent Socialist and Catholic leaders. This event produced a PPI backlash against Facta, and his government fell without the solution it had been created to encourage. For a brief time it seemed that Parliament would install a Center-Left government committed to curbing Fascist excesses, but this hope evaporated amid Mussolini's threats of civil war and the divisions among his enemies. The reformists resolved to support an anti-Fascist cabinet, and in a clamorous development, Turati consulted the king. Nothing came of these efforts. PSI executive organs denounced the reformist parliamentarians, and the Catholic right wing rejected cooperating with the Socialists, as did Sturzo. Consultations revealed that no agreement on resolving the crisis by naming an authoritative prime minister existed. As a result, Facta headed a new cabinet and again awaited a more permanent solution.

The failure to craft an anti-Fascist compromise strengthened Mussolini. This truth became clear during the July 31–August 2, 1922, "legalitarian" general strike. Originally conceived as pressure in favor of a Giolitti-Turati cabinet, a "labor alliance" of anti-Fascist unions formed the previous February called the strike to demonstrate against Fascist terror. Badly organized, the strikers were no match for armed *squadristi* who attacked them in the name of national solidarity, frequently in the company of police. The Fascists broke the strike and exploited the occasion to destroy labor organizations, burn their enemies' property, and expel Socialist city administrations.

The disastrous legalitarian strike and Facta's reconfirmation opened the road to power for Mussolini. The labor alliance crumbled, and in October the CGL severed its ties with the Socialist Party. The Fascists now added to their control of the land the political domination of all the major cities in the North and Center. More important, the political establishment concluded that there could be no solution to the country's turmoil without Fascist participation in a governmental coalition. Giolitti and other liberal leaders agreed; in the PPI, tensions between the pro-Fascist right and the anti-Fascist left wing increased. In response to these developments and to its intensified internal debate on collaboration, the PSI ripped itself in half at its Nineteenth Congress, October 1–4, 1922. With the help of the "third internationalists," the maximalists barely managed to expel the reformists, who formed the Unitary Socialist Party (PSU) under the leadership of Turati and Giacomo Matteotti. The Marxist movement was now split into three competing parties, the intransigent PSI and PCI viewing fascism as signaling the approach of the proletariat's dictatorship and the PSU advocating collaboration with democratic groups to defeat Mussolini. If PSI and PCI policy continued to be suicidal, however, the PSU had arrived at its governmental appointment too late because the PPI and the liberals were now primarily interested in cooperating with Mussolini and not the Socialists. Defeated in the field, split, and shorn of their labor support, the Socialists no longer presented an effective opposition to fascism.

Mussolini's success, however, meant that he had to act quickly. With the "Bolshevik" threat smashed, his bourgeois allies might soon tire of supporting an expensive and now unnecessary repressive organization and would favor maintaining order by means of a strengthened traditional government. During the next two months, Mussolini skillfully balanced military moves and the desire of establishment politicians to cooperate with him. At the same time, he cleverly combined the differences of fascism's two wings. One, led by Dino Grandi, pressed him to come to power "legally" by taking advantage of a governmental coalition; the other, headed by Balbo, Farinacci, and Michele Bianchi, preferred the "insurrectional" approach, that is, a "March on Rome" from the provinces as perfected by the marches of local leaders on various Italian cities. Mussolini understood that only a mixture of these methods would work because the army could easily defeat a Fascist coup attempt; he intensified the delicate task of convincing the army and its leader, the king, not to intervene against a coup that would be in their own interest.

In a complex series of maneuvers, Mussolini dangled both the "legal" and "military" solutions before friend and foe. He negotiated with liberal leaders clamoring to form a governing coalition with him, but, unwilling to accept a subordinate position, he stalled agreement. Mussolini most feared the most discussed solution, a Giolitti-led cabinet: Mussolini considered Giolitti the liberal statesman most likely to order the military to stop a Fascist coup d'état. Mussolini also played up to the king by attenuating fascism's republican propensities, but he suggested that, by accepting only the monarchy and not the monarch, if Victor Emanuel opposed him he would replace the king with his more glamorous cousin, the Duke of Aosta. Counterbalancing these political maneuvers, in October Fascist leaders carried out an August decision of their Central Committee to form a unified military command of Fascist forces. This move amounted to formal creation of an illegal private army, whose organizational criteria Mussolini's newspaper published on October 3 and 12, 1922. The government did not react.

Mussolini masterfully managed the complicated and confused situation that now ensued. Gabriele D'Annunzio still rivaled him and enjoyed a strong following even among Fascists. During talks with liberal politicians, the poet agreed with Facta that a large demonstration of war veterans would take place in Rome on November 4, anniversary of the Italian victory in World War I. Rumor had it that D'Annunzio planned a ceremony to reconcile the country's opposing forces, close the continuing dispute over the war, and create the basis for a new government, perhaps headed by Giolitti. After an unsuccessful attempt to work out his differences with D'Annunzio, Mussolini decided to hold a march on Rome a week before the scheduled "reconciliation."

On October 16, Mussolini met in Rome with the military heads of fascism—Balbo, Bianchi, Cesare Maria De Vecchi, Emilio De Bono, and others. Mussolini declared that a parliamentary solution to the country's crisis was imminent and that the resolution would damage fascism; he insisted that the time for a military takeover of the capital had arrived. He proposed moving immediately following a Fascist congress scheduled for Naples on October 24, which would both give the Fascists momentum and create a diversion. De Vecchi, head of the Turinese Fascists and a captain, and De Bono, a retired general, objected that Fascist forces were not ready, but Mussolini insisted. According to De Vecchi, Mussolini said that D'Annunzio and Giolitti had planned a clamorous act of reconciliation for November 4—an embrace at the Tomb of the Unknown Soldier. Mussolini believed the theatrical gesture would work and produce a Giolitti cabinet, "and you know that with Giolitti it is better to think of other things." Insisting that the government was "rotten" and that the time had come to act, Mussolini won out. Over the next two days, the Fascist leaders made military plans for the March on Rome.

At the Naples congress, the exact date of the march and other details were ironed out. Mussolini and the *quadrumvirs* who led the military action understood that they would be defeated if the army was called out. They moved to obviate that possibility. On October 25, Mussolini took the train for Milan, stopping at Rome to consult with pro-Fascist Masonic army elements who had influence with the king. The next few days were marked by a series of intense consultations, which have not yet been fully reconstructed, with influential personages.

Writing to the king at his vacation retreat, Facta first expressed doubt about a Fascist insurrection, then said that the government was ready to meet it. He tried desperately to reach a political solution that would bring the Fascists into a ruling coalition. Mussolini played along, indirectly helped by Giolitti's refusal to be rushed; some influential Fascists believed that the best that could be achieved was a cabinet consisting of Fascists and Nationalists and headed by Salandra, but Mussolini preferred the weaker Facta and dragged out the negotiations. There are indications that on October 26 Mussolini agreed to a new Facta government with Fascist participation (the documents have not been found), but later the same day Bianchi stated that only a Mussolini-led cabinet could resolve the crisis.

Perhaps convinced that he had an agreement with Mussolini, Facta sent a soothing telegram to the king at 12:10 AM on October 27, but asked him to come to Rome. As Victor Emanuel boarded a train to the capital, the first signs of Fascist military activity appeared, along with army preparations to meet it. During the day, negotiations with Mussolini for a new government broke down definitively. At the Rome station, Facta briefed the king on the day's developments, and Victor Emanuel expressed irritation that he had to make decisions under the pressure of Fascist rifles. Between 9:00 and 10:00 PM, at the king's Roman villa, Facta pointed out that the king could declare martial law but apparently did not make a strong argument. Facta then went to his hotel to sleep.

At midnight, the prime minister was awakened and told of further Fascist military action. At 5:30 AM, October 28, the cabinet convened. That night at the War Ministry, some cabinet members complained that Fascists occupied strategic sites as a result of the army's failure to act, and an army representative lamented the lack of orders. The cabinet proceeded to draft a proclamation of martial law; Facta consulted the king, who agreed to sign the declaration the next morning. The cabinet voted unanimously to declare a state of siege, informed the police and military commanders of the decision, and revised the text. At 8:30 AM, posters plastered in Rome announced martial law. At 9:00, Facta presented the decree to Victor Emanuel for his signature; surprisingly, Victor Emanuel refused to sign. There is some dispute as to whether a second meeting took place, but at 11:30, Facta resigned and telegrams went out countermanding the orders to institute martial law.

What accounts for the king's refusal? Much later he would argue that he feared civil war would result, but this explanation seems to have been concocted to justify the king during a referendum on the monarchy after World War II. Other accounts tell of secret meetings with his advisers and supposed doubts that the army, infiltrated by Fascist sympathizers, would fight, but no evidence exists that the military—fiercely loyal to the Savoys—would have refused to follow orders. Most probably, the king concluded that had he employed the army to stop the Fascists, he would have prolonged the chaotic situation in Italy and encouraged a vacuum on the right that would have favored a leftist revival. Even though irritated by Fascist military action, Victor Emanuel knew that the political establishment believed some form of Fascist participation in government to be inevitable, and he himself considered it a stabilizing force. Given these factors, he opted for the solution he believed would stabilize the political situation for a while.

More important, the monarch's refusal to sign the martial law decree in the face of a unanimous vote by the government reveals a fatal flaw in the Italian Constitution. In the West, constitutional development tended to weaken the executive. Italy participated in this trend, but it had not developed as fully as in Britain and France. Furthermore, the postwar political instability exacerbated this defect. It seems likely that Giolitti, more authoritative than Facta, or a prime minister with a strong parliamentary majority would have been successful in securing the king's assent to martial law. As in 1915, when he supported Italian entrance into the war, the king sided with conservative coteries against the legally constituted order.

Victor Emanuel preferred Salandra to Mussolini as the head of a cabinet, even if such a government would have included Fascists in important positions. As indicated, some Fascists such as De Vecchi did not believe a Mussolini-led cabinet possible. More politically astute than they, Mussolini adamantly held out for an official mandate to form a government. The king gave in. On the evening of October 29, 1922, Mussolini took a sleeper train for Rome. His cabinet, supported by Nationalists, PPI (against Sturzo's wishes), and liberals, included five Fascists in the most important posts (Mussolini headed the cabinet and the powerful interior and foreign ministries), three pro-Fascists (war, navy, and education), and seven Fascist undersecretaries; liberals, democrats, and Catholics completed the picture.

Fascist power in the government was out of all proportion to the PNF's representation in the Chamber of Deputies, but the cabinet was presented as the victory of the young generation that had fought and died for the country in war over the decrepit politicians. From this point on, the discredited Parliament steadily lost power and ceased being the center of political decision-making. Many deputies voted for the Mussolini government because they believed that they retained the power to vote the cabinet out of office should they wish to do so—but this possibility became increasingly theoretical, and the country no longer had a fully functioning parliamentary regime. "In this sense, on October 29–30, 1922, in Italy a coup d'état occurred which broke the continuity of the parliamentary-constitutional tradition, even if it did not formally violate the letter of the *Statuto* issued by Charles Albert."

On October 30, the squads flooded into Rome and other cities, terrorizing and killing their enemies, sacking their meeting places, devastating their homes, and dismembering their organizations. With the government in Mussolini's hands, they became the country's real rulers. In doing so, they created a new style and began an era not only in Italy but also in Europe.

It is frequently stated that Mussolini did not create a dictatorship until 1926 or even later. However, while it is true that the Fascist regime was not fully structured until that year, there can be little doubt that the Fascist dictatorship existed by October 1922 when Mussolini took over the government, that Fascist squads controlled the country, and that only army intervention could have defeated them. A common view also holds that the Nazis under Hitler achieved power faster—another flawed and dangerous interpretation if one considers that Italian fascism achieved power in only three years (1919–1922) compared to fourteen for the Nazis (1919–1933). The more sophisticated use of power by the Fascists perhaps accounts for this mistaken view. It is worth noting that in Germany, as in Italy with the Fascists, the army could have ended the Nazi regime but chose not to do so.

CHAPTER SIXTEEN

Mussolini's Italy

Despite serious problems before World War I, the Italian constitutional system made notable progress toward democracy. By the 1850s, Piedmontese—and after unification Italian—ministers were responsible to Parliament, even though the king retained an important voice in governmental affairs. The French achieved this ministerial responsibility definitively only in 1877, although the executive power was much weaker. In Italy, the Senate appointed by the king under the Statuto never had more than gadfly status, in contrast to Britain's House of Lords, until 1911. Germany, Austria-Hungary, and Russia failed to develop ministerial responsibility before World War I. After that conflict, Italians probably enjoyed more civil liberties than the citizens of most European countries and the United States. In fact, excessive liberty and the economic and social effects of the war help explain the reaction of 1921–1922 and the rise of fascism. The events of those years reversed the country's steady progress toward parliamentary democracy and were a radical departure from the recent past.

Consolidating the Regime

On November 16, 1922, Mussolini asked the Chamber of Deputies for a vote of confidence. The Duce's creation of a coalition cabinet convinced traditional politicians anxious to ignore reality that the March on Rome signified only the installation of a cabinet capable of restoring order, one they could vote out of office whenever they wished. But although right-wing liberals such as Salandra saw Mussolini as heading a restoration government, and left-liberal leaders advocated patience until Fascist mistakes induced Parliament to topple Mussolini, the Duce presented the March on Rome as a revolution and his request for confirmation only a courtesy. He remarked: "I could have bolted Parliament shut and constituted a government made up exclusively of Fascists. I could have: but I do not, at least for now, choose to do so."

Liberal and Catholic deputies ignored his speech in the confidence debate, choosing to emphasize Mussolini's promise to restore law and order. PSU leader Filippo Turati denounced Mussolini, but Communists and PSI Socialists continued to underestimate him and muted their response. On November 17, liberals, Catholics, and small democratic groups joined Fascists and Nationalists to give Mussolini a 306 to 116 majority.

For the next year and a half, Mussolini maneuvered to outwit his opponents and consolidate his rule. On December 3, 1922, the Chamber voted the government full powers for a year to confront the economic crisis and reduce the bloated bureaucracy. The Fascists exploited the law to reorganize the state administration, fire their opponents, and gain control of the bureaucracy. Moreover, Mussolini established institutions foreshadowing the formal creation of a one-party state. On December 15, 1922, Fascist chiefs instituted the Fascist Grand Council, which met on that date to solve the problem of the squads. On January 11, 1923, the *Popolo d'Italia* announced the names of those who had the right to sit on the Grand Council; these persons included National Fascist Party Directorate members, Fascist ministers and other officials, and governmental functionaries such as the head of the police (*pubblica sicurezza*). Besides those officials sitting on the Council by right, no set rule determined who could participate in the deliberations, and Mussolini reserved the right to summon others whose presence he might find useful on an ad hoc basis. Thus the Grand Council assumed both party and state functions; it strengthened Mussolini's control over an unruly Fascist Party, enunciated principles, and drafted legislation consolidating his power and organizing the regime. Other changes in membership occurred before the Council's existence was formalized by a law of 1928, but it lost power, for the reason soon to be discussed.

The Grand Council resolved the problem of the squads. Their wanton violence had long threatened fascism's respectability, and their independence challenged Mussolini's control of the movement. With socialism's defeat removing the necessity for open violence, the Duce, heading a cabinet pledged to restore law and order, could no longer be seen as sanctioning squadrista violence. In addition, Mussolini had to act quickly because the army and non-Fascist conservatives were pressuring him to "normalize" the squads, which they correctly perceived as an irregular (and rival) armed force. Mussolini had his own problems with the squads and hoped to assert control, but did not favor eliminating them because he still needed an independent military arm to continue intimidating his opponents and consolidate his power. The Fascist Grand Council resolved these issues by formally dissolving the squads and instituting the Voluntary Militia for National Security (MVSN), a decision ratified by royal decree. Composed of former squad members and conserving Fascist symbols, the MVSN's mission was to protect the "October Revolution." This restructuring permitted fierce attacks—this time state-sanctioned—against fascism's enemies, which intensified in 1923 and 1924 and forced them underground or into exile.

Used to their independence, local Fascist Ras resisted Mussolini's "normalization" attempts. Along with the merger with the Nationalists in March 1923, these contrasts caused a crisis in the Fascist Party. Mussolini supported the "revisionist" current led by Giuseppe Bottai and Massimo Rocca. These leaders argued that fascism had to be transformed from a combat organization into a movement capable of renewing the nation. This task implied the advent of a new ruling class that would accept and make use of competent people from all sectors of Italian society. Opposing them, the "intransigent" wing led by Ras such as Roberto Farinacci fought "normalization" and advocated a "second wave" of the Fascist revolution to destroy what was left of liberal Italy, including the remnants of Socialist, Communist, and Catholic organizations. As was his wont, Mussolini switched his support to this second movement when he needed its military might.

The instability caused by adopting proportional representation in 1919 produced widespread demands for its modification by Fascists and liberal politicians. A bill drafted by Mussolini's undersecretary, Giacomo Acerbo, proposed giving two-thirds of the seats in the Chamber to an electoral coalition achieving a plurality, provided it received 25 percent of the total votes cast; the remaining one-third would be distributed proportionately among the other parties. The left-wing parties opposed passage, and conservatives supported it, but the real struggle occurred within the pivotal PPI. Most of this party supported proportional representation, including Sturzo and others who wished to continue collaborating with Mussolini's government. Since Catholic defection on this issue would cause the bill to fail, Mussolini enlisted the Vatican's aid to block the PPI from voting against the Acerbo bill, or at least to split the organization. By making important concessions to the Church, he hoped to convince the Vatican that it did not need a Catholic party, or at least to encourage the PPI's right wing to support him. On January 20, 1923, the Duce and Vatican secretary of state Cardinal Pietro Gasparri met secretly; Mussolini agreed to continue the bailout of the Catholic Banco di Roma, and the Vatican replaced the bank's directors, strong supporters of the Sturzo wing.

Shortly afterward, the PPI right wing, with Vatican support, called for continued collaboration with the Mussolini government and sought expulsion of Mussolini's enemies within the organization on the grounds that they sympathized with subversive parties. After a heated debate at its April congress in Turin, the delegates approved "conditional collaboration," meaning continued support for the government but defense of full proportional representation. Mussolini responded by dropping Catholic representatives from his cabinet, intensifying Fascist violence against Catholic organizations, and initiating an anti-Catholic press campaign. Supported by the Vatican, right-wing Catholic periodicals attacked the party leadership and pressured Sturzo to resign as secretary. Mussolini hoped to obtain Sturzo's resignation before debate on the Acerbo bill and achieved his objective on July 10, 1923. Five days later, the Chamber accepted the Acerbo bill; several right-wing PPI deputies bolted discipline, voted in favor of the bill, and were later expelled. Their close links with the pope, however, further alienated the Vatican; Mussolini had skillfully prepared the ground for the pope's abandonment of the Catholic Party.

The political forces now faced new elections, called for April 1924. In addition to controlling the government apparatus, the Fascists enjoyed a great advantage because of the economy's rebound and Mussolini's diplomatic success in negotiating the cession of Fiume to Italy. The Fascists also agreed with prominent liberals, such as Salandra and former Prime Minister Orlando, former PPI politicians, and other non-Fascist politicians, on a single electoral list. These allies attracted many votes to the *listone* (big list) and gave the Fascists respectability. Fascist opponents failed to present a united front. The PSI, racked by an internal dispute on whether to fuse with the PCI, underwent a new split in 1923. The PCI offered to join a united list, but the PSU, pushing for a coalition of all democratic forces and reunion with the PSI, branded the Communists "unwitting" accomplices of fascism and rejected collaboration.

These factors, along with Fascist violence, Mussolini's control of the voting machinery, and state intervention, facilitated a Fascist victory. The Fascist-led electoral coalition won 64.9 percent of the votes and two-thirds of the seats in the Chamber. Nevertheless, the elections revealed strong opposition to fascism despite Fascist terror; in the industrialized areas of North Italy, the opposition lists outpolled the Fascist-led coalition.

Even the large Fascist majority achieved in the elections failed to assure Mussolini of a docile Chamber of Deputies, and his enemies exhibited a growing combativeness. The PSU secretary, Giacomo Matteotti, gave a well-researched and effective speech contending that Fascist violence had invalidated the recent elections and demanding new ones. Republicans, Catholics, and liberal monarchists took up Matteotti's cry. On June 10, 1924, Matteotti disappeared.

The facts of Matteotti's disappearance soon became known. The concierge of a nearby apartment house noticed five men waiting in a car; suspecting that the men were thieves, he jotted down the license plate number. The police traced the car to the editor of a Fascist newspaper that had links to the secretary of state for the Interior Ministry. The leader of the special squad was Amerigo Dumini, a Tuscan Fascist with a criminal record who received a salary from Cesare Rossi, head of Mussolini's press office. The squad members belonged to the "Fascist *checka*," a secret police organized by Fascist Party administrative secretary Giovanni Marinelli.

Questions immediately arose as to the kidnappers' intent and Mussolini's responsibility. Dumini stated that the squad did not intend to murder Matteotti but to "teach him a lesson" by beating him. The crime's circumstances and Mussolini's attempt to cover up the disappearance contradicted this explanation. As to Mussolini's involvement, the Duce later contended that the affair caused him so much trouble that only his "worst enemy" could have conceived it. No documents demonstrating Mussolini's direct involvement in the crime have been found, but most historians agree that Mussolini created the conditions under which the crime occurred.

The Matteotti affair ended by consolidating Mussolini's power. A wave of revulsion swept Italy, affecting Fascists and non-Fascists. The police made arrests, and when details of the case emerged, most people assumed that Matteotti's outspoken opposition to fascism had caused his murder, even though his body was not discovered until August. Hoping to prevent his non-Fascist allies from deserting the coalition, Mussolini denied involvement in Matteotti's disappearance, said he had given strict orders for a thorough investigation that would punish the culprits, promised that he would purge fascism's unruly elements, dropped from his government all officials implicated in the case, and expressed the hope that a national reconciliation would emerge from the affair. At the apparent behest of the king and his non-Fascist partners, Mussolini relinquished the Interior Ministry to Luigi Federzoni, a Nationalist leader and the monarch's confidant. On June 30, the Chamber and Senate accorded Mussolini a vote of confidence.

Encouraged by the turn of public opinion against the government, the opposition took its case to the country. In what became known as the "Aventine Secession," Mussolini's enemies hoped to focus the nation's moral condemnation of Mussolini by boycotting the Chamber. There followed an intense press campaign by the opposition's remaining periodicals that kept the Matteotti affair before the public, which for a time promised to be effective. The strategy, however, was doomed to fail because its success depended on the king to dismiss Mussolini as prime minister, but the monarch refused because the Duce had won a vote of confidence and because he feared that removal of the cabinet would revive leftist fortunes. In the meantime, despite his conciliatory words, a new wave of violence began when Mussolini swung his support to the intransigents within the PNF. Given Fascist military domination of the country, an attempt at insurrection would have been suicidal, and the labor movement refused Gramsci's proposal for a general strike because defeat was certain. Moreover, the opposition's absence from the Chamber made Mussolini's survival easier.

The struggle entered a new phase after Matteotti's body was discovered on August 16. The protracted crisis raised the possibility of a union of Mussolini's enemies and defection by his liberal allies. Turati offered to coordinate action with the Catholics, a proposal PPI Secretary Alcide De Gasperi and Luigi Sturzo seri-ously considered. The Vatican vetoed the alliance, but Mussolini pressured the Vatican to force Sturzo to leave Italy. The Vatican complied, and Sturzo departed the country on October 25, 1924, for a twenty-two-year exile. Mussolini's more radical opponents fared no better. Gramsci proposed transforming the Aventine into an "antiparliament" from which a revolutionary appeal would be made to the nation. The other anti-Fascist forces rejected the proposal as dangerous, and the Communists reentered the Chamber in 1925.

Opposition tactics failed to shake the Duce's liberal allies, although the Con-findustria (the manufacturers' association), which had financed the Fascist coali-tion's list in the 1924 elections, switched to an attitude of prudent reserve despite pressure by prominent liberal leaders to condemn fascism. In October, a congress of liberals voted for a return to legality, respect for the division of powers, main-tenance of the constitutional order, the end of private armies, and respect for la-bor organizations, but no concrete action followed this strong statement, and Salandra's followers remained in Mussolini's cabinet. Mussolini's more deter-mined liberal opponents joined together in a "National Union" headed by monarchist Giovanni Amendola, who was later beaten to death by the Fascists. On December 27, 1924, the National Union's newspaper, *Il Mondo*, began publish-ing a memorandum by Cesare Rossi, who had been involved in the Matteotti af-fair, accusing Mussolini of personally having ordered many acts of violence and, by implication, of having done the same in Matteotti's murder. The publication of Rossi's document created an enormous impression, coming on the heels of uncertainty within the Fascist-led coalition, the resignation of Italo Balbo as in-terim head of the MVSN following proof that he had ordered beatings, the attempt of a group of moderate Fascists to present a motion requesting the coun-try's normalization, and rumors that Victor Emanuel planned either a return to a liberal government or the institution of a military one. Salandra finally withdrew his support from the cabinet, but other non-Fascist government members did not. Confronted by the military ministers' support for Mussolini and cowed by the Duce's promise to employ force against an eventual successor, the cabinet stuck by him at a meeting on December 30.

These events illustrate how Mussolini's ability to stay in power depended on his military control of the country. Only his fear that Victor Emanuel and the army might turn against him had made him cautious. By the end of 1924, how-ever, the political aftermath of the Matteotti murder had made Mussolini more dependent on the squads, whose leaders feared that indecisive action might lead to his downfall and to their own arrest. Fascist leaders intensified their violence and demanded that Mussolini drop his "weak" policies and finish off the opposi-tion once and for all. Mussolini promised to silence the opposition when the Chamber reopened on January 3, 1925.

On that day, Mussolini made a famous speech accepting moral responsibility for Matteotti's murder and challenged the opposition to move against him. Then he reshuffled his cabinet and appointed new Fascist ministers known for their support of the monarchy in order to gain the confidence of Victor Emanuel, rumored to be lukewarm toward him. In a series of shrewd concessions, Mussolini won the support of the army and industrialists but balanced this policy with concessions to fascism's intransigent wing, which ushered in a new period of violence against fascism's enemies. These actions prepared the way for measures to consolidate the regime that the government introduced between January 1925 and the end of 1926 and that changed the country's constitutional structure and reversed the course of its democratic tradition. The boycotting of the Chamber by Mussolini's opponents facilitated passage of the legislation.

ADMINISTRATION, ECONOMICS, LABOR, 1925 TO 1929

In 1925 and 1926, four attempts on Mussolini's life occurred, which the Duce exploited to pass and systematize repressive legislation. Liberal icon Luigi Albertini was removed as editor of the *Corriere della Sera* in November 1925, and this newspaper passed under Fascist control along with the rest of the independent press. In 1925 and 1926, the government suppressed all opposition parties and associations, including the Masons, and expelled the Aventine deputies from the Chamber. In September 1926, Mussolini appointed the super-efficient Arturo Bocchini as national police chief and gave him new repressive tools. In November and December, the government received wide power to confine persons who subverted the political and social order or who allegedly conspired to do so. To meet the growing exile opposition, government officials gained the power to review and annul passports, to fire on persons attempting to leave the country illegally, and to deprive Italians abroad of their citizenship and property. The government also instituted the death penalty for assassination attempts against government and royal family members and established a special tribunal to try persons committing or contemplating political crimes against the Fascist regime.

New legislation modified the constitutional order and strengthened Mussolini's personal position. In December 1925, parliamentary control over cabinets evaporated with the transformation of the prime minister into the "Head of the Government," responsible to the king and no longer to Parliament. In addition to losing the right to determine who would become prime minister, the Chamber lost its power to influence the choice of individual ministers, who were now nominated by Mussolini and appointed by the king. Mussolini eliminated Parliament's legislative initiative by gaining control of its agenda. In January 1926, a

PORTRAITS

ARTURO BOCCHINI
"Vice Duce"

ᔫᔪ

Ironically, and unlike Hitler, Mussolini did not turn over control of the Italian population to special party police forces but to the ordinary police. When the Duce took over the country, he worked closely with the carabinieri, but later realized that the carabinieri would always owe their major loyalty to the king. He turned to the civilian police located in the Interior Ministry's Direzione Generale della Pubblica Sicurezza (Public Security) to exercise political control over the Italians. This branch of the police was motivated to support him primarily by its traditional opposition to left-wing subversion and by its belief that cooperating with Mussolini was the best way to block hothead Fascists who advocated a "second wave" of the Fascist revolution.

In 1925 and 1926, a wave of assassination attempts against Mussolini occurred. These attempts led to the emergence of a career police official, Arturo Bocchini, whom the Duce made chief of police. Born in San Giorgio di Sannio (Benevento) on February 12, 1880, Bocchini was not a Fascist. (When asked whether he was a Fascist, he answered, "Sure I am, since I was in fasce [diapers]," a play on words that has remained famous.) Bocchini, son of a doctor, received a degree from the University of Naples. In 1903, he began working for the Interior Ministry, eventually advancing to the rank of prefect in some of Italy's most troublesome cities until Mussolini tapped him in 1926; he remained chief of police until his death in Rome on November 20, 1940. The power he wielded in this position earned him the nickname of "Vice Duce."

Bocchini performed his task with efficiency, intelligence, and surprising moderation. He restructured the Italian police and established a wide network of informants to keep tabs on the country's mood and the regime's opponents, but he was not brutal.

Bocchini served the regime as a career civil servant, not as a Fascist. He differed with the Duce's foreign policy, disliked the Germans, and did not favor Italy's entrance into World War II. A meeting with SS head Heinrich Himmler in 1938 was reportedly icy, and unconfirmed accounts that he planned to have Mussolini arrested before he could bring Italy into war still circulate. "Don Arturo" died before he could witness the disaster that the Duce's policy caused the country. After his death, persistent rumors that he had left secret archives made the rounds, but none were ever found.

measure ended Parliament's power over the state administration by authorizing the government to enforce decisions after consulting the Council of State. In February, a law replaced local elected administrations with appointed officials subordinated to the prefects—the *podestà*. In 1928, provincial administration came under similar control, and local autonomy disappeared.

Mussolini also triumphed over the Fascist hard-liners, who aimed at destroying all pre-Fascist institutions. Mussolini preferred to employ the police against his enemies rather than the squads that besmirched his image at home and abroad, and unlike his enemies, Mussolini favored compromise with existing groups whose support he felt was necessary to maintain him in power. In 1926, the Duce forced intransigent leader Farinacci to resign and replaced him as secretary general of the Fascist Party with the more malleable Ras from Brescia, Augusto Turati (not to be confused with Socialist leader Filippo Turati). Turati eliminated all elected party officials, replaced them with appointees, purged the PNF of violent squadristi, and transformed the party into a highly centralized and pliable instrument of Mussolini's will. The organization lost its unruly character, the percentage of workers and peasants declined, and it became more middle-class.

Mussolini also pursued a middle-class policy in economics, the touchstone of his regime's success. Between 1922 and 1925, Alberto De Stefani, a free-trader, ran Fascist economic policy as minister of finance. The European economy staged a recovery from World War I during this period; in Italy, previous economic policy, the temporary disappearance of German competition, the low value of the lira, and low wages stimulated exports and contributed to an impressive increase in production. De Stefani aimed to please large industrialists and the Church and did so by repealing the obligation to register stock, putting the telephone system and other industries into private hands, adjusting the tariff to help industry, relinquishing the state monopoly in life insurance, and abandoning an inquiry on war profits. These steps identified De Stefani's tenure with laissez-faire economic policy and won praise at home and abroad. However, De Stefani continued previous policies to salvage the banks and industrial concerns hit hardest by the earlier economic crisis. Combining interventionist with laissez-faire principles proved a powerful combination that revived the economy and allowed the finance minister to balance the budget.

In 1925, the relatively stable lira began a precipitous decline. International speculation against currencies not backed by the gold standard caused this fall. Within the country, the decline produced inflation, a drop in real wages, and labor agitation—and a stock market boom. De Stefani attempted to stem the crisis by restricting credit and choking off speculation in stocks. As a result, the Confindustria asked that he be replaced with a person in whom they had greater confidence. On July 8, Count Giuseppe Volpi di Misurata, a successful businessman who had held a series of government posts, replaced De Stefani.

Volpi unblocked negotiations with the United States over the war debt question. The United States provided Italy with short-term favorable conditions for repayment and opened the spigot of American loans that the Fascists used to achieve a stabilized lira, but a new international monetary crisis touched off another spiral of decline beginning in April 1926. As the exchange rate fell to 155 against the British pound and 30.54 against the dollar, Mussolini feared that the lira's collapse would threaten the regime. He resolved to stabilize the lira at 90 to the pound, its rate when he took office in 1922. Beginning in August, the government instituted a series of deflationary measures and negotiated a hefty loan from the Morgan Bank. The lira rose to 92.46 to the pound and 19 to the dollar on December 21, 1927, at which point the Italian currency returned to the gold standard.

The lira's revaluation at a high rate made Italian products expensive when international prices were declining and aggravated the economic situation. Export industries suffered, and credit restrictions hurt agriculture and commerce. The government took measures to help large banks and big firms by placing orders, granting tax breaks and favorable contracts, and increasing protective tariffs. Foreshadowing future developments, the government directly intervened in the economic sector by facilitating mergers, favoring rationalization, and cutting producer costs by reducing worker salaries. In 1927, for example, the government decided on a 20 percent reduction in salaries with the argument that lower prices compensated the workers for these cuts, but this was only partially true. By 1929, real wages had fallen substantially (see Table 16.1).

The revaluation crisis proved decisive for the Fascist labor movement, which had tried to improve working conditions and wages under its leader, former revolutionary syndicalist Edmondo Rossoni. Rossoni aimed at strengthening the workers' position by absorbing the CGL and the Catholic labor unions into his organization, the Confederazione Generale dei Sindacati Fascisti, and to win employers' recognition for it as the sole representative of labor. His ultimate goal was a "corporate" system to enhance national unity by including workers and employers in the same union. This project faced stiff opposition from employers, who preferred to keep workers divided among different labor organizations. Mussolini, who blew hot and cold toward the workers, gradually came to favor the employers in order to consolidate his power. On December 19, 1923, the employers scored a victory against Rossoni in the "Palazzo Chigi Pact": they successfully put off Rossoni's goal of a single employer-employee organization by establishing a privileged but not an exclusive relationship between employers and Fascist unions.

The tensions between the Fascist labor movement and the industrialists culminated in March 1925. The monetary crisis had already lowered the standard of living for workers and stimulated labor agitation among the metal workers. During talks for a new contract, the industrialists resisted workers' demands. On March 12, in the northern industrial city of Brescia, Fascist leader Augusto Turati

Table 16.1

Real Wage Indices for Interwar Italy, 1919–1940 (1913 = 100)

Year	Wage	Year	Wage
1919	93.1	1930	119.0
1920	114.4	1931	121.6
1921	127.0	1932	118.4
1922	123.6	1933	120.8
1923	116.0	1934	124.2
1924	112.6	1935	117.8
1925	111.8	1936	108.8
1926	111.5	1937	103.8
1927	120.8	1938	100.5
1928	120.7	1939	105.7
1929	116.0	1940	107.8

initiated a strike that rapidly spread to Milan and Turin, where Communist labor leaders received strong backing. Alarmed at the strength of the labor movement, Mussolini halted the strike by ordering wage increases, but he resolved to break what was left of the non-Fascist labor movement and to tame the Fascist labor organizations.

On October 2, representatives of the Confindustria and of Fascist unions signed the Palazzo Vidoni Pact, which provided for their reciprocal recognition as representatives of employers and employees. Over the next two years, enabling legislation implemented this apparently favorable decision but defanged the labor movement. Only Fascist unions could legally negotiate and enforce contracts, and previous contracts were voided. These measures forced independent labor unions to dissolve in 1926 and 1927. The Confindustria became formally Fascist, and its president and secretary entered the Fascist Grand Council, thus sealing the alliance with the government. In 1926, laws drafted by former Nationalist and "right" Fascist theoretician Alfredo Rocco prohibited strikes and lockouts and mentioned "corporations" for the first time. These were defined as central organs linking workers' and employers' organizations with the purpose of increasing production and facilitating dispute resolution. A "Labor Magistracy" was established as a court of appeal in case of deadlock. The Fascist Party had a mediating role in helping resolve labor disputes. These changes nailed down strong business support for the government during the revaluation crisis and the worldwide Great Depression, but at the cost of further reducing the standard of living for employees.

In agriculture, relations between Rossoni and the employers' organization, the Confagricoltura, were so difficult that the Fascists established their own employers' association. As the disagreements in industry were resolved, however, government pressure produced similar patterns on the land, and the attempts of Rossoni and other "left" Fascists to win gains for small landholders and for workers failed. In 1925, the Duce announced the "Battle of the Grain," one of the regime's more spectacular propaganda campaigns. For reasons of prestige and self-defense in case of war, Mussolini tried to make the country self-sufficient in foodstuffs. The government encouraged investment and improvements in a campaign to increase grain production. It hoped to achieve this goal by increasing yield per acre without reducing production for other crops. The campaign cut Italy's grain imports substantially, allowing Mussolini to claim "victory"; bringing more land into production and shifting away from other crops, however, not increased yield per unit, accounted for the greater production of grain. The exportation of more lucrative products suffered, and the collapse of international food prices forced producers to become more efficient by killing their animals and introducing tractors and modern chemical fertilizers. Small landholders who had contracted debts to pay for their land fell behind and lost their possessions, a reverse of the previous trend toward small landholding. In contrast, large landholders consolidated their position.

On April 21, 1927, the government published the "Labor Charter" with great fanfare. This document stated the right of labor to good working conditions, equitable wages, and social security; it also proclaimed private initiative the most efficient way of serving the country's interests, but promised state intervention in the economy when necessary for the good of the nation. This last statement was an important one on which the regime acted during the Depression, but the charter remained primarily a statement of principle as applied to workers. Indeed, tensions continued, and in 1928 the Fascists further weakened Rossoni's labor movement by splitting his single national confederation of unions into six organizations corresponding to those of the employers.

The same year witnessed fundamental constitutional changes to deal with the country's new political reality. The Fascist Grand Council altered the method of electing the Chamber of Deputies. The number of deputies was reduced to 400, no longer individually elected. The Council drew up a national list of 400 persons recommended by the employers', employees', and other associations. The list was then presented to the voters, who either accepted it or rejected it. Inspired by Alfredo Rocco, this law changed the basis of representation from an individual one to one based on a person's economic role in society and transformed Parliament into a rubber stamp.

The Grand Council also merged Fascist and state institutions by formalizing its own role in government. This step sealed the Council's decline because Mussolini ensured his control over the institution. Nonetheless, this measure had important results because the Grand Council gained a voice, however theoretical, in the succession to the throne, in naming an eventual successor to Mussolini, and in other prerogatives hitherto reserved to the monarchy. The move damaged the king's prestige and strained relations between fascism and the monarchy. Most importantly, in 1943 the Grand Council had an important role in Mussolini's ouster.

Completing the construction of the Fascist state, on February 11, 1929, Mussolini signed the "Lateran Accords" with the Vatican. These agreements formally ended the dispute with the papacy that had resulted from the annexation of the Papal State during the Risorgimento. The Accords created the independent state of Vatican City in Rome, paid the pope a large sum to compensate him for the annexed territories, and regulated the religious affairs of the country.

The Lateran Accords had vast implications. Among the Italian masses and in the international community, the Duce received credit for having settled the annexation dispute, a development that cemented his regime at home and abroad. A thankful pope declared that Providence had introduced him to Mussolini. The Holy Father's blessing prompted the leading scholar of Italian Catholicism, Arturo Carlo Jemolo, to interpret the agreements as "the last nail in the coffin of Italian liberty." In addition, the Accords reversed the lay character that the Risorgimento had bequeathed to the Italian state. By surrendering control over matrimony, allowing religious instruction in secondary public schools, giving the Church censorship powers over free expression in the Holy City, and renouncing other rights, the Fascists created major problems for the Italian state and colored its future character.

In 1929, however, this long-range result would have seemed paradoxical. Mussolini believed that he had relinquished nothing and, having signed the Accords, attacked the Church in an attempt to curb its political and social power and influence over the country's youth. This campaign ended in 1931 with an apparent victory for Mussolini; thereafter, at least until the anti-Semitic laws of 1938, the Church supported the regime in domestic and foreign affairs. Seven years after coming to power, openly opposed by no one but an increasingly isolated group of exiles, Mussolini had achieved unparalleled stability at home and new respect abroad.

THE GREAT DEPRESSION

The great world economic crisis struck when the effects of revaluation had not been completely absorbed by the Italian economy. As in other countries, the Depression hit Italian industry hard, increasing unemployment and decreasing working hours. The government responded by encouraging a new round of salary decreases, but the price drop and the institution of additional compensation for large families cushioned the blow. Real salaries for industrial workers who remained employed—already cut during the revaluation crisis—consequently did not fall significantly as a result of the Depression. For the unemployed, who received support for only ninety days, conditions were bleak. To increase employment and production, the government reduced the workweek to forty hours and instituted new tariff measures to help industry. To cushion the Depression's social impact, the government expanded and rationalized a system of social security that had originated in the 1880s. This system included accident, old age, and health insurance, as well as maternity benefits.

The regime also undertook a vast public works program, a showpiece of the regime much ballyhooed abroad. This policy included building housing and roads, bringing electricity into areas that lacked it, and, above all, reclaiming land. This ambitious program failed to produce the desired results because the regime concentrated its resources on helping industry weather the Depression and, later, on rearmament. As a consequence, the government reduced its public works funds, reclaiming only about 10 percent of the land that needed to be drained and irrigated.

On the land, the Depression had less impact than in industry, but it worsened chronically poor conditions caused by underemployment, the Battle of the Grain, government favoritism toward industry, and the collapse of international trade. These economic developments created tensions that caused serious strikes and tumults despite police repression. The government responded with the "ruralization" policy. Justified ideologically in the name of a high rural ideal, the government instituted laws to stem the movement of people from the land and smaller cities into large urban centers. Fascist officials hoped to decrease the concentration of the disaffected poor and unemployed in the cities, a source of opposition and in the past a reservoir for the Socialist and Communist Parties. This population movement, however, was a long-term trend that preceded fascism and would follow it.

The economic crisis produced particularly interesting developments in commerce and industry and their relationship with the government. Italian banks were of the "mixed" variety: that is, they collected deposits and invested them in commercial endeavors. Unwilling to sustain major losses during the Depression, the banks bought up shares to maintain prices. By 1931, large banks held one-third of large and medium Italian firms, but as the crisis deepened, they came close to failing and called for government help.

Mussolini turned for advice to Alberto Beneduce. A banker and a non-Fascist immune to pressure from Fascist hierarchs with links to bankers, Beneduce opposed the mixed banking system. An October 31, 1931, agreement resulted in the shifting of the banks' commercial holdings to companies controlled by the banks themselves—with the costs transferred to the Bank of Italy. The next month witnessed the creation of an agency empowered to make loans to ailing companies, the Istituto Mobiliare Italiano (IMI). In 1932, however, the economic crisis worsened substantially, revealing the inadequacy of these measures.

In January 1933, Beneduce and the new finance minister, Guido Jung, founded a new state agency: the Istituto per la Ricostruzione Industriale (IRI). Originally conceived to arrange long-term financing of industries in major difficulty and as a means of stimulating economic recovery, IRI was supposed to buy up the depressed companies in the banks' portfolios and liquidate them. Instead, IRI developed into a major new departure in Italian economic development, with far-reaching consequences. IRI acquired the commercial holdings of the major banks and, in the process, achieved control of the banks themselves and of other companies. Although it sold some of the holdings, IRI discovered that many of its new acquisitions could not be disposed of. In addition, as the Duce embarked on a series of wars, the state wished to keep in its hands the basic industries necessary for the rearmament effort. These considerations led to the development and rational organization of IRI companies in important sectors of the economy such as steelmaking, shipbuilding, and communications. By the time of its permanent establishment in 1937, IRI had evolved into a modern holding company under public control and employed the most advanced private enterprise techniques.

IRI's ownership of about one-fifth of the outstanding stock in Italian companies led historian Rosario Romeo to remark that after 1936 the state in Italy managed a greater proportion of industry than any European country except the Soviet Union. The state had always taken a strong economic role in Italy, but now it was a major player financing industry, creating new firms, owning companies, and operating like a private entrepreneur. The taxpayer bore the cost of absorbing companies battered by the Great Depression, but public intervention through IRI stimulated industry in northern Italy to improve production methods so much that Italian industry in some areas at least matched the most advanced European industrial standards. This development created a strong base that greatly contributed to the "economic miracle" that occurred following fascism's fall.

In 1935, preparations for the Ethiopian War forced the Duce to make adjustments in the economy. The government floated a series of loans to finance the conflict. The costs of economic intervention, increased interest payments, and war expenditures produced large budget deficits. In October 1936, Mussolini devalued the lira to bring the currency into line with the pound and the dollar. Prices rose despite attempts to control them, and unions obtained salary increases in 1936, 1937, and 1939. Since inflation remained relatively modest between

Table 16.2

Average Yearly Production of Electrical Energy in
Giolittian and Fascist Italy (in millions of kilowatt hours)

1901–1910	752
1911–1920	3,192
1921–1930	7,640
1931–1940	14,158

Table 16.3

Average Annual Capital Formation in the
Industrial Sector (Plant, Equipment, etc.) During
the Giolittian and Fascist Periods (in millions of 1938 lire)

1901–1910	7,945
1911–1920	8,312
1921–1930	14,634
1931–1940	17,968

1935 and 1939, a general economic recovery accompanied by increased industrial production occurred during these years. The nation's gross national product rose, in 1938 lire, from 140 billion in 1936 to 162 billion, and national income went from 126 billion to almost 148 billion lire. Although agriculture remained static, unemployment in the industrial sector fell and real salaries rose slightly.

Institution of the "autarchy" policy in 1936 contributed to this development. Announced by Mussolini as a response to League of Nations sanctions over Ethiopia and accompanied by a great propaganda campaign, this policy had its origins during the Great Depression. Under the pressure of war, Mussolini sought to transform the system into a kind of economic plan for the country involving currency controls, an austerity program, the substitution of Italian products for imported ones where possible, control of imported raw materials by large firms and state agencies, government involvement in the development of new products and processes, control of manufacturing from start to finish, and an intensified search for new sources of energy by state agencies such as the Azienda Generale Italiana Petroli (AGIP).

In the light of later statistics, Fascist economic policies had their failures, particularly in agriculture and real wages. But those policies also stimulated important modern industries such as electricity, steel, engineering, chemicals, and artificial fibers. Italy's profile began to resemble that of the modern European countries to a greater degree than in the past. Between the end of the Ethiopian conflict and World War II, autarchy seemed to be a success as well, and in 1939 exports exceeded imports for the first time since 1871. Before the Duce embarked on his warlike adventures, fascism's policies and ideology appeared brilliant and, for many Depression-era Europeans and Americans, a model to emulate.

SOCIETY, IDEOLOGY, AND CULTURE, 1930 TO 1940

Fascism's enemies had always described its ideology as a hodgepodge, an analysis that occasioned public debates among Fascist and anti-Fascist intellectuals beginning in the 1920s and among historians afterward. The view of fascism as a bogus ideology unworthy of consideration as a thought system prevailed after World War II. In the 1960s, however, when Italian historian Renzo De Felice began publication of a massive biography of Mussolini, he argued, in this and other writings, that the development of Mussolini's ideology was a subject worthy of serious consideration. More important, because of De Felice's work, as well as that of later historians, fascism could be viewed as a "leftist" movement—or at least a movement with leftist roots—which contradicted the interpretation of fascism as a reactionary movement.

Italian historians launched an intense attack on De Felice in the press, but the attempt to dismiss his views failed. Instead, his views produced an interesting historical debate. According to Israeli scholar Zeev Sternhell, for example, fascism emerged from a late nineteenth- and twentieth-century European rejection of the rationalistic and materialistic aspects of Marxism and individualistic liberalism ultimately derived from the Enlightenment. Because of reformist domination of socialism, the proletariat worked within the existing political system. In short, the proletariat renounced revolution. However, some Socialists remained revolutionary, namely the revolutionary syndicalists, and they discovered the nation as a revolutionary agent: "Having to choose between a proletarian but moderate socialism and a nonproletarian but revolutionary and national socialism, they opted for the nonproletarian revolution, the national revolution."

Sternhell thus sees fascism as grounded in European civilization and in leftist thought. In his opinion, fascism emerged from the melding of the revolutionary revision of Marxism, as operated by French and Italian revolutionary syndicalists, with Enrico Corradini's Nationalism and with Futurist aesthetics. This combination gave fascism its character of cultural and political revolt, which Sternhell believes was the essence of fascism already by 1910 before the movement adopted its name. As for the argument that it was not a coherent ideology, he writes: "Let there be no doubt about it: fascism's intellectual baggage enabled it to travel alone, and its theoretical content was neither less homogeneous nor more homogeneous than that of liberalism or socialism. Nor were the inconsistencies and contradictions greater in number or more profound than those which had existed in liberal or socialist thought for a hundred years." Sternhell concludes that fascism was an alternative to socialism and liberalism. Ironically, this is also the way the Fascists saw themselves.

By the 1930s, fascism had been in power for ten years and felt the need for a more systematic statement of its ideology so that it could explain itself to the outside world, a task undertaken by sophisticated thinkers such as philosopher Giovanni Gentile and Nationalist theoretician Alfredo Rocco. Judging from the regime's actions, this ideological framework functioned primarily as window dressing for conservative economic and social policies, but the ideas expressed during frequently passionate debates and their links to other ideologies of this troubled period help to understand the inner mechanisms of the movement.

In a comprehensive statement published in 1932, Mussolini described fascism's early doctrine simply as "action." He condemned Marxism's economic materialism as "an absurd delusion." He denounced liberalism and democracy, which he and other Fascist theoreticians lumped together with socialism, because they emphasized the individual over the community. According to these doctrines, Fascists argued, society "is merely a sum total of individuals." Paradoxically, these doctrines generated communism, which submerges the individual within the community. They claimed that fascism represented a "third way," because it recognized the community as supreme but left ample space to individual initiative. Unlike the other ideologies, fascism believed in the objective inequality of individuals and therefore emphasized "heroism" and "sentiment." Fascism combined state superiority and individual enhancement, without the false freedom found in the liberal and Communist countries.

These last elements ultimately derived from Nationalist ideology, but the Fascists adopted other Nationalist principles that had a major impact on their movement: Italy as a "proletarian nation," the "class struggle" among nations, and the inevitability of war. As noted in chapter 13, the Nationalists projected the Marxist class struggle onto the international plane as the struggle between rich and poor nations. The Fascists updated this idea into the fight between the "have-nots" and the "plutocratic" countries, and the concept had internal repercussions. The Nationalists believed that internal unity had to be achieved to prepare Italy for the coming "revolutionary" war against the rich nations. This vision prompted the formation of institutions to bolster the government by mobilizing the masses, to be discussed later. This quest for unity could be seen in Rocco's prohibition of strikes and lockouts and in the "Corporate State."

A 1926 law alluded to "corporations" but did not institute them because of the employers' opposition. With the Great Depression, however, Fascist unionists pressed for formal institution of the much-heralded corporations and a clear definition of their structure and functions. Between 1930 and 1934, a vigorous debate on the issue occurred among Fascist intellectuals, many of whom interpreted the corporations as the concrete embodiment of the Fascist "third way." To the conservative view that the corporations be simple coordinating bodies, philosopher Ugo Spirito countered that corporations set up by the state should take over ownership of firms, integrate the workers as full-scale partners in production, and leave entrepreneurs in a managerial capacity. Spirito argued that this solution would mark the end of the class struggle and fulfill fascism's promises, but he was denounced as a "Bolshevik." Spirito's "left Fascist" colleague Giuseppe Bottai adopted a middle position between these "conservative" and "radical" conceptions.

A law of February 5, 1934, set up the corporations and produced a conservative win. Twenty-two corporations were created to cover all sectors of production: agriculture, commerce, services, and industry. In the end, the corporations turned out to be councils in which employer and employee organizations enjoyed equal representation despite the numerical superiority of workers. Theoretically, in each corporation employers and employees sat down together to determine production and settle differences between workers and capitalists, with government representatives present to protect state interests. The Fascists claimed that they had officially ended the class struggle. In effect, however, the corporations had little power and normally ratified government proposals generated by the employers' associations. Completing this Corporate State, a 1938 law abolished the Chamber of Deputies and created the Chamber of Fasces and Corporations, composed of Fascist Party officials and members of the National Council of the Corporations. Members of the Chamber became so by virtue of their office, eliminating the need for elections to a national representative body. In theory, the Corporate State altered the basis of representation from the individual to productive members of society and fulfilled the Fascist view of economic self-government and national unity. In practice, a PNF-business alliance ran the country.

Besides setting up the Corporate State, the Fascists sought support by creating various institutions in the 1920s; these became important tools for the mobilization of public opinion and in the attempted transformation of Italians into militant Fascists. The Opera Nazionale Balilla (ONB) regimented boys and girls from six to twenty-one in seven youth organizations. These young people wore uniforms, marched in a military manner, and participated in organized group activities. Mussolini considered the ONB the training ground of the Fascist of the future, and it became a model for the Hitler Youth. To control future intellectuals, university students were obliged to join the Gioventù Universitaria Fascista (GUF). This organization provided scarce results for "fascistization" because, even though Mussolini forced university professors to sign an oath of allegiance to the regime, higher education remained relatively free from political interference.

As with higher education, the Fascists also substantially failed to "fascistize" the secondary schools, reformed by Giovanni Gentile in 1923. Gentile's major innovations were a more rigorous selection process for the best schools, institution of a stiff national examination for graduation, and establishment of the scientific lycée alongside the *liceo classico*. Gentile's reforms applied principles that had been discussed during the liberal era and were not specifically Fascist. Primary schools were more heavily propagandized than secondary schools and universities, with the inculcation of Fascist and Nationalist principles and the overt glorification of Il Duce. The Opera Nazionale Dopolavoro (OND) rounded out the Fascist socialization network. This leisure-time organization arranged discounts for theaters and cinema and provided vacations, tours, and sports events at reduced prices. The OND had precursors in Italy, came into contact with millions of workers, and was the regime's most successful institution of this kind. The OND served as a model for the Nazi "Strength Through Joy" organization.

By the 1930s, the Fascist Party also emphasized socialization. In 1930, Mussolini demoted Augusto Turati and installed Achille Starace as secretary. An unintelligent and obsequious tool of Mussolini, he implemented the Duce's policy of reducing the once obstreperous PNF to a bland and unthreatening body. At the same time, Starace attempted to impose on the Italians the spirit and "discipline" of ancient Rome, in the words of Philip Cannistraro, by "substituting the handshake with the Roman salute, by adopting the *passo romano* [goose step], by introducing mass marches and parades, and by [implementing] a host of minute and frequently ridiculous details." On October 29, 1932, Fascist Party membership, which had been closed, was reopened and greatly expanded. Unlike Nazi Germany and Communist Russia, membership in the PNF meant little because it was necessary for many positions. As if to emphasize the party's social function, the ONB was put under an umbrella organization, the Gioventù Italiana del Littorio (GIL), and absorbed by the party in 1937. The party had scant political significance, which helps explain why it did not intervene to save Mussolini when he fell in 1943.

Fascism's treatment of women also illustrates its ambivalent social policies. In general, attitudes toward women did not differ to a great degree from those of the democratic countries during the period. Conflict existed because of a desire to use female workers in building up the nation's economic base while suppressing the liberation that greater economic security implied. During the 1920s, fascism praised women and argued for recognizing their rights and duties within the nation, just as it did for men. It attempted to "nationalize" women, as it had men, by creating special organizations and by expanding maternity leave and other social security benefits specific to women. During the 1930s, however, the Depression and the country's foreign adventures made policy on this issue more consistent with Fascist style, which glorified virile and warlike masculinity. Since the Duce required more soldiers and a larger population to claim more territory, he encouraged women to stay home and have babies. The state gave medals to mothers who bore a large number of children. To increase productivity and profits, the government tolerated young women working at low wages, but discriminated against them as they got older to force them back into the home. Fascist propaganda discouraged viewing work or the professions as a means of liberation for women. Furthermore, since male unemployment created more serious problems for the regime, it reduced the number of women in the more remunerative jobs by encouraging them to return to the home or to enter the traditional low-paying women's jobs that men refused to do. In September 1938, the regime passed a law that mandated a cutback of female workers in state and private offices to 10 percent of their total staff. Despite such measures, however, "in the 1930s, over one-quarter of Italy's work force was female, and one woman out of every four between the ages of fourteen and sixty-five was economically active."

The 1930s witnessed the increased application of technology for propaganda, although to a lesser degree than one might imagine. The radio, favored by the regime but of slow diffusion in the 1920s, profited from government intervention in the 1930s, but the number of sets in use in Italy still trailed behind Britain, the United States, and Germany. The cinema, a field in which the country had once led, languished behind foreign and especially American films, which dominated at the box office. In 1931, a new law encouraged domestic production under government supervision, and later the Cinecittà studios were built in Rome. These events aided the Italian film industry and set the conditions for future development, but it still remained behind in its own market. Ironically, censorship seemed to have little effect; this period was the seedtime of the postwar flowering of Italian directors. Surprisingly, the regime made only a few propaganda films. The regime preferred to exploit the weekly newsreel for propaganda because private theaters were obliged to show them; Mussolini personally participated in their editing. In 1935, press and propaganda affairs, radio, cinema, and other means of communication were put under the umbrella of a new Ministry for Press and Propaganda, later renamed the Ministry of Popular Culture (Minculpop). In this way, the regime hoped to rationalize modern technology to create the "new Fascist man."

In literature, the regime also exercised a weak censorship. Prominent intellectuals exhibited their resistance by translating American novels dealing with social issues, and publishing houses became hotbeds of opposition. Officials discouraged such translations but did not crack down unless political opposition was overt. Until the anti-Semitic campaigns of the 1930s, Mussolini's Jewish mistress, Margherita Sarfatti—"a vigorous champion of modern, international currents in cultural life"—served as the regime's unofficial "dictator of culture," according to Philip Cannistraro and Brian Sullivan. The regime never adopted an official artistic style; instead, it indirectly controlled artists through a combination of labor unions, government purchases, and a network of regional and national exhibitions. Mussolini considered architecture, which was heavily dependent on public construction projects, the most important of the arts, but building design ranged from classical to the most modern international styles.

Whether because of personality characteristics, the pressure of war, or his increasing isolation from those around him, in the 1930s the Duce accentuated his personal power. Slogans such as "Mussolini Is Always Right" and "Believe, Obey, Fight" covered Italian buildings. Mussolini chafed at the king's formal supremacy and talked about seizing the first occasion to abolish the monarchy. He eliminated potential rivals such as the popular Italo Balbo, the chief of the air force who was famous for conducting mass flights across the Atlantic, by giving them honorable jobs without real power. In 1933 and later, he reshuffled the cabinet several times, taking the military ministries for himself. Despite this apparent control, Mussolini failed to achieve operational direction of the armed forces, which remained in the hands of military undersecretaries. He also became more narrowly nationalistic and chauvinistic as he attempted to rid Italy of foreign influences. This policy culminated in the anti-Semitic campaign and the racial laws of 1938.

Fascist anti-Semitism has remained controversial. On the one hand, anti-Semitism had no deep roots in Italian society or in the Fascist movement; there were many Jewish Fascists, and the idea of racial superiority seems to have been based on "spirit" rather than biology. Mussolini himself had had more than one Jewish mistress, famously condemned Nazi anti-Semitic policies, and allowed fleeing German Jews to use Italy as a transit point to Palestine; during World War II, Italian occupying armies protected Jews from the Germans, sometimes opposing Mussolini's orders. However, through no fault of their own, Italian Jews lost basic rights and suffered because of the racial laws, though not on the scale of the suffering of Jews in Germany or the German-occupied areas.

In 1937 and 1938, an anti-Semitic faction became prominent in Italian fascism, but Mussolini refused to sanction a campaign against Italian Jews, who numbered around 50,000. This faction wished to cement Italian-German relations and identified Jews variously with the bourgeoisie, liberalism, socialism, and communism. The "left" Fascist Bottai prominently opposed Jews, but the most virulent anti-Semite was the ex-priest Giovanni Preziosi. After May 1938, Mussolini gave the go-ahead for an anti-Semitic campaign. He may have been motivated by a visit to Rome by Hitler and by a desire to increase his power by decisively influencing the Italian character. The Duce was particularly taken with the idea of transforming the Italians into a "warrior" race, a concept that had prompted the prohibition of racial interaction in Italian East Africa. A racist journal was founded, *La difesa della razza*, and in September 1938, laws prohibiting foreign Jews from entering Italy, banning Jews from the teaching profession, and excluding them from receiving an education in public secondary schools were passed. More serious provisions, including a ban on intermarriage, exclusion from the army and public jobs, and a limit on Jewish economic activities, followed in November. A host of confusing exceptions accompanied these laws, allowing many individuals to escape their effect.

Contrary to the Duce's expectations, a wave of disgust and passive resistance followed enactment of the anti-Semitic laws, despite their acceptance by party hacks and some intellectuals. The anti-Semitic campaign surprised the country and prompted many people to turn against fascism. This reaction was a symptom of the country's growing disenchantment with a movement that had been in power for almost twenty years. Even though the opposition was primarily passive at this point, by 1940 increasing isolation from the nation characterized fascism.

In recent years, historical literature has been published criticizing Fascist anti-Semitism and attempting to make it an inherent part of Italian Fascist culture. Perhaps this is a backlash to a favorable view of Italian actions in favor of Jews during World War II. There is no question that the anti-Semitic laws were discriminatory and caused great hardship and that after Mussolini's overthrow in 1943 and the creation of a puppet republic under German suzerainty in northern Italy anti-Semites such as Giovanni Preziosi gained a free rein to attack Jews and turn them over to the Germans. However, taken as a whole and compared to the actions of the Germans and their allies (including the Vichy French and the Croatians), Italian efforts to rescue or otherwise protect the lives of Jews in Italy and in their occupation areas should be recognized.

RESISTANCE

Mussolini's victory in the 1920s immediately ushered in resistance. Opponents who chose to remain in Italy and who dropped out of political activity were closely watched and occasionally jailed, but they were relatively undisturbed. Many of these opponents participated in the Resistance during World War II and returned to political prominence after Mussolini's fall. Many political leaders emigrated and carried on the fight from foreign soil. The center of this exile community was Paris, although Communist leaders such as Palmiro Togliatti fled to Moscow, and other European and American cities counted active exile communities. The exile leaders reorganized their movements abroad and in Paris established the Concentrazione Antifascista, an umbrella organization to fight Mussolini and to warn other countries against the spread of fascism. Until Hitler's rise, however, foreigners, including leftists, ignored these warnings and interpreted fascism as a purely Italian phenomenon. The exiles became increasingly isolated in their host countries through the activities of the Italian consulates and by the host governments, who wooed Mussolini and were embarrassed by the exiles' presence. In addition, exile groups were infiltrated by the secret Fascist police, the OVRA,* who stimulated disagreements among the exiles.

Exile organizations primarily operated outside Italy at first by disseminating information, but later they attacked prominent Italian figures traveling abroad. The Communists established the first and most robust clandestine network, and later this activity led to increased Communist influence among the Italian masses and helps explain Communist strength when Mussolini was overthrown. However, they were not the only group to pose resistance. Organizations such as Giustizia e Libertà (GL, Justice and Liberty) led by Socialist-leaning Carlo Rosselli, demanded greater aggressiveness in fighting fascism within the country. Operatives of these organizations, including future Socialist presidents of the Republic Giuseppe Saragat and Sandro Pertini, infiltrated Italy, usually to be apprehended by the efficient Italian police, who periodically delivered heavy blows to the domestic underground organizations. These defeats failed to break the spirit of the anti-Fascist movement.

International events altered this perspective. Nazism's threat to the Soviet Union spurred Soviet-backed Communist parties to cooperate with their former Socialist rivals. Italian Communists and Socialists formed a Popular Front on the French model, and the exiles were less isolated as a result of Mussolini's growing cooperation with Hitler and his more aggressive foreign policy. When the Spanish Civil War broke out, Carlo Rosselli spearheaded an Italian exile force to combat Mussolini's intervention. Rosselli's view of Spain as a training ground for fighters who would later overthrow fascism in Italy threatened the regime, and it

---

*This acronym had the purpose of terrifying opponents. Some experts believe the term is meaningless; others say it derived from [Pi]ovra, Octopus, supposedly to signify that the secret police was omnipresent. Still others think it stands for Opera Vigilanza Repressione Antifascista, or some variant thereof.

had him assassinated by a French Fascist organization, along with his brother Nello, on June 10, 1937.

Despite these activities, only war could dislodge Mussolini. Fascism's opponents could maneuver only within the shadows of international politics, rearranging their alliances and alignments in preparation for the day when the fall of Mussolini's Italy at the hands of foreign armies would permit them to return to their homeland.

WHAT IS FASCISM?

In the decades following the end of fascism, historians have sought a greater understanding and a definition of the Fascist phenomenon, both to understand a major twentieth-century movement and to guard against its possible return to power.

A precise understanding of fascism has been hard to come by because of the complexities of the movement and because this field of study has been particularly affected by political considerations. In the earliest view of fascism, the Left argued that fascism was the reactionary movement of capital to suppress a workers' movement that was coming too close to achieving power. In accomplishing this aim, as Italian Communist leader Palmiro Togliatti put it, Fascists established a mass movement of the Right. The Communists argued that fascism was the last stage of capitalism and its appearance signaled its imminent fall; this theory had nefarious results, because it encouraged Communists to focus on the wrong enemies, such as the Socialists.

Gradually, however, fuller and more articulated interpretations came to the fore because fascism did not make an appearance only in Italy. A strong trend among historians has been to define "generic fascism"—that is, to identify certain characteristics that Fascist movements had in common. This technique involves a quest for similar ideas and actions undertaken by Fascist parties in different countries, making a list, and then determining that "fascism" is any movement that exhibits a certain number of those characteristics. This method is unusual, not having been applied to any other political movement or ideology. Why apply it exclusively to fascism? In addition, this method has yielded paradoxical results: either many movements can be defined as "Fascist" or only the Italian and the German ones can. Nevertheless, trying to isolate characteristics of "generic fascism" and then applying them to different movements to determine whether they qualify as "fascist" has become important for political scientists and historians. In general, they distinguish between the two countries in which fascism came to power, Italy and Germany, and those in which it remained a movement.

What are some of the most important characteristics of fascism as seen by political scientists and historians? In contrast to the contention that fascism does not have an ideology, recent scholarship generally agrees that it does. In Italy and in other countries, the movement has had theoreticians whose writings and speeches can be examined and analyzed for the enunciation of Fascist principles. The enemies of fascism have considered these manifestations "propaganda," but this contention has been challenged on the grounds that fascism has a "style" that is easily confused with propaganda but, taken as a whole, is relevant to its ideology. This "style" includes marches, rallies, and symbols, which were certainly present in the Italian variant that served as a model for other fascisms. Indeed, these aspects of fascism have been interpreted—particularly by historian Emilio Gentile—as a "civic religion," although some political scientists insist on the difference between a "political ideology" and a "political religion" because of the "religious" aspects a secular ideology can acquire when attempting to regenerate society. Scholars have given credence to fascism's claim to be "revolutionary" by focusing on its desire to remake, regenerate, and renew the nation by remaking its people. This principle is called "palingenesis," or rebirth. In fascism, the palingenetic "myth" is combined with another important principle necessary to its appeal: whipping up the people through nationalism. Nationalism has a long history in the West, but scholars have labeled the type of extreme nationalism identified with fascism as "populist ultra-nationalism."

All of these characteristics were present in Italy and in some other countries before the rise of fascism, but certain conditions must be present for fascism to come to power and effect a transition from a movement to a regime. These conditions may be summarized as those present after a great crisis that threatens the collapse of a society, such as occurred in Italy after the strain of World War I. Historically, however, when fascism comes to power, it has not been able to renew society, for a variety of reasons, and, depending on the situation in different countries, takes on different forms. In order to understand fascism in its different permutations, political scientists and historians have examined conditions in different countries, where they discover fascism's relationship to the Right, to racism, to modernization, and to other aspects of society.

Newer interpretations of the complexity that was fascism thus show greater promise than the views that were current during the period of its greatest diffusion. Historians and political scientists have argued for a methodology that considers fascism on its own terms. With regard to Italy, some historians object to the tendency to dismiss the Italian movement as a garden-variety dictatorship that enunciated certain principles but did not implement them and had no intention of doing so. For example, the Italian Fascists declared that they were *totalitarian*, a term first used by its enemies in the 1920s, but many scholars (following the lead of philosopher Hannah Arendt) deny that the Italians either were totalitarian or attempted to become so. In reaction to this tendency, a school of historians led by Emilio Gentile argues that Italian Fascist rhetoric must be taken seriously and that the Fascists were serious about implementing their ideas. Noting the recent emphasis on ideology, this school insists that ideology is only one dimension of Fascist reality and that fascism should be analyzed through the study of its "institutional" and "organizational" dimensions—that is, in terms of how it actually functioned. This analysis is the key to a true understanding of Italian fascism.

Gentile attributes three novel principles to Italian fascism, emphasizing their wide-ranging influence on twentieth-century history. According to Gentile's work *Fascismo: storia e interpretazione*, Italian fascism was the first revolutionary nationalist movement with the clear intention of taking power in order to destroy liberal democracy and of building a new state in order to regenerate the nation. It accomplished this goal by organizing itself as a "militia-party" constantly on a war footing. In addition, the National Fascist Party was the first to have understood the power of myth and to have brought it into the realm of political power. It did this through the "sacralization of politics," that is, by creating a "political religion" and by institutionalizing its "myths, rites, symbols, and commandments." This explains such typical Fascist innovations—imposed on the masses—as the wearing of uniforms, the use of the fasces and other symbols, the shouted slogans, the huge demonstrations, and the myth of the Duce and of "the Nation" that became the hallmark of fascism and of an era. Finally, because of the extension of these principles to political and social life, Italian fascism was the first movement characterized, from its beginnings, by *totalitarianism*, a term that was only later extended to Nazism and communism, and then only by analogy to Italian fascism.

For the new historiography, the qualities that marked Italian fascism made it a new, modern, twentieth-century movement that should not be confused with socialism and that had mass political appeal. It may be that a new model of fascism will be constructed around these attributes. Thus, for good or ill, the old model of fascism as essentially a reactionary capitalist movement bent on destroying the workers' movement no longer holds under the interpretations elaborated since De Felice began his groundbreaking research. The study of Italian fascism has become one of the most fertile in European historiography. With the passage of time, scholars and the general public may acquire a more intimate and accurate understanding of one of the twentieth century's most complex and perplexing movements.

CHAPTER SEVENTEEN

World War II
and the Resistance

F ASCISM HAD IMPORTANT REPERCUSSIONS FOR ITALIANS AND FOR THE world. In discussing Fascist foreign policy, historians debate whether the aims and policies of fascism represented an essential continuation of pre-Fascist Italy's foreign policy or a radical departure.

THE RADICALIZATION OF FOREIGN POLICY

Surface similarities exist between Fascist and pre-Fascist foreign policy. Italy had embarked on colonial adventures, nationalism had been a potent force, and inconsistency had marked Italian diplomacy before Mussolini. However, imperialism and nationalism characterized all the great powers, and Italy's weakness made it sensitive to alterations in the balance of power. Italian foreign policy before fascism operated within the European diplomatic mainstream.

With Mussolini, Italian foreign policy changed because fascism's ideology affected foreign policy. Extremist nationalism, once the province of the small Nationalist Association, now absorbed by fascism, became official policy, favoring expansionism, generating unreasonable demands, and taking the country out of the diplomatic mainstream. Fascism's exploitation of nationalism to mobilize the masses increasingly fed on itself, for failure to make touted gains could destabilize the regime. The regime consequently intensified existing resentments for domestic reasons, particularly the idea that Italy had been cheated of the fruits of victory in World War I and should have colonies because the country was overpopulated. Mussolini's anti-Bolshevism and his disdain for democracy complicated the foreign policy picture, prompting him to aid reactionary and pro-Fascist movements in Europe and driving up tensions. To these elements should be added objective ones that affected international relations, such as rising unemployment during the 1930s and the closing of immigration by the United States, which reduced an important safety valve. Moreover, Mussolini's personal style, including threats, bombast, and quick mood changes, shocked European diplomats. As in domestic affairs, Benito Mussolini was prepared to do anything to achieve his ends. Before World War I, liberal democrats who shared common viewpoints determined Europe's diplomacy, but fascism radically altered this consensus.

The Fascists aimed to revise the Paris peace settlement following World War I, a desire that would probably have been strongly felt even by non-Fascist governments. The Versailles settlement had left Italy unsatisfied territorially and by prostrating Germany had made France supreme on the Continent. With Britain supporting France, there was no possibility of constituting a second camp that Italy might join to redress the "mutilated victory." This anomalous situation, combined with a Fascist regime that glorified war and violence, proved fatal to the European system, for although Italy lacked the strength to alter the status quo unilaterally, a resurgent and vengeful Germany bent upon doing so would find an ally in a Fascist Italy.

Between 1922 and 1925, Fascist foreign policy generally followed pre-Fascist lines. Despite his tough talk, only the Corfu incident in 1923 caused a crisis. Mussolini ordered the navy to take the Greek island after several Italians helping the League of Nations mark the Albanian border were assassinated by Greek bandits, but he evacuated Corfu after Greece met his conditions for reparations. In 1924, Mussolini also signed an agreement with Yugoslavia that gave Fiume to Italy. This initial "good behavior," however, did not mean that the Duce had given up his desire to alter the European status quo.

The consolidation of Mussolini's rule between 1925 and 1926 affected foreign affairs. The transformation of Paris into a hotbed of exile antifascism strained relations with France. Moreover, Italy challenged France's dominance in eastern Europe by opposing France's allies—the "Little Entente" of Yugoslavia, Czechoslovakia, and Romania. Italy supported the claims of another revisionist power, Hungary, against the Little Entente by signing a Hungarian pact in 1927 and supplying arms and other aid to pro-Fascist Hungarian groups. Italy also aimed at dismembering Yugoslavia, a French ally, by financing and arming anti-Serb Croatian separatists. In addition, Italy and Yugoslavia competed in Albania, prompting Mussolini to transform the small Balkan state into an Italian protectorate.

Given the relatively stable international situation in the 1920s and Italy's lack of power to alter the status quo, Italian policy oscillated from revisionism to conciliation. During the tenure of Dino Grandi as Fascist foreign minister from 1929 to 1932, Italian diplomacy emphasized stabilization over revisionism. At the Geneva disarmament conference in 1932, Grandi proposed an "arms moratorium" that would reduce Germany's military inferiority and eventually produce parity among the major powers. This step might have enhanced Italy's position by reestablishing two European "camps," an Italian aim.

Grandi hoped to barter Italian support for France against Germany to gain colonial concessions, but he ran into opposition because Mussolini was too impatient to wait for his policy to yield results. In 1932, the Duce took over the Foreign Ministry and appointed Fulvio Suvich as his undersecretary. Fascist policy alternated between demanding change by violent means and presenting itself as the champion of a just and negotiated alteration of the European status quo, which helps explain why the Western powers downplayed Fascist rhetoric and considered it to be for internal consumption. But Hitler's rise to power and the Depression's economic effects allowed fascism to pursue its destabilizing foreign policy aims.

Mussolini viewed Hitler with a combination of apprehension and hope. On the one hand, Hitler's admiration flattered him, but on the other, Germany was a powerful force to be reckoned with. German resurgence presented Italy with a familiar choice: either join with Germany or go with Britain and France. In judging which option would pay the most, Mussolini did not make his selection quickly or, initially, on ideological grounds. In fact, Italo-German relations started off badly. In 1934, Hitler attempted to absorb Austria (*Anschluss*). Austrian opponents of "union" asked in vain for Franco-British support. Concrete help came instead from Italy, which was understandably anxious to keep Germany far from its northeastern border. On March 17, at the signing of the Rome Protocols by Italy, Austria, and Hungary, Rome publicly declared that it would defend Austria from invasion. A meeting between Hitler and Mussolini followed, which left the Italian unimpressed. On July 25, a Nazi *putsch* occurred in Vienna, and Dollfuss was assassinated. Mussolini mobilized four divisions and sent them to the Austrian border, while the French and British remained inactive. Hitler immediately retreated.

As relations with Germany cooled, those with France improved. Anxiety over Hitler's rise made the French more conciliatory in an attempt to gain Italian support against Germany. Jean-Louis Barthou, the hard-line French foreign minister, favored a Franco-Italian rapprochement over Yugoslavia, a policy that his successor, Pierre Laval, carried forward. A convinced partisan of Italo-French cooperation to fight Hitler's rising bellicosity, Laval signed a series of accords with Mussolini during a Rome visit from January 4 to 7, 1935, that resolved several outstanding problems between the two countries. These written accords reveal that Italy made various concessions and accepted some worthless African territory to settle its claims against France. The mystery of why Mussolini would accept such a bad deal is explained by his contention that Laval assured him that France would give Italy a free hand in Ethiopia. Laval later denied the contention, but the evidence favors Mussolini.

Convinced that he had a French agreement not to oppose a conquest of Ethiopia, Mussolini sought British acquiescence. This enterprise proved more difficult, since the British feared Hitler less than the French did. In April 1935, Italian, French, and British representatives met at Stresa in hopes of renewing the old wartime alliance after Hitler's attempt to seize Austria and his declaration, in violation of the Versailles Treaty, that Germany would reinstate compulsory military service. Nevertheless, the British, citing public opinion, refused to sanction an Italian takeover. Mussolini did not take their answer seriously, given that the British possessed the world's largest colonial empire and British interests in the area made their opposition seem like sour grapes. Furthermore, the British did not make their intentions clear should the Italians attack Ethiopia, and their signing of a naval agreement with Germany safeguarding their own interests encouraged Mussolini to go ahead. In June 1935, Anthony Eden went to Rome but failed to resolve the question. Tensions escalated and a war scare ensued. However, the British navy calculated that it would take heavy losses in a confrontation with the Italian fleet, and Mussolini charged ahead.

Three reasons for attacking Ethiopia seem to have been paramount in the Duce's mind: the perceived economic advantages for Italy in taking over a land rich in natural resources; the domestic prestige that would accrue to him from conquering a land adaptable to Italian colonization (unlike the other Italian colonies); and the belief that the new international situation —the British Admiralty was distracted by the Japanese in the Far East—provided him with a unique opportunity. In addition, fascism emphasized nationalism and glorified war and violence, and Ethiopia presented it with the opportunity to test its theories. Mussolini believed that, having mobilized the masses and brought them to a fever pitch, his regime would be jeopardized if he did not achieve a concrete result. Finally, the effects of the Depression lingered, and war would increase employment and stimulate the economy. The war would represent the high point of his regime's popularity.

Following border incidents in 1934, Italian military preparations commenced in earnest. When the Italians invaded Ethiopia in October 1935, the League of Nations imposed economic sanctions. These sanctions were serious, but the failure to add petroleum to the list and Italy's continuing ability to trade with nations not belonging to the League, especially the United States, encouraged the Italians. In the meantime, the military effort went well, despite widespread predictions to the contrary because of the difficult terrain and logistical concerns. The use of modern weapons and the extensive employment of mustard gas and terror turned out to be effective, though expensive from a financial and public relations point of view. Only guerrilla tactics would have helped the outgunned Ethiopians, but Emperor Haile Selassie avoided them. In December 1935, there was an attempt to end the conflict by granting Italy ample concessions in the Hoare-Laval proposals; Mussolini agreed to consider them, but the political backlash in

Britain caused their quick withdrawal. By May 1936, the Italians took the Ethiopian capital and the emperor fled. On May 9, Mussolini proclaimed the empire.

Although thoroughly condemned outside the country, the Ethiopian victory increased Mussolini's prestige in Italy because he had stared down the British and won an important military success. But the conquest of Ethiopia also had wide-ranging negative effects: it worsened Europe's international crisis, destroyed the League's influence, encouraged new adventures, increased the Duce's contempt for the democracies, made him turn against the Western powers, and pushed him into Hitler's arms.

THE STRANGE EVOLUTION OF AN ALLIANCE

Italo-German relations improved during the Ethiopian conflict because of Mussolini's worsening relations with Britain and France. Furthermore, with Europe's attention riveted on Ethiopia, and fearing that a quick Italian victory would deprive him of the opportunity, Hitler had announced remilitarization of the Rhineland in March. This move took some pressure off Mussolini and marked the beginning of de facto collaboration between the two dictators. Trying to assuage the Western powers, Hitler had declared his readiness to rejoin the League, but this move would have obligated him to institute sanctions against Italy. Responding to Italian protestations, Hitler promised to delay reentering the League until after the war; in return, Italy refused to approve a motion condemning Germany's action. Shortly thereafter, and in response to the Communist Popular Front policy, the Italian and German police officially began cooperating against their Socialist and Communist enemies. This agreement signaled the beginning of a common policy eventually focused upon anticommunism, antidemocracy, and, finally, anti-Semitism.

In June 1936, Mussolini appointed his pro-German son-in-law Galeazzo Ciano as foreign minister. In the summer, Italy and Germany independently decided to intervene in the Spanish Civil War on the rebel side against the Popular Front Republican government. Intervention brought Italy and Germany closer together. The German foreign minister visited Rome in the fall and signed several accords with the Italians. The Germans agreed that the Mediterranean basin was to be considered an Italian sphere. The Duce defined this new collaboration as the "Axis." With German strength apparently behind him, Mussolini publicly challenged the British, who had dominated the Mediterranean since the eighteenth century, and claimed that the British were trying to "suffocate" the Italians in their own sea.

Unexpected Republican resistance and mounting evidence of Soviet activity in the Mediterranean stimulated massive Italian intervention in Spain in 1937, which further cemented relations with Nazi Germany. Motivated by fear that the Popular Front French and Spanish governments would collaborate against fascism, the Duce poured in men and equipment but failed to win a decisive victory. The Italians met an embarrassing defeat at Guadalajara, a failure that was exceeded only by the battle's political significance. For the first time, Mussolini's Fascist armies had been stopped, partly at the hands of Italian anti-Fascists. The Civil War became a war of attrition, bogging the Italians down in a long, drawn-out fight that ended only in 1939. The Duce's continued involvement in the conflict and Italian submarine action heightened tensions with Britain and France. The chances of a rapprochement diminished, and he became friendlier to Germany. Hitler had written in *Mein Kampf* that Germany should split the World War I coalition by separating Italy from it, and he was succeeding, despite the Duce's wariness. In 1937, Hitler proposed a military alliance with Italy, but Mussolini hesitated to take the radical step of linking up militarily with Nazi Germany.

In March 1938, Nazi Germany absorbed Austria, a move the Italians had blocked in 1934. Unlike Mussolini's previous response, friendliness between the two dictators and the Italian isolation produced by the Ethiopian War precluded Mussolini from intervening. Hitler guaranteed the Brenner Pass as Italy's border, but Italians recognized *Anschluss* as a defeat for them, despite Mussolini's attempt to put a good face on the affair, and his popularity plunged.

Preoccupied with Italy's accelerating drift toward Germany, Britain and France attempted a rapprochement, but it was too little too late. The League lifted sanctions on July 15, 1936, and in January 1937 Britain and Italy reached a so-called Gentlemen's Agreement on maintaining the status quo in the Mediterranean. Mussolini hoped to win Franco-British recognition of the empire and authorized Dino Grandi, the Italian ambassador in London, to open negotiations aiming at a general understanding. On April 16, 1938, the two countries resolved several important problems affecting their relations. British recognition of the empire followed, but this success could not be duplicated with France.

In September 1938, Mussolini played an important role at the Munich Conference, which resolved the Czechoslovak crisis of that year. Hitler's demands for immediate cession of the German-speaking areas of Czechoslovakia made war seem likely, but Mussolini played a key part in a compromise solution. Widely perceived as a peacemaker, the Duce received general applause. But the weakness demonstrated by the democracies during the crisis encouraged Mussolini to be tough in achieving a French agreement. In November, staged demonstrations demanded the restoration of the former Italian territories of Corsica, Nice, and Savoy, as well as takeover of the French colony of Tunisia, where many Italians had settled. The Duce apparently intended to prepare the ground for settlement of outstanding questions with France in Africa, but his unorthodox methods backfired. Anti-Italian demonstrations shook France, making it difficult for

French diplomats to respond to Italian requests. Mussolini realized that if France resorted to military action, Italy would face the attack alone because the British would not support him and no military pact with Germany existed. The choice that Mussolini's foreign policy presented Italy stood out in all its striking clarity: either the Duce would have to sign an alliance with Hitler or he would have to abandon Hitler and become friendlier to Britain and France. This second selection, however, was highly improbable for several reasons. It would contrast glaringly with his recent policies and damage his personal prestige. It would put him in the anomalous position of allying with countries whose internal composition conflicted with his own; because of fascism's evolution, by 1938 this consideration, though not insuperable, had become significant. Politics, past behavior, and the internal contrasts between his regime and the democracies made the second choice highly improbable.

Consequently, Mussolini moved toward a German military alliance, even though the Germans made it difficult for him. In March 1939, the Germans irritated the Duce by occupying Bohemia and Moravia. Clearly, Mussolini's risky foreign policy had so far benefited only Germany; the galling corollary was that the Duce appeared unable to duplicate the spectacular gains of his onetime disciple. In April, Mussolini ordered his army to occupy Albania, which had been an Italian protectorate, ironically as a response to possible German expansion in the Balkans. The British, who had rushed to guarantee Poland's boundaries in the wake of Hitler's occupation of Bohemia and Moravia, now guaranteed Greece against an Italian attack and opened talks with Turkey. These moves convinced Mussolini that he urgently needed a military pact with Germany.

In the Italo-German talks concerning an alliance, Mussolini and Ciano made it abundantly clear that Italy would not be prepared for a major war for at least three or four years. The Germans readily agreed to such a condition, and on May 22, 1939, the two countries signed the "Pact of Steel." Unlike traditional alliances, this pact did not limit mutual aid to cases of attack by a third power. The Duce had foolishly committed Italy to go to war on Germany's side even if Germany initiated a conflict; he also naively believed Hitler's assurances that he would not precipitate a war for at least three years.

By signing the German pact, Mussolini reversed traditional Italian foreign policy and threw caution to the wind by abandoning his country's freedom of action, by committing Italy to follow another power into a war, by disregarding the British navy, which was dominant in the Mediterranean and capable of striking the long and vulnerable Italian coastline, and by turning against the French, who shared powerful cultural traditions with Italians.

Furthermore, Hitler's word meant little, even to the people he professed to admire. As the Polish crisis heated up, Mussolini repeatedly tried to convince Hitler to back off. When World War II broke out on September 1, 1939, over the issue of the German minority living in the "Polish Corridor," the Italians reacted with consternation. Foreign Minister Ciano, formerly pro-German, accused the Germans of lying to and tricking the Italians. He argued that since Italy had made it clear that it would be several years before it could be prepared for war, German provocations had absolved Italy from its obligations under the Pact of Steel. Fearing for the country and the regime, important Fascist hierarchs, including Grandi, Bottai, Balbo, and De Bono, agreed and advocated disengaging from Hitler. Even pro-German hierarchs were prepared to follow the Duce's lead should he abandon Hitler. A struggle now began to win Mussolini over. Mussolini's mood shifted erratically from disengagement because of German betrayal to intervention on the grounds of "honor." He found it humiliating, after his own boasts and threats of war, not to follow Hitler. Moreover, he never dreamed that Hitler would crush France so quickly, and he calculated that events favored a German success from which he could draw advantages. The Soviet-German "Non-Aggression Pact" pointed to a probable British and French accommodation with Hitler after these two powers had made a good show of not abandoning Poland. However, the lack of military preparedness made Mussolini cautious. He attempted to restrain Hitler, but if the Germans won a quick victory, he wanted a share of the spoils. As time went on, the Duce concluded that in the event of a short war, the lack of Italian military preparation would matter little. The maximum gain at least cost would come by staying out of the conflict but keeping his German connection; if Nazi victory was fast and certain, he would intervene.

Mussolini accomplished the first part of his plan by reminding Hitler that their talks had contemplated war only after 1942. Consequently, the Duce would be willing to fulfill his obligations if the Germans supplied the war matériel that Italy lacked. Hitler asked for a list detailing Italian needs, and Ciano drew up one that, he remarked in his diary, "would kill a bull, if he could read it." When Hitler received the request, he acknowledged that Germany could not meet the Italian requests and stated that he understood Italy's position. Mussolini then declared not neutrality but "nonbelligerence," an ominous term that suggested he would enter the war under the right conditions.

Terrified that they might have to participate in the conflict on the side of the hated Germans, the Italian people rejoiced at the decision. The anti-German wing of Italian fascism campaigned to disengage Italy from the Nazis. Unless a German defeat was imminent, however, all hope of keeping the country out of war was vain. The carefully crafted term "nonbelligerence"—as opposed to "neutrality"—signified continued adherence to the German alliance in view of further developments. As Hitler piled up victory after victory, Mussolini remained loyal to him—and none of the hierarchs could contest the Duce. Mussolini had hitched his star too closely to Hitler to pull away, and he was determined to achieve spectacular gains by military means, according to Fascist doctrine. Furthermore, abandoning Germany would have meant altering the nature of fascism to effect a rapid rapprochement with the democracies. This policy would have implied a sudden reversal of his attitude concerning the "decadent" democracies and suggested a need for domestic reforms that would have transformed his dictatorship into a more conventional conservative regime. Finally, turning against Hitler would likely provoke German military retaliation. In the end, the Duce's own domestic and foreign policies combined to spur him to enter the war on the German side.

THE UNPREPARED WAR

As impressive Nazi victories continued, Mussolini's reluctance to intervene ended. On May 10, 1940, the Germans launched a successful offensive that brought France to its knees within a month. At this point, the question of Italian military preparation became secondary for the Duce because he believed the war would soon end. By the time the deficiencies in the Italian armed forces could be made good, the opportunities offered by a German victory would have passed. In a meeting with military leaders on May 29, Mussolini is reported by Badoglio to have answered the objections of his generals to enter the conflict with the assertion that the war was over and that he needed only a few thousand dead to participate in the peace discussions. Mussolini's conviction that the war would end quickly is further substantiated by his demobilization of military units shortly after he entered the conflict because he wanted the men to return to industry and take advantage of the economic opportunities presented by the war's imminent end!

In his conviction that the war would be a brief one, the Duce began discussing hypothetical dates for Italian intervention—each closer at hand. The ideal time would be late enough to be certain that Britain and France were really defeated, but early enough to substantiate a claim that he had made an important contribution to victory. Mussolini's military advisers had serious misgivings about his decisions but did not express them forcefully to the Duce. Mussolini rejected appeals from the British, French, and Americans to keep out of the conflict and declared war on Britain and France on June 10, 1940.

Italy's extreme unpreparedness, in addition to military errors made by the Duce or generated by Fascist ideology, explains the poor Italian performance in World War II. The previous wars in Ethiopia and Spain had consumed great quantities of war matériel, and other equipment had been handed over to Franco or remained in East Africa. A large proportion of the lost equipment did not begin to be replaced in significant amounts until the 1938–1939 budget cycle, later than the other European belligerents had begun rearming. Moreover, because

Italian industry could not match that of the other European powers, Italy produced the needed arms at a much slower rate. Although Mussolini initially believed that Italy would be ready for war in 1943, it soon became clear that the country could not meet even that target. Finally, financial constraints remained severe. It has been estimated that the Italians spent only 10 percent of the amount of the German total on arms. Faced with the major problems of financing arms acquisitions, of increasing production, and of paying for the great quantities of raw materials that had to be imported to sustain a first-class rearmament program, the government resolved only the first dilemma.

These problems placed a great burden on the armed forces. The army had modernization plans, but owing to financial considerations and the country's limited industrial capacity, they were never carried out. The land forces began the war armed with rifles designed in 1891, a lack of modern artillery, and only light tankettes. The modern idea of *blitzkrieg* was discussed but only partially realized by altering the division structure; without application of the doctrine's other elements, the change only increased the units' vulnerability to attack. In addition, the army suffered from "fascistization" attempts, which, though never completely successful, produced favoritism.

Because the air force was new, modern, romantic, and focused on individual initiative, the Fascists considered it their particular preserve. Led by the dashing Italo Balbo, the air force undertook highly visible prestige flights under his command and won important international competitions during the interwar years, but its great pretensions were accompanied by even greater weaknesses. Even though the Italians possessed in Giulio Douhet perhaps the first theorist in the modern employment of air power, the air force stressed individual derring-do, failed to put modern projects into mass production, slacked off from a technical viewpoint in the years immediately preceding the war, and exhibited a highly competitive spirit with regard to the other armed forces. During World War II, this last point contributed to a lack of coordination with the army and the navy and gravely hampered war operations. Furthermore, Balbo and his successor, Giuseppe Valle, were inclined to exaggerate the numbers and quality of aircraft, and these boasts led to a false sense of security. For example, in 1939, the air force undersecretary claimed more than 5,340 aircraft, but Valle's successor, Francesco Pricolo, stated that only 650 bombers and 190 fighters were in good fighting condition. When the war began, the Italian air force was probably comparable to France's—which had been unable to stand up to the Germans—and inferior to England's.

The navy had a claim to being the most efficient fighting force. It had built itself up considerably during the interwar period and had most successfully resisted Fascist attempts to influence it. Despite these notable accomplishments, however, a heavy-handed rigidity hampered the navy's technical development. Its weaknesses included poor antiaircraft defenses, no air arm of its own and a lack of coordination with the air force, no radar, and a lack of fuel. Although the navy fought well and frequently imaginatively with new and effective weapons such as the midget submarine, its commanders realized that it faced a losing battle against its traditional ally, the British fleet, which was three times as large.

Mussolini's inept leadership compounded the armed forces' weaknesses. In March 1940, Mussolini had delineated a defensive posture for an eventual Italian war effort, reflecting his desire to save his strength to take advantage of a German breakthrough. Since he and the Italian commanders did not trust their German allies, the Duce rejected coordination with the Germans and planned on an independent "parallel" war. The Italians opened hostilities by attacking France, already reeling from the German offensive. Italian unpreparedness took its toll, and the campaign failed. The Italians also attacked the British in the Mediterranean, North Africa, and East Africa, all with scarce results. From the beginning, Mussolini demonstrated a fatal propensity to scatter his forces. He held back badly needed men and equipment from North Africa—important for the capture of the Suez Canal, which would have allowed East Africa to be resupplied—because he wished to take over the Balkans. Hitler, however, vetoed Mussolini's plans: he feared giving the British an excuse for setting up bases there, providing the Soviets with a pretext to get involved, and hampering the delivery of supplies to the Reich. Later, Mussolini insisted on sending an Italian army to fight in Russia. Such a force could not make a decisive contribution there, but the men and equipment might have made a difference in North Africa, or at least given the British a harder time. The need to give attention to several major theaters of operation, including the Balkans, Russia, and North and East Africa, not only weakened the army's action everywhere but rendered it incapable of defending the homeland.

Soon after Hitler vetoed Mussolini's plans in the Balkans, he moved into Romania. This action infuriated the Duce, and he vowed to retaliate by attacking Greece. He exclaimed: "Hitler always presents me with a fait accompli. This time, I'll do the same thing. He'll find out from the newspapers that I have occupied Greece."

The Greek attack turned out to be a grave blunder. The invasion was not seriously planned because Mussolini pushed it forward in great haste to prevent Hitler from vetoing the operation. The chiefs of staff of all the services opposed the invasion and made their reasons known to chief of staff Pietro Badoglio, who agreed in private but did not present their opposition forcefully to the Duce. Military disaster resulted. The Italian move meant that the British could set up Greek bases from which to bomb southern Italy and the vital Romanian oil fields; when the Germans intervened, setting the Balkans aflame, the Nazis were forced to postpone the attack on Russia. With the Italians still reeling from the Greek debacle, the British unleashed a great North African offensive in January 1941 that inflicted dangerous defeats on them. Italian East Africa, cut off from resupply, capitulated by November 1941, despite a heroic resistance. These developments spelled the end of Italy's "parallel war," and the Germans descended to rescue the Italians in North Africa as well. From now on, the conflict became a German-directed war. The Italian army and diplomatic service, however, honorably resisted repeated demands by their allies to hand over Jews in their occupation zones for transport to concentration camps; despite their own military inferiority, they spared no effort to protect them.

After American intervention, the tide of war turned; on July 10, 1943, the Anglo-Americans landed in Sicily.

This development stunned a country already hard hit by the war. The conflict had reduced real salaries to subsistence level. Starvation threatened great numbers of people, especially city dwellers. Lengthy work shifts in war-related industries, the flourishing black market, and the extremely cold winter of 1942 caused mounting unrest and claimed many lives. Allied bombardments destroyed houses, killed and maimed citizens, and caused intolerable living conditions. Rising popular disaffection with Mussolini and the war alarmed government authorities, who felt it necessary to make some economic concessions. These proved inadequate, however, and in March 1943 widespread strikes broke out in Turin, Milan, and other important industrial centers—the only ones to affect Axis or occupied Europe during the war. Economic distress was the major cause of these strikes, but Communist, Socialist, and anti-Fascist activity during these actions alarmed Italian authorities and the Germans. Although the industrialists granted pay raises after the strikes, disaffection remained widespread.

The strikes provided big business and other supporters of fascism with a good reason to back away from Mussolini. As the war went sour, important Fascist hierarchs became convinced that Mussolini's removal from power was essential to disengage Italy from Germany and to forestall a catastrophe. The Duce could be dislodged only with the king's support because the monarch retained supreme constitutional authority and the army's loyalty. Even though dispirited by defeat, the army was still formidable enough to carry off a coup d'état against Mussolini. These conditions produced a bloc of Fascist hierarchs favoring an appeal to the king to take control of the country. This group, which included Grandi, Ciano, Bottai, Federzoni, De Vecchi, and De Bono, communicated its disaffection to the king. In a report to SS commander Heinrich Himmler, SS colonel Eugen Dollmann commented that in case of a conflict with the king, Mussolini "could only count on about 150 bodyguards armed with pistols."

The revolt against Mussolini occurred at a dramatic meeting of the Fascist Grand Council that lasted from 5:15 PM on July 24, 1943, to 2:40 AM the next day.

PORTRAITS

DINO GRANDI
"Non-Fascist" Fascist

∽∞∾

The man who presented what amounted to a motion of no confidence in Mussolini at the famous Fascist Grand Council meeting of July 24–25, 1943, was a close ally of the Duce from the beginning of the movement.

Dino Grandi, perhaps the most polished and respected Fascist, was born at Mordano (Bologna) on June 4, 1895. He came from a well-off peasant family with leftist sympathies and was an altar boy. Originally a Socialist sympathizer, he became attracted to Benito Mussolini and his Fascist movement. In October 1920, the "Reds" destroyed his office, after which he became a hard-line Fascist and one of the movement's most active local leaders. He later became a moderate who advocated traditional policies and even suggested alliances with more traditional political forces because he considered fascism a transitory phenomenon.

Unhappy with this attitude, Mussolini cast him into the political wilderness until 1924, when he became vice president of the Chamber of Deputies. Mussolini appointed him undersecretary of foreign affairs in 1925 and, on September 12, 1929, foreign minister.

On July 20, 1932, Mussolini took over control of the Foreign Ministry and named Grandi ambassador to England. During his seven years in London, Grandi made close and permanent contacts with the most important British officials, who appreciated his sophisticated diplomacy. Unlike Mussolini, Grandi gained a real understanding of international realities and the limits of Italian action. Grandi frequently acted independently of Rome, disregarding or ignoring Mussolini's directives. The Duce came to the verge of removing Grandi, but considered him too valuable. Grandi's behind-the-scenes diplomacy, for example, was responsible for the favorable terms of the Hoare-Laval proposals and for the failure of petroleum to appear on the list of items that the League had prohibited Italy from receiving during the Ethiopian conflict. In 1936 and 1937, Grandi engineered a rapprochement between Britain and Italy and in 1938 was behind Neville Chamberlain's appeal to Mussolini that resulted in the Munich Conference, which postponed World War II. Grandi believed that if war came, Italy should participate on the Anglo-French side against Germany. For this reason, when Mussolini signed the "Pact of Steel" with Hitler, he recalled Grandi from London in deference to his ally.

When the conflict went badly for Italy, Grandi entered into conversations with the king about the possibility of removing Mussolini. Grandi's motion, in contrast to another one under discussion, was important for its reference to the Constitution, which provided the king with legal cover to remove the Duce.

In January 1944, a Fascist court in Verona sentenced Grandi to death in absentia. In 1947, a special court investigating Fascist officials also issued a death sentence against him. Grandi, however, had already escaped to São Paolo, Brazil, where he engaged in successful business ventures. Returning to Italy in the 1950s, he established a model agricultural enterprise and avoided politics. He died peacefully in Bologna, on May 21, 1988—at age ninety-three—the last Fascist-era hierarch.

In preparation for the meeting, Grandi drew up a motion that called upon the Duce to surrender his powers to the king for the country's good. Grandi had hoped to secure Mussolini's acceptance of the motion's substance without convoking the Grand Council, but the Duce refused on the grounds that the Germans possessed a "secret weapon" that would reverse the conflict's fortunes. The Grand Council meeting produced heated debate and acceptance of Grandi's motion by a vote of 19 to 7.

Mussolini's behavior has puzzled observers because he could have refused to convoke the Fascist Grand Council, as he had refused to do since December 1939, and because he seems to have been particularly passive during the attempt to remove him. But the session seems to have had its origins in Mussolini's attempts to quell internal opposition following the defeat of his armies. As to his passiveness, he appears to have had no option; besides convincing his own men to retain him, he could only have made a humiliating appeal to his German allies for protection.

After the vote, Mussolini had no choice but to bring the motion to Victor Emanuel III and to convince the sovereign to accept a compromise. He made an appointment to see the king at 5:00 PM on July 25. At 11:00 AM that day, the king had already appointed Badoglio head of a military government without informing the Duce, and plans were drawn up for army units, the carabinieri, and the police to occupy key ministries, communication centers, and strategic locations in the capital. When Mussolini arrived for the appointment, a car carrying his bodyguards remained outside the gate as he drove in to talk with Victor Emanuel. At the meeting, the monarch informed the Duce that he had decided to replace him with Badoglio. As the shocked Mussolini walked out of the villa, two carabinieri requested that he follow them for his own protection. The Duce was ushered into an ambulance and arrested.

Finding their communications cut and feeling dispirited and disoriented, Mussolini's remaining Fascist supporters dispersed—fleeing to the German embassy, submitting to arrest, or surrendering. Neither the Fascist Party nor the militia rose to defend the Duce during the ensuing uprisings and demonstrations that shook the country. Crowds destroyed Fascist Party offices and symbols and demanded an end to the war. Workers walked off their jobs and listened to anti-Fascist orators released from the jails. The Badoglio government dissolved the PNF and repealed Fascist measures, but it feared that the demonstrations would develop into a Communist or Republican-led revolution, and it ordered the armed forces to fire on the demonstrators.

Besides suppressing a possible revolution, Badoglio and the king faced the major problems of avoiding German retaliation and preserving the dynasty. Furious with Mussolini's overthrow, Hitler wanted to order the immediate arrest of the "traitors," but his advisers persuaded him to wait until German forces could move into Italy. To calm the Germans, Badoglio announced on July 25 that "the war continues." Badoglio rejected immediate abandonment of the German alliance—insistently demanded by newly reconstituted anti-Fascist associations and the people—on the grounds that doing so would provoke a harsh German military response. In fact, had the government quickly turned against the Germans while the Italians had military superiority in central and southern Italy, it probably would have succeeded in acquiring control of at least a large part of the country, sparing the Italians great suffering and the Allies a year's hard fighting. Instead, several high-level meetings between Italian and German officials took place at which they reciprocally attempted to deceive each other by agreeing that they were still allies.

Badoglio also initiated talks with the Anglo-Americans, stalling for time because of the feared German reaction and irritating the Allies as well. Among other things, the delay prevented a coordinated attack with Allied airborne troops to save the capital from German occupation. At the same time, Badoglio and the king did nothing to stop German troops from pouring into Italy or to prepare the army for a military confrontation with them. No orders went out to the forces in the field, and the government informed them that an armistice had been arranged with the Allies only when it was too late to react. The announcement of an armistice with the Allies on September 8, 1943, provoked a German attack. Italian troops around Rome resisted the Germans for a time, but the lack of orders made the fight futile. While the battle raged, the king, the royal family, and Badoglio fled ignominiously to Allied-occupied Brindisi. The Germans also suddenly attacked their former allies in the various occupation areas, and the army dissolved. Some soldiers left for home, others fought the Germans until overwhelmed and taken prisoner or executed, and others joined the Resistance in Italy or in the countries where they were stationed. On the Greek island of Cephalonia, fierce fighting occurred between Italians and Germans, and the German army (not Nazis) brutally executed the survivors after they surrendered. These dramatic events set the stage for the Resistance, the elimination of the monarchy, and the establishment of the Republic.

THE RESISTANCE

On September 12, 1943, German commando Otto Skorzeny liberated Mussolini from his mountaintop prison in a daring rescue. Hitler then set up the Duce in German-occupied Italy, transformed into the puppet Italian Social Republic (RSI), commonly called the Salò Republic. Here the dispirited Mussolini attempted to create a functioning state but failed. His anger with the "bourgeoisie" for having overthrown him led to the reemergence of his youthful anticapitalism. The most rabid Fascists followed Mussolini to his truncated domain and zealously cooperated with the Nazis in their hunt for opponents, who were executed. Among those Mussolini had killed were his former foreign minister and son-in-law, Galeazzo Ciano, and others who had voted against him at the Grand Council meeting of July 25 who could be apprehended. In all of German-occupied Italy, the hunt for Jews and their deportation to German concentration camps began, along with non-Jewish Italians.

The disasters that fascism caused created perhaps the most widespread and influential Resistance movement of occupied western Europe. This movement had its origins in the opposition that had built up against fascism beginning in the 1920s. In October 1941 in Toulouse, an alliance between Socialists, Communists, and GL (Justice and Liberty) strengthened cooperation among the major anti-Fascist exile parties. As the war turned against the Axis, anti-Fascists set up committees representing Socialists, Communists, liberals, Christian Democrats, "Demoliberali" (the old Radicals), and Actionists (the GL political party). As Mussolini settled into the RSI, local Committees of National Liberation (CLNs) took charge of the Resistance and centralized themselves under more important committees in Rome—headed by the moderate Ivanoe Bonomi—and a radical Milanese body, the Committee of National Liberation for North Italy (CLNAI), for the North. The Rome committee delegated the armed struggle to a military junta composed of Luigi Longo, a Communist; Sandro Pertini, a Socialist; and Riccardo Bauer, an Actionist. These committees operated under extreme danger and were distrusted by the British, who pursued an openly pro-monarchist policy, and the Americans, who were particularly suspicious of their Communist or leftist orientation.

In January 1944, the Socialists, Communists, and Actionists proposed abolition of the monarchy but encountered predictable resistance from the Christian Democrats and other conservative CLN parties. Unable to secure an endorsement of their policy, the Left parties requested Victor Emanuel's abdication and the establishment of an openly anti-Fascist government; the king refused but, responding to increasing pressure, indicated that he would yield his powers to his son Humbert upon the liberation of Rome. On March 14, however, the Soviet Union formally recognized the Badoglio government. Following through on this policy, the Communist leader, Palmiro Togliatti, returned from exile in Moscow, announced the postponement of the "institutional problem," and advocated a Badoglio-led unity cabinet to drive the Germans out of Italy. Togliatti downplayed the PCI's revolutionary image and set the stage for a "new party" willing to compromise and come to power within a democratic context. This "svolta di Salerno" shocked the country and ignited a fierce debate among leftists, given Badoglio's long collaboration with fascism and his role in Italy's intervention in the war. With the "svolta" came a reshuffling of the Badoglio cabinet in April 1944 and promises by the weakened leftists to delay demands for major social reforms until war's end. The Allies imposed these concessions because they were anxious to preserve the social order.

With Rome's liberation in June 1944 and the transfer of powers from the king to his son (with the title of "lieutenant-general of the realm") came a Socialist decision to reverse the conservative tide by eliminating Badoglio and setting up a cabinet responsible to the CLN. The Socialists demanded that ministers swear allegiance to the CLN, not Humbert, that a law convening a Constituent Assembly be adopted immediately, and that an anti-Fascist civilian take over the War Ministry. This crisis culminated in the replacement of Badoglio by Bonomi, but the Communists and conservatives united to thwart the other Socialist requests.

In the meantime, the military ranks of the Resistance swelled. The movement acquired a social dimension that raised the specter of class war by virtue of the contact it established with peasants and workers. For the moment, the focus was on expelling the Germans, as Nazi-Fascist atrocities—including the slaughter of innocent civilians, the deportation of Italian workers, and the rounding up of Jews—created mass revulsion. In conjunction with the victorious Allied march up the peninsula, an insurrection was touched off in northern Italy by the CLNAI on April 25, 1945. On April 27, Mussolini and his mistress, Claretta Petacci, previously captured by partisans while trying to escape Italy, were executed by partisan commander "Valerio" (Walter Audisio); their bodies were later exposed to the crowd's scorn at a gas station in Milan where fifteen hostages had been executed by the Fascists. Estimates indicate that 40,000 Resistance fighters lost their lives in Italy and that between 12,000 and 15,000 Fascists were killed after the April insurrection that marked the end of hostilities, with other estimates as high as 30,000. Journalist Giampaolo Pansa has claimed that the Communists exploited their military superiority and the chaos following the war's end to kill thousands of non-Fascist Resistance fighters in order to eliminate as many rivals as possible for the future political control of the country.

In the euphoria of liberation, the CLNAI revived demands for a purge of Fascists and demanded the end of the Bonomi cabinet. Bonomi could not withstand this "wind from the North." Partisan commander Ferruccio Parri replaced him as prime minister, with Socialist leader Pietro Nenni as vice premier and minister for the Constituent Assembly, Togliatti as justice minister, and Christian Democrat Alcide De Gasperi as foreign minister. The government's program included punishing Fascist supporters, reconstructing the Italian economy, redistributing the wealth, an exchange of the currency, a graduated income tax, a capital tax, and allocation of raw materials in a manner favoring small firms over large.

This program raised havoc among conservatives. Communists and Socialists had a preeminent position within the Resistance movement, and they had achieved considerable local power, but the partisans were no match for the Allied armies, which controlled the peninsula militarily and politically and, despite the partisan contribution, had won the war. In addition, although personally respected, Parri belonged to the Action Party, composed of intellectuals with scant popular support and on its way to extinction. Business interests not only opposed the government's program but also feared continued occupation of factories by workers and partisans, who claimed to have saved them from destruction by the Germans. This tense situation spelled the end of the Parri government, which fell under Allied and conservative pressure. On a visit to Italy, the Italian-American banker A. P. Giannini criticized Parri and warned that American loans essential for the country's survival would not be forthcoming as long as partisans occupied the factories. Allied support aided the liberals in bringing the cabinet down. In the succeeding cabinets headed by De Gasperi, the liberals attained a stranglehold over economic policy.

Many Italians who fought in the Resistance believed it would be the starting point of a social revolution. Probably this hope was doomed from the beginning because Allied armies dominated the country. Indirect Allied support allowed the conservatives to postpone indefinitely the economic provisions of the Parri government, end the purge of former Fascists and regular administrative officials tainted by fascism, and replace CLN-nominated local authorities with traditional officials. Whether or not a revolutionary situation—or even the conditions for radical reforms—ever existed, it ended with Parri's fall, which "marked the comeback of all the old conservative forces in Italian society."

PART SIX

The Republic

CHAPTER EIGHTEEN

The Structure of Postwar Italy

F ASCISM AND WORLD WAR II LEFT ITALY A TROUBLED LEGACY. NOT ONLY had the war been lost in an inglorious manner, but the country's participation in the conflict had had no moral or diplomatic justification. In addition, the Resistance prolonged the aspects of civil warfare initiated by the Fascist regime in 1922. The division of Italy into two regimes—German-controlled in the North and Allied-dominated in the South—increased confusion and exacerbated animosity among Italians. The creation of an Italian army in the South to fight alongside the Allies, designed to refurbish Italy's image, helped perpetuate the stereotype of Italian "treachery," and the Resistance, even though it did much to save Italian honor, hardly reversed hostile Western opinion. Indeed, the Communist-dominated Resistance caused the Allied victors considerable worry.

The Resistance, however, allowed anti-Fascists to claim credit for overthrowing Mussolini and the mission of ruling Italy. But twin fears threatened the future—a Fascist resurgence or a Soviet-style dictatorship. Right and Left evaluated these threats and their implications differently, and their contrasting judgments determined the country's postwar destiny.

A DEVASTATED LAND—AND THE "GOLDEN AGE"

To contemporaries, Italy at war's end presented a desolate picture. Combat deaths had been fewer than in World War I, but the bombings and fierce fighting on Italian territory more than made up the difference among civilians, and 1.5 million deportees and prisoners of war were not finally repatriated until 1947. Of the 31 million rooms available to the population before the conflict, 6.7 million had been either destroyed or damaged. In the North, electricity functioned 90 percent of the time, but in the South it was less than 45 percent and in parts of the Center, where the worst fighting had occurred, electricity was available only 3 percent of the time. Another crucial economic sector, transport, had been hard hit: the once-proud merchant marine was reduced to one-tenth of its prewar size, the railway system worked at 40 percent efficiency, and the trucking industry operated at 35 percent. The economic indexes reflected this situation. With 1938 equal to 100, in 1945 the index for industrial production stood at 29; the corresponding figure for agriculture was 63, and for national income 51.9. The black market flourished, and starvation stalked the civilian population.

In reality, statistics painted the country's portrait inaccurately. The pre-Fascist and Fascist periods had created a robust industrial infrastructure. The success of the Fascist regime in bringing industry and production methods up to European standards has already been noted. Northern industry had survived German plans to transfer or destroy it, thanks to the efforts first of the RSI (Italian Social Republic) economics minister, Angelo Tarchi, and then the Resistance. According to the minister of reconstruction, Meuccio Ruini, lack of raw materials, transport, and other collateral elements accounted for the low index of industrial production, not destroyed plant; he estimated that production would have been at 75 to 80 percent of the 1938 figure had it not been for those factors, which were more easily corrected than rebuilding factories.

In addition to plant, the previous regime had bequeathed a legacy of ambitious projects, trained engineers, skilled workers, and a low-wage labor force. In the 1930s and 1940s, the workers' depressed buying power and the wartime economy had handicapped industry's ability to expand to its potential. After World War II, the new Western economic order imposed by the United States—which produced a sixfold increase in international trade between 1950 and 1970—created the premise for removal of these limits. Italian success in achieving a moderate, pro-Western democratic regime allowed Italian industry to exploit its solid base and to become a leader in the Atlantic world's unprecedented economic development. The massive movement of low-wage workers from the South to the North, from less efficient enterprises to more modern ones, and from agriculture to industry also provided a great reserve of labor that enormously enhanced the competitiveness of Italian industry on the world market. In real terms, Italian GNP (gross national product) increased at a yearly average of about 5 percent between 1950 and 1980. This figure surpassed the corresponding figures for the United States and Britain, matched those of France and Germany, and eventually built the country into the world's fifth-largest industrial power. A revolution half a century in the making, and based on the restoration of democracy, this "economic miracle" transformed the country.

The Anti-Fascist Alliance Breaks Up

The six anti-Fascist parties of the Committees of National Liberation collaborated in the government from the last two years of the war until May 1947. Two of them, the Action Party and the Demoliberals, did not survive the immediate postwar era. The Liberal Party (Partito Liberale Italiano, PLI), although small, inherited a great European tradition and, through its most noted economist and a future president of the republic, Luigi Einaudi, dominated economic policy in the immediate postwar period.

The Christian Democrats (DC), heirs of Luigi Sturzo's *popolari*, emerged as the largest Italian party under the leadership of Alcide De Gasperi, the last PPI (Italian Popular Party) secretary. Reborn in 1942, the Catholic Party believed that Christian values could resolve modern society's tensions. It supported small property holders and small business and opposed big capitalists. It sank deep roots into Italian society by founding an association of peasant landowners, the Coldiretti (under Paolo Bonomi), and a Christian workers' association (Associazioni Cristiane Lavoratori Italiani, ACLI). These institutions, soon joined by the 2 million–strong Catholic Action organization, and the Vatican's support established the party's credentials as a mass organization. The DC's appeal to the poor, along with traditional Catholic concern for the disinherited and the robust left-wing Catholic ideology of philosopher Giuseppe Dossetti, appealed also to Communists and Socialists, who theorized a working-class alliance regardless of party affiliation. The uncertain Communist attitude toward small property holders and Catholic hostility to the Soviet system, however, made Catholics the sworn enemies of Communists and their Socialist allies. An incalculable advantage for the DC was De Gasperi himself, a shrewd moderate who stood between a Vatican hoping to impose its wishes and the DC left. De Gasperi's willingness to compromise with secular political groups and the powerful Christian Democratic appeal within Italian society induced industrialists to deemphasize their traditional Liberal connections and link up with the DC to combat communism.

Strong Marxist influence stemming from the Communist role in the Resistance represented the real novelty of postwar Italian politics and society. During the first postwar era, leftist Socialists and Communists had pursued a policy of intransigence and verbal revolution that had contributed to the rise of fascism. Now Communists and Socialists participated in the government and, dissuaded by the presence of Allied troops, Togliatti vetoed the Socialist idea of a revolution based on popular Resistance organizations. He advocated a new party capable of appealing to the masses, arguing that a revolution was impossible in Allied-controlled Western Europe. Whether this principle was Togliatti's or imposed by Stalin, as argued by historian Sergio Bertelli, is a matter of dispute, but influential and rank-and-file hard-line Communists accepted the policy as a method of obtaining an electoral majority based on reform while adhering to a secret revolutionary agenda. Communist officials denied this "double-track" policy, but even Togliatti's attitude appeared ambivalent, as illustrated by a speech to the Constituent Assembly during which he renounced violence, but only for "today." At

PORTRAITS

ÁLCIDE DE GÁSPERI
Architect of Reconstruction

ഛഛ

At the end of World War II, Italy had the good fortune to have at its helm one of the outstanding European statesmen who came to the fore after the conflict. Alcide De Gasperi rebuilt his country, put it solidly in the Atlantic camp, and has gone down in history as a father of united Europe.

Born on April 3, 1881, at Pieve Tesino (Trentino) of middle-class parents in what was then Austria-Hungary, Alcide De Gasperi graduated from the University of Vienna in 1905. De Gasperi was active in the Catholic social movement of the Italian-speaking Trentino and fought for its administrative autonomy in the Austrian Parliament, to which he won election in 1911.

After World War I, the Trentino became part of Italy. De Gasperi entered Don Luigi Sturzo's Popular Party (PPI) and in 1921 was elected to the Italian Parliament. He advocated PPI collaboration with reformist Socialists to block Mussolini's coming to power, but Pope Pius XI vetoed the idea. During the Matteotti crisis, he participated in the Aventine Secession and lost his parliamentary seat. The police arrested him in 1927; after his release in 1929, he began work in the Vatican library, becoming its secretary despite Mussolini's attempts to have him fired. In 1942, he took steps to revive the PPI, calling the new formation the Christian Democratic Party.

In December 1945, De Gasperi became prime minister. He presided over the referendum that ended the monarchy and made Italy a republic on June 2, 1946, was premier during the discussions for a new Italian constitution, and negotiated a peace treaty with the Allies.

In May 1947, De Gasperi traveled to the United States and returned home with a promise of American aid to help reconstruct his country. De Gasperi reorganized his cabinet, excluding the Communists and Nenni Socialists. There followed a difficult political campaign leading up to the crucial elections of April 1948, which he won. De Gasperi made use of Catholic Action (a politically active and influential lay Catholic group) and the influence of the Catholic Church to win the balloting, but considered his party an organization of the center that would eventually move to the left.

During his tenure, which lasted until the summer of 1953, De Gasperi made many controversial decisions. In 1949, he endorsed Italian entrance into NATO despite a vociferous campaign against it by the Popular Front parties. By favoring a mixed economy and agrarian reform, he lost liberal support. De Gasperi also made the country an important actor in the move toward European unity when he brought Italy into the European Coal and Steel Community and the Council of Europe. In 1953, De Gasperi favored a new law that would have awarded the parties that received 50.01 percent of the vote a premium in Parliament, but the Left denounced it as the "swindle law."

De Gasperi's coalition failed to win a stable majority in the 1953 elections. De Gasperi died on August 19, 1954, in Sella Valsugana and was buried in the Church of San Lorenzo Outside-the-Walls.

any rate, in 1948 it seemed to friend and foe alike that the Marxist parties had an excellent shot at winning a majority in free elections.

The Socialist Party regenerated itself after fascism's fall, despite the heavy burden it carried of having failed to stop Mussolini's rise. As minister for the Constituent Assembly in the De Gasperi cabinet, Pietro Nenni was instrumental in setting a date for national elections and securing a referendum on whether the monarchy should be eliminated. Another Socialist, Interior Minister Giuseppe Romita, reduced the banditry and political violence that plagued postwar Italy, ensuring peaceful conditions for elections and countering a powerful argument for their possible postponement or nullification. On June 2, 1946, the referendum and national elections for a Constituent Assembly took place; they instituted a republic and established the Socialist Party as the country's most popular leftist organization.

The Socialists proved unable to maintain their position for three major reasons: the Communist connection, the Socialists' divisions, and the inability to match the financial support that the big powers funneled to their Catholic and Communist rivals. Led by Giuseppe Saragat, the Socialist right wing believed the Socialist Party should sever its alliance with the PCI and become explicitly social democratic, as had the parties in other Western European countries. Convinced that there would be a resurgence of fascism if Communists and Socialists were divided, Nenni rejected this idea and advocated instead a Popular Front alliance, as had been constituted in France in 1935. This debate produced a disastrous split in January 1947 at a Socialist congress held in Rome. Saragat founded the Social Democratic Party (PSDI), which over the years became a splinter organization tied to the government. With his great rival out of the party, Nenni and his ally Rodolfo Morandi established the Popular Front alliance with the Communists and reversed Socialist tradition by reorganizing the PSI on the Communist Party model—a dictatorial organization in which no one could question leadership decisions. The Communists quickly seized advantage of the divisions to wrest control of the leftist labor union, the Confederazione Generale Italiana di Lavoro (CGIL), and the League of Cooperatives and Mutual Aid Societies. With PCI domination of the PSI, hope for substantial middle-class support for the Socialists evaporated, and they lived on handouts from the well-heeled Communists subsidized by the Soviet Union. In Italy, contrary to what happened in the rest of Western Europe, the Communists achieved political and intellectual hegemony on the left.

These developments reflected the international situation, where the wartime alliance between the Western powers and the Soviet Union had given way to the Cold War. According to James Miller, U.S. policy after World War II focused on a postwar world based on stabilization and democracy. The Americans could not allow a Soviet-dominated force to come to power in Italy, a country with historical ties to the United States and strategically placed astride the Mediterranean with its close proximity to the oil-rich Middle East. Understanding that the Socialists were unavailable for dialogue and viewing an extremist government as a blow to their design for political stabilization and economic prosperity, the Americans turned to the Christian Democrats.

The superpowers' Italian struggle culminated in 1947 and 1948. In January 1947, the head of the Italian government, De Gasperi, visited the United States without Foreign Minister Nenni. There is a difference of opinion as to whether the decision to oust the Marxist parties from the government was made explicit during De Gasperi's trip, was implicit in his talks with American officials, or emerged as an outright condition of further American financial aid. In May, De Gasperi ousted the Communists and Socialists from the cabinet. In October, the Soviets established the new Communist International, the Cominform, which chastised the Italian and the French parties for being too prone to compromise and initiated a period of greater confrontation: "The era of antifascist coalitions was over and that of the Cold War had begun."

In response to the virulent Popular Front electoral campaign against the United States, the American embassy in Rome estimated the Front's electoral strength at 40 percent and judged the Italian situation "extremely dangerous." Aware of massive Russian aid to the PCI—Ambassador James Dunn reported a Communist electoral budget of 3 billion lire in the three northern industrial provinces alone—and convinced that the Communists harbored insurrectionary designs, Secretary of Defense James Forrestal, supported by President Harry Truman, authorized clandestine action. Fitting within the Truman Doctrine's general framework, Italy became the major theater of American intervention. In November 1947, the National Security Council (NSC) recommended an interruption in the rate of American troop withdrawals if the Communists took power anywhere in Italy before December 15. The NSC also authorized Central Intelligence Agency (CIA) operations in Italy. An installment of $10 million secretly entered a fund for anti-Communist activities, for bribes, and for influencing elections. Aid arrived through other avenues as well. In view of the crucial national elections scheduled for April 18, 1948, American officials threatened a cutoff of aid should the Front win and stimulated a letter-writing campaign by Italian Americans to their relatives in Italy.

Front leaders believed they had an excellent chance for victory, but the campaign by the Christian Democrats and their American supporters proved extremely effective. Revulsion against Communist totalitarianism and the conviction of many voters that they risked putting another dictatorship in place worked against the Front, as did the threat of reduced aid. The same period witnessed the overthrow of the Czech government and the establishment of Communist regimes in Eastern

Europe by the Red Army, and this Soviet activity influenced the Italian elections. When the results came in, the Christian Democrats alone had won 48.4 percent of the vote, which allowed them to rule without allies if they wished. The Popular Front did much poorer than expected, capturing only 31 percent of the vote. The Socialist share of this figure came to only 10 percent, bringing it even more forcefully under PCI domination and cementing the "Italian anomaly": a Communist Party that was much larger than the Socialist.

The 1948 elections ended the immediate postwar era. The anti-Fascist alliance had broken up, and given the fear of a Communist takeover and American opposition to a Communist presence in the government, the DC remained the fulcrum of politics in Italy for the next forty-five years.

The Structure of Postwar Italy

On June 2, 1946, a close vote in an institutional referendum had eliminated the monarchy and established a republic. The voters also elected a Constituent Assembly to govern the country and draft a constitution. This body overwhelmingly approved the new constitution on December 22, 1947, stipulating that it should take effect on January 1, 1948.

The major forces represented in the Constituent Assembly and their percentages were: Christian Democrats, 35.2; Socialists, 20.7; and Communists, 18.9. This split guaranteed that the new constitution would be a product of compromise. The document incorporated democratic and social principles enunciated in other postwar European constitutions, reestablished where possible the governmental structure of pre-Fascist Italy, and instituted measures to prevent a relapse into dictatorship.

Since the leftist parties were unable to transmute the Resistance into the revolution to which they had constantly appealed, the Constituent Assembly allowed them to write the hope of future change into the constitution. For this reason, and because of the strong leftist affinity with Catholic social thought, social principles protecting less-advantaged citizens were written into the constitution. Theoretically, this incorporation permitted the Left to pass specific legislation making those principles real should it receive enough support in the country; practically, however, it embarrassed future cabinets, whose actions could never measure up to the principles.

The constitution declared Italy a democratic republic "founded on labor," gave sovereignty to the people, promised social equality, and proclaimed that citizens and groups possessed inviolable rights. In accordance with the evolution of Western political thought, it pledged to demolish economic and social obstacles that hindered workers from effectively participating in the country's political and economic order, blocked personal development, and prevented the attainment of true equality. To achieve these goals, the constitution refused to accord private property the status of an absolute right, recognizing it but emphasizing its social obligations and limitations. Furthermore, although favoring free initiative, the constitution provided for nationalization of important industries on the grounds of utility and allowed for the possibility of a massive land reform program. Included also was a promise of full employment. In short, the constitution provided for a mixed economy with a large dose of public participation and the basis of a welfare state; in this it continued the work of previous regimes but went beyond them.

Besides these principles dear to Marxist and Catholic thinkers alike, the Constituent Assembly accepted provisions designed to please the Catholics. The most important made the Lateran Accords of 1929 an integral part of the constitution. Besides the anomaly of incorporating a treaty with a foreign state into a country's constitution, this move created major problems for the future by blocking divorce until 1970–1974, sanctioning the heavy interference of the Church in public education, violating the rights of former clergy, and discriminating against other religions. Fearing criticism and alienation of Catholic opinion, the Communists split with their Socialist allies and voted with the Christian Democrats in favor of instituting into law this most backward aspect of the constitution. Bowing to another Catholic concern, the Assembly also adopted provisions favoring the family.

In the political arena, the constitution followed the principle of restoring pre-Fascist institutions where possible, modernizing them where necessary, and attempting to create a governmental structure that would resist the creation of a future dictatorship. Essentially, this technique involved creating a weak governmental structure that no one group could dominate, thus opening the road to inefficiency. This principle is at the origin of the famous governmental instability of the republic, which, however, did not prevent the political longevity of individuals and the shifting of political power to the parties.

To begin, the new constitution differed from the 1848 Statuto in being a "closed" document that could no longer be modified by ordinary legislation passed by Parliament. The Fascists had manipulated the Statuto through the legislative process to build their dictatorship. The new republican instrument resembled the American constitution rather than the British in that legislation had to be judged for its adherence to constitutional principles. This structure mandated a high court to make these decisions, the Constitutional Court— a new body consisting of fifteen judges sitting for a limited term and chosen separately by the president of the republic, Parliament, and high judicial groups. In effect, this provision weakened the Parliament when compared to the pre-Fascist period.

As before, Parliament consisted of two bodies. The Chamber of Deputies was reinstituted practically as it had existed before Mussolini. The Chamber consists of 630 members, and its usual term is five years, but it can be dissolved earlier and new elections held under certain conditions. The Senate, previously appointed by the king, became elective. Consisting of 315 senators, the Senate's functions parallel those of the Chamber; since there has never been a clear rationale for its existence, the reform and even elimination of the Senate has been a constant theme of debate in postwar Italy. Although the Senate is theoretically entitled to a longer term, it is dissolved along with the Chamber of Deputies. The powers of the Italian Parliament resemble those of the Third and Fourth French Republics: the body is responsible for legislation, approves the budget, ratifies treaties, declares war, and conducts investigations into important matters. Its most important function, however, is to create a government and to vote confidence in it.

Officially the government or cabinet is known as the Council of Ministers, and its head carries the title of President of the Council of Ministers (referred to herein as the prime minister, or the premier, to avoid confusion with the president of the republic). In accordance with the principle of avoiding a future dictatorship, the constitutional framers reversed Fascist practice and made the cabinet dependent on parliamentary whim. The republican cabinet has thus been a weak institution. The prime minister-designate is nominated by the president of the republic after a wide round of consultations. Although the president is bound to nominate the person with the most obvious chance of success, the Italian political system and the constitution provide some leeway and confer more prominence on the Italian president than did the corresponding offices in Germany and in the Fourth French Republic, which ended in 1958. Once chosen, the cabinet must obtain a vote of confidence (a majority vote) in both houses. Far from determining the cabinet's policy, the prime minister is the first among equals and rules by consensus; this is a difficult and frequently impossible task given the cabinet's usual composition of temporarily allied parties and/or factions continually jockeying for position. The government has no fixed term and can be formally overthrown at any time by a no-confidence vote in either house. Add to this factor "pure" proportional representation, in force until 1992, which produced only slender majorities; factionalized parties and secret voting, which permitted deputies to take cover while voting against major legislation, perhaps sanctioned by their own party, without fear of political retribution; and the exclusion of a large bloc of representatives for the formation and support of governments (Socialist and Communist up to 1963, for the Socialists, Communist thereafter), and the premise was set for governmental instability throughout the Cold War. Pure proportional representation (described later) allowed representation of very small groups in Parliament and caused great instability; not until the explosion of a serious corruption scandal did the Italians modify it in 1992 (and several times thereafter), making 75 percent of Parliament subject to election by a majority. If a cabinet lost a vote of confidence in Parliament, the old government remained as a caretaker unable to take major policy decisions while the interminable process of forming a new government, frequently with the prospect of only a brief life, began anew. Within this context, however, the parties were able to create a surprising measure of de facto stability, as explained in chapter 19.

The voting system that was set up at the republic's beginning and that underwent continual change after 1992–1993 encouraged instability in national and local administrations (although local elections were modified to ensure more stability). Concern about being able to give different political views a voice in Parliament and in local government after twenty years of Fascist repression explains why the Italians established pure proportional representation. A complex formula saw that parties were represented according to the number of votes they received in the country as a whole, not just in a particular electoral district. No 5 percent barrier to representation existed, as in Germany (although barriers of different kinds were later established). Citizens voted for lists presented by parties, not for candidates, although they could express preferences within those lists (limited to one in 1991 and later eliminated). This procedure gave party establishments immense power because they determined who got onto the lists and the prominence of their positions within those lists. In addition, since no one party held a majority, with the exception of the DC from 1948 to 1953, coalition governments became the rule. Small parties wielded power disproportionate to their numbers because a shift of a few votes could prevent a cabinet from coming to power, maintaining power, or fulfilling its legislative program. Despite attempts to redress this problem in the 1990s, the electoral law under which the 2006 elections were held presented this problem again with a vengeance.

To form a government, a prime minister-designate must negotiate with several parties large and small. Each of these parties has its own treasured items to insert into the government's program and its favorite ministries (government departments). The whole process was extremely complicated during the Cold War because the large Communist Party and, until the late 1950s, the Socialist Party, as well as the neo-Fascist Movimento Sociale Italiano (MSI), were frozen out of ruling coalitions because they were considered undemocratic. This factor enhanced the role of parties with as small as 2 or 3 percent representation. Further complicating this already complex procedure, the parties were usually divided into several feuding currents that might oppose their party's participation in a cabinet for different reasons. Frequently it was impossible to determine a party's position until after a congress that thrashed out competing principles—and often not even then, which meant holding another assembly. Even if a party agreed to vote for a government, that support might evaporate at any time and bring down a cabinet. Despite strong party discipline, parliamentary rules allowing secret votes on crucial issues provided cover for "snipers" in the ruling coalition who wished to shoot down a cabinet against their own party hierarchy's wishes, and a party could always split.

At the local level, this procedure had to be repeated in electing the legislative councils, executive committees, and mayors of the provinces (equivalents of the French departments, but centering on a major capital) and communes and introduced instability there as well. More characteristic of local government was the state's failure to fulfill the constitution's promise of decentralization. Moreover, the prefect, a central government representative dating back to Napoleonic times who had wide powers to interfere with and dissolve local government institutions and to influence elections, hindered local autonomy. Although the prefect's powers tended to diminish over the years, he/she remained a powerful figure. Another unfulfilled promise was partially satisfied in 1970 when equivalents of American state government, the regional governments, were instituted—but their powers have still not been finally defined. Promised in the constitution as a reaction to Fascist centralization, the government refused to establish regional governments because the Communists controlled strategic regions in Central Italy—the Red Belt—and their fate became a major issue during discussions that brought the Socialists into the governing coalition in August 1960.

The failure to institute regional autonomy illustrates a major problem with the 1948 constitution. The Constituent Assembly left many of the principles enunciated in the constitution to be implemented later by enabling legislation. As the long delay in establishing the regions shows, crucial parts of the document were enacted late or not at all. In addition to the delay in setting up regional governments, the Constitutional Court began operations only in 1956, and the magistrates' self-governing body, the Consiglio Superiore della Magistratura (CSM), had to wait until 1958. A related but more serious issue in realizing the constitution's democratic principles was the failure to alter important laws adopted during fascism. Thus, Fascist legislation in criminal matters remained in effect and was modified only piecemeal by specific Constitutional Court decisions before it was finally replaced in 1990; the civil code, although it fared better, was similar.

The Constituent Assembly instituted the president of the republic as the head of state. Elected by a two-thirds majority on any of the first three ballots, with only a majority required thereafter by the Chamber of Deputies and the Senate sitting together, the president resembles a constitutional monarch. The powers of the office are ill defined, and it increases in prominence when Parliament is gridlocked or its prestige is low. The president's right to return legislation for reconsideration, to dissolve Parliament, and to influence the choice of a prime minister-designate is conditioned by the political situation. Furthermore, the constitution provides that to be valid the ministers or the premier must countersign the president's acts. The president's real power stems from his long term of office (seven years), his irremovability (except by impeachment), his ability to persuade, his chairmanship of important bodies such as the CSM, and his supposed position above petty politics.

Rounding out republican Italy's governmental structure is the legal system. Based on career judges who advance on the basis of examinations and qualifications, the magistracy governs itself through the previously noted CSM. The legal system's organization makes the judiciary a more independent and aggressive power than it is in other Western democracies, including the United States. The Constituent Assembly favored independence in order to create another roadblock to possible dictatorship. But although this feature has allowed magistrates to pursue investigations free from interference, it has also produced highly politicized judges who are responsible to no one but themselves, not even the minister of justice. The judges have created their own partisan groups, further compromising the justice system's impartiality.

The method of dispensing justice has exacerbated the tendency toward lack of impartiality, despite lip service to that ideal. There is a very close association between prosecuting attorneys (the *pubblico ministero*), who are magistrates serving in that capacity, and other judges. Furthermore, indictments are handed down not by grand juries but by an investigating judge (the *giudice istruttore*). These magistrates investigate alleged criminal behavior in secret with the help of their favorite police force—competing police forces being another safeguard, at the cost of inefficiency, against a revival of dictatorship. Prosecutors frequently and selectively leak evidence against a defendant, whose guilt the press then publicly proclaims. Moreover, allegations of police brutality have been rife in postwar Italy. In addition to the cozy relationship among police, prosecutors, and judges, there is no real protection against being forced to testify against oneself, no habeas corpus, no guarantee of a speedy trial, and no hard exclusion of hearsay evidence. A favorite technique of investigators is to hold defendants in jail until they implicate others. A defendant's presumption of innocence is at best vague; until lately, Italian law allowed the verdict of "acquitted for lack of proof," a provision that subjected the accused to another trial on the same charge if frustrated prosecutors believed that new proof establishing guilt had been gathered. Crimes punishing free speech, such as criticism of public officials, established institutions, and the pope, have only recently fallen into abeyance.

Although the legal system's insensitivity to civil rights symbolizes the contradiction between the constitution's promises and its reality, the republic has important gains to its credit. It established a generous welfare system, a modern economy in much of the country, and a democratic environment that—despite occasionally sensational cases—has allowed the most diverse opinions to flourish. For interconnected international and domestic reasons, however, the republic has been unable to correct its major deficiencies over time, and this failure threatens its viability, especially after establishment of a common currency and the advent of globalization.

CHAPTER NINETEEN

Postwar Politics: "Imperfect Bipolarism"

T HE EXCLUSION OF THE COMMUNIST PARTY (PCI) FROM THE RULING coalition during the Cold War meant that the Christian Democratic (DC) Party and its allies had a steady majority in Parliament. But as time went on, electoral losses for the DC-led bloc, combined with PCI increases, made the governmental system more unstable, even after the Socialists joined the ruling coalition in the 1960s. These conditions produced a gridlocked political situation that political scientist Giorgio Galli labeled "imperfect bipolarism": because of domestic and international fears that the Communists and their supporters would establish a Soviet-style dictatorship and ally Italy with the Soviet Union should they be entrusted with any degree of governmental participation, the alternation of power became impossible. Because Communists and not Socialists dominated the Italian left, Italy became a "blocked democracy." The long tenure in office of DC-led coalitions favored the inefficiency and corruption that produced the republic's major crises.

CENTRISM

Following World War II, the major items of business for Italy were negotiating a peace treaty, rebuilding a political system, and reconstructing the economy. The first question found a relatively rapid resolution, and the second proved the thorniest; both will be the subject of this chapter. As discussed in chapter 20, the republic would complete the third task beyond everyone's wildest expectations.

Even though the peace treaty allowed the country to put the war behind it because most of the questions were settled, its terms deluded many anti-Fascists because they had expected their opposition to Mussolini, their role in the Resistance, and Italian support of the Allies in the South to placate the antagonism of their country's former enemies.

The territorial provisions of the settlement signed on February 10, 1947, caused the most consternation. Italy lost all of its colonies, a bitter blow, although a blessing considering the money that the country had wasted on them. French border rectifications also hurt Italian pride, but they were minor—and French attempts to annex larger areas were thwarted. In the Northeast, Italy retained its 1919 boundaries despite an Austrian claim. The area in dispute, the South Tyrol, included an ethnic Austrian majority that had prompted Hitler to annex it during the war; later, Italians and Austrians worked out an agreement to respect *Südtiroler* rights, which brought peace to the region despite tensions and periodic flare-ups. The Italian border with Yugoslavia was a different question. The Italian population had been expelled from the prewar boundary areas closest to Yugoslavia and many Italians were murdered; even more menacing, however, the Russians and Italian Communist leader Togliatti supported Marshal Josip Broz Tito's exaggerated claims on the entire region of Venezia Giulia. The Allies drew various lines based on ethnicity; the Italians claimed the most favorable but were forced to accept the least favorable. This solution, exacerbated by an agreement to divide Trieste into Allied and Yugoslav occupation zones, outraged Italians. The emotional dispute occasioned several serious crises with the Americans and Yugoslavs before it was finally resolved in October 1954.

The other peace provisions caused emotional pain but were less significant. The country had to pay reparations, and Italian assets in some countries were also lost. The Italian argument that they had made a substantial financial contribution to the Nazi defeat was rejected; in addition, the country's gold reserve, which had been stolen by the Germans and recovered by the Allies, was not returned intact. The United States, Britain, and France renounced reparations in 1945, but the Soviet Union and the smaller countries making claims against Italy refused to do so. In the context of postwar economic recovery and American aid, however, the economic provisions of the peace had minor practical significance.

The other volatile issue involved limits on the Italian military establishment and the breakup of the Italian fleet. Despite De Gasperi's contention that putting restrictions on fortifications and military hardware and limiting the Italian army—including carabinieri—to 250,000, the navy to 25,000, and the air force to 200 combat planes left the country defenseless, the Allies forced the Italians to accept them. The defense clauses had little practical significance, given the change in the world's military configuration and extension of the American nuclear umbrella to protect the country.

Having disposed of World War II's diplomatic heredity, the country turned to ordinary administration. As mentioned, the DC won a majority of the seats in the Chamber of Deputies in the 1948 elections. De Gasperi could have formed a cabinet consisting exclusively of DC members, as his party's right wing demanded.

De Gasperi wisely resisted this temptation and created instead a Center coalition including, besides the DC, the small secular parties—Liberals (PLI) and the moderate leftist Republicans (PRI) and Social Democrats (PSDI).

This coalition faced a difficult situation. Excluded from power, Communists and Socialists attacked the government at every turn. They vigorously supported Soviet foreign policy, most notably by conducting a raucous campaign in the country and in Parliament against Italian entrance into the North Atlantic Treaty Organization (NATO) in 1949. Socialist leaders publicly approved of the Communist takeover in Czechoslovakia and, symbol of their subservience to the Communists and Soviet foreign policy, also criticized Marshall Plan aid as an instrument of American domination. They called protest strikes and attempted to stop the delivery of supplies. These policies demonstrated Communist manipulation of the labor movement and produced strains in the CGIL, the labor union reorganized in June 1944 to represent workers of all political shades. In July 1948, a general strike was called to protest the attempted assassination of PCI head Palmiro Togliatti. Many Communist workers considered the strike a call to revolution, and the party had to pull them back. Communist policies caused non-Communist labor leaders to break with the Communists and their Socialist allies. Over the next year, a series of splits occurred, and by 1950 the three unions that were to dominate the postwar era had emerged: the Communist-controlled Confederazione Generale Italiana di Lavoro (CGIL), which included the Socialists; the Catholic-influenced Confederazione Italiana dei Sindacati dei Lavoratori (CISL); and the smaller Unione Italiana del Lavoro (UIL), which represented primarily Republicans and Social Democrats.

Communist stimulation of labor protest and escalating unrest caused by unemployment and peasant demands for land prompted a strong reaction. The Christian Democrat interior minister, Mario Scelba, forbade propaganda in the workplace and organized special police squads that specialized in beating up recalcitrant workers. Although these policies further alienated the Left, they brought De Gasperi no peace from conservatives, including Christian Democrats, who demanded that he put down the agitation with even greater firmness and that he outlaw the Communist Party. Conservatives also denounced the prime minister's attempt to address peasant demands through land reform, and their opposition limited its scope. These developments estranged the moderate leftists in the coalition, who also resented the manner in which Christian Democrats appointed members of their party to head public corporations and government-controlled agencies; this policy initiated a perverse tradition that, over the life of the republic, parceled out crucial public-sector jobs according to party affiliation and influence in governing coalitions (*lottizzazione*) rather than on merit.

The small parties generally voted for the cabinets, even though, given DC control of Parliament, the Christian Democrats could have managed without these votes, but as the 1950s progressed by-elections pointed toward a slipping Catholic majority. The Vatican and Catholic Action—led by Pope Pius XII and Luigi Gedda—intensified their intervention in secular affairs. The Church claimed credit for the DC victory of 1948; given the weak DC organization, the party depended on parish priests and Catholic Action committees to organize the voters and get them to the polls. Because of their role, bishops and other clergy felt authorized to influence the choice of important state managers and public policy. This activity further alienated the DC's lay allies and embarrassed De Gasperi, who favored state independence from the Church and, in the words of political scientist Norman Kogan, "fought a hard battle against the clericalization of Italian life."

This struggle culminated after the local elections of 1951–1952, in which the DC share of the vote dropped to 35.1 percent (compared with 48.5 in 1948). On the right, the neo-Fascist Movimento Sociale Italiano (MSI) had absorbed the votes of the Uomo Qualunque (Any Man)—a Fascist-oriented movement opposing all politicians—and along with the Monarchist Party (PNM) tripled its votes. At the same time, the Socialists picked up greater electoral support. These developments led Gedda to propose an alliance with the Extreme Right in Rome and the South. De Gasperi bitterly fought the deal, realizing that a victory in local Rome elections on that basis would produce a powerful demand for a similar coalition on the national level. De Gasperi believed that the DC had a future only if it pursued a progressive social policy. He won the struggle, and the Center coalition formula prevailed, but the fight greatly weakened both De Gasperi and the DC.

The decline in DC support during the 1951–1952 elections indicated that the stable majority possessed by the Center parties would disappear during the 1953 parliamentary contest and that governmental instability would result. To forestall this development, the centrist coalition proposed to alter the electoral system so that the alliance of parties receiving one vote more than 50 percent would receive an "electoral bonus," bringing their seats in the Chamber up to two-thirds of the total. Because of the supposed resemblance of this provision to the Acerbo law, which had been instrumental in consolidating Mussolini's power in 1924, the proposal touched off a bitter brawl in the country and in Parliament. Baptizing the bill the "swindle law," the Left initiated a major campaign against it, but influential moderates such as lawyer Piero Calamandrei also opposed it. The law passed in Parliament after an animated debate, but moderate opponents blocked its implementation by forming an independent group that attracted just enough support during the elections to keep the Center coalition's share of the vote to 49.85 percent.

The predictions of those who had forecast instability came true. Although the Center coalition received a slight majority of seats in Parliament, it lacked a viable majority. All the government parties lost support, and divisions within the individual parties and disputes among them increased in the postelectoral attempt to assign blame. Combined with the increased votes for the Communists and the Extreme Right, these conflicts guaranteed the formation of weak governments. Even Alcide De Gasperi failed to put a cabinet together and retired from politics. A year later he died.

Despite the similarity of the electoral bonus and the Acerbo law, the persons who suggested the 1953 proposal had personally suffered from Fascist repression and, despite leftist accusations, did not plan a return to fascism. Given the instability to which the country has been subject since 1953, other electoral mechanisms that awarded some kind of electoral premium were put forward at different times. The loud voice that the Italian system gave to political minorities encouraged extreme fragmentation, a tendency that—except for the call of history—might have been eliminated in 1953 if a compromise had been worked out.

THE LONG TRAVAIL OF THE CENTER-LEFT

The instability generated by the 1953 elections made widening the governing coalition an urgent matter. Two solutions existed—bringing in either the Extreme Right or the Socialists. Christian Democrats were divided on this issue. As indicated, Gedda wished to ally with the MSI and the Monarchists, but the DC left wing, influenced by the long tradition of Catholic social thought, favored an "opening to the Left" with the Socialists. This solution, however, faced serious obstacles. The social thinkers of the Catholic left did not control the DC. Could they win the backing of the party, and if they did, would the conservatives go along? DC conservatives adamantly opposed the Socialists because of their affiliation with the Communists and distrusted them. Along with the Liberals—who would be ousted if the Socialists joined the coalition—the conservatives argued that the PSI would not renounce the Communist alliance, and if they did, Socialist Party members would not go along. Worse, conservatives regarded Nenni as a "Trojan Horse" for PCI influence and eventual membership in the government.

In their struggle, the DC conservatives had powerful allies: the Vatican and the United States. Pope Pius XII had attempted to help Gedda. For fear that Communists and Socialists would take Italy out of NATO, the United States officially opposed the opening to the Left, even though the American embassy's first secretary, George Lister, quietly made contact with Socialist representatives with the approval of Ambassador James Zellerbach. Liberal Party leader Giovanni Malagodi's contacts in the Rome embassy, however, stiffened the back of American diplomats, and the Republican administration of President Dwight Eisenhower seemed unlikely to lift the American "veto."

Pietro Nenni had believed that the Popular Front of which he was a part would win in 1948. The defeat of that year damaged his party more than the Communists. Because of superior Communist organization and the manner in which seats were distributed, PSI representation in Parliament declined drastically. Nenni recognized the election as a disaster and contemplated abandoning the alliance, but he had to move gradually; his party had become subordinate within the labor movement, depended on the Communists for financial support, and, in effect, had become a PCI satellite.

The elections of 1953 brought Nenni an opportunity to resolve his dilemma. If he withdrew from the Communist alliance, not only would his party regain its independence, but he would strengthen Italian democracy by increasing governmental stability and widen its base by bringing part of the working class to the republic's support. As a condition of this operation's success, however, he demanded domestic reforms that would reduce the gap between rich and poor and regional imbalances, bring about land reform, industrialize the South, institute rational economic planning, make electoral modifications, create regional governments, and nationalize the electrical industry (a conservative fortress). In foreign affairs, Nenni asked for a more "defensive" interpretation of NATO to gain party support.

The Socialist leader launched these ideas in March 1955 at the Congress of Turin. His party apparently accepted his new policy, although the PSI, controlled by the apparatus, greeted it without understanding its implications. But the death of Rodolfo Morandi, who dominated the party bureaucracy with an iron hand and seemed to support Nenni during this phase, spelled trouble. In April, Nenni shrewdly maneuvered to attain the election of a Christian Democrat friendly to the Center-Left, Giovanni Gronchi, to the presidency of the republic. Between 1955 and 1956, Socialist prestige grew remarkably with successes in local elections, the attainment of several important Socialist-sponsored measures, moves to loosen ties with the Communists, and, most important, a meeting with Giuseppe Saragat during which Saragat and Nenni agreed to merge their parties. In 1956 came the Khrushchev report on Stalin's crimes at the Twentieth Congress of the Communist Party of the Soviet Union (CPSU), the Hungarian Revolution, and the Soviet repression. These events caused great consternation among Italian leftists, which Nenni hoped to harness to his cause. Nenni denounced the invasion and wrote a series of articles maintaining that the dictatorial aspects of communism could not be attributed to a person but to the system.

From this high point, however, Nenni's problems began. Togliatti feared isolation and fought back. Talks to implement the PSI-PSDI merger stalled, and the

PSI's pro-Communist left wing mobilized against Nenni. At the Congress of Venice in February 1957, the PSI left wing dramatically demonstrated its power by electing a Central Committee opposed to the opening to the Left, even as the delegates approved Nenni's Center-Left policy. Two years of complex maneuvering followed while Nenni attempted to secure control of his party. At the Naples congress in January 1959, he received a 58.3 percent vote of support. Though this majority seemed comfortable, his opponents were far from defeated.

These developments allowed conservative Christian Democrats and American diplomats resisting the Center-Left to argue that even if Nenni had dropped his philo-communism, his party would not follow him. The DC left had won the position of secretary with Amintore Fanfani, who sympathized with the Socialist aims and hoped to transform the DC into a modern mass party with a progressive program. But Catholic conservatives blocked attempts at dialogue with the Socialists and favored maintaining the DC's traditional policies and structure, based on financial contributions from private industrialists and an organization rooted in the parishes and Catholic Action. Thus, a struggle paralleling the one in the PSI raged within the DC. Hampered by disappointments in the 1958 elections, a feeble majority in the party, and a scandal, Fanfani was forced to resign as prime minister and secretary. His faction, based on the ideas of progressive Catholic thinker Giuseppe Dossetti, dissolved and was replaced by a looser coalition of DC leaders, known as the "Dorotei," headed by Aldo Moro.

This confused infighting was reflected in Parliament and the country. The cabinet Fanfani had headed sympathized with the Center-Left, and his resignation made it extremely difficult to find agreement. President Gronchi gave Fernando Tambroni a mandate to form a government. Tambroni had recently defended Fanfani, but because he was anxious to achieve a majority on his own, he haggled with the Left and, secretly, with the Right. Astoundingly, on April 3, 1960, he accepted MSI support in a confidence vote in the Chamber. Ten cabinet ministers resigned in protest, but since no other majority existed, Tambroni survived for the moment.

Although Tambroni said that his government would handle only routine administrative matters until a more permanent solution to the crisis could be found, his actions spoke differently. He pledged strong government and took steps to increase his popularity with the business community and middle classes. During the delicate international period following the downing of a U.S. U2 spy plane and the resulting clamorous breakup of the Geneva Summit, Tambroni projected the image of a strong leader. Rumor had it that he had established a secret police and awaited radicalization of the political situation to "save" the country. Furthermore, Tambroni's dependence on MSI votes conditioned his action toward the neo-Fascists, who in June scheduled a congress for Genoa. The city, a major Resistance center against the Fascists, considered this development a provocation. Spontaneous strikes and riots protesting the congress began in the port city on June 30 and spread across the country. Tambroni mobilized massive police forces, but the resulting street battles ended his government. The emergency allowed Moro to press the DC for Tambroni's substitution by Fanfani. Moro secured parliamentary support from Social Democrats, Liberals, and Republicans and the abstention of Socialists and Monarchists. Tambroni resigned on July 19, 1960.

The new Fanfani cabinet—labeled the "parallel convergences"—produced several important Socialist-inspired reforms, but these did not result in PSI gains. Local elections resulted in a PSI decline and a PCI increase, which commentators attributed to leftist Socialist voters crossing over to help the Communists. Lack of an electoral breakthrough complicated the next step toward a Center-Left coalition—the establishment of local four-party Center-Left administrations (DC, PSI, PRI, PSDI), foreshadowing a national coalition. As the price of cooperation, Christian Democrats demanded an immediate end to local Socialist coalitions with the Communists, but political realities dictated gradual disengagement. The Church intervened when Cardinal Giuseppe Siri brutally informed Moro that the bishops would not condone DC collaboration with the PSI until the Socialists had guaranteed their independence from the Communists.

At this point, the elections of liberal Pope John XXIII in 1958 and President John F. Kennedy in 1960 influenced the struggle for the Center-Left. The pope imposed a pro-Center-Left policy on the Church and silenced anti-Socialist conservatives in the DC. The American position was more complex. Given the many crises that the new administration had to resolve, it did not immediately stifle anti-Center-Left opponents in the Rome embassy, the State Department, and the CIA. Kennedy, however, gave carte blanche to presidential adviser Arthur M. Schlesinger Jr. to support the Center-Left. A well-known historian of the United States, Schlesinger had learned to love Italy through contact at Harvard University with anti-Fascist exile Gaetano Salvemini. The next three years witnessed a complicated struggle within the American diplomatic establishment between forces—flanked by their respective Italian allies—that favored or opposed the opening to the Left.

Maneuvering in Italy paralleled these developments. The attraction of communism for left-wing PSI leaders and voters allowed the PCI to whittle away at the Socialist electorate, and DC leader Moro had trouble keeping his right wing in check. In February 1962, the Socialists agreed on an advanced program to be implemented by Fanfani and supported him in Parliament by abstaining in the vote on his cabinet. With Socialist encouragement, this cabinet nationalized the electric power companies, imposed a new withholding tax on stock dividends, made school attendance until age fourteen obligatory, and passed other reforms. This activity, however, alienated conservatives and did not satisfy leftist Socialists, who were upset because the nationalization of electric companies provided compensation for the owners and failed to organize the industry in a way that attacked capitalism. The withholding tax closed an important loophole but frightened investors, prompting a massive flight of capital abroad. In addition, the Communists moved to sabotage the Socialist-DC agreement by encouraging the unions to strike. The resulting wage increases fueled inflation, which caused more disorder and further weakened the government.

The unrest exacerbated the political situation as well. Discussions that were to have brought Socialist representatives into the cabinet increased the infighting, which continued up to November 22, 1963. Only the shock of Kennedy's assassination induced the last Socialist holdout, Riccardo Lombardi, to give in, and an agreement was reached to form a cabinet that included Socialists. This action caused the PSI left wing to split off and form a new, pro-Communist party, the Partito Socialista di Unità Proletaria (PSIUP). In this dangerous situation, DC secretary Moro negotiated with the unions to moderate their demands and soften the economic crisis, but they refused. On May 27, 1964, a Rome newspaper published a letter in which the treasury minister predicted economic collapse if the government did not drop its Socialist-inspired reform program. The divisions prompted the government to resign and to review the political agreements.

During the discussions, Moro pleaded with Nenni to slow down the pace of reforms, but the party refused. Negotiations dragged on until July 17, when the Socialists suddenly agreed to a new cabinet that would put less emphasis on reform.

What accounts for this strange capitulation? Nenni indicated at the time that if the Socialists had not given in, there would have been a rightist coup d'état. During the crisis, president Antonio Segni took the highly unusual step of consulting with military commanders and Senate president Cesare Merzagora, the vocal advocate of an emergency government. In 1971, a parliamentary investigation confirmed that a plan had been drawn up in 1964 by general Giovanni De Lorenzo, the commander of Servizio Informazione Forze Armate (SIFAR), the Italian secret service, to provoke disorders to serve as an excuse to gain military control of the country. This plan, of which American military commanders were informed, included setting up detention camps and arresting prominent leftist politicians in and out of the government. According to some scholars, the fear of a coup convinced Nenni to jettison his reform program to save Italian democracy.

Did a serious possibility of a coup exist, or did Center-Left opponents merely exploit the threat? The answer is still debated, but one thing seems clear: opposition to the Center-Left from both Extreme Right and Extreme Left helped degrade a program of reforms from a plan to correct the country's social ills into a political deal.

This development had dire consequences for the future. Despite notable legislative achievements, especially in the labor field, between 1964 and 1968 the Socialists no longer possessed the countervailing power they needed to convince their Center-Left allies to implement significant reforms and thus failed to renew the basis of Italian politics. Disappointment among the electorate followed. Hammered by Communist charges of Socialist betrayal, the Socialist share of votes nosedived in the May 1968 general elections; as a result, recently reunited Socialists and Social Democrats redivided, and the PSI adopted, once more, a politically disastrous pro-Communist policy. These developments foreshadowed a new, tumultuous era.

Years of Lead

With the breakdown of political cooperation came the intense turmoil that characterized Italian life in the 1970s. The unrest affected the entire Western world, but Italy more so. The student protests that struck France and Germany in May 1968 had a long prelude in Italy in 1967 and lasted longer. The students went from criticism of the failure to reform education—an unfulfilled Center-Left plank— to a virulent attack on the political system and society. Riots also shook the South, whose problems the gridlocked Center-Left failed to resolve. In October 1969—the "Hot Autumn"—the three major unions initiated a long series of rancorous strikes for higher wages, better working conditions, and reforms. Parliament prepared to adopt reforms in response to the agitation when the reaction arrived. On December 12, 1969, terrorists planted four bombs in Milan and Rome, killing thirteen people. Thus began the so-called strategy of tension, supposedly implemented by occult rightist forces that aimed to create the impression of leftist violence, which in turn would justify a takeover by conservative forces. Political violence, armed confrontations, and conspiracies to overthrow the republic continued unabated over the next years. Combined with hot political battles over divorce and various scandals, Italy seemed to be falling apart.

In 1973, two foreign events profoundly influenced the country: the Yom Kippur War, with its resulting oil embargo, and Salvador Allende's overthrow in Chile. The oil embargo occasioned draconian conservation measures that shut down recreation facilities at night, restricted automobile circulation, and set off fifteen years of drastic inflation, jeopardizing the energy-short country's economy. Chilean events provoked an important rethinking of PCI strategy by its secretary, Enrico Berlinguer. To defeat the reactionary forces threatening Italian democracy, to cure Italy's ancient ills, and to ensure Italian economic development, Berlinguer offered a "historic compromise" among the progressive forces that represented the majority of Italy's population—Catholics included.

ENRICO BERLINGUER
Euro-Communist

~~~

Noted for his intelligence and his subtle political reasoning, Enrico Berlinguer will probably remain most famous for weaning the Italian Communist Party (PCI) away from the Soviet Union. Berlinguer thus led a movement that, had it been accepted, might have democratized and saved communism.

Berlinguer had strange antecedents for a Communist. He came from a noble Sardinian family that had excellent political contacts. Berlinguer's grandfather was a friend of both Giuseppe Garibaldi and Giuseppe Mazzini. His father, Mario, went to school with Palmiro Togliatti, the postwar Italian Communist secretary. Enrico, born in Sassari, Sardinia, on May 25, 1922, had one brother, Giovanni, also a Communist, and was a cousin of two Christian Democrats who became prime ministers and presidents. Berlinguer married Letizia Laurenti on September 26, 1957, and fathered four children.

Berlinguer joined the Communist Party in 1943; in 1945, Togliatti named him a member of the Central Committee. Berlinguer rose to the position of secretary in the Communist Youth Federation (FGCI) in 1949. In 1968, he won election to Parliament. In 1969, he became vice secretary of the PCI, but soon ran the party because the party secretary, Luigi Longo, suffered poor health. Berlinguer became party secretary in 1972, a post he held until his death.

Berlinguer objected to Soviet control of the PCI and proposed independent policies. These included the "historic compromise" and "Eurocommunism." The first policy called for a coalition between Communists and Catholics. The second, Eurocommunism, definitively stated in 1977, was an attempt at agreement with other Western European Communist parties to establish a new, democratic communism independent of Moscow.

In 1968, Berlinguer informed Soviet leader Leonid Brezhnev that the Italian Communists did not agree with his military repression of Czechoslovakia. In 1976, he reiterated the PCI's independence, saying that he believed in pluralism, that the Italian Communists aimed at building a different kind of socialism in Italy, and that he felt safe under NATO's protection. In 1980, he condemned the Soviet invasion of Afghanistan.

Berlinguer's *strappo* (rip or tear) encountered criticism in the PCI and from political enemies who believed that he moved too slowly and that he remained a Communist at heart. Most people, however, believed Berlinguer to be both sincere and courageous.

At a large political gathering in Padua on June 7, 1984, a brain hemorrhage suddenly cut Berlinguer down. He died on June 11. Public figures from the world over and a million ordinary people flocked to his funeral in Piazza San Giovanni in Rome.

This proposal continued a long Communist evolution away from Soviet control and toward Westernization. Berlinguer indicated that he was willing to play by democratic rules, favor pluralism, and accept NATO; this was "Eurocommunism," a democratic "Western" communism. This policy made the PCI attractive to Westerners and increased Communist votes in Italy. At the same time, extreme leftists, influenced by mythical revolutionary leaders Mao Zedong and Che Guevara, viewed the PCI as having been absorbed by the capitalist political structure and had nowhere to go. Convinced as well that the country had to be rescued by military means from the regressive forces behind the strategy of tension, they turned to terrorism.

Fueled by the failure to reform Italian society during the late 1960s, terrorists found sympathy in Italian society, and their movement achieved proportions unseen in other modern Western democracies. The incidence of violence, kneecappings, and murder escalated by the mid-1970s. By 1977, terrorism, labor agitation, economic distress, social unrest, and the appearance of a raucous "extraparliamentary left" had created a national emergency. Political instability worsened. As Communist votes approached the DC total, it seemed necessary to "unfreeze" the Communist electorate, excluded from the ruling coalition and now necessary for governmental stability, and to convince workers to accept economic sacrifices. The Communists agreed because Italian democracy seemed to be in danger, and they joined the "national solidarity" coalition. The PCI contracted not to vote against a cabinet headed by DC leader Giulio Andreotti. This was the culmination of "consensus" politics—in which Communists and Catholics had unofficially cooperated despite their public differences. Reflecting its enhanced role, and supported by DC secretary Moro, in late 1977 and 1978 the PCI negotiated for full equality within the coalition and eventual membership in the cabinet. Despite an official rebuke from the United States on January 12, 1978, these discussions culminated in agreement that an Andreotti cabinet would be supported by a parliamentary array that openly included the Communists.

At the same time, in Turin, the trial of Renato Curcio, founder of the Red Brigades, and his colleagues opened a new round of attacks on the state by leftist guerrillas. In a textbook-perfect military operation, Red Brigades terrorists kidnapped Moro in Rome on March 16, 1978, killing his five-man escort. The suspicious timing of this operation on the eve of the official Communist entrance into the governing coalition fueled speculation about the real motives of the kidnappers. If they meant to block the operation, however, they failed, because the Andreotti cabinet attained confirmation as agreed. After "interrogating" Moro, the Red Brigades offered to exchange him for thirteen jailed terrorists, but the government refused. When talks broke down, the terrorists killed Moro and symbolically left his body midway between DC and PCI headquarters in Rome.

The Communist experiment as an open member of the governing coalition damaged the party. The cabinet implemented unpopular austerity measures, but the economy worsened, as did unemployment and crime. The PCI, locked in the coalition, could not avoid its share of blame, but when it asked for representation in the cabinet to have some control over policy, the request was rejected. Despite declared PCI autonomy from Moscow, many Italians were still unwilling to entrust PCI members with power. Finally, in January 1979, the PCI officially withdrew from the ruling coalition—although under-the-counter collaboration continued—badly bruised by the experience.

POLITICAL REVIVAL—AND FALSE DAWN

Had the historic compromise succeeded, the Socialists would have been damaged the most; their pro-Communist policies had already cost them support because the PSI was no longer the balance of power, and the leftist electorate preferred to vote directly for the stronger PCI if no policy differences existed. In the 1972 and 1976 national elections, the PSI vote share remained stuck at its historic low of 9.6 percent. In July 1976, a revolt occurred at a Central Committee meeting at the Midas Hotel in Rome: younger leaders removed their older brethren from power and installed Bettino Craxi as PSI secretary. Craxi was not expected to last long, but by 1980 he had defeated his numerous internal enemies and established an iron control over the party. He ended cooperation with the Communists. In both the intellectual and the popular press, Socialist intellectuals argued against the democratic credentials of the PCI by demolishing the idea that Antonio Gramsci had established a democratic brand of communism, as the Communists maintained. On the contrary, the Socialists claimed that only the PSI had inherited the Italian social democratic tradition. Proclaiming Socialist independence from the Communists represented the first step in Craxi's goal of ending Communist hegemony of the Left and reversing the "Italian anomaly," that is, a large Communist Party and a small Socialist Party.

Craxi hoped to achieve these results by increasing Socialist prominence and importance in governmental affairs. He put forward his own candidacy for prime minister and pushed Socialist candidates for key institutional positions. In 1978, after the resignation of scandal-ridden Giovanni Leone, Craxi intervened decisively to secure Sandro Pertini's election as president of the republic. Pertini, an old freedom fighter, turned out to be an enormously popular choice and enhanced the Socialist image. But attaining the premiership seemed an insurmountable task. Since the DC, as the largest party, had a permanent claim on the office, Craxi put forward the theory of "alternation" of the premiership within the coalition. In the ensuing political maneuvering, the Socialist secretary demonstrated himself to be a brilliant tactician and took on the Christian Democrats as well as the Communists. Craxi was stymied in his drive to become prime minister in June 1981, when Republican Giovanni Spadolini became the first non-DC premier in thirty-five years. Despite the achievements of Spadolini's government, his party proved too small to retain the office for long. In the 1983 elections, the Socialists increased their votes slightly, but the DC suffered an electoral defeat by dropping 5.4 percent. This set the stage for a Craxi-led cabinet.

Despite his abrasive personality, Craxi proved himself an excellent governmental leader. He presented a well-articulated, broad, and specific program reinforcing the issues with which his party had gone to the polls. Beginning with crucial economic questions, his government proposed lowering the inflation rate from 15 percent in 1983 to 10 percent in 1984. The government hoped to accomplish this goal by reducing the deficit from 16 percent of GNP to 15 percent. Two-thirds of the deficit reduction would come from reduced public spending, and increased revenues would account for the rest. Acting on another inflation factor, the government proposed limiting salary increases to the inflation rate, slowing wage indexation, and discouraging price rises.

To avoid labor trouble, previous governments had sought agreement with the PCI before instituting economic policy, making it impossible to alter the system that produced the double-digit inflation threatening the country. Craxi's "decisionism" ended this consensus politics and caused a harsh reaction from the Communists, who resented their displacement at the center of Italian politics by their erstwhile subordinates. The Communists rejected out of hand a proposal to slow the *scala mobile*—the automatic cost-of-living increases that economists had long identified as a major contributor to spiraling inflation. They set out to topple the cabinet through strikes and stiff parliamentary opposition. The government stood its ground, and the PCI discovered itself politically isolated; the law was applied, and the inflation rate fell dramatically. Refusing to accept its defeat, the PCI forced a national referendum on the question of the scala mobile. On June 11, 1984, Berlinguer died suddenly, and later in the month a sympathy vote for the PCI during the European elections resulted in the Communists receiving a higher share of the vote than did the DC. Communist leaders mistook this development for the long-awaited *sorpasso* (overtaking) of the DC, but their party lost the ensuing referendum and the local elections by significant margins. Their opposition appeared as pique toward effective government, and their electoral slide, begun during the "national solidarity" period, accelerated.

Combined with the defeat of leftist terrorism—exemplified by the brilliant rescue of American General James Lee Dozier during the administration of Giovanni Spadolini—Craxi's stunning victory on economic policy signaled a change

MAP 19.1 ITALIAN REGIONAL DIVISIONS, 1985

in the country's style. Absenteeism, strikes, low productivity, tax evasion, bloated state industry, and incredible deficits attached to social services had become legendary during the previous fifteen years. These problems could not suddenly disappear, but the nation altered its work habits and seriously discussed the more difficult issues confronting it. Between 1985 and 1986, absenteeism declined, and time lost because of strikes diminished to among the lowest in Europe. At the same time, the government successfully encouraged industrial reconversion, productivity increased, industry registered higher profits, and progress was made on privatization. In another shift, employers seemed to be achieving their long-desired linkage of salary and productivity increases. These developments, combined with the drop in oil prices, led Carlo Azeglio Ciampi, chairman of the Bank of Italy, to declare that the back of inflation had been broken. Italy's new economic flowering resulted in a sustained stock market boom that doubled the value of shares in four months and attracted heavy foreign investment.

In addition to its activity in the economic sphere, the government streamlined the legislative process and put institutional reform on the table. Fighting among the parties blocked all serious reform, however, a mistake that would debilitate them in the 1990s. The government also signed a new concordat with the Vatican that enhanced the Church's position in religious education but ended state salaries for the clergy and instituted as a new funding mechanism a check-off system on income tax forms that later became controversial. Craxi also pursued a more active foreign policy than before. The sending of an Italian contingent in 1983 to Lebanon had signaled a willingness to shoulder greater international responsibility in areas close to the country. Now Craxi made frequent trips to foreign capitals and regularly corresponded with President Ronald Reagan, demonstrating a tendency to negotiate with the Americans on more equal terms than his predecessors. The Socialists were instrumental in the acceptance of American cruise missiles on Italian soil, a move that encouraged other European countries to accept them and that contributed to the end of the Soviet Union. Craxi, however, displeased the Americans by adopting a more independent policy in the Middle East. He called for talks with the PLO chairman, Yasser Arafat, who, he argued, stood ready to renounce terrorism and formally recognize Israel. Craxi also promoted an active Mediterranean policy and established an informal entente with Spain, ruled by his Socialist counterpart Filipe González. Craxi's insistence on Italian jurisdiction in the *Achille Lauro* affair and the standoff with American troops—who, he claimed, violated Italian sovereignty by landing in Sicily to capture the terrorists—greatly increased his popularity in Italy, even among Communists, by displeasing the Americans. At the Tokyo Economic Summit in May 1986, Craxi insisted on Italy's entrance into the "Club of Five," which made the world's most important economic decisions, and won his case. The new course in foreign policy met with general approval.

When the Craxi government resigned in 1987 after a record tenure in office, the Socialist leader seemed dominant in Italian politics. He chastised the Vatican for its interference in Italian affairs, attacked judges for their easy arrest propensities, successfully pushed for the sending of Italian warships to the Persian Gulf to protect the shipping lanes, and sponsored a series of victorious national referendums. Despite this activity, the 1987 national elections failed to reward Craxi with the electoral breakthrough he had always predicted, but the PSI vote share did increase and the party seemed more attractive for women and young people. The PCI, on the other hand, continued its electoral slide, failed to appeal to youth, and seemed to be falling apart. An influential segment of the leadership wished to link up with the Socialist leader and reach an agreement with him. A fierce battle within the PCI leadership sanctioned the existence of two official factions and shattered the antique Leninist principle of "democratic centralism," which imposed unity by suffocating debate. Reversal of the Italian anomaly appeared within reach as Communist vote share declined.

At this point, however, Craxi began making a series of bad mistakes. He left office with the promise to reform the PSI—his Achilles' heel—by strengthening its structure, promoting internal dialogue, and weeding out the persistent corruption problem that seriously compromised its image and proved his eventual undoing. Instead, he left the party as it was. Believing the Communists dead, Craxi attempted to cannibalize the PCI instead of reaching agreement with party leaders who agreed with his policies, but he made the mistake of refusing to force early elections to take advantage of the collapse of international communism. This failure allowed the Italian Communists to regroup, cut themselves free of association with the Soviet Union, and change their name; they emerged seriously damaged, but not destroyed as a political force. In an egregious and useless statement, Craxi opposed a 1991 referendum designed to reduce corruption in elections. His denigration of the referendum backfired because of his arrogant invitation to Italian citizens not to vote but to "go to the beach." This statement was unpopular and turned the vote into a referendum against him.

Craxi's major strategic error, however, proved to be the deal he made with the Christian Democrats that was designed to ensure his return to the office in which he had proved so successful. He agreed with DC leaders that he would back them in keeping the premiership during the life of the legislature, 1987 to 1992, in exchange for their support of him for the five years of the legislature that would follow. As the world rapidly changed with the fall of the Berlin Wall and the end of the Soviet Union, Craxi openly adopted the old politics of wheeling and dealing he had, ironically, refused when he was weak. His support in the country rested on the belief that, despite his arrogance, he was the only politician capable of implementing a serious reform program that could renew the nation. However, his shift to a cozy DC alliance destroyed that contention and revealed him as playing "politics as usual," a stance Italians increasingly rejected.

The elections of April 5 and 6, 1992, produced a political upheaval. The Christian Democrats lost 5 percent of their vote; the Democratic Party of the Left (PDS), which had succeeded the PCI, received 16 percent; and the hard-line rump, Rifondazione Comunista (PRC), took 5.5 percent. The Socialist vote remained stable, and the difference with the PDS was minimal. But the real story was that the four-party ruling coalition retained only a slender majority and that the Lega Lombarda (Lombard League, later the Northern League)—an antigovernment force advocating drastic political changes and a federal Italy—in receiving 9 percent nationwide, had become the North's largest party and continued to grow. The political basis for Craxi's deal was gone, and a major corruption scandal, which would deprive him of the office of premier and secretary and sweep away all the old parties, was on the horizon. With the Cold War over, the postwar politics of "imperfect bipolarism" ended.

CHAPTER TWENTY

The Economic
Miracle and Its Effects

ITALY'S STUNNING ECONOMIC PERFORMANCE CONTRASTED WITH AND counterbalanced the negative politics of imperfect bipolarism. The industrial base constructed during the Fascist period and a large labor reserve, which meant low wages for workers, allowed the Italians to take advantage of the high degree of international economic cooperation that produced a boom of unprecedented proportions after World War II, primarily in the industrial sector. This "economic miracle" and its benefits fostered the view that Christian Democratic leadership, in contrast to that of the Communists, guaranteed democracy, participation in Western multilateral organizations, and continued economic development. Italians complained about the government's imperviousness to reform, but the economic miracle kept the DC in power.

RECONSTRUCTION,
ECONOMIC GROWTH, MIRACLE

The end of hostilities allowed the first postwar governments to tackle the problem of reconstruction. The presence of Communist and Socialist representatives in the early postwar cabinets had little influence on economic policy, but their exclusion after May 1947 guaranteed resolution of the most pressing questions through classic economics. Luigi Einaudi, budget minister in the fourth De Gasperi cabinet, was primarily responsible for economic policy.

Among the many urgent economic problems, inflation predominated. To fight the war, the Fascist government had frozen prices and wages in June 1940, but prices doubled by late 1942 anyway. After Mussolini's overthrow in 1943, German economic demands on the Salò Republic, the infusion by the Allies of "amlire" in the South to pay for their needs, and wartime hoarding caused inflation to explode. The price index (1938 = 100) rose from 273 in 1943 to 1,215 in 1944 to 2,392 in 1945, and real wages dropped 75 percent. In the North, the German repressive apparatus controlled inflation better, but by war's end real wages had still fallen 50 percent from their 1938 level. In 1945–1946, prices stabilized as the government floated loans and confidence in the lira seemed restored.

Strong inflationary pressures on the lira soon resumed because of government spending, continued price supports for flour, the failure of a plan to replace the old currency, pressure from labor for cost-of-living increases, and the sabotage of a proposed capital levy tax. The dollar rose to 900 lire (from an official rate of 225) by May 1947, setting off a new round of credit expansion, government deficits, and rising prices. By the spring of 1947, the annualized rate of inflation reached 50 percent, and the wholesale price index rose to 6,200 by September.

The government responded by instituting a deflationary policy, restricting credit, and encouraging the return of capital that had fled abroad. Companies that had hoarded goods in anticipation of rising prices brought them out for fear of losing money. The wholesale price index began a steady fall, and in 1950 dropped to 5,000. Foreign reserves increased dramatically because of the return of Italian capital and aid from the European Recovery Program (Marshall Plan), which also stimulated foreign investment. In September 1949, the lira was stabilized at 625 to the dollar, where it remained until the 1970s.

By itself, the improved monetary situation did not resolve the nation's foreign trade problems because the war had practically destroyed Italy's gold and foreign currency reserves. As a result, the country lacked funds to replace damaged plant, to purchase raw materials for industry, and to pay for foodstuffs to keep its population from starving. This situation, common to war-devastated Europe, required American intervention. The United States initially extended aid to Italy through the United Nations Relief and Rehabilitation Administration (UNRRA) and the Foreign Economic Administration and, in 1947, provided credits with Argentina for buying food and ships. This assistance tided Italy over until more systematic aid reached it through the Marshall Plan. American aid accounted for $1.75 billion of the total $2 billion received by the Italians between 1943 and 1947. Seventy percent of this aid went to industry, railways, and public works and encouraged "a more rational development of the economy." The Italians repaid all their American loans by July 1962.

The Italians speeded recovery by reversing previous trade policy and by inserting their country into the international trading system created after World War II. Trade liberalization, as favored by the United States, marked postwar Western economic policy. Italy dropped quotas or loosened restrictions on imports from countries belonging to the Organization of European Economic Cooperation (OEEC), even though Italian tariffs remained higher than those of its European trading partners.

In addition to liberalizing trade regulations, the Italians were among the founders of the key multinational organizations on which the new European trading system was based. These included the European Coal and Steel Community (ECSC), which, on February 10, 1953, created free trade among member nations (Italy, West Germany, France, Belgium, Luxembourg, and the Netherlands) in coal and ferrous metals. An English participant at the sessions establishing the organization remarked that the noisiest representatives were the Italians, "and they don't even have any coal or iron." The country was also a founding member of the European Economic Community (EEC, the Common Market, later called the European Community, EC, and then the European Union, EU). Europe recognized Italy's importance in this initiative by selecting Rome as the site to sign the treaty establishing the EEC. Taking effect on January 1, 1958, the EEC successfully established free trade among its members and looked forward to complete economic integration and common political and foreign policies.

These measures and the advantages of a solid economic base and cheap labor transformed Italy from an agricultural country into a world industrial power. The index of industrial production tells this story. The index reached 102 in 1948 from a base of 100 in 1938; in 1953, it hit 164; from a new base of 1953 = 100, the index went to 196 in 1961. The mechanical industry (automobiles, railway stock, tractors, shipbuilding, airplanes, and electrical equipment, including appliances, calculating and office machines, and typewriters), ferrous metal production (at which the country became efficient despite the lack of raw materials), road building, electricity, chemicals, and the petrochemical industry all expanded at a tremendous rate. Private enterprises, such as Fiat and Olivetti, and the public companies changed the country's physiognomy. By 1960, industry accounted for 46.6 percent of national income, compared with 34.2 percent between 1936 and 1940. According to the 1961 census, industry employed 38 percent of the working population and the service sector 32 percent; agricultural workers had declined to 30 percent.

Rounding out the "economic miracle," the gross domestic product (GDP) increased at a yearly average of 6.5 percent between 1958 and 1963; the comparable figure for industry was 8 percent, the highest rate since unification. Exports took off as well, increasing at an average of 14.5 percent a year. The percentage of Italian products exported to the EEC went from 23 percent in 1955 to 40.2 percent in 1965. By 1967, the country had become the world's third-largest producer of refrigerators and Europe's largest manufacturer of washing machines and dishwashers. With the remarkable jump in production and exports came wage increases that touched off a boom in private consumption, further stimulating the economy.

The negative effects of this rapid economic development could have been mitigated by economic planning, a concept widely discussed throughout Europe following World War II. In Italy, however, economic planning had radical implications rejected by politicians. The Socialist minister for industry and commerce from July 1946 to May 1947, Rodolfo Morandi, conceived of economic planning as a transition to socialism, but he ran afoul of both the DC and the PCI. In fact, because Communists labeled planning within a capitalist system useless, the DC had a greater influence in this area. Catholic economist Pasquale Saraceno argued that Church thinking sanctioned state intervention to correct social and other imbalances caused by the free market. The Christian Democrats accepted his premises but shied away from their implications: state enforcement of production levels and equitable income distribution. The issue came to the fore again later, pressed by Christian Democrat Ezio Vanoni and the Socialists, but political opposition blocked economic planning.

Planning objectives were instead loosely set by the powerful public companies established under fascism; controlling a large part of the Italian economy under the republic, these companies determined where investments would be made. The South served as a prime example of this policy, which ultimately failed to redress the economic imbalance with the North. In 1957, the government mandated that the Istituto per la Ricostruzione Industriale (IRI) concentrate 40 percent of its total investment and 60 percent of its investment in industrial plant in the South; the idea was to kick off economic development in the region by greatly improving the infrastructure and building model industries in the region.

IRI had become an enormous holding company with major interests in all sectors of the economy—from shipbuilding to steelmaking, from roads to airlines, from banking to communications. Another public corporation established by the Fascists, the Azienda Generale Italiana Petroli (AGIP), was transformed in 1953 by its director, Enrico Mattei, into a gigantic company for the hydrocarbon sector. This Ente Nazionale Idrocarburi (ENI) aggressively developed Italian natural gas deposits and the petrochemical industry. It became an international power by defending the economic interests of oil-rich Arab and African states and challenging the Western oil companies that, Mattei believed, exploited them. Mattei's activities—combined with creation of a state monopoly of electric power, Ente Nazionale per l'Energia Elettrica (ENEL), during the Center-Left—assured Italy of cheap supplies of energy, which fueled its amazing postwar industrial development.

Besides its involvement in industry, the government intervened in agriculture by pouring in funds to repair war damage done to plant, livestock, and machines and by investing in land reclamation and improvements. To satisfy the traditional peasant land hunger, beginning in 1950 the government passed a series of reforms that applied to the regions where need was greatest. The laws allowed the expropriation of land from large landowners—who were paid by government bonds—and the sale of the land to peasants under favorable conditions. A series of other

PORTRAITS

ENRICO MATTEI
Murder of a Manager?

State industry played a great part in fueling Italy's extraordinary postwar economic development. The Italians pioneered a new type of company: the state firm operating under the direction of exceptional managers with wide autonomy and great political clout. One of these companies was the giant hydrocarbons concern, Ente Nazionale Idrocarburi (ENI), founded by Enrico Mattei.

Born the son of a junior carabiniere officer in 1906 in Acqualagna (Pesaro), Mattei began work in a mattress factory and later started his own chemical firm geared to the textile and leather industries. Following the Italian surrender of September 8, 1943, Mattei joined the Resistance movement and led with distinction a partisan band of leftist Catholics.

On May 12, 1945, the Committee of National Liberation made him head of Azienda Generale Italiana Petroli (AGIP) with the assignment of shutting the firm down. AGIP had been founded during the Fascist period to seek petroleum reserves in Italy and lessen the country's dependence on imported oil. Instead of closing AGIP, however, Mattei restructured it and in 1949 made the spectacular announcement that the company had discovered large reserves of natural gas and oil. As a result, AGIP received an exclusive concession to continue searching for and to market the oil it discovered. Even at this early stage, Mattei polarized Italian politics, with leftists supporting him and conservatives opposing his activities. To gain support in the country, Mattei branched out,

bribed the parties, and circumvented the rusty bureaucracy. He also controlled newspapers in order to influence public opinion. His homey style and his aggressiveness in trying to build up Italy's importance in the area of petroleum exploration made Mattei very popular.

Legislation in 1953 enlarged and consolidated his holdings with the creation of Ente Nazionale Idrocarburi (ENI), into which he folded AGIP. ENI allowed him to become a major player on the international petroleum scene controlled by the Americans and the British. Shut out of the most lucrative oil concessions by the "Seven Sisters," he gained the right to prospect in promising areas by offering Middle Eastern countries a 75–25 percent split instead of the standard 50–50 percent split given by the major oil companies. Mattei also negotiated for a pipeline to bring oil from the Soviet Union to Italy, and in 1960 he declared that the American oil monopoly was over. These actions irritated the American government, then in the throes of the Cold War.

Not surprisingly, Mattei received death threats. He suspected the CIA and other secret services enough to surround himself only with trusted bodyguards he had known from his partisan days. On October 27, 1962, his plane crashed while coming in for a landing at the Milan airport, killing Mattei, his pilot, and an American journalist. Officially, the crash was ruled an accident, but books, films, and later statements made by Italian officials pointed to murder.

laws provided more economic benefits for peasants. Because of conservative opposition, these laws were not comprehensive, nor did they eliminate all the problems, but by 1950 agriculture had recovered from the damage caused by war, and exportation of agricultural products resumed. The Center-Left implemented further measures favoring peasants, but the great draw of industry and tertiary economic activities induced many of them to abandon the land.

The failure to slow this movement and the attempt of government planners to industrialize the South proved to be errors. As national income rose to European levels, the country ran an enormous deficit to import expensive agricultural items, which, with proper encouragement, the South might have supplied.

Insufficient attention to agricultural development was one aspect of the republic's inability to resolve the problem of the South despite great expenditure and some successes. Besides attempting to industrialize the region through public company intervention, on August 10, 1950, the state instituted a special fund to improve economic conditions there. The Cassa per il Mezzogiorno spent enormous sums on the development of a badly needed transportation system (including roads), land reclamation projects, and, most important, tourism. Though there were definite improvements, the return was not proportional to the amounts spent. The Cassa proved subject to political pressure and corruption, and the equipment and know-how for industrialization came from the North, ironically stimulating that region's economy. The North has continued to increase its economic development at a higher rate than the South. Not only did the South continue to lose its most active population to northern migration, but infrastructure problems, such as the lack of water, hampered the South's growth.

Poor economic conditions, combined with the influx of government money, exacerbated the region's exploitation by organized crime. Criminal organizations such as the Mafia and the Camorra became more entrenched by siphoning off Cassa funds earmarked for economic development. Moreover, they expanded their activities to the North and to different economic sectors. The inefficiency and corruption of the state's southern operation produced resentment and rebellion in the North. Northerners had to put up with discriminatory economic policies favoring the South; the wealth they produced was grabbed by the central government through heavy taxation. This wealth frequently went to help organized crime and to create a vast welfare network (*stato assistenzialista*) based on clientelistic relationships and controlled by criminal elements and corrupt politicians. Organized crime used its gains to finance corrupt organizations and the traditional parties, whose vote-getting capabilities were strengthened by their unholy alliance with organized crime and by their ability to dole out government jobs and welfare benefits. In this way, politicians beholden to criminals increased their influence over the country and procured more funds for the South to keep the process going. As a result, many northerners believed that the South dragged the entire country down and favored breaking the cycle. The Lega Lombarda (later called the Lega Nord or Northern League), discussed in the next chapter, advocated a "federalism" bordering on separatism to cure these ills and revolutionized Italian politics.

Indeed, the spread of criminal associations to the most advanced parts of the country to take advantage of the greater economic advantages in those areas presented uniquely modern problems. Easier communications and Italy's participation in international trade organizations facilitated the worldwide cooperation of Italian and foreign crime syndicates. The world narcotics trade enriched the Mafia and created a serious drug problem; this development produced an explosion of petty crime throughout the country and contributed to the spread of AIDS in the North. These developments further strained the overburdened national health system. Furthermore, as discussed in the next section, organized crime seriously affected the political and business climate. These are some ways in which Italy's amazing economic development, which has brought great advantages, has also produced novel and grave problems.

SOCIAL TRANSFORMATION

Italy's unprecedented expansion has more traditionally negative sides. It has been estimated that between 1951 and 1971, interregional migration totaled over 9 million, outpacing the emigration to Germany and Switzerland that had been the earliest destinations of southern workers. In fleeing the South, the emigrants abandoned agricultural land, overcrowded big cities and their hinterlands, and polluted the environment. The automobile manufacturing city of Turin—a good example of the country's drastic urbanization—increased from about 719,000 in 1951 to 1.25 million inhabitants in 1967, and its immediate suburbs grew by 80 percent. Unhampered growth combined with new wealth pouring into the country set off an uncontrolled housing boom and real estate speculation that compromised the environment in urban and rural areas. Even though the law provided for planned development, bureaucratic inefficiency, corruption, and the free rein for private initiative often resulted in wholesale violations of aesthetic principles and safety norms.

Facing low wages and discrimination, southern emigrants lived in shantytowns in overcrowded and unhealthy conditions. Besides housing, their numbers overwhelmed the social services of the North—including health services and education—which already had been barely adequate.

As the economic miracle accelerated, however, successful trade union agitation won wage increases and raised cost-of-living adjustments to the point that raises for workers outstripped both the rate of inflation and increases for salaried professional workers. Inspired by the Center-Left, the "Brodolini reform" revolutionized relations in the workplace by mandating important rights for workers, vastly strengthening job security, and reducing employer control. Italian workers enjoyed long vacations and maternity leaves, generous severance packages, and a low retirement age. Outside the workplace, new working-class housing went up in large quantities, and, despite strains, the educational system gradually integrated emigrant children into northern society. In the 1970s, social services were greatly expanded, and the Italian welfare state became one of the most generous in Europe. Despite serious inefficiencies and long delays in securing services, the system supplied a safety net that provided basic care from cradle to grave. By the 1980s and 1990s, extended benefits and the poor administration of this system accounted for major expenses in the state's escalating public debt, and governments took action to control costs. For southern workers, however, "the terrible period of uprooting and transition seemed to have been worth it; a new life had begun."

The South remained much behind the booming North into the twenty-first century. While the North went on to pioneer modern forms of production and found it necessary to import workers from other countries, unemployment in the South and the islands stood at over 20 percent. Ironically, because of welfare state benefits, southerners did not find it economically advantageous to move north to take advantage of employment opportunities there. As more Italian workers moved into the service sector, agriculture accounted for a greater percentage of employment in the South than in the North and Center, signifying a less modern economy. All the statistics gauging economic progress showed that the South trailed; even more worrying, the gap with the North increased. Despite its progress, therefore, Italy proved unable to resolve the age-old disparity that divided the country. Indeed, the South qualified for aid that the EU provided for Europe's least-advanced regions.

Nevertheless, postwar social and economic transformation affected the entire population. The Italian business class, both public and private, underwent a major overhaul, adopting modern business techniques frequently learned in American universities. Highly efficient and profitable small firms in such areas as shoe manufacturing brought a flood of wealth even into the provinces. White-collar employment increased from 9.8 to 17.1 percent between 1951 and 1971, at a par with other advanced countries, a trend that accelerated into the 1990s. By 1971, the percentage of industrial and building workers taken together exceeded Britain and France. This activity greatly increased per capita income; with a base of 100 in 1950, it reached 234 in 1970, compared with 136 for France and 134 for Britain; starting from a lower level, this faster increase brought Italy up to the most-advanced European standards. Thanks to the economic miracle, greater numbers of Italians than ever before could afford washing machines, dishwashers, telephones, television sets, cars, long vacations, and expensive foods. The famous Fiat 600 motorized the country as the number of automobiles rose from 342,000 in 1950 to 4.67 million in 1964. In terms of durable goods, Italy became a "saturated" country by the 1980s (see Table 20.1).

This injection of new wealth had profound social effects. The increase in leisure time created a greater demand for periodical literature and books, even if the nation still lagged behind other European countries. Daily newspapers such as *La Repubblica*, established in 1976, and weeklies such as *L'Espresso* and *Panorama* joined the older *Corriere della Sera* in replacing the party press in the formation of public opinion because the best writers preferred to write for them, regardless of their own political affiliation. In the 1970s, the revolutionary press flourished, contributing to the radical climate of the age, only to disappear rapidly, with the notable exception of *Il Manifesto*. *Rotocalchi* (illustrated magazines) for women, such as *Annabella* and *Amica*, proliferated and greatly increased in circulation.

Television was also instrumental in forming popular opinion, in altering existing values, and in uniting the country linguistically. Introduced in the late 1950s, limited to evening hours and to one official station, the medium had an explosive development as private sets became common and private stations invaded the airways. *Tribuna Politica* provided equal time for politicians during elections to explain their ideas. Quiz shows taken from American models and providing

Table 20.1

Annual Production of Selected Consumer Goods, 1987–1992

	Automobiles*	Refrigerators (Noncommercial)	Washing machines (Noncommercial)	Dishwashers (Noncommercial)	Color televisions
1987	1,912,232	3,767,006	4,140,481	614,597	2,054,887
1988	2,114,108	3,942,495	4,368,157	783,279	2,262,058
1989	2,224,602	4,082,478	4,337,681	746,193	2,380,702
1990	2,120,879	3,971,645	4,339,188	742,906	2,332,602
1991	1,878,561	4,155,481	5,028,676	893,279	2,433,607
1992	1,681,555	4,010,639	5,132,477	883,106	2,149,854

* For civilian use only; excludes motor scooters, motorcycles, trucks, and buses

fabulous prizes became extremely popular and helped spread a consumer mentality. Advertising was an integral part of this process, even though the government tried to control it by setting standards; this effort gave rise to *Carosello*, an advertising program that became the most popular television show in Italy, after which Italian children went to bed. But the state gave up its attempts at regulation, and consumerism triumphed. By 1996, 64 percent of Italians owned a second television set. In the same year, out of 1,000 northerners, 312 owned sets; in the South, the figure was 220.

On the negative side, drug addiction, overdoses, and HIV infections, once rare, became more common. By 2000, an estimated 142,000 addicts were in treatment centers. Italians had caught up with the front-runners in illegal drug use.

Along with the development of a consumer society came less religiosity. A 1988 survey found that only 35 percent of Italians went to church. In the early 1960s, church attendance was more characteristic of women than men, but in later years the number of women going to church declined drastically. In the 1950s, Catholic teaching had repressed sexual behavior, but by the 1980s Italian women appeared as free as their European sisters. With increasing wealth, the size of the Italian family shrank, as did the number of extended families. Between 1971 and 1997, the average Italian household went from 3.3 people to 2.69, and the percentage of single-resident households rose from 10.6 percent to 21.3. These changes helped elevate the status of women, who had long been relegated to an inferior social and economic position. For example, the infidelities of husbands were winked at, but those of wives were legally punishable. Relationships between men and women were graphically depicted in two classic Pietro Germi films, *Divorce Italian Style* (i.e., murder) and *Seduced and Abandoned*. In the latter film, a Sicilian man seduces a woman but refuses to marry her because she is no longer a virgin—and he gets his mother's support. Attitudes toward women during this period were reflected in statistics showing that fewer Italian women worked outside the home than in other European countries.

Feminist movements, however, had been present on the Italian political scene since the 1890s. In the early republic, the Communist-dominated Union of Italian Women (UDI) had been an important PCI flanking organization; Christian Democratic women had also decisively contributed to their party's electoral victories. Women's concerns, however, had been subordinated to those of men in both instances, even though the abolition of legalized prostitution was a victory for women and a divorce law passed in 1970 was confirmed by a hard-fought 1974 referendum. The 1970s witnessed the birth of an aggressive feminist movement that brought women's issues forcefully to the nation's attention. Under feminist pressure, several major pieces of legislation passed. These included a reform of family law establishing equality of the sexes (1975), parity with men in the workplace (1977), and legalized abortion (1978). This last, hotly debated measure provided free abortions through the national health care system, although a "conscientious objector" provision for doctors opposing abortions limited the law's effectiveness. Unfortunately, the efficacy of Italian law was frequently limited by poor implementation.

With birth control also legal, and with consumer values firmly entrenched, Italy's birthrate in the 1990s fell to the lowest of any country in the world. The lower birthrate, an educational system that mandates free preschool care and free obligatory schooling up to age sixteen, and a generous paid leave policy for pregnant women and mothers with young children have all enabled women to work outside the home in greater numbers. Italian higher education has also remained substantially free. Despite organizational and funding problems, this factor, combined with liberalized access, has brought about an increase in the proportion of Italians, including women, holding advanced degrees, although in 2007 statistics showed that the country trailed in the percentage of the population receiving degrees. Once economically "visible" primarily as industrial workers and peasants, Italian women have now become a crucial presence in the professions and in politics.

The Italian birthrate collapse had numerous other sides of the coin. The question of how the immigrants who flooded into the country would change Italian culture, its religious and secular values, caused concern among religious and lay leaders. The drop had ominous consequences for Italy's bloated welfare and pension systems. The time loomed when only one worker would be supporting one pensioner—with all the social and economic consequences that implied. Typical of Italy, for example, demographic projections showed that in Bologna, by 2020, twenty-five adults over fifty, including one over eighty, would be present for every child under five. Without an immediate and significant increase in the birthrate or immigration, it was difficult to see how such problems could be resolved.

A New Phenomenon: Immigration

As Italy entered the twenty-first century, the country faced an increasingly difficult issue that confronted all of Europe but that also held out hope of resolving the problem of an aging population: immigration. Because of its economic success, Italy had ceased being a land of emigrants, and waves of immigrants were reaching Italian shores. These included immigrants from Eastern Europe, particularly Poland, the former Yugoslavia, Albania, and Romania. Gianni Amelio's film *Lamerica*, about Albania, emphasizes the irony of the change in Italy's condition. Immigrants also arrived from North Africa and more distant countries such as the Philippines, Somalia, Sri Lanka, Bangladesh, China, Ethiopia, Morocco, and the Kurdish parts of Turkey.

Although the percentage of new immigrants into Italy remains below that of Germany and France—it had grown rapidly to 5 percent in 2008—they have strained social services such as health and education. In general, Italians remain more tolerant than other Europeans, but the immigrants still face serious problems. Many Albanians have turned to crime, causing strong resentment and press attacks. Chinese immigrants to Florence entered the leather industry, a traditional specialty, causing Florentines to complain that shoddy Chinese workmanship was ruining their reputation, and disorders have occasionally occurred. In Rome, so many Chinese have moved into the Piazza Vittorio Emanuele II area that it has became the new "Chinatown," their willingness to work for low wages driving out local merchants. "Chinatown" and Muslim quarters have also developed in Milan, where neither group had ever existed. The police have found it difficult to penetrate Chinese ranks to contain crime, while the large number of Muslim immigrants and the establishment of mosques in Italian cities increase fears of terrorism and, when the police crack down, charges of discrimination.

Italy's long coastline, humanitarian tradition, and liberal asylum policy have made it an attractive landing point for immigrants who wish to settle there or who aim at joining relatives elsewhere in Europe—this is especially true for Kurds heading for Germany. For a while, its EU partners kept Italy out of the Schengen agreement that allows persons in one EU country to pass into the others without a passport and without going through customs controls. Once Italy met the conditions for membership, however, more illegal immigrants have been arriving in leaky boats, frequently brought by smugglers who charge exorbitant fees and throw them overboard when chased by the coast guard. Some immigrants purposely scuttle their boats, knowing that the navy will rescue them. Italy has attempted with some success to stem the tide of immigration by giving aid to the home countries, especially those in Eastern Europe. Also, the agreement in 2003 by which most of the Eastern European countries would enter the EU in 2004, with others to follow, gave hope that the flow would be regulated, but in Romania's case the flood swelled. Immigration from Africa has increased, and the debate on illegal immigration drew international attention in 2003 when Bossi stated that the Italian navy should fire on boats bringing immigrants to Italian shores. A Northern League spot on YouTube shows a rape, gives statistics, and concludes: "We want to be safer in our own country!" One of its posters for the 2008 elections shows a picture of a Native American with the caption: "They weren't able to regulate immigration and now they live on reservations! Think about it."

There is, however, another side to the question. Italy needs many of the immigrants. Ironically, northern industry, being short of labor, which the immigrants supply, supports immigration for that reason. Southern farms require help as well, since Italians refuse to do the jobs requiring hard physical labor. As the Italian population has stagnated with one of the lowest birthrates in the world, Parliament passed legislative measures to increase it by providing economic incentives. These actions, however, will take years to give results, and when the Center-Right gained a majority in Parliament, it passed measures that have had the opposite effect. In the meantime, Italy's population would have fallen had it not been for immigration. These facts have increased Italy's need for workers and for persons to take care of old people, which, in turn, stimulates immigration.

A 2008 report on births revealed that the birthrate for Italian women took the most dramatic plunge among fifteen EU countries between 1960 and 2007, from 2.41 to 1.29. (The average birthrate for those countries, also low, fell from 2.59 to 1.50.) A falling birthrate is a common phenomenon among industrialized countries, but the drop in the Italian rate has caused particular concern. In 2008, one in ten babies was born to immigrants, the number of births rising from 48,925 in 2004 to 57,925 in 2008. The percentage of babies born to foreign women increased from 1.7 percent in 1995 to 11.4 percent in 2007. The average annual growth of immigrants in the country was calculated at 325,000. If this rate continues, in ten years the immigrant population will double, and by 2050 immigrants will represent between 17 and 20 percent of the population. At the same time, the Center-Right government passed legislation in 2004 making it practically impossible for women unable to become pregnant to receive advanced fertility treatment in Italy, which was formerly noted for its research in this field. This law, which reflects the Catholic Church's increasing influence in Italian politics and society, has contributed to the declining birthrate. It is estimated that in the four years following passage of the "Legge 40," as it is known, births declined by 2.78 percent and that the number of Italian women going abroad to get fertility treatment increased by 200 percent. As a consequence of these developments, the number of births among Italian women fell from 519,731 in 2004 to 505,202 in 2007.

The low birthrate among Italian women, combined with increasing immigration, is rapidly changing Italian society into a diverse and multicultural one at the beginning of the twenty-first century. The new immigrants are not only racially diverse but have different religions; indeed, they are helping to create a new Italy. Ironically, Italy, the target of Muslim invasions since the eighth century, has seen a different kind of "invasion" as its Muslim population burgeons. In the country's major cities, flourishing mosques have become a common sight, as in the rest of Europe. The Roman Catholic hierarchy emphasizes the differences between Islam and the country's Catholic traditions, arousing the protests of immigrants and their supporters. Government officials speculate about when Italian schools—which teach Catholicism—will have to begin teaching the

Muslim religion. Citizens and the media debate how terrorism imported from the Middle East might affect Muslim communities in Italy and what the response will be. They fear the spread of violence, inspired by the Palestine-Israeli conflict, to Italian cities. Indeed, many Italians, especially on the Left, sympathize with the Palestinians, causing friction with Jewish Italians and prime minister Silvio Berlusconi, who has taken a strong pro-Israel stance. The foreign minister in Romano Prodi's short-lived government, Massimo D'Alema, was more pro-Arab, and fueled the debate.

In practice, Italian institutions have implemented regulations in harmony with EU policy to regulate the inflow of immigrants, combat illegal immigration, and integrate the new minorities.

The number of foreign (non-EU) workers to be accepted into Italy is set yearly. In 2007, this number was 170,000, while a number of 80,000 seasonal workers was set for 2008. The Interior Ministry under Giuliano Amato revolutionized the application procedures by putting them completely online, thus greatly reducing the time involved. Besides work, family reunification is a prime reason for legal immigration into Italy. The ministry has attempted to streamline all immigration procedures by creating a single desk for immigration (including family reunification and asylum for political or religious reasons) located in the different Italian provinces in the prefects' offices.

Immigration was regulated by a law of July 30, 2002, the Bossi-Fini law. Although criticized at the time of its passage, when the Center-Right was in power, it essentially follows the lines of previous Center-Left legislation in this area; ironically, it has been heavily criticized by the labor-hungry industrialists of the country's prosperous Northeast. This legislation stipulates the expulsion of illegal immigrants by the police chief of an area after confirmation of the order by a judge and after procedures for the establishment of identification and arrangements for safe travel have been made. These immigrants have to be held in Centers for Temporary Stay and Assistance (CTSAs), which provide health care and social aid, food, clean conditions, language and cultural help, and other services. The maximum length illegal aliens can stay in these centers pending the completion of procedures designed to return them to their home countries is sixty days.

Perhaps more important than these measures, however, are those that have been taken to integrate new immigrants into Italian society. The law's stated goal is to help those groups "who are animated by a desire to safeguard their culture and their religious and linguistic traditions." Accordingly, Italy favors the integration of immigrants through outlawing discrimination, notifying immigrants about the opportunities the country offers them, disseminating important information relating to their rights and duties, and informing them about relevant economic, social, religious and recreational activities. In order to let immigrants know about these initiatives and to promote the creation of a harmonious multiracial society, the Interior Ministry started the Civis Project through RAI (the state broadcasting company). This project, approved by the EU, has the task of helping immigrants adjust to Italy and informing Italians through television and radio broadcasts and through the Internet (in seven foreign languages) of the immigrant condition and emphasizing their contribution to Italy's society and economy.

Besides this multimedia informational effort, Italy has established institutions to simplify and speed the integration of immigrants. The most important are the Territorial Councils for Immigration. These councils, set up by a presidential decree of December 18, 1999, consist of representatives of the state, the region, local governing bodies, chambers of commerce, workers' associations, employers, local groups active in providing assistance to immigrants, and local immigrant groups. They are headquartered in the offices of the prefect, who chairs them. These councils have a number of tasks, including monitoring the number of aliens in an area and the local capacity to absorb them, fostering close cooperation among different institutions, serving as consultative organs regarding immigrant needs, planning social integration policies suited to different local conditions, and implementing effective measures for assistance. According to the Interior Ministry, "They constitute a real resource for solving together with different institutional and non-institutional subjects, issues related to migration, as well as for promoting integration initiatives and sending proposals, which are worked out on the local scale, to the 'centre.'"

Since the Muslim community presents a particular challenge, the Interior Ministry set up the "Council [*Consulta*] for Italian Islam," on September 10, 2005. This is a consultative body charged with doing research, understanding the condition of Italian Muslims, forming opinions, and elaborating proposals to the ministry for facilitating institutional dialogue between the Muslim community and the state in order to facilitate the integration of Muslims into Italian society. Members of the council include scholars and experts on Islam who contribute to the dialogue on how to blend the values of Muslims and those of the Italian Republic. The council meets whenever important issues arise, but at least three times a year. The fact that the minister of the interior chairs the council and that Italian officials at the highest levels are regularly invited to attend the sessions demonstrates how important it is to Italian governments.

A MATURING, BUT ANOMALOUS, ECONOMY

In the 1970s, the Italian economy went through numerous crises that paralleled the political unrest. Labor agitation ignited by the 1969 Hot Autumn, the oil crisis, and a rapid rise in real wages touched off double-digit inflation that continued for fifteen years. Before 1969, for example, real wages increased in Italy at about the same rate as in other Organization for Economic Cooperation and Development (OECD) countries, 10 percent a year; in the 1970s, the annual increase jumped to between 20 and 25 percent, double the OECD rate, and was no longer matched by increases in productivity. The resulting inflation outstripped the other advanced European countries and the United States, reaching a high of 21 percent in 1980, and remained substantially above the rate for the other highly industrialized countries. In 1983, when Craxi's Socialist-led government took office, inflation was still at 15 percent. At the same time, economic growth languished, scoring in the negative numbers in 1982 and 1983.

Craxi's tenure signaled a return to prosperity. The Socialist leader was helped by a decline in oil prices and a worldwide recovery, but he came to office with the goal of preparing the country to share in this recovery, already foreshadowed on the horizon. Political stability, redressing the balance between business and labor by reducing worker excesses, measures encouraging business, and the *scala mobile* referendum, discussed in the previous chapter, brought inflation down to 4.6 percent in 1987 and productivity into line once again with the increase in real wages. Growth rates also took off, averaging over 2.5 percent per year from 1983 to 1987 compared with under 1 percent during the previous four years. The stock market soared, allowing capitalization to quadruple, and major business restructuring occurred—industry became more efficient and profitability increased dramatically. Fiat engaged in a seesaw battle with Volkswagen for the position of largest European automobile manufacturing concern; clothing and shoes rode the reputation for Italian design to world prominence; and engineering firms prospered. Names such as Benetton, Armani, Valentino, De Benedetti, Gardini, and Berlusconi became familiar throughout Europe and in the United States. Public industry restructured itself under IRI's Romano Prodi and ENI's Franco Reviglio, became profitable again, and undertook privatization initiatives.

As a result of this "second" economic miracle, the Italians claimed to have surpassed the United Kingdom as the world's fifth-largest economy in 1987. Despite British denials, later figures confirmed the Italian contention, if the large underground economy was counted. Italy's statistical profile resembled that of the advanced European countries—a sharp decline in agricultural employment, a slower one in industry, a rapid rise in the tertiary sector, and an increase in female employment (50 percent since 1972) (see Table 20.3). As in the rest of Europe, the country's economic development resulted in a great influx of immigrants, especially from Africa, who were willing to take jobs that Italians no longer wished to perform.

The size of Italy's underground economy is one sign that the Italian economy remains anomalous with respect to the other economically developed countries,

Table 20.2

Gross Production of Electrical Energy, 1986–1991 (in millions of kilowatt hours)

1986	193,330
1987	201,372
1988	203,561
1989	210,750
1990	216,891
1991	222,041

Table 20.3

Percentage Employment by Economic Sector

Year	Agriculture	Industry	Services
1971	20.1	39.5	40.4
1981	13.3	37.2	49.5
1982	12.3	36.7	51.0
1983	12.3	25.8	51.9
1984	11.8	34.1	54.1
1985	11.1	33.2	55.7
1986	10.7	32.7	56.6
1987	10.4	32.2	57.4
1988	9.8	32.2	58.1
1989	9.3	32.2	58.6
1990	8.7	32.4	58.8
1991	8.4	32.0	59.5
1992	8.1	32.0	59.9

despite the country's accelerating modernization. Usually "black" economies have the purpose of circumventing taxes and fringe benefits paid by employers, thus exploiting workers. The first intention is present in Italy, but the second—though it is certainly a factor—also served to increase worker income by ensuring an extra job (*doppio lavoro*). The phenomenon of the worker who gets off early or continually calls in sick to "moonlight" while receiving generous paid benefits from a first job is more widespread than in other countries. The underground economy causes a great loss of tax revenue for the state.

The tax structure is another anomalous feature of the Italian economy. First, it provides a moral justification for evasion. There are more than 200 taxes in Italy that, if paid according to law, would quickly bankrupt the ordinary citizen. Second, compounding this situation is the confusion and inefficiency of the tax collection system, which makes it difficult to know when and how taxes should be paid. Nevertheless, Italians do pay heavy taxes, and when governments have undertaken austerity measures, the extra revenues have usually exceeded their expectations.

One group, storekeepers, successfully resisted paying its full share of taxes, usually by doing a cash business and greatly underestimating receipts. This situation resulted in strong resentment on the part of salaried workers, who claimed that they paid an unfair proportion of taxes. In an attempt to redress this situation, in 1983 the government mandated that shopkeepers install electronic cash registers and give receipts for purchases. Although these enforcement measures undoubtedly helped, they have not resolved the problem. The ability to evade taxes and the protection that shopkeepers receive from their associations have preserved small shops from the decline that has occurred in other parts of the industrialized world. As a result, Italy has the highest density of small shops in Europe, causing some critics to maintain that the country has an inefficient distribution system despite the changes that came slowly in the late 1990s.

The phenomenon of the old and the new existing side by side characterizes the Italian economy, but the inefficiency of public services hampers modernization and contrasts starkly with sectors—such as computers, textiles, steel, and automobiles—that are among the most advanced in the world. Most evident to the casual observer is the poor state of the mails. Italians adapt by making greater use of fax machines and private couriers, but Italy has not kept pace with the communications revolution on a level with other European countries. The country has a high density of cell phones, however, and the Internet is coming into ever-greater use.

More seriously, a slow and inefficient bureaucracy has handicapped the Italian ability to compete in an increasingly globalized world economy. Legislation to reform the bureaucracy has been passed but not enforced, and basic services such as health care not only cost the taxpayer more but have degraded over time and, in certain areas, threatened to break down. Myriad documents requiring great expenditure of time and effort are required for the simplest operations. This reality favors corruption as private citizens, businesspeople, and even public servants attempt to get around regulations unanimously judged to be ridiculous and useless. The corruption increases costs, contributes significantly to the massive

Table 20.4

GDP and Gross Wage per Full-Time
Labor Unit (in thousands of current lire)

Year	GDP per F.T. labor unit	Gross wages per F.T. labor unit
1986	39,494	18,865
1987	43,002	20,540
1988	47,321	22,296
1989	51,694	23,881
1990	56,382	26,475
1991	60,835	28,793
1992	64,842	30,214

increase in the public debt, and damages the efficiency of Italian enterprises; it also contributed to the outbreak of a major scandal in 1992 that drastically altered the political scene.

The public debt, though always high, increased steeply during the Craxi years and continued its rise after his tenure. By 1985, it had reached almost 85 percent of GDP, compared to 48.5 percent for the United States, and by the 1990s it surpassed 100 percent. The resulting need for the state to borrow spurred it to offer attractive yields, at first tax-free and then taxed at a favorable rate. Investors earned more in absolute safety by buying government bonds than by investing in productive enterprises and risking their money. Public borrowing thus soaked up capital that might otherwise have been invested in the private sector and bloated the debt even more until new instruments were introduced.

The enormous debt weakened the lira and hampered Italian efforts to become fully integrated into the EU (which formally came into existence in 1984 because of changes in the treaties of the European Community). This issue and the linked problem of Italy's habitually high deficit became particularly important for Italy because, in December 1991, in Maastricht, Holland, the EU members decided to create a common currency, later called the euro. The Maastricht Treaty set up strict criteria according to which the budget deficit of countries aspiring to join the single currency could not exceed 3 percent. Most Europeans believed that Italy could not fulfill the criteria and therefore would not be among those eligible to adopt the common currency on the first round. The Italians, however, strongly supported the EU, and its leaders made it a point of honor for the Italians, among the founding members of the Union, to become eligible for the new currency when the other major nations did so—fearing otherwise that the country's image and economy would suffer. Romano Prodi, who became prime minister at the head of a Left-Center coalition following the 1996 elections, instituted a drastic austerity program with the support of most political factions. In May 1998, Italy was certified as having met the Maastricht conditions for entering the new monetary union (officially known as the European Monetary Union, or EMU) at the same time as its major partners. Despite the austerity imposed by Maastricht, many Italians hoped that the EU would force them to adopt difficult measures they otherwise would be politically unable to implement, However, the creation of a tariff-free zone after December 31, 1992, caused Italian companies that had been used to government subsidies much trouble. Given the inefficiencies of some industrial sectors and the inability of government substantially to reform public services, Italian firms found it difficult to adjust to the new economic realities of increased competition and globalization.

The most efficient economic concerns have been centered in the North, especially in Milan and the Veneto. A new model of a highly efficient cottage industry using computers, for example, sprouted in the Veneto; these new firms were strongly oriented to the export trade and transformed the economy and labor relations of the region. Paradoxically, however, this economic revolution highlighted another of Italy's anomalies. Although, as mentioned earlier, Italy's statistical profile approaches that of advanced Europe, this is an average boosted by the stunning progress of the North. The South remains one of Europe's most backward areas economically. Compared to the North and the Center, unemployment has remained high (frequently surpassing 20 percent), more persons work without benefits, and the workforce is still declining. In the South, fewer women are employed outside the home, family size is larger, more young people leave school to take menial jobs or seek low-paying state positions, demeaning public assistance is more widespread, and over 18 percent of the population subsists below the poverty line compared with under 7 percent for the other regions. Besides the psychological wounds this situation inflicts on southerners, it makes Italy less competitive in a more open Europe and has provoked the northern revolt against the stato assistenzialista discussed earlier.

In addition to the frustrations of the Italian South, the extent of organized criminal activity is also anomalous in a modern country with a thriving economy. In 1986, officials estimated that organized crime profits accounted for about 12.5 percent of GDP. To protect this investment from state offensives, criminal organizations committed a series of spectacular crimes, including the murders of Carlo Alberto Dalla Chiesa, who had defeated the terrorists, and Mafia-fighters Giovanni Falcone and Paolo Borsellino. The state struck back by adopting laws that make it easier to fight criminal activity, conducting maxi-trials, exposing connections between politicians and criminals, and successfully capturing major leaders. Despite this activity, in 1986 an anti-Mafia official claimed that three southern provinces were no longer under the full control of the state. Whether this assessment was accurate or not, by the late 1980s the state had initiated a vigorous counterattack against the criminal organizations and had scored significant successes that continued into the twenty-first century. Italian officials claimed, however, that Italian organized crime was expanding its activities into Eastern Europe and Russia as a result of its defeats in Italy. Concern increased that Italian criminal organizations would find it easier to penetrate other Western European countries as a result of the EU's elimination of border controls. The so-called Schengen agreement, of which Italy is a signatory, allows people from one area of the EU to travel freely to any other without a passport.

Moreover, the enormous Italian public sector itself constitutes an anomaly. Its size represents greater state intervention in the economy than is the case in other countries. Despite the crucial role that public companies had in Italy's economic growth, they became inefficient, usually because of political corruption. Their size and importance made them targets of the parties, which milked them for political contributions in return for public works contracts. The political scandal that erupted in 1992, which involved public activity, brought insistent demands for privatization beyond that accomplished during the Craxi era. Italians have struggled to achieve a proper balance between state intervention and private initiative, but how or at what point equilibrium would be attained have remained unclear. However, since privatization and less government intervention in the economy is a major EU goal, Italy was committed to implementing these principles.

The introduction of the euro in 2002, globalization, and the worldwide economic crisis in the early years of the twenty-first century have underscored the grim problems that Italy faces as a result of failing to reform its economic and political systems. While the Italians have done better by "muddling through" than they had dared to hope, they reached the point in 2008 where they could not put off reforms much longer. Italy's growing problems have made reforming the economic and political systems the most urgent matters on the national agenda. The big question is whether Italians will succeed or whether the country will be condemned to decline in the future.

CHAPTER TWENTY-ONE

A Style for the Republic

Sociologist Francesco Alberoni has written: "Italians do not have an ethical tradition, but an esthetic one. . . . They would be lost if they were not able to save themselves through good form and good taste."

In modern times, the republic has enabled this aesthetic tradition to become supreme. Emerging from a detested dictatorship and devastated psychologically by participation in an immoral war, the country achieved a positive image, despite its perennially troubled political atmosphere, through the culture that the republic allowed to flourish.

Cinema

Harking back to a remarkable cinematic tradition, postwar Italian cinema incorporated a new cultural style. Directors of the "Neorealistic" school, such as Roberto Rossellini, Vittorio De Sica, and Luchino Visconti, focused on contemporary Italian problems and characters taken from ordinary life and made Italian film world-famous.

Ironically, this movement's seeds can be found in the Fascist period. For example, Alessandro Blasetti's *1860*, made in 1934, gives an unromantic view of Garibaldi's fight for Italian unity and as such influenced the development of neorealism. Blasetti, who had the sympathy of the Fascist regime, nevertheless displeased it on occasion. Fascists rejected one of his films on fascism, and another movie, *La corona di ferro* (The Iron Crown), brought the remark from Nazi propaganda chief Josef Goebbels that in Germany Blasetti would have been shot.

That neorealism had its roots in the Fascist period can also be seen by the biographies of the major directors of that school. Roberto Rossellini, who opened the Neorealist period with his masterpiece *Open City* (1945), was born in Rome in 1906 and worked at the Istituto Luce, which produced government newsreels. He also worked on a famous propaganda film, *Renato Serra pilota* (Renato Serra, Pilot), and on a trilogy of films on the war in Europe. *Open City*, shot in German-occupied Rome, tells the story of Roman resisters against the Nazi occupation. Based on the true story of a priest executed by the Germans for his resistance activities, Rossellini's priest, Don Pietro, helps a Communist engineer (Manfredi) who is opposing the Nazis. But the film also shows the resistance at the popular level. In a dramatic scene that has remained fixed in the annals of cinematic history, a woman of the lower classes, Pina (played by the famous actress Anna Magnani), is killed by German machine guns in front of her little son. Her lover—the boy's father and a resistance fighter—was being taken away by the Germans, and they kill her when she tries to prevent the deportation. At the end of the movie, Manfredi is tortured and killed because he will not give up his fellow resisters, and Don Pietro is executed by a firing squad before the eyes of Pina's little boy. *Open City* won a prize at the Cannes Film Festival in 1946 and international audiences acclaimed it. Rossellini went on to make two other masterpieces dealing with the war. He later made more headlines because of his affair with Swedish actress Ingrid Bergman, whom he later married. After his early successes, he made several films that were failures. However, two of his later works stand out: *General Della Rovere* (1959) and *The Rise of Louis XIV*, made for French television in 1967.

In an unusual twist, *General Della Rovere* starred Vittorio De Sica. De Sica began his career as an actor but is renowned as one of the best Neorealist directors. De Sica helped pioneer neorealism in a 1943 film and reached his apogee with four films that appeared in quick succession: *Shoeshine* (1946), *Bicycle Thief* (1949)—both of which received an Oscar—*Miracle in Milan* (1951), and *Umberto D.* (1952), all produced by the legendary Cesare Zavattini. These films tell about the desperate social and economic conditions in Italy immediately after the war. De Sica's later films do not come up to the standards of his earlier work, but two well-received films, *Yesterday, Today, and Tomorrow* (1963) and *The Garden of the Finzi-Continis* (1971), won Oscars.

Luchino Visconti, an aristocratic Milanese who had worked in Paris with the great director Jean Renoir and was influenced by Blasetti, directed the first Neorealist masterpiece in 1942: *Obsession*, considered a "Resistance" film and made just before Mussolini's fall. Visconti, whose film was based on James Cain's novel *The Postman Always Rings Twice*, "achieved . . . a magnificent linkage between his tragic protagonists and their environment" and showed the importance international currents had in the movement. Arrested in 1943 for his partisan activities, Visconti returned to filmmaking in 1948 with *La Terra Trema* (The Earth Shakes), another Neorealist masterpiece based on the famous Giovanni Verga novel *I Malavoglia* (The House by the Medlar Tree). In 1954, he directed *Senso* (Feeling), a look at the Risorgimento without rose-colored glasses and based on a short story of the same title. Perhaps his best- known masterpiece, however, is *Rocco and His Brothers* (1960). This film examines the breakdown of a peasant family when it moves to the big city, a crisis that affected millions of people during the economic and social transformation that occurred in postwar Italy. His most famous later films include *The Leopard*, based on the extraordinary novel about the Risorgimento of the same title, and *The Damned*, about the rise of Nazism in Germany and the event known as the "Night of the Long Knives." Visconti scrupulously portrayed history on his sets and was noted for his absolute fidelity in portraying past eras.

The Neorealist cinema had a greater commercial and artistic impact abroad than in Italy, which remained dominated by Hollywood productions. Even after 1951, when an Italian-American accord curbed imports and allowed more Italian films to be exported to the United States, American films predominated at the Italian box office; nevertheless, Italian Neorealist works had a lasting cultural influence in the cinematic field.

Italy's best-known director, Federico Fellini, also had his cinematic roots in the 1940s. Born in Rimini, on the Adriatic coast, on January 20, 1920, Fellini earned his first money as a teenager drawing caricatures for a movie house and for tourists. In January 1939, he moved to Rome, ostensibly to study law, but there he came into contact with the world of acting and the cinema. He began by writing gags for movies and during the war started collaborating on screenplays. In 1943, he met his wife—and future star in his movies—actress Giulietta Masina. His rise to fame started when he wrote screenplays for some of Rossellini's most famous films, including *Open City*, and for other directors.

The 1950s witnessed Fellini's emergence as a renowned director. In 1952, he directed *The White Sheik*, a film about the dreams of a character from the provinces. *I Vitelloni* (The Loafers) (1953) brought him international fame. This film discusses the carefree and disordered lives of five friends who come into sudden contact with reality. Films such as *The Nights of Cabiria* and *La Strada*, which won an Oscar for best foreign film, solidified his reputation and set the stage for his 1960s masterpieces: *La Dolce Vita*, *8½*, and *Juliet of the Spirits*. *La Dolce Vita* symbolized an era of growing leisure but decaying morals. A journalist (Marcello), played by Marcello Mastroianni, accompanies a visiting beautiful star (Swedish actress Anita Ekberg) around Rome. He becomes infatuated with her, and the visit culminates in a famous scene in which the actress takes a nocturnal splash in Rome's Trevi Fountain. Marcello confesses his feelings for the actress, but the next day everything melts away with the sun and the anger of the actress's boyfriend. This story and Marcello's relationship with a friend who commits suicide illustrate the frivolousness of the "sweet life." In the partly autobiographical *8½*, Fellini's best film, the famous director Giulio Anselmi (Marcello Mastroianni) battles his producers and the press, both anxious to know where he stands on his latest film. Giulio, however, is in the throes of an artistic crisis and cannot work on it. At the same time, he is pressured by his wife, who is tired of his affairs, and by his friends. Even the arrival of his mistress brings no relief. Giulio dreams about how he would like his life to be while he is pressured by the mundane demands of his fans and friends. He cannot do anything. He panics, but when things seem utterly lost, he regains his artistic clarity and his creative force. Fellini's $8\frac{1}{2}$ ends with a famous circus tune in which everyone participates, and Giulio's film finally begins.

Fellini's later movies include *Amarcord* (I Remember), a haunting depiction of life under fascism, and films on the cultural and political milieu of the 1970s and 1980s. Nino Rota, who became a world-renowned composer for the cinema, wrote the music for Fellini's films. He also wrote the music for the *Godfather* films, for one of which he won an Oscar in 1975 for best score.

Spurred by this fame, the Italian film industry reorganized itself in the late 1950s. In the 1960s, producers financed not only "art" films but also "serious" comedies such as Mario Monicelli's *The Organizer* (1963), which is about the early Socialist and labor movements. (In addition to being a theater critic, Monicelli's father Tommaso was a well-known Socialist in early 1900s Milan.) Monicelli directed acclaimed comedies such as *L'Armata Brancaleone* (Brancaleone's Army) (1965), which won many prizes. Pietro Germi, whose *Divorce Italian Style* and *Seduced and Abandoned* have already been noted, won international praise. The son of a worker and a tailor, Germi died early of hepatitis, depriving the Italian cinema of one of its most sophisticated practitioners. Director Sergio Leone originated the "spaghetti westerns" that made Clint Eastwood a superstar. The music composer for these movies, Ennio Morricone, composed over 300 scores for films, and on February 25, 2007, the Academy of Motion Picture Arts and Sciences awarded him an honorary Academy Award for his lifework. Leone also directed a commentary on American life and crime, *Once Upon a Time in America*. Success of this kind allowed Italian production companies to break into the middle-class market and to capture a wide international audience—and to increase their share of the home box office with respect to Hollywood's take, which declined to 15 percent.

In the 1970s, the crisis that struck Italian society affected the film industry. As the economic picture for Italian cinema became less rosy, however, the Italian presence on the international cinematic scene remained strong. Italian filmmakers explored alienation in modern life and political issues of concern during that period. These directors included Michelangelo Antonioni (*L'Avventura, Blow-Up, Red Desert*), Pier Paolo Pasolini (*Pigpen, Teorema, Salò*), and Bernardo Bertolucci, who was once Pasolini's assistant (*Last Tango in Paris, The Conformist, 1900*). Pasolini, noted also for his literary works, stirred up intense debate with his films and his homosexual lifestyle. Bertolucci's first great film, *Before the Revolution*, told the story of a man's vain attempt to break free from the bourgeois life. His *Last Tango in Paris*, censured in Italy and denounced abroad for its sex scenes, was notable for its technique—its male star, Marlon Brando, made up his lines as he went along. *The Conformist*, loosely based on the novel by Alberto Moravia, tells the story of Marcello, who tries to expiate a crime he believes he has committed by helping the Fascist secret police murder his old professor. *1900* is a panoramic view of the epic class struggle in Bertolucci's native region and of the rise of fascism. As in literature, fascism and the Resistance provided favorite themes for Italian filmmakers, inspiring, among others, Lina Wertmuller's *Love and Anarchy*, Bertolucci's *The Spider's Stratagem*, and the Taviani brothers' *The Night of the Shooting Stars*. Marco Leto's award-winning *La villeggiatura* (The Vacation) portrays a gloomy picture of life under the Fascist dictatorship. The Italian political and social situation also came under scrutiny in the films of Elio Petri (*Investigation of a Citizen Above Suspicion*), Ettore Scola (*We All Loved Each Other Very Much*), and Francesco Rosi (*Three Brothers* and *Excellent Cadavers*). Lina Wertmuller, who had worked with Fellini, directed *The Seduction of Mimi*, a complex film in which social mores, politics, and the Mafia are all brilliantly intertwined. Her *Swept Away* explored the class struggle and the battle between the sexes.

Faced by renewed American domination in the motion picture field, Italian cinema continued to experience an economic crisis into the 1980s and beyond, although there was some recovery. Filmmakers turned to television and international cooperation to continue making high-quality products, such as Bertolucci's *The Last Emperor*, which won nine Oscars, *Cinema Paradiso*, *Mediterraneo*, and *Life Is Beautiful*, which won Oscars for best picture in 1989, 1991, and 1997, respectively. Despite its inability to compete in the contemporary high-budget, action-oriented movie climate, Italian film retained a strong presence on the international cultural circuit in this best-known art form of contemporary Italy.

LITERATURE

Besides cinema, literary endeavor brought a high profile to the Italy of the republic. Three world-class poets who had done important work during the interwar period remained very active after the war. Widely regarded as deserving a Nobel Prize, Giuseppe Ungaretti did not receive that honor, possibly for political reasons, but collected a host of other awards. Noted for shearing Italian poetry of rhetoric and metaphor, his work translated into many languages, Ungaretti lectured in foreign countries, including the United States, and was one of the strongest influences in modern poetry.

The prestigious Nobel Prize that had eluded Ungaretti was awarded to two of his contemporaries. Salvatore Quasimodo, brother-in-law of novelist Elio Vittorini, won the prize in 1959. Quasimodo claimed to be the real founder of hermetic poetry, a form in which the poet has to face himself without referring to conventional cultural standards. Quasimodo, who was educated in the sciences, was not able to escape the influence of his native Sicily even though he left it. Eugenio Montale, the 1975 Nobel Prize winner and one of the founders of an influential political journal, *Il Mondo*, dabbled in politics only briefly and "was probably the profoundest poetic interpreter of the drama of twentieth-century man, with his existential anguish and his victimization by events and movements." These three poets testify to the extraordinary presence of Italian poetry on the twentieth-century stage.

As in poetry, prominent novelists who wrote during the Fascist period continued publishing during the republic. Unlike the poets, however, their writings bore directly on the political situation. Fascism—opposition to it first, the Resistance after, and as an evil to be guarded against later—thus served as a prime stimulant to literary production. Indeed, publishing houses had served as centers of anti-Fascist activities, and many of the writers associated with them were Communists, although some later turned against the movement. Ironically—given the writers' future anti-American stance—this "resistance" to fascism frequently took the form of translating into Italian the American novels of the 1930s that dealt with social issues (for example, John Steinbeck's *Grapes of Wrath*) and, as in cinema, exposed many Italian writers to international currents.

Among the novelists who criticized fascism and whose work had international repercussions was Alberto Moravia, who had burst onto the literary scene with a masterpiece that condemned Fascist values: *The Time of Indifference*. Moravia, publishing at the rate of about a novel a year, continued to comment on the ills of modern society into his eighties. *The Conformist*, a book loosely based on the murder of the anti-Fascist Rosselli brothers by the secret police, and one of Moravia's later works, *Two Women*, became classic films. Carlo Levi, a left-wing painter condemned to "internal exile" in a poor southern region, profited from his experience to write *Christ Stopped at Eboli*, one of the most famous characterizations of the oppressive Fascist climate. Ignazio Silone, a Communist who later repudiated the movement, also condemned Fascist oppression in *Fontamara* and gave a picture of the underground in *Bread and Wine*. This last novel also raised important moral issues and demonstrated increasing disillusionment with communism. In his later works, Silone was preoccupied with the relationship of Christianity and politics in society. In the late 1990s, Silone became the object of an attempt to brand him as an informer for the Fascist police, but the case was refuted and the debate remained open.

Another world-class novelist had a continuing influence on the literary scene during the republic, the Sicilian Elio Vittorini. Vittorini exercised this sway thanks to his collaboration with important literary reviews and his connections with major Italian publishers. He opposed the Mussolini regime and translated American authors into Italian during the Fascist period as a way of criticizing it—ironically, in view of his Communist militancy. In fact, during the war, Vittorini participated in the Resistance and later became editor of the Communist daily newspaper *Unità*. Vittorini's novel *Il garofano rosso* (The Red Carnation) was condemned as subversive by the government. His more noted *Conversazione in Sicilia* (Conversations in Sicily) combines "the energy of political commitment with a strikingly effective technique." Perhaps, most important, Vittorini's *Uomini e no* (Men and Not Men), a stark portrayal of Milanese partisans fighting the Nazis, heavily influenced by Hemingway's style, served as a prototype for a major postwar Italian movement, the Resistance novel.

With the war and censorship over by the late 1940s, Italy witnessed an "explosion" of novels dealing with the Resistance. One of the best writers was the former partisan fighter Beppe Fenoglio. Fenoglio, the son of a butcher who died prematurely at age forty-one, was influenced by American literature. He had trouble publishing his works at first, thanks also to the opposition of Vittorini, but he remains famous as one of the most important practitioners of the Resistance novel. His most famous work is *Il partigiano Johnny* (Johnny the Partisan). In addition to Fenoglio, the country's best writers—Vasco Pratolini, Cesare Pavese, Italo Calvino, Carlo Cassola, and Guido Piovene—wrote important works. Renata Viganò published *L'Agnese va a morire* (Agnese Goes to Her Death), an examination of a woman's road to antifascism and the Resistance.

Fueled by an enduring tradition of high-level literary journals, Italian literature continued to demonstrate great vitality in the postwar decades. Its preoccupation with national, social, and political issues was illustrated in Giuseppe di Lampedusa's 1958 international literary sensation, *The Leopard*. Later transformed into a film by Visconti, this novel describes Sicily at the time of Garibaldi's landing in 1860 and contends that the old Italian elites hijacked the Risorgimento and turned it to their own purposes. Vasco Pratolini is best known for his description of Florentine life, but demonstrated a flair for the historical novel with contemporary implications in *Metello*, a novel of early socialism. The Sicilian novelist Leonardo Sciascia won international acclaim for a series of brilliant novels unmasking the Mafia's operations, as well as for his political novels. Giorgio Bassani examined the effects of the anti-Semitic legislation and the war on Italian Jews in Ferrara in *The Garden of the Finzi-Continis*, popularized outside of Italy by the De Sica movie of the same name. On this same theme, the autobiographical works of former concentration camp inmate Primo Levi have been translated and widely covered by the American press. (Interviews with Levi by American novelist Philip Roth had an important impact in the United States.) Two of his most famous works are *Survival in Auschwitz* and *The Reawakening*. Another novel, *The Truce*, was made into a movie by Francesco Rosi.

Other prominent writers of the republican period who gained worldwide fame include Carlo Emilio Gadda and Umberto Eco. The most famous novels of Gadda, an electronics engineer who at first failed to make a living from his literary production, are the much-acclaimed *La cognizione del dolore* (Acquainted with Grief) and the crime story set in Rome, *Quer pasticciaccio brutto di via Merulana* (That Awful Mess on the Via Merulana). Umberto Eco burst on the international scene as author of *The Name of the Rose*, an international best-seller made into a well-known film. Italo Calvino was famous for his novels portraying a less concrete world and for his *Italian Folk Tales*. In 1997, the unorthodox and highly political playwright Dario Fo won the Nobel Prize for literature. Pier Paolo Pasolini and Edoardo De Filippo illustrate another postwar literary trend that is now a dying tradition—literature written in dialect.

The republic's lively literary atmosphere allowed female writers to come into their own, building on the tradition of female novelists discussed in chapter 13. The best female novelist to emerge in contemporary Italy was Elsa Morante, the wife of Alberto Moravia. She produced a number of important works, but her most ambitious is *History: A Novel*. Creating a literary sensation when it was first published in 1974, this work tells the story of Useppe—born as the result of the rape of his mother by a German soldier during the occupation of Rome—and of his family lacerated by war. It has been judged a masterpiece on the model of nineteenth-century Russian novels. The works of Oriana Fallaci, a prominent newspaperwoman, have been translated into English; her novels and other writings relied heavily on her journalism, as did those of Matilde Serao. More in the traditional mode of a novelist, but emphasizing memorialistic material, are the books of Natalia Ginzburg, a member of a prominent Turinese Jewish family. Other prominent female novelists include Dacia Maraini and Anna Banti, whose novels remain untranslated into English.

DESIGN AND FASHION, SCIENCE AND TECHNOLOGY

Besides literature and cinema, two related areas have spread Italy's fame during the republic: design and fashion. Attractive design of modern industrial products must be ranked among the major reasons why Italian products have had such great appeal on the world market. This activity includes everything, as the catalog of one exhibition put it, "from the spoon to the city." The products of large companies such as Olivetti and Fiat and design outfits such as Kartell (plastics), Artemide (lamps), and Brionvega (electronics) illustrate the reputation that the country has gained in this field, which has become an essential part of modern marketing.

In addition to advanced design, fashion has become a byword for Italy during the republic. Names such as Armani, Versace, Prada, Krizia, Valentino, Fendi, Mila Schön, and Ferrè are known the world over. Gianni Versace, tragically murdered outside his home in South Beach (Miami), Florida, on July 23, 1997, winner of many prestigious awards, built a fashion empire worth over $800 million in ten years. Fendi, opened by Edoardo and Adele Fendi in 1925, began as a small store specializing in fur and leather goods and grew to world renown through the efforts of the founders' five daughters.

Style was not the only element that made these firms and those like them important. In the 1980s, Italy became the third-largest world manufacturer of apparel, with production amounting to $20 billion. Much of this production was exported, making the sector into the industrialized world's largest export-oriented business. The clothing industry's development is a tribute not only to the country's aesthetic sense but also to its adaptability and its technological and organizational know-how. In the 1970s, the industry began reorganizing to meet the demands of the "mass individualism of post-industrial society" by combining modern inventions with artisan techniques and imagination. Benetton became a pioneer in making clothing practically to order through the use of computers. Italian firms were leaders in the application of CAD-CAM (computer-aided design–computer-aided manufacturing) techniques. In twelve years, CAD-CAM systems increased at an annual 48 percent rate, so that by 1987 they accounted for 50 percent of market potential. As a result of this massive effort, apparel exports increased 700 percent from 1976 to 1987.

This advanced technology also indicated the country's position at the cutting edge of modern technology. An example of this increasingly close interconnection between science and technology has been the development of new materials. In this field, Giulio Natta of the Milan Polytechnic won the 1963 Nobel Prize in chemistry for his research on high polymers, essential for the production of plastic.

Another field in which Italy has distinguished itself is nuclear physics. As with electromagnetism, discussed in chapter 13, research in this area cuts across political regimes and dates back to 1927, when physicist Orso Mario Corbino transformed the University of Rome's physics institute at Via Panisperna 89A into a world-class institution. Corbino approached Mussolini for financing and assembled a brilliant team of nuclear physicists who ranked among the best in the world—the "Via Panisperna Boys." The star of the institute was Enrico Fermi, who won the 1938 Nobel Prize in physics and was unusual among physicists because he excelled in both theory and experimentation. In 1933, he published a fundamental paper describing the "weak interactive force." His statistics were very important for quantum mechanics; after he left Italy and went to the United States in January 1939 in protest against Italian anti-Semitic legislation (his wife was Jewish), his research in Rome on "slow neutrons" culminated at the University of Chicago in the first controlled nuclear chain reaction. Italian scientists who came to the United States during the same period, including Emilio Segrè, founded a school of nuclear physics based on his work. In the Soviet Union, Fermi's physics was propagated by Bruno Pontecorvo, another member of his group who fled to the East in 1950 in a clamorous early incident of the Cold War. Continuing Italian research in the field of the weak interactive force resulted in another Nobel in physics for Carlo Rubbia in 1984.

On January 1, 1989, Rubbia took over as director-general of the Conseil Européen pour Recherches Nucléaires (CERN), the leading European nuclear research center in Geneva, for a five-year term. By then, nuclear research had become internationalized—with the collaboration of Italian scientists. Paralleling Italian interest in multilateral economic organizations after World War II, physicist Edoardo Amaldi, youngest of the Via Panisperna Boys, realized that modern nuclear physics would be impossible without great economic resources. This reality dictated the pooling of European money and talent, he believed, if Europe was to be in a position to compete with the United States. Amaldi's powerful advocacy of a European nuclear research facility culminated in the foundation of CERN.

Indeed, during the years of the economic miracle, increasing internationalization became the hallmark of modern science. Scientists such as Rubbia and Riccardo Giacconi, winner of the 2002 Nobel Prize in physics "for pioneering contributions to astrophysics, which have led to the discovery of cosmic X-ray sources," moved comfortably from Italian posts to European and American ones, and back again. Other examples of this tendency include Rita Levi-Montalcini, 1986 Nobel Prize winner in medicine. Levi-Montalcini spent thirty years in the United States, although her prize-winning research began in Turin. Amazingly, two of Levi-Montalcini's classmates at the University of Turin, who also worked abroad for many years, also won Nobel Prizes in medicine. Salvador Luria shared the prize in 1969 for his research on viruses that infect bacteria instead of ordinary cells, work that the Nobel Committee stated "set the solid foundations on which modern molecular biology rests" and greatly advanced the understanding of genetics and of diseases caused by viruses. Renato Dulbecco shared the 1975 Nobel Prize in medicine. His groundbreaking work on virus replication advanced knowledge on the mechanism of tumor growth and cancer.

PORTRAITS

EMILIO SEGRÈ
Bombs and Books

The period between World War I and World War II was the golden age of Italian physics. Led by Enrico Fermi and the group he established in Rome, scientists made fundamental discoveries about the atomic nucleus. The increasing domestic repression, the Ethiopian War, and the anti-Jewish legislation had devastating effects on Italian science. One important result, however, was that the scattering of Italian nuclear scientists aided in the invention of the atomic bomb and nuclear power and in the creation of new physics schools in the United States, England, and the Soviet Union.

One of the major exiles from the Italian scientific community was Emilio Segrè. Segrè was born in Tivoli, outside Rome, on February 1, 1905. Segrè decided to study physics under Fermi, even though his mother fretted about her son's choosing a profession that paid poorly and offered little opportunity for steady employment. Segrè became a member of the famous "Via Panisperna Boys," buying samples of all the natural elements so the group could bombard them with neutrons and observe the results. At the time, this task was not as simple as it sounds; Segrè scoured the shops of Rome with cash in his pocket until he found a merchant who was well stocked and knowledgeable. This person, Signor Troccoli, enjoyed speaking Latin with Segrè.

During his work with the Fermi group, Segrè worked with the most famous physicists of the period. Segrè was in the United States in 1938 when the Fascist anti-Jewish legislation was passed. Unwilling to return to Italy, he approached scientist Ernest O. Lawrence, who offered him a job as a research assistant at the Berkeley Radiation Laboratory (the famous "Rad Lab"), even though Segrè was a professor at the University of Palermo. Lawrence proposed a salary that Segrè accepted. In his gratitude, he told Lawrence that he was a Jew and could not return home—at which point Lawrence promptly reduced his salary.

At Berkeley, Segrè codiscovered a new element and plutonium–239, which was fissionable and was used for atomic weapons. During World War II, Segrè worked as a group leader on the Manhattan Project, making an important discovery in 1944: his demonstration that the plutonium bomb as originally designed would not work because of impurities caused a shake-up in the lab.

Emilio Segrè is credited with a number of important discoveries in nuclear physics, and in 1959 he was awarded the Nobel Prize in physics (with Owen Chamberlain) for the discovery of the anti-proton. Segrè became an American citizen in 1944, taught physics at several American universities, including Columbia and Berkeley, and returned to Rome in 1974 as a professor of nuclear physics. He died on April 22, 1989, of a heart attack.

Segrè published histories of science and his informative memoirs, *A Mind Always in Motion*. He also left a large photographic archive documenting the history of modern science.

PORTRAITS

RITA LEVI-MONTALCINI
"A Concept Out of Apparent Chaos"

〜〜〜

R ita Levi-Montalcini illustrates how a person can overcome severe adversity in many areas to produce excellence.

Levi-Montalcini was born in Turin on April 22, 1909, along with her twin, Paola, who became a noted painter. Her father made the decisions and believed that women should not pursue professional careers. While still young, Rita decided that she did not fit into her father's image of women. She asked him whether she could go to the university, and in eight months she had completed the necessary work in Latin, Greek, and mathematics that would qualify her to enter the University of Turin. At the university, she studied with two classmates who later won Nobel Prizes, and she received her degree in medicine in 1936.

In 1938, Mussolini instituted the racial laws barring Jews from pursuing academic or professional careers. Levi-Montalcini, torn between a career in medicine and a career in neurobiological research, wrote that the laws made the decision for her. She set up a small lab in her bedroom so that she could work without need for support from the outside world.

The German occupation of Italy in September 1943 forced her family to flee to Florence, where they linked up with the partisans and lived underground. With Florence's liberation in August 1944, Levi-Montalcini served as a doctor at a refugee camp, ministering to the victims of infectious diseases spread as a result of the fighting. In 1947, she received an invitation to continue her research on chick embryos at Washington University in St. Louis. Levi-Montalcini, who expected to stay for twelve months, would remain in St. Louis for over thirty years, climbing the academic ladder, establishing a research center in Rome, and heading several prestigious research centers.

The most notable result of her research came in 1951–1952, when she discovered nerve growth factor (NGF), crucial for the growth and differentiation of nerve cells. With her colleague Stanley Cohen, she continued her research on NGF for the next thirty years; later studies would demonstrate that it had a wider range and played a more important role than originally believed. As a result of her work, she won the 1986 Nobel Prize in medicine (with Cohen). As the Nobel Committee put it: "The discovery of NGF in the beginning of the 1950's is a fascinating example of how a skilled observer can create a concept out of apparent chaos."

Since she received her prize, Rita Levi-Montalcini has continued to be amazingly active into her nineties. She oversees important research institutes, has written four best sellers, serves as a life senator, and has established a family foundation fostering education, peace, personal development, and nondiscriminatory values.

Italy thus benefited greatly from the republic's openness and encouragement of economic and cultural ties with other countries—and has made significant contributions in these crucial areas. However, there has been a constant debate about the low level of research support for Italian scientists, resulting in a significant "brain drain" in favor of foreign countries such as the United States. Italy does a poor job in financing research and development; one international report pegged its support in this area just above that of Greece. This situation has produced resentment, in addition to the "brain drain" of scientists fleeing the country for better opportunities abroad. Different governments have pledged more help but have not been true to their word. Support for higher education has also fallen even as it has been restructured. Given the weak support for research, it is remarkable that groundbreaking research is still done in the country.

Euro-Marxism

Another area in which Italy became notable in the postwar era was in the elaboration of Marxist theory, a field in which Europeans distinguished themselves.

The publication of Antonio Gramsci's *Prison Notebooks* after World War II was an Italian and European event. The Fascists imprisoned Gramsci, a founder of the Italian Communist Party, and released him shortly before his death. In his cell, Gramsci wrote a series of notebooks published in five volumes between 1948 and 1951. The *Notebooks* opened up a new cultural debate, but later came under attack because Communist Party secretary Palmiro Togliatti edited them to remove references to material considered harmful to communism.

According to Italian Marxist thinkers, while in a Fascist prison cell, Gramsci painfully worked out a new brand of Marxism that did not ignore the Western, and Italian, democratic and cultural traditions. They presented Gramsci as elaborating a new theory that the Italian Communists would follow in order to gain power while at the same time affirming democracy. This meant, in effect, that the Communists would use electoral methods to win control of the government. They would do so, these theoreticians contended, with the support of both northern workers and southern peasants. Because of this support, communism-in-power would aim at implementing idealistic values such as social justice. Through the medium of Gramsci, the Communist challenge to existing society appeared as the challenge of idealism to the capitalist order, though within a democratic context.

This kind of thinking underpinned the most innovative policies of the Italian Communist Party, particularly during the tenure of Enrico Berlinguer as secretary. These policies included the right of the PCI to go its own way, independently of the Soviet Union, as Berlinguer claimed at the Fourth Congress of the Communist

Party of the Soviet Union in 1971. It also underlay his attempt to forge an alliance of Communist parties in the West ("Eurocommunism") and his proposal to ally with Catholic Italian workers who followed the lead of the Christian Democratic Party—the "Historic Compromise."

The Italian Communist interpretation of Gramsci's writings thus helped to propel the PCI in a direction that made it a supporter of Italian democracy and a point of reference for Western Communists, leftists, and Communists in the Eastern Bloc hoping to push Soviet-style communism in a more democratic direction. After the end of international communism between 1989 and 1991, Berlinguer's example served as a stimulus for Italian Communists in the transition to postcommunism. Italy was the only Western democracy in which postcommunism became an important part of the political landscape and in which former Communists occupied the country's highest offices of prime minister and president.

CHAPTER TWENTY-TWO

The
"Bloodless Revolution"

I N 1992, A DRASTIC SHAKE-UP OF ITALY'S POLITICAL AND ECONOMIC SYSTEM, labeled the "bloodless revolution," began. It caught commentators completely by surprise, but if imperfect bipolarism had marked republican politics, international communism's collapse and the Cold War's end were bound to produce extreme consequences. Confronted with the choice of losing their liberty or tolerating a "blocked" political system that encouraged corruption, Italians had selected the latter; with the threat to their freedom gone, they no longer had to face this dismal choice.

THE END OF THE ITALIAN COMMUNIST PARTY

Several key developments preceding the general elections in 1992 signaled important changes in the Italian political equilibrium. The first put intense pressure on the Italian Communist Party. In 1989, the revolution against Soviet power in Eastern Europe and the Red Chinese massacre in Tiananmen Square forced the PCI to distance itself further from Moscow than in the past. PCI secretary Achille Occhetto decided to change his party's name and apply for admission into the Socialist International. Led by prestigious party founder Pietro Ingrao and former secretary Alessandro Natta, the hard-liners objected because, they argued, PCI traditions differed from those of the "People's Republics." The long debate over these issues and grave internal opposition to Occhetto's leadership from hard-liners and Communist "reformists" (*miglioristi*) presaged a split. With the selection of a new name, the Democratic Party of the Left (PDS), the hard-liners broke off and formed Rifondazione Comunista (PRC).

International communism's fall caused a grave crisis not only for the PCI but also for the Christian Democrats. Their status as an anti-Communist bulwark had allowed them to block progressive reforms advocated by their Socialist and smaller allies. The odd contrast between a modern economy and inefficient public services and the brazen exploitation of state resources for political gain fueled the rise of a new political force in the North, Lega Lombarda (the Lombard League, also known as the Northern League). This organization accused Rome of incompetence and of running the country for the benefit of southerners at the expense of northerners. The Lombard League rapidly gained support, at Christian Democratic expense.

The general elections of April 5 and 6, 1992, focused all these elements and produced a political earthquake. The DC dropped 5 percent, a big change in Italian elections. The League won over 9 percent of the vote, making it the largest party in Milan, the country's industrial and financial heartland, and later local elections would confirm it as the largest northern party. The PDS received 16 percent of the vote, and the hard-line Rifondazione 5.5 percent. The four-party coalition that ruled Italy before the elections no longer had a stable majority.

THE SCANDALS: TANGENTOPOLI

Given the bankruptcy of international communism, the maintenance of PSI vote share, and Bettino Craxi's blank check from DC leaders who had promised to support him in the new legislature, Craxi claimed the prime minister's office. But Craxi soon faced a serious crisis. In February 1992, a Milanese businessman had complained to the authorities that money had been extorted from him by a local Socialist. Officials conducted an investigation that uncovered an incredible network of bribes that businesspeople paid to politicians to obtain public works contracts. Although further investigation revealed that all of the political parties were involved, the scandal had the greatest effect on the Socialists. In the summer of 1992, recently elected president Oscar Luigi Scalfaro refused to commission Craxi to form a government. His reason: if the scandal ever involved the Socialist leader personally, the republic itself would be endangered. After a long crisis, Giuliano Amato, Craxi's second-in-command, became prime minister.

Magistrates based in Milan launched "Operation Clean Hands" to get to the root of the corruption. Important members of the Milan "pool" had come out of the 1968 movement, although Antonio Di Pietro, the lead magistrate, had a conservative background. It was well known that bribery had been widespread and accepted as a necessary evil, but the judges charged that the system reached up to the highest levels of the party hierarchies, which were thus vulnerable. There was even talk of establishing a political system in which the magistrates would predominate. The main target was the country's most visible politician, Bettino Craxi. He was particularly vulnerable because he kept control of party affairs in his own hands, because of his campaign against the Communists, and because his brashness had alienated the political elite.

As the investigation progressed, Craxi was charged with corruption in a host of cases. He had allegedly stashed away funds in foreign bank accounts and used them to support his political endeavors and for personal use. Because he trusted no one, he personally collected many of the payments. This technique made it easier to target him than other politicians and parties. The Communists, for example, ran a much tighter organization than did the Socialists, and their treasurer insisted that he had used the money skimmed off the top of public works projects for himself and not for the party. Socialist secretary Craxi defended himself by stating that taking funds from publicly financed projects was normal procedure in the Italian political system because it was the only manner in which parties could realistically finance themselves, given inadequate public funding. He claimed that it was a necessary way to raise funds to fight the well-heeled Communists, who received large subsidies from the Soviet Union.

Craxi was the only major Italian politician to admit that he took money from public projects in order to finance his party, although it quickly became clear that all Italian parties did the same and that skimming was a normal and time-honored method of raising money. Public opinion gave Craxi some points for being forthright, but he had admitted the charges. Although many charges were dismissed on appeal, some stuck. As a result, Craxi fled Italy for Hammamet, Tunisia, where he had a summer home. He claimed that he was ill (he had diabetes) and that the magistrates wished to jail him to deny him medical attention.

From Hammamet, he periodically released statements commenting on Italian affairs, but his capacity to influence Italian politics ended. His death on January 19, 2000, sparked a debate about his role. Some observers and the general public viewed him as a corrupt politician, but others saw him as a fighter who had struggled to modernize Italian politics. While all parties took payoffs, the Socialists had gone too far and had acquired a reputation for corruption that Craxi did not reverse after he returned as party secretary following his long tenure as prime minister. His old enemies, now ex-Communists, condemned him and went overboard in labeling all Socialists as corrupt. This attitude boomeranged because many Socialist voters resented this blanket characterization and moved to the political Right, a trend that the most intelligent PDS leaders tried unsuccessfully to stanch. The allegations of corruption at the highest political levels hardly stopped with Craxi and the Socialists. Former DC secretaries and prime ministers, including Arnaldo Forlani and Giulio Andreotti, and leaders of the smaller parties such as Republican Giorgio La Malfa were also implicated. Investigations demonstrated that the PCI and PDS had also participated in the widespread system of payoffs and kickbacks. In Milan, called Tangentopoli (variously translated as "Kickback City" and "Bribesville"), payoffs were divided among all the ruling parties, including the PCI, according to a preset formula. The political crisis, the enormous deficit, and an international recession created a national emergency that Prime Minister Amato successfully met by imposing a drastic austerity program and new taxes.

What factors accounted for the enormous bribery scandal? First, the system of "imperfect bipolarism" had encouraged corruption by preventing alternation in government and allowing the DC to dominate for forty-five years. In addition, the financing of the PCI by the Soviet Union and of the DC and its allies by the United States during the Cold War had also spurred corruption. Besides the direct subsidies Moscow provided, the Soviet Union required Italian companies doing business with Soviet-dominated Eastern Europe to contribute a percentage of the proceeds to firms controlled by the PCI; at the same time, American unions funneled money to anti-Communist forces. The non-Communist parties competed by exploiting their ability to influence public enterprise through the governing coalition by demanding kickbacks from private companies seeking contracts from the vast public sector. A campaign financing law failed to break this vicious cycle because of the insufficient funds allocated to political activity. Consequently, illegal methods escalated during the 1980s, when politics became much more expensive. Furthermore, given the complexity of Italian law, contradictory legislation, and an oppressive bureaucracy, it became essential to buy political influence to accomplish anything in the economic sphere. Some of Italy's most famous business leaders, including Olivetti's Carlo De Benedetti and Fiat's Cesare Romiti, testified to this fact when they became enmeshed in the scandal. Bribes were necessary to conduct business even on the smallest scale. Not surprisingly, the enormous sums of cash siphoned off from state coffers not only went to pay for political expenses and to grease contracts but also to increase funds in personal bank accounts. Payoffs became the glue linking political fundraising and economic activity and generated personal wealth for politicians and business leaders as a by-product. The ostentation of this wealth was well covered in the press and caused great resentment among the public.

Rapid-fire and continuous revelations of the enormous funds involved and the personal profiteering inflamed public opinion. The most spectacular example was the Enimont affair. This scandal involved manipulation of the state company Ente Nazionale Idrocarburi (ENI) by private concerns in the formation of a gigantic chemical company, producing great losses for taxpayers. The parties and companies involved reportedly split the resulting profits. As investigation into these clamorous allegations proceeded, Gabriele Cagliari, former ENI head, and Raul Gardini, chief of the Ferruzzi group, committed suicide.

Effects of the Scandals

Several issues important for Italy's future arose out of the scandals: the deficit, privatization, civil rights, and political dislocation. Although there were payoffs in all countries (similar scandals broke out in Germany and France), the scandals in Italy broke when corruption there raised the cost of public works beyond that of other countries to the point that these costs contributed dramatically to the country's ballooning deficit and had a negative influence on the economy. Italians hoped that the greater stringency and oversight of public spending resulting from the scandals would reduce the excessive costs of public works. However, when publicity over the corruption dampened the willingness of companies to bid on public works, building stalled. Even though, when bids did come in, they were at first about 40 percent below pre-scandal levels, the expectation of great reductions in the cost of public works did not materialize over the long run. Indeed, during the next decade corruption increased.

The scandals convinced many Italians that the government was too heavily involved in the economy and that public companies were particularly vulnerable to extortion by political forces. This attitude, reinforced by European Union policy, promoted an increased drive for privatization and a debate about the proper balance between the private and public sectors. On one side of the discussion were those Italians who believed that private business was more efficient than public enterprises and that the government should reduce its influence on the economy. On the other side were state companies such as IRI and ENI that had had a crucial role in the country's spectacular development. In general, however, all admitted the need for reform of public enterprises but feared that private entrepreneurs would gain too much from privatization. Interestingly, in Italy the Left favored privatization and privatized large public concerns such as ENEL, the state company that dominated electric energy.

The Ills of the Justice System

Another major issue that arose from the scandals was whether a highly politicized justice system traditionally insensitive to civil rights could resolve the questions raised by the scandals. The most prominent figures in the scandals were targeted through an instrument designed to protect their civil rights, the *avviso di garanzia*—notification that a person's name had come up during an investigation and that the person was suspected of a crime and should obtain legal representation. Most of the politicians enmeshed in the scandals were not immediately indicted, would not be tried for years, and would not be convicted of the serious crimes charged by magistrates. However, the press proclaimed them guilty, and they were destroyed politically after receiving the avviso. Leaking allegations to the press was a favorite method by which magistrates "burned" political leaders and ended their careers.

Moreover, in violation of basic Western legal norms, Italian magistrates arrested people and incarcerated them until they "named names." This procedure produced extraordinary numbers of names, a host of conspiracy theories, clamorous miscarriages of justice, little evidence, and few convictions. It also prompted high-profile suicides, such as the death in July 1993 of the ex-head of ENI, Gabriele Cagliari, who was confined in prison under intolerable conditions because he would not "talk." This episode raised the ire of the justice minister, Giovanni Conso, against the investigating magistrates, but the Italian system gave him no control over their activities; nor could Parliament do much. A chorus of protests drowned legislative proposals to guarantee the rights of the accused—such as the right not to testify against oneself and restraining officials from leaking sensitive material to the press. In later years, a reaction set in among both the public and politicians to the methods used by the magistrates, dividing Italians into *giustizialisti* and *garantisti*—those who demanded summary "justice" and advocates of civil rights. While there was some improvement, Parliament remained unable to institute proper limits on the anomalous political role of Italian magistrates. Even more pernicious, as it continued out of control, the Italian justice system also proved incapable of rendering everyday service for Italian citizens, who frequently waited ten or fifteen years for the resolution of ordinary court cases. This situation made it common for the strong to abuse the weak in the everyday dealings of society by exploiting the outrageous but normal delays of a broken justice system.

POLITICAL REFORMS

The events of the "bloodless revolution" had rapid and dramatic political repercussions. So many members of Parliament came under investigation that there was a loss of confidence in that institution. This reality, in turn, prompted deputies and senators to yield to a seemingly irresistible popular consensus, as formally expressed on April 18, 1993, in a series of referendums calling for fundamental changes in the electoral system. The proportional representation instituted following World War II, once considered sacred, was overhauled. Citizens could now elect mayors directly, and other provisions ensured that the winner would have majorities in the city councils. In the Senate, a winner-take-all system on one ballot was instituted, but there were fears that if many candidates ran in a

PORTRAITS

GABRIELE CAGLIARI
Italian Justice
᠁ↄ∘ↄ᠁

A lthough the political earthquake that followed the scandals of 1993 was "bloodless," it did leave deaths in its wake. The judges who orchestrated the political changes used the justice system and the jails to accomplish their aims. Their technique was to jail suspects until they "talked" and named their accomplices, a practice that has continued. They jailed their victims and kept them incarcerated on the grounds that, if left free, they could cover up evidence of their guilt. However, the conditions under which the suspects were kept were degrading, inhuman, and psychologically debilitating. These conditions usually quickly broke the spirit of persons who had never had contact with the brutal penal system, in which defense lawyers had litte power. The civil rights violations committed in Italy during this period would have put other Western countries to shame.

One of the most prominent victims of this technique was the sixty-seven-year-old manager of Ente Nazionale Idrocarburi (ENI), the state authority for hydrocarbons founded by Enrico Mattei. Gabriele Cagliari was accused of hiding funds for the use of political parties. He was arrested, questioned, and held for four months. At the end of his last round of questioning, state prosecutor Fabio De Pasquale promised Cagliari in the presence of his lawyer that he would release him from prison and put him under house arrest. De Pasquale then changed his mind without informing anyone and took off for a pleasant summer vacation in Calabria.

On July 20, 1993, Cagliari was discovered in his cell, dead, a plastic bag over his head.

Before he died, Cagliari wrote a letter of farewell to his family. The letter encapsulated the criticisms that have since been made about the techniques of the bloodless revolution—the criminalization of practices once considered normal and applied only to some, the violation of civil rights, the barbaric treatment of suspects. Cagliari wrote: "I am convinced that the magistrates consider prison nothing more than an instrument necessary for their job, for psychological torture, where cases can, indifferently, either mature or become moldy, even if they concern a person's life."

district a person could be elected with an insignificant number of votes. A similar winner-take-all system was also adopted for 75 percent of the Chamber of Deputies, although 25 percent would continue to be elected by proportional representation; so out of favor was proportional representation that this last provision aroused loud protest. The electoral law was changed only on December 31, 2005, when a worse one was adopted. To discourage the political fragmentation that plagued Italy, the new legislation favored the formation of electoral coalitions and required that a party or coalition receive a minimum of 4 percent before it could be represented in Parliament. This provision, however, did not allay fears that the splintering of political forces would worsen. Even before the first national elections under the new system were held, there were calls for changes. Despite agreements among the different political forces in the country, these changes did not come about by 2003, but two major coalitions—Center-Left and Center-Right—emerged.

In addition to overturning the electoral system, the bloodless revolution produced the indictments, arrests, or implication in illegalities of more than 3,000 of Italy's most famous politicians and business leaders. As a result, the parties of the old ruling coalition imploded. Hit hard by charges of corruption and Mafia collusion and by the revolt of its own Mario Segni—who initiated the referendum movement to change the electoral system—the once-dominant Christian Democratic Party dissolved.

After a series of complex maneuvers over several years, the Catholics divided into several parties. In 1994, a group under the leadership of Pier Ferdinando Casini, unhappy with the Catholic alliance with the ex-Communists, broke off to form the Centro Cristiano Democratico (Democratic Christian Center, CCD). This new party allied with small and medium-sized businesses. It wished to reform the "machinery of the state," to change the economy to make it more efficient, and to resolve the problem of excessive state subsidies for people who did not need them. Although it supported social programs, the CCD defined itself as "liberal-democratic" and joined the Center-Right coalition, whose principles it considered more congenial to its own than those of the Center-Left. Another Catholic group, the Unione Democristiano di Centro (Christian Democratic Union of the Center, UDC), influenced by the ideas of Rocco Buttiglione, also joined the Center-Right. Buttiglione, a philosopher and university professor, emphasized social thought, but the UDC's leaders pledged to remain in the political center. These parties would undergo further changes in the future.

On March 22 to March 24, 2002, another (mostly) Catholic organization came into being, uniting Catholics in different organizations and Greens (a party primarily concerned with environmental issues)—the Margherita (Daisy). This political formation pledged to bring "a new cultural and civil vision of democracy and liberty." The Margherita supported a government based on multilateralism but emphasized the orderly and just evolution of globalization. It advocated modifying the rules of commerce to help the poorer nations and redistributing resources among countries to bring about a balanced economic development. According to the Margherita, these necessities made it imperative to work out a new international structure. This formation brought together groups that had inherited most strongly the Christian Democratic concern with social issues. The

Margherita elected Francesco Rutelli, the Center-Left standard-bearer in the May 2001 elections, as president and joined the Center-Left coalition. It accentuated its links to the ex-Communists.

Although the DC had broken up into a series of small parties, the Catholics retained a powerful influence in Italian politics. As members of both major coalitions, they conditioned the policies of the Center-Left and Center-Right, given the delicate balance in both political formations. Besides the parties mentioned, another ex-Christian Democrat, Romano Prodi, became prime minister when the Center-Left coalition known as the Ulivo (Olive Tree) won the 1996 elections. In fact, Catholics occupied important institutional offices and cabinet positions after the Center-Left victory in 1996 and following the Center-Right win in 2001.

The ex-Communists had a different evolution. Luckily, they had confronted their crisis before Tangentopoli. They had not only severed their ties with world communism before its collapse but adopted a new name (PDS) that omitted the term "Communist" and chosen a new symbol—a big oak tree with large roots that enclosed a diminutive Communist hammer and sickle that quickly disappeared. Presenting itself as a moderate leftist party, PDS strategy aimed at creating a broad coalition that it could lead to power. The PDS later tried to absorb the scattered Socialist elements. Led by Massimo D'Alema, this operation failed despite the co-optation of some former Socialist leaders, but the party changed its name to Democratic Leftists (Democratici di sinistra, DS) as a result.

The main Communist rival on the Left, the Socialist Party, disappeared. It was unable, for example, to elect a single city councilor in Milan, its former stronghold, and its rank and file deserted in droves. New PSI secretaries struggled to revive the party but failed in a hostile political climate. At a congress held from November 11 to 13, 1994, the Socialist Party formally dissolved itself, with some prominent Socialist leaders moving toward the PDS-dominated coalition. A new, small organization called Socialdemocratici Italiani (Italian Social Democrats, SDI) appeared under Enrico Boselli. This group presented itself as the heir to the rich Socialist tradition. It joined the leftist coalition and remained independent of ex-Communist influence, but failed to grow.

As the political crisis worsened and an economic recession hit full force, Italy established a government of "technicians" under former Bank of Italy governor and future president Carlo Azeglio Ciampi. Charged with remaining "above politics," providing stability, beginning the task of reforming the country's most serious ills, and presiding over elections to be held under the revamped voting system, Ciampi governed during unruly times and gained the popularity that later led to his election as president. His government confronted the privatization issue directly, managed the first local elections under the new voting law, carried on a renewed war against the Mafia, adopted economic austerity measures, cut government spending, and instituted a hiring freeze and other measures to gain control of the bloated bureaucracy. His government did well in foreign policy, receiving widespread international approval when it criticized the American propensity to use force in Somalia.

The aim of the political reforms was to pressure the nation's politicians into producing practical results in the local and national arenas. From now on, if they won and performed poorly, the voters would have a specific party or coalition to blame and would vote it out. As in other countries, that party would have to reorganize itself while its successors ruled and took advantage of the opportunity to prove their competence. With the Cold War's close, Italy was no longer a frontier area between the two great powers, nor was it a "blocked democracy," as the so-called First Republic had been. From now on, Italians would be free to make immediate changes if they believed that the persons governing them did a bad job or were corrupt. That newfound ability and the decimation of the old political elite constituted the real bloodless revolution.

Politically, besides the disappearance of the old parties, the major political result of the bloodless revolution appeared to be the intensification an earlier trend: once-radical ideologies battling for Italy's center. In the heat of political realignment, several crucial questions emerged. Was it possible that the PDS might emerge as the mainstay of a moderate, Left-leaning coalition while the Movimento Sociale Italiano (MSI), formerly neo-Fascist, evolved into a respectable conservative force? Would the PDS and an increased MSI share of the vote hold in the future, or did their performance primarily represent a protest? Would their need for electoral alliances stimulate both parties to change further and to compromise with other political forces? Both movements were aware of these issues and openly discussed them. If a serious, moderate, mass conservative movement eventually emerged in Italy, it would be the first time since unification—when conservatism was discredited because of its identification with the Austrians and the old states.

The most interesting question being asked was: would the Italian political system force the extremes to evolve to the point that they would become moderate leftists and conservatives presenting the country with meaningful choices and alternating in power without threatening democracy? The electoral reforms had encouraged the development of coalitions, and alternation in power of blocs leaning either to the Left or to the Right would be a major change in Italian politics. However, the future had other surprises in store besides the end of the old political system. The MSI would not be the major party on the Right even as it struggled to overcome its Fascist heritage; on the Left, the PDS, which would continue to be important but not predominant, would merge into a new political formation.

CHAPTER TWENTY-THREE

The Berlusconi Phenomenon

T HE GREATEST POLITICAL SURPRISE AFTER TANGENTOPOLI APPEARED ON the Right, where Silvio Berlusconi conjured up a political movement practically out of thin air. The son of a bank employee, Berlusconi was a self-made man who had once worked as a singer on cruise ships and who qualified at the time as Italy's richest man, his fortune estimated at $10 billion. He had made money in real estate and then went into television, with Bettino Craxi's encouragement. Italy's state television network (RAI) was divided into patronage havens for the Christian Democrats, Socialists, and Communists. (This system, called *lottizzazione*, division of the spoils, affected other areas of public endeavor as well.) Parliament had struggled for decades without success to regulate and modernize the industry. Berlusconi launched several television stations, purchased American television programs that successfully competed with the staid state television, and soon controlled Italy's three private networks. The advertising revenue made Berlusconi rich, and he branched out into other areas, including publishing. These activities raised concern that he had too much influence over public opinion. The Berlusconi empire included film production, insurance and financial services, publicity, video rentals, telephones, and a major soccer team.

Berlusconi believed that despite the collapse of international communism, the Italian ex-Communists still embraced their antidemocratic ideals and threatened his interests. Since the polls put them on track to win the next elections, he entered politics and created a new political party modeled on his soccer club network.

New Political Forces

The first national elections to be held under the newly instituted electoral reforms loomed as a watershed in the republic's history. Scheduled for spring 1994, the balloting was crucial because of the rapid decline of the traditional parties and the rise of the Lombard League. The League received much of its support from small businesspeople, many of whom were former Communists who had lost their jobs and taken their *liquidazione* (a cash payment made by Italian firms to workers who lost their jobs) to establish small companies that introduced state-of-the-art technology.

The League exploited antisouthern sentiment by charging that the South received unfair subsidies from the central government, the funds for which came from industrious northern taxpayers. These "handouts" fostered a culture of laziness and dependence, the League charged, which, when combined with the inefficiency and corruption of the Rome bureaucracy, damaged the economy of the North. The Lombard League leader Umberto Bossi expressed himself in immoderate, violent, and racist tones against southern Italians and the growing wave of immigrants flooding into the country. The League attracted support in Lombardy—the country's most economically advanced area and one that, thanks to its dense population, sent a large bloc to Parliament—because it tapped into a vast reservoir of resentment issuing from high taxes, inefficient public services, and the Tangentopoli scandal. Bossi drew condemnation for his intemperate rhetoric and his demand that Italy be split up into different states. The League roiled Italian politics, and representatives of the armed forces indicated they might intervene if the League was on the winning side in the next elections and were given important posts in the cabinet. However, although Bossi did not moderate his rhetoric, in later years the League was absorbed into Berlusconi's Center-Right—not without clamorous developments—and advocated the country's decentralization, a long-discussed principle that Italians were ready to accept (although not as the League had initially proposed it).

There was another big surprise: the success of the neo-Fascist Movimento Sociale Italiano. The MSI did not run as part of any coalition but emerged as the largest vote-getter. These results indicated that voters were rewarding political organizations that had been cut out of the ruling coalition and therefore not involved in the corruption scandal. Furthermore, the MSI had experienced a parallel development to what had happened to the Communists. Over the years a long struggle had taken place between Pino Rauti, an unrepentant Fascist, and Gianfranco Fini, who acknowledged the MSI's origins but who pressed the party to distance itself from them. Fini, born in 1952 and too young to have experienced fascism, became MSI secretary and struggled to bring the MSI into the Italian mainstream. By deemphasizing the MSI's Fascist roots and presenting his party as conservative, Fini appealed to non-Fascist voters fed up with the Left. As part of this evolution, on November 24, 2003, on a trip to Israel, Fini denounced the 1938 anti-Semitic laws as "infamous." Finally, Fini transformed the MSI into Alleanza Nazionale (AN, National Alliance), which he presented as moderately conservative.

PORTRAITS

GIANFRANCO FINI
Post-Fascist

⟶∿∿⟵

Born in Bologna on January 3, 1952, Ginafranco Fini's parents were Fascists. In 1969, he got into a fight when Extreme Left youngsters tried to prevent him from entering a cinema projecting his hero John Wayne's film *The Green Berets*. Fini stated that he became interested in rightist politics from that moment, later heading the youth movement of the Neo-Fascist MSI party. In 1987, he became party secretary. In 1993, following the Tangentopoli scandal—which opened up new horizons for parties, such as the MSI, that had been shunned by national politics—Fini ran for mayor of Rome. He lost the election, but his endorsement by Silvio Berlusconi and high vote total of 49.6 percent in the second ballot made him a national figure.

Fini became convinced that the party had to downplay its Fascist past and become more moderate if it was to aspire to power on the national scene. In 1994–1995, the party merged with some Liberal and Christian Democratic leaders and claimed to have become a traditional Western conservative party. The party dissolved itself and was replaced with a new organization called National Alliance (AN). At the same time, Berlusconi entered Italian politics and Fini allied with him despite strong disagreements with Umberto Bossi's Northern League. With Berlusconi's victory, AN sent a contingent to join the short-lived new government. In 1996, early elections were won by Berlusconi's coalition, of which AN was a part. Fini emerged as vice premier and later became foreign minister.

Fini continued trying to moderate his party, backing off after calling Mussolini a great statesman and saying that the anti-Semitism of the twentieth century was absolute evil. Fini's relationship with Berlusconi has frequently been stormy, but the two have always managed to patch things up. Fini enthusiastically adhered to Berlusconi's new People of Liberty Party (PDL, which will be formed by the merging of Forza Italia and AN), which defeated the Center-Left's Democratic Party in the 2008 elections. On April 30, 2008, Fini was elected president of the Chamber of Deputies, the first post-Fascist to hold the Italian state's third-highest post. His inaugural speech combined moderation and conciliation, signaling the acceptance by post-Fascism of the defeat of Nazi fascism in World War II, and its links with working people, whose "labor day," observed on May 1, was associated primarily with the Left.

As has been the case with post-communism, Fini's transition to post-fascism came at the cost of splits. Thanks to Fini, most neo-Fascists have become part of the Italian and European political mainstream.

The most significant outcome of the destruction of the old parties was the rise of Silvio Berlusconi. The elections of March 27–28, 1994, produced clamorous and unexpected results. The leftist coalition, the "Progressive Pole" led by the PDS, grouped together parties that traditionally identified themselves as leftist organizations, while the flamboyant Berlusconi entered the political fight by organizing an existing network of fan clubs supporting a soccer team he owned; he named his party Forza Italia (Go Italy). Berlusconi skillfully exploited his three private television stations to advocate greater privatization, drastically lower taxes, and a smaller governmental role in economic life. He promised that these measures would produce a great number of jobs and an end to the economic recession. Forza Italia's social base included for the most part persons who had recently become wealthy or who had otherwise done well in the new Italy, not big business, which was tied politically and economically to the Left.

Berlusconi worked hard to form a coalition out of the disparate Lombard League, which demanded the division of Italy into three republics, and AN, which retained belief in a centralized state. In addition, the crude Bossi and the sophisticated Fini disliked each other. The desire to win trumped these and other differences, and Berlusconi, Bossi, and Fini formed a Center-Right coalition, the "Liberty Pole."

The election results surprised everyone. The Liberty Pole won an absolute majority of seats in the Chamber of Deputies, 366 out of 630. In the Senate, the Right fell only three votes short of an absolute majority. (Since the voting age in the Senate is twenty-five, compared with eighteen in the Chamber, this result suggested that the youth vote went for the Liberty Pole.) The unresolved issues within the Center-Right coalition, however, came to the fore after the elections.

Berlusconi became prime minister after difficult negotiations among the troubled allies, but he had a very hard time with Bossi. The allegations against Berlusconi of conflict of interest and bribery with relation to his vast business holdings also heated the political atmosphere and threatened the survival of both his cabinet and the coalition. Berlusconi's critics emphasized that as prime minister he had an important say in who ran the state television stations, and that created a conflict of interest because of his ownership of Italy's private television networks. The conflict-of-interest issue never went away and haunted Berlusconi's politics. The new cabinet led an uneasy existence, and in December 1994 Bossi defected from the coalition and presented a no-confidence motion. It was widely rumored that President Oscar Luigi Scalfaro, a former member of the left wing of the old Christian Democratic Party, was behind Bossi's move.

In response to Bossi's abandonment of the Center-Right coalition, Berlusconi resigned and demanded new elections because the coalition that the voters had endorsed no longer existed.

THE OLIVE TREE AND THE CENTER-LEFT

President Scalfaro refused to call new elections, and a cabinet of technicians headed by former central banker Lamberto Dini replaced Berlusconi. Supported by the Left and the League, this government ruled for about a year and attempted to address the economic decline in Italy caused by globalization and competition from countries with cheaper labor. In the meantime, the magistrates brought Berlusconi up on bribery charges linked to his business activities; this and his squabbles with Fini further weakened him. Berlusconi's difficulties gave new hope to the Center-Left, which reorganized itself under an umbrella group, the Ulivo (Olive Tree); led by the former Christian Democrat Romano Prodi, the Ulivo's major organizational support was in the PDS.

In the national elections of April 1996, a higher abstention rate than during the previous election in the South and Forza Italia's political inexperience contributed to a narrow Ulivo election victory. However, while the Ulivo commanded a majority in the Senate, in the Chamber of Deputies Prodi's new Center-Left cabinet depended on Rifondazione Comunista (PRC)—unrepentant Communists whose unwillingness to reform labor legislation and pension laws impeded the country's modernization and reduction of its massive public debt.

Nevertheless, it was vital to decrease the country's deficit so that Italy could meet the stringent Maastricht criteria for the European Union's projected single currency, the euro. To accomplish this feat the Prodi government had to cut social services, particularly health care and pensions (where there was widespread fraud), and give industry more economic incentives and freedom to adapt to changing conditions through downsizing and other measures. The PRC and the unions demanded more government services, increased taxation, and an uncompromising defense of workers' rights. The labor unions backed the PRC to the hilt. This conflict spelled trouble for Prodi's cabinet on several fronts, with the PRC threatening to bring the government down if it did not get its way.

Despite these difficulties, Prodi made meeting the Maastricht criteria his government's top priority and confounded prevailing European opinion that Italy would not qualify for the euro with the first-tier nations. Berlusconi had proposed austerity measures that provoked mass demonstrations by organized labor, but with a Center-Left cabinet forced to take similar action, the unions deemphasized strikes, choosing instead to negotiate, oppose, and attempt to delay changes ad infinitum. Prodi underscored the blow to Italy's prestige and economic development should it fail to be among the first wave of countries qualifying for the euro and convinced the Italian people, who accepted economic stringency measures to reduce the high deficit. The government's budgetary measures and a special "Eurotax" drastically decreased the proportion of debt to GDP.

These changes came despite fierce opposition from the Extreme Left. On October 9, the PRC withdrew its support of the cabinet, claiming that Prodi's austerity budget demanded too many sacrifices from workers and pensioners. An immediate and overwhelming backlash resulted. With the deficit declining from 6.7 percent of GDP to 3.1 percent or less, and inflation dropping to 1.7 percent by the summer of 1997, Italians credited Prodi with a remarkable achievement in bringing Italy to within striking distance of the single European currency. Faxes protesting against Rifondazione flooded party headquarters, and crowds booed its leader, Fausto Bertinotti, at public appearances in the "Red Belt." The public opinion backlash forced the PRC to backtrack, and it renewed its support.

During 1998, the government's austerity policy brought the Italian deficit down to 2.7 percent of GDP. The Italian economy still needed to reduce welfare state expenses, but in May the country was certified as having fulfilled the criteria for entrance into the first tier of nations adopting the euro.

This new "economic miracle" marked the greatest achievement of the Prodi government and the Center-Left coalition, but on the all-crucial issues of pension reform and structural changes to the country's bloated welfare system, PRC and union opposition eventually won out over public opinion.

The Center-Left also failed to achieve significant political reform. Italian political leaders concurred that reforms instituted following the Tangentopoli scandals were incomplete and had not brought stability to the Italian political system. The Center-Left and Center-Right agreed to seek consensus on reliable mechanisms to ensure greater stability and alternation in government (bipolarism). They established the "Bicamerale"—a bicameral commission representing all political forces to adopt and implement constitutional reforms.

If anything, on the question of representation, the ruling coalition was even more divided than on economic and social policy. More stability meant less representation for small parties, reducing their capacity to utilize a handful of votes to bring down governments. Rifondazione Comunista and other small parties were therefore unlikely to support reforms that would decrease their influence.

There was disagreement on other issues as well. Another proposed reform would have strengthened the presidency by allowing the people to elect a president on the American or French model or the prime minister directly. The PRC condemned such direct elections as "Caesarism" and threatened to block proceedings; in the words of Armando Cossutta: "We will present hundreds of amendments." The other wild card was the Lombard League. Bossi, advocating immediate secession, had proclaimed a new "country" in northern Italy ("Padania"). In the summer of 1996, he called for a demonstration of one million persons in the North in favor of this new entity. When this appeal fell flat, Bossi's attraction diminished. The League remained a small party and, like the PRC, tried to block the Bicamerale's reforms.

Nevertheless, on June 30, 1997, the larger parties represented on the Bicamerale agreed to present reforms to Parliament, by a lopsided vote of 51 to 9 (three abstentions). The commission proposed a president similar to the French president ("semipresidentialism"), elected directly by the people, with greater powers in the foreign policy and defense areas. In the domestic arena, the president would be able to dissolve Parliament and call for new elections after six months if, upon election, he or she did not like the existing political majority. If parliamentary elections produced a majority unwelcome to the president during the term of office, the president would have to wait a year before dissolving Parliament. The president would name the prime minister, who had to have a majority in Parliament. The Bicamerale also proposed modifying the 1993 electoral law in that there would be two ballots. On the first, voters would elect 55 percent of the representatives according to the winner-take-all formula (down from 75 percent) and 25 percent by proportional representation. Voters would choose the remaining 20 percent on a second ballot in which only candidates from the two coalitions that received the largest number of votes in the first ballot would be allowed to participate. The Bicamerale also proposed a federal system for Italy.

This agreement unraveled over differences on how to reform the justice system. Berlusconi demanded that two tracks be established for magistrates, one for judges and one for prosecutors. The ability of Italian magistrates to serve as both led to frequent abuses. Berlusconi requested guarantees regarding his own legal woes, the origins of which he regarded as political. In fact, Berlusconi was convicted twice for bribing tax inspectors who were investigating his business affairs. He was fined $5.6 million and given combined jail sentences of five years, but he appealed and won public sympathy because many people blamed Italy's contradictory laws for his problems. Berlusconi's popularity had its ups and downs during this period because he put his personal problems before the country's, but another reason for the Bicamerale's failure was the fear on the Left that Berlusconi might have won a popular election for president had the Bicamerale's reforms gone into effect.

THE INSTABILITY OF THE CENTER-LEFT

As time went on, divisions within the Center-Left coalition increased. For example, Berlusconi's ownership of Italy's major television networks and his influence over RAI should he become prime minister made it imperative to resolve the conflict-of-interest question. However, despite its majority, the Center-Left never passed a conflict-of-interest law because many of its members were more interested in eliminating Berlusconi as a rival than in resolving the issue. In addition, the tensions between the PRC and Prodi escalated. In October 1998, a PRC conference rejected the government's proposed 1999 budget because it mandated too many cuts in order to institute the euro, failed to implement a thirty-five-hour work-week, and did not address the high southern unemployment rate. This rejection meant that the PRC would vote against the government, causing it to fall; however, a segment of the party led by Armando Cossutta objected for fear of opening the way for a Center-Right cabinet. Cossutta's faction split from the main organization and established the Partito dei Comunisti Italiani (Party of the Italian Communists, PDCI), which voted in favor of Prodi. However, the government fell by one vote (313 to 312).

Negotiations for a new cabinet led by Prodi failed, and on October 21, 1999, Massimo D'Alema, secretary of the largest party in the Center-Left coalition, was sworn into office as prime minister—the first ex-Communist to head the government of a major Western country. D'Alema pledged to continue his predecessor's strong pro-Europe policy and made an attempt at reform through Giuliano Amato, who was unsuccessful.

Economic policy was another source of dissension. In July 2000, the European Central Bank cautioned Italy to reduce its expenses. The government proved unable to reform the bloated pension system because of noisy opposition by its union and Communist partners. Aside from an ongoing privatization effort, major reforms never materialized, and D'Alema faced more opposition in his own coalition. On April 17, 2000, local elections resulted in a defeat for the Center-Left that proved fatal to D'Alema, and he resigned. Giuliano Amato formed a new government and unsuccessfully sought a compromise with Berlusconi on reform. With new elections on the horizon in 2001, there was no incentive for the Center-Right to compromise because the increasingly fractious nature of the governing coalition reduced its chances of winning.

BERLUSCONI'S VICTORY

The disarray in the Center-Left coalition proved fatal in the national elections of May 2001. The Center-Right (Casa delle Libertà, the "House of Liberties") presented a different picture. Berlusconi had wooed Umberto Bossi back into the coalition, mindful of polls showing that a coalition of Forza Italia, AN, and the Lombard League (in addition to several small parties) would garner 60 percent of the vote. Berlusconi exuded confidence that this time he could hold Bossi in the coalition because Bossi's alliance reversal of 1994 had not benefited him and he had learned his lesson.

Berlusconi's legal and conflict-of-interest troubles intrigued the international media but did not affect most Italian voters. Berlusconi loudly claimed that

PORTRAITS

MÁSSIMO D'ÁLEMÁ
Post-Communist

⟊⟊∾

M assimo D'Alema is among the most noted of Italy's professional politicians who helped engineer the transition of the Italian Communist Party to postcommunism and who have been prominently involved in all of its various transmutations. He is clever and intelligent and evokes extremes of respect and condemnation in different sectors of the country. When the Center-Left is in power, it seems that it cannot do without D'Alema as a prominent member of the government. D'Alema served as the first prime minister of a major Western nation after the fall of international communism, was a candidate for president, and served as foreign minister in the Prodi cabinet.

Born in Rome on April 20, 1949, Massimo D'Alema came from a Communist family and "breathed politics" since his youth. He participated in the Communist Youth Federation (FGCI) and served as its national secretary from 1975 to 1980. In 1968, D'Alema participated in the youth revolts and traveled to Prague just as the Soviets invaded the country. In an interview, he claimed that the invasion had a major impact on his life.

In 1979, D'Alema entered the PCI's Central Committee, in 1983 the Directorate, and in 1986 the Secretariat. In 1987, he won election to the Chamber of Deputies, and he has been continuously reelected since then. He also edited the party newspaper, *L'Unità*. In 1994, he took over as the national secretary of the Democratic Party of the Left (PDS) and engineered its merger with other groups that produced the DS (Democratic Leftists). On February 5, 1997, he was elected president of the parliamentary commission for institutional reform (the Bicamerale) and served as prime minister from October 21, 1998, to April 2000.

A slight person with a serious outlook and a lover of sailing and soccer, Massimo D'Alema does not hesitate to speak his mind. When he became prime minister, he released an interview with the *New York Times* that offended official Washington. His support of measures cutting the welfare state raised the ire of unions and the unemployed and provoked demonstrations against him despite his history as a Communist.

When the Center-Right won the elections of 2001, D'Alema spent his time out of power building a positive image among European leftists, projected primarily by his work as head of a foundation, Italianieuropei, which publishes a journal that has the same name and carries the subtitle *Bimonthly of Italian Reformism*. As foreign minister in the short-lived Prodi cabinet (May 17, 2006, until January 24, 2008, when it lost a vote of confidence in the Senate and remained in office only for routine business), he followed a policy that was friendlier to the EU and to the Arabs than did his predecessor.

When the Democratic Party led by former Rome mayor Walter Veltroni lost the 2008 elections and he came under attack in his own organization, it was widely rumored that D'Alema was maneuvering to replace him as party secretary.

politically motivated left-wing magistrates were trying to drive him out of politics, and the experience of Italians with the politicized and inefficient justice system and the unfair tax structure both worked in his favor. Although Berlusconi had been found guilty on various charges involving bribery and tax evasion, he had won on appeal (sometimes because the statute of limitations had run out). Berlusconi's campaign borrowed some elements from American politics, such as issuing a "contract" with Italians in which he promised to lower taxes, create a million new jobs, increase minimum pensions, initiate great public works projects, and pass anticrime measures. If he did not deliver on four of these five promises within the five-year period of the next legislature, he promised on television, he would not run again. Berlusconi repeated his pledge in full-page advertisements in the country's major newspapers and in mailings to all Italian families, and on May 13, 2001, the Center-Right won a strong majority in the Chamber of Deputies and in the Senate.

THE BERLUSCONI GOVERNMENT

During the electoral campaign, Berlusconi had promised to modernize Italy. On June 11, 2001, after a series of negotiations with his political allies, the Berlusconi cabinet was sworn in. Composed of political allies and technicians, the Center-Right cabinet promised to be stable and likely to last the entire legislature thanks to its command of a majority in both houses.

Besides Berlusconi as prime minister, the cabinet included his two most important allies in visible positions: Gianfranco Fini as vice premier and Umberto Bossi as minister for institutional reform and devolution. In this position, Bossi could work on giving more power to the regions, as was happening in France, Britain, and Spain. Presumably he would work merely for decentralization, but he still made intemperate remarks that embarrassed the country and presented ideas on decentralization that caused his allies to balk. Bossi and Fini continued to dislike each other, and the cabinet proved fractious. Berlusconi tried to rein Bossi in, but the prime minister himself was soon revealed to be a nontraditional and controversial figure who had little self-control and whose misstatements roiled Italy and Europe.

The cabinet's most important test would be in the economic field, where Berlusconi tapped a fifty-four-year-old professor from the North to be "superminister" of economics and finance: Giulio Tremonti. Tremonti exuded optimism, defining Italy as "a spring ready to be released." His economic proposals included: reducing taxes on businesses that reinvested their profits and hired more people; following the European model for work contracts, which gave employers greater flexibility than Italian practice; instituting measures to encourage the underground economy to become legal; encouraging the investment of venture capital in modern economic enterprises; eliminating the estate tax; regulating firms not represented on the stock exchange; reducing bureaucratic procedure with the goal of eliminating 190 million documents; instituting a vast program of infrastructure modernization; and allowing homeowners to restructure their homes inside without government interference. Other items designed to stimulate the economy and reduce government interference in business accompanied these proposals.

Because of the global recession that began in 2001, it proved difficult to assess the efficacy of these measures. The Italian economy worsened, following a global pattern. Increased imports of cheap Chinese goods into the country provided difficult competition for industry. The physical introduction of the euro on January 1, 2002, produced a burst of inflation that experts considered temporary, and the country flirted with exceeding the maximum 3 percent deficit mandated by the EU. In fact, both Germany and France did go over the limit. Furthermore, the euro prevented the strategic currency devaluations that the Italians had used in the past to perk up their economy. The Center-Right coalition thus failed to deliver on the promises it had made during the election campaign, but there was some moderate progress toward the goals outlined by the government. Tremonti's policies were in the European mainstream: they reduced somewhat the presence of the government in the economy, as advocated by the EU. According to Tremonti, the Center-Right aimed at "liberal neutrality" in the economy. This goal would stand or fall depending on the global economy and EU management of Europe's predicament.

In 2002, the country's economic quandary was best represented by the emergency that hit Italy's largest private-sector employer and biggest manufacturer, Fiat. This icon of Italian industrialism slipped from the position of Europe's largest automaker in 1989 to seventh in 2003. Facing increasing competition in Italy because of the disappearance of tariffs, Fiat's market share went from 60 percent in 1986 to under one-third. To remedy this situation, the company laid off over 8,000 employees in 2002, mostly in Italy, and in 2003 announced plans to lay off an additional 12,300 worldwide. These and other measures had turned the company around by 2007 without significant government intervention.

The Berlusconi government quickly encountered the hostility of intellectuals and of organized labor for its labor policies, and it failed to institute pension reform, a recalcitrant issue that past and future governments were unable to tame. Perhaps the most contentious issue was the "Biagi Law," passed by the Center-Right in 2003. Marco Biagi, a professor of labor law at the University of Modena, was a government consultant who advocated measures introducing greater flexibility into the Italian labor market as a means of increasing employment. The Extreme Left detested him as antiworker, and on March 19, 2002, the "New Red Brigades" assassinated him. On February 14, 2003, however, Parliament enacted his proposals into law. The Biagi law regulated the idea of the "independent contractor," reviled in Italy, where workers aimed at and expected a permanent position. Under the law, employers could hire people for a limited time and let them go without giving them a permanent job. The law's opponents have condemned it for increasing the number of *precariati*—those workers without a permanent contract who can be let go at any time when a project is finished and then rehired if needed, thus increasing economic insecurity. Critics have also contended that the law allows employers to evade social security system payments and to pay low wages. Its defenders have praised the flexibility it introduced into the labor market and credit it with increasing employment. This law has remained very controversial in Italy.

During the summer of 2001, the Berlusconi government faced its first big domestic test. The summit of the world's richest nations, the G8, met in Genoa in July. Anticapitalist protesters objecting to increasing globalization flocked to the city from all over Europe—anarchists, so-called no-globals, leftist Catholics, diehard Communists. Most of the protesters were peaceful, but a minority rioted, burned, and looted. For two days, Genoa resembled a war zone, with many protesters wounded and one killed by a paramilitary carabiniere who feared for his life. The violence of the protesters made public opinion sympathetic to the government, until the police raided the headquarters of the peaceful protesters, whom they suspected of harboring rioters. The rioters followed a policy of blending with peaceful demonstrators to confuse the police. This incident embarrassed the government, alienated sectors of public opinion, and wound up in the courts.

Besides the events in Genoa, other divisive issues surfaced. The government and the Center-Left blamed each other for the failure to agree on reforms. Berlusconi, who had promised a law on conflict of interest in the first one hundred days of his tenure, failed to deliver. A controversy opened up in the state television sector, where the prime minister had a say in appointing members of the governing board, opening himself up to charges of weakening state television in favor of his networks.

The justice system continued to be a serious source of conflict. Both the majority and the opposition believed that the pendulum of power had swung too far toward the magistrates and that the balance with the politicians should be redressed; despite their differences, on November 10, 1999, both coalitions compromised on procedures to make trials fairer. They agreed that trials would occur before impartial judges and that defense and prosecution lawyers would be on an equal footing. The defense would have the right to cross-examine witnesses, and a guilty verdict could not be based on the declarations of witnesses who could not be cross-examined by the defense. A new law provided that defendants had to be accorded the time and opportunity to organize a defense and that prosecutors could not exploit the media in their attempts to win convictions. The role of hearsay testimony, however, remained a major issue of contention.

As prime minister, Berlusconi continued his efforts to institute separate career tracks for prosecutors and judges. The opposition accused him of being motivated by his own legal troubles, and Berlusconi continued to charge that left-wing magistrates were out to get him and his closest associates. The high points of this conflict included a dispute over instituting European procedures to extradite suspected criminals, which Berlusconi blocked and which attracted international disapprobation. Majority and opposition fought over a Berlusconi-backed measure instituting changes of venue when defendants charged that judges in a case were biased. This measure passed in Parliament over the opposition's protests. When Berlusconi tried to have his bribery trial regarding his takeover of a major food company shifted from Milan, however, Italy's highest court refused to do so. Berlusconi's supporters responded by passing a bill that granted immunity from prosecution to Italy's five highest constitutional officers while they were in office, again over loud opposition protests. This law, signed by Italy's respected President Carlo Azeglio Ciampi, stopped a high-profile corruption trial against the prime minister, but it brought protests that attracted international attention. Italy's highest court blocked implementation on constitutional grounds, but Berlusconi—at the head of a new government in 2008—corrected the errors and it was accepted.

A prime reason for the hasty passage of the law was to avoid embarrassing the country during the Italian term of the EU's rotating presidency, beginning in July 2003. The Italian presidency came at a particularly delicate point in the EU's development because a draft of the European Constitution—in which Giuliano Amato played a prominent role as vice president of the European constitutional convention—had recently been published.

Berlusconi's appearance before the EU Parliament turned out to be a public relations disaster. The prime minister's wealth, conflict of interest, legal problems, and strong support for the Americans during the Iraq War made him a controversial figure all over Europe. European leftist leaders attacked him in the press as being unfit to head the EU. In the Parliament, a German left-wing member of the German Socialist Party (SPD) told him so openly. The undiplomatic and abrasive Berlusconi responded sharply that he knew of a person shooting a documentary on the Holocaust and that his German critic would be perfect for the role of a kapo (a concentration camp official). This remark brought universal condemnation, and the German prime minister demanded an apology. Berlusconi responded that his remark had been ironic, and he quickly spoke to his German colleague, who declared the incident closed.

At the same time, the tensions among Berlusconi's allies escalated, particularly between Fini and Bossi, but also with the Casa delle Libertà's smaller Catholic allies. The arguments ranged from the Lombard League's plan for the devolution of power to the regions, opposed by AN, to an amnesty supported by Berlusconi but opposed by the justice minister, a League member. Berlusconi and Forza Italia favored the amnesty as a means of closing the books on the period of Italian terrorism and demonstrating that they did not ask for changes in the justice system only for themselves. Most important, a fight broke out over the proposed budget. Tremonti, with an ever-watchful eye on EU demands to keep the deficit under control, sought to keep spending under control and favored pension reform. AN sought funds in favor of Italians abroad, and the League objected to proposed pension changes that would gradually increase the age of retirement from fifty-eight to sixty-five. An irritated Berlusconi expended much energy keeping his fractious allies in line.

These incidents weakened the government, and midterm local elections went against the Center-Right. There were questions as to how Berlusconi's abrasive governing style, his legal woes, his conflict of interest, his gaffes, and a bad international press would affect his chances of winning the next general election in 2006.

FOREIGN POLICY

Berlusconi's negative image proved particularly ironic in light of the Center-Right's policy, followed since 1996, of bolstering Italy's prestige and conducting a foreign policy more in line with its economic importance.

In January 1996, a pyramid scheme touched off widespread revolts in Albania, located across the Adriatic from the heel of the Italian boot. As Albania fell apart, tens of thousands of Albanians took off for Italy, flooding the country and compounding the already serious immigration problem. In response, the Italians put together and led a European force into Albania to restore order, to stem the tide of illegal immigrants, to provide humanitarian relief, and to encourage peace for new elections. The PRC opposed the expedition and voted against it in the Chamber of Deputies, which would have brought down the Prodi government had Berlusconi not agreed to support it. The Italian mission settled the country, winning praise from American President Bill Clinton. A similar development occurred in 1999, when a crisis in the former Yugoslav province of Kosovo dominated international politics. The government of Massimo D'Alema allowed the United States to use its Aviano airbase to bomb Yugoslavia, and Italian planes also participated in the operation. The Communists in D'Alema's cabinet and elements of the prime minister's own party protested, but the government received strong encouragement from Berlusconi.

As prime minister, Berlusconi aimed to increase Italy's international influence. He intensified Italy's ties with the United States, openly declaring his admiration for the Americans, his gratitude for their role in World War II, and his friendship for President George W. Bush. With the destruction of the World Trade Center in New York City on September 11, 2001, relations with the United States became closer because most Italians strongly sympathized with the Americans. In addition, Italy, which had successfully confronted a major terrorist threat during the heyday of the Red Brigades, feared a resurgence of terrorism. Many Muslims had immigrated to the country, and the police discovered close connections with Middle Eastern terrorists and various plots. This conjunction of both government and people in support of the United States was unusual given the strength of the Catholic and Communist traditions (both vociferously anticapitalist) and antiwar movements that considered the Americans imperialists.

Berlusconi's clear majority in both houses altered the political situation because the defection of small groups no longer threatened government stability. Like most countries, Italy supported the American invasion of Afghanistan and sent a force of *Alpini* (elite mountain troops) to Afghanistan to fight the deposed Taliban and to aid the search for Osama bin Laden. It also played a part in the diplomacy through the former Afghan king, who had been in Roman exile for many years.

Circumstances differed in 2002 and 2003. Italian public opinion vocally opposed the invasion of Iraq by the United States and Britain. Despite widespread antiwar feelings among Italians, Berlusconi supported the United States, although he called for a United Nations endorsement. Suspicion of Berlusconi's policies was rife because respected Foreign Minister Renato Ruggiero (a "technician") had resigned over differences with the prime minister, and Berlusconi had taken over the Foreign Ministry himself. Berlusconi's strong pro-Americanism put him at odds with the large peace movement and with Germany and France. While both of those countries refused to send troops to Iraq, the Italians sent a contingent that was the third largest, with the mission of training the police and engaging in peacekeeping operations. In November 2003, a car bomb killed nineteen Italians (including two civilians) in Nassiria, Iraq. While Berlusconi reaffirmed Italian determination to remain in Iraq, the massacre reinforced Italians' feelings of national identity. His Italian adversaries accused him of distancing Italy from the EU, but he gained credibility with the United States. Berlusconi attempted to conduct diplomacy at a high level in order to bolster his country's prestige, and his activism in the foreign policy field attracted attention. In one week in February 2003, he flew to Washington, D.C., to meet with President Bush, to London to talk with British Prime Minister Tony Blair, and to Moscow to convince Russian President Vladimir Putin to support the Iraq operation. Claiming a special relationship with Putin, Berlusconi took credit for adding Russia to the G7 and for making it an associate of NATO. At an EU summit in 2003, he announced that he favored Russia's entrance into the Union, a position his partners did not relish. Berlusconi's political opponents considered his claims of success exaggerated, but for good or ill, he succeeded in shining the international spotlight on Italy. The press criticized his activities, but Italy's stock with the United States rose appreciably. In the next few years, with insurrection in Iraq mounting and in view of elections in 2006, Berlusconi announced a phased withdrawal of Italian troops in the country, a move soon followed by other allies.

AN INCONCLUSIVE RESULT

In April 2005, midterm elections produced a significant loss for the Center-Right. Polls also indicated that the Berlusconi coalition was at a disadvantage in the upcoming general elections. In an attempt to prevent a loss, the ruling coalition exploited its control of both houses of Parliament to pass an electoral law that it believed would help it win the next national elections. Parliament and the president accepted the new legislation in December 2005. The main features of this complex law were its return to proportionality and its encouragement of small parties to join coalitions with parties with which they had little in common. The legislation contained so many complicated features that its author called it a *porcata* (a mildly distasteful term indicating that it was a mess), and the Italians, with their propensity for Latinisms, baptized it the "Porcellum." The Center-Left (the "Unione") promised to repeal the legislation if it won the elections. The other feature that affected the 2006 elections was passage of a measure that allowed Italians living abroad to vote for their own representatives. This law passed at the insistence of the right wing of the ruling coalition because it mistakenly assumed that Italians abroad would vote for it.

Despite early polls showing the Unione with a comfortable lead, the elections held on April 9 and 10, 2006, produced very close results. In the Chamber of Deputies, a difference of about .07 percent in the popular vote gave the Center-Left an electoral bonus and a working majority of 340 seats to 277. In the Senate, however, it was a different story. Without the votes of Italians living abroad, the Center Right had a one-seat advantage, but the Unione won four out of the six seats allocated to that group, giving it a two-seat majority there (the electoral bonus worked on a regional basis in the Senate) and shaky control of that house. Unione leader Romano Prodi became prime minister claiming that his government would last for five years. This was unlikely because, with such a small advantage in the Senate, the government had to rely on the erratic support of the unelected life senators. The other serious problem for the Center-Left was the coalition's disparate nature, counting as it did unruly small parties, including the two Communist organizations that had caused Prodi so much trouble during his previous stint as prime minister, and a splinter Christian Democratic group called the UDEUR headed by Clemente Mastella, who became justice minister; in all, the cabinet included nine parties. The small parties promised to behave themselves and signed a 280-page agreement drafted by Prodi, but the odds were that the Prodi cabinet would not last long.

THE PRODI GOVERNMENT

The major accomplishments of the Prodi cabinet in its year-and-a-half life were economic, but even here it presented a mixed record. Tommaso Padoa-Schioppa, minister for the economy and finance, was an internationally respected economist and a "founding father" of the euro; he instituted policies curbing tax evasion that brought an unexpected flood of new funds into the treasury. The fiscal deficit of 4.4 percent inherited from Berlusconi in 2006 fell to 1.9 percent in 2007, while the all-important export sector increased 17 percent. The public debt as a percentage of GDP also fell. Corporate taxes were reduced, and the government liberalized some protected economic sectors. These results brought praise from the EU commissioner for economic and monetary affairs. However, the deficit's decline was due to extremely unpopular increases that brought taxes as a percentage of GDP to 43.3, the highest rate since 1997, when a special tax was instituted to bring Italy into the euro bloc. This development added to an increase in inflation and contributed to strong disapproval of government policies from which the Center-Left never recovered. The overall inflation rate reached 2.9 percent on an annualized basis in February 2008, but the percentage increases for staples were much greater (bread, 12.5 percent; pasta, 14.4 percent; dairy products, 7.3 percent). Higher international oil prices resulted in increases of 13.1 percent for unleaded gas and 16.9 percent for diesel fuel. High inflation and low economic growth augmented popular discontent against Center-Left policies. Italy's economic growth for 2007 was just 1.5 percent, below the EU average of 2.6 percent, and the International Monetary Fund (IMF) estimated 2008 growth at just 0.3 percent. Moreover, high-profile problems dogged the nation as the number of strikes remained substantially higher and wages lower than in the other advanced Western countries. The troubles of the national airline, Alitalia, whose losses had cost the country a fortune over the years, led to high-profile negotiations for its sale and a national debate over whether it should be sold to foreigners, and a trash crisis engulfed the region around Naples. The Center-Left thus ran afoul of the difficult economic times facing the West as well as an image problem.

The malaise that permeated Italy in 2007 made international headlines when a strongly critical article in the *New York Times* describing Italy as poor and old appeared on December 22, 2007. Families could not reach the end of the month on their salaries, and the ages of politicians and even beauty contest judges were advanced, the reporter claimed. The article cited Spain as having overtaken Italy (a debatable claim that the Spanish prime minister had made earlier), described Greece as breathing down Italy's neck, and quoted an industrialist as saying that Italy was going "backwards." The article concluded with a series of statistics showing that the country lagged behind other European countries economically, was afflicted by strikes, was becoming older, and, in general, was declining. As for the Center-Left, the piece focused on an incident in the piazza outside the prime minister's offices in which a citizen accused Prodi of "ruining us all." The *Times* article caused a furor in Italy, and as the British press picked up the theme. Berlusconi and the Center-Right attacked the Center-Left as incompetent and as having shamed the country before the entire world.

The Center-Right kept up a relentless criticism of the cabinet because it claimed that the Center-Left no longer had a majority and no legitimacy to rule. The basis for this charge was that Prodi had to work hard to keep his Extreme Left allies in line, especially its representatives in the cabinet who opposed important legislation and threatened to join street demonstrations against the government when it adopted provisions with which they disagreed. Moreover, Prodi's majority in the Senate, tenuous at best, had faded. His coalition lost several confidence votes and had to rely on life senators to retain a majority, which the Center-Right attacked as undemocratic. Many observers speculated that the cabinet would not last beyond January 2008. In that month, the magistrates attacked the small UDEUR, a party in the ruling coalition that accounted for 1.9 percent of the total vote and whose head was the justice minister, Clemente Mastella. The magistrates arrested his wife, swooped down on the party, and accused Mastella of corruption. An angry Mastella resigned as justice minister and withdrew from the coalition. The government then lost a confidence vote in the Senate on January 24. In March 2008, the charges against Mastella were dropped as other judges ruled that the dispute had arisen from the justice minister's attempt to transfer a magistrate.

President Giorgio Napolitano hoped to avoid new elections by appointing a government that would change the electoral law and then manage the new elections, but Berlusconi refused to go along, either with this solution or with a "Grand Coalition" government on the German model. New elections were then called for April 13 and 14, 2008. After these events and the publication of a bestselling book revealing the income and privileges of members of Parliament and other politicians, popular opinion of Italian leaders reached a new low.

PARTY CONSOLIDATION

It became clear during these events that the electoral law and the party structure encouraged governmental instability. This realization led to changes in the Italian political system that seemed to favor consolidation and greater clarity. The former Communists (DS, the Democratic Leftists) and the Catholics in the Center-Left (the Margherita or Daisy Party) began a process of consolidation into a new party. They hoped to combine the strengths of both organizations, an assumption that public opinion polls repeatedly confirmed. DS Secretary Piero Fassino spurred the process on, as did Francesco Rutelli, representing the Margherita. The two parties created the Partito Democratico (Democratic Party, PD), which dropped all official affiliation with Marxism. Walter Veltroni, the popular Rome mayor and former Communist who had proclaimed himself a "Kennedyite," emerged as party leader.

Interestingly, public opinion polls gave this party a greater share of the vote if it did not ally with or include the Extreme Left parties. Veltroni announced that the PD would not ally with them, and in the run-up to the new elections the Extreme Left parties (including the Communist parties and the Greens) formed their own coalition, the "Rainbow Left." The PD coalesced with Antonio Di Pietro's small "Italy's Values" party.

Similar developments occurred in the Center-Right. Berlusconi announced that he would dissolve Forza Italia and form a new party, the Popolo della Libertà (People of Liberty, PDL). Even though he had been quarreling with Fini, the two quickly made up, and Fini agreed to fold AN into the PDL. He announced that the PDL would make an alliance with the Lombard League but that it refused to ally with a small Christian Democratic Party (the UDC), whose leader, Pierferdinando Casini, ran independently.

The last months of 2007 and January 2008 were taken up by talks between Veltroni and Berlusconi in hopes of reforming the electoral law. These discussions seemed to progress until the Prodi cabinet fell, after which Berlusconi announced that he preferred to hold the new elections under the old law passed during his previous administration.

FROM BERLUSCONI TO BERLUSCONI

The Porcellum boded ill for the elections held on April 13 and 14, 2008. In order to create working majorities, the law gave an "electoral bonus" to the coalition that won the most votes in the Chamber of Deputies and in the Senate. For the Chamber, the votes were counted nationwide and seats distributed proportionately,

PORTRAITS

WALTER VELTRONI
Partito Democratico

༄ঙ০০৳

Walter Veltroni was selected as leader of the newly established Partito Democratico (Democratic Party), the major Center-Left organization, with over 75 percent of the vote after a primary election on October 14, 2007. Primaries are a fresh phenomenon in Italy, and the new party—a 2007 merger of former Communists and former Christian Democrats—believed that a popular vote would confer an important mandate on its new leader.

Born in Rome on July 3, 1955, Veltroni is the son of an Italian journalist and the daughter of the Slovenian ambassador to the Vatican during World War II. He began as a Communist, and was elected, in 1987, to Parliament and served as a vice premier. In 1988, he became a member of the party's secretariat and helped the Italian Communist Party transition to post-communism. He has downplayed his Communist past and claimed to be a follower of John F. Kennedy. From 1992 to 1996, he edited *L'Unità*, the former Communist daily later inked to the Democratic Party of the Left (PDS) and the Democratic Leftists (DS), successor organizations of the Communist Party. He was elected mayor of Rome in 2001; in 2006, he was reelected in a landslide. In 2005, he visited Senator Barack Obama in the United States and became one of his earliest supporters. He wrote the preface to the Italian edition of Obama's book *The Audacity of Hope* and adopted his slogan, "Yes, we can," as watchwords in his own campaign for the Italian elections of 2008.

Veltroni became very popular during his tenure as mayor of Rome. He won the support of the Vatican and came to be seen as a compromiser. He instituted reforms designed to improve municipal services for ordinary citizens and tourists and successfully revived the cultural life of the city, making it once again an international mecca. Under him, Rome took the leadership in deploying buses that run on clean fuel and banning motor vehicles from large areas of the city center. Veltroni instituted a new Roman film festival, and the "Auditorium," a multifunction musical complex designed by Italian architect Renzo Piana has been a huge cultural success.

On February 13, 2008, Veltroni resigned as mayor to run the campaign for the April national elections against former prime minister Silvio Berlusconi. While praised for his tendency to compromise, he has been criticized for taking both sides of important issues and baptized *ma anche* ("but also"). The Center-Left met defeat in the national elections and in the Rome mayoral election. These defeats raised questions about Veltroni's leadership and his ability to survive as leader of the Democratic Party.

except that the coalition with the most votes received a working majority in that house (340 seats). Coalitions had to receive at least 4 percent of the vote to be represented in the Chamber of Deputies. Achieving victory in the Senate was much more complicated. Senate elections were held on a regional, not a national, basis, and the vote was divided in such a manner as to result in a majority of 55 percent in the electoral colleges of the regions. In order to be represented in the Senate, coalitions had to win at least 8 percent of the vote in a region. Different coalitions consisting of different parties (some of them perhaps not running for the Chamber) ran in the different regions, complicating the Senate contests. Furthermore, in both the Chamber and the Senate, parties running within coalitions had to win a minimum percentage of the votes. It was thus very difficult to achieve a majority in the Senate (as the 2006 elections had demonstrated), and polls indicated that the likely result would be a Berlusconi victory in the Chamber and a tie or weak majority for him in the Senate.

Instead, the 2008 election results astounded observers: they gave the Berlusconi coalition a comfortable majority in both houses. The other astonishing result was the disappearance of the Extreme Left parties. The Rainbow Left parties won only 3.08 percent of the vote, not enough to be represented in the Chamber of Deputies, and they failed as well to elect a single senator. For the first time since the foundation of the Italian Republic, Communists would not be present in Parliament. Other small parties of the Right and the Left (including the Socialists) also failed to win any representation, and politicians who had long been icons of Italian politics did not get elected.

A major surprise was the excellent showing made by Bossi's Lombard League, which had been declining. Running within the Berlusconi coalition, this party doubled its votes. The 2008 elections demonstrated that the Italian political system—long beset by instability caused by the excessive representation of and power wielded by a host of small parties—had slowly evolved into something resembling the bipolar structure characteristic of other Western democracies. There were now two large parties on the Center-Right and the Center-Left that attracted the forces of different parts of the political spectrum. The Left-Center coalition included only one small party allied with the PD, while the PDL coalesced with the Lega Lombarda and a small party; only Casini's UDC survived, barely, running alone under its own symbol.

Analyses of the 2008 elections revealed some features that might prove important for the country's future. The humiliating defeat of the Extreme Left parties came about in their core areas of strength. A post-election poll revealed that except for small businesspeople, workers were the largest category voting for the Lombard League (11.3 percent). There were contrasting interpretations of this outcome. Some pollsters contended that workers abandoned the Extreme Left for

Bossi's League. The reason for this result, they argued, was that the League had become mainstream by evolving a "second generation" of leaders who were more respectable and more sophisticated than Bossi. Another analysis of voting patterns reached a different conclusion. It indicated that while some former Extreme Left supporters voted for the League, most of their votes went to the Partito Democratico, while most of the League gain came from former Forza Italia voters. Nevertheless, Berlusconi's PDL won big. It defeated Veltroni's PD among all categories except white-collar workers. For example, Berlusconi's party overpowered Veltroni among housewives by a hefty twenty percentage points (47.9 percent to 27.9 percent).

While Berlusconi's victory among traditional groups supporting the Right is comprehensible, what factors explain the depth of his victory in the 2008 elections? One contributing cause was the behavior of the Extreme Left representation in the Prodi cabinet: continually obstructing the government's actions, leftist ministers constantly attacked the cabinet of which they were a part. However, more fundamental reasons that are bound to have profound effects in the future also help explain the shift.

Globalization was a critical factor. With the decline of the Italian economy in a context of global crisis, workers feared for their jobs because of increasing competition from China, India, and other parts of the developing world. The crisis of Alitalia and the Naples trash scandal, with its attendant riots, smearing of Italy's image, and damage to the region's agricultural income brought the issue of Italian decline into the international spotlight. The elections revealed a split between the workers and their union leaders, especially the largest union (CGIL), linked with the Left. Indeed, following the elections, the leader of the Industrialists' Association remarked that the workers were closer to the industrialists than to their own unions. The Prodi period had been characterized by significant labor strife that seemed to damage the country's productivity. Ironically, the antiglobal movement, the extreme left of the Extreme Left, supported the Lombard League because of its focus on social issues, its populism, and its emphasis on local identity. Northern workers also responded to the League's call for reforms such as "fiscal federalism," ill defined but attractive during the electoral campaign.

Intimately linked to globalization, and hurting both the Center-Left and Extreme Left parties, were the immigration and criminality issues. In 2007, an Italian woman was murdered in Rome by a Romanian. The reaction rapidly became international as Fascist elements attacked Romanians. Interior Minister Giuliano Amato prepared a decree that made the expulsion of communitarian citizens easier. (Romania became an EU member in 2007.) This decree received the cabinet's approval, but the Extreme Left (part of the government that endorsed the decree) created obstacles in Parliament, and the legislation failed. Amato revised the decree, which eventually received parliamentary approval, but the Extreme Left's reluctance to fight criminality made the issue a major liability for both the Extreme and Center Left in the elections. Several other well-publicized criminal attacks by immigrants exacerbated the situation despite Amato's contention that overall crime had declined. The League seized control of the crime issue, which helped explain its strong electoral showing. In the discussions setting up the new Berlusconi cabinet, the League continued its campaign on this issue by demanding control of not only the Reform Ministry but the Ministry of the Interior, which controls the police. Blue-collar workers, normally supporters of the Left, were not immune to the Center-Right's anticrime campaign and protectionist evocations. Post-election interviews revealed that even recent immigrants who had become legalized were attracted to the Center-Right coalition because it promised to protect their jobs from competition from new immigrants. The crime issue also was a major factor in the local elections, particularly the victory of the Center-Right in Rome. In that city, Gianni Alemanno defeated former mayor and Margherita leader Francesco Rutelli in the mayoral election. Berlusconi exulted upon hearing the news, and Fini called it "the most beautiful victory" of the elections.

After the voting, Silvio Berlusconi enunciated his program. He promised to keep open the dialogue he had begun before the elections with the Center-Left in an effort to pass reforms; if the PD would add its votes to those of the governing majority, the reforms would be unstoppable. He promised to work to solve the Alitalia problem by bringing in Italian businesspeople and by opening talks with foreign airlines open to a partnership with, not a takeover of, the Italian airline. In an attempt to blunt the trash problems of Naples, he announced that he would hold several cabinet sessions a week in that city until the problem had been resolved. He pledged to do away with the local real estate tax on homes, abolish taxes on overtime, institute productivity bonuses, and provide a childbearing incentive of 1,000 euros.

There was no word, however, on possible repeal of the "Legge 40." Labeled by Dr. Alessandro Di Gregorio, head of a Turin fertility center, "a law that takes us back to the Middle Ages" (*La Repubblica*, April 26, 2008), this law, by making it next to impossible for Italian women to receive fertility treatment in Italy, had a negative impact on the birthrate. The law represented very graphically the increased influence of the Catholic Church in Italian affairs. While this subject caused great concern among commentators and, increasingly, among the public, it seemed unlikely that much could be done about it because the Center-Right was anxious to be viewed as part of the European Catholic movement while the Center-Left Democratic Party included a large contingent of Catholics and showed no stomach to confront the Church. In fact, when the majority challenged in Parliament the ruling of the country's highest court affirming the right of a father to take off life support his daughter who had been in a vegetative state for sixteen years, the Partito Democratico chose not to vote on the issue.

The new Berlusconi cabinet was sworn in on May 8, 2008. Responding to complaints that Italian cabinets had become bloated, the new government counted only twenty-one ministers, of whom nine had no portfolio, and four were women. For the major posts, Berlusconi tapped familiar names who had served in his earlier cabinets: Giulio Tremonti, economics minister; the Lombard League's Roberto Maroni, interior minister; and Franco Frattini at the Foreign Ministry had all served in the same posts before. The Reform Ministry, coveted by the League, went to Umberto Bossi. Berlusconi had to perform a delicate balancing act to satisfy the demands of his various partners, but seemed to have succeeded.

Political commentators noted that Berlusconi had won the 2008 elections—unlike those held in 2001—without making wild, impossible-to-keep promises. There was general agreement that the cavaliere's five-year tenure in power until 2006 had not accomplished very much, that he had spent much of his time defending himself from the magistrates, and that he had left Italy in poor economic shape. In 2008, the country found itself in a worse situation because important reforms had not been passed and the international economic crisis had become severe. In 2008, there was a sense that Italy was at the brink of disaster, that drastic action had to be taken, and that Berlusconi again had five years in which to improve the country's economy and adopt needed reforms. In an apparent recognition of his challenging task, Berlusconi promised many difficult years ahead. As in 2001, he had a comfortable majority that he could use to implement reforms, although his own partner, the Lombard League, might cause him trouble. But could he pass essential reforms and revive the country's fortunes this time?

At the beginning of the eighteenth century, Italy was a land subject to change through military invasion. In the twenty-first, observers wonder whether Berlusconi can succeed in fulfilling his promises or whether his new tenure in office will be as lackluster as his last. In the second half of the twentieth century, Italy shared with the West the benefits and problems of industrialization, free trade, and globalization, but its inability to reform itself hampered its economic development to an alarming degree. The twenty-first century world is changing at a pace unseen before, and Italy is struggling to keep up with the transformations and compete efficiently in a new world. Only the future will show the impact of the alterations in the political system in 2008 on the country's destiny.

Bibliographical Essay

S INCE CONVENIENT BIBLIOGRAPHIES ON ITALY FROM THE EIGHTEENTH
century to the present are not readily available, this essay has been designed with
several purposes in mind. The works cited in English will allow undergraduates who
are writing papers and have little or no familiarity with Italian to find documentation
on the major themes discussed in the various chapters. General as well as specific
works have been included so that a person interested in Italian history can become
familiar with the general history of a period or topic before proceeding to a more detailed analysis of particular questions. This technique may also prove useful for general readers. For graduate students or scholars interested in different periods, the
most useful works in Italian have been included.

Before considering books connected to specific chapters, several useful reference
publications may be mentioned. There are two good historical dictionaries that provide brief biographies of major characters and discussions of minor personages, institutions, publications, and movements that would otherwise be difficult to find, along
with indications for further reading. They are Frank J. Coppa, editor-in-chief, *Dictionary of Modern Italian History* (Westport, 1985), and Philip V. Cannistraro, editor-
in-chief, *Historical Dictionary of Fascist Italy* (Westport, 1982). Roland Sarti's *Italy: A
Reference Guide from the Renaissance to the Present* (New York, 2004) provides valuable information on important people, ideas, and events in Italian history. It also
gives brief narratives and a chronology of major events.

Convenient short bibliographies worth noting are Frank J. Coppa and William
Roberts, *Modern Italian History: An Annotated Bibliography* (New York, 1990), which
begins in the eighteenth century; Charles F. Delzell, *Italy in the Twentieth Century*,
American Historical Association pamphlet 428 (Washington, D.C., 1980); and Clara
Lovett, *Contemporary Italy: A Selective Bibliography* (Washington, D.C., 1985). Essays
on recent American books on Italy and valuable memoirs of Americans involved in
Italy are in Borden W. Painter Jr., ed., *Perspectives on Italy* (Hartford, 1992), a special
issue of the *Cesare Barbieri Courier*, based at Trinity College, Hartford, Connecticut.
Another good resource is Martin J. Bull, *Contemporary Italy: A Research Guide* (Westport, 1996). Lists of works, including recent books, articles, papers, dissertations, and

works in progress, may be found in the annual *Newsletter of the Society for Italian Historical Studies* (Boston College), edited by Alan Reinerman. An equivalent publication discusses recent works primarily in political science: the *Newsletter of the Conference Group on Italian Politics and Society*.

Attention has also been paid to women. See Rinaldina Russell's *Italian Women Writers: A Bio-Bibliographical Sourcebook* (Westport, 1994) and *The Feminist Encyclopedia to Italian Literature* (Westport, 1997).

It is important to remember that the Internet has become an increasingly valuable—if not indispensable—resource for research, if used properly and in conjunction with more traditional sources. For example, the Italian Chamber of Deputies, the Senate, the Prime Minister's Office, political parties, and even minor political groupings have websites that can be profitably consulted. The same is true of libraries and archives, in addition to other organizations interested in Italian history. WorldCat is a basic resource for finding books, and H-Italy (http://www.h-net.org/reviews/showlist.cgi?sort=rev&lists=H-Italy), part of H-Net, is important for reviews of recent books.

Introduction:
From "School of Europe" to Conquered Land

For the history of Italian heretics, see the classic work by Delio Cantimori, *Eretici italiani del Cinquecento* (Florence, 1967), and his short and brilliant *Prospettive di storia ereticale italiana del Cinquecento* (Bari, 1960). Eric Cochrane and John Tedeschi summarize Cantimori's work and its influence in "Delio Cantimori: Historian," *Journal of Modern History* 39, no. 4 (December 1967): 438–445. In English, Barry Collett, *Italian Benedictine Scholars and the Reformation* (Oxford, 1985), tells of the failure of a congregation of monks to resolve the schism between Catholics and Protestants. Nicholas Terpstra, ed., *The Politics of Ritual Kinship: Confraternities and Social Order in Early Modern Italy* (New York, 2000), is a collection of scholarly chapters discussing the role of religious confraternities during the seventeenth century. Marie-Louise Roden discusses the complexities of papal politics in *Church Politics in Seventeenth-Century Rome* (Stockholm, 2000). A special issue of the *Journal of Modern History* discusses questions related to the rise of the state in Renaissance Italy: "The Origins of the State in Italy, 1300–1600," vol. 67, supplement (December 1995).

The pessimistic view of the post-Renaissance is represented mostly by Italians. See Benedetto Croce, *Storia dell'Italia moderna*, 5th ed. (Bari, 1967); Giorgio Candeloro, *Storia dell'Italia moderna*, 2d ed., vol. 1 (Milan, 1966); and Guido Quazza, *La decadenza italiana nella storia europea* (Milan, 1971). A more balanced view and rich detail is provided by Romolo Quazza, *Preponderanza Spagnuola (1559–1700)* (Milan, 1950). The revisionists are represented by Eric Cochrane, *Florence in the Forgotten Centuries* (Chicago, 1973), an exciting voyage through the years under consideration, and more explicitly in his *Italy 1530–1630* (London and New York, 1988), edited posthumously by Julius Kirschner. R. Burr Litchfield's *Emergence of a Bureaucracy: The Florentine Patricians 1530–1790* (Princeton, 1986) essentially concurs with Cochrane. Domenico Sella, *Crisis and Continuity: The Economy of Spanish Lombardy in the Seventeenth Century* (Cambridge, Mass., 1979), provides a reasoned argument against "refeudalization" and a judicious interpretation of the economic crisis of the period. Antonio Calabria discusses decline in Naples in *The Cost of Empire: The Finances of the Kingdom of Naples in the Time of Spanish Rule* (New York, 1991). Richard Tilden Rapp examines the meaning of decline in his *Industry and Economic Decline in Seventeenth-Century Venice* (Cambridge, U.K., 1979), while the essays in Brian Pullan, ed., *Crisis and Change in the Venetian Economy in the Sixteenth and Seventeenth Centuries* (London, 1968), are fundamental for an understanding of the period. In *Shipbuilders of the Venetian Arsenal: Workers and Workplace in the Preindustrial City* (Baltimore, 1991), Robert C. Davis discusses the role of ordinary workers and their families in Venice. *Venice Reconsidered*, edited by John Jeffries Martin and Dennis Romano (Baltimore, 2000), presents some of the new research on society and culture and questions some previous conclusions; it is also an example of the literature that can be found on the individual city-states. John Marino, ed., *Early Modern Italy, 1550–1796* (Oxford, 2002), collects essays discussing the most important aspects of Italian life during the period. Finally, the Einaudi *Storia d'Italia*, vol. 2, pt. 2 (Turin, 1974), provides a comprehensive survey of the period and its antecedents, including a good economic overview.

Chapter 1: The Italian Enlightenment

Although English-language historians have not devoted much attention to the Italian Enlightenment, a host of works exist in Italian, only the most important of which can be listed here. The fundamental work on this period is Franco Venturi's multivolume *Settecento riformatore* (Turin, 1969), which discusses in detail Enlightenment activity in the Italian states and traces European connections. This work has been only partially translated, but students may get a taste of Venturi's style in the excellent *Italy and the Enlightenment* (London, 1972). Venturi's views have influenced all modern scholarship on the eighteenth century, as may be seen by Dino Carpanetto and Giuseppe Ricuperati, who present an exquisitely balanced survey, including a discussion of the historiographical problem, in *Italy in the Age of Reason, 1685–1789* (London, 1987), and the early chapters of Stuart Woolf, *A History of Italy* (London, 1979), which provide an excellent introduction to the period. In January 2004, a conference coinciding with the tenth anniversary of Venturi's death was held; see John Davis and David I. Kerzer, eds., *The Culture of Enlightenment and Reform in Eighteenth-Century Italy* (Abingdon, U.K., 2005). Woolf's *The Poor in Western Europe in the Eighteenth and Nineteenth Centuries* (London, 1986) also focuses on Italy. Giorgio Candeloro concentrates on the crisis of the Italian states in volume 1 of his *Storia dell'Italia moderna*, 2d ed. (Milan, 1966). The articles in Daniela Frigo, ed., *Politics and Diplomacy in*

Early Modern Italy (Cambridge, U.K., 2000) examine the diplomacy of the smaller Italian states.

For particular areas, consult Eric Cochrane, *Tradition and Enlightenment in the Tuscan Academies, 1690–1800* (Chicago, 1961), for a peek at the intense Tuscan intellectual life. Mario Mattolini, *Il principe illuminato, Pietro Leopoldo* (Florence, 1981), is a rare work on Peter Leopold and Tuscany during this period. Caroline Castiglione, *Patrons and Adversaries: Nobles and Villagers in Italian Politics, 1640–1760* (New York, 2005), discusses the struggle between the Barberini family and the villages they ruled. Jeffrey Collins, *Papacy and Politics in Eighteenth-Century Rome* (Cambridge, U.K., 2004), examines Pope Pius VI and his relationship to the arts. Benedetto Croce's insights in his classic *History of the Kingdom of Naples* (Chicago, 1970) have been modified but are still provocative. On intellectual women in this era, see Gabriella Berti Logan, "The Desire to Contribute: An Eighteenth-Century Italian Woman of Science," *American Historical Review* 99, no. 3 (June 1994): 785–812. Consult also Paul Oskar Kristeller, "Learned Women in Early Modern Italy: Humanists and University Scholars," in Patricia H. Labalme, ed., *Beyond Their Sex: Learned Women of the European Past* (New York, 1980). Vincenzo Ferrone has examined Newton's legacy in *The Intellectual Roots of the Italian Enlightenment: Newtonian Science, Religion, and Politics in the Eighteenth Century* (Atlantic Highlands, 1995). For the influence of Italian intellectuals in other parts of Europe, see Sherer West, ed., *Italian Culture in Northern Europe in the Eighteenth Century* (Cambridge, U.K., 1999).

Harold Acton's *The Bourbons of Naples* (London, 1956) includes an interesting, detailed, and sympathetic synopsis of the period. Naples during the reign of Maria Carolina is the subject of Rafaelle Del Puglia's *La regina di Napoli: il regno di Maria Carolina dal Vesuvio alla Sicilia* (Pavia, 1989). A more general history is John Davis, *Enlightened Illusions: Naples and Its Kingdom in the Age of Reform and Revolution* (New York, 2003). Mario Giannattasio has written a work spanning the Kingdom of Naples from this period to that of Murat, discussed in chapters 2 and 3, *Le due Caroline: il regno di Napoli tra Carolina di Borbone e Carolina Murat* (Naples, 1999). Much has been written on the most important Neapolitan thinker of this period; a good example is Cecilia Miller, *Giambattista Vico: Imagination and Historical Knowledge* (New York, 1993). Books on the career of another important, more traditionally Enlightenment, thinker—Gaetano Filangieri—include Marcello T. Maestro, *Gaetano Filangieri and His Science of Legislation* (Philadelphia, 1976), and Gerardo Ruggiero, *Filangieri: un uomo, una famiglia, un amore nella Napoli del Settecento* (Naples, 1999).

A good account of Sicilian society and the attempts at reform is in *A History of Sicily: Modern Sicily After 1713* by Denis Mack Smith (London, 1968). More detailed accounts of Neapolitan reform efforts under Caracciolo may be found in the following works: Benito Li Vigni, *Il Vicerè: Domenico Caracciolo, un riformatore nella Sicilia del Settecento* (Naples, 1992); Mauro Bonanno, *Il rivoluzionario: Domenico Caracciolo e il riformismo in Sicilia: 1781–1786* (Acireale, 1998); and Francesco Brancato, *Il Caracciolo e il suo tentativo di riforme in Sicilia* (Palermo, 1995). Franco Venturi gives an intimate look at life in Venice in his short but provocative *Venezia nel 700* (Turin,

1980). In English, Frederic C. Lane's *Venice: A Maritime Republic* (Baltimore, 1973) and William H. McNeill's *Venice: The Hinge of Europe* (Chicago, 1974) are concerned with the glory days but have short chapters on the eighteenth century. On the Lombard land survey and its implications, see Daniel Klang, *Tax Reform in Eighteenth-Century Lombardy* (New York, 1977); on the nobility, see J. M. Roberts, "Lombardy," in Albert Goodwin, ed., *The European Nobility in the Eighteenth Century* (London, 1953): 60–82. Alexander I. Grab argues that the Austrians in Lombardy were interested in reform only for the added power it might bring them and that they essentially failed. See his articles, "The Politics of Subsistence: The Liberalization of Grain Commerce in Austrian Lombardy Under Enlightened Despotism," *Journal of Modern History* 57 (June 1985): 185–210; "Enlightened Absolutism and Common Lands Enclosure: The Case of Austrian Lombardy," *Agricultural History* 63, no. 1 (Winter 1989): 49–72; and "Enlightened Despotism and State Building: The Case of Austrian Lombardy," in *Austrian History Yearbook* (Minneapolis, 1989): 43–72. See also his *La politica del pane* (Milan, 1986), which discusses deregulation of the grain trade. Further information on particular areas may be found in Venturi's *Italy and the Enlightenment*, previously cited. Daniel Klang discusses *Tax Reform in Eighteenth-Century Lombardy* (Boulder, 1977). On Trieste, see Lois C. Dubin, *The Port Jews of Habsburg Trieste: Absolutist Politics and Enlightenment Culture* (Stanford, 1999).

On daily life, the best book is the short, comprehensive, and insightful *Daily Life in Eighteenth-Century Italy* (New York, 1963) by Maurice Vaussard. An interesting work describing how opera reflected the changing culture and ideas of the time is Martha Feldman's *Opera and Sovereignty* (Chicago, 2007). Though concerned primarily with the nineteenth century, Woolf's *The Poor in Western Europe in the Eighteenth and Nineteenth Centuries*, previously cited, discusses the eighteenth century and has an excellent introduction analyzing the parameters of the problem. Books by foreigners telling about their travels in Italy are prime sources for our knowledge of daily life during this period. These include Johann Wolfgang von Goethe, *Italian Journey* (New York, 1989); Arthur Young, *Travels During the Years 1787, 1788, and 1789* (London, 1794); and Frank Brady and Frederick A. Pottle, eds., *Boswell on the Grand Tour: Italy, Corsica, and France* (London, 1955).

On the question of growing national feeling, Emiliana Noether's *Seeds of Italian Nationalism, 1700–1815* (New York, 1951) makes the case for the importance of the eighteenth century. On Muratori's role, consult Comitato per le Onoranze a L. A. Muratori nel Bicentenario dalla Morte, *Miscellanea di studi muratoriani* (Modena, 1951).

CHAPTER 2: ITALY AND THE FRENCH REVOLUTION

The essays collected in John A. Davis, ed., *Italy in the Nineteenth Century* (New York, 2000), include good material on the period discussed in this chapter and on the entire nineteenth century. Despite the appearance of this book, French revolutionary and Napoleonic Italy have suffered from a scarcity of works and research, and the period would reward investigators who decide to dedicate time and energy to the topic. The English-language literature is particularly thin, although more has been done in recent years. Considerable work is still needed on the social and economic implications of the reforms of this period, particularly in the South, and the same could be said for the counterrevolutionary movements.

Some of the works cited for chapter 1, including Croce (*History of the Kingdom of Naples*), Woolf (*A History of Italy*), Acton (*The Bourbons of Naples*), and Candeloro (*Storia dell'Italia moderna*), have good discussions of this period. Michael Broers, *The Napoleonic Empire in Italy, 1796–1814* (New York, 2005), is a general history. Anna Maria Rao has published a comprehensive history of the Italian exiles in France and their relationship to French ideas and activities: *Esuli: l'emigrazione politica italiana in Francia, 1792–1802* (Naples, 1992). R. M. Johnston, *The Napoleonic Empire in Southern Italy*, 2 vols. (London, 1904), is old but still useful, as is Guglielmo Ferrero, *Avventura: Bonaparte in Italia (1796–1797)* (Milan, 1947). Angus Heriot, *The French in Italy, 1796–1799* (London, 1957), is short on insights but good on gossip. Giovanni Pillinini discusses Jacobinism in Venice in his *1797: Venezia "giacobina"* (Venice, 1997). Giorgio Vaccarino, *I patrioti "anarchistes" e l'idea dell'unità italiana* (Turin, 1955), is an excellent account of the beginning of the idea of Italian unity during the period. Not much secondary literature exists on the Cispadane Republic, but there are documentary collections. On the Cisalpine Republic, see the general work by Giorgio Boccolari, *La Repubblica Cisalpina* (Florence, 1969). On particular issues, see Umberto Marcelli, *La vendita dei beni nazionali nella Repubblica Cisalpina*, 2d ed. (Bologna, 1973), and Manlio Paganella, *Alle origini dell'unità d'Italia: il progetto politico-costituzionale di Melchiorre Gioa* (Milan, 1999). For the relationship between the French and the Republic, consult Carlo Zaghi, *Il Direttorio francese e la Repubblica Cisalpina* (Rome, 1992). The creation of an army by Napoleon has received attention for its positive and negative effects on Italian society and on future ideas of unity. See Frederick C. Schneid, *Soldiers of Napoleon's Kingdom of Italy: Army, State, and Society, 1800–1815* (Boulder, 1995), a view of the army's relationship to society and the Risorgimento. Schneid has also published *Napoleon's Italian Campaigns 1805–1815* (Westport, 2002). Similar themes are treated in depth by Alexander Grab, "Army, State, and Society: Conscription and Desertion in Napoleonic Italy (1802–1814)," *Journal of Modern History* 67 (March 1995): 25–54; "La formation de l'armée italienne à l'époque de la Republique Italienne (1802–1804)," *Revue de l'Institut Napoleon* 162 (1994): 29–50; and "State Power, Brigandage, and Rural Resistance in Napoleonic Italy," *European History Quarterly* 25 (January 1995): 39–70. "La politica finanziaria nella Repubblica e nel Regno d'Italia sotto Napoleone (1802–1814)," in *L'Italia nell'età napoleonica* (Milan, 1998), examines the result of military expenses on the finances of the Republic and Kingdom of Italy. Armando Frumento, *Il Regno d'Italia Napoleonico: siderurgia, combustibili, armamenti ed economia, 1805–1814* (Milan, 1991), discusses the economy. Georges Bourgin, *Italie et Napoléon, 1796–1814* (Paris, 1936), is an insightful short account. Grab has also published *Napoleon and the Transformation of Europe* (Basingstoke, 2002). The economic life of this period is explored by Evgenij V. Tarle, *La vita economica dell'Italia nell'età napoleonica* (Turin, 1950). John A. Davis has published an interesting work on *Conflict and Control: Law and Order in Nineteenth-Century Italy* (Atlantic Highlands, 1988), which considers the issue from 1790 to 1900. See also Steven C. Hughes, *Crime, Disorder, and the Risorgimento* (New York, 1994), which uses Bologna as a case study in the development of a modern police force. Pietro Colletta's *Storia del reame di Napoli* (Florence, 1962) is a classic account, as is Vincenzo Cuoco's history of the Neapolitan counterrevolution of 1799, *Saggio storico sulla rivoluzione di Napoli* (Milan, 1806). Several general works treat different aspects of the Neapolitan revolution. These include Claudia Petraccone, *Napoli nel 1799* (Naples, 1989), an examination of the bourgeoisie and the nobility; Mario Proto, *Il Mezzogiorno e la rivoluzione napoletana del 1799* (Manduria, 1999), a more general treatment; John Davis, *Naples and Napoleon* (Oxford, 2006), an attempt to put the revolution into a European context; and Anna Maria Rao, *Napoli 1799 fra storia e storiografia* (Naples, 2002), a collection of articles from a conference drawing lessons from the Neapolitan revolution. Documents on the role of Admiral Nelson have been published; see H. C. Gutteridge, *Nelson and the Neapolitan Revolution: Documents Relating to the Suppression of the Jacobin Revolution at Naples, June 1799* (London, 1903). On the Neapolitan revolution and counterrevolution, see also Benedetto Croce, *La rivoluzione napoletana del 1799* (Bari, 1961). The amazing story of Cardinal Ruffo is told in Giovanni Ruffo, *Il cardinale Fabrizio Ruffo tra psicologia e storia: l'uomo, il politico, il sanfedista* (Catanzaro, 1999), and in Domenico Petromasi, *Alla riconquista del Regno: la marcia del cardinale Ruffo dalle Calabrie a Napoli* (Naples, 1994). On different aspects of his role, see Peter Nichols, *La notte comincia ancora una volta: atti del Convegno Fabrizio Ruffo fra storia ed immaginario: San Lucido 27–28 luglio 1984* (Cosenza, 1985). On Rome, Gerard Pelletier, *Rome et la Revolution Française* (Rome, 2004), discusses politics, theology, and the papacy up to 1799, while Michael Broers, *Politics and Religion in Napoleonic Italy* (Microsoft Reader eBooks), examines the cultural conflict created by French reforms and the causes of the fight between Napoleon and Pius VII. Scholarly articles cover the reigns of both popes during the French revolutionary era in Marino Mengozzi's *I pontificati di Pio VI e Pio VII* (Cesena, 2001). E. E. Y. Hales, *The Emperor and the Pope* (New York, 1978), is a more general history.

For resistance to French rule after the Neapolitan revolution, see Milton Findley, *The Most Monstrous of Wars* (Columbia, 1996), an account of the guerrilla war against the French and their supporters between 1806 and 1811 that, according to the author, foreshadowed the uprising in Spain. The case of a Tuscan reformer through the Enlightenment and the Napoleonic periods is examined by Renato Pasta, *The Making of a Notable: Giovanni Fabbroni Between Enlightened Absolutism and Napoleonic Administration* (Princeton, 1985). Melzi d'Eril has received some attention in the historical literature. See Francesco Melzi d'Eril, *Francesco Melzi d'Eril, 1753–1816: Milanese scomodo e grande uomo di stato visto da un lontano pronipote* (Florence, 2000). Nino Del Bianco sees him in terms of a missed opportunity; see his *Franceso Melzi d'Eril: la grande occasione perduta agli albori dell'indipendenza nell'Italia napoleonica* (Milan, 2002).

Further literature on the historiographical question discussed at the beginning of this chapter may be found in Emiliana Noether, "The Transition from the Enlightenment to the Risorgimento: A Question of Historical Interpretation," in Frank J. Coppa, ed., *Studies in Modern Italian History from the Risorgimento to the Republic* (New York, 1986).

CHAPTER 3: THE FIRST WAR FOR ITALIAN UNITY

The events discussed in this chapter suffer even more from neglect than those of chapter 2. Very little exists in English, and foreign-language works are mostly old, dating from the nineteenth and early twentieth centuries.

On Eugène Beauharnais, see Carola Oman, *Napoleon's Viceroy: Eugène di Beauharnais* (London, 1966). On Eugène's military significance, consult Robert M. Epstein, *Prince Eugène at War, 1809: A Study of the Role of Prince Eugène de Beauharnais in the Franco-Austrian War of 1809* (Arlington, 1984), and, more germane to this chapter, George Nofziger and Marco Gioannini, *The Defense of the Napoleonic Kingdom of Northern Italy* (Westport, 2002). In his PhD dissertation, "The Administration of the Kingdom of Italy Under Eugène Beauharnais, 1805–1814" (Ann Arbor, 1978), Ert J. Gunn discusses the administration of Prince Eugène's realm. The best work on Murat is still Angela Valente, *Murat e l'Italia meridionale*, 2d ed. (Turin, 1965). More recently, there is Jean Tulard, *Murat* (Paris, 1999). Antonio Spinoza's *Murat* (Milan, 1984) is a biography that portrays the cavalry general as the most adventurous of the rulers set up by Napoleon. In French, see *Joachim Murat, Roi de Naples: la dernière annèe de règne*, 5 vols. (Paris, 1909), and H. Weill, *Le prince Eugène et Murat*, 5 vols. (Paris, 1902). See Johnston (*The Napoleonic Empire in Southern Italy*) and Colletta (*Storia del reame di Napoli*). The war itself is examined by Pietro Colletta, *La campagna d'Italia di Gioacchino Murat* (Turin, 1982). The latter part of Murat's reign is examined by E. Ohnmeiss and F. Corromeo, *Giocchino Murat e la fine della dominazione napoleonica in Italia* (Lugano, 1991), while Franco Cortese discusses his end in *Sbarco, cattura e fuciliazione di Gioaccino Murat a Pizzo Calabro nel 1815* (Cosenza, 2006). There is ample literature on the carbonari, but, again, it is usually old; see A. Ottolini, *La Carboneria dalle origini ai primi moti insurrezionali (1797–1817)* (Modena, 1936); a more recent account is R. J. Rath, "The Carbonari: Their Origins, Initiation Rites, and Aims," *American Historical Review* 69 (1964). On events in the North, see D. Spadoni, *Milano e la congiura militare nel 1814 per l'indipendenza italiana*, 3 vols. (Modena, 1936); Spadoni is also the author of "Nel centenario del proclama di Rimini," in *Rassegna Storica del Risorgimento* (1915). On British policy, see C. K. Webster, *The Foreign Policy of Castlereagh, 1812–1822*, 2 vols. (London, 1931–1934); H. M. Lackland, "The Failure of the Constitutional Experiment in Sicily, 1813–1814," and "Lord Bentinck in Sicily, 1811–1812," both in *English Historical Review* (1926 and 1927); and C. W. Crawley, "England and the Sicilian Constitution of 1812," *English Historical Review* (1940).

CHAPTER 4: A "GEOGRAPHICAL EXPRESSION"

On the diplomatic side of the Restoration, two older works are still useful: René Albrecht-Carrié, *A Diplomatic History of Europe Since the Congress of Vienna* (New York, 1973), and C. K. Webster, *The Congress of Vienna 1814–1815* (London, 1919). Guiliano Procacci, *Storia degli italiani* (Bari, 1993), gives a good account of this period. An interesting article on the diplomatic rivalry between Austria and Russia in Italy is Alan J. Reinerman's "Metternich, Alexander I, and the Russian Challenge in Italy," *Journal of Modern History* 46, no. 2 (June 1974): 20–38. On the intellectual side, Ettore Alberoni's *Storia delle dottrine politiche in Italia* (Milan, 1985) presents a succinct history of political theory during this time. Pietro Colletta's *Storia del reame di Napoli* (Florence, 1962) is a classic with a chapter treating this period. On the early Restoration in the North, see R. J. Rath, *The Provisional Austrian Regime in Lombardy-Venetia, 1814–1815* (Austin, 1969); on Austrian relations with the papacy, see Alan Reinerman, *Between Conflict and Cooperation 1809–1830*, vol. 1 of *Austria and the Papacy in the Age of Metternich* (Washington, D.C., 1979). On the Restoration in Rome, see Massimo Petrocchi, *La Restaurazione romana (1815–1823)* (Florence, 1943). On the Kingdom of Sardinia, see the collection of scholarly papers by Maria Barbara Bertini, *Ombre e luci della Restaurazione* (Rome, 1997). Margaret O'Dwyer's *The Papacy in the Age of Napoleon and the Restoration, 1800–1823* (Lanham, 1985) comes into the Restoration era. John Tracy Ellis's *Cardinal Consalvi and Anglo-Papal Relations 1814–1824* (Washington, D.C., 1942) is an older but still excellent account of Consalvi's diplomacy. On Consalvi, see as well John Martin, *Cardinal Consalvi* (New York, 1987), and the essays in Convegno interregionale di Storia del Risorgimento, *Atti del Convegno interregionale di Storia del Risorgimento: Pio VII e il cardinale Consalvi: un tentativo di riforma nello Stato Pontificio* (Viterbo, 1981). Good cultural insights may be found in Benedetto Croce, *Una famiglia di patrioti* (Bari, 1927), and *Storia della storiografia italiana nel secolo decimonono*, 2 vols. (Bari, 1921). In English, see Christopher Cairns, *Italian Literature* (London, 1977), a general work that includes good brief discussions of the dominant themes of the literature of this period. Useful information on Sicily is in M. I. Finley, Denis Mack Smith, and Christopher Duggan, *A History of Sicily* (New York, 1987).

CHAPTER 5: FAILED REVOLUTIONS: THE 1820S AND 1830S

The most comprehensive work in English on the Neapolitan Revolution is still George T. Romani's *The Neapolitan Revolution of 1820–1821* (Evanston, 1950). In Italian, consult Michele De Vivo, *I moti di Napoli e di Palermo del 1820–1821* (Florence, 1968). Giorgio Spini has discussed the Spanish Revolution's role in the Italian revolutions of 1820–1821 in *Mito e realtà della Spagna nelle rivoluzioni italiane del 1820–1821* (Rome, 1950). For an indication of some of the constitutional issues, see Paolo Pastori, *Gioacchino Ventura di Raulica e la costituzione napoletana del 1820* (Florence,

1968). The role of the Papal State is examined in Joseph Hugh Brody, *Rome and the Neapolitan Revolution of 1820–1821* (New York, 1937). Chapters on the revolution can be found in Acton's *The Bourbons of Naples* and in Croce's *History of the Kingdom of Naples,* previously cited. A discussion of Restoration culture, the secret societies, and the revolutions of this period is in Stuart Woolf, *A History of Italy, 1700–1860* (London, 1979), and Harry Hearder, *Italy in the Age of the Risorgimento, 1790–1870* (New York, 1983). George Martin, *The Red Shirt and the Cross of Savoy* (New York, 1969), shows particular insight into the problems of the period. See the previously cited works also on the Piedmontese agitation of 1821 and on the 1831 revolutions. Giorgio Candeloro, *Storia dell'Italia moderna,* vol. 2 (Milan, 1962), is excellent, as is Nino Valeri, ed., *Storia d'Italia,* vol. 3 (Turin, 1965), whereas great detail and an especially good section on the Italian exiles of this period may be found in Cesare Spellanzon, *Storia del Risorgimento e dell'unità d'Italia,* vol. 2 (Milan, 1934), which covers Italy up to the eve of the 1848 revolutions. Istituto per la storia del Risorgimento italiano, *L'Italia tra rivoluzione e riforme, 1831–1846* (Rome, 1994), is a collective volume on the desire of some Italian states during the period for mild administrative reform. Alan Reinerman has studied how the first effort of the powers to reform the Papal State failed, in "The Concert Baffles: The Roman Conference of 1831 and the Reform of the Papal States," *International History Review* 5, no. 1 (1983): 20–38.

There are many memoirs, local histories, and literary works on the carbonari, many dating from the nineteenth century, that the reader will easily find. See, for example, Felice Foresti, *The Fate of the Carbonari Society: The Memoirs of Felice Foresti* (New York, 1932). On the 1831 revolutions, particularly useful works are Paolo Emilio Faggioni, *I moti carbonari del 1831* (Florence, 1968), and E. Ohnmeiss, *Dai moti carbonari a Ciro Menotti* (Vignola, 1991).

The standard works on Buonarroti are Armando Saitta, *Filippo Buonarroti,* 2 vols. (Rome, 1950), and Alessandro Galante Garrone, *Filippo Buonarroti e i rivoluzionari dell'Ottocento* (Turin, 1951). In English, see Arthur Lehning's articles, "Buonarroti and His Secret Societies," *International Review of Social History* 1 (1956): 112–140; "Buonarroti's Ideas on Communism and Dictatorship," *International Review of Social History* 2 (1957): 266–287; and Elizabeth Eisenstein, *The First Professional Revolutionist: Filippo Michele Buonarroti* (Cambridge, Mass., 1959).

Chapter 6: Three Models for Unification

Mazzini was fortunate in finding English-language scholars who studied his work, but after a period of intense interest he would be neglected for a long time. A new interest arose in his ideas toward the end of the twentieth century, and this interest accelerated as the two-hundredth anniversary of his birth approached in 2005. Worldwide celebrations in honor of the Italian patriot were held in that year. Denis Mack Smith's *Mazzini* (New Haven, 1994), followed by Roland Sarti, *Mazzini: A Life for the Religion of Politics* (Westport, 1997), seem to have begun the trend. Salvo Mastellone has been very active in highlighting Mazzini not only as an Italian but as a European figure. See the book he edited, *Giuseppe Mazzini: la vittoria della democrazia* (Milan, 2005). Other books by Mastellone on Mazzini include *La democrazia etica di Mazzini (1837–1847)* (Rome, 2000); *Mazzini e gli scrittori politici europei, 1837–1857* (Florence, 2005); and *Mazzini e Linton: una democrazia europea (1845–1855)* (Florence, 2007). In English, see his *Mazzini and Marx* (Westport, 2003), in which he emphasizes Mazzini's influence in England and on the writing of the *Communist Manifesto*. Other important works include Bruno Gatta, *Mazzini: una vita per un sogno* (Naples, 2002), and Pietro Galletto, *Mazzini nella vita e nella storia* (Treviso, 2005). In-depth analyses of his role in Italy include Bruno Ficcadenti, *Il Partito Mazziniano italiano* (Pisa, 1999), and a collective work on his action in the Italian and international democratic movement: Stefania Bonanni, *Pensiero e azione* (Rome, 2006). As time goes on, neglected aspects of his life are being brought to light, such as the involvement of women in Mazzinianism. See Sonia Amarena, *Donne mazziniane, donne repubblicane* (Imola, 2003), and Liviana Gazzetta, *Giorgina Saffi: contributo alla storia del mazzinianesimo femminile* (Milan, 2003). The classic work by Gaetano Salvemini, *Mazzini*, is an essential starting point for an understanding of Mazzini's thought. Gwilym O. Griffith, author of *Mazzini: Prophet of Modern Europe* (New York, 1970), quotes Lloyd George's statement about Mazzini—"How right he was!"—which summarizes the book's main thesis. E. E. Y. Hales, *Mazzini and the Secret Societies: The Making of a Myth* (London, 1956), rightly emphasizes Mazzini's "shock value" to the existing Italian order. An older but excellent treatment of Mazzini is Bolton King's *Mazzini* (London, 1903). The author was able to speak to persons who had known Mazzini intimately, yet he succeeded in providing an objective study. It can be stated that Mazzini both accepted foreign influences and had an impact in other countries. An aspect of this interaction has been examined by Joseph Rossi, *The Image of America in Mazzini's Writings* (Madison, 1954). Mazzini's writings have been collected and published, and a good, albeit brief, sampling may be found in N. Gangulee, ed., *Giuseppe Mazzini: Selected Writings* (Westport, 1974). On the central "religiosity" of Mazzini's thought, see the essay on Mazzini in John MacCunn, *Six Radical Thinkers* (New York, 1964). Italian counts many works on Mazzini. Emilia Morelli, *Giuseppe Mazzini: quasi una biografia* (Rome, 1984), emphasizes the point that Mazzini's religiosity was both the force behind and the brake upon his entire activity. In English, Roland Sarti, in his full-fledged biography, *Mazzini: A Life for the Religion of Politics* (Westport, 1997), agrees: "Insistence on the unity of religion and politics separates Mazzini from the political mainstream of his time and ours." Salvo Mastellone's *Mazzini e la "Giovane Italia,"* 2 vols. (Pisa, 1960), is a particularly fertile work that discusses the modern revolutionary method found in Mazzini's thought. Mastellone has also done a close textual analysis demonstrating that Marx's *Manifesto of the Communist Party* was partially a direct response to Mazzini's criticisms: Salvo Mastellone, ed., *Giuseppe Mazzini: pensieri sulla democrazia in Europa* (Milan, 1997). Mastellone has also written *Mazzini's Ethical Democracy (1837–1847)* (Westport, 2004). Franco Della Peruta, *Mazzini e i rivoluzionari italiani* (Milan, 1974), is another important work on the subject.

Gioberti's works and numerous letters have been published. There are several good, older biographies dedicated to him. A. Anzilotti's *Gioberti* (Florence, 1922) is a positive work; Adolfo Omodeo, *Vincenzo Gioberti e la sua evoluzione politica* (Turin, 1941), takes a more complex view, according to which Gioberti used neo-Guelphism as an instrument to impart movement to the Italian situation. Omodeo's argument that Gioberti was able to mobilize moderate public opinion, in addition to a discussion of Balbo, may be found in his far-reaching work *L'età del Risorgimento italiano* (Naples, 1946). A more recent biography is Giorgio Rumi, *Gioberti* (Bologna, 1999). Several books also discuss his thought. See Marcello Muste, *La scienza ideale: filosofia e politica in Vincenzo Gioberti* (Catanzaro, 2000), and Mario Sancipriano, *Vincenzo Gioberti: progetti etico-politico nel Risorgimento* (Rome, 1997). The proceedings of a conference held on Gioberti have been published in Giuseppe Riconda and Gianluca Cuozzo, *Giornata giobertiana* (Turin, 2000). Besides the works by Gioberti and Balbo mentioned in the text, see Gioberti's *Del Rinnovamento civile d'Italia*, 3 vols. (Bari, 1968), and Balbo's *Sommario della storia d'Italia* (Milan, 1927). The relevant portions of Stuart Woolf's previously cited *A History of Italy, 1700–1860* are excellent on the discussion of alternative plans for Italian unification.

Developments in the Papal State in the period before Pius IX are cogently discussed by Alan Reinerman in *Revolution and Reaction, 1830–1838*, vol. 2 of *Austria and the Papacy in the Age of Metternich* (Washington, D.C., 1989). G. F. H. Berkeley, in *Italy in the Making*, vol. 1, *1815 to 1846*, and vol. 2, *June 1846 to 1 January 1848* (Cambridge, U.K., 1968), provides an informative and interesting account of events of the period, as does the older work by William Roscoe Thayer, *The Dawn of Italian Independence*, vol. 1 (Boston, 1893). These last two works are also valuable for the views of English-language historiography during the periods in which they were written.

Books on Charles Albert are few and far between. A popular but careful historian, Silvio Bertoldi, has written *Il re che tentò di fare l'Italia: vita di Carlo Alberto di Savoia* (Milan, 2000). Filippo Ambrosini has published *Carlo Alberto re* (Turin, 2004), and Marziano Brignoli's *Carlo Alberto ultimo re di Sardegna, 1798–1849* (Milan, 2007) completes the picture of a troubled king. On foreign policy, see F. Lemmi, *La politica estera di Carlo Alberto nei suoi primi anni di regno* (Florence, 1928), while N. Radolico, *Carlo Alberto negli anni di regno 1831–1843* (Florence, 1930), discusses most of his reign. The chapter on Charles Albert in Rosario Romeo, *Dal Piemonte sabauda all'Italia liberale* (Turin, 1964), gives the best insight on developments during this period. Political changes during Charles Albert's reign are covered by Narciso Nada, *Storia del regno di Carlo Alberto dal 1831 al 1848: dallo Stato assoluto allo Stato costituzionale* (Turin, 1980), and by Umberto Levra, *Il Piemonte alle soglie del 1848* (Turin, 1999). Renato Balduzzi, *L'altro Piemonte nell'età di Carlo Alberto* (n.p., 2001), collects essays on the Piemontese provinces.

Chapter 7: The Revolutions of 1848: The Great Shakeout

Priscilla Robertson's *Revolutions of 1848: A Social History* (Princeton, 1971) is an excellent work that puts the Italian revolutions into the European context. G. F. H. Berkeley, *January 1st 1848 to November 16, 1848*, vol. 3 of *Italy in the Making* (Cambridge, U.K. 1940), covers the revolutions in great detail. William Roscoe Thayer, *The Dawn of Italian Independence*, vol. 2 (Boston, 1893), gives a stirring account that may seem out-moded but, like Berkeley's work, conveys a real portrait of the passions of the period. Thayer's work is particularly colorful in describing the reign of Pope Gregory XVI, the developments of which can also be followed in Domenico De Marco, *Il tramonto dello stato pontificio: il papato di Gregorio XVI* (Naples, 1992). Kent Roberts Greenfield presents long-term economic and political developments in *Economics and Liberalism in the Risorgimento: A Study in Nationalism in Lombardy, 1814–1848* (Baltimore, 1965). George Martin's previously cited *The Red Shirt and the Cross of Savoy* has sev-eral good chapters on events of the period. In Italian, Candeloro, *Storia d'Italia*, vol. 3, is entirely devoted to the revolutions and their implications, while another excellent account is in Nino Valeri, ed., *Storia d'Italia*, vol. 3 (Turin, 1965). Luigi Salvatorelli, ed., *Prima e dopo il Quarantotto* (Turin, 1948), a collection of essays from different jour-nals, is excellent on the implications of the revolutions.

Besides politics, Mazzini led an interesting personal life. See Livio Pivano, *Mazzini e Giuditta Sidoli* (Modena, 1936). His love letters to Sidoli have also been published, in Giuseppe Mazzini, *Lettere d'amore* (Genoa, 1922). Mauro Ferri has concentrated on Mazzini's role during the Roman Republic in *Giuseppe Mazzini nell'assemblea della Repubblica Romana* (Rome, 2005). On his life in exile, see Stringfellow Barr, *Portrait of an Exile* (New York, 1935), and see Paolo Lingua, *Mazzini il riformista* (Genoa, 1992), on Mazzini's last years and thinking on social issues.

On particular persons, besides D'Azeglio's *Ultimi casi*, see his extremely important memoirs: Massimo D'Azeglio, *I miei ricordi* (Turin, 1965). On Cattaneo's role, see Clara Lovett, *Carlo Cattaneo and the Politics of the Risorgimento, 1820–1860* (The Hague, 1972), and Cattaneo's own memoirs of this period, Carlo Cattaneo, *Dell'insur-rezione di Milano nel 1848 e della successiva guerra: memorie* (Milan, 1973). Giuseppe Armani has published *Carlo Cattaneo* (Milan, 1997); Cattaneo is the subject of Franco Della Peruta, *Carlo Cattaneo politico* (Milan, 2001), and again, *I Volti di Carlo Cattaneo (1801–1869)* (Milan, 2001). Maria Corona Corrias has published *Carlo Cattaneo: temi e interpretazioni* (Florence, 2003); Lauretta Collucci discusses Cattaneo as a historical figure in *Carlo Cattaneo nella storiografia* (Milan, 2004). On Pius IX, see E. E. Y. Hales, *Pio Nono: A Study in European Politics and Religion in the Nineteenth Century* (Garden City, 1954), a very sympathetic biography, and the later biography by Frank Coppa, *Pope Pius IX: Crusader in a Secular Age* (Boston, 1979). For a more detailed work, con-sult Giacomo Martina, *Pio IX*, 3 vols. (Rome, 1974–1990). Luigi Armando Giovagni fo-cuses more narrowly on Pius's rule up to 1849 in *Dalla elezione di Pio IX alla caduta della Repubblica romana* (Chiavari, 1975). Roberto De Mattei concentrates on Pius from 1846 until his death in *Pius IX* (Leominster, 2004). *Pio IX e la distruzione della Repubblica Romana* by August Rossi (Rome, 2001) considers that event a "black day" in the papacy's history. Giuseppe Campolieti, *Il re Bomba* (Milan, 1991), discusses Fer-dinand II's opposition to a united Italy, and Francesco Di Giovini discusses the king and his period in *L'età di re Ferdinando (1830–1859)* (Naples, 2006). Christopher Hib-bert's *Garibaldi and His Enemies: The Clash of Arms and Personalities in the Making of*

Italy (London, 1965) is readable and deals with Garibaldi's defense of Rome, while the classic account is George McCauley Trevelyan's *Garibaldi's Defense of the Roman Republic* (New York, 1907). Alfonso Scirocco's *Garibaldi: Citizen of the World* (Princeton, 2007) bills itself as a biography but concentrates on his military life. Luci Riall's *Garibaldi: Invention of a Hero* (New Haven, 2007) argues somewhat unconvincingly that Garibaldi was built up into a hero after his death. In *Anita Garibaldi: A Biography* (Westport, 2001), Anthony Valerio has done an excellent job in bringing to life the role of Garibaldi's wife in Rome and in the general's life. Works on Manin and Venice during this period have been scarcer. George M. Trevelyan's older work, *Manin and the Venetian Revolution of 1848* (London, 1923), is still useful, as is Paul Ginsborg's *Daniele Manin and the Venetian Revolution of 1848–1849* (Cambridge, U.K., 1979), although the latter is marred by its overtly Marxist viewpoint. Pietro Golletto has written on the same subject in *La vita di Daniele Manin e l'epopea veneziana del 1848–1849* (Treviso, 1999). On the exiles in England, see M. C. Wicks, *The Italian Exiles in London, 1816–1848* (Manchester, 1937).

CHAPTER 8: CAVOUR AND THE PIEDMONTESE SOLUTION

A number of good general histories of the Risorgimento cover the events discussed in this chapter. Edgar Holt, *Risorgimento: The Making of Italy, 1815–1870* (New York, 1970), provides a detailed and well-organized story. Bolton King's *History of Italian Unity* (New York, 1967) is an old but still useful work. A more recent overview, Harry Hearder, *Italy in the Age of the Risorgimento, 1790–1870* (London and New York, 1983), is valuable for its discussion of varying interpretations and the culture of the movement. Derek Beales, *The Risorgimento and the Unification of Italy*, vol. 2 (New York, 1971), has a stimulating and comprehensive introduction and reprints a number of important documents. Another excellent book of documents is Denis Mack Smith, ed., *The Making of Italy, 1796–1870* (New York, 1968). A short work that may be profitably consulted is Massimo Salvadori, *Cavour and the Unification of Italy* (New York, 1961).

Patrick O'Clery has published *La rivoluzione italiana* (Milan, 2000), a book on how Italy was made. Another interesting work is Albert Ascoli and Krystyna Von Henneberg, *Making and Remaking Italy* (Oxford, 2001), a work that discusses national identity. Gilles Pecout and Roberto Balzani see the Risorgimento as a long movement that made contemporary Italy; see *Il lungo Risorgimento* (Milan, 2000). Daniel Ziblatt considers the question of state building in Risorgimento Italy along with Germany in *Structuring the State: The Formation of Italy and Germany and the Puzzle of Federalism* (Princeton, 2006). The documents relevant to Plombières, along with an intelligent introductory essay, have been published by Mack Walker, ed., *Plombières: Secret Diplomacy and the Rebirth of Italy* (New York, 1968). Two brilliant works by A. J. P. Taylor explain both the Italian and European diplomatic context of the era: *The Italian Problem in European Diplomacy* (Manchester, 1934), and *The Struggle for Mastery in Europe, 1848–1918* (London, 1954). Other aspects of the diplomacy of the period as it relates to Italy may be found in Nello Rosselli, *Inghilterra e regno di Sardegna dal 1815 al 1847* (Turin, 1954), and the interesting book by Giuseppe Berti, *Russia e stati italiani nel Risorgimento* (Turin, 1957).

As might be expected, there are many works on the most important individuals of the Risorgimento that are fundamental to an understanding of the age. The best and most exhaustive biography of Cavour and his times is Rosario Romeo, *Cavour e il suo tempo*, 3 vols. (Bari, 1984). In English, the massive and sympathetic work by William R. Thayer, *The Life and Times of Cavour*, 2 vols. (New York, 1971), is still useful. Maurice Paleologue's *Cavour* (New York, 1927) provides a flattering portrait of Cavour as a statesman, while A. J. Whyte's *The Political Life and Letters of Cavour, 1848–1861* (Westport, 1975) connects his parliamentary career to his diplomacy. Denis Mack Smith's *Cavour* (London, 1985) is unfriendly to the Piedmontese statesman. Frank J. Coppa has written a short biography, *Camillo di Cavour* (New York, 1973). By analyzing the relationship between *Cavour and Garibaldi 1860* (Cambridge, 1954), Denis Mack Smith has concluded that it could not be assumed in 1860 that a monarchist unitary state was the only solution that might emerge from the revolution. But Harry Hearder, *Cavour* (London and New York, 1994), presents the Piedmontese leader as a subtle statesman who, in practice, had "no alternative" to imposing a unitary state on Italy. Filippo Ambrosini, *Camillo Cavour* (Turin, 2005), considers him the greatest statesman in Italian history. J. A. R. Marriott's lectures on the three major figures of the period, *The Makers of Modern Italy* (London, 1889), are still valuable.

Besides Cavour, Garibaldi has attracted the attention of English-speaking historians. George MacCaulay Trevelyan wrote three classic works: *Garibaldi's Defense of the Roman Republic* (London, 1907), previously cited; *Garibaldi and the Thousand* (London, 1909); and *Garibaldi and the Making of Italy* (London, 1919). More recent biographies include Paul Frischauer, *Garibaldi: The Man and the Nation* (New York, 1935); David Larg, *Giuseppe Garibaldi* (New York, 1970); Peter de Polnay, *Garibaldi: The Man and the Legend* (New York, 1961); Christopher Hibbert, *Garibaldi and His Enemies* (London, 1965), a readable account; and Jasper Ridley, *Garibaldi* (New York, 1974), which is perhaps the best. Denis Mack Smith has also written an excellent short biography, *Garibaldi: A Great Life in Brief* (New York, 1956). Ugo Carcassi interprets him as a revolutionary in *Garibaldi* (Sassari, 2001). Antonella Grignola and Paolo Ceccoli, in *Garibaldi* (Florence, 2005), see him dedicating his life to liberty. Garibaldi's "obsessions" have been examined by Daniel Pick, *Rome or Death* (London, 2006), and, one might say, by Luca Goldoni, *Garibaldi: l'amante dei due mondi* (Milan, 2003). Alfonso Scirocco's *Garibaldi: Citizen of the World* (Princeton, 2007) devotes a lot of space to his military career. Garibaldi's memoirs have also been published as *The Memoirs of Garibaldi*, edited by Alexandre Dumas (New York, 1931). An idea of Garibaldi's military genius may be gleaned from Andrea Viotti, *Garibaldi: The Revolutionary and His Men* (Dorset, 1979). For Garibaldi in "art and history," see the reproductions in *Garibaldi: arte e storia* (Florence, 1982). On military aspects of the Risorgimento, Piero Pieri, *Storia militare del Risorgimento: Guerre e insurrezioni* (Turin, 1962), cogently argues that Risorgimento military history demonstrates heroism and illustrates the capacity of the Italian people for sacrifice; especially interesting is his contention that the Risorgimento was accompanied by a valuable theoretical literature on using all the vital forces of a nation in the struggle for freedom. In addition to Pieri, Frank Coppa has published a good account of *The Origins of the Italian Wars of Independence* (London and New York, 1992).

For some of the other characters in the story, see Denis Mack Smith, *Victor Emanuel, Cavour, and the Risorgimento* (London, 1971); Clara Lovett, *Giuseppe Ferrari and the Italian Revolution* (Chapel Hill, 1979); C. Ambrosoli and Silvia Rota Ghibaudi, *Giuseppe Ferrari e il nuovo stato italiano (convegno internazionale, Luino, 5–6 ottobre 1990)* (Milan, 1992); William Hancock, *Ricasoli and the Risorgimento in Tuscany* (New York, 1969); Giuliana Biagioli, *Il modello del proprietario imprenditore nella Toscana dell'Ottocento* (Florence, 2000); and Michael St. John Packe, *The Bombs of Orsini* (London, 1957) and *Orsini: The Story of a Conspirator* (Boston, 1958). Those who dissented from the way in which Italy was unified were also important. See Ugo Dotti, *I dissidenti del Risorgimento: Cattaneo, Ferrari, Pisacane* (Rome, 1975). The most radical of these dissidents was Pisacane. For more information on him, see Nello Rosselli, *Carlo Pisacane nel Risorgimento italiano* (Turin, 1977), a classic account by the historian murdered with his brother by the Fascists in 1937; and Gustavo Padiglione, *Eran trecento: Carlo Pisacane: un eroe romantico fra amore e rivoluzione* (Florence, 1998). The 1859 war has been analyzed by Arnold Blumberg, *A Carefully Planned Accident: The Italian War of 1859* (London, 1990).

For views of Italian events outside of Italy, see Howard R. Marraro, *American Opinion on the Unification of Italy, 1846–1861* (New York, 1932); Harry W. Rudman, *Italian Nationalism and English Letters* (New York, 1940); and A. William Salomone, "The Nineteenth-Century Discovery of Italy: An Essay in American Cultural History: Prolegomena to a Historiographical Problem," *American Historical Review* 73, no. 5 (June 1968): 1359–1391.

On the activity of the democrats in the South, see the fundamental work by Franco Della Peruta, *I democratici e la rivoluzione italiana* (Milan, 1958), and Giuseppe Berti, *I democratici e l'iniziativa meridionale nel Risorgimento* (Milan, 1962). In *Il pensiero politico di Carlo Pisacane* (Turin, 1995), L. La Puma argues that the Neapolitan Socialist's political ideas foreshadowed Marx's historical materialism. Raymond Grew wrote the definitive *A Sterner Plan for Italian Unity: The Italian National Society in the Risorgimento* (Princeton, 1963).

For more general interpretations of the Risorgimento, Luigi Salvatorelli argues that the Risorgimento was spiritual in addition to material and sought a "new" Italy; see *The Risorgimento: Thought and Action* (New York, 1970). The fundamental Marxist interpretation of the Risorgimento as a "failed" revolution may be found in Antonio Gramsci, *Il Risorgimento* (Turin, 1955), while Rosario Romeo's *Risorgimento e capitalismo* (Bari, 1963) offers a brilliant rebuttal to the thesis. One may also consult Rosario Bottari, *Rosario Romeo e il Risorgimento in Sicilia* (Soveria Manelli, 2002), which considers the historiography. Good contributions to the historical debate may be found in A. William Salomone, "Statecraft and Ideology in the Risorgimento," in Edward R. Tannenbaum and Emiliana Noether, *Modern Italy: A Topical History Since 1861* (New York, 1974); see also Salomone, "The Risorgimento Between Ideology and History: The Political Myth of *rivoluzione mancata*," H. Stuart Hughes, "The Aftermath of the Risorgimento in Four Successive Interpretations," and Raymond Grew, "How Success Spoiled the Risorgimento," all conveniently grouped in A. William Salomone, *Italy from the Risorgimento to Fascism: An Inquiry into the Origins of the Totalitarian State* (New York, 1970). Walter Maturi's *Interpretazioni del Risorgimento: lezioni di storia e storiografia* (Turin, 1962) is an excellent and detailed history of Risorgimento interpretations from thinkers of the period up to Mack Smith. Zeffiro Ciuffoletti, *Stato senza nazione* (Naples, 1993), argues that an Italian "nation" did not exist at the beginning of the process of unification and that the state had to create one. The book edited by John A. Davis and Paul Ginsborg, *Society and Politics in the Age of the Risorgimento: Essays in Honour of Denis Mack Smith* (Cambridge, U.K., 1991), brings together the interpretations of British and Italian experts. Finally, Nicholas Doumanis, *Italy* (London, 2001), part of a series called "Inventing the Nation," attempts to put Italian nationalism into a wider context, from prehistory to the present. He argues that Italy was a creation of Piedmontese foreign policy.

CHAPTER 9: CAVOUR'S HEIRS: THE "RIGHT" REIGNS

Piero Raggi has investigated the volunteers who defended Rome for Pius IX between 1860 and 1870 in *La nona crociata* (Ravenna, 2002). The pope did not reconcile himself to the loss of Rome and plotted to take it back. On this issue, see David I. Kerzer, *Prisoner of the Vatican* (Boston, 2004).

Works in English on the period of the Right's rule are few. The general works mentioned previously can be consulted. In keeping with the book's tone, Denis Mack Smith's *Italy: A Modern History* (Ann Arbor, 1959) provides a generally negative interpretation of the Right's tenure. Volume 4 of Giovanni Sabbatucci and Domenico Vitotto's *Storia d'Italia* (Rome, 1997) provides essays on the broad sweep of Italian history from unification to fascism. On the economic problems and policies during this period, Shepard B. Clough's *The Economic History of Modern Italy* (New York, 1964) gives a balanced and impartial account. A more recent survey of economic history beginning from this period is Vera Zamagni, *The Economic History of Italy, 1860–1990* (New York, 1993). A series of well-connected (and difficult to find) documents in translation, readings, and comments on Italian developments from this era and others are in Shepard B. Clough and Salvatore Saladino, *A History of Modern Italy: Documents, Readings, and Commentary* (New York, 1968). A quantitative analysis of Italian democrats, the social context, and their significance and activities in the new kingdom can be found in Clara Lovett, *The Democratic Movement in Italy, 1830–1876* (Cambridge, Mass., 1982). John Whittam's discussion of this period in *The Politics of the Italian Army, 1861–1918* (London, 1977) is a convincing description of the difficulties of establishing a national army. A wider discussion of the army and its role before World War I, relevant also for succeeding chapters, may be found in John Gooch, *Army, State and Society in Italy, 1870–1915* (New York, 1989). On the Papal State, Frank J. Coppa's *Cardinal Giacomo Antonelli and Papal Politics in European Affairs* (New York, 1990) argues that the policies for which Antonelli was condemned were really the pope's. An interesting view of how the papal infallibility doctrine came about is August Hasler, *How the Pope Became Infallible: Pius IX and the Politics of Persuasion* (Garden City, 1981).

In Italian, the discussion on this period in Nino Valeri, ed., *Storia d'Italia*, vol. 4 (Turin, 1965), is complete, balanced, and richly illustrated. Volumes 5 and 6 of Candeloro's *Storia d'Italia moderna* (Milan, 1968, 1970) also give a detailed and excellent account. Raffaella Gherardi, *L'arte del compromesso: la politica della mediazione nell'Italia liberale* (Bologna, 1993), argues that the statesmen of the Right, such as Minghetti, were practical rather than ideological and that liberals of both the Right and the Left stood ready to compromise. Along with Nicola Matteucci, Gherardi has also published *Marco Minghetti, statista e pensatore politico: dalla realtà italiana alla dimensione europea* (Bologna, 1988). Giuseppe Caputo has studied Minghetti's thought on the Church in *La libertà della Chiesa nel pensiero di Marco Minghetti* (Milan, 1965). See Società Libera, *Marco Minghetti e le sue opere* (Milan, 2001), an analysis of his thought and action by well-known scholars. On Quintino Sella, see the essays collected in Cristina Vernizzi, *Quintino Sella tra politica e cultura, 1827–1884* (n.p., 1986), and Pier Luigi Bassignana, *Quintino Sella* (Turin, 2006). Two books are useful in understanding the action of the Church in Italian society during this period: Angelo Gambasin, *Il movimento sociale nell'Opera dei congressi (1874–1904)* (Rome, 1958), and Giovenale Dotta, *La nascita del movimento cattolico a Torino e l'Opera dei congressi (1870–1891)* (Alessandria, 1999). Marco Invernizzi opens up the question of whether the Catholics and the Opera dei congressi threatened Italian unity in *I cattolici contro l'unità d'Italia? L'Opera dei Congressi (1874–1904)* (Casale Monferrato, 2002).

On some of the economic issues, see G. Are, *Il problema dello sviluppo industriale nell'età della Destra* (Pisa, 1965), and Luciano Cafagna, "Industrialismo e politica economica dopo l'unità d'Italia," in *Annali dell'Istituto Giangiacomo Feltrinelli* (Milan, 1962): 150–182; Romeo's previously cited *Risorgimento e capitalismo* includes a section on this period. Mario Isnenghi, *I luoghi della memoria: personaggi e date dell'Italia unità* (Rome, 1997), discusses the period immediately following unification. On Sicily during this era, see Paolo Alatri, *Lotte politiche in Sicilia sotto il governo della Destra (1866–1874)* (Turin, 1954). The most concise story of the "brigandage" phenomenon is Franco Molfese's *Storia del brigantaggio dopo l'Unità* (Milan, 1966).

CHAPTER 10: TWO "PARLIAMENTARY DICTATORS"

The developments discussed in this chapter are, again, unfortunately not well covered in English, although a general discussion may be found in the relevant sections of

Christopher Seton-Watson's excellent *Italy from Liberalism to Fascism, 1870–1925* (London, 1967). Another general work, Christopher Duggan's *A Concise History of Italy* (Cambridge, 1994), suffers from the attempt to impose on all of Italian history a single, overwhelming theme above all others: disunity. Besides the works cited in this section, more follow in the next section of this essay, which is devoted to a discussion of more specific problems during this rich and understudied period. Giampiero Carocci's *Agostino Depretis e la politica interna italiana dal 1876 al 1887* (Turin, 1956) is a detailed study not only of Depretis but of the Italian politics of the period. Emilia Morelli has written an account of three important prime ministers of the period, including Depretis: *G. Lanza, A. Depretis, B. Cairoli* (Rome, 1990). On Giovanni Nicotera's policies, see Marco de Nicolò, *Trasformismo, autoritarismo, meridionalismo: il ministro dell'interno Giovanni Nicotera* (Bologna, 2001). Carlo Vallauri discusses Zanardelli's activities in *La politica liberale di Giuseppe Zanardelli dal 1876 al 1878* (Milan, 1967), while the biography of the man who conducted the survey of southern social conditions may still be consulted with profit: Stefano Jacini, *Un conservatore rurale della nuova Italia*, 2 vols. (Bari, 1926). The papers of a conference on Zanardelli have been published in Francesco Barbagallo and Roberto Chiarini, *Giuseppe Zanardelli: atti del convegno, Brescia 19, 30 settembre 1983, Pavia, 1 ottobre 1983* (Milan, 1985), but it is unfortunate that this important figure does not have more attention devoted to him.

On international affairs, Federico Chabod's classic *Storia della politica estera italiana dal 1870 al 1896*, 2 vols. (Bari, 1965) is notable for its documentation and fundamental for an understanding of the entire period. Luigi Salvatorelli's discussion of the Triple Alliance, *La Triplice Alleanza: Storia diplomatica, 1877–1912* (Milan, 1939), provides a clear view of the diplomatic issues involved.

Massimo Grillandi's *Crispi* (Turin, 1969) is a detailed biography, but see the more recent Christopher Duggan's *Francesco Crispi, 1818–1901: From Nation to Nationalism* (New York, 2002) and D. Adorni's *L'Italia crispina: riforme e repressione: 1887–1896* (Florence, 2002). Nicolò Inglese's short biography, *Crispi* (Milan, 1961), is less satisfactory but still worth consulting. Earlier works include a balanced interpretation of the controversial statesman by the distinguished Arturo Carlo Jemolo, *Crispi* (Florence, 1921), and a favorable one by Gioacchino Volpe, *Francesco Crispi* (Venice, 1928). The high points of the domestic problem faced by Crispi are recounted in Giuseppe Astuto, *Crispi e lo stato d'assedio in Sicilia* (Milan, 1999), and Fausto Fonzi, *Crispi e lo "stato di Milano"* (Milan, 1965), which tells about the growth of opposition in Italy's economic capital that finally did him in. Much primary material relating to Crispi has been published, including speeches and memoirs. See in English translation his *Memoirs*, 3 vols. (London, 1912–1914).

The fundamental work on the African venture and Italian imperialism of the Crispi period has been written by Roberto Battaglia, *La prima guerra d'Africa* (Turin, 1958), which includes a detailed account of the Battle of Adowa. On the battle itself, see Angelo Del Boca and D. Adorni, *Adua: le ragioni di una sconfitta* (Rome, 1997), and Nicola La Banca, *In Marcia verso Adua* (Turin, 1993). For an English-language view of the international implications of Italian actions in Africa, consult Arthur Marsden, "Salisbury and the Italians in 1896," *Journal of Modern History* 40, no. 1 (March 1968): 91–117. On Italian policy in the area after the Crispi period, see the well-documented work by Alberto Aquarone, *Dopo Adua: Politica e amministrazione coloniale* (Rome, 1989). Although more valuable for information on the later periods of his life, Giovanni Giolitti's *Memoirs of My Life* (London, 1923) can be consulted for his views of Crispi's involvement in East Africa. On the first Giolitti cabinet, the best source is Gastone Manacorda, "Il primo ministero Giolitti," pt. 1, *Studi Storici* 2, no. 1 (January–March 1961): 88–103, and pt. 2, *Studi Storici* 3, no. 1 (January–March 1963): 106–120.

CHAPTER 11: SOCIAL AND ECONOMIC DILEMMAS

The economic and social themes discussed in this chapter are fairly well covered in the literature. Gianni Toniolo's *An Economic History of Liberal Italy 1850–1918* (London and New York, 1990) is an excellent, clear, and brief treatment of the entire period covered by the author. Consult also Giovanni Federico, *The Economic Development of Italy Since 1870* (Aldershot, 1994). On the agricultural crisis, see Emilio Sereni, *Il capitalismo nelle campagne, 1860–1900* (Turin, 1947), and P. D'Angiolini, "L'Italia al termine della crisi agraria della fine del secolo XIX," *Nuova Rivista Storica* 3–4 (1969): 323–365. Clough's *Economic History of Italy*, previously cited, provides a clear exposition of Italian economic development in its international context during this period. On public finance, see Isidore Sachs, *L'Italie, ses finances et son developpement économique 1859–1884* (Paris, 1885). Good general works covering the Italian economy of this period include Epicarmo Corbino, *Annali dell'economia italiana*, 5 vols. (Città di Castello, 1938); Gino Luzzatto, *L'economia italiana dal 1861 al 1914* (Milan, 1963); and, by the same author, "L'economia italiana nel primo decennio dell'unità," in *Rassegna storica del Risorgimento* (1957). For local finances, see F. Volpi, *Le finanze dei comuni e delle province del Regno d'Italia, 1860–1890* (Turin, 1962); fiscal policy is examined in G. Parravini, *La politica fiscale e le entrate effettive del Regno d'Italia, 1860–1890* (Rome, 1958). The role of foreign investments is considered by Luigi De Rosa, *Iniziativa e capitale straniero nell'industria metalmeccanica del Mezzogiorno, 1840–1904* (Naples, 1968), and B. Gille, *Les investissments français en Italie (1815–1914)* (Turin, 1968). Gian Luigi Basini's *L'industralizzazione di una provincia contadina: Reggio Emilia, 1861–1940* (Rome, 1995) is an account of one province's modernization. Francesca Polese, *Alla ricerca di un'industria nuova* (Venice, 2004), discusses the origins of the Pirelli industrial empire. Jonathan Morris, *The Political Economy of Shopkeeping in Milan, 1886–1922* (Cambridge, U.K., 1993), examines the very important category of small shopkeepers in Milan during the liberal period; small shopkeepers are still an important element in Italian economic and political affairs.

Sandro Rogari addresses agricultural developments in his book on the first farmers' organization and its influence, *Proprietà fondiaria e modernizzazione: la società degli agricoltori italiani, 1895–1920* (Turin, 1994). Roland Sarti's *Long Live the Strong* (Amherst, 1985) is a case study of a rural society in the Apennine Mountains and how it adapted to different conditions down to the present times.

Giovanni Gozzini, *Il segreto dell'elemosina* (Florence, 1993), studies poverty and the organization of charity in Florence between 1800 and 1870. David I. Kertzer analyzes the issue of child abandonment in the midnineteenth century and the Church's role in *Sacrifices for Honor* (Boston, 1993).

On the question of economic growth and the tariff, see Alexander Gerschenkron, "Notes on the Rate of Industrial Growth in Italy, 1881–1913," *Journal of Economic History* (December 1955). Rosario Romeo provides a different version in *Breve storia della grande industria in Italia, 1861–1961* (Bologna, 1972). See also D. Morelli, *Il protezionismo industriale in Italia dall'unificazione del Regno* (Milan, 1920), and M. Calzavarini, "Il protezionismo industriale e la tariffa dognale del 1887," *Clio* (1966). A good general idea of the issues involved in the economic question may be gained by reading Walt W. Rostow, *The Stages of Economic Growth* (Cambridge, U.K., 1960), and Alexander Gerschenkron, *Economic Backwardness in Historical Perspective* (Cambridge, Mass., 1962). A number of essays on the relevant questions are collected in A. Caracciolo, *La formazione dell'Italia industriale* (Bari, 1963). For an idea of the contribution by Marxist historians to the interpretation of the economics of this period, see *Problemi dell'Unità d'Italia: atti del II convegno di studi gramsciani tenuto a Roma nei giorni 19–21 marzo 1960* (Rome, 1966). Luciano Cafagna's "L'industrializzazione italiana: la formazione di una 'base industriale' fra il 1896 e il 1914," *Studi Storici* 3–4 (1961): 690–724, discusses the issue of retarded economic development. On the relationship between agricultural development and industry, see Renato Zangheri, "Agricoltura e sviluppo del capitalismo: problemi storiografici," *Studi Storici* 3–2 (1968): 531–563. Good studies on particular industries are too numerous to cite here, but a good review of the literature is G. Mori, "La storia dell'industria italiana contemporanea nei saggi, nelle ricerche e nelle pubblicazioni giubilari di questo dopoguerra," *Annali dell'Istituto Giangiacomo Feltrinelli* 2 (1959): 264–366.

The literature on the North-South question is also abundant. On Jacini's investigation, see Alberto Caracciolo, *L'inchiesta agraria Jacini* (Turin, 1976). See Shepard B. Clough and Carlo Livi, "Economic Growth in Italy: An Analysis of the Uneven Development of North and South," *Journal of Economic History* (September 1956): 334–349. Gustav Schachter, *The Italian South: Economic Development in Mediterranean Europe* (New York, 1965), gives an excellent perspective on the problem. Rosario Villari, *Il Sud nella storia d'Italia*, 2 vols. (Bari, 1966), has put together a very good anthology of writings on the subject. Luciano Cafagna discusses the *Dualismo e sviluppo nella storia d'Italia* (Venice, 1989). The demographic issues are discussed by Giuseppe Galasso in his essay "Lo sviluppo demografico del Mezzogiorno prima e dopo l'unità," in his *Mezzogiorno medievale e moderno* (Turin, 1965); and by M. Boldrini, "Un secolo di sviluppo della popolazione italiana," in *L'economia italiana dal 1861 al 1961* (Milan, 1961). In English, see Robert Dickinson, *The Population Problem of Southern Italy: An Essay in Social Geography* (Syracuse, 1955). Good statistics on emigration may be found in *Annuario statistico dell'emigrazione italiana dal 1876 al 1925, con notizie sull'emigrazione negli anni 1869–1875* (Rome, 1926). General statistics relating to the South are in Svimez, *Statistiche sul Mezzogiorno d'Italia 1861–1953* (Rome, 1954), and Svimez, *Un secolo di statistiche italiane: Nord e Sud 1861–1961* (Rome, 1961). Frank Snowden, *Naples in the Time of Cholera, 1884–1911* (Cambridge, U.K., 1995), outlines the state's response to cholera outbreaks in Naples in 1884 and 1911. On southerners who returned and their impact, a theme emphasized by Gaetano Salvemini, see Dino Cinel, *The National Integration of Italian Return Migration, 1870–1929* (Cambridge, U.K., 1991).

Although the Mafia has attracted attention and there is a rich mine of memoirs and descriptions of social conditions, this important period is less well covered by scholars. See the relevant portions of Denis Mack Smith, *A History of Sicily: Modern Sicily After 1713* (London, 1968); Giuseppe Alongi, *La maffia* [sic] (Florence, 1886); and Raimondo Catanzaro, *Il delitto come impresa: storia sociale della mafia* (Padua, 1988). Greater insight into the Mafia phenomenon may be gained through Eric Hobsbawm, *Primitive Rebels* (Manchester, 1959), and Anton Blok, *The Mafia of a Sicilian Village* (Prospect Heights, 1988). For a history of the Mafia, see Salvatore F. Romano, *Storia della mafia* (Milan, 1963). The Mafia's organization is described in Henner Hess, *Mafia and Mafiosi: The Structure of Power* (Lexington, 1973). An excellent history of the island during this period is Francesco De Stefano and Francesco Luigi Oddo, *Storia della Sicilia dal 1860 al 1910* (Bari, 1963).

On the Catholic movement, see the classic work by Arturo Carlo Jemolo, *Chiesa e stato in Italia dalla unificazione a Giovanni XXIII* (Turin, 1965); Gabriele De Rosa, *L'Azione Cattolica: storia politica dal 1874 al 1904* (Bari, 1953); and Fausto Fonzi, *I cattolici e la società italiana dopo l'unità* (Rome, 1953). Giorgio Candeloro's *Il movimento cattolico in Italia* (Rome, 1953) is an excellent work, while Giovanni Spadolini's *L'opposizione cattolica da Porta Pia al '98* (Florence, 1961) is the classic comprehensive history of the subject during the years under consideration. S. Secco Suardo concentrates on the intransigents in *I cattolici intransigenti* (Brescia, 1962), while Sandor Agócs examines the ideology and action of Catholic social activists in *The Troubled Origins of the Italian Catholic Labor Movement, 1878–1914* (Detroit, 1988). On Toniolo, see Romano Molesti, *Giuseppe Toniolo: il pensiero e l'opera* (Milan, 2005), and Domenico Sorrentino, *L'economista di Dio: Giuseppe Toniolo* (Rome, 2001). On Murri, see Sergio Zoppi, *Dalla Rerum Novarum alla democrazia cristiana di Murri* (Bologna, 1991), and Maurilio Guasco, *Il pensiero politico di Romolo Murri* (Ancona, 1993). On Meda, see Gabriele De Rosa, *Filippo Meda e l'età liberale* (Florence, 1959); the collected papers of a conference on Meda edited by Mario Belardinelli, *Filippo Meda: tra economia, società e politica* (Milan, 1991); and Alfredo Canevero, *Filippo Meda: l'intransigente che portò i cattolici nello stato* (Milan, 2003). Giorgio Spini, ed., *Studi sull'evangelismo italiano tra otto e novecento* (Turin, 1994), is a collection of wide-ranging essays that cover Italian Protestantism in the nineteenth and twentieth centuries. The school system is discussed by D. Bertoni Jovine, *La scuola italiana dal 1870 ai giorni nostri* (Rome, 1958).

The anarchist movement has been examined with great acumen by Pier Carlo Masini in *Storia degli anarchici italiani: da Bakunin a Malatesta* (Milan, 1969) and *Sto-*

ria degli anarchici nell'epoca degli attentati (Milan, 1981). The best general history of Italian anarchism during this period in English is Nunzio Pernicone's *Italian Anarchism, 1864–1892* (Princeton, 1993). There is also the groundbreaking older work by Richard Hostetter, *Origins (1860–1882)*, vol. 1 of *The Italian Socialist Movement* (New York, 1958). Bakunin's relationship with the Italians is the subject of a book by T. R. Ravindranathan, *Bakunin and the Italians* (Montreal, 1988). Aldo Romano's *Storia del movimento socialista italiano*, 3 vols. (Turin, 1954–1956) exhibits a strong anti-Bakunin viewpoint. A general view of anarchism is Enzo Santarelli, *Il socialismo anarchico in Italia* (Milan, 1959). The early congresses of the fledgling Italian labor movement are the subject of Gastone Manacorda's *Il movimento operaio italiano attraverso i suoi congressi, 1853–1892* (Rome, 1953). Franco Della Peruta has examined the failure of anarchist methods in "La banda del Matese e il fallimento della teoria anarchica della moderna 'jacquerie' in Italia," *Movimento Operaio* 3 (1954). The Radical Democrats have been examined by Giovanni Spadolini, *I radicali dell'Ottocento* (Florence, 1960), and by Stefano Merli, "La democrazia radicale in Italia (1866–1898)," *Movimento Operaio* 1 (1955). Important documentation on the movement has also been published: Liliana Delle Nogare and Stefano Merli, eds., *L'Italia Radicale: carteggi di Felice Cavallotti, 1867–1898* (Milan, 1959); S. Ganci, ed., *Democrazia e socialismo in Italia: carteggi di Napoleone Colajanni, 1878–1898* (Milan, 1959); and, especially, Pier Carlo Masini, ed., *La scapigliatura democratica: carteggi di Arcangelo Ghisleri, 1875–1890* (Milan, 1960).

For the early Socialist movement, see Elio Conti, *Le origini del socialismo a Firenze (1860–1880)* (Rome, 1950); Felice Anzi, *Il movimento operaio socialista italiano (1882–1894)* (Rome, 1946); and, by the same author, *Origini e funzioni delle camere del lavoro* (Milan, n.d.). General considerations on Costa can be found in A. Berselli, ed., *Andrea Costa nella storia del socialismo italiano* (Bologna, 1982); the story of his party in the Romagna is told in Manuel Gonzales, *Andrea Costa and the Rise of Socialism in the Romagna* (Washington, D.C., 1980). Stefano Merli has published a collection of legal defenses by left-wing defendants, *Autodifiese di militanti operai e democratici italiani davanti ai Tribunali* (Milan, 1958). Ernesto Ragionieri has studied the influence of German social democracy on Italian Socialists in *Socialdemocrazia tedesca e socialisti italiani 1875–1895* (Milan, 1961). Luigi Cortesi's book, *La costituzione del partito socialista italiano* (Milan, 1962), tells the story of the PSI's foundation. Cortesi has also published a compendium of Turati's early works, *Turati giovane: scapigliatura, positivismo, marxismo* (Milan, 1962). The most monumental and detailed work on early socialism is the collected work edited by Giovanni Sabbatucci, *Storia del socialismo italiano*, vol. 1, *Dalle origini alla svolta di fine secolo* (Rome, 1981). The Sicilian *fasci* are examined in detail by Gastone Manacorda et al., *I fasci siciliani*, 2 vols. (Bari, 1975). For Anna Kuliscioff's early life as a Russian revolutionary, see Franco Venturi's excellent article, "Anna Kuliscioff e la sua attività rivoluzionaria in Russia," *Movimento Operaio* 4 (March–April 1952): 277–286; see also the documents on Costa in the same issue. Kuliscioff's letters to Costa, with an excellent introduction, have been published as *Lettere d'amore a Andrea Costa, 1880–1909* (Milan, 1976). Marina Addis Saba's

Anna Kuliscioff: vita politica e passione privata (Milan, 1993) is a full-length biography. There are also the proceedings of a conference on her action: Fondazione Brodolini, *Anna Kuliscioff e l'età del riformismo* (Rome, 1978), and a political biography by Paolo Pilllitieri, *Anna Kuliscioff* (Venice, 1986). On Antonio Labriola, the most important Marxist philosopher of this age, see Luigi Dal Pane, *Antonio Labriola, la vita e il pensiero* (Rome, 1935), and, by the same author, *Antonio Labriola nella politica e nella cultura italiana* (Turin, 1975). See also Gian Piero Orsello, *Antonio Labriola* (Milan, 2003). A contemporary work with living profiles of the Socialists of this period is Alfredo Angiolini, *Socialismo e socialisti in Italia* (Florence, 1900).

The following chapters in Edward R. Tannenbaum and Emiliana P. Noether, eds., *Modern Italy: A Topical History Since 1861* (New York, 1974), offer good surveys on the issues considered in this chapter during and beyond the time span considered: Denis Mack Smith, "Regionalism," pp. 125–146; Jon S. Cohen, "Economic Growth," pp. 171–196; Nunzio Pernicone, "The Italian Labor Movement," pp. 197–230; Edward R. Tannenbaum, "Education," pp. 231–253; and Raymond Grew, "Catholicism in a Changing Italy," pp. 254–273.

CHAPTER 12: THE RISE OF SOCIALISM AND THE GIOLITTIAN ERA

The political, economic, and social questions of the years from 1900 to 1914 have given rise to a rich historical literature. The translation of Giolitti's memoirs has been previously cited, but the original version, *Memorie della mia vita* (Milan, 1967), is far superior. In addition, Giolitti's parliamentary and extraparliamentary speeches have been published, and most interesting is the archival collection of his correspondence with the prefects and crucial political leaders: Istituto Giangiacomo Feltrinelli, *Dalle carte di Giovanni Giolitti: quarant'anni di politica italiana*, 3 vols. (Milan, 1962). The role of Zanardelli in the government of 1901 has been treated by Roberto Chiarini, *Alle Origini dell'età giolittiana: la svolta liberale del governo Zanardelli-Giolitti, 1901–1903* (Venice, 2003). Biographies of Giolitti are not plentiful in Italian. The most complete is the balanced Nino Valeri, *Giolitti* (Turin, 1972). Valeri, however, keeps in mind Giolitti's later role in the rise of fascism; a more recent attempt to look at Giolitti according to the statesman's own objectives is Sergio Romano, *Giolitti: lo stile del potere* (Milan, 1989). The best political biography in English, thoroughly researched and complete, is Alexander De Grand's *The Hunchback's Tailor: Giovanni Giolitti and Liberal Italy from the Challenge of Mass Politics to the Rise of Fascism, 1882–1922* (Westport, 2001). Consult also Aldo Alessandro Mola, *Giolitti: lo statista della nuova Italia* (Milan, 2003), and, by the same author, *La svolta di Giolitti* (Foggia, 2000).

The best biographies produced after Salomone's "rehabilitation" of Giolitti, overly influenced by this event but still essential for an understanding of the historiographical debate, are Giovanni Ansaldo, *Il ministro della buona vita* (Milan, 1949), and the work by Giolitti's friend Gaetano Natale, *Giolitti e gli italiani* (Milan, 1949). The pamphlet by Alfredo Frassati, *Giolitti* (Florence, 1959), gives a quick overview. On reevaluation of Giolitti and Italian politics during the period, the essential work is A. William Salomone, *Italy in the Giolittian Era: Italian Democracy in the Making 1900–1914*, 2d ed. (Philadelphia, 1960). This edition retains Salvemini's famous "Introductory Essay" and is enriched by a new section, "Giolittian Italy Revisited," bringing the discussion up to 1960. Salvemini's *Il ministro della mala vita* can be found along with his other writings on Giolittian Italy in Elio Apih, ed., *Gaetano Salvemini: il ministro della mala vita e altri scritti sull'Italia giolittiana*, opere 4, vol. 1 (Milan, 1966). Salvemini's theses are at the origin of Antonio Gramsci's negative criticisms about an explicit northern "deal" between Giolitti and the Socialists to the South's detriment, a contention that can be found in Gramsci's *Il Risorgimento* (Turin, 1955). For the development of this thesis in Marxist hands, compare Palmiro Togliatti's scurrilous "Turatiana," in *Stato Operaio* (April 1932), and the same author's sophisms on the issue, after the publication of Salomone's book, in his *Discorso su Giolitti* (Rome, 1950). An author who believes that this conjunction between the reformists and Giolitti did not come about, at least not in the terms proposed by Communist historiography, is Brunello Vegezzi, *Giolitti e Turati: un incontro mancato*, 2 vols. (Milan and Naples, 1976). Two useful collected works on Giolitti may round out various aspects of his tenure, *Istituzioni e metodi politici dell'età giolittiana* (Turin, 1979) and *L'Italia di Giolitti* (Milan, 1981). A balanced work is Emilio Gentile's *Le origini dell'Italia contemporanea: l'età giolittiana* (Rome, 2003).

The attempt to give a more articulated interpretation of the Giolittian period is achieved by Giampiero Carocci, *Giolitti e l'età giolittiana* (Turin, 1961), who argues that the Giolittian period arose from a need to liquidate the heavy-handed governmental methods of the nineteenth century. The most successful attempt to view the age in its own terms by examining in depth the details of governmental action and their relation to Italian life of the period has been made by Alberto Aquarone in *L'Italia giolittiana (1896–1915)* (Bologna, 1981) and in the posthumously published *Tre capitoli sull'Italia giolittiana* (Bologna, 1987). Aquarone also made an excellent exposition of his historical method in "A Closing Commentary: Problems of Democracy and the Quest for Identity," in Tannenbaum and Noether, eds., *Modern Italy: A Topical History Since 1861*, pp. 355–376. An excellent and more popular treatment of the Giolittian "world" is given by Giovanni Spadolini, *Il mondo di Giolitti* (Florence, 1970). Ronald S. Cunsolo brings the historiographical issues up to date in "The Great Debate on Prime Minister Giovanni Giolitti and Giolittian Italy," *Canadian Review of Studies in Nationalism* 18, nos. 1–2 (1991): 95–115. Denis Mack Smith discusses the kings of united Italy in *Italy and Its Monarchy* (New Haven, 1989). Louise A. Tilly, *Politics and Class in Milan, 1881–1901* (Oxford, 1991), is an analysis of workers in Milan and the formation of a working-class consciousness there.

On the economic aspects of the Giolittian era, see Frank J. Coppa's positive treatment of Giolitti's policies in *Economics and Politics in the Giolittian Age* (Washington, D.C., 1971). For the effects of tariff policy, see the same author's "The Italian Tariff and the Conflict Between Agriculture and Industry: The Commercial Policy of Liberal Italy, 1860–1922," *Journal of Economic History* 4 (1970). Coppa has also published an essay on Giolittian policies in the South in Coppa, "Giolitti and the *Mezzogiorno*," *Studies in Modern Italian History*, pp. 59–78. A more strictly economic history is the excellent work by Valerio Castronovo that treats the entire period after unity but is particularly good on the early twentieth century, "La storia economica," in the Einaudi *Storia d'Italia: dall'Unità a oggi*, vol. 4 (Turin, 1975). Luciano Cafagna discusses the formation of a modern industry during the period in "La formazione di una 'base industriale' fra il 1896 e il 1914," *Studi Storici* 3–4 (July–December 1961): 690–724, previously cited. General histories include the older but still useful Epicarmo Corbino, *Annali della economia italiana (1861–1915)*, previously cited; Alberto Caracciolo, ed., *La formazione dell'Italia industriale*, 3d ed. (Bari, 1972); Rodolfo Morandi, *Storia della grande industria in Italia* (Turin, 1966); and Rosario Romeo, *Breve storia della grande industria in Italia* (Bologna, 1972). For economics and the changing nature of Italian imperialism, see Richard A. Webster, *Industrial Imperialism in Italy, 1908–1915* (Berkeley and Los Angeles, 1975; consult also the more extensive Italian edition). On industrial workers, Duccio Bigazzi's *Il portello: operai, tecnici e imprenditori all'Alfa Romeo 1906–1926* (Milan, 1988) is especially good on the workforce of one of Italy's most famous automobile firms.

For the effect of the Libyan War on the Giolittian system's breakdown, see Ronald Cunsolo, "Libya, Italian Nationalism, and the Revolt Against Giolitti," *Journal of Modern History* (June 1965), and, by the same author, "Libya and the Undoing of the Giolittian System," in Coppa, ed., *Studies in Modern Italian History*, pp. 79–102. Maurizio degl'Innocenti has linked the Libyan War, Socialist policies, and the collapse of the Giolittian system in *Il socialismo italiano e la guerra di Libia* (Rome, 1976). For the changes in Mussolini and Italian socialism as a result of Red Week, see Spencer Di Scala, "'Red Week' 1914: Prelude to War and Revolution," in *Studies in Modern Italian History*, pp. 123–133. Connections between the prewar revolutionary syndicalist movement and Fascist personalities may be found in David D. Roberts, *The Syndicalist Tradition and Italian Fascism* (Chapel Hill, 1979), and in Renzo De Felice's first volume of Mussolini's life, *Mussolini il rivoluzionario* (Turin, 1965). On Sidney Sonnino, see Geoffrey Haywood, *Failure of a Dream: Sidney Sonnino and the Rise and Fall of Liberal Italy 1847–1922* (Florence, 1999); Pier Luigi Ballini, *Sidney Sonnino e il suo tempo* (Florence, 2000); Rolando Nieri, *Costituzione e problemi sociali: il pensiero politico di Sidney Sonnino* (Pisa, 2000); and Emanuela Minuto, *Il partito dei parlamentari: Sidney Sonnino e le istituzioni rappresentative (1900–1906)* (Florence, 2004). Sonnino's diary and papers have been published by Laterza. On the concrete workings of liberal Italy, see Susan Ashley, *Making Liberalism Work: The Italian Experience, 1860–1914* (Westport, 2003).

On socialism in general, Gaetano Arfé has written a good history up to 1926, *Storia del socialismo italiano (1892–1926)* (Turin, 1965), while Antonio Landolfi's work, *Storia del Psi* (Milan, 1990), integrates the latest research. The most detailed work is Giovanni Sabbatucci, ed., *Storia del socialismo italiano*, vol. 2, *L'Età Giolittiana (1900–1914)* (Palermo, 1981). Z. Ciuffoletti, M. Degl'Innocenti, and G. Sabbatucci's *Storia del PSI: 1. Le origini e l'età giolittiana* (Bari, 1992) attempts to tell the history of the PSI from an integrated political and social viewpoint utilizing the latest scholarship. Other older, general histories include Giacomo Perticone, *Linee di storia del socialismo*, 2d ed. (Milan, 1944); Leo Valiani, *Questioni di storia del socialismo* (Turin, 1958); and the insightful essay by the same author, "Il partito socialista italiano dal 1900 al 1918," *Rivista Storica Italiana* 75 (1963). Maurizio Degl'Innocenti's study of early Socialist structures, *Geografia e istituzioni del socialismo italiano* (Naples, 1983), is a valuable contribution to the field. The correspondence of Engels with Turati and Kuliscioff, along with other writings, may be found in Gianni Bosio, ed., *Karl Marx–Friedrich Engels: scritti italiani* (Milan and Rome, 1955).

The historiographical "rehabilitation" of Turati and a discussion of the movement's policies and problems may be found in Spencer Di Scala, *Dilemmas of Italian Socialism: The Politics of Filippo Turati* (Amherst, 1980). See also the introduction and preface to the Italian edition, *Filippo Turati: le origini della democrazia in Italia* (Milan, 2007). Fulvio Conti's *L'Italia dei democratici: sinistra risorgimentale, massoneria e associazionismo fra Otto e Novecento* (Milan, 2000) gives an idea of the Italian leftist milieu in general. Letterario Bruguglio, *Turati 1892: origini e caratteri del Psi* (Milan, 1982), discusses Turati and the beginnings of the Socialist Party. Carlo Rosselli, *Filippo Turati e il movimento socialista italiano* (Rome, 1968), is a classic account by a critical admirer of Turati's who was murdered by the Fascists. James Edward Miller discusses the nature of the prewar PSI and Mussolini's "innovations" in *From Elite to Mass Politics: Italian Socialism in the Giolittian Era, 1900–1914* (Kent, 1990). Turati's connections with European Socialists has been examined by Maurizio Degl'Innocenti, *Filippo Turati e il socialismo europeo* (Naples, 1985). For Turati and the crisis of reformism, consult Daniele Nino, *Filippo Turati: autonomia socialista e crisi del riformismo* (Naples, 1997). The correspondence between Turati and Kuliscioff, indispensable for an understanding of this and the period up to Mussolini's takeover, has been published in *Carteggio*, 7 vols. (Turin, 1949–1978). Other correspondence may be found in Alessandro Schiavi, ed., *Filippo Turati attraverso le lettere di corrispondenti (1880–1925)* (Bari, 1947) and *Esilio e morte di Filippo Turati* (Rome, 1956); other letters between Turati and Kuliscioff have also appeared; see Filippo Turati and Anna Kuliscioff, *Amore e socialismo: un carteggio inedito* (Scandicci, 2001). Collections of Turati speeches at party congresses and some interesting writings are in *Le vie maestre del socialismo*, 2d ed. (Naples, 1966). Schiavi also published a short biography of Turati, *Filippo Turati* (Rome, 1955), and of his companion, *Anna Kuliscioff* (Rome, 1955). Marina Addis Saba's *Anna Kuliscioff: vita privata e passione politica*, previously cited, is a rare biography of the feminist and Socialist leader. There is also Maria Casalini, *La signorna del socialismo italiano* (Rome, 1987); and, in English, Claire La Vigna, *Anna Kuliscioff: From Russian Populism to Italian Socialism* (New York, 1991), and Beverly Tanner Springer, *Anna Kuliscioff: Russian Revolutionist and Italian Feminist* (Westport, 1981). Franco Catalano's *Filippo Turati* (Milan, 1957) is basically an overview. Two more recent long biographies of Turati may be useful for information but are biased and not very satisfactory: Renato Monteleone, *Turati* (Turin, 1987), and Franco Livorsi, *Turati* (Milan, 1984). On Kuliscioff, see also the collection edited by Turati on the occasion of her death, *Anna Kuliscioff, in memoria: a Lei, agli intimi a me* (Milan, 1926). The essays in *Anna Kuliscioff e l'età del riformismo* (Rome, 1978) provide an excellent idea of her influence on Italian socialism. Claire La Vigna's essay "Anna Kuliscioff in Italy," *Italian Quarterly* 20, nos. 77–78 (Summer–Fall 1976): 65–85, is a synthetic summary of her action in Italy. A sense of Turati's local political action and its relationship to national questions may be achieved by consulting Spencer Di Scala, "Filippo Turati, the Milanese Schism, and the Reconquest of the Italian Socialist Party, 1901–1909," *Il Politico* (March 1979): 153–163. Giuseppe Mammarella takes up the specific action of reformists and revolutionaries in *Riformisti e rivoluzionari nel partito socialista italiano, 1900–1912* (Padua, 1968), a question also examined by Brunello Vigezzi in *Il PSI: le riforme e la rivoluzione (1898–1915)* (Florence, 1981).

Less controversial than Turati, Bissolati has been treated better by historians; see, for example, Ugoberto Alfassio Grimaldi and Gherardo Bozzeti, *Bissolati* (Milan, 1983), and Raffaele Colapietra, *Leonida Bissolati* (Milan, 1958). See also the book by Bissolati's collaborator, Ivanoe Bonomi, *Leonida Bissolati e il movimento socialista in Italia* (Milan, 1929). Bonomi's role has been examined by Luigi Cortesi, *Ivanoe Bonomi e la socialdemocrazia italiana: profilo biografico* (Salerno, 1971), and by Luigi Cavazzoli, *Ivanoe Bonomi riformatore* (Manduria, 2005). An examination of Arturo Labriola's revolutionary syndicalism is Dora Marucco's *Arturo Labriola e il sindacalismo rivoluzionario* (Turin, 1970). Gaetano Salvemini's influence on the Socialist movement may be measured by his collected writings on the South during this period collected by Gaetano Arfé, *Gaetano Salvemini: movimento socialista e questione meridionale,* opere 4, vol. 2 (Milan, 1963), and Massimo Salvadori, *Gaetano Salvemini* (Turin, 1963). Essential for an understanding of Salvemini's thinking are the most complete editions of his correspondence and an anthology of his writings of this period, edited by Enzo Tagliacozzo and Sergio Bucchi, *Carteggio 1894–1902* (Bari, 1988) and *Carteggio 1912–1914* (Bari, 1984), and *Gaetano Salvemini: socialismo riformismo democrazia* (Bari, 1990). The book by Charles Killinger, *Gaetano Salvemini: A Biography* (Westport, 2002), is the best in any language.

On the Socialist congresses, a compendium has been published by Franco Pedone, *Il partito socialista italiano nei suoi congressi,* 4 vols. (Milan, 1963). Gaetano Arfé has published an informative history of the Socialist Party daily up to 1940, *Storia dell' Avanti!,* 2 vols. (Milan, 1956–1958). On the most important Socialist newspaper, see also Piero V. Scorti, *Storia dell'Avanti! 1896–1986* (Milan, 1986), and Gherardo Bozzetti, *Mussolini direttore dell'Avanti!* (Milan, 1979), which examines Mussolini's editorship.

The Italian labor movement has received attention from Daniel Horowitz, *The Italian Labor Movement* (Cambridge, Mass., 1963), and Maurice Neufield, *Italy: School for Awakening Countries* (Ithaca, 1961). Carlo Cartiglia's view of the period's pioneer labor leader, *Rinaldo Rigola e il sindacalismo riformista in Italia* (Milan, 1976), is overly colored by Rigola's naive actions during the Fascist period. The documents of the Socialist labor union have been conveniently collected by Luciana Marchetti, *La Confederazione Generale del Lavoro negli atti, nei documenti, nei congressi 1906–1926* (Milan, 1962). Adolfo Pepe has written a history of the CGL up to the Libyan War, *Storia della*

Confederazione Generale del Lavoro dalla fondazione alla guerra di Libia, 1905–1911 (Bari, 1972). Elda Gentili Zappi's *If Eight Hours Seem Too Few: Mobilization of Women Workers in the Italian Rice Fields* (Albany, 1991) examines the attempts of Socialist leagues to find support among female workers. An exhaustive description of peasant conditions is provided by Giuliano Procacci, "Geografia e struttura del movimento contadino della valle padana nel suo periodo formativo (1901–1906)," *Studi Storici* 5, no. 1 (January–March 1964).

The 1898 crisis is analyzed by Umberto Levra, *Il colpo di stato della borghesia: la crisi politica di fine secolo in Italia, 1896–1898* (Milan, 1975). The social and political changes in Italy's most advanced industrial city during the same period are examined by Louise Tilly, *Politics and Class in Milan* (New York, 1992), and Volker Hunecke, "Comune e classe operaia a Milano (1858–1898)," *Studi Storici* 18, no. 3 (July–September 1983). Luigi Pelloux's memoirs, *Quelques souvenirs de ma vie* (Rome, 1967), are a fundamental and underutilized source. For insights on the operations of Parliament, see Salvatore Saladino's essay, "Parliamentary Politics in the Liberal Era," in Tannenbaum and Noether, eds., *Modern Italy: A Topical History*, pp. 27–51, and the general history by the same author, *Italy from Unification to 1919* (New York, 1970).

On the Catholic movement, besides the works previously cited, see Giovanni Spadolini's very informative *Giolitti e i cattolici 1901–1914* (Florence, 1960) and Gabriele De Rosa's biography of a major leader of the period, *Filippo Meda e l'età liberale* (Florence, 1959). For an overview of the relationship between Socialists, Catholics, and Giolitti, there is Spencer Di Scala, "Socialists and Catholics in the Giolittian Era," *La Parola del Popolo* 28, no. 69 (March–April 1977): 54–56. See also Frank J. Coppa, "Giolitti and the Gentiloni Pact Between Myth and Reality," *Catholic Historical Review* 53, no. 2 (July 1967): 217–228, which argues that the "pact" has been misinterpreted.

CHAPTER 13: THE CULTURE OF THE NEW ITALY

Material on private lives during this period must be culled from a variety of sources, especially correspondence, periodicals, and novels. In English, the short piece by R. J. B. Bosworth, "The Opening of the Victor Emmanuel Monument," *Italian Quarterly* 18, no. 71 (Winter 1975): 78–87, gives a taste of life in 1911. A good overview of the demographic growth and the changes taking place in the cities is provided by Luigi De Rosa, "Urbanization and Industrialization in Italy (1861–1921)," *Journal of European Economic History* 17, no. 3 (Winter 1988): 467–490. Aldo Alessandro Mola's *1882–1912: Fare gli italiani: una società nuova in uno Stato vecchio* (Turin, 1975) combines social analysis with documents and statistics. The multivolume Einaudi history of Italy includes two large volumes of relevance to this and other sections regarding social history and the development of science and technology: Franco Della Peruta, ed., *Storia d'Italia: annali 7: malattia e medicina* (Turin, 1984), and Gianni Micheli, ed., *Storia d'Italia: annali 3: scienza e tecnica nella cultura e nella società dal Rinascimento a oggi* (Turin, 1980). Mary Gibson discusses prostitution during this period in

Prostitution and the State in Italy, 1860–1915 (New Brunswick, 1986). Gibson has also produced a rare work on an important founder of criminology, *Born to Crime: Cesare Lombroso and the Origins of Biological Criminology* (Westport, 2002). Steven C. Hughes has put dueling in its social, political, and gender context in *Politics of the Sword* (Columbus, 2007). The book edited by Edward Muir and Guido Ruggiero, *Sex and Gender in Historical Perspective* (Baltimore and London, 1990), includes one essay on the social relationships and the role of women during the time period discussed in this chapter.

A number of general works examine the literature of this period. The best include the collection of Benedetto Croce's essays, *La letteratura della nuova Italia*, 6 vols. (Bari, 1967); Gaetano Mariani and Mario Petrucciani, eds., *Letteratura contemporanea italiana* (Rome, 1979), vols. 1 and 2, which also include a discussion of dialectical literature; and the massive Gianni Grana, ed., *Novecento*, 10 vols. (Milan, 1980), which provides the economic and social context of the literature examined. Emilio Cecchi's *Letteratura italiana del Novecento* (Milan, 1972) is a high-level work, while Alfredo Galletti's *Il Novecento*, 4th ed. (Milan, 1967) in the *Storia letteraria d'Italia* multivolume set gives a particularly detailed view of this period. Piero Bigongiari, *Poesia italiana del Novecento* (Milan, 1978), provides an introduction to poetry. Brief histories such as J. H. Whitfield, *A Short History of Italian Literature* (Westport, 1960), are less satisfactory but may serve as an introduction. Svevo is a particularly interesting writer who has attracted attention. See Beno Weiss, *Italo Svevo* (New York, 1987), Joseph Cary, *A Ghost in Trieste* (Chicago, 1993), and Giuliana Minghetti, *In the Shadow of the Mammoth: Italo Svevo and the Emergence of Modernism* (Toronto, 2002).

Works on the music of this period and biographies of the musicians cited are readily available, but an unusually good chapter on Verdi's politics may be found in Paul Robinson, *Opera and Ideas* (New York, 1985). An attempt to give a complete portrait of the great composer, faults and all, is Mary Jane Philips Matz, *Verdi: A Biography* (New York, 1994).

Specialized works on Italian painting of the age may be consulted. Albert Boime, *The Art of the Macchia and the Risorgimento: Representing Culture and Nationalism in Nineteenth-Century Italy* (Chicago, 1993), attempts a reevaluation of the international reputation of the Macchiaioli. In English also, Lionello Venturi's critical study, *Italian Painting* (New York, 1952), has a section on this period, while James Thrall Soby and Alfred H. Barr, *Twentieth-Century Italian Art*, 2 vols. (New York, 1949), is more complete. Good general works include Emily Braun, ed., *Italian Art in the Twentieth Century* (Munich and London, 1989), Corrado Maltese, *Storia dell'arte in Italia, 1785–1943* (Turin, 1960), and Pontus Hulten and Germano Celant, eds., *Arte Italiana: presenze 1900–1945* (Milan, 1989). See also Dario Cecchi's full-scale biography of painter *Giovanni Boldini* (Turin, 1962).

On futurism, consult Giusi Baldissoni, *Filippo Tommaso Marinetti* (Milan, 1986), which combines biography and criticism. Isabella Gherarducci, *Il futurismo* (Rome, 1984), gives good criticisms and readings, while Anna Elena Giammarco's *Le forme poetiche nei futuristi* (Rome, 1977) is a short analytical work on the poetry. Willard Bohn also discusses poetry, in *Italian Futurist Poetry* (Toronto, 2005). See as well Ester Coen, *Umberto Boccioni* (New York, 1988), Claudia Salaris, *Storia del futurismo* (Rome, 1985), and Pontus Hulten, ed., *Futurismo e futurismi* (Milan, 1986). Other general works include Richard Humphreys, *Futurism* (New York, 1999), Caroline Tisdall and Angelo Bozzola, *Futurism* (New York, 1978), Rosa Trillo Clough, *Futurism: The Story of a Modern Art Movement: A New Approach* (New York, 1961), and Marjorie Perloff, *The Futurist Moment: Avant-Garde, Avant Guerre, and the Language of Rupture* (Chicago, 1986). Look at Sylvia Martin, *Futurism* (London, 2005), and Giovanni Lista, *Futurism* (Paris, 2001). Besides the famous manifesto of 1909, Futurists produced many others, collected by Umbro Apollonio, *Futurist Manifestos* (New York, 1973). More specialized works include Christiana J. Taylor, *Futurism: Politics, Painting, and Performance* (Ann Arbor, 1979); the essays collected by Laura Matteoli Rossi, *Boccioni's Materia* (New York, 2004); and Giovanni Lista, *Futurist and Photography* (London, 2001).

On architecture, see Richard A. Etlin, *Modernism in Italian Architecture, 1890–1940* (Cambridge, Mass., 1991), and Esther da Costa, *The Work of Antonio Sant'Elia: Retreat into the Future* (New Haven, 1995).

Catalogs of exhibitions can sometimes be a good introduction to art; some that might be profitably consulted are: Maria Cristina Gozzoli and Fernando Mazzocca, *Hayez* (Milan, n.d.); *Arte moderna in Italia, 1915–1935* (Florence, 1967); Commisariato Generale d'Italia per l'Expo '86, *Futur-Balla* (Milan, 1986); Maurizio Calvesi, *Boccioni prefuturista* (Milan, 1983); and Maurizio Fagiolo dell'Arco, *Severini prima e dopo l'opera* (Florence, 1983).

An idea of the Italian cinema within the general cinematic context may be gleaned in Gianni Rondolino, *Storia del cinema*, vol. 1 (Turin, 1977). General histories that consider this period, among others, include Pierre Leprophon, *The Italian Cinema* (London, 1972), and Carlo Lizzani, *Il cinema italiano, 1895–1979*, vol. 1 (Rome, 1979). Useful specific works on the early days of Italian filmmaking are: Aldo Bernardini, *Cinema muto italiano: industria e organizzazione dello spettacolo, 1905–1909* (Rome, 1981), *Cinema muto italiano: arte, divismo e mercato, 1910–1914* (Rome, 1982), and *Cinema muto italiano: ambiente, spettacoli e spettatori, 1896–1904* (Bari, 1980); Roberto Paolella, *Storia del cinema muto* (Naples, 1956); Mario Verdone, *Cinema e letteratura del futurismo* (Rome, 1968); and Riccardo Redi, *Ti parlerò d'amore: cinema italiano fra muto e sonoro* (Turin, 1986). The film journal *Bianco e Nero* published a thorough review of Italian films of the 1920s in its issues of 1980 and 1981.

Emiliana P. Noether contributed an essay on "Italian Intellectuals" in Tannenbaum and Noether, eds., *Modern Italy: A Topical History,* which may serve as a general introduction to the period. Leone Bortone's chapter, "La cultura politica," in Nino Valeri, *Storia d'Italia*, vol. 4 (Turin, 1965), is an incisive and exhaustive summary. Catholic modernism, with rich chapters on Italy and an analysis of Fogazzaro's important novel *Il Santo*, is considered by Michele Ranchetti, *The Catholic Modernists: A Study of the Religious Reform Movement* (London, 1969). Richard Drake, *Byzantium for Rome:*

The Politics of Nostalgia in Umbertian Italy, 1878–1900 (Chapel Hill, 1980), is best at tracing the development of intellectual resentment during this period and pointing out its link with the rest of Europe. In his long chapter on Italy in *The Generation of 1914* (Cambridge, Mass., 1979), Robert Wohl makes the link more apparent and establishes a connection with fascism. Walter L. Adamson examines the relationship of "modernist" culture in Florence—as expressed in journals such as *La Voce*—and Fascist ideology and rhetoric in *Avant-Garde Florence: From Modernism to Fascism* (Cambridge, Mass., 1993). Emilio Gentile's *La grande Italia* (Milan, 1997) describes the development of the idea of a great role for Italy from the Crispi period forward, leading to a culture linked to nationalism and fascism.

Works providing an intimate view of the Nationalists are Enrico Corradini, *Discorsi politici, 1902–1923* (Florence, 1923), *Il nazionalismo italiano* (Milan, 1914), *L'ora di Tripoli* (Milan, 1911), and Pier Ludovico Occhini, *Enrico Corradini e la nuova coscienza nazionale* (Florence, 1925). An explanation of Nationalist desires is in Alfredo Rocco, *Che cosa vogliono i nazionalisti* (Padua, 1914), while a "balance sheet" is drawn up by Romain Raniero, *Da Oriani a Corradini* (Milan, 2003). Giovanni Papini and Giuseppe Prezzolini explain their later nationalism in *Vecchio e nuovo nazionalismo* (Milan, 1914). Papini's autobiography, *Un uomo finito* (Florence, 1974), gives a precious insight into the workings of the mind of a rightist intellectual of this period. For an example of Nationalist views on Libya, look at P. Vinassa de Regny, *Libya Italica* (Milan, 1913), and Giuseppe Piazza, *La nostra terra promessa* (Rome, 1911); for an excellent contemporary analysis of the Nationalist role during this period, consult Gaetano Salvemini, *Come siamo andati in Libia* (Florence, 1914). Ronald S. Cunsolo combines interpretation and readings in *Italian Nationalism from Its Origins to World War II* (Malabar, 1990). The best work on the Nationalist Association is Alexander De Grand, *The Italian Nationalist Association and the Rise of Fascism in Italy* (Lincoln, 1978), while an excellent essay in English on the rise of a "new" right in Italy is Salvatore Saladino's essay in Hans Rogger and Eugen Weber, *The European Right: A Historical Profile* (Berkeley and Los Angeles, 1966).

On D'Annunzio, see the biographies by Philippe Jullian, *D'Annunzio* (London, 1972), and the still useful Tom Antongini, *D'Annunzio* (New York, 1971). The D'Annunzio phenomenon has also been analyzed by Jared Becker, *Nationalism and Culture: Gabriele D'Annunzio and Italy After the Risorgimento* (New York, 1994), Paolo Valerio, *Gabriele D'Annunzio: The Dark Flame* (New Haven, 1992), and Anthony Rhodes, *D'Annunzio: The Poet as Superman* (New York, 1960). For a short critical introduction and guide to D'Annunzio's work, consult Anco Marzio Mutterle, *Gabriele D'Annunzio* (Florence, 1980).

Many good studies exist in English on Mosca and Pareto, and their works have also been translated. An excellent short introduction to Gaetano Mosca is Ettore A. Albertoni, *Mosca and the Theory of Elitism* (Oxford, 1985), and Mauro Fotia, *Il liberalismo incompiuto* (Milan, 2001); for an introduction to Pareto, see Joseph Lopreato, *Vilfredo Pareto* (New York, 1965). Francesco Mancuso has published *Gaetano Mosca e la tradizione del costituzionalismo* (Naples, 1999). There is a good introduction by S. E.

Finer in his edition of *Vilfredo Pareto: Sociological Writings* (New York, 1966). The essays in James H. Meisel, ed., *Pareto and Mosca* (Englewood Cliffs, 1965), are excellent and highly recommended. Richard Bellamy takes the long view in *Modern Italian Social Theory: Ideology and Politics from Pareto to the Present* (Stanford, 1987). On Robert Michels's work and his connection with Italy, see the chapter putting that writer in Italian and German context in Arthur Mitzman, *Sociology and Estrangement* (New York, 1973). See also Juan J. Linz, *Robert Michels, Political Sociology, and the Future of Democracy* (New Brunswick, 2006). Armand Patrucco has produced an excellent study on the effects of Mosca's and Pareto's thought within the general context of the criticism of the parliamentary system, *The Critics of the Italian Parliamentary System, 1860–1915* (New York and London, 1992). Other books considering the influence of this school, from different viewpoints, are Robert A. Nye, *The Anti-Democratic Sources of Elite Theory: Pareto, Mosca, Michels* (London, 1977), Norberto Bobbio, *On Mosca and Bobbio* (Geneva, 1977), and Robertino Ghiringhelli and Ettore A. Alberoni, *Elitism and Democracy: Mosca, Pareto, and Michels* (Milan, 1992). On Croce's importance for Western thought, see H. Stuart Hughes, *Consciousness and Society* (New York, 1961); for an assessment of the philosopher, there is David D. Roberts, *Benedetto Croce and the Uses of Historicism* (Berkeley, 1987). Norberto Bobbio's *Ideological Profile of Twentieth-Century Italy* (Princeton, 1995), the translation of a 1969 book, provides a good general outlook on political thought of the period.

Italian science during this period is not well covered, except for Alessandro Volta. See Giuliano Pancaldi, *Volta: Science and Culture in the Age of Enlightenment* (Princeton, 2003), and Alberto Gigli Berzolari, *Alessandro Volta e la cultura scientifica e tecnologica tra '700 e '800* (Milan, 1993), in addition to commemorations and published proceedings of conferences. There is little on Righi, but see Antonio Rostagni, *Augusto Righi e la sua opera a mezzo secolo dalla scomparsa, 11 dicembre 1911* (Rome, 1972). On Marconi, there is *Signor Marconi's Magic Box* (London, 2003), the story of how he began the "radio revolution," and the reminiscences of his daughter, Degna Marconi, *My Father, Marconi* (Toronto, 2001).

Chapter 14: World War I and the Red Biennium

Students wishing to understand the general diplomatic situation before and during World War I would do well to consult the previously cited classic by A. J. P. Taylor, *The Struggle for Mastery in Europe, 1848–1918*. The best book on the diplomatic issues leading up to and during the Libyan War is still William C. Askew, *Europe and Italy's Acquisition of Libya, 1911–1912* (Durham, 1942). In addition to general European diplomacy and the war's outbreak, Italy's position is exceptionally well analyzed by Luigi Albertini, who was editor of the country's major newspaper and knew many of the Italian protagonists personally. His magisterial work has been translated as *The Origins of the War of 1914*, 3 vols. (Oxford, 1965). Albertini was an important figure in Italy, and his memoirs, *Venti anni di vita politica*, 2 vols. (Bologna, 1969), may be consulted with profit on all issues of the day. The military aspects of Italy's connection with the Triple Alliance are treated in Fortunato Minniti, *Esercito e politica da Porta Pia alla Triplice alleanza* (Rome, 1984). Rino Longhitano, *Antonino di San Giuliano* (Milan, 1954), is a rare work on the Italian foreign minister. R. J. B. Bosworth's *Italy, the Least of the Great Powers: Italian Foreign Policy Before the First World War* (London, 1979) is marred by the author's attempt to establish too close a "continuity" between the foreign policy of Liberal and of Fascist Italy, but it is nevertheless an interesting and informative book. Bosworth's collaborative effort with Sergio Romano examining Italian foreign policy from 1860 to 1985, *La politica estera italiana 1860–1985* (Bologna, 1991), includes some excellent essays and others that are less useful. Bosworth has also published a short work on *Italy and the Approach of the First World War* (London, 1983), but see also Roy Price, "Italy and the Outbreak of the First World War," *Cambridge Historical Journal* 11, no. 2 (1954): 219–227. Also in English there is W. A. Renzi's account of the neutrality period, *In the Shadow of the Sword: Italy's Neutrality and Entrance into the Great War, 1914–1915* (New York, 1987). Balanced views on Italian foreign policy by a protagonist are in Leonida Bissolati, *La politica estera dell'Italia dal 1897 al 1920* (Milan, 1923). Gaetano Salvemini's *La politica estera dell'Italia* (Florence, 1944) is a good work by one of Italy's leading historians. William C. Askew's "The Austro-Italian Antagonism, 1896–1914," in Lillian Parker Wallace, ed., *Power, Public Opinion, and Diplomacy* (New York, 1968), is an outstanding overview of the Austro-Italian relationship and the issues dividing the two "allies." Askew has also published "Foreign Policy and Diplomacy After Unification," in the previously cited Tannenbaum and Noether, *Modern Italy: A Topical History*. On Albania, Renzo Falaschi combines interpretation with an interesting set of Italian documents (translated also into English) up to 1921 in *Ismail Kemal Bey Vlora: il pensiero e l'opera attraverso i documenti italiani* (Rome, 1985). James Burgwyn has published two valuable articles on Italian diplomatic activity in the Balkans on the eve of war and during the conflict, "Sonnino e la diplomazia italiana del tempo di guerra nei Balcani nel 1915," *Storia Contemporanea* 16, no. 1 (February 1985): 113–137, and "Italy's Balkan Policy 1915–1917: Albania, Greece, and the Epirus Question," *Storia delle relazioni internazionali* 2, no. 1 (1986): 3–61. The excellent book by John Thayer, *Italy and the Great War* (Madison and Milwaukee, 1964), provides a probing analysis of the Italian cultural milieu during the interventionist debate and in the period before the war.

The best work examining Italy's neutrality from all aspects is Brunello Vigezzi's *L'Italia neutrale*, vol. 1 of the massive *L'Italia di fronte alla prima guerra mondiale* (Milan and Naples, 1966), while Isacco Artom's *Iniziative neutralistiche della diplomazia italiana nel 1870 e nel 1915* (Turin, 1954) is useful for the diplomacy of the neutrality period. Relations with Germany during neutrality are expertly examined in Alberto Monticone, *La Germania e la neutralità italiana 1914–1915* (Bologna, 1971). Leo Valiani's *Il partito socialista italiano nel periodo della neutralità 1914–1915* (Milan, 1963) is a classic work on the Socialist Party during months of neutrality. For the impact of the interventionist crisis on the parliamentary system, see Spencer Di Scala, "Parliamentary Socialists, the Statuto, and the Giolittian System," *Australian Journal of Politics and History* 25, no. 2 (August 1979): 157–168. Mario Toscano, a prominent diplomatic historian, examines the negotiations and the Pact of London in *Il patto di Londra* (Bologna, 1934). H. James Burgwyn revises earlier notions of Italy's foreign policy under Sonnino in *The Legend of the Mutilated Victory: Italy, the Great War, and the Paris Peace Conference, 1915–1919* (Westport, 1993). Of the writings left by the protagonists, consult Sidney Sonnino, *Diario 1914–1916* (Bari, 1972); Antonio Salandra, *La neutralità italiana: ricordi e pensieri* (Milan, 1928) and *L'intervento 1915* (Milan, 1930); G. B. Gifuni, ed., *Il diario di Salandra* (Milan, 1969); Ferdinando Martini, *Diario 1914–1918* (Milan, 1966); and Giolitti's memoirs, *Memorie della mia vita*, previously cited. On Salandra, see Tommaso Nardella, *Antonio Salandra* (Manduria, 1996). See also Brunello Vigezzi, *I problemi della neutralità e della guerra nel carteggio Salandra-Sonnino* (Milan, 1962). Documents relevant to Giolitti are in *Dalle carte di Giovanni Giolitti: Quarant'anni di politica italiana*, vol. 3, previously cited. The official documents relating to intervention have been published by Augusto Torre, ed., *I documenti diplomatici italiani*, series 4, vol. 12, and series 5, vol. 1 (Rome, 1954).

The best military history of the war on the Italian side is Piero Pieri, *L'Italia nella prima guerra mondiale 1915–1918* (Turin, 1965); see also Emilio Faldella, *La grande guerra* (Milan, 1965), and the official history, Ufficio storico dello Stato maggiore dell'Esercito, *L'esercito italiano nella grande guerra 1915–1918* (Rome, 1927–1967). The best book in English explaining the military situation on the Italian front is John R. Schindler, *Isonzo: The Forgotten Sacrifice of the Great War* (Westport, 2001). Books on the Italian commanders that are useful are Gianni Roca, *Cadorna* (Milan, 1985); Luigi Gratton, *Armando Diaz: Duca della Vittoria: da Caporetto a Vittorio Veneto* (Foggia, 2001); and Angelo Mangone, *Diaz* (Milan, 1987). Piero Melograni has written the best political history of the country during World War I, *Storia politica della grande guerra* (Bari, 1969). An excellent work that captures the essence of the war effort and the country during the conflict is Mario Silvestri, *Isonzo 1917* (Turin, 1965). Mario Morselli has examined the Caporetto defeat in *Caporetto 1917: Victory or Defeat* (New York, 2001). Rino Alessi, *Dall'Isonzo al Piave: lettere clandestine di un corrispondente di guerra* (Milan, 1966), gives a picture of the climate after Caporetto.

On the Italian participation at Versailles, the best work in English is still René Albrecht-Carrié, *Italy at the Paris Peace Conference* (New York, 1938). For the dispute with Yugoslavia, see Dragoljub Zivojinovic, *America, Italy, and the Birth of Yugoslavia (1917–1919)* (Boulder, 1972). For an analysis of the conference and the mutilated victory, there is James Burgwyn, *The Legend of the Mutilated Victory* (Westport, 1993). A good source on the economic aftermath of the war, with a host of relevant statistics, is the previously cited Clough, *The Economic History of Italy*. The work by Douglas Forsyth, *Monetary and Financial Policy and the Crisis of Liberal Italy* (New York, 1993), gives a good overview of the problems and their effects. See also the relevant chapters of Rolf Petri, *Storia economica d'Italia: dalla grande guerra al miracolo economico, 1918–1963* (Bologna, 2002), and Peter Hertner and Giorgio Mori, *La transizione dall'economia di guerra all'economia di pace in Italia e in Germania dopo la Prima Guerra Mondiale* (Bologna, 1983). On the relationship between economic and social issues during the period, see Luigi Einaudi, *La condotta economica e gli effetti sociali della guerra italiana* (Bari, 1933). Electoral statistics for the period are in Istituto Centrale Statistica e Ministero per la Costituente, *Compendio delle statistiche elettorale italiane dal 1848 al 1934*, 2 vols. (Rome, 1947), while economic statistics may be found in Ministero dell'economia nazionale, *Annuario statistico italiano*, 2d series, vol. 8, *1919–1921* (Rome, 1925). On the Socialist Party during the Red Biennium, consult Gaetano Arfé, *Storia del socialismo italiano 1892–1926* (Turin, 1966). A Socialist protagonist, Pietro Nenni, wrote the excellent *Storia di quattro anni 1919–1922* (Milan, 1927). Debates in the Socialist congresses can be followed in Luigi Cortesi, *Il socialismo italiano tra riforme e rivoluzione* (Bari, 1969). A contemporary, Francesco Magri, followed the factory councils in *La crisi industriale e il controllo operaio* (Milan, 1922). Giovanni Pesce, *Da Lenin a Mussolini* (Rome, 1928), describes the impact of the Russian Revolution. The question of revolution is analyzed by Franco Felice, *Serrati, Bordiga, Gramsci, e il problema della rivoluzione in Italia, 1919–1920* (Bari, 1971). On the workers, see G. Maione, *Il biennio rosso* (Bologna, 1975), and on the stiffening attitude of the employers to the disorders, M. Abrate, *La lotta sindacale nella industrializzione in Italia 1906–1926* (Turin, 1968).

CHAPTER 15: THE RISE OF FASCISM

The interpretations of fascism's rise to power and its development have attracted enormous interest and given rise to heated polemics. Important questions include whether the liberal state had reached the end of its rope and whether fascism was inherent in Italian society or came about as a result of the war and its aftermath. Before coming to conclusions on such issues, it behooves the reader to become thoroughly versed in the complex developments of the period.

Economic affairs may be studied in Clough's *The Economic History of Italy* and Forsyth's *Monetary and Financial Policy*, both previously cited, while the section on this period in Valerio Castronovo's "La storia economica," in *Storia d'Italia*, vol. 4, *Dall'unità a oggi*, I (Turin, 1975), is particularly useful.

Roberto Vivarelli's *Dopoguerra in Italia e l'avvento del fascismo (1918–1922)*, vol. 1, *Dalla fine della guerra all'impresa di Fiume* (Naples, 1967) is a very impressive and complete work that links events in Italy to the democratic interventionism of the United States and to the Communist Revolution. The same author's *Storia delle origini del fascismo: l'Italia dalla grande guerra alla marcia su Roma*, 2 vols. (Bologna, 1991), distinguishes between "good" and "bad" nationalism. On the Fiume affair and its links to fascism, see Michael Ledeen, *The First Duce: D'Annunzio at Fiume* (Baltimore, 1977). Federico Chabod, *L'Italia contemporanea* (Turin, 1961), argues that fascism was a completely new movement holding none of the principles that had previously determined the political struggle. Chabod and Vivarelli believe that in the period under discussion are to be found the origins of contemporary Italy, and they emphasize the country's disillusion with the war despite its victory. This is a theme developed by Gaetano Salvemini in his Harvard lectures, published as *The Origins of*

Fascism in Italy (New York, 1973), and in the earlier *The Fascist Dictatorship in Italy* (London, 1928). Ironically, G. A. Borgese, Salvemini's fellow exile and a professor at the University of Chicago, sought the roots of fascism in the remote Italian past in his *Goliath: The March of Fascism* (New York, 1937). Though not going back quite so far, Vivarelli also found it necessary to go further into the past in pursuing the reasons for the collapse of liberal institutions in his *Il fallimento del liberalismo* (Bologna, 1981). For more information on this point, Nino Valeri reviews the literature relating to the relationship between liberalism and fascism in his *Tradizione liberale e fascismo* (Florence, 1972).

For other views of fascism's rise to power, see the classic and extraordinarily clear Angelo Tasca, *Nascita e avvento del fascismo*, 2 vols. (Bari, 1965). This period is also covered by the controversial but convincing and informative Renzo De Felice, *La conquista del potere 1921–1925*, vol. 1 of *Mussolini il fascista* (Turin, 1966).

Many protagonists of these years have left important works. An analysis by a leftist opponent is Pietro Nenni, *La lotta di classe in Italia* (Milan, 1987). Luigi Sturzo published *Italy and Fascism* (New York, 1967). The anarchist leader Armando Borghi has left his memoirs, *Mezzo secolo di anarchia* (Naples, 1954). The former revolutionary syndicalist who served in Giolitti's cabinet, Arturo Labriola, published *Le due politiche: fascismo e riformismo* (Naples, 1924). Giolitti's memoirs have been previously cited, but see also the letters on fascism published by Gabriele De Rosa in *Venti anni di politica nelle carte di Camillo Corradini* (Rome, 1957). Ivanoe Bonomi's recollection of this period is *From Socialism to Fascism* (London, 1924); see also Roberto Vivarelli, "Bonomi e il fascismo in alcuni documenti inediti," *Rivista Storica Italiana* (March 1960). On the Bonomi government's economic policy, see the work of the minister for industry, Bortolo Belotti, *La politica economica del ministero Bonomi* (Milan, 1923). On the Banca di Sconto affair, consult the musings of its head, Cesare Rossi, *L'assalto alla Banca di Sconto: Colloqui con Angelo Pogliani* (Milan, 1950). D'Annunzio before fascism is examined in Romain Raniero and Stefano Galli, *L'Italia e la "Grande Vigilia"* (Milan, 2007). An important memoir that presents critical documents relating to the March on Rome is Effrem Ferraris, *La marcia su Roma veduta dal Viminale* (Rome, 1946). For the Fascists, see Benito Mussolini, *Tempi della rivoluzione fascista* (Milan, 1930), and, for a flavor of the squads, the diaries of Italo Balbo, *Diario 1922* (Milan, 1932), and of Umberto Banchelli, *Le memorie di un fascista* (Florence, 1922). For the origins of the Fascist Party, see Direzione del Partito Nazionale Fascista, *Le origini e lo sviluppo del fascismo* (Rome, 1928).

On leftist party activities, in addition to general histories, see the relevant sections of Alexander De Grand's parallel history of the Socialist and Communist parties, *The Italian Left in the Twentieth Century* (Bloomington and Indianapolis, 1989). See also De Grand's study of Angelo Tasca, *In Stalin's Shadow* (DeKalb, 1986). Serrati's politics are examined by Tommaso Detti, *Serrati e la formazione del Partito Comunista d'Italia* (Rome, 1972). On Turati, see *Le vie maestre del socialismo* (Naples, 1966) and *Turati-Kuliscioff: carteggio*, vol. 5 (Turin, 1953), both previously cited. The Socialist congresses of this period are summarized by Franco Pedone, *Il Partito Socialista Italiano nei suoi congressi*, vol. 3 (Milan, 1963), but see especially Direzione del Partito Socialista Italiano,

Resoconto stenografico del XVII Congresso Nazionale: Livorno 1921 (Milan, 1963). The Matteotti affair is analyzed by Mauro Canali, *Il delitto Matteotti: affarismo e politica nel primo governo Mussolini* (Bologna, 1997); Matteotti's career can be followed in Carlo Carini, *Giacomo Matteotti: idee giuridiche e azione politica* (Florence, 1984). For the "Arditi del Popolo," see Eros Francescangeli, *Arditi del Popolo: Argo Secondari e la prima organizzazione antifascista (1917–1922)* (Rome, 2000).

The birth and early life of the Communist Party is chronicled by Paolo Spriano, *Da Bordiga a Gramsci*, vol. 1 of *Storia del Partito Comunista Italiano* (Turin, 1967); on the formation of the Communist Party, an essential work is Palmiro Togliatti, *La formazione del gruppo dirigente del Partito Comunista Italiano nel 1923–1924* (Rome, 1971). Many works have been written on Gramsci. James Martin attempts an introduction, *Gramsci's Political Analysis: A Critical Introduction* (New York, 1998). See also John Cammett's fine work, *Antonio Gramsci and the Origins of Italian Communism* (Stanford, 1967), and Martin Clark, *Antonio Gramsci and the Revolution That Failed* (New Haven, 1977). Richard Bellamy and Darrow Schecter have published a short work on *Gramsci and the Italian State* (Manchester, 1993), which seeks to place the Communist leader within his Italian context. Dante Germino, *Antonio Gramsci: Architect of a New Politics* (Baton Rouge, 1990), argues that Gramsci owes his importance to his vision of a "new politics of the excluded." For analyses of his idea of hegemony, consult Walter L. Adamson, *Hegemony and Revolution: A Study of Antonio Gramsci's Political and Cultural Theory* (Berkeley, 1980), and Joseph V. Femia, *Gramsci's Political Thought: Hegemony, Consciousness, and the Revolutionary Process* (Oxford, 1981). Maurice A. Finocchiaro has instead focused on another aspect, *Gramsci and the History of Dialectical Thought* (Cambridge, U.K., 1988). An interesting attempt to link the values and ideas of Gramsci and Turati has been made by Lelio Lagorio and Giancarlo Lehner, *Turati e Gramsci per il socialismo* (Milan, 1987).

For studies on the Catholic movement during this period, see John N. Maloney, *The Emergence of Political Catholicism in Italy* (London, 1977), and two works on Luigi Sturzo—a biography and an analysis of his thought: Francesco Piva and Francesco Malgeri, *Vita di Luigi Sturzo* (Rome, 1972), and Giorgio Campanini, *Il pensiero politico di Luigi Sturzo* (Caltanisetta, 2001).

Several good local studies exist on agrarian fascism. For an overview of local fascism and bolshevism, see Alexander De Grand's essay "Bolshevik and Fascist Attacks on the Liberal State, 1919–1922," in Frank Coppa, ed., *Studies in Modern Italian History* (New York, 1986). Paul Corner's *Fascism in Ferrara 1915–1925* (London, 1975) is a fine study. Frank M. Snowden connects the class struggle in Apulia at the beginning of the century up to 1922 in *Violence and Great Estates in the South of Italy* (Cambridge, U.K., 1986). Two studies of fascism in Brescia are Paolo Corsini's massive *Il feudo di Augusto Turati* (Milan, 1988) and Alice Kelikian's brief *Town and Country Under Fascism: The Transformation of Brescia 1915–1926* (Oxford, 1986). Frank Demers has produced a good study on *Le origini del fascismo a Cremona* (Bari, 1979). N. Onofri's *La strage di Palazzo d'Accursio: origine e nascita del fascismo bolognese* (Milan, 1980) examines the origins of fascism in Bologna, while Anthony Cardoza, *Agrarian Elites and Italian Fascism* (Princeton, 1982), links agrarian fascism in Bologna to a new group of commercial farmers who became more important after 1900. Other good studies of local Fascist movements include Raffaele Colapietra, *Napoli tra dopoguerra e fascismo* (Milan, 1962); R. Bernabei, *Fascismo e nazionalismo in Campania* (Rome, 1975); M. Francini, *Primo dopoguerra e origini del fascismo a Pistoia* (Milan, 1976); R. Cantagalli, *Storia del fascismo fiorentino 1919–1925* (Florence, 1972); M. Vaini, *Le origini del fascismo a Mantova* (Rome, 1961); and S. Colarizi, *Dopoguerra e fascismo in Puglia 1919–1926* (Bari, 1971).

On all of the events considered in this section, see the relevant parts in Paolo Calzini et al., eds., *Fascismo e antifascismo (1918–1936): lezioni e testimonianze* (Milan, 1963). Guido Neppi Modona's work on the Italian magistracy also considers its role in the rise of fascism, *Sciopero, potere politico e magistratura 1870–1922* (Bari, 1969). The Fascist labor movement is examined in Ferdinando Cordova, *Le origini dei sindacati fascisti 1918–1926* (Bari, 1974). On the crises leading up to the March on Rome, and the march itself, consult Danilo Venerusso, *La vigilia del fascismo: il primo ministero Facta e la crisi dello Stato liberale in Italia* (Bologna, 1968); Marcello Soleri, *Memorie* (Turin, 1949); Cesare Maria De Vecchi, "Mussolini vero: memorie," in the weekly *Tempo* (November–December 1959); Cesare Rossi, *Trentatre vicende mussoliniane* (Milan, 1958); and Antonino Repaci, *La marcia su Roma* (Milan, 1972). Giulia Albanese has also written on "the March": *La marcia su Roma* (Rome, 2006). Dahlia S. Elazar has written a specialized work on fascism from 1919 to 1922: *The Making of Fascism* (Westport, 2001). David D. Roberts tries to put totalitarianism into context in his *The Totalitarian Experiment in Twentieth-Century Europe* (London, 2006). Roberts has also tried to link twentieth-century ideas, politics, and fascism in his *Historicism and Fascism in Modern Italy* (Toronto, 2007).

Although biographies of Mussolini are listed in the bibliography for the next chapter, a useful brief biography may be mentioned here: Anthony Cardoza, *Benito Mussolini: The First Fascist* (New York, 2006). For the early Mussolini, see Paul O'Brien, *Mussolini in the First World War: The Soldier, the Journalist, the Fascist* (New York, 2005). For the evolution of Italian Fascist ideology, there is Emilio Gentile's *The Origins of Fascist Ideology, 1918–1925* (New York, 2005). Alberto De Bernardi has posed fascism as a "modern dictatorship," a problem that requires more exploration than generally has been the case: *Una dittatura moderna: il fascismo come problema storico* (Milan, 2001). Another interesting question is the relationship between futurism and fascism, examined by Valerio Zecchini, *Futurismo e fascismo: manifesti e programmi* (Bologna, 2000). On the relationships among futurism, nationalism, and fascism, see Emilio Gentile, *The Struggle for Modernity* (Westport, 2003). More about the Fascist "left," mentioned in this chapter, can be gleaned from Giuseppe Parlato, *La sinistra fascista: un progetto mancato* (Bologna, 2000).

CHAPTER 16: MUSSOLINI'S ITALY

Whoever treads into the field of Italian Fascist history will find a bewildering array of literature on practically every aspect of the *ventennio*, most of it emotionally charged and viewed from different angles that generally depend on the political viewpoint of the author.

Books written on fascism during Mussolini's regime in Italy or outside must generally be approached with caution, since many of them were justifications of the regime. The best of them, however, are still useful and also give an idea of how fascism justified itself. For example, the book of a reputable historian, Giaocchino Volpe, *L'Italia in cammino* (Milan, 1927), argues that important developments of Giolittian Italy had a positive outcome in fascism. Anti-Mussolini literature must also be used with caution because it gives an opposite viewpoint, although here as well the best can be used profitably to understand the views of Mussolini's enemies. An example is Gaudens Megaro's critical biography, *Mussolini in the Making* (Boston, 1938), which sought to rebut Mussolini's apologists. A notable exception to the more polemical literature, despite his opposition to Mussolini and his feisty style, are the books of Gaetano Salvemini, now collected in his general works that have been previously cited. His best works in English are *The Fascist Dictatorship in Italy* (New York, 1967) and *Under the Axe of Fascism* (New York, 1936). Other early treatments of the Fascist phenomenon that still have value include Herbert W. Schneider, *Making the Fascist State* (New York, 1968); Herman Finer, *Mussolini's Italy* (New York, 1965); Carl T. Schmidt, *Italy Under Fascism* (New York, 1939) and *The Plough and the Sword* (New York, 1938); William G. Welk, *Fascist Economic Policy* (Cambridge, Mass., 1938); and Frances Keene, ed., *Neither Liberty nor Bread* (Port Washington, 1940).

Bibliographical articles include Emiliana Noether, "Italy Reviews Its Fascist Past," *American Historical Review* 51 (July 1956): 877–899; Charles Delzell, "Italian Historical Scholarship: A Decade of Recovery and Development," *Journal of Modern History* 29 (December 1956), 374–388; "Benito Mussolini: A Guide to the Bibliographical Literature," *Journal of Modern History* 35 (December 1963); and "Mussolini's Italy Twenty Years After," *Journal of Modern History* 38 (March 1966): 53–58. Marxist interpretations of fascism may be found in John Cammett, "Communist Theories of Fascism, 1920–1935," *Science and Society* 31 (Spring 1967): 149–163. Charles S. Maier's "Some Recent Studies of Fascism," *Journal of Modern History* 48 (September 1976): 506–521, examines a number of historians writing about Italian and German fascism.

To get an idea of the specific events of this period, consulting a general history is recommended. These range from multivolume works to short books. The best in each of these categories are: Luigi Salvatorelli and Giovanni Mira, *Storia d'Italia nel periodo fascista* (Turin, 1964), an unusually complete and balanced treatment; Danilo Veneruso, *L'Italia fascista (1922–1945)* (Bologna, 1981), vol. 5 in the author's history of Italy from unity to the Republic, is less detailed but still very useful. In the short category, there are: Alexander De Grand, *Italian Fascism* (Lincoln and London, 1989), noted for its clarity of organization and its theory of "hyphenated fascisms"; Alan Cassels, *Fascist Italy* (Arlington Heights, 1985); Elizabeth Wiskemann, *Fascism in Italy: Its Development and Influence* (New York, 1969); and S. William Halperin, *Mussolini and Italian Fascism* (New York, 1964). Introductory works also include John Whittam's *Fascist Italy* (New York, 1995) and Martin Blinkhorn's *Mussolini and Fascist Italy*

(London, 1994). Philip Morgan's *Italian Fascism, 1915–1945* (New York, 2004) and Martin Blinkhorn's *Mussolini and Fascist Italy* (New York, 2006) are good general histories. Emilio Gentile, *Fascismo: storia e interpretazione* (Rome, 2002), has made a major contribution to the interpretation of fascism by demonstrating that the Fascists were serious about their ideas and in their attempt to implement them. To keep all the characters straight, it might be handy to have a copy of Philip V. Cannistraro, ed., *Historical Dictionary of Fascist Italy* (Westport, 1982), mentioned at the beginning of this essay. *The Dictionary of Modern Italian History* (Westport, 1985), edited by Frank J. Coppa, picks up some people not mentioned in the previous reference work and is useful for important actors of the entire period covered in this book.

Documentary collections include the fundamental collection of Mussolini's speeches and writings, edited by Edoardo and Duilio Susmel, *Opera omnia di Benito Mussolini*, 36 vols. (Florence, 1961). In English, an idea of the Fascist "mystique" may be gleaned from Adrian Lyttelton, ed., *Italian Fascisms from Pareto to Gentile* (New York, 1973), which has a good introduction by the editor. Important documents are published in Benito Mussolini, *Fascism: Doctrine and Institutions* (New York, 1968). Interviews that had a major impact during the Fascist period are collected in Emil Ludwig, *Talks with Mussolini* (Boston, 1933). Charles F. Delzell has edited *Mediterranean Fascism, 1919–1945* (New York, 1970), which has many difficult-to-find documents on Italy. A good collection of translated articles reflecting some of the best Italian scholarship on fascism is Roland Sarti, ed., *The Ax Within: Italian Fascism in Action* (New York, 1974), while A. William Salomone's *Italy from the Risorgimento to Fascism* (New York, 1970) tackles the question of origins. Domenico Settembrini's excellent book deserves greater notice; he argues for the kinship between fascism and communism in *Fascismo controrivoluzione imperfetta* (Florence, 1978).

Biographies are a fundamental part of modern scholarship on fascism, especially those of Mussolini. The most important work here is Renzo De Felice's massive, multivolume *Mussolini* (Turin, 1966–1993). De Felice considers Mussolini in the context of his times, trying to give him a fair hearing and going into minute detail to explain his actions. Not surprisingly, this method has raised controversial issues and numerous debates. De Felice argues, for example, that fascism was forward-looking, but that Nazism was quite different and backward-looking. De Felice also distinguishes between the positive effects of fascism as a movement and its negative effects as a regime and maintains that Mussolini's policies achieved "consensus" in the Italy of the 1930s. Some scholars, particularly of the Left, have accused De Felice of whitewashing the Duce, but De Felice held his own and, despite the controversies he generated, renewed the discourse on interpreting fascism. The last, incomplete, volume of De Felice's biography appeared posthumously: *Mussolini l'alleato: III: la guerra civile* (Turin, 1997). The controversy that might have greeted this book was instead focused on a long interview by De Felice that preceded it in which the author maintained that the Resistance had much more limited popular support than the Left maintained and that Mussolini was killed on orders from Winston Churchill. The interview was published as Pasquale Chessa, ed., *Rosso e nero* (Milan, 1995). The debate's parameters may be found in the Italian press, but De Felice puts them into sharp relief in his *Intervista sul fascismo* (Bari, 1975), edited by Michael A. Ledeen (published in an English translation, *Fascism: An Informal Introduction to Its Theory and Practice* (New Brunswick, 1976). Ledeen has also written an article on De Felice's views, "Renzo De Felice and the Controversy over Italian Fascism," *Journal of Contemporary History* 11 (October 1976): 269–282. Other assessments in English of De Felice's work are Borden W. Painter Jr., "Renzo De Felice and the Historiography of Italian Fascism," *American Historical Review* 95, no. 2 (April 1990): 391–405, and a sympathetic study of his influence by Emilio Gentile, "Fascism in Italian Historiography: In Search of an Individual Historical Identity," *Journal of Contemporary History* 21 (1986): 179–208. Gentile has also written *Renzo De Felice: lo storico e il personaggio* (Rome, 2003). A special issue of the *Italian Quarterly*, edited by Spencer M. Di Scala, was devoted to "Renzo De Felice and the Problem of Italian Fascism"(nos. 141–142, Summer–Fall 1999). Views of Mussolini and fascism that can be contrasted to those of De Felice have been written by R. J. B. Bosworth in *Mussolini* (London, 2002) and *Mussolini's Italy: Life Under the Dictatorship, 1915–1945* (New York, 2006). See also Martin Clark's biography, *Mussolini* (New York, 2005).

For a neutral, although not sympathetic, view of Mussolini, see Gaspare Giudice's *Benito Mussolini* (Turin, 1971). A sympathetic biography instead is Giorgio Pini and Duilio Susmel, *Mussolini: l'uomo e l'opera*, 4 vols. (Florence, 1963). In English, Denis Mack Smith's *Mussolini* (New York, 1982) adopts a very negative and critical attitude, making him De Felice's counterpoint. Ivone Kirkpatrick's *Mussolini: A Study in Power* (New York, 1964) still stands out as a notable work. Paolo Monelli, *Mussolini: The Intimate Life of a Demagogue* (New York, 1954), is well worth reading for its insights into Mussolini's personality. Mussolini's widow has provided interesting glimpses of family life in Rachele Mussolini, *Mussolini: An Intimate Biography* (New York, 1977). Laura Fermi's *Mussolini* (Chicago, 1961) is readable but of little scholarly value. Other biographies that might be consulted are Christopher Hibbert, *Il Duce* (Boston, 1962); Richard Collier, *Duce!* (London, 1971); and Richard Lyttle, *Il Duce* (New York, 1987). R. J. B. Bosworth has published the previously-mentioned biography, *Mussolini*, and an interpretative essay, *The Italian Dictatorship: Problems and Perspectives in the Interpretation of Mussolini* (New York, 1998). Nicholas Farrell, *Mussolini: A New Life* (London, 2003), is a revisionist biography.

In addition to Mussolini, see biographies of the hierarchs, especially Claudio Segrè, *Italo Balbo: A Fascist Life* (Berkeley, 1987). Paolo Nello's two-volume biography—*Dino Grandi: la formazione di un leader fascista* (Bologna, 1987) and *Un fedele disubbidiente: Dino Grandi da Palazzo Chigi al 25 luglio* (Bologna, 1993)—discusses the career of one of the most important Fascist leaders and his impact on Italy's foreign policy. A full-fledged biography of the "philosopher" of fascism emphasizes the complexity of his subject: Gabriele Turi, *Giovanni Gentile* (Florence, 1995). On intellectuals and their association with the regime, A. James Gregor has considered some little-studied personages in English: *Mussolini's Intellectuals: Fascist Political and Social Thought* (Princeton, 2005). Philip V. Cannistraro and Brian Sullivan's *Il Duce's Other Woman* (New York,

1993) is a work on Margherita Sarfatti that also provides an excellent view of the milieu in which Mussolini was formed and of the cultural politics of fascism. On the same topic, see Marla Susan Stone, *The Patron State: Culture and Politics in Fascist Italy* (Princeton, 1998). Stone rightly argues that no simple formula defines culture during this period, which was instead marked by diversity and contradiction. Sarfatti authored a hagiographic biography of Mussolini, *The Life of Benito Mussolini* (New York, 1925). See as well Emily Braun's *Mario Sironi and Italian Modernism: Art and Politics Under Fascism* (Cambridge, U.K., 2000). An important intellectual's role is considered by Fabio Fernando Rizi, *Benedetto Croce and Italian Fascism* (Toronto, 2003). On Bottai, see the interesting review of his ideas by Alexander De Grand, *Bottai e la cultura fascista* (Bari, 1978). Another author, Giordano Bruno Guerri, *Giuseppe Bottai: un fascista critico* (Milan, 1976), argues that Bottai was the only Fascist who had an organic view of the hypothetical state that fascism wished to construct. See also Bottai's own *Venti anni e un giorno* (Milan, 1949) and *Diario* (Milan, 1988). For another hierarch, see Harry Fornari, *Mussolini's Gadfly: Roberto Farinacci* (Nashville, 1971).

On the consolidation of the regime, the most noted work in English is Adrian Lyttleton, *The Seizure of Power* (New York, 2004). In Italian, Giuseppe Rossini, *Il delitto Matteotti tra il Viminale e l'Aventino* (Bologna, 1966), and Ariane Landuyt, *Le sinistre e l'Aventino* (Milan, 1973), confront the same theme. Doug Thompson, *State Control in Fascist Italy: Culture and Conformity, 1925–1943* (Manchester, 1991), discusses the transition from violent coercion during the early phase of fascism to nonviolent control of the country through legislation, mass organizations, and propaganda. On the organization of the Fascist state, the best work is Alberto Aquarone, *L'organizzazione dello stato totalitario*, 2 vols. (Turin, 1965).

On the papacy and the Catholics during this period, see Francesco Margiotta Broglio, *Italia e Santa Sede dalla grande guerra alla conciliazione* (Bari, 1966), and, most important, Gabriele De Rosa, *Il partito popolare italiano*, vol. 2 of *Storia del movimento cattolico in Italia* (Bari, 1966). In English, there are P. Kent, *The Pope and the Duce: The International Impact of the Lateran Agreements* (London, 1981), and J. F. Pollard, *The Vatican and Italian Fascism, 1929–1932* (Cambridge, U.K., 1985). Richard Webster's *The Cross and the Fasces* (Stanford, 1960) discusses Christian democracy's relations with fascism. The regime's suppression of the Catholic missionary organization Opera Bonomelli is discussed in Philip V. Cannistraro and Gianfausto Rosoli, *Emigrazione, chiesa e fascismo: lo scioglimento dell' Opera Bonomelli (1922–1928)* (Rome, 1979). The reaction of big business to fascism is discussed in some of the general works cited in this essay for the previous period. More specific works include Piero Melograni, *Gli industriali e Mussolini* (Milan, 1972), Roland Sarti, *Fascism and the Industrial Leadership in Italy, 1919–1940* (Berkeley, 1971), and Ernesto Rossi, *Padroni del vapore e fascismo* (Bari, 1966). On the army's attitude, see Giorgio Rochat, *L'esercito italiano da Vittorio Veneto a Mussolini 1919–1925* (Bari, 1967).

In addition to De Grand's general treatment, previously cited, the leftist parties during this period are covered in detail by Ariane Landuyt, *Le sinistre e l'Aventino,* already cited, Giovanni Sabbatucci, *I socialisti nella crisi dello Stato liberale (1918–1926),* vol. 3 of the general history of Italian socialism previously cited; Paolo Spriano, *Storia del partito comunista*, vol. 1, previously cited; Vittorio Vidotto, *Il Partito Comunista Italiano dalle origini al 1946* (Bologna, 1975), who publishes important documents relating to the PCI; Palmiro Togliatti, *La formazione del gruppo dirigente del Partito Comunista Italiano*, cited; and Giorgio Amendola, *Storia del Partito Comunista Italiano, 1921–1943* (Rome, 1978). Alexander De Grand has also published a book on Angelo Tasca, *In Stalin's Shadow*, previously cited. See Giuseppe Fiori's biography of the PCI founder, *Antonio Gramsci: Life of a Revolutionary* (New York, 1971). Simona Colarizi has examined the more moderate democrats in *I democratici all'opposizione: Giovanni Amendola e l'unione nazionale, 1922–1926* (Bologna, 1973). Continued opposition to fascism is discussed by Emilio Gentile, *Fascismo e antifascismo: i partiti italiani fra le due guerre* (Florence, 2000); Jean McClure Mudge examines opposition to Mussolini in Italy and the United States in *The Poet and the Dictator: Lauro de Bosis Resists Fascism in Italy and America* (Westport, 2002). The life of Carlo Rosselli, killed by Mussolini's henchmen in France, is analyzed by Stanislao G. Pugliese, *Carlo Rosselli: Socialist Heretic and Antifascist Exile* (Cambridge, Mass., 2000). For the influence of the Rosselli brothers, see Lauro Rossi, *Politica, valori, idealità: Carlo e Nello Rosselli: maestri dell'Italia civile* (Rome, 2003). On the issue of censorship, see Guido Bonsaver, *Censorship and Literature in Fascist Italy* (Toronto, 2007), and George Talbot, *Censorship in Fascist Italy* (New York, 2007).

On Fascist economic policies and their results, see Giuseppe Toniolo, ed., *Lo sviluppo economico italiano 1861–1940* (Bari, 1973); Giorgio Mori, *Il capitalismo industriale in Italia* (Rome, 1977); and Ernesto Cianci, *Nascita dello Stato imprenditoriale in Italia* (Milan, 1977). Marco Maraffi, *Politica ed economia in Italia: la vicenda dell'impresa pubblica dagli anni trenta agli anni cinquanta* (Bologna, 1990), takes the story of Italy's public firms from the 1930s to the 1950s. Giampiero Carocci's short *Italian Fascism* (Harmondsworth, 1974) is at its most interesting on economic affairs. Federico Caprotti has written on the land reclamation projects and the cities built during the regime; his book, *Internal Colonialism in Italy, 1930–1939* (Youngstown, 2007), is at its strongest when discussing technical issues. Borden Painter has examined Fascist urban policies in Rome in *Mussolini's Rome: Rebuilding the Eternal City* (New York, 2005), and Emilio Gentile has looked at the monuments that fascism left behind in *Fascismo di pietra* (Rome, 2007). On the Corporate State, see the articles collected by Luigi Lojacono, *Le corporazioni fasciste* (Milan, 1935), and the works of Alfredo Rocco, *Scritti e discorsi politici*, 3 vols. (Milan, 1938). A good examination of Rocco is Paolo Ungari, *Alfredo Rocco e l'ideologia giuridica del fascismo* (Brescia, 1963). On Fascist attempts to mobilize the masses, see the fundamental work by Philip V. Cannistraro, *La fabbrica del consenso: fascismo e mass media* (Bari, 1975), and Victoria De Grazia, *The Culture of Consent* (New York, 1981). A discussion of how the youth was mobilized is in Tracy Koon, *Believe, Obey, Fight: Political Socialization of Youth in Fascist Italy, 1922–1943* (Chapel Hill, 1985). Philip V. Cannistraro, "The Radio in Fascist Italy," *Journal of European Studies* 2, no. 2 (June 1972): 127–154, and "Mussolini's Cultural Revolution," *Journal of Contemporary History* 7, nos. 3–4 (July–October

1972): 115–139, analyze the themes and goals of Fascist cultural policy. Edward Tannenbaum's book *The Fascist Experience* (New York, 1972) delves deeply into popular culture. On a related theme, see Luisa Passerini, *Fascism in Popular Memory: The Cultural Experience of the Turin Working Class* (Cambridge, U.K., 1987). Ruggero Zangrandi, *Il lungo viaggio attraverso il fascismo* (Milan, 1972), gives a good idea of what it was like to live under fascism. Mussolini's attempt to eradicate the Mafia is studied by Christopher Duggan, *Fascism and the Mafia* (New Haven, 1989). Fascism's appeal to youth is discussed in Michael Ledeen, *Universal Fascism* (New York, 1972). Renzo De Felice, *Intelletuali di fronte al fascismo* (Rome, 1985), details how some prominent intellectuals reacted to fascism. Cultural aspects are examined by Edwin P. Hoyt, *Making the Fascist Self: The Political Culture of Interwar Italy* (Ithaca, 1997). Alexander De Grand has written on "Women Under Italian Fascism," *Historical Journal* 19 (1976): 647–688, while Victoria De Grazia has published a more ample treatment, *How Fascism Ruled Women* (Berkeley, 1992). Gigliola Gori has written *Italian Fascism and the Female Body: Sport, Submissive Women, and Strong Mothers* (New York, 2004). See also Eugenia Paulicelli, *Fashion Under Fascism* (New York, 2004). Perry R. Willson, *The Clockwork Factory: Women and Work in Fascist Italy* (New York, 1994), traces women's work experience in a specific setting. Michela De Giorgio, *Le italiane dall'unità a oggi: modelli culturali e comportamenti sociali* (Rome, 1993), is an overview of Italian women but concentrates on the liberal and Fascist periods. Perry Willson has examined *Peasant Women and Politics in Fascist Italy* (London, 2002). David G. Horn, *Social Bodies: Science, Reproduction, and Italian Modernity* (Princeton, 1994), is an analysis of Fascist demographic policy. See also Elizabeth Dixon Whitaker, *Measuring Mamma's Milk* (Ann Arbor, 2000). Ruth Ben Ghiat has written *Fascist Modernities: Italy 1922–1945* (Berkeley, 2001). Edward Tannenbaum's article on education in Tannenbaum and Noether, eds., *Modern Italy*, pp. 231–253, treats education in general but gives a good synopsis of the Fascist period. Science during this period has been reviewed by Roberto Maiocchi in *Scienza italiana e razzismo fascista* (Florence, 1999), *Gli scienziati del Duce* (Milan, 2003), and *Scienza e fascismo* (Rome, 2004). The specific case of Fermi and his group has been examined by Spencer M. Di Scala, "Science and Fascism: The Case of Enrico Fermi," *Totalitarian Movements and Political Religions* 6, no. 2 (September 2005): 199–211.

On other aspects of popular culture, Mino Argentieri has written on the newsreels, *L'occhio del regime* (Florence, 1979), and Alberto Monticone has studied the radio during the period, *Il fascismo al microfono* (Rome, 1978). Gianni Isola, *Abbassa la tua radio: storia dell'ascolto radiofontico nell'Italia fascista* (Florence, 1990), examines the impact of radio on the Italians during the Fascist era. On film during this period, consult Gian Piero Brunetti, *Cinema italiano tra le due guerre: fascismo e politica cinematografica* (Milan, 1975), and, in English, Marcia Landy argues that the postwar cinema had its origins in the Fascist era in her *Fascism on Film* (Princeton, 1986). James Hay, *Popular Film Culture in Fascist Italy* (Bloomington, 1987), also sees a "verist" culture in the filmmaking of the 1930s. See also Jacqueline Reich and Piero Garofalo, eds., *(Re)viewing Fascism: Fascism and Film* (Bloomington, 2002).

On the PNF, the only full-length study in English, Dante Germino's *The Italian Fascist Party in Power* (Minneapolis, 1959), emphasizes the "social" aspect of the party but is outdated; Emilio Gentile has published *Storia del Partito Fascista 1919–1922* (Rome and Bari, 1989). How the party was organized and how it functioned in practice is the subject of Ricciotti Lazzero's *Il Partito Nazionale Fascista* (Milan, 1985).

Fascism's appeal in other countries may be seen in John Diggins, *Mussolini and Fascism: The View from America* (Princeton, 1972), and Alastair Hamilton, *The Appeal of Fascism* (London, 1971). Relations between the United States and Italy up to the Ethiopian War are examined by Claudia Damiani, *Mussolini e gli Stati Uniti 1922–1935* (Bologna, 1980). On England, see Claudia Badoli, *Exporting Fascism* (New York, 2003).

As might be expected, the interpretation of fascism has generated considerable heat. A general introduction to this subject is provided by Renzo De Felice, *Interpretations of Fascism* (Cambridge, Mass., 1977); see also his *Il fascismo: le interpretazioni dei contemporanei e degli storici* (Bari, 1970). Federico Chabod, one of Italy's major historians, emphasized the conditions and the state of mind that produced the Fascist victory in the previously cited *L'Italia contemporanea* (Turin, 1961). The idea of "modernization" has also been discussed as a contributor to fascism. See Roland Sarti, "Fascist Modernization in Italy: Traditional or Revolutionary?" *American Historical Review* 75 (April 1970): 1029–1045. Emilio Gentile, *Le origini dell'ideologia fascista* (Rome and Bari, 1975), has argued for a coherent ideological content to fascism, while Zeev Sternhell, with Mario Sznajder and Maia Asheri, *The Birth of Fascist Ideology: From Cultural Rebellion to Political Revolution* (Princeton, 1994), contend that fascism was grounded in European civilization and was a coherent ideological opponent of both Marxism and liberalism. Gentile has also written *The Sacralization of Politics in Fascist Italy* (Cambridge, Mass., 1996), a book examining the "religious" symbolism of fascism, and has contributed to the modernization debate with a collection of essays, *The Struggle for Modernity: Nationalism, Futurism, and Fascism* (Westport, 2003).

A controversial view on the subject of ideology that has generally not been well received but deserves consideration is developed by A. James Gregor, *The Ideology of Fascism* (New York, 1969), and *Italian Fascism and Developmental Dictatorship* (Princeton, 1979). A good book to read to become acquainted with the Marxist viewpoint is Palmiro Togliatti's *Lectures on Fascism* (New York, 1976). Marxist views have been challenged by Rosario Romeo, *Italia moderna fra storia e storiografia* (Bari, 1977), and *L'Italia unita e la prima guerra mondiale* (Bari, 1978). Gino Germani, *Authoritarianism, Fascism, and National Populism* (New Brunswick, 1975), views fascism as a form of modern authoritarianism, while Charles Maier, *Recasting Bourgeois Europe* (Princeton, 1975), sees similar patterns of interest group representation in several European countries. A balanced view of Fascist ideology is given by Pier Giorgio Zunino, *L'ideologia del fascismo* (Bologna, 1985). A good article on the historiography of fascism (along with interesting documents) may be found in "Mussolini and Italian Fascism," a special issue of the *Cesare Barbieri Courier* (Hartford, 1980).

On the Jews during the Fascist period, the major work is still the older Renzo De Felice, *Storia degli ebrei italiani sotto il fascismo*, 4th ed. (Turin, 1988). Michele Sarfatti,

Gli ebrei nell'Italia fascista: vicende, identità, persecuzione (Turin, 2000), takes a harder look. Other books on the same topic are the informative Enzo Collotti, *Il fascismo e gli ebrei* (Rome, 2003), which discusses the racial laws, and the collected essays in Camera dei Deputati, *La persecuzione delgi Ebrei durante il fascismo* (Rome, 1998). Mario Toscano's *Ebraismo e antisemitismo in Italia* (Milan, 2003) is a survey from 1848 to the Six-Day War. Stanislao G. Pugliese has edited *The Most Ancient of Minorities: The Jews of Italy* (Westport, 2002). For relations between the popes and the Jews, consult David I. Kertzer, *Popes Against the Jews* (New York, 2001). A different view is taken by Matteo L. Napolitano and Andrea Tornielli, *Il Papa che salvo' gli Ebrei* (Casale Monferrato, 2004). Meir Michaelis, *Mussolini and the Jews: German-Italian Relations and the Jewish Question in Italy* (Oxford, 1978), takes a harsher stand on Mussolini and the regime. A comparative view of Italian reaction to Nazi racial policies is offered in Ivo Herzer, ed., *The Italian Refuge* (Washington, D.C., 1989). Susan Zuccotti's *The Italians and the Holocaust* (New York, 1987) makes use of many interviews and concludes that the record was mixed. Alexander Stille, *Benevolence and Betrayal: Five Italian Jewish Families Under Fascism* (New York, 1991), successfully strives to provide a view of ordinary Jews during the Fascist period, including an examination of Jews who were an intimate part of the Fascist movement from the beginning. Daniel Carpi, *Between Mussolini and Hitler* (Hanover, 1994), details the unwillingness of Italian diplomats and soldiers to work with Vichy and Nazi plans to round up Jews for elimination. Covering a longer period is H. Stuart Hughes, *Prisoners of Hope: The Silver Age of the Italian Jews, 1924–1974* (Cambridge, Mass., 1983). On the question of racism in the colonies, the most interesting work is Luigi Preti, *I miti dell'impero e della razza nell'Italia degli anni '30* (Rome, 1965). The conjunction between the two is discussed in Gene Bernardini, "Origins and Development of Racial Antisemitism in Fascist Italy," *Journal of Modern History* 49 (September 1977): 431–453. Aaron Gilette believes that racial ideology had deeper roots than is generally acknowledged in his *Racial Theories in Fascist Italy* (New York, 2002). Maria Pichetto looks at the ideas of two anti-Semites, *Alle radici dell'odio: Preziosi e Benigni antisemiti* (Milan, 1983). Joshua D. Zimmerman's *Jews in Italy Under Fascist and Nazi Rule, 1922–1945* (New York, 2005) collects the thoughts of scholars on this topic. Wiley Feinstein, *The Civilization of the Holocaust in Italy* (Madison, 2003), considers roots.

A sampling of the views and actions of the Fascist opposition may be gleaned from the following: Istituto Socialista di studi storici, *L'emigrazione socialista nella lotta contro il fascismo (1926–1939)* (Florence, 1982); Gaetano Arfé, *Storia dell'Avanti! 1926–1940* (Milan, 1968); Stefano Merli, ed., "La ricostruzione del movimento socialista in Italia e la lotta contro il fascismo dal 1934 alla seconda guerra mondiale," *Annali Feltrinelli* 5 (1962); Giuseppe Tamburrano, *Pietro Nenni* (Bari, 1986); Aldo Garosci, *La vita di Carlo Rosselli* (Florence, 1977); Lelio Basso, ed., *Le riviste di Piero Gobetti* (Milan, 1961); Giovanni Spadolini, *Gobetti: Un'idea dell'Italia* (Milan, 1993), a collection of Spadolini's writings on this anti-Fascist martyr; Paolo Spriano, *Gli anni della clandestinità* (Turin, 1969), which is vol. 2 of his general history of the PCI; Pietro Secchia, "L'azione svolta dal partito comunista in Italia durante il fascismo, 1926–1932," *Annali Feltrinelli* 2 (1969); Aldo Garosci, *Storia dei fuorusciti* (Bari, 1958); Frank Rosengarten,

The Italian Antifascist Press (Cleveland, 1968); Santi Fedele, *Storia della concentrazione antifascista 1927–1934* (Milan, 1976); and Pier Giorgio Zunino, *La questione cattolica nella sinistra italiana (1919–1945)*, 2 vols. (Bologna, 1975–1977). Stanislao G. Pugliese has published a wide-ranging account, *Fascism, Anti-Fascism, and the Resistance in Italy, 1919 to the Present* (Lanham, 2004). Roger Griffen's *The Nature of Fascism* (New York, 1993) has a good discussion of generic fascism and its applications to Fascist studies.

CHAPTER 17: WORLD WAR II AND THE RESISTANCE

The fundamental documents on foreign policy in this era and in earlier years, *I documenti diplomatici italiani*, were published by the Ministry of Foreign Affairs (Rome, 1952–1953 and 1954–1965). Another essential source for this period are the diaries of Galeazzo Ciano, *Ciano's Diary, 1939–1943* (London, 1947), and *Ciano's Hidden Diaries, 1937–1938* (London, 1952).

Alan Cassels has written a good account in English on *Mussolini's Early Diplomacy* (Princeton, 1970) and has also edited *Italian Foreign Policy, 1918–1945: A Guide to Research and Research Materials* (Wilmington, 1991). Works in Italian that cover a similar period are Giorgio Rumi, *Alle origini della politica estera fascista 1918–1923* (Bari, 1968); Ennio Di Nolfo, *Mussolini e la politica estera italiana 1919–1933* (Padua, 1960); and Giampiero Carocci, *La politica estera dell'Italia fascista* (Bari, 1969). H. James Burgwyn has written the comprehensive *Italian Foreign Policy in the Interwar Period, 1918–1940* (Westport, 1997); Burgwyn argues that ideology did not drive Mussolini's foreign policy. Books that make the case for Mussolini's aggressiveness and willingness to engage in war include MacGregor Knox, *Mussolini Unleashed, 1939–1941: Politics and Strategy in Fascist Italy's Last War* (Cambridge, U.K., 1982) and *Common Destiny: Dictatorship, Foreign Policy, and War in Fascist Italy and Nazi Germany* (Cambridge, U.K., 2000). Knox has also published *Hitler's Italian Allies: Royal Armed Forces, Fascist Regime, and the War of 1940–1943* (New York, 2000). G. Bruce Strang, *On the Fiery March: Mussolini Prepares for War* (Westport, 2003), argues that an ultranationalist and social Darwinist mentality drove Mussolini to war. Robert Mallett, *Mussolini and the Origins of the Second World War, 1933–1940* (London, 2003), argues that the Duce consciously took advantage of Hitler's rise and the instability it caused for expansionist ends.

Several older accounts of Fascist foreign policy are still solid and very important: Gaetano Salvemini, *Prelude to World War II* (New York, 1954); Elizabeth Wiskemann, *The Rome-Berlin Axis* (London, 1969); Mario Toscano, *The Origins of the Pact of Steel* (Baltimore, 1967); and Maxwell H. H. Macartney and Paul Cremona, *Italy's Foreign and Colonial Policy, 1914–1937* (London, 1938). Denis Mack Smith's *Mussolini's Roman Empire* (New York, 1976) labels Mussolini's foreign policy as senseless. There are two good essays on this period in Gordon Craig and Felix Gilbert, eds., *The Diplomats* (Princeton, 1953). A comprehensive and balanced work on the subject is Rosaria

Quartararo's *Roma tra Londra e Berlino: politica estera fascista dal 1930 al 1940* (Rome, 1980). Richard Lamb has examined Mussolini's attempt to make Italy a world player in *Mussolini as a Diplomat: Il Duce's Italy on the World Stage* (New York, 1999), and written on the Duce's relationship with the British in *Mussolini and the British* (London, 1997).

On specialized diplomatic topics, there is an interesting book on Mussolini's attempt to bring Germany back into a "normal" relationship with the other powers, Konrad Jarausch, *The Four Power Pact* (Madison, 1965). William I. Shorrock's *From Ally to Enemy: The Enigma of Fascist Italy in French Diplomacy* (Kent, 1988), while good on France, is less satisfactory on Italy. Angelo Del Boca, *Gli italiani in Africa orientale* (Bari, 1979), provides a comprehensive discussion of the Italians in East Africa. Claudio Segrè discusses Libya during this period in *Fourth Shore: The Italian Colonization of Libya* (Chicago, 1975). Robert L. Hess discusses *Italian Colonialism in Somalia* (Chicago, 1966). Many works have been written on the Ethiopian venture, but readers must remain aware of pro- or anti-Mussolini bias, especially in older books. The best book in English is George Baer, *The Coming of the Italian-Ethiopian War* (Cambridge, Mass., 1967); another account is Frank Hardie, *The Abyssinian Crisis* (London, 1974); see also the older work by Geoffrey Garratt, *Mussolini's Roman Empire* (New York, 1938). Franklin D. Laurens discusses the French position in *France and the Italo-Ethiopian Crisis, 1935–1936* (The Hague, 1968). On Italian colonial policies in Ethiopia, consult Haile M. Larebo, *Italian Land Policy in Ethiopia, 1935–1941* (New York, 1994), and Alberto Sbacchi, *Ethiopia Under Mussolini: Fascism and the Colonial Experience* (London, 1989). Larebo's study is interesting because he believes that Italy, at great expense, bequeathed Ethiopia the basis of a modern infrastructure. On the military and political preparations for the campaign, the most useful works are Giorgio Rochat, *Militari e politici nella preparazione della campagna d'Etiopia* (Milan, 1961), and A. J. Barker, *The Civilizing Mission* (London, 1968). For contemporary first-person accounts of the war, there are Emilio De Bono, *La conquista dell'impero* (Rome, 1937); Pietro Badoglio, *La guerra d'Etiopia* (Milan, 1936); Rodolfo Graziani, *Il fronte sud* (Milan, 1938); and Quirino Armellini, *Con Badoglio in Etiopia* (Milan, 1937). Some wider implications of the Ethiopian War are discussed by George Baer, *Test Case: Italy, Ethiopia, and the League of Nations* (Stanford, 1976), and Esmonde Robertson, *Mussolini as Empire-Builder* (London, 1977), discusses the European situation.

On Italian intervention in the Spanish Civil War, John Coverdale, *Italian Intervention in the Spanish Civil War* (Princeton, 1975), is a good account in English that tends to debunk some of the myths in American academic circles about the supposed ineffectiveness of the effort. A good Italian work on the same theme is G. Ranzato, *Rivoluzione e guerra civile in Spagna 1931–1939* (Turin, 1975). Mediterranean issues and the outbreak of the war are discussed by Reynolds M. Salerno, *Vital Crossroads: Mediterranean Origins of the Second World War, 1935–1940* (Ithaca, 2002).

For the best discussion of the state of the Italian armed forces on the eve of Italy's entrance into World War II, see Lucio Ceva, "Le forze armate," in *Storia della società italiana dall'unità a oggi* (Turin, 1981). The army's historical office has also published an "official" history, Ufficio storico dello stato maggiore dell'esercito, *La politica militare italiana tra la 1a e la 2a guerra mondiale* (Rome, 1954); see also Emilio Canevari, *La guerra italiana: retroscena della disfatta*, 2 vols. (Rome, 1948), and L. Mazzetti, *La politica militare italiana tra le due guerre mondiali* (Salerno, 1974). John Joseph Timothy Sweet has written on the mechanization of the Italian army and why it did not work; briefly, the Italians understood the intellectual aspects of modern tank warfare and established mechanized forces, but the society could not sustain the forces. The book is a commentary not only on mechanization but on why the army did poorly: *Iron Arm: The Mechanization of Mussolini's Army, 1920–1940* (Mechanicsburg, 2007). On the navy, see Ufficio storico della marina, *La marina italiana nella seconda guerra mondiale* (Rome, 1972); on the air force, consult G. Santoro, *L'aeronautica nella seconda guerra mondiale*, 2 vols. (Rome, 1957). James J. Sadovich, *The Italian Navy in World War II* (Westport, 1994), is a revisionist view arguing that, given the lack of material resources, the navy did not do too badly in the conflict. See also Jack Greene et al., *Mare Nostrum: The War in the Mediterranean: Being a Study on the Aspects of the Italian Navy and Air Forces with Comments on the German and Allied War Contribution in the Mediterranean and North African Fighting in World War II* (Watsonville, 1990). For an understanding of the role that industrial production had in losing the war, there is Carlo Favagrossa, *Perchè perdemmo la guerra: Mussolini e la produzione bellica* (Milan, 1946).

On the war operations themselves, there exists a host of memoirs written by the main characters on particular episodes or areas; except for Pietro Badoglio, whose views are, for good or ill, fundamental, *Italy in the Second World War* (London, 1948), the accounts are too numerous to mention here. Good scholarly accounts of the general war effort are given by Giorgio Bocca, *Storia d'Italia nella guerra fascista 1940–1943* (Bari, 1969), Emilio Faldella, *L'Italia nella seconda guerra mondiale: revisioni di giudizi* (Bologna, 1959), and Lucio Ceva, *La condotta italiana della guerra* (Milan, 1975); Ceva has also written a general history, *Storia delle forze armate in Italia* (Turin, 1999), as has Piero Melograni, *La guerra degli italiani 1940–1945* (Novara, 2006). Nino Arena has published a book that seeks to understand the technical reasons for Italy's defeat: *L'Italia in guerra: retroscena tecnico della disfatta* (Parma, 1997). Alberto Aquarone has written an article demonstrating how unpopular Italian intervention in the war was in the country, "Lo spirito pubblico in Italia alla vigilia della seconda guerra mondiale," *Nord e Sud* 11 (January 1964): 117–125. Philip S. Jowett concentrates on the army itself in *The Italian Army, 1940–1945* (Oxford, 2000–2001). Davide Rodogno has concentrated on Italy's occupation areas in *Fascism's European Empire* (Cambridge, U.K., 2006), and James Burgwyn has written *Empire of the Adriatic: Mussolini's Conquest of Yugoslavia, 1941–1943* (New York, 2005). Philip Morgan has reconsidered the Italian war effort in *The Fall of Mussolini: Italy, the Italians, and the Second World War* (New York, 2007). For the armed forces of the Salò Republic, consult Pier Paolo Battistelli and Andrea Molinari, *Le forze armate della RSI* (Bresso, 2007); for their role on the Allied side, see Giuliano Manzari, *La partecipazione delle forze armate alla guerra di liberazione e di Resistenza* (Rome, 2003).

During World War II, the Italian armed forces and diplomats distinguished themselves by refusing demands by their German allies and satellite states to hand over the Jews in their occupation areas for extermination. They were the only officials of an Axis country to save *foreign* Jews on a large scale. See in this regard Jonathan Steinberg, *All or Nothing: The Axis and the Holocaust 1941–1943* (London, 1990), and Leon Poliakov and Jacques Sabille, *Jews Under the Italian Occupation* (Paris, 1955), which also supplies important documentation. There is also the remarkable story of a private Italian citizen in Budapest who masqueraded as the Spanish consul and saved many Hungarian Jews; see Enrico Deaglio, *La banalità del bene: storia di Giorgio Perlasca*, 12th ed. (Milan, 2002). Although Susan Zuccotti's *Under His Very Windows* (New Haven, 2000) is concerned primarily with the Vatican and its policies toward the Holocaust, the book has an Italian dimension.

The last phases of the Fascist regime, the March 1943 strikes, have been examined by Roberto Finzi, *L'unità operaia contro il fascismo: gli scioperi del marzo '43* (Bologna, 1974). Gianfranco Bianchi's *Perchè e come cadde il fascismo* (Milan, 1982) is a detailed account of the preparations for Mussolini's overthrow on July 25, 1943. There are firsthand accounts of the Duce's fall, including Mussolini's *The Fall of Mussolini* (Westport, 1975), and Dino Grandi, *25 luglio: quarant'anni dopo* (Bologna, 1983). In 1994, debate raged on documents purporting to be Mussolini's secret diaries, but the jury is still out on their authenticity. Fundamental for an understanding of the relationship between Mussolini and Hitler and of the Salò Republic during this period is F. W. Deakin, *The Brutal Friendship: Mussolini, Hitler, and the Fall of Italian Fascism* (London, 1962), and Dino Alfieri, *Dictators Face to Face* (New York, 1955), while Giorgio Bocca's *La repubblica di Mussolini* (Bari, 1977) is also an excellent account. See also Ray Moseley, *Mussolini: The Last 600 Days of il Duce* (Dallas, 2004). On the breakup of the Axis, see Friedrich-Karl von Plehwe, *The End of an Alliance: Rome's Defection from the Axis in 1943* (London and New York, 1971). On the German reaction, see Gerhard Schreiber, *La vendetta tedesca, 1943–1945: le rappresaglie naziste in Italia* (Milan, 2000). G. Mayda discusses the persecution of Jews under Salò in *Ebrei sotto Salò* (Milan, 1978). There has been increasing interest in the role of women in the Salò Republic; see Ulderico Munzi, *Donne di Salò* (Milan, 1999). On the period between fascism's fall and the armistice, good accounts include Melton Davis, *Who Defends Rome?* (New York, 1972); Ruggero Zangrandi, *1943: 25 luglio–8 settembre* (Milan, 1964); Mario Toscano, *Dal 25 luglio all'8 settembre* (Florence, 1966); Peter Tomkins, *Italy Betrayed* (New York, 1966); and Robert Katz, *The Battle for Rome* (New York, 2003). Silvio Bertoldi's *La guerra parallela: 8 settembre 1943–25 aprile 1945: le voci delle due Italie a confronto* (Milan, 1966) is an illuminating collection of testimony by Resistance and RSI officials. The RSI's military predicament is analyzed by Nino Arena, *RSI: forze armate della Repubblica sociale italiana: la guerra in Italia 1943* (Parma, 1999), and Silvio Bertoldi, *Soldati a Salò: l'ultimo esercito di Mussolini* (Milan, 1995). For the debate on Salò after the war, consult Giosè Rimanelli, *Discorso con l'altro: Salò, la guerra civile e l'Italia del dopoguerra* (Milan, 2000). D. Ellwood's *Italy, 1943–1945* (Leicester, 1985) is a good secondary source on the same period. On the debate over the armistice and its results, see Carlo Pinzani, "L'8 settembre: elementi di ipotesi per un giudizio storico," *Studi Storici* 13, no. 2 (April–June 1972): 289–337, and Elena Agarossi, *A Nation Collapses: The Italian Surrender of September 1943* (Cambridge, U.K., 2000), the English translation of the book originally published in 1985. An account of the Italian "co-belligerency" period when the South cooperated with the Allies is Aldo Alessandro Mola, *La Cobelligeranza italiana nella lotta di liberazione dell'Europa: atti del convegno internazionale* (Milano, 1984; Rome, 1986). An excellent account of Mussolini's end is given by two protagonists, Pier Luigi delle Stelle (Pedro) and Urbano Lazzaro (Bill), *Dongo: la fine di Mussolini* (Milan, 1962). The person actually responsible for killing Mussolini, Walter Audisio, has published *In nome del popolo italiano* (Milan, 1975).

The best book in English on the Resistance remains Charles Delzell's *Mussolini's Enemies* (New York, 1974), a complete work that also covers the early opposition. See also Maria Wilhelm, *The Other Italy: Italian Resistance in World War II* (New York, 1988). Patrick Gallo's *For Love and Country* (Lanham, 2003) is a general work. Gallo has also written *Enemies: Mussolini and the Anti-Fascists* (n.p., 2002), which covers the period before the war. On the role of women, consult Jane Slaughter, *Women in the Italian Resistance* (Denver, 1997), and Daniella Gagliani, *Donne, guerra, politica* (Bologna, 2000), on the experience and memory of Italian women. Marina Addis Saba has chosen an interesting topic in her *La scelta: ragazze partigiane, ragazze di Salò* (Rome, 2005). Besides the works mentioned in chapter 16, which carry over into the time period discussed in this chapter, see Frank Rosengarten, *Silvio Trentin dall'interventismo alla Resistenza* (Milan, 1980). Accounts of the Resistance abound, but the classic account of the movement in all its aspects is Roberto Battaglia's *Storia della Resistenza italiana, 8 settembre 1943–25 aprile 1945* (Turin, 1964). Claudio Pavone's *Una guerra civile* (Milan, 1992) is a breakthrough work on the Resistance because it introduces the concept of the Resistance as a civil war in addition to its character as a war of liberation and a class conflict. See also, in this regard, Cesare Bermani, *Il nemico interno: guerra civile e lotta di classe in Italia: 1943–1976* (Rome, 1997), and Nuto Revelli and Michele Calandri, *Le due guerre: guerra fascista e guerra partigiana* (Turin, 2003). Giorgio Bocca's *Storia dell'Italia partigiana* (Bari, 1977) is also excellent, while a good brief overview in English may be attained in Guido Quazza, "The Politics of the Italian Resistance," in Stuart J. Woolf, *The Rebirth of Italy, 1943–1950* (London, 1972). The passion of the Resistance comes out in full force in Piero Malvezzi and Giovanni Pirelli, eds., *Lettere di condannati a morte della Resistenza italiana* (Turin, 1965). Luigi Longo, head of the Communist forces, has published *Un popolo alla macchia* (Rome, 1974). On the northern Resistance movement and its aims, see Franco Catalano, *Storia del CLNAI* (Bari, 1956). Santo Peli, *Storia della Resistenza in Italia* (Turin, 2006), is a general history, while his *La Resistenza in Italia* (Turin, 2004) is an overview of history and criticism on the topic. There was the famous resistance of Naples, which is discussed by Renato Caserta, *Ai due lati della barricata: la Resistenza a Napoli e le Quattro giornate* (Naples, 2003). For political developments during the waning days of the war, see Palmiro Togliatti, *La politica di Salerno* (Rome, 1969); Aurelio Lepre, *Storia della svolta di Salerno* (Rome, 1966); and Giulio Andreotti, *Concerto a sei voci* (Rome,

1945). Interesting also is the treatment of Italian-Soviet relations at the end of the war up to the Popular Front elections by Roberto Marozzo, *La politica estera italiana e l'Unione Sovietica, 1944–1948* (Rome, 1985). Relations with the Allies during this period are cogently examined by Norman Kogan, *Italy and the Allies* (Cambridge, Mass., 1956), while the relationship between foreign and domestic affairs is analyzed by Elena Agarossi, *L'Italia nella sconfitta: politica interna e situazione internazionale durante la seconda guerra mondiale* (Naples, 1985). Roy Palmer Domenico explains what happened to Italian Fascist leaders after World War II in *Italian Fascists on Trial* (Chapel Hill, 1991). What has made Giampaolo Pansa's book, *Il sangue dei vinti: quello che accadde in Italia dopo il 25 aprile* (Milan, 2003), so controversial is not only his high estimates of the dead but also his contention that the Communists killed many non-Fascists in an attempt to consolidate their control of the country after the war. See also his *La grande bugia* (Milan, 2006). Renzo De Felice, *Rosso e Nero* (Milan, 1995), created great controversy when it came out because it challenged the standard view of the insurrection of a whole people against the Nazi-Fascists.

On the Parri government and its aftermath, see Enzo Piscitelli, *Da Parri a De Gasperi: storia del dopoguerra 1945–1948* (Milan, 1975), and Archivio dello Stato, *Il governo Parri: atti del convegno: Roma, 13 e 14 dicembre 1994* (Rome, 1995). Memoirs about Parri, a Resistance fighter, have also been written, including Aldo Aniasi, *Parri: l'avventura umana, militare, politco di Maurizio* (Turin, 1991).

CHAPTER 18: THE STRUCTURE OF POSTWAR ITALY

Some of the issues discussed in this chapter are well treated in Woolf, ed., *The Rebirth of Italy*, previously cited. General economic developments are examined in Clough, *The Economic History of Modern Italy*, previously cited; Valerio Castronovo, *Storia d'Italia*, vol. 4 of *Dall'Unità a oggi* (Turin, 1975); and Michele Salvati's lucid *Economia e politica in Italia dal dopoguerra a oggi* (Milan, 1984). Important essays are also to be found in Frank J. Coppa and Margherita Repetto-Alaia, *The Formation of the Italian Republic: Proceedings of the International Symposium on Postwar Italy* (New York, 1993). Important party documents are readily available in Gabriele De Rosa, *I partiti politici in Italia* (Bergamo, 1981). Peter Lange has edited a useful bibliography, *Studies on Italy 1943–1975: Select Bibliography of American and British Materials in Political Science, Economics, Sociology, and Anthropology* (Turin, 1977). Another bibliography for postwar Italy is Roland Sarti, ed., *A Select Bibliography of English-Language Books on Modern Italian History* (Amherst, 1989).

Elisa Carillo has published a good biography of Alcide De Gasperi, *De Gasperi: The Long Apprenticeship* (Notre Dame, 1965). A later biography is Rosa Parolini, *De Gasperi: una vita per la libertà* (Milan, 1974). His life under the Hapsburg Empire has been examined by Stefano Trinchese, *L'altro De Gasperi* (Rome, 2006). More than his life, scholars have tended to concentrate on De Gasperi's policies. See the following works: Alfredo Canavero, *Alcide De Gasperi: il trentino che ricostruì l'Italia a fondò l'Europa* (Milan, 1997); Giulio Andreotti, *De Gasperi e la ricostruzione* (Rome, 1974); Giuseppe Rossini, *De Gasperi e l'età del centrismo, 1947–1953: atti del Convegno di studio organizzatio dal Dipartimento cultura, scuola e informazione della Direzione centrale della D.C., Lucca 4–6 marzo 1982* (Rome, 1984); Enrico Nassi, *Alcide De Gasperi: l'utopia del centro* (Florence, 1997); and Pietro Scoppola, *La proposta politica di De Gasperi* (Bologna, 1977). Piero Craveri has published a massive biography, *De Gasperi* (Bologna, 2006). A number of books detail his European influence; see, for example, Eckart Conze, Gustavo Corni, and Paolo Pombeni, *De Gasperi: un percorso europeo* (Bologna, 2006). An important account of De Gasperi's 1947 trip to the United States is Alberto Tarchiani, *America-Italia: le dieci giornate di De Gasperi negli Stati Uniti* (Milan, 1947). De Gasperi's foreign policy in general is discussed by Giuseppe Petrilli, *La politica estera ed europea di De Gasperi* (Rome, 1975).

Pietro Nenni's diaries for this period are a precious resource; see *Tempo di guerra fredda: diari 1943–1956* (Milan, 1981). The standard biography is Giuseppe Tamburrano, *Pietro Nenni* (Manduria, 2000). On the Socialist Party, see Giovanni Sabbatucci, ed., *Storia del socialismo italiano*, vol. 5 (Rome, 1981), and, in English, the relevant chapters in Spencer M. Di Scala, *Renewing Italian Socialism: Nenni to Craxi* (New York, 1988).

For the Communists, in addition to the works cited later, see Gianmaria Bottino and Aldo Brandirali, *La linea politica dei comunisti nella Resistenza e nel dopoguerra, 1943–1953* (Milan, 1974), Livio Maitan, *Teoria e politica comunista nel dopoguerra* (Milan, 1959), and Marcello Flores, *Fronte poplare e democrazia progressiva* (Rome, 1973). In English, Communist strategy during the postwar period can be followed in Donald Sassoon, *The Strategy of the Italian Communist Party from the Resistance to the Historic Compromise* (New York, 1981). Alastair Davidson discusses the same topic in *The Theory and Practice of Italian Communism* (London, 1982). For the relationship between the Communists and the workers of Italy's most important city in the immediate postwar period, consult Tom Behan, *The Long Awaited Moment: The Working Class and the Italian Communist Party in Milan, 1945–1948* (New York, 1997). Stephen Gundle has examined how the Communists confronted the issue of mass politics and culture that began during the immediate postwar period with the extension of the suffrage and more efficient means of communication: *Between Hollywood and Moscow: The Italian Communists and the Challenge of Mass Culture* (Durham, 2000). Giuseppe Mammarella, *Il partito comunista italiano, 1945–1975* (Florence, 1976) is a general history. Simon Serfaty and Lawrence Gray's *The Italian Communist Party: Yesterday, Today, and Tomorrow* (Westport, 1980) includes a good section on the early postwar period. Italo De Feo, *Diario politico, 1943–1948* (Milan, 1973), contains interesting interpretations of PCI policies during these years. Many people wondered how the Communists of such a Catholic country as Italy handled religion. On this topic, see David I. Kertzer, *Comrades and Christians: Religion and Political Struggle in Communist Italy* (Cambridge, U.K., 1980). Nello Ajello discusses the attraction that the PCI had for non-Communist intellectuals in *Intelletuali e PCI 1944–1958* (Rome and Bari, 1979). A trenchant examination of the PCI's "double-track" politics by a number of prominent critics is in Mario Baccianini, ed., *Le ceneri di Togliatti* (Rome, 1991).

The debate on whether Togliatti or Stalin first believed that revolution was impossible in Italy, thus imposing the "new party" policy, is referred to in an interesting review of Di Scala, *Renewing Italian Socialism,* by Sergio Bertelli, "Quando Togliatti a Mosca sognava l'abbraccio mortale," *Messaggero veneto* (June 25, 1991). On the general influence of Stalinism on the Italian left, see *Lo stalinismo nella sinistra italiana: atti del convegno organizato da Mondoperaio: Roma 16–17 marzo 1988* (Rome, 1988), and the debate to which it gave rise in the Italian press of the period. Since the end of the Soviet Union, documents have been published on the relationship between Togliatti and Stalin; see Elena Agarossi and Victor Zasvlasky, *Togliatti e Stalin: il PCI e la politica estera staliniana negli archivi di Mosca* (Bologna, 2007). Readers can find ample literature on Togliatti and various aspects of Communist policy; see also the biography by Aldo Agosti, *Togliatti: un uomo di frontiera* (Turin, 2003). Togliatti gave an amnesty to Fascists when he was justice minister. On this question, see Mimmo Franzinelli, *L'amnistia Togliatti: 22 giugno 1946: colpo di spugno sui crimini fascisti* (Milan, 2006). This measure was part of his attempt to absorb former Fascists into the Communist Party. On this point, see Spencer Di Scala, "Resistance Mythology," *Journal of Modern Italian Studies* 4, no. 1 (Spring 1999). Ugo Finetti's *La Resistenza cancellata* (Milan, 2004) explains how the Resistance was politicized and used after the war.

On Christian Democracy, see Silvio Lanaro and Mario Isneghi, eds., *La Democrazia Cristiana dal fascismo al 18 aprile* (Venice, 1978); see also the older but still useful Mario Einaudi and François Gaguel, *Christian Democracy in Italy and France* (Notre Dame, 1952); Richard Webster, *Christian Democracy in Italy, 1860–1960* (London, 1961); and the chapters on this period in the more complete Giorgio Galli, *Storia della D.C.* (Bari, 1978). A detailed general history of the Christian Democratic Party is Francesco Malgeri, *Storia della Democrazia cristiana,* 5 vols. (Rome, 1987–1989); see also his *L'Italia democristiana* (Rome, 2005). For the Christian Democrat role in Italian reconstruction, see Silvana Casmirri, *Un'economia per la ricostruzione: riflessione teorica e azione politica dei cattolici italiani (1943–1956)* (Rome, 2000). There are a number of books that examine various aspects of Dosetti's life, but, generally, see the collection of papers in Giuseppe Alberigo et al., *Giuseppe Dossetti: un itinerario spirituale* (Venice, 2006).

There are general considerations of the all-important 1948 elections. Robert Ventresca, *From Fascism to Democracy: Culture and Politics in the Italian Elections of 1948* (Toronto, 2004), puts a heavy emphasis on the role of religion, and Marco Innocenti stresses the duel between De Gasperi and Togliatti, *L'Italia del 1948: quando De Gasperi battè Togliatti* (Milan, 1997). See also Luigi Gedda, *18 aprile 1948: memorie inedite dell'artefice della sconfitta del Fronte Popolare* (Milan, 1998). A study of the basis of Christian Democratic power in Italian society—crucial in the 1948 victory and beyond—has been published by Mariuccia Salvati, *Stato e industria nella ricostruzione: alle origini del potere democristiano, 1944–1949* (Milan, 1982). Santi Fedele, *Fronte popolare: la sinistra e le elezioni del 18 aprile 1948* (Milan, 1978), analyzes the Left during the 1948 elections. The best work on the Uomo Qualunque, a right-wing movement that rapidly appeared and disappeared during the immediate postwar years, is Sandro Setta, *L'Uomo Qualunque 1944–1948* (Rome and Bari, 1975).

The right-wing threat to democracy—mainly epitomized by the neo-Fascist MSI—confronted during the early postwar period is analyzed by Franco Ferraresi, *Threats to Democracy: The Radical Right in Italy After the War* (Princeton, 1996), and Giorgio Bocca, *Il filo nero* (Milan, 1995). Since the MSI's exclusion from politics served it well after 1992, because it could not have participated in the corrupt politics that characterized the DC era, it is important to study its attributes. See Piero Ignazi, *Il polo escluso: profilo del Movimento sociale italiano* (Bologna, 1989). For a general history of the Italian right after World War II, see Federico Gennaccari, *Italia tricolore 1946–1989* (Rome, 2006).

Books on U.S. policy toward Italy in the immediate postwar period include James Edward Miller, *The United States and Italy 1940–1950* (Chapel Hill, 1986), and John Lamberton Harper, *America and the Reconstruction of Italy* (Cambridge, U.K., 1986). H. Stuart Hughes's *The United States and Italy* (Cambridge, Mass., 1979) is an older work that is still useful. Important documents for this period may be found in U.S. Department of State, *Western Europe*, vol. 3 of *Foreign Relations of the United States, 1948* (Washington, D.C., 1974), and later volumes. On CIA involvement in Italian affairs, see Trevor Barnes, "The Secret Cold War: The CIA and American Foreign Policy in Europe, 1946–1956," *Historical Journal* 24, no. 2 (June 1981), and William Colby, *Honorable Men* (New York, 1978).

The documentary history of the Constituent Assembly is *La Costituzione della Repubblica nei lavori preparatori dell'Assemblea Costitutente*, 8 vols. (Rome, 1976). Pietro Scoppola puts the constitution in context in a short but trenchant volume, *Gli anni della Costituente fra politica e storia* (Bologna, 1980). On the Italian constitution, see Enzo Cheli, *La riforma mancata: tradizione e innovazione nella Costituzione italiana* (Bologna, 2000). Two books in English give an excellent idea of the structure and working of Italy's government and administration in the postwar situation; John Clarke Adams and Paolo Barile's *The Government of Republican Italy* (Boston, 1966) is the more detailed, while Dante Germino and Stefano Passigli's *The Government and Politics of Contemporary Italy* (New York, 1968) is the more readable. David Hine's *Governing Italy: The Politics of Governed Pluralism* (Oxford, 1993) is a welcome addition to the literature and brings the story beyond the two earlier works. See also Norman Kogan, *The Government of Italy* (New York, 1962). Antonio Lombardo's work, *La grande riforma: governo, istituzioni, partiti* (Milan, 1984), gives a good synopsis of the government, parties, and chief areas for reform. Robert C. Fried has described the bureaucracy and the prefects in *The Italian Prefects: A Study in Administrative Politics* (New Haven, 1963). Two other important institutions in Italian society are examined in R. Canosa and P. Federico, *La magistratura in Italia dal 1945 a oggi* (Bologna, 1974), and R. Canosa, *La polizia in Italia dal 1945 a oggi* (Bologna, 1976).

CHAPTER 19: POSTWAR POLITICS: "IMPERFECT BIPOLARISM"

There are a number of English-language general histories concentrating on Italy's postwar political history. Roy Palmer Domenico's *Remaking Italy in the Twentieth*

Century (Lanham, 2002) is a concise treatment. Patrick McCarthy, ed., *Italy Since 1945* (Oxford, 2000), collects essays on the most important themes of the postwar period. Norman Kogan, *A Political History of Italy: The Postwar Years* (New York, 1983), excels for its tone and coverage. The general treatment by Frederic Spotts and Theodor Wieser, *Italy, a Difficult Democracy: A Survey of Italian Politics* (Cambridge, U.K., 1986), is also a very good treatment in a book of manageable length. John Earle's *Italy in the 1970s* (London, 1975) provides an overview of this period. A book that takes a partisan viewpoint but that can be used profitably for its emphasis on Italian society is Paul Ginsborg's *A History of Contemporary Italy: Society and Politics, 1943–1988* (London, 1990). See also his *Italy and Its Discontents: Family, Civil Society, State, 1980–2001* (New York, 2003). Much information can also be gleaned from Donald Sassoon, *Contemporary Italy: Politics, Economy, and Society Since 1945* (London and New York, 1986), but it is less satisfactory. Coppa and Repetto-Alaia's previously cited edited work, *The Formation of the Italian Republic*, includes several incisive essays on the questions this chapter deals with.

In Italian, general works include Antonio Gambino, *Storia del dopoguerra dalla liberazione al potere DC* (Bari, 1975). On De Gasperi during this period, see his daughter's biography, *De Gasperi uomo solo* (Milan, 1964) by Maria Romana Catti De Gasperi, who has also published a documentary collection, *De Gasperi scrive* (Brescia, 1974). Leo Valiani's *L'avvento di De Gasperi* (Turin, 1949) is an early view by an influential thinker. Books describing De Gasperi's policies include Pietro Scoppola, *La proposta politica di De Gasperi* (Bologna, 1978), and Andreotti, *De Gasperi e il suo tempo*, cited earlier. For the "early" DC and the issues with which it was concerned, see Gianni Baget Bozzo, a priest and an influential political commentator, *Il partito cristiano al potere: la DC di De Gasperi e di Dossetti, 1945–1954* (Florence, 1974), and, by the same author, *Il partito cristiano e l'apertura a sinistra: la DC di Fanfani e di Moro, 1954–1962* (Florence, 1977) and *Aldo Moro: il politico nella crisi, 1962–1973* (Florence, 1983). The excellent general history of the DC by Giorgio Galli, already cited, is fundamental for this and later periods: *Storia della democrazia cristiana*. Another general history that can be profitably consulted and that comes down until the end of the party is Agostino Giovagnoli, *Il partito italiano: la Democrazia Cristiana dal 1942 al 1994* (Rome, 1996). For political relationships among all major parties during these years, and their policies, the first volume of Pietro Nenni's diaries is a fundamental source, *Tempo di guerra fredda: diari, 1943–1956* (Milan, 1981).

Studies—mostly the province of political scientists—that seek to understand the nature of the DC's dominance include Robert Leonardi and Douglas Wertman, *Italian Christian Democracy: The Politics of Dominance* (New York, 1989), and two books by Alan S. Zuckerman, *Political Clienteles in Power: Party Factions and Cabinet Coalitions in Italy* (Beverly Hills, 1975) and *The Politics of Faction: Christian Democratic Rule in Italy* (New Brunswick, 1979).

The Tambroni affair is the subject of Phillip E. Cooke's *Luglio 1960: Tambroni e la repressione fallita* (Milan, 2000).

As mentioned in the text, Giorgio Galli has interpreted the politics of this period as one of "imperfect bipolarism." See his *Il bipartismo imperfetto: comunisti e democristiani in Italia* (Bologna, 1967) and *Dal bipartismo imperfetto alla possibile alternativa* (Bologna, 1975). Domenico Settembrini has focused on an interesting theme running through Italian history that should be taken into consideration when analyzing postwar Italian politics, *Storia dell'idea antiborghese in Italia, 1860–1989* (Rome and Bari, 1991). Joseph La Palombara's *Democracy Italian Style* (New Haven, 1987) views Italian politics as spectacle, but seems unconvincing.

The attempted assassination of Togliatti and its impact is examined by Carlo Maria Lomartire, *Insurrezione: 14 giugno 1948: l'attentato a Togliatti e la tentazione rivoluzionaria* (Milan, 2006). There are several interesting books in English by political scientists on the postwar Communists. They include Donald Blackmer, *Unity in Diversity: Italian Communism and the Communist World* (Cambridge, Mass., 1968); Sidney Tarrow, *Peasant Communism in Southern Italy* (New Haven, 1967); Donald Blackmer and Sidney Tarrow, *Communism in Italy and France* (Princeton, 1975); and Donald Blackmer and Annie Kriegel, *The International Role of the Communist Parties of Italy and France* (Cambridge, Mass., 1975). Most of the essays in the previously cited Serfaty and Gray, *The Italian Communist Party*, deal with the period covered in this chapter. Albertina Vittoria has published a general history of the PCI from its foundation to its dissolution: *Storia del PCI 1921–1991* (Rome, 2006). The "different" nature of the PCI is argued in a long interview format in Giorgio Napolitano and Eric Hobsbawm, *The Italian Road to Socialism* (Westport, 1977). Stephen Hellman discusses the historic compromise in *Italian Communism in Transition: The Rise and Fall of the Historic Compromise in Turin, 1970–1980* (New York, 1988). Relations between the Americans and the Italian Communists are treated by Mario Margiocco, *Stati Uniti e PCI 1943–1980* (Rome, 1981). The Communist approach to mass politics between 1943 and 1991 has been treated in Stephen Gundle's *Between Hollywood and Moscow* (Durham, 2000). The changes in the Italian Communist Party, the difference between that organization and other Western Communist organizations, and the possibility that it might enter the government are topics that have long fascinated observers. See in this regard, as a prelude, Grant Amyot, *The Italian Communist Party: The Crisis of the Popular Front* (New York, 1981), but more particularly Leonard Weinberg, *The Transformation of Italian Communism* (New Brunswick, 1995); James Ruscoe, *On the Threshold of Government: The Italian Communist Party, 1976–1981* (New York, 1982); and John A. Baker, *Italian Communism: The Road to Legitimacy and Autonomy* (Washington, D.C., 1989). For Italian Communist policy and the European Left, see Vassilis Fouskas, *Italy, Europe, the Left: The Transformation of Italian Communism and the European Imperative* (Brookfield, 1998).

A detailed analysis in English of Socialist policy of the postwar period and the American view during the Kennedy period, including important interviews, is Spencer M. Di Scala, *Renewing Italian Socialism* (New York, 1988). In Italian, see vols. 5 and 6 of Giovanni Sabbatucci, ed., *Storia del socialismo italiano* (Rome, 1981). A short but excellent history is Giorgio Galli, *Storia del socialismo italiano* (Bari, 1983). Antonio Landolfi has published both an excellent analysis of the sociological base of Italian socialism, *Il socialismo italiano: strutture comportamenti valori* (Cosenza, 1977), and a general history of the party, *Storia del PSI*, cited previously. Nenni's diaries are, again, a fundamental source, *Gli anni del centro-sinistra: diari 1957–1966* (Milan, 1982), and *I conti con la storia: diari 1967–1971* (Milan, 1983). Interpretations of Nenni's work, including a contribution by Arthur M. Schlesinger, are in Fondazione Pietro Nenni, *Nenni dieci anni dopo* (Rome, 1990). Spencer M. Di Scala, *Italian Socialism: Between Politics and History* (Amherst, 1996), collects essays written by distinguished Italian and American historians and protagonists in the hundred-year history of the Socialist movement in Italy; the contributions include firsthand accounts that have themselves become historical documents. Excellent insights on the relationship between the United States and Italy during the Center-Left in particular and on the entire postwar period in general are provided by a collaborator of Schlesinger's who interviewed most of the important personages involved, Leo J. Wollemborg, *Stelle, strisce e tricolore: trent'anni di vicende politiche fra Roma e Washington* (Milan, 1983). The best analysis of the Center-Left period has been written by Giuseppe Tamburrano, *Storia e cronaca del centro-sinistra* (Milan, 1990).

Insights on the role of economic planning can be obtained from Joseph La Palombara, *Italy: The Politics of Planning* (Syracuse, 1966), and Valdo Spini, *I socialisti e la politica di piano (1945–1964)* (Florence, 1982). The Social Democrats are discussed in Giuseppe Averardi, *I socialisti democratici da Palazzo Barberini alla scissione del 4 luglio 1969* (Milan, 1977).

Italian labor is treated by Maurice Neufeld, *Italy: School for Awakening Countries* (Ithaca, 1961); Daniel L. Horowitz, *The Italian Labor Movement* (Cambridge, Mass., 1963); Joseph La Palombara, *The Italian Labor Movement* (Ithaca, 1957); and Joan Barkan, *Visions of Emancipation: The Italian Workers' Movement Since 1945* (New York, 1984). Union strategy is examined by Peter Lange, George Ross, and Maurizio Vannicelli, *Unions, Change, and Crisis: French and Italian Union Strategy and the Political Economy, 1945–1980* (London, 1982). Electoral and political analysis is found in Howard R. Penniman, ed., *Italy at the Polls: The Parliamentary Elections of 1976* (Washington, D.C., 1977), in later books in the same series, and in Robert Leonardi and Raffaella Y. Nanetti, *Italian Politics: A Review*, vol. 1 (London, 1986), which is also an ongoing series. Giorgio Galli and Alfonso Prandi analyze *Patterns of Political Participation in Italy* (New Haven, 1970). Several books by political scientists examining political attitudes, party operations, techniques, and representation have been published; they include Robert Putnam, *Beliefs of Politicians: Conflict and Democracy in Britain and Italy* (New Haven, 1973); Sidney Tarrow, *Between Center and Periphery: Grassroots Politicians in Italy and France* (New Haven, 1977); Giuseppe Di Palma, *Surviving Without Governing: The Italian Parties in Parliament* (Berkeley, 1977); and Samuel H. Barnes, *Representation in Italy: Institutionalized Tradition and Electoral Choice* (Chicago, 1977).

Sidney Tarrow, in *Democracy and Disorder: Protest and Politics in Italy 1965–1975* (New York, 1989), ties unrest in Italy to similar agitation in Europe and believes it strengthened Italian democracy. Luciano Pellicani has written an excellent book on the terrorist mentality in general, *I rivoluzionari di professione* (Florence, 1975).

Richard Drake links modern terrorism to intellectual tradition in *The Revolutionary Mystique and Terrorism in Contemporary Italy* (Bloomington, 1989). Drake has written *Apostles and Agitators: Italy's Marxist Revolutionary Tradition* (Cambridge, Mass., 2003), a book that unravels the mystery of why ideological terrorism had so much appeal in the Italy of the 1970s and why it remains a potential threat. Robert C. Meade Jr., *Red Brigades: The Story of Italian Terrorism* (New York, 1990), deals primarily with the Moro case; he is adequate on the facts but weak on interpretation. Carla Mosca and Rossana Rossanda's *Mario Moretti Brigate Rosse: una storia italiana* (Milan, 1994) is a book-length interview of one of the most notorious Red Brigades leaders and kidnapper of Aldo Moro. A graphic description of one of the many kidnappings that afflicted Italian life during this period is Curtis Bill Pepper, *Kidnapped! Seventeen Days of Terror* (New York, 1978). The best work in Italian on terrorism is Giorgio Bocca, *Il terrorismo italiano, 1970–1982* (Milan, 1986). Two autobiographical works by leftists convey very well the climate of the time: Oreste Scalzone, *Biennio Rosso '68–'69: figure e passaggi di una stagione rivoluzionaria* (Milan, 1988), and Mario Capanna, *Formidabili quegli anni* (Milan, 1988). Bocca has written a book on the Moro case, *Moro: una tragedia italiana* (Milan, 1978), while Galli has taken up the question of possible involvement of the right wing in the Italian political crisis, *La crisi Italiana e la destra internazionale* (Milan, 1974). The best book in English on the Moro murder is Richard Drake, *The Aldo Moro Murder Case* (Cambridge, Mass., 1995). On the theme of possible American intervention in Italian affairs, the books by Roberto Faenza, *Il malaffare* (Milan, 1978), and by Roberto Faenza and Marco Fini, *Gli americani in Italia* (Milan, 1978), are interesting but contain a goodly dose of imagination.

For the 1980s, see the papers in Giuseppe De Palma and Philip Siegelman, *Italy in the 1980s: Paradoxes of a Dual Society* (San Francisco, 1983), which analyze the country's contradictions at the beginning of the decade. For an analysis of the relationship between Communists and Socialists just before that decade, see Giuliano Amato and Luciano Cafagna, *Duello a sinistra: socialisti e comunisti nei lunghi anni '70* (Bologna, 1982). The Socialist attack on the undemocratic nature of Antonio Gramsci's ideology and of Italian Communist roots is contained in *Egemonia e democrazia: Gramsci e la questione comunista nel dibattito di Mondoperaio* (Rome, 1977), and in Craxi's famous article on the same theme, "Il vangelo socialista," *L'Espresso*, August 27, 1978. Good works on Craxi, his policies, and the nature of his influence include Guido Gerosa, *Craxi: il potere e la stampa* (Milan, 1984), and Antonio Ghirelli, *L'effetto Craxi* (Milan, 1982). The "rise" of Craxi can be followed in Eugenio Scalfari, *L'anno di Craxi (o di Berlinguer)* (Milan, 1984), while newspaper articles on him have been collected by Ugo Intini in *Tutti gli angoli di Craxi* (Milan, 1984). The Craxi government's program and goals were published by the Presidenza del Consiglio dei Ministri, *Il governo Craxi* (Rome, 1983). Press reaction has been collected in *Craxi in prima pagina* (n.p., 1984). Since Craxi's death in 2000, there have been attempts to his career into historical context. Massimo Pini, *Craxi: una vita, un'era politica* (Milan, 2006), is an exhaustive biography. Simona Colarizi, *La cruna dell'ago: Craxi, il partito socialista e la crisi della Repubblica* (Rome, 2005), attempts to explain the crisis of the "First Republic." Luigi Musella's *Craxi* (Rome, 2007) gives readers a good outline of his life, career, aims, and end. Ugo Intini, a close collaborator of Craxi's, has published *Craxi: una storia socialista* (Rome, 2000).

On foreign policy issues, see the views of two protagonists, Alberto Tarchiani, *Dieci anni tra Roma e Washington* (Milan, 1955), and Carlo Sforza, *Cinque anni a Palazzo Chigi: la politica estera italiana dal 1947 al 1951* (Rome, 1952). Giovanni Di Capua presents a clear exposition of political attitudes surrounding Italy's entrance into NATO: *Come l'Italia aderì al Patto Atlantico* (Rome, 1971). On the issue of South Tyrol, see Mario Toscano's *Alto Adige, South Tyrol: Italy's Frontier with the German World* (Baltimore, 1975). Alessandro Brogi, *L'Italia e l'egemonia nel Mediterraneo* (Florence, 1996), tells of Italy's attempt at a policy of dialogue with Arab nationalism. There is a stimulating essay on the republic's foreign policy by Christopher Seton-Watson in Richard J. B. Bosworth and Sergio Romano, *La politica estera italiana 1860–1985* (Bologna, 1991). An ample section is devoted to foreign policy during the Craxi period in A. Benzoni, R. Gritti, and A. Landolfi, *La dimensione internazionale del socialismo italiano: 100 anni di politica estera del PSI* (Rome, 1993). Andrea Spiri, ed., *Bettino Craxi, il socialismo europeo e il sistema internazionale* (Venice, 2006), collects the papers of an international conference on Craxi's foreign policy held in Milan in 2005.

CHAPTER 20: THE ECONOMIC MIRACLE AND ITS EFFECTS

Besides Clough, *The Economic History of Modern Italy*, and Castronovo, "La storia economica," already cited, two older works on postwar Italian economic development may be mentioned as retaining their usefulness. These are Muriel Grindrod, *The Rebuilding of Italy: Politics and Economics* (London, 1955), and Vera Lutz, *Italy: A Study in Economic Development* (London, 1962). Rolf Petri has written a general history of the Italian economy from the end of World War I to 1918: *Storia economica d'Italia: dalla grande guerra al miracolo economico, 1918–1963* (Bologna, 2002). Agostino Giovagnoli writes about Italy's position in the world immediately after the war in *L'Italia nel nuovo ordine mondiale: politica ed economia dal 1945 al 1947* (Milan, 2000). Juan Carlos Oliva Martinez looks at the domestic and international factors in the economic stabilization of postwar Italy: *La stabilizzazione del 1947* (Rome, 2006). The "economic miracle" is analyzed by Antonio Cardini, *Il miracolo economico italiano, 1958–1963* (Bologna, 2006). Chiarella Esposito, *America's Feeble Weapon: Funding the Marshall Plan in France and Italy, 1948–1950* (Westport, 1994), is a study of the economic aid so essential to Italy's postwar recovery. See also a treatment of the effects of the plan on southern Italy in Manrico Gesummaria, *Piano Marshall e Mezzogiorno* (Atripalda, 2003). For a general discussion of American aid after World War II, there is Claudia Villani, *Il prezzo della stabilità: gli aiuti americani all'Italia, 1953–1961* (Bari, 2007). Pasquale Saraceno, one of the country's major economists, has spoken out on the Reconstruction in *Intervista sulla Ricostruzione 1943–1953* (Rome and Bari, 1977). The papers of a conference on his thought regarding the South has been published; see Diomede Ivone, *Cultura Stato e Mezzogiorno nel pensiero di Pasquale Saraceno* (Naples, 2004). F. Roy Willis, *Italy Chooses Europe* (New York, 1971), discusses the issues with regard to Italian membership in multilateral trade organizations. Robert M. Stern, *Foreign Trade and Economic Growth in Italy* (New York, 1967), focuses on the role of exports in Italian economic growth. General economic developments for the period may be followed in Salvati, *Economia e politica in Italia*, previously cited; Giuliano Amato, *Economia, politica e istituzioni in Italia* (Bologna, 1976); Napoleone Colajanni, *Riconversione grande impresa partecipazioni statali* (Milan, 1976); and Augusto Graziani, ed., *L'economia Italiana 1945–1970* (Bologna, 1972). A good short essay is Luigi De Rosa's "Italy's Second Industrial Revolution," in Coppa, ed., *Studies in Modern Italian History*, previously cited. For Communist economic views, see Eugenio Peggio, *La crisi economica italiana* (Milan, 1976), and Sergio Garavini, *Crisi economica e ristrutturazzione industriale* (Rome, 1974). Raffaella Y. Nanetti argues that Italy's success in responding to the economic crisis of the 1970s was a "unique response," one that involved institutional decentralization: *Growth and Territorial Policies: The Italian Model of Social Capitalism* (London and New York, 1988). Edith Kurzweil, *Italian Entrepreneurs: Rearguard of Progress* (New York, 1983), looks on the Italian entrepreneurs of the 1970s acting as innovators and adapting to new social and economic conditions.

Good treatments of economic and societal issues are also in the general works by Paul Ginsborg and Donald Sassoon, cited in chapter 19. Works in Italian encompassing all aspects of the Italian Republic, including treatments of economic, social, and cultural issues, are Silvio Lanaro, *Storia dell'Italia repubblicana dalla fine della guerra agli anni novanta* (Venice, 1992), and the more concrete Aurelio Lepre, *Storia della prima repubblica: l'Italia dal 1942 al 1992* (Bologna, 1993). Excellent detailed essays on different aspects of Italian society, including women, youth, custom, culture, and ideology, may be found in *Dal '68 a oggi: come siamo e come eravamo* (Rome and Bari, 1979). General living conditions are discussed in two older books, now surpassed but useful as a picture of their times—news correspondent Irving R. Levine's *Main Street, Italy* (New York, 1963) and Andrew Bryant's *The Italians: How They Live and Work* (New York, 1971). The economic state of the Italian population is examined by Luigi Cannari and G. D'Alessio, *La richezza degli italiani* (Bologna, 2006); the authors discuss such questions as what is meant by "rich" and where the Italians fit in compared to other countries. The papers in Luca Baldissara's *Le radici della crisi* (Rome, 2001) analyze the Italian crises of the late 1960s and 1970s. An examination of cultural stereotypes and economic realities may be found in the essays collected in Carlo Chiarenza and William L. Vance, eds., *Immaginari a confronto* (Venice, 1992). The links between the state and the private economy is examined by Grant Amyot, *Business, the State, and Economic Policy: The Case of Italy* (New York, 2004). Cristina Nardi Spiller analyzes the postwar economy from the viewpoint of prices in *The Dynamics of the Price Structure and the Business Cycle: The Italian Evidence from 1945 to 2000*

(New York, 2003). Maurizio Ferrara and Elisabetta Gualimini discuss *Rescued by Europe? Social and Labor Market Reforms in Italy from Maastricht to Berlusconi* (Amsterdam, 2004). The papers collected in Massimo Di Matteo and Paolo Piacentini, *The Italian Economy at the Dawn of the Twenty-first Century* (Aldershot, 2003), review the economy since the end of World War II.

Women's issues are treated in Maria Michetti, Margherita Repetto, and Luciana Viviani, *Udi laboratorio e politica delle donne* (Rome, 1984), and in Franca Pieroni Bortolotti, *Sul movimento politico delle donne* (Rome, 1987). See also the paper and response between Paola Gaiotti de Biase and Margherita Repetto Alaia, "The Impact of Women's Political and Social Activity in Postwar Italy," in Coppa and Repetto-Alaia's previously cited *The Formation of the Italian Republic*, and Repetto-Alaia's paper in *Italian Socialism: Between Politics and History*, cited in chapter 19. For the 1970s, see *La donna e le scelte della società italiana per gli anni '70* (Rome, 1971); R. Spagnoletti, ed., *I movimenti femministi in Italia* (Rome, 1971); and B. Frabotta, *Femminismo e lotta di classe in Italia (1970–1973)* (Rome, 1973). Maria Teresa Silvestrini, Caterina Simiand, and Simona Urso, *Donne e politica: la presenza femminile nei partiti politici dell'Italia repubblicana: Torino 1945–1990* (Milan, 2005) is a detailed work. Rosa Rossi has written an interesting essay on language as it relates to women, *Le parole delle donne* (Rome, 1978). Judith Adler Hellman has examined Italian feminism in *Journeys Among Women: Feminism in Five Italian Cities* (New York, 1988). Other aspects of women's issues and roles in postwar Italy are examined in the books of Ann Cornelisen, most especially *Women of the Shadows* (Boston, 1976). On feminism and the women's movement, in English, see Lucia Chiavola Birnbaum, *Liberazione Della Donna: Feminism in Italy* (Middletown, 1986). On women in various aspects of contemporary Italian culture, see Maria Cicioni and Nicolle Prunster, *Visions and Revisions: Women and Italian Culture* (Providence and Oxford, 1993), and Giuliana Bruno and Maria Nadott, eds., *Off Screen: Women and Film in Italy* (London and New York, 1988), which is primarily concerned with the post–World War II era but contains flashbacks to earlier periods. Elizabeth L. Krause has published a case study trying to understand the reasons for the drop in the Italian birthrate and its effects on a family-oriented society; see *A Crisis of Births: Population Politics and Family Making in Italy* (Belmont, 2005).

Immigration is beginning to be considered in some English-language books, but a wide literature has already appeared in Italian. Charles Richards has a chapter on immigration in his book, *The New Italians* (London, 1995). There is an essay on Tunisians in Italy in Floya Anthias and Gabriella Lazaridis, eds., *Into the Margins: Migration and Exclusion in Southern Europe* (Aldershot, 1999). Francesca Froy and Giuguere, eds., *From Immigration to Integration* (Paris, 2006), includes a chapter on services in Italy. For a larger treatment, see Manfred Werth, *Immigration of Citizens from Third Countries into the Southern Member States of the EEC* (Luxembourg, 1991). The general phenomenon of immigration into Italy is considered in Luca Einaudi, *Le politiche dell'immigrazione dall'Unità a oggi* (Rome, 2007). Sante Matteo and Stefano Bellucci have concentrated on Africa in a book of collected essays: *Africa Italia: due continenti si avvcinano* (Santarcangelo di Romagna, 1999). Corrado Bonifazi has written *L'emigrazione straniera in Italia* (Bologna, 1998). Some works discuss immigration and conflict; see Enzo Bartocci and Vittorio Cotesta, *L'identità italiana* (Rome, 1999); Vittorio Cotesta, *La cittadella assediata* (Rome, 1992); and Leone Iraci Fedeli, *Razzismo e immigrazione: il caso Italia* (Rome, 1990). Marzio Bargagli discusses crime and immigration in *Immigrazione e criminalità in Italia* (Bologna, 1998). There is also a literature that considers the future impact of immigration and integration; see Laura Bergnach and Emidio Sussi, *Minoranze etniche ed immigrazione* (Milan, 1993); Antonio Golini, *L'immigrazione straniera: indicatori e misure di integrazione* (Bologna, 2006); Livia Turco and Paola Tavella, *I nuovi italiani: l'immigrazione, i pregiudizi, la convivenza* (Milan, 2005); Consiglio Regionale, Lombardia, *Immigrazione e integrazione* (Milan, 1999); Roberto Marini, *Immigrazione e società multiculturale* (Milan, 2004); and Maurizio Ambrosini and Stefano Molina, *Seconde generazioni: un'introduzione al futuro dell'immigrazione in Italia* (Turin, 2004). The economic impact is considered in Enrico Pugliese, *Rapporto immigrazione: lavoro, sindacati, società* (Rome, 2000), and Maria Concetta Chiuri et al., *L'esercito degli invisibli: aspetti economici dell'immigrazione clandestina* (Bologna, 2007). The Chinese immigration has been considered by Giovanni Campana et al., *L'immigrazione silenziosa: le comunità cinesi in Italia* (Turin, 1994); the Albanian by Giovanna Da Molin, *L'immigrazione albanese in Puglila: saggi interdisciplinari* (Bari, 1999); and the Polish by Marco Martinelli, *Immigrazione dei Polacchi a Roma* (Rome, 1998). Giuseppe Barile considers the important wave of immigration into Milan in *Tra due rive: la nuova immigrazione a Milano* (Milan, 1994). See also Massimiliano Melilli, *Mi chamo Ali: identità e integrazione* (Rome, 2003). On the demographic statistics cited, see "Italia, saldo demografico attivo," *La Repubblica*, April 26, 2008.

The South is amply considered in the works cited earlier on the topic of economics; on the region's particular problems, see, in addition, Paquale Saraceno, "La politica di sviluppo di un'area sottosviluppato nell'esperienza italiana," in Augusto Graziani, ed., *L'economia italiana 1945–1970* (Bologna, 1972); Judith Chubb, *Patronage, Power, and Poverty in Southern Italy* (Cambridge, U.K., 1982); and Raimondo Catanzaro, "Mafia, economia e sistema politico," in U. Ascoli and R. Catanzaro, eds., *La società italiana degli anni Ottanta* (Bari, 1987). Salvatore Cafiero examines state intervention in the region in *Storia dell'intervento straordinario nell'Mezzogiorno, 1950–1993* (Manduria, 2000), while the issue can be seen from the industrialist viewpoint in A. L. Denitto, *Confindustria e Mezzogiorno, 1950–1958* (Galatina, 2001). A broad view of the South and Sicily and their modern problems can be understood through the essays collected by Giuseppe Giarrizzo, ed., *Mezzogiorno senza meridionalismo: la Sicilia, lo sviluppo, il potere* (Venice, 1992). A classic work on the Mafia and its roots is Michele Pantaleone's *Mafia e politica 1943–1962* (Turin, 1962). On Mafia structure and organization, refer also to the works cited in chapter 11. The best treatment of the current structure of the Sicilian Mafia is Pino Arlacchi, *Men of Dishonor: Inside the Sicilian Mafia* (New York, 1993). The Mafia and its effect on southern development has been examined in Antonio La Spina's book, *Mafia, legalità debole e sviluppo del Mezzogiorno* (Bologna, 2005). Important works by the protagonists of the fight against the Mafia include Giuseppe Ayla, *La guerra dei giusti: i giudici, la mafia, la politica* (Milan, 1993), and Giovanni Falcone, *Cose di cosa nostra* (Milan, 1993).

CHAPTER 21: A STYLE FOR THE REPUBLIC

Books on Italian film are plentiful in both Italian and English, although the English-language works tend toward more specialized topics. Director Martin Scorsese produced his own narrative on the effect that Italian filmmakers from the Neorealist period had on his own works in *Il mio viaggio in Italia* (My Trip to Italy), two discs, in English, distributed by Buena Vista Home Entertainment, 2003. Packed with information, Peter Bondanella's book *Italian Cinema from Neorealism to the Present* (New York, 1990) is a good general history in English and includes a valuable bibliography. Mary P. Wood's *Italian Cinema* (New York, 2005) is a complete history. Millicent Marcus examines *Italian Film in the Light of Neorealism* (Princeton, 1986) and the links with literary theory. She also has an interesting work linking the cinema to the Holocaust, *Italian Film in the Shadow of Auschwitz* (Toronto, 2007). An author who believes that neorealism had a fundamental influence on Italian cinema is John J. Michalczyk in his examination of *The Italian Political Filmmakers* (London and Toronto, 1986). Angela Dalle Vacche, *The Body in the Mirror: Shapes of History in Italian Cinema* (Princeton, 1992), explores how the uniqueness of Italian culture emerged onto the screen. Carlo Testa links Italian cinema and literature in *Italian Cinema and Modern European Literatures, 1945–2000* (Westport, 2002). Robert S. Dombowski links several art forms in his postwar consideration of *Italy: Fiction, Poetry, Theater, Film Since 1950* (Middle Village, 2000). Angelo Restivo connects film to the economic miracle in *The Cinema of Economic Miracles: Visuality and Modernization in the Italian Art Film* (Durham, 2002).

In Italian, Gian Piero Brunetta's massive *Storia del cinema italiano 1945–1982* (Rome, 1982) examines the topic from every conceivable angle and completes the job with a vast bibliography and excellent photographs. See also Lino Miccichè's multi-volume *Storia del cinema italiano* (Venice, 2001–).Briefer treatments include director Carlo Lizzani's *Il cinema italiano, 1895–1979* (Rome, 1979) and Bruno Torri's *Cinema italiano dalla realtà alle metafore* (Palermo, 1973). Franca Faldini and Goffredo Fofi have collected the comments of directors and actors in *L'avventurosa storia del cinema italiano raccontata dai suoi protagonisti 1935–1959* (Milan, 1979); Massimo Mida and Lorenzo Quaglietti focus on the transition from Fascist filmmaking to neorealism, reproducing essential documents, in *Dai telefoni bianchi al neorealismo* (Rome and Bari, 1980). Early neorealism has been analyzed in a publication of the association for Resistance film, *Neorealismo DOC: i film del 1948* (Turin, 1995). Sara Cortellazzo and Massimo Quaglia examine film and the Resistance in *Cinema e Resistenza* (Turin, 2005). The cinema of the Reconstruction period is analyzed in Fabio Carlini and Maurizio Gusso, *I sogni nel cassetto* (Milan, 2001). Political and economic aspects are emphasized in Lorenzo Quaglietti's *Storia economico-politica del cinema italiano 1945–1980* (Rome, 1980).

Books on individual Italian directors are plentiful, and only a sampling is given here. As might be expected, Rossellini has drawn much attention; see Tag Gallagher, *The Adventures of Roberto Rossellini: His Life and Films* (New York, 1998), and Peter E. Bondanella, *The Films of Roberto Rossellini* (Cambridge, U.K., 1993). Sidney Gottlieb has edited essays on *Open City* in a book entitled *Roberto Rossellini's Rome Open City* (New York, 2004). Another edited work is David Forgacs et al., *Roberto Rossellini: Magician of the Real* (London, 2000). The life and work of Vittorio De Sica has been examined in a number of good books; these include Bert Cardullo, *Vittorio De Sica: Director, Actor, Screenwriter* (Jefferson, 2002), and, more widely, Giuglielmo Moneti, *Neorealismo fra tradizione e rivoluzione: Visconti, De Sica e Zavattini: verso nuove esperienze cinematografiche della realtà* (Siena, 1999). There is also the collection of essays edited by Stephen Snyder and Howard Curie, *Vittorio De Sica: Contemporary Perspectives* (Toronto, 2000). Books on Visconti are plentiful; see Henry Bacon, *Visconti: Explorations of Beauty and Decay* (Cambridge, U.K., 1998), and Lino Miccichè, *Luchino Visconti: un profilo critico* (Venice, 1996). Visconti's best films are discussed by Geoffrey Newall-Smith, *Luchino Visconti* (London, 2003). There is also a disc, *Luchino Visconti* (Image Entertainment, 1999), with the testimonies of people who knew him. On Fellini, consult Charlotte Chandler, *I, Fellini* (New York, 1995); Peter E. Bondanella, *The Cinema of Federico Fellini* (Princeton, 1992); and Frank Burke, *Fellini's Films: From Postwar to Postmodern* (New York, 1996). Film critic Tullio Kecizh has published a biography, *Federico Fellini: His Life and Work* (New York, 2006); Peter Bondanella discusses his most famous films in *The Films of Federico Fellini* (Cambridge, U.K., 2002). There are also the collected essays in Frank Burke et al., *Federico Fellini: Contemporary Perspectives* (Toronto, 2002).

A mine of information on modern Italian cinema, art, literature, and culture in general, including the themes discussed in this chapter, may be found in English in the pages of the *Italian Quarterly*, for which a convenient index for articles up to 1971 has been published separately.

Good introductions to the lives and works of the three poets mentioned in this chapter are Frederic J. Jones, *Giuseppe Ungaretti: Poet and Critic* (Edinburgh, 1977); Leone Piccioni, *Vita di Ungaretti* (Milan, 1979); Walter Mauro, *Vita di Giuseppe Ungaretti* (Albano, 2006); Rebecca J. West, *Eugenio Montale: Poet on the Edge* (Cambridge, Mass., 1981); G. Singh, *Eugenio Montale: A Critical Study of His Poetry, Prose, and Criticism* (New Haven, 1973); and Michele Tondo, *Salvatore Quasimodo* (Milan, 1971). Books that make comparisons include Alberto Bertoni and Jonathan Sisco, *Montale vs. Ungaretti* (Rome, 2003), and Giorgi Baroni, *Tempo e tempo: Ungaretti e Quasimodo* (Milan, 2002).

General histories of Italian literature usually include a discussion of the period examined in this chapter. The best treatment of the postwar era is Gaetano Mariani and Mario Petrucciani's *Letteratura italiana contemporanea*, vol. 3 (Rome, 1982); Alberto Asor Rosa, ed., *Letteratura italiana: storia e geografia*, vol. 3, *L'età contemporanea* (Turin, 1989), is a detailed treatment that is heavy on social considerations, organized by region and literary category. Other good works include Romano Luperini, *Il Novecento: apparati ideologici ceto intelletuale sistemi formali nella letteratura italiana contemporanea* (Turin, 1985). On female writers, see the collected work edited by Santo L. Aric, *Contemporary Women Writers in Italy: A Modern Renaissance* (Amherst, 1990).

Short sections on Italian design may be found in English in Stephen Bayley, Philippe Garver, and Deyan Sudjic, *Style and Design* (New York, 1986). The scope and influence of Italian industrial design can be gleaned from the following catalogs with both English and Italian texts: Piero Sartozo, *Italian Revolution: Design in Italian Society in the Eighties* (Milan, 1982); *Compasso d'oro* (Milan, 1985); *Dal cucchaio alla città: From the Spoon to the City* (Milan, 1983); and *Design Process: Olivetti 1908–1978* (Milan, 1979). See Giampiero Bosoni, *Brevetti del design italiano: 1946–1965: Original Patents of Italian Design: 1946–1965* (Rome, 2000), and Silvana Annicchiarico and Augusto Morello, *Il design in Italia: 1945–2000* (Rome, 2001). For an indication of the role of Italian fashion, see *Moda Italia: Creativity and Technology in the Italian Fashion System* (Milan, 1988), the catalog of an exhibition held in New York City under the auspices of the Italian Institute for Foreign Trade (ICE). On fashion, see Valerie Steele, *Fashion, Italian Style* (New York, 2003). For an American connection, see Nicola White, *Reconstructing Italian Fashion: America and the Development of the Italian Fashion Industry* (New York, 2000).

Works on science in the republic are scarce, and the topic must be researched from many sources. The same is also true for more prominent scientists such as Enrico Fermi, who is due for a good, full-scale biography. Fermi's wife has written a book telling of their life together, *Atoms in the Family: My Life with Enrico Fermi* (Chicago, 1954), while his collaborator Emilio Segrè attempted to put Fermi's lifework into focus in *Enrico Fermi: Physicist* (Chicago, 1970).

Antonio Gramsci is probably the modern Italian thinker on whom the most has been written. Steve Jones, *Antonio Gramsci* (New York, 2006) is a good introduction. For a thorough bibliography, see John Cammett's *Bibliografia gramsciana* (Rome, 1989 and 1991) and the supplements published in 1992 and 1995. Cammett also wrote a groundbreaking study of Gramsci, *Antonio Gramsci and the Origins of Italian Communism* (Stanford, 1967). A good biography is Giuseppe Fiori, *Antonio Gramsci: Life of a Revolutionary* (New York, 1973). Roger Simon's introduction to Gramsci's thought, *Gramsci's Political Thought: An Introduction* (London, 1991), is a good starting point for readers to acquaint themselves with the Communist philosopher. Richard Bellamy and Darrow Schecter's book, *Gramsci and the Italian State* (Manchester, 1993), puts Gramsci into political context. Benedetto Fontana examines one of Gramsci's most influential concepts in *Hegemony and Power* (Minneapolis, 1993), and Adam David Morton discusses both hegemony and the "passive revolution" in *Unraveling Gramsci* (London, 2007). Deb J. Hill examines education and Gramsci's continuing influence in *Hegemony and Education: Gramsci, Post-Marxism, and Radical Democracy Revisited* (Lanham, 2007). Various aspects of Gramsci are discussed in the essays collected by Andreas Bieler and Adam Morton, *Images of Gramsci: Connections and Contentions in Political Theory and International Relations* (London, 2006).

For general themes in Italian culture, consult: Anna Maria Torriglia, *Broken Time, Fragmented Space: A Cultural Map for Postwar Italy* (Toronto, 2002); D. Forgacs, *Italian Culture in the Industrial Era, 1880–1980* (Manchester, 1990); and D. Forgacs and R. Lumley, eds., *Italian Cultural Studies* (Oxford, 1996). Zygmunt G. Baranski and Rebecca J. West's *The Cambridge Companion to Modern Italian Culture* (Cambridge, U.K., 2001) is a collection of essays on the topic. Finally, see Fillippo Ceccarelli, *Lo stomaco della Repubblica: cibo e potere in Italia dal 1945 al 2000* (Milan, 2000).

CHAPTER 22: THE "BLOODLESS REVOLUTION"

The discussion in this chapter relies heavily on the press and on talks with Italian scholars and politicians, since the events are so close to the present. The Italian press is to be used with caution in anticipation of thoughtful scholarly works that will analyze the rapid-fire events of the "bloodless revolution." Italian scholars have not been quick to publish historical works on the subject, and few have been free of polemics. A work that makes a good start in putting Craxi and the events during this period into historical perspective is Arturo Gismondi, *La lunga strada per Hammamet: Craxi e I poteri forti* (Milan, 2000). Gismondi argues that Craxi attempted to introduce a "modern" Left into Italy and that his defeat has weakened leftists. For different reasons, the English-language press has also been quite poor on the issues, but the *New York Times* and *The New Yorker* have carried articles. Two serious articles are Angelo Codevilla, "A Second Italian Republic?" *Foreign Affairs* (Summer 1992), and John W. Holmes, "Can Italy Change Yet Remain Stable?" *Mediterranean Quarterly* (Spring 1993). Michael Ledeen's "Italy's Great Purge," *American Spectator* (October 1993), gives a good account of the Italian situation up to that date, but is overly preoccupied with American politics. The *Financial Times*, a British publication, has closely followed events. The following articles by Spencer Di Scala, in the *Christian Science Monitor*, may prove helpful for an analysis up to the dates when they were published: "Italy's Embattled Left," February 13, 1990; "Italy's Political Upheaval," April 15, 1992; and "Italian Political Reform Needs More Than 'Clean Hands,'" April 15, 1993. In October 1992, despite the cool reaction of Bettino Craxi, a conference on the scandals and their significance was held at the initiative of the group responsible for publishing the party's ideological review, *Mondoperaio*. The conference reports are published in the November 1992 issue of the journal.

A number of works examining the causes and results of the bloodless revolution have appeared. Stanton H. Burnett and Luca Mantovani's *The Italian Guillotine: Operation Clean Hands and the Overthrow of Italy's First Republic* (Lanham, 1998) is an excellent account of the tactics utilized by the magistrates that has not received the attention it deserves. Luigi Preti has written *La crisi della giustizia in Italia: i casi Craxi, Andreotti, Berlusconi* (Milan, 2000). On the investigation into the corruption scandal, see Enrico Nascimbeni and Andrea Pamparana, *Le mani pulite: l'inchiesta di Milano sulle tangenti* (Milan, 1992). For the judges' version, consult Gian Carlo Caselli et al.,

La vera storia d'Italia (Naples, 1995). Ennio Di Nolfo's *La Repubblica delle speranze e degli inganni: l'Italia dalla caduta del fascismo al crollo della Democrazia cristiana* (Florence, 1996) gives an indication of the delusion suffered by intellectuals. Sergio Turone, in *Corrotti e corrottori, dall'unità d'Italia alla P2* (Rome, 1984) and *Politica ladra* (Rome, 1992), and Donatella Della Porta, in *Lo scambio occulto* (Bologna, 1992), discuss the general theme of corruption in Italy. Vittorio Bufacchi and Simon Burgess, in *Italy Since 1989* (New York, 1998), discuss events in the country and give interpretations. The fall of the "regime" is examined in *Il crollo: Andreotti, Craxi e il loro regime* (Rome, 1993). The crisis of the Italian parties during Tangentopoli is discussed in Maurizio Cotta and Pierangelo Isernia, *Il gigante dai piedi d'argilla* (Bologna, 1996). Sergio Romano, *L'Italia scappata di mano* (Milan, 1993), gives some interesting ideas on its origins and developments. Giorgio Bocca, *Metropolis: Milano nella tempesta* (Milan, 1993), gives what purports to be the history of the real Tangentopoli ("Kickback City"). Gianpaolo Pansa, *L'anno dei barbari: diario cattivo di come la crisi dei partiti ci ha regalato l'incognita leghista* (Milan, 1993) is the warning of a well-known journalist not to go from the frying pan into the fire. Luciano Cafagna also warned forcefully of the potential dangers resulting from the reaction to Tangentopoli in *La grande slavina: l'Italia verso la crisi della democrazia* (Venice, 1993). Patrick McCarthy's *The Crisis of the Italian State* (New York, 1995) is an attempt to put the events of 1992–1993 into historical perspective. Scholars discuss party finance and corruption in different countries, including Italy, in Robert Williams, *Party Finance and Political Corruption* (New York, 2000). The essays in Donatella Della Porta and Yves Meny's *Democracy and Corruption in Europe* (London, 1997) discuss corruption in other European countries, and those in Jeffrey Ian Ross, *Varieties of State Crime and Its Control* (Monsey, 2000), help put Italian corruption into a general context.

Books examining developments of the 1990s in Italian politics include Stephen Hellman and Gianfranco Pasquino, eds., *Italian Politics: A Review* (Kent and Worcester, 1992); Robert D. Putnam, *Making Democracy Work: Civic Traditions in Modern Italy* (Princeton, 1993); Mauro Calise, ed., *Come cambiano i partiti* (Bologna, 1992); Gianfranco Pasquino and Patrick McCarthy, eds., *The End of Post-war Politics in Italy: The Landmark 1992 Elections* (Boulder, 1993); Carol Mershon and Gianfranco Pasquino, eds., *Italian Politics: Ending the First Republic* (Boulder, 1994); and Mark Gilbert, *The Italian Revolution: The Ignominious End of Politics, Italian Style* (Boulder, 1994). Matt Frei has published *Getting the Boot: Italy's Unfinished Revolution* (New York, 1995). Works with an "institutional" focus include Sebastiano Messina, *La grande riforma* (Rome and Bari, n.d.). Anna Chimenti has written a work on the role of the referendum in contemporary politics, *Storia dei referendum* (Rome and Bari, 1993), while Primo di Nicola has published a work on an influential promoter of referendums, *Mario Segni* (Milan, 1992). The role of the referendum is also examined in Marcello Fedele's *Democrazia referendaria: l'Italia dal primato dei partiti al trionfo dell'opinione pubblica* (Rome, 1994). For a discussion of the last Parliament of the "First" Republic, see Luca Ridolfi, *L'ultimo parliamento* (Rome, 1993). Alan Friedman's *Spider's Web* (New York, 1993) discusses the role of the Banca Nazionale del Lavoro in arming Iraq and gives a good idea of the links between Italian domestic politics, corruption, and foreign affairs. An excellent work on Craxi's political "demise" and the reasons for it is Antonio Padellaro and Giuseppe Tamburrano, *Processo a Craxi: ascesa e declino di un leader* (Milan, 1993). Tamburrano, one of Craxi's earliest and harshest critics, is notable for his balanced tone in this book. Besides the Socialist and Communist Parties, this period also witnessed the end of the DC; on this topic, see Franco Massimo, *Tutti a casa: il crepuscolo di mamma DC* (Milan, 1993). Achille Occhetto, the person who led the Italian Communists into the post-Communist era, has published his reflections and judgments as *Il sentimento e la ragione* (Milan, 1994).

CHAPTER 23: THE BERLUSCONI PHENOMENON

Ilvo Diamante has published a solid work on the Lombard League and the sources of its power, *La Lega: geografia, storia e sociologia di un nuovo soggetto politico* (Rome, 1993). This book also has a bibliography valuable for the study of this new phenomenon. Other books on the League include Umberto Bossi and Daniele Vimercati's *La Rivoluzione* (Milan, 1993), a clear exposition of the League's ideology and history; Luigi De Marchi's *Perchè la Lega* (Milan, 1993), an attempt to put the League and its ideas into world context; and Giulio Savelli's *Che cosa vuole la Lega* (Milan, 1992), which seeks to explain the reasons for the League's rise. For the League's "ideology," see the various works of and interviews with Gianfranco Miglio, erstwhile official League "philosopher." His books include *Per un Italia "federale"* (Milan, 1990), *Disobbedienza civile* (Milan, 1993), *Una repubblica migliore per gli italiani* (Milan, 1983), and *Cosi andata a finire* (Milan, 1993).

On the South, examined in light of the League's growing influence, see Isaia Sales, *Leghisti e sudisti* (Rome and Bari, 1993). Shorter treatments examining the issue of whether the League is a "federalist" phenomenon are James P. Cross's "The Lega Lombarda: A Spring Protest or the Seeds of Federalism?" *Italian Politics and Society* 32 (Winter 1990–1991); and Michael Thompson's "From Canoux to Bossi: The Roots of Northern Regionalist Politics," *Italian Politics and Society* 39 (Spring 1993).

The evolution of the Movimento Sociale Italiano (MSI) into the Alleanza Nazionale (AN) may be followed in a series of works, including Piero Ignazi, *Postfascisti? Dal Movimento Sociale Italiano ad Alleanza Nazionale* (Bologna, 1994); Paolo Nello, *Il partito della fiamma: la destra in Italia dal MSI ad AN* (Pisa, 1998); and Marco Tarchi, *Dal MSI ad AN: organizzazione e strategia* (Bologna, 1997).

A number of books by rightist protagonists reflecting their own movement, usually printed by small publishers, are worth the effort of reading. Some interesting ones include Nino Tripodi's *Fascismo così: problemi di un tempo ritrovato* (Rome, 1984), which seeks to reinterpret fascism in light of contemporary problems, and Adalberto Baldoni's *Noi rivoluzionari: la Destra e il "caso italiano" Appunti per una storia 1960–1986* (Rome, 1986), which argues against the political isolation of the Right. Giano Accame maintains that it is possible to heal the divisions of Italian society by rediscovering fascism's "red" roots in his work with an apparently paradoxical title, *Il fascismo immenso e rosso* (Rome, 1990); this is the continuation of a theme found in the same author's *Socialismo tricolore* (Novara, 1983). There are also two books jointly written by rightists and leftists that seek to open a dialogue: E. Landolfi and F. M. D'Asaro, *Socialismo e nazione* (Rome, 1985), and Adalberto Badaloni and Sandro Provvisionato, *La notte più lunga della repubblica: sinistra e destra ideologie, estremismi, lotta armata (1968–1989)* (Rome, 1989).

Some books have appeared on the later period and on Berlusconi's rise. See Ginsborg, *Italy and Its Discontents: Family, Civil Society, State, 1980–2001*, previously cited; this book continues the work of his earlier social history and includes an appendix with a wealth of statistics. Ginsborg has also published *Silvio Berlusconi: Television, Power, and Patrimony* (New York, 2004), originally published as *Berlusconi: ambizioni patrimoniali in una democrazia mediatica* (Turin, 2003). In this brief work, Ginsborg considers Berlusconi a "prototype" because he combines vast wealth and charisma. Pino Corrias, Massimo Gramellini, and Curzio Malatesta's *1994 Colpo Grosso* (Milan, 1994) is the story of Berlusconi's amazing climb to power and victory in the 1994 elections. Giovanni Ruggeri and Mario Guarino's *Berlusconi: Inchiesta sul Signor TV* (Milan, 1994) is an unfriendly journalistic "investigation" of Berlusconi's political and financial connections and a good example of the passion that the new leader engendered. Giuseppe Fiori's *Il Venditore* (Milan, 1995) concentrates on Berlusconi's business affairs, and particularly on his company Fininvest. Alessandro Stille is also critical in *The Sack of Rome: How a Beautiful European Country with a Fabled History and a Storied Culture Was Taken Over by a Man Named Silvio Berlusconi* (New York, 2006). The international press devoted a fair amount of attention, not all of it balanced, to Italian affairs following the first elections after the new reforms. For a good idea of the fiscal problems facing the new government, see "Berlusconi Confronts a Critical Challenge over Fiscal Reform," *Wall Street Journal*, August 25, 1994. Finally, the political "geography" of the "Second Republic" is examined by Paolo De Lalla Millul, *Topografia politica della Seconda Repubblica 1: la Destra* (Naples, 1994). Political scientist Gianfranco Pasquino has examined the 2001 election in *Dall'Ulivo al governo Berlusconi: le elezioni del 13 maggio 2001* (Bologna, 2002). Consult also J. L. Newell, ed., *The Italian General Election of 2001* (Manchester, 2002).

Two important protagonists of the political struggles following the 1996 elections have published books. Massimo D'Alema's *La grande occasione* (Milan, 1997) is an important work because it reveals the workings of the Bicamerale and how and why it reached its decisions. Fausto Bertinotti, *Le due sinistre* (Milan, 1997), explains and defends PRC policies. Enzo Bettiza's criticism of the Ulivo's foreign policy, "A cavallo dell'anatra zoppo," *La Stampa*, August 17, 1997, is a rare, cogently argued sally into the dilemmas of Italian diplomacy at the time. The Iraq War saw the intensification of anti-Americanism, but the phenomenon has a long history. A good work explaining the views fueling this is Massimo Teodori's *Maledetti americani: destra, sinistra e cattolici: storia del pregiudizio antiamericano* (Milan, 2002). The May–June 2002 and May–June 2003 issues of *Mondoperaio* contain articles on the same question.

The essays in Francesco Tuccari, ed., *Il governo Berlusconi: le parole, I fatti, I rischi* (Rome, 2002), give the views of a number of scholars eight months after the Berlusconi cabinet took office. An important issue, Berlusconi's relationship to the justice system, can be examined in David Lane's *Berlusconi's Shadow: Crime, Justice, and the Pursuit of Power* (London, 2004). Giovanni Sabbatucci, *Il trasformismo come sistema: saggio sulla storia politica dell'Italia unita* (Rome, 2003), takes a more general view and includes chapters on the transformation of the Italian political system. Giano Accame, *Una storia della repubblica: dalla fine della monarchia a oggi* (Milan, 2000), attempts a general history from 1945. Roy Palmer Domenico, *Remaking Italy in the Twentieth Century*, cited, is a reflective book with a synopsis of the most recent issues and concerns.

The book that describes the "perks" of Italian politicians and caused a sensation in Italy is Sergio Rizzo and Gian Antonio Stella, *La Casta: così i politici italiani sono diventati intoccabili* (Milan, 2007).The article in the *New York Times* that caused a stir in Italy is Richard Owen, "The Dolce Vita Turns Sour as Italy Faces Up to Being Old and Poor," December 22, 2007. The question of the Catholic Church's increasing intervention in the state's affairs during the Prodi and Berlusconi administrations loomed as a potentially crucial point of debate. One book, for example, argued that the Church cost Italian citizens much more to maintain than the political establishment that came under so much criticism in 2007 and 2008. See Curzio Maltese, *La Questua: quanto costa la Chiesa agli italiani* (Milan, 2008). The well-respected commentator Sergio Romano wrote a more reflective work, *Libera Chiesa: Libero Stato? Il Vaticano e l'Italia da Pio IX a Benedetto XVI*.

About the
Book and Author

T HE PREVIOUS EDITIONS OF *ITALY: FROM REVOLUTION TO REPUBLIC, 1700 to the Present* filled a serious gap in the field by synthesizing modern Italian history and placing it in a fully European context. In this new edition, Spencer Di Scala has updated the book's content and detailed bibliographical essay and has considered developments up to the general elections of 2008. He assesses the progress of the "Second Republic," the fundamental changes that are occurring in the country's political structure, the performance of the center-right and center-left coalitions, the economic crisis brought about by globalization, and the prospects for reform at a critical juncture in the country's history. Di Scala discusses the impact on Italy of its entrance into the Euro zone, the country's struggle to maintain its economic position in the twenty-first century, and whether it can achieve a foreign policy more in keeping with its economic clout as the world's fifth or sixth largest producer. Presenting the history of modern Italy from the eighteenth century to the present, this book begins with a brief introduction to the legacy of the Renaissance and the seventeenth century. Di Scala also critically reexamines traditional historical interpretations and assumptions. The "European context" ranges from the Enlightenment to unity, to liberalism, to the South, to Fascism, and to the republic. This new edition includes expanded examinations of contemporary Italy's economic, social, and cultural developments while providing a picture of how ordinary Italians live. It emphasizes globalization, the country's transformation from a land of emigration to one of immigration and the problems brought about by this condition, and the country's growing cultural importance in the contemporary era. Di Scala discusses the role of women and gives ample attention to the Italian South, not only in terms of the "problems" of that region but also in terms of its active participation in the historical and cultural life of the nation. Cast in a clear and lively style that appeals to students, Di Scala's work builds on its strong contribution to the field by incorporating the most recent scholarly contributions in his analyses. The book includes a rich bibliographic essay, completely updated for this edition, designed to guide undergraduate and graduate students to further reading on the various topics under consideration.

Spencer M. Di Scala is professor of history and History Graduate Program Director at the University of Massachusetts Boston. He received his Ph.D. from Columbia University, has held several Fulbright fellowships to Italy, both as a student and as a professor, and has been named a *Commendatore* in the Order of Merit of the Italian Republic. He is the author of numerous scholarly books and articles on Italian and European politics and culture, serves on the editorial boards of scholarly journals, and has received national and regional awards for his teaching and innovative pedagogy.

Index